Strategic International Management

Dirk Morschett · Hanna Schramm-Klein ·
Joachim Zentes

Strategic International Management

Text and Cases

3rd Edition

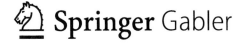 **Springer** Gabler

Dirk Morschett
University of Fribourg
Fribourg, Switzerland

Joachim Zentes
Saarland University
Saarbrücken, Germany

Hanna Schramm-Klein
University of Siegen
Siegen, Germany

ISBN 978-3-658-07883-6
DOI 10.1007/978-3-658-07884-3

ISBN 978-3-658-07884-3 (eBook)

Library of Congress Control Number: 2014959424

Springer Gabler

Springer-Verlag GmbH Berlin Heidelberg is part of Springer Science+Business Media (www.springer.com)

Preface

In this third edition, all chapters have been updated, new chapters integrated, all case studies revised and recent data were integrated. The concept, as it is described below, remained unchanged.

Over the last few decades, international activities of companies have gained dramatically in importance. Empirical evidence for this statement can be found, for instance, in the rapid growth of world trade and in foreign direct investment flows as well as in the high share of intra-company trade on total world trade, indicating the relevance of cross-border value creation processes. Courses on International Management have, thus, become an integral part of most management studies at universities today and dedicated Masters and MBA programmes on International Management have emerged in recent years.

Concept and Overview of this Book

This book intends to give a compact overview of the most relevant concepts and developments in International Management. Various strategy concepts of internationally active companies and their implementation in practice are the core of this book. It is not designed as a traditional textbook or a collection of case studies, but tries to combine both. The book introduces the complex and manifold questions of International Management in the form of 23 lessons that give a thematic overview of key issues and illustrates each topic by providing a comprehensive case study.

The book is divided into six major parts. Part I ("Introduction to Strategic International Management") lays the foundation by explaining basic concepts and theories of International Management. The growing importance of emerging country multinationals will be taken into account. In Part II, the influence of the external environment on Multinational Corporations (MNCs) is described, looking into market barriers and regional integration, the competitive advantage of nations and the influence of country culture. Part III focuses on the coordination of internationally dispersed activities in a Multinational Corporation. An overview of formal and informal instruments is given and some coordination instruments are discussed in more detail. Another core decision with regard to international activities, the foreign operation mode, is dealt with in Part IV. After an overview of the basic types of foreign operation modes, the three main options – market, cooperation and hierarchies – are explained in individual chapters. In this third edition export modes now also receive special attention. Part V is devoted to specific value chain activities, production & sourcing, R&D and marketing. At last, human resource management and international control are discussed as highly relevant business functions in Part VI of the book.

Teaching and Learning

The book is primarily aimed at students at the beginning of their Masters studies who major in Business Administration, International Management, Strategic Management or related fields. In addition, practitioners who seek compact and practice-oriented information on international strategy concepts can benefit from the book. The case studies accompany each lesson in such a way that they provide additional content and a specific application of the individual lessons on the one hand. They are part of the explanation of the topic, but they also lead to suggested discussion subjects and questions in order to deepen the understanding of the topic.

Instructors are provided with additional resources. A set of PowerPoint slides can be downloaded from the publisher's website (www.gabler.de). Furthermore, for each case study, a solution draft can be obtained.

Acknowledgements

A textbook with cases cannot be written without the active support and cooperation of the selected companies. Thus, first of all we appreciate the help of the companies and their representatives who have willingly supported us in the development of the case studies.

At Gabler we thank Barbara Roscher who accompanied and supported our concept for this book from the beginning.

At the universities where the three authors are teaching and researching International Management, we would in particular like to thank Darlene Whitaker (Saarland University) for the preparation of case studies as well as for copyediting the book. We also acknowledge the assistance of Marta Kramarek and Matthias Schu from the University of Fribourg, Kim Kathrin Kunze, Gunnar Mau, Florian Neus, Robér Rollin and Sascha Steinmann from the University of Siegen, and Tatjana Freer, Daniel Keßler, Victoria Lonnes and Benjamin Ney from the Saarland University, who have all prepared specific case studies.

Fribourg, Siegen and Saarbrücken, October 2014

DIRK MORSCHETT   HANNA SCHRAMM-KLEIN   JOACHIM ZENTES

Contents

Contents

Dirk Morschett is Professor of International Management at the University of Fribourg, Switzerland. He holds the Chair of International Management and is responsible for the Master of Arts in European Business. He is in the directorate of the Centre for European Studies at the University of Fribourg and visiting lecturer in several Master and MBA programmes at universities in Switzerland and abroad.

Hanna Schramm-Klein is Professor of Marketing at the University of Siegen, Germany. She holds a Chair in Business Administration, especially Marketing, and is visiting lecturer in several Master and MBA programmes at universities in Germany and abroad.

Joachim Zentes is Professor of Management and Marketing at the Saarland University, Saarbrücken, Germany. He is Director of the H.I.Ma. (Institute for Commerce & International Marketing) and Director of the Europa-Institut at the Saarland University. He holds a Chair in Business Administration, especially Foreign Trade and International Management. Joachim Zentes is a member of various boards of directors and advisory boards in Germany and abroad.

Basic Definitions

Globalisation – the growing integration of economies around the world and companies' increasing cross-border activities – is one of the most intensively discussed topics of recent decades. Such cross-border activities of companies take various forms:

- *International trade* has risen strongly during recent decades. More importantly, worldwide exports are consistently growing more strongly than worldwide gross domestic product (GDP). This proves that the world's GDP is increasingly produced and consumed in cross-border processes. For companies, as well as for countries, international trade can be *exports*, i.e. selling merchandise and services to customers in other countries, or *imports*, i.e. buying merchandise and services from suppliers in other countries. — *Exports and Imports*

- In addition, companies have increasingly undertaken *foreign direct investment (FDI)*, for example establishing production plants abroad. Over the past two decades, global FDI flows have increased twice as fast as global GDP. Under the definition of most international organisations and statistical offices, FDI refers to an investment made to acquire a lasting interest in enterprises operating outside of the economy of the investor. The investor's assumed objective is to gain an effective voice in the management of the enterprise. FDI can take the form of transferring equity capital or reinvestment of foreign earnings, among others. Usually, a threshold of 10% of equity ownership is used to qualify an investment as FDI. Below that threshold, the term "portfolio investment" is used, which represents passive holdings of foreign financial assets such as foreign stocks or bonds. — *Foreign Direct Investment*

The link between FDI and international trade becomes clear through the fact that about one-third of worldwide trade is undertaken as intra-company trade. This is clear evidence of the enormous relevance of the cross-border value chains of Multinational Corporations with production facilities in different countries. The most recent World Investment Report by UNCTAD even argues that global value chains coordinated by Multinational Corporations account for approximately 80% of global trade (UNCTAD 2013, p. x).

It is this international dispersion of activities that ultimately characterises a Multinational Corporation (MNC). We use the term MNC very broadly, referring to *any company with routine cross-border activities*. More particularly, following an old definition from the United Nations that is also employed by — *Multinational Corporation (MNC)*

Bartlett/Beamish (2014, p. 2), we see an MNC as "an enterprise (a) comprising *entities* in two or more countries, regardless of the legal form and fields of activity of those entities, (b) which operates under a system of decision-making permitting coherent policies and a common strategy through one or more decision-making centres, (c) in which the entities are so linked, *by ownership or otherwise*, that one or more of them may be able to exercise a significant influence over the activities of the others, and, in particular, to share knowledge, resources and responsibilities with others" (United Nations 1984, p. 2).

It is not relevant which legal form the entity has, only that "active, coordinated management of operations in different countries, as the key differentiating characteristic of an MNC" (Bartlett/Beamish 2014, p. 3) is possible. And those entities are not necessarily production plants; they could be just sales subsidiaries or other activities. While some authors demand certain quantitative thresholds for an MNC, (e.g. entities in a certain number of foreign countries, a certain percentage of employees abroad, share of foreign sales or direct investment) we consider those thresholds to be arbitrary. It should be noted that the UN applies the term *transnational corporation* (TNC) with the same meaning in its reports (e.g. UNCTAD).

When characterising those corporations' activities and highlighting their relevance for the world economy, UNCTAD states: "[Global Value Chains] are typically coordinated by TNCs, with cross-border trade of inputs and outputs taking place within their networks of affiliates, contractual partners and arm's-length suppliers." (UNCTAD 2013, p. xxii)

Foreign Subsidiaries International operations do not necessarily have to be internalised. Instead, contractual cooperation or joint ventures are viable alternatives to wholly-owned foreign subsidiaries. As a consequence, subsidiaries are not necessarily wholly-owned. Instead, we understand a *foreign subsidiary* to be "any operational unit controlled by the MNC and situated outside the home country" (Birkinshaw/Hood/Jonsson 1998, p. 224). For international business (IB), the main criterion is not ownership (even though it will be the usual form of control) but the possibility to exercise influence. For example, in an MNC network, a contract manufacturer or a long-time supplier may deliver a strategic contribution to the MNC's performance and, thus, such entities must also be "managed", an adequate location must be chosen, their conduct needs to be influenced for the sake of the MNC, etc.

It has to be noted, though, that some authors only use the term "subsidiary" when there is a certain degree of equity ownership. This understanding of subsidiary (or, synonymous, "affiliate") is exemplified by UNCTAD's definition (2004, p. 44): "A *foreign affiliate* or direct investment enterprise is an incorporated or unincorporated enterprise in which a foreign direct investor, resident in another economy, owns a stake that permits a lasting interest in the management of that enterprise (an equity stake of 10% for an incorporated enterprise or its equivalent for an unincorporated enterprise)."

For International Management, three main dimensions need to be decided and managed: the configuration, coordination and operation mode of the international activities.

■ A major characteristic of MNCs is that they are active in more than one country. This is simultaneously an advantage and a challenge. The specific characteristics of a country therefore play a role in the selection of locations. *Configuration* refers to the location where each value chain activity is performed, including the number of locations (Porter 1986, p. 17).

Configuration

■ Those dispersed activities must be integrated to ensure that all subsidiaries contribute to the MNC's objectives and achieve synergy effects where possible. *Coordination* can be defined as the process of integrating activities that remain dispersed across subsidiaries (Martinez/Jarillo 1991, p. 431). "A mechanism of coordination is any administrative tool for achieving integration among different units within an organisation, i.e. to align a number of dispersed and yet interdependent international activities" (Martinez/Jarillo 1989, p. 490).

Coordination

■ As has already been established, MNCs can exploit country-specific advantages in a foreign country through other methods than establishing a wholly-owned subsidiary. For example, production in a foreign country could be carried out via a licensing agreement with a local manufacturing company. A *foreign operation mode* can be defined as an institutional arrangement or organisational arrangement that is used for organising and conducting an international business transaction, such as manufacturing goods, servicing customers or sourcing various inputs (Andersen 1997, p. 29; Welch/Benito/Petersen 2007, p. 18).

Foreign Operation Modes

References

ANDERSEN, O. (1997): Internationalization and Market Entry Mode: A Review of Theories and Conceptual Framework, in: Management International Review, Vol. 27, No. 2, pp. 27-42.

BARTLETT, C.A.; BEAMISH, P.W. (2014): Transnational Management: Text, Cases, and Readings in Cross-Border Management, 7th ed., Boston, McGraw-Hill.

BIRKINSHAW, J.; HOOD, N.; JONSSON, S. (1998): Building Firm-specific Advantages in Multinational Corporations: The Role of Subsidiary Initiative, in: Strategic Management Journal, Vol. 19, No. 3, pp. 221-241.

MARTINEZ, J.; JARILLO, J. (1989): The Evolution of Research on Coordination Mechanisms in Multinational Corporations, in: Journal of International Business Studies, Vol. 20, No. 3, pp. 489-514.

MARTINEZ, J.; JARILLO, J. (1991): Coordination Demands of International Strategies, in: Journal of International Business Studies, Vol. 22, No. 3, pp. 429-444.

PORTER, M.E. (1986): Changing Patterns of International Competition, in: California Management Review, Vol. 28, No. 2, pp. 9-40.

UNCTAD (2004): Development and Globalization 2004: Fact & Figures, Geneva.

UNCTAD (2013): World Investment Report 2013: Global Value Chains: Investment and Trade for Development, Geneva.

UNITED NATIONS (1984): Work Related to the Definition of Transnational Corporations: Question of the Definition of Transnational Corporations, Report of the Secretariat, E/C.10/1984/17, New York.

WELCH, L.; BENITO, G.; PETERSEN, B. (2007): Foreign Operation Methods: Theory – Analysis – Strategy, Glos, Edward Elgar Publishing.

Part I

Introduction to

Strategic International

Management

Chapter 1

Multinational Corporations as Networks

The complexity of Multinational Corporations (MNCs) regarding multiple geographical markets and the dispersed activities within the company often renders centralised management models ineffective and inefficient. Knowledging the increased relevance of foreign subsidiaries and the observation that some subsidiaries assume strategic roles within the MNC lead to a conceptualisation of the MNC as a network. In this Chapter, the network perspective of the MNC is explained, nodes and linkages in the network are described and the contribution of this perspective to understanding the modern MNC is demonstrated.

From Centralised Hubs to Integrated Networks

From the early 1980s, the limitations of hierarchical models of the company with regard to their capability to manage the complexity of a Multinational Corporation (MNC) became obvious in the course of increasing internationalisation, the emergence of more and more MNCs, and the constantly rising relevance of foreign subsidiaries. Studies by scholars such as Prahalad, Doz, Bartlett and various others revealed that top management in the home country had more and more problems in effectively and efficiently processing and understanding the vast amount of information necessary to coordinate the MNC.

MNC management is confronted with the challenge of designing systems that allow flexible responses to the very heterogeneous context in which the different subsidiaries have to compete. It is also necessary to sense the diverse opportunities and demands that the MNC faces, and to simultaneously ensure the necessary coherence to act as one company, to achieve global scale effects by specialising their subsidiaries' activities and to exploiting synergy potential. In a sophisticated and differentiated configuration of specialised assets and responsibilities, the interdependence of worldwide units increases, and an *integrated network structure* becomes necessary to coordinate the dispersed activities. In this network model, management regards each of the worldwide units as a potential source of ideas, skills, capabilities, and knowledge that can be used to benefit the entire organisation. Efficient local plants may be converted into production sites with worldwide responsibility, and innovative organisational units may become the MNC's centres of competence for a particular product or process (Bartlett/Beamish 2014, pp. 284-285).

The Integrated Network Model

To understand this modern type of network model better, Figure 1.1 contrasts it with two alternative models, the *centralised hub,* a traditional model in which the foreign subsidiaries merely implement central decisions and have no autonomy, and the *decentralised federation,* a multinational model with great autonomy of the subsidiaries, but only weak linkages within the MNC, which acts mainly as a holding company. While national subsidiaries in decentralised federations enjoy considerable *independence* from the headquarters, those in centralised hubs remain strongly *dependent* on the parent company. Integrated networks are *interdependent* organisations, with dispersed, and specialised, but coordinated interrelationships between the units. Such networks result in a so-called *decentralised centralisation,* i.e., the activities are globally integrated and aligned. Subsidiaries are not necessarily coordinated by the headquarters but in some cases and for some products, by another foreign subsidiary (Birkinshaw/Morrison 1995, p. 734).

Figure 1.1 | *Alternative Models of the MNC*

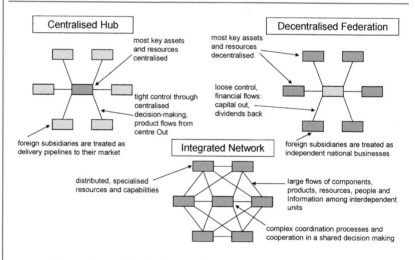

Source: Adapted from Bartlett/Beamish 2014, p. 281, p. 285.

From the 1980s onwards, more and more scholars started to model the MNC as *a network.* The "transnational organisation" (Bartlett/Ghoshal 1989), the "heterarchy" (Hedlund 1986), and the "differentiated network" (Nohria/Ghoshal 1997) are just a few examples. While there are many differences in detail, all these models recommend organising the MNC as an integrated network of dispersed organisational units.

Networks consist of *nodes* (in this case mainly foreign subsidiaries) and *linkages* between those nodes (like coordination relationships, product flows, communication, etc.). Some of the nodes, i.e. of the foreign subsidiaries, achieve – due to unique resources, capabilities and competences, for example – a crucial influence on the decisions of the MNC and foreign subsidiaries can assume "strategic roles" (see Chapter 3). Competitive advantages of the MNC are not necessarily developed in the home country any longer and then transferred and exploited in foreign countries, but can be established by single foreign subsidiaries or through cooperation in the whole MNC network. *Learning* becomes necessary to create and diffuse knowledge quickly within the MNC (Schmid/Kutschker 2003, pp. 163-164). *Nodes and Linkages*

Heterogeneity between Foreign Subsidiaries

The network perspective of the MNC acknowledges that foreign subsidiaries are and should be heterogeneous: "to be truly effective, multinational corporations should be differentiated" (Nohria/Ghoshal 1997, p. xv). Looking at the British MNC *BP*, which is described in detail in the case study at the end of this Chapter, one can see that the company is active in more than 80 countries. Some foreign subsidiaries (e.g. in Iran) were established more than 100 years ago, but others are just a few years old. Some foreign subsidiaries mainly carry out, for instance, oil exploration, while others focus on distribution (e.g. selling fuel via a network of gas stations). Some only employ a few people, while in the UK, the company has about 10,000 employees. Some work in slow-growing countries of Western Europe, others in fast-growing emerging economies like India. Some are wholly-owned and some are operated in partnerships with other companies.

The *BP* example demonstrates that subsidiaries can be distinguished by many different criteria. Heterogeneous characteristics of subsidiaries include, inter alia (Morschett 2007): *Subsidiary Characteristics*

- value-added activities carried out by the subsidiary, extend from single activities (e.g. only sales) to full value chains

- dominant motives for the establishment of the country subsidiary, for example, resource seeking or market seeking (see Chapter 4)

- available resources and capabilities of the subsidiary

- local conditions of the host country, e.g. political and economic situation

- degree of horizontal and vertical product and communication flows with other subsidiaries and the headquarters

- control and influence of the headquarters

- national, regional or worldwide responsibility of the subsidiary

- age of the foreign subsidiary or time frame of belonging to the MNC (in the case of an acquisition)

- size of the subsidiary (sales, employees, financial assets, etc.)

- performance of the subsidiary.

The role typologies of International Management (see Chapter 3) are an attempt to categorise subsidiary roles following some of these characteristics.

Subsidiaries as Centres of Excellence

Network models also assume that subsidiaries can become "centres of excellence" (or *competence centres*) for the MNC. A centre of excellence is "an organizational unit that embodies a set of capabilities that has been explicitly recognized by the firm as an important source of value creation, with the intention that these capabilities be leveraged by and/or disseminated to other parts of the firm" (Frost/Birkinshaw/Ensign 2002, p. 997). Studies have shown that most MNCs have foreign subsidiaries adopting the role of centres of excellence (Schmid/Bäurle/Kutschker 1999, pp. 108-109). Such centres of excellence play a highly strategic role in the MNC network.

High Autonomy and Strong Integration A high level of competence is an obvious prerequisite for this role and centres of excellence are characterised by simultaneous appearance of *high autonomy*, because a relatively high degree of freedom is necessary to deploy its competences effectively, and *strong integration* in the MNC to ensure that the competence is available to other country subsidiaries as well (Forsgren/Pedersen 1997). Centres of excellence can concern products or processes or functions of the MNC (Frost/Birkinshaw/Ensign 2002, pp. 998-1000). It becomes increasingly obvious, though, that the concept of a centre of excellence is not an all or nothing situation, but rather a continuum, i.e., each subsidiary may act to a certain (but different) level as a centre of excellence within its MNC.

Flows in the MNC Network

The network perspective of the MNC illustrates it as a combination of nodes and linkages. Those linkages include potential superordination and subordination in the headquarters-subsidiary relations and coordination relationships that might be more or less centralised. Sometimes, coordination might not be achieved through the corporate headquarters in the home country, but rather from a superordinate subsidiary that acts as the regional head-quarters.

Linkages in the network also encompass a number of different transactions among units located in different countries. Hence, the MNC can also be thought of as a *network of capital, product, and knowledge flows* between organisational units (Gupta/Govindarajan 1991, p. 770). In the network perspective, it becomes evident that, *instead of unidirectional flows* of products, components and know-how from the headquarters to the foreign subsidiaries, there are *bidirectional and reciprocal flows* and interdependencies. Not only are there *vertical linkages* between the headquarters and each subsidiary, but increasingly, there are *horizontal relations* between the subsidiaries, concerning both product flows and employees and knowledge exchange.

A Network of Capital, Product and Knowledge Flows

For example, a French sales subsidiary of the German car manufacturer *BMW* mainly receives product inflows, while the German factories exporting to other countries are a source for product outflows. The US factory of *BMW* which sells its vehicles to Mexico demonstrates horizontal product flows. In cross-border production processes (see Chapter 19), components are produced in different countries and often transported to a subsidiary that assembles the finished products. Similarly, dispersed R&D activities and innovation processes are only possible through substantial vertical and/or horizontal knowledge flows (see Chapter 20).

Generally, these flows within the MNC may have different magnitudes and different directions, and the transactional perspective increases the number of potentially heterogeneous characteristics of MNC subsidiaries, since substantial differences across subsidiaries within the same MNC will exist. The role typologies (see Chapter 3) attempt to capture some of these differences systematically.

Intra- and Inter-organisational Networks

As mentioned in the introductory section, MNCs comprise entities in two or more countries, regardless of the legal forms and fields of activity of those entities. It is not relevant what legal form the entity has, but only that "active, coordinated management of operations in different countries, as the key differentiating characteristic of a MNE" (Bartlett/Beamish 2014, p. 3) is possible. An MNC must own or control value-adding activities in more than one country (Dunning 1993). Given that *subsidiary* is defined "as any operational unit controlled by the MNC and situated outside the home country" (Birkinshaw/Hood/Jonsson 1998, p. 224), foreign subsidiaries are not necessarily wholly-owned. The enormous relevance of cooperative operation modes (see Part IV of this book), like licensing, joint ventures, franchising, etc., necessitates the inclusion of these internationalisation modes in the conceptualisation of an MNC.

Figure 1.2   *The MNC as an Intra- and Inter-Organisational Network*

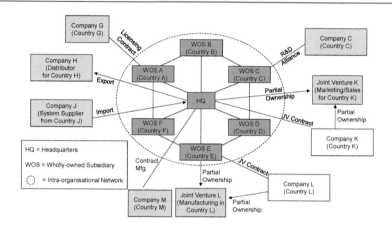

Source: Adapted from Schmid/Kutschker 2003, p. 165.

As an example of the potential complexity, Figure 1.2 illustrates the MNC network, consisting of wholly-owned subsidiaries and other foreign activities that are closely linked to the company, by partial ownership, contracts or otherwise.

Increasing Relevance of Inter-organisational Networks

From Market Capitalism to Alliance Capitalism

Thus, it is not only the company itself that is more and more structured as a network. Networks, as *stable relational systems* between different organisational units, have grown tremendously in relevance over the last few decades. Cooperative arrangements between companies are becoming very common, and some authors have called this a change from "market capitalism" to "alliance capitalism" (Dunning 1997).

Cooperation as Hybrid Operation Modes

Cooperation, as hybrid arrangements between the transaction forms of "market" and "hierarchy", seem to combine the advantages of both extremes and help to compensate for the weaknesses of both (Das/Teng 1999). Bartlett and Ghoshal, who originally developed their network model with the perspective of a purely intra-organisational network, recognised later that this perspective is too narrow and has to be expanded to include the inter-organisational network (Ghoshal/Bartlett 1991). This perspective acknowledges that the MNC is involved in *strategic alliances* with other companies.

Blurry Boundaries of the MNC

With this perspective, however, the idea that an MNC has clearly defined boundaries becomes disputable (Nohria/Ghoshal 1997, p. 19). While one could merely see the external network (inter-organisational) as an extension of the internal (intra-organisational) network, a clear separation between both becomes almost impossible (Morschett 2007). For example, while a close and long-time customer would usually still be regarded as part of the inter-organisational network, a 95%-owned foreign company would usually be seen as part of the intra-organisational network. Whether majority-owned subsidiaries, parity joint-ventures or contract manufacturers that manufacture a company's product with a fixed long-term contract are "internal" or "external", cannot however be stated categorically. One could even argue that MNC networks like this do not even have clearly defined boundaries (Hakansson/Johanson 1988, p. 370). A *"boundaryless corporation"* (Picot/Reichwald/Wigand 2003) might well be the consequence.

However, for practical reasons, it is frequently necessary to define the boundaries, but this is necessarily subjective and depends on the purpose of the exercise. Some authors suggest that the *perceived identity* of the organisational units might be decisive: "We argue that normative integration is the glue that holds differentiated networks together as entities called firms. [...] it is the distinctive codes of communication shared by the members of the multinational that truly demarcate the boundaries of the organization" (Nohria/Ghoshal 1997, p. 6).

Corporate (Internal) and Local (External) Embeddedness

If, for analytical reasons, one still tries to distinguish between the internal and the external network, a foreign subsidiary is linked to the MNC headquarters and to other subsidiaries, i.e. to the internal or corporate network.

Furthermore, the local network of the foreign subsidiary is relevant. Critical resources of the subsidiary are linked to the subsidiary's specific relationships with customers, suppliers and other counterparts (Andersson/Forsgren 1996). This local network is a powerful resource and often plays an equally strong role for the operative activities of the subsidiary and even for the strategic competitiveness of the subsidiary, as part of the relationship with the rest of the MNC. Regarding, for instance, the know-how that is relevant for the subsidiary, not only the knowledge transfer from the rest of the MNC, e.g. from the headquarters is important, but also the ques-

Local Network as Resource

tion of how new, locally relevant knowledge is created within the subsidiary. Here, the external, local network of the subsidiary is a strategic source for subsidiary-specific advantages. These "network resources" of each subsidiary can enhance the competitiveness of the MNC as a whole, because they influence the competitiveness of each subsidiary in its local market and also – by transferring of knowledge to peer subsidiaries – the capabilities of the company network (Andersson/Forsgren/Holm 2002). As mentioned above, the presence in heterogeneous local contexts can be seen as a basic advantage of MNCs, compared with purely national players. Thus, one can also consider *the foreign subsidiary as an important connection*, a "linking pin", between the external, local network in a host country and the internal company network (Andersson/Forsgren/Holm 2002, p. 992).

Embeddedness

To work successfully in a network, each subsidiary is *embedded* in relationships with other actors (Andersson/Forsgren 1996). This basically refers to an adaptation of the resources of the subsidiary to its specific network, i.e. other network actors. The adaptation includes specific investment, technical adaptations of production processes, adaptations of the product design, etc. This embeddedness must occur regarding the local network in the host country ("local embeddedness"), but also for the linkage of the subsidiary to the rest of the MNC, i.e. to the intra-organisational network ("corporate embeddedness"). However, this *dual embeddedness* might lead to conflict. The subsidiary is exposed to *different internal and external stakeholders* who usually try to influence its behaviour in accordance with their own interests. Different contexts can lead to tension, which creates a *dilemma* within the MNC. A strong local embeddedness of the subsidiary can enhance its competitiveness and also the knowledge creation of the MNC in total. Furthermore, the local embeddedness enhances the absorptive capacity of the subsidiary for new local knowledge. However, this local embeddedness often reduces the embeddedness in the corporation and thus diminishes the potential influence of headquarters (Andersson/Forsgren 1996).

Tension between Local Environment and Corporate Integration

Ultimately, this dilemma is a consequence of the basic challenges for an MNC, and captured particularly in the discussion of the integration/responsiveness-framework (see Chapter 2). Greater responsiveness to local conditions and stronger internal integration are potentially two forces in tension that have to be optimally resolved in the MNC.

Coordinating the MNC Network

With increasing complexity of the MNC, and the dual tendency to disperse activities to differentiated subsidiaries around the world, with simultaneous competitive pressure to coordinate these widespread activities, managers recognise that the organisational structure is insufficient to manage the challenging tasks facing the network. In addition to the formal structure of the company – which is still a powerful instrument – other instruments, including processes, communication channels, decision-making loci and interpersonal relationships become necessary for coordination. In particular, more subtle and informal coordination mechanisms are seen as relevant for coordinating MNC networks (Martinez/Jarillo 1989, p. 489).

The Structure of the MNC as a Differentiated Network   *Figure 1.3*

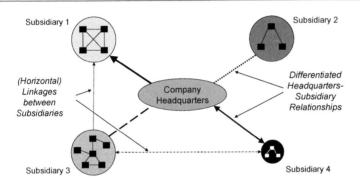

Source: Adapted from Nohria/Ghoshal 1997, p. 14.

One shortcoming of the company's organisational structure as a means of coordinating the MNC lies in heterogeneity. All subsidiaries are confronted with the same MNC structure, but within a differentiated network, "variations within such MNCs can be as great as variations across them" (Nohria/Ghoshal 1997, p. 12).

Subsidiaries, as mentioned, have different tasks, resources and competences. They also have different internal structures. Thus, as shown in the model of the integrated network, horizontal linkages between subsidiaries emerge and they are beneficial. Direct horizontal links between subsidiaries, however, make central coordination from the headquarters even more complicated. In all, the *headquarters-subsidiary relationships* must be heterogeneous as well. Stronger centralisation of decisions for certain subsidiaries and more autonomy for other subsidiaries might be sufficient. Formal and standardised procedures might be well suited for production subsidiaries but counterproductive for R&D subsidiaries, and so on. Thus, flexible and more complex coordination mechanisms become necessary. Frequently, the delegation of decision-making power to dispersed organisational units is suggested, in combination with coordination via a strong corporate culture, i.e. *normative*

Complex and Differentiated Coordination

15

integration (Bartlett/Ghoshal 1987; Buckley 1996, p. 32). To stimulate horizontal transactions between subsidiaries, informal communication by means of creating of a network of personal and informal contacts among managers across different units of the company is seen as crucial. Generally, in order to implement complex strategies that result from interrelated, multiple-country, specialised activities around the world, an enormous coordination effort is needed. Thus, all types of coordination instruments, formal and structural, plus informal and more subtle mechanisms, are needed (Martinez/Jarillo 1989, p. 492). The different coordination mechanisms are discussed in more detail in Part III of this book.

Persisting Important Role of Headquarters

However, even in the model of the differentiated network, headquarters still exist and have a somewhat hierarchical position in the network. While the heterarchical models have become prominent, most empirical studies still reveal greater a higher power in the headquarters, mostly in the home country. The network model in its extreme, i.e., a network of equally powerful organisational units with extreme decentralisation of strategic decisions to different subsidiaries and no hierarchical power in the centre, is *more of an ideal-type* in the literature than a common phenomenon in reality (Morschett 2007). "Notwithstanding the fact that MNCs are indeed becoming 'heterarchies' [...] i.e., integrated complex networks with significant devolution of authority and responsibility to the subsidiaries, the parent corporation continues to serve" (Gupta/Govindarajan 2000, p. 483) at least as a *primus inter pares*, and usually as the strongest unit concerning knowledge generation, decision power, etc.

Conclusion and Outlook

Originally, the network perspective was only used for a specific type of MNC model, in which all foreign subsidiaries have relatively high autonomy, specialised assets and competences which they leverage for the total MNC (see Figure 1.1).

Every MNC is a Network

It becomes evident, however, that many elements of a network, including relationships with internal and external actors, some degree of horizontal linkages and specialised tasks, some heterogeneous characteristics of the subsidiaries and transactional exchange between different organisational units in different countries, are not features of a specific MNC type but, to some degree, of all MNCs. One can thus conclude that "every MNC is a network" (Gupta/Govindarajan 2000, p. 491), even if it may, in many cases, still be reasonable to concentrate some key resources and capabilities in the home country. In any event, the network perspective is very useful for understanding the MNC.

Case Study: British Petroleum*

Profile, History, and Status Quo

In 1901, the English entrepreneur William D'Arcy acquired an exclusive right to search for oil in South-West Persia (modern Iran). After years of unsuccessful searching, in 1908, the chief explorer Reynolds announced in a telegram sent to D'Arcy, who was about to go bankrupt, an immense oil discovery. The *Anglo-Persian Oil Company* started business within a year and would become *British Petroleum* (*BP*) in 1954.

First Oil Discovery of Anglo-Persian

With the rise of the automobile, *Anglo-Persian* expanded its business to the mainland of Europe and the USA in the 1920s and 1930s. Thus, the number of *BP*-labelled petrol pumps or service stations increased from 69 in 1921 to more than 6,000 in 1925. In the post-war era, *Anglo-Iranian* invested mainly in refineries and new marketing efforts in Europe. It took the company several years to find new large oil reservoirs – in 1969 on the Prudhoe Bay in Alaska and in 1970 offshore in the North Sea. Those discoveries were crucial to the survival of *BP*, because almost every oil-rich nation in the Middle East, including Iran where the company once concentrated its complete strategy, was about to nationalise its resources. Hence, *BP* learnt its strategy lesson with regard to configuration for the future. Over the last few decades, *BP plc.* grew into one of the largest vertically integrated energy groups in the world.

Rise of BP

A dramatic event in 2010 changed the future of *BP* and put its existence at risk. On April 20th, 2010, a gas release and subsequent explosion occurred on the Deepwater Horizon oil rig working for *BP* in the Gulf of Mexico. Eleven people died as a result of the accident. For three months, the oil well spilled enormous amounts in the sea. It is now estimated that more than 3 million barrels of oil were released; the accident is one of the largest environmental disasters ever. Enormous costs for *BP* are the consequence. The company has to compensate and participate in measures to limit the environmental impact, including fighting the spill, removing and dispersing the oil offshore, protecting the shoreline and clean-up activities of the oil that came ashore. Legitimate claims by local businesses (e.g. fishermen), individuals, government agencies, etc., have to be fulfilled. A trust has been set up with a value of 20 billion USD to make sure that the funds are available in the long-run.

Deepwater Horizon Oil Spill

---

* Sources used for this case study include the corporate websites and various annual reports, investor-relations presentations, as well as explicitly cited sources.

*Divesting 50
Billion USD
of Assets*

After the oil spill, *BP* announced a huge divestment programme to compensate its liabilities related to the accident. By spring 2014, the company had completed the sales of assets of 38 billion USD and announced a further 10 billion USD divestment to be completed by the end of 2015. Thus, within less than 5 years, *BP* drastically downsized and it will have carried out a divestment of almost 50 billion USD.

*Second Largest
Company in the
UK*

Still, with revenues of 390 billion USD in 2013, more than 80,000 employees, and operations in 80 countries, *BP* today is one of the largest MNCs in the world and the second largest British company with a stake of 19.75% in the Russian giant *Rosneft*. It maintains an extensive network of exploration, production, refining and sales operations worldwide (see Figure 1.4).

Figure 1.4

Geographic Spread and Functional Diversity of BP's Worldwide Operations (as of Dec. 31, 2013; without Operations of Rosneft)

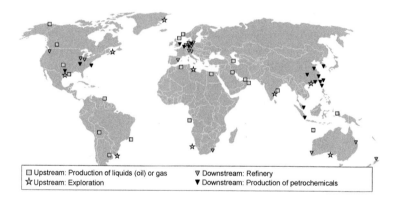

Source: BP 2014a, pp. 4-5.

The Value Chain of BP

*BP's Vertical
Integration*

BP is a vertically integrated, globally distributed company network. It has operations in all stages of the oil and gas value chain, including the exploration and extraction of crude oil and gas, the transportation and trade in oil and gas, the manufacturing stage, including refining of fuels, lubricants and petrochemicals, and, ultimately marketing and sales activities which involve selling the refined petrol through almost 18,000 service stations globally (see Figure 1.5). Usually, the first two stages in the value chain are categorised as "upstream" activities, the last two stages are seen as "downstream" activities. The midstream activities are, in the organisation of *BP*, combined with the upstream activities.

Figure 1.5

Value Chain of BP

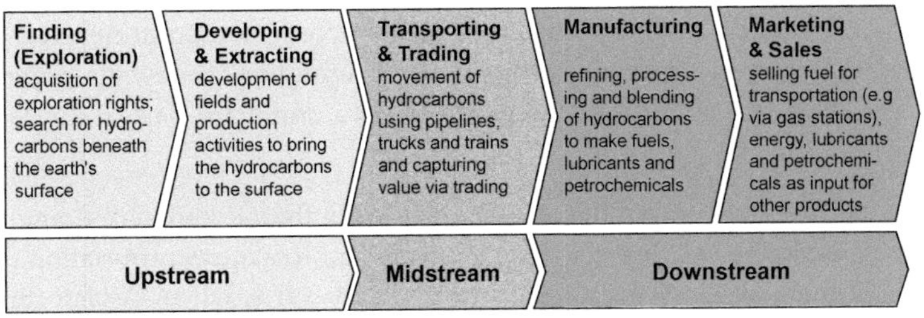

Finding (Exploration) acquisition of exploration rights; search for hydro-carbons beneath the earth's surface	Developing & Extracting development of fields and production activities to bring the hydrocarbons to the surface	Transporting & Trading movement of hydrocarbons using pipelines, trucks and trains and capturing value via trading	Manufacturing refining, process-ing and blending of hydrocarbons to make fuels, lubricants and petrochemicals	Marketing & Sales selling fuel for transportation (e.g via gas stations), energy, lubricants and petrochemi-cals as input for other products
Upstream		Midstream	Downstream	

Source: Adapted from BP 2014a, pp. 2-3.

From the above value chain, it already becomes evident that the *multinational network* of *BP* is highly heterogeneous and that the different activities in the different stages have very different requirements:

■ The configuration of *upstream activities* is strongly determined by where the natural resources are found and were they can be exploited most profitably. The locations are often in developing countries and in politi-cally unstable environments. Concerning the external partners, these are often state-owned or at least with close relationships to the respective governments who tend to keep a strong influence on their energy re-serves. *(Following Natural Resources)*

■ Concerning the *downstream activities*, the configuration is strongly influ-enced by demand patterns. For fuel, for example, the countries of Europe and the USA are important sales markets. Since these activities need to be carried out close to the market (e.g. via networks of service stations), they are often also done in partnerships, e.g. via franchising. Similarly, petrochemicals which are used as inputs for other products are mainly sold in the industrialised countries. *(Following Customers)*

■ These two differing selection criteria for the locations for upstream and downstream activities manifest themselves in a *wide-spread company net-work*. Midstream activities are needed as *links* between those locations. Their geographic locations are therefore almost predetermined, but *BP* does not necessarily have to carry out those activities itself. Huge logis-tics companies have fleets of tankers that distribute oil worldwide. How-ever, it is in particular where highly specific assets are necessary (see *(Linking Up-stream and Downstream)*

19

Chapter 6 for the explanation of *asset specificity*), that *BP* has to invest it-self in the midstream activities, e.g. with pipelines which connect oil and gas fields which are exploited by *BP* to customers or ports.

Upstream - Exploration and Production

International
Sourcing

The oil industry is an example of how the access to natural resources is a main influence factor on the company's configuration. Today, the proved oil reserves are spread around the world (with a dominant part in the Middle East).

Country Risks

One can see until today that the country risks that accompany doing business in unstable political regions can even lead to state expropriation or the danger thereof. This was the case in the early 1970s when *Gaddafi* came to power through a military coup in Libya and nationalised *BP*'s oil operation. In 2008, *BP* struggled with its Russian joint venture *TNK-BP*. Here, the Russian shareholders had tried to take control of the company, and it seemed that the administration in Russia was joining forces with the Russian oligarchs against *BP*. Still, in resource-rich countries, *BP* needs to pursue strategic alliances with such local partners. Nowadays, in countries like Russia or Azerbaijan, these are often state-owned companies. Another mutual benefit of collaboration is that the huge investment risks (with very late pay-offs), which are often associated with those projects, can be shared.

Change in Strategy since 2010

The accident in the Gulf of Mexico has led to a substantial reorganisation and reconfiguration of *BP*'s upstream business. The recent strategy of *BP* in this respect is "value over volume". For example, this meant divesting many non-core assets in the upstream portfolio and maintaining in particular those in which *BP* has particular capabilities, e.g. in deepwater oil reserves. Since 2010, *BP* has reduced its operated installations worldwide by more than half and the operated wells by 35%. Geographically, this meant refocusing on larger units. For example, *BP* has divested many of its smaller upstream operations, e.g. in Vietnam or Columbia. The main objective is to reduce the network "by focussing our investment into the key regions that are also the higher margin regions of our portfolio" (McKay 2014). This means reducing the exposure to low-margin assets and keeping the more profitable ones. The investment focus of *BP* in its upstream projects and operations is now on four key regions: Angola, Azerbaijan, the Gulf of Mexico and the North Sea.

Separating the Onshore Business in the USA

Another major strategic change was recently announced. In March 2014, *BP* informed the public that it would "separate" its US onshore oil and gas business, the so called "US Lower 48". This mainly refers to the shale oil and shale gas business, a technological innovation which drastically changes the business. *BP* faces a dilemma in this business: Participating in the shale oil and gas exploitation is important for the long-term upstream strategy, because "Lower 48 will remain at the forefront of innovation, and drive global learning in unconventionals for the foreseeable future" (McKay 2014). "Unconventional" gas reserves are basically synonymous with shale reserves. However, currently, this business is not very profitable for many of the larger oil companies. An analysis has shown that *BP* underperforms in this activity, partly because of its corporate structure and processes. Many players in this part of the industry are smaller, independent companies which are able to move and decide quicker than a large MNC as *BP*. Separating the management for the US onshore business, including different governance processes, would allow it to compete better, because it could improve speed of innovation and decision making. The business should, though, still remain part of *BP*'s network (Dudley 2014; McKay 2014). Outside observers have a more critical perspective on this separation. They argue that *BP* has the declared objective to become smaller and more profitable. Thus, separating the operations could, at least at first sight, increase the profit margin of the remaining *BP* activities. The separation even raises the question of whether this could be a step towards divesting these operations (Scheck/Fowler 2014).

Midstream - Efficient Bridges from Production to Refining

To connect the production locations of gas and oil with the refineries, the hydrocarbons need to be transported. This is done via different transport mechanisms, often pipelines. Such pipelines are huge projects, often running across different countries and of high economic and political relevance to these countries. One example of such a pipeline is the 1,768-kilometre *Baku-Tbilisi-Ceyhan Pipeline* (BTC) from Azerbaijan at the oil-rich Caspian Sea through Georgia and Turkey to a terminal at the Turkish coast that commenced operation in 2005. The *BTC* pipeline was a challenging engineering project justified by the aim of bypassing the politically unstable territories of Russia and Iran – a cost-efficient and reliable logistic to the Western markets. The pipeline is owned by a consortium of several oil producers; the largest shareholders are *BP* (with about 30%) and the *State Oil Company of Azerbaijan* (*SOCAR*) with 25%. It is operated by *BP*. *Pipelines as Joint Projects*

In Alaska, an agreement for another major midstream project was signed in 2014. This project is so big that it needs the involvement of several companies. For a feasibility study in the so-called *"Alaska LNG export project"*, *BP* works together with *ExxonMobil* and *Conoco-Phillips* who also own gas fields in Alaska, the pipeline company *TransCanada* and the *State of Alaska* to analyse the possibility to commercialise Alaskan gas through "liquified natural *Liquified Gas from Alaska* gas". This project would require building a massive plant to cleanse the produced gas in the vicinity of the gas fields, almost 900 miles of pipeline across Alaska to Nikiski and then the construction of a liquefaction plant, storage facilities and a tanker terminal. The estimated costs for the project are between 45 and 65 billion USD. Again, several companies and – as often in the case of natural resources – the state are involved.

Downstream - Refining and Marketing

BP not only concentrates on finding and extracting oil and gas but also on extending its business down the value chain to refining oil, marketing and distributing petrol and other products to the consumer. Since the Second World War, *BP* has invested heavily in international sales expansion. Moreover, within what was long its second major business segment for a long time, investments in *refineries* in Germany, but also in France and Italy were undertaken. To further expand its downstream business, *BP* sought several large M&As. In 1987, the company acquired the remaining shares of *Sohio*, an American oil company with refineries and a service station network, which was incorporated into *BP America*. In 1998, *BP* merged with *Amoco* to deal with the tough competition by combining their global operations and hence, the largest producer of oil and gas in the USA was formed. Soon, *Amoco's* service stations were re-branded as *BP*. Furthermore in 2000, *BP* was joined by *ARCO*, an American oil company with a large network of pipelines, chemical plants, refineries and over 900 outlets trading as *"ampm"*. Thereafter, all service stations of the *BP Group* on the West side of the Rocky Mountains were branded as *ARCO*. However, in the course of its divestment programme, *ARCO* was sold in 2013 to *Tesoro* from Texas, a refiner and marketer of petroleum products in the Western part of the USA.

Castrol, a producer of lubricants especially for automotive and aeroplane engines, has belonged to the *BP Group* since 2000. *Aral*, with its very modern service station network, became part of the *BP Group* in 2002 and *BP* decided to keep the *Aral* brand. The 630 German *BP* stations were rebranded with the familiar *Aral* blue and white.

Service Stations Often in Alliances

BP now concentrates many of its activities in Europe and the USA on these main brands. The company was also looking for new markets, however, and now operates 850 retail stations in China, in joint ventures with its local partners *Sinopec* and *Petrochina*. In marketing and distribution, joint ventures and alliances are very common. In the UK, as another example, *BP* works in a partnership with *Marks & Spencer*. This retail company has opened 170 of its *"Simply Food"* stores at *BP* forecourts to combine the strengths of an extensive roadside network of *BP* with those of a well-known retailer. In many other countries around the world, the gas stations through which *BP* sells fuels are operated by franchisees, independent entrepreneurs who are allowed to use the *BP* brand and adhere to the *BP* brands and standards. In all, there are 17,800 retail stations operated under the different *BP* brands worldwide, but many of them not by *BP* itself.

A major move in *BPs* downstream business is the divestment of refineries. Since 2000, *BP* has sold 13 refineries, reducing its capacity by almost 40%. It now only operates nine refineries and five joint venture refineries, which are operated by remaining partners. This is part of the strategy to increase the corporate profit margins, since the refining stage is relatively less profitable than the marketing stage. In fact, *BP* now follows a *refining deficit strategy*. It outsources its refining activities to others, reducing its own level of vertical integration and thus enters into even more crucial network partnerships.

Moving Towards a Refining Deficit

Partnerships of BP

As *BP* itself points out, companies in the oil and gas industry must have a broad *network* of close business partnerships. Impressively, in 2013, 54% of the 373 million hours worked by *BP* were carried out by contractors. Concerning the coordination of this network, *BP*'s operating management system includes requirements and practices for working with contractors and the company expects its contractors to adhere consistently to *BP*'s code of conduct when they work on *BP*'s behalf (*BP* 2014b). The strategy to develop deeper, longer-term relationships with fewer partners is relatively new.

Contractors

Furthermore, *BP* operates many different joint ventures with different levels of shareholding in them which in turn determine its influence or control over the joint venture. When *BP* operates the joint venture, its operating management system applies to the operations of the joint venture as well. However, about 46% of upstream production and 13% of its refining capacity in 2013 were from joint ventures for which *BP* is not the operator (BP 2014b).

Joint Ventures

The Minority Stake in Rosneft and a Conflict within the Network

Since 2003, *BP*'s operations in Russia were conducted via the joint venture *TNK-BP* with a consortium of Russian partners, *AAR* (*Alfa Group, Access Industries, Renova*). This was a major part of *BP*'s global network, representing almost one fourth of *BP*'s production and one fifth of its total reserves in 2007. The conflicts within the joint venture have been mentioned above, but eventually they were revolved. However, in 2011, a new, critical problem emerged. *BP* was intending to close a mega-deal with the Russian oil giant *Rosneft* to explore the oil reserves in the Arctic region. But *AAR* managed to

One Joint Venture with 25% of BP's Business

block this deal through a British court because these activities would have compelled with the *TNK-BP* operations. *AAR* rightfully claimed that *BP's* proposed rival joint venture with *Rosneft* would have breached the shareholder agreement governing *TNK-BP* (Webb 2011). This demonstrates the potential conflicts within company networks and potential networks.

Getting a Stake in Rosneft

One year later, *Rosneft*, which is said to be controlled by the Kremlin, announced that it would take over *TNK-BP* from its owners. The deal was completed in spring 2013. *Rosneft* paid *AAR* in cash for their half of *TNK-BP*, 27.7 billion USD. *BP* received 12.5 billion USD in cash and 18.5% *Rosneft* shares. Including the previously owned shares, *BP* now holds 19.75% of *Rosneft*, today the largest oil producer in volume in the world. The relevance of this minority stake (and, thereby, making *Rosneft* a node in *BP's* international network) for *BP* is very high:

New Future in Russia

■ Given the enormous relevance of the reserves in Russia, the CEO of *BP*, Bob Dudley, called the completion of the deal with *Rosneft* a "New Future in Russia" (Dudley 2014, p. 10).

■ Without *Rosneft*, *BP* has dropped in the international ranking of oil producers to No. 5, with 2.3 million barrel per day (and 11.4 billion barrels of proved reserves). Together with the stake in *Rosneft*, *BP* is still the No. 2 in the world with 3.2 million barrel production per day and 18 billion barrels of proved reserves. Thus, via this network partner, *BP* has increased production by 40% and its proved reserves by almost 60%.

■ With this strategic alliance and ownership, *BP* hoped for a preferential treatment and more exclusive deals with *Rosneft* in Russia. However, in the first year after the deal, *Rosneft* has signed a number of agreements with other major oil companies which caused some disappointment among *BP* shareholders.

Joint Venture with Rosneft Amidst Sanctions

However, this changed in May 2014, when *Rosneft* and *BP* signed an exclusive agreement to explore "unconventional oil" in Central Russia in a joint venture which is owned 51% by *Rosneft* and 49% by *BP*. Moscow is hoping to replicate the shale oil boom from the USA and to be able to exploit its own reserves. As *Reuters* (2014) reported *BP's* CEO Dudley saying: "President (Putin) has urged us today to invest into shale oil". Furthermore, it is noteworthy that the signing of the agreement happened amidst the sanctions against Russia following the annexion of the Crimea. *Rosneft's* CEO Igor Sechin is personally being targeted by US sanctions because he is a close ally of President Putin. Putin himself attended the signing ceremony.

Summary and Outlook

BP is one of the largest MNCs in the world, but now finds itself in midst of drastic change with continued enormous divestments, restructuring and focusing its worldwide activities – risk management in particular, of the upstream business.

BP has a global network of subsidiaries with different roles for the company, often focusing on one part of the value chain. Some of them are for oil or gas exploration, some of them are dedicated to refining or transporting oil or gas, and some focus on the sale of fuels via gas service stations. Many of these activities are carried out in partnerships with are institutionalised in different modes. Ranging from consortiums with other oil companies (for example, the BTC pipeline) to a minority stake in one of the largest companies in the world, *Rosneft*, to many joint ventures which are operated by *BP* or by other partners and other contractual relationships for the production or refinery of hydrocarbons – the case of *BP* clearly demonstrates how the activities of a modern MNC are carried out within a network of wholly-owned subsidiaries, partly-owned subsidiaries and external partnerships.

Questions

1. One of the major strategic moves of *BP* in the last few years was the transition with *Rosneft*, giving the company access to huge oil and gas reserves in Russia. Discuss the benefits, disadvantages and risks of this partnership.

2. In 2003, the joint venture *TNK-BP* was formed, which is an example of all the challenges associated with the petroleum industry in a politically unstable country. Describe and analyse the problems that *BP* was experiencing with this Russian engagement.

3. To sell fuel, *BP* has gas stations in many countries. Describe this retail network and the partnerships that *BP* has formed in different countries in order to build and maintain this network. What are the benefits and risks?

Hints

1. Media articles about the conflicts within TNK-*BP* can be found, inter alia, at www.ft.com.

2. Focus on the largest countries in which *BP* sells fuel and investigate the franchising agreements and other partnerships. Information can be found, inter alia, at the corporate website.

References

ANDERSSON, U.; FORSGREN, M. (1996): Subsidiary Embeddedness and Control in the Multinational Corporation, in: International Business Review, Vol. 5, No. 5, pp. 487-508.

ANDERSSON, U.; FORSGREN, M.; HOLM, U. (2002): The Strategic Impact of External Networks: Subsidiary Performance and Competence Development in the Multinational Corporation, in: Strategic Management Journal, Vol. 23, No. 11, pp. 979-996.

BARTLETT, C.A.; BEAMISH, P.W. (2014): Transnational Management: Text, Cases, and Readings in Cross-Border Management, 7th ed., Boston, McGraw-Hill.

BARTLETT, C.A.; GHOSHAL, S. (1987): Managing Across Borders: New Strategic Requirements, in: Sloan Management Review, Vol. 28, No. 4, pp. 7-17.

BARTLETT, C.A.; GHOSHAL, S. (1989): Managing Across Borders: The Transnational Solution, Boston, McGraw-Hill.

BIRKINSHAW, J.; MORRISON, A.J. (1995): Configurations of Strategy and Structure in Subsidiaries of Multinational Corporations, in: Journal of International Business Studies, Vol. 26, No. 4, pp. 729-753.

BIRKINSHAW, J.; HOOD, N.; JONSSON, S. (1998): Building Firm-specific Advantages in Multinational Corporations: The Role of Subsidiary Initiative, in: Strategic Management Journal, Vol. 19, No. 3, pp. 221-241.

BP (2014a): Strategic Report 2013, London.

BP (2014b): Website of BP Corporation, http://www.BP.com, accessed on July 10, 2014.

BUCKLEY, P. (1996): The Role of Management in International Business Theory: A Meta-analysis and Integration of the Literature on International Business and International Management, in: Management International Review, Vol. 35, No. 1 Special Issue, pp. 7-54.

DAS, T.; TENG, B. (1999): Managing Risks in Strategic Alliances, in: Academy of Management Executive, Vol. 13, No. 4, pp. 50-62.

DUDLEY, B. (2014): The BP Proposition: Investor Update March 2014, ww.bp.com/content/dam/bp/pdf/investors/Investor_update_2014_presentati on.pdf, accessed on July 24, 2014.

DUNNING, J. (1993): Multinational Enterprise and the Global Economy, New York, Addison-Wesley.

DUNNING, J. (1997): Alliance Capitalism in Global Business, London, Routledge.

FORSGREN, M.; PEDERSEN, T. (1997): Centres of Excellence in Multinational Companies: The Case of Denmark, Working Paper 2/1997, Institute of International Economics and Management, Copenhagen Business School, Copenhagen.

FROST, T.; BIRKINSHAW, J.; ENSIGN, P. (2002): Centers of Excellence in Multinational Corporations, in: Strategic Management Journal, Vol. 23, No. 11, pp. 997-1018.

GHOSHAL, S.; BARTLETT, C.A. (1991): The Multinational Corporation as an Interorganizational Network, in: Academy of Management Review, Vol. 16, No. 4, pp. 768-792.

GUPTA, A.K.; GOVINDARAJAN, V. (1991): Knowledge Flows and the Structure of Control within Multinational Corporations, in: Academy of Management Review, Vol. 16, No. 4, pp. 768-792.

GUPTA, A.K.; GOVINDARAJAN, V. (2000): Knowledge Flows within Multinational Corporations, in: Strategic Management Journal, Vol. 21, No. 4, pp. 473-496.

HAKANSSON, H.; JOHANSON, J. (1988): Formal and Informal Cooperation Strategies in International Industrial Networks, in: CONTRACTOR, F.; LORANGE, P. (Eds.): Cooperative Strategies in International Business, New York, Emerald Group, pp. 369-379.

HEDLUND, G. (1986): The Hypermodern MNC: A Heterarchy?, in: Human Resource Management, Vol. 25, No. 1, pp. 9-35.

MARSON, J. (2013): Rosneft Completes $55 Billion Takeover of TNK-BP, http://online.wsj.com/news/articles/SB10001424127887324103504578374184188808640, accessed on July 3, 2014.

MARTINEZ, J.; JARILLO, J. (1989): The Evolution of Research on Coordination Mechanisms in Multinational Corporations, in: Journal of International Business Studies, Vol. 20, No. 3, pp. 489-514.

1

MCKAY, I. (2014): BP Investor Update of the Chief Executive Upstream, http://www.bp.com/content/dam/bp/pdf/investors/Investor_Update_script_s lides_v2.pdf , accessed on August 08, 2014.

MORSCHETT, D. (2007): Institutionalisierung und Koordination von Aus- landseinheiten: Analyse von Industrie- und Dienstleistungsunternehmen, Wiesbaden, Gabler.

NOHRIA, N.; GHOSHAL, S. (1997): The Differentiated Network: Organizing Multinational Corporations for Value Creation, San Francisco, Jossey-Bass.

PICOT, A.; REICHWALD, R.; WIGAND, R. (2003): Die grenzenlose Unter- nehmung, 5th ed., Wiesbaden, Gabler.

REUTERS (2014): Rosneft, BP Agree to Explore for Shale Oil in Russia Amid Sanctions, http://www.reuters.com/article/2014/05/24/us-russia-forum-ros- neft- idUSBREA4N07R20140524, accessed on August 08, 2014.

SCHECK, J.; FOWLER, T. (2014): BP to Carve Out U.S. Onshore Assets, http://online.wsj.com/news/articles/SB10001424052702303630904579418880723703334, accessed on June 22, 2014.

SCHMID, S.; KUTSCHKER, M. (2003): Rollentypologien für ausländische Tochtergesellschaften in Multinationalen Unternehmungen, in: HOLT- BRÜGGE, D. (Ed.): Management Multinationaler Unternehmungen, Heidel- berg, Physica-Verlag, pp. 161-182.

SCHMID, S.; BÄURLE, I.; KUTSCHKER, M. (1999): Ausländische Tochterge- sellschaften als Kompetenzzentren: Ergebnisse einer empirischen Untersu- chung, in: KUTSCHKER, M. (Ed.): Management verteilter Kompetenzen in multinationalen Unternehmen: Tagungsband der Wissenschaftlichen Kom- mission "Internationales Management", Wiesbaden, Gabler, pp. 100-126.

WEBB, T. (2011): BP's Russian Deal with Rosneft Blocked by Court, http://www.the guardian.com/business/2011/mar/24/bp-russian-deal-rosneft- blocked-court, accessed on July 17, 2014.

Chapter 2

The Integration/Responsiveness- and the AAA-Frameworks

MNCs are exposed to two sets of strategic forces to which they must respond but which are at least partly conflicting, namely forces for global integration and forces for local responsiveness. In the Integration/Responsiveness-framework (I/R-framework), a fourfold typology of MNCs has been proposed based on the differing strengths of the two forces. More recently, the AAA-framework, comprising adaptation, aggregation and arbitrage, has been proposed as an improved concept to describe MNC strategies. Both frameworks are described in detail in this Chapter.

Forces for Global Integration and Forces for Local Responsiveness

One of the most influential typologies of MNCs stems from the studies by Doz, Prahalad, Bartlett and Ghoshal in the 1970s and 1980s. The tension between external forces towards adaptation to the local environment in the different host countries ("local responsiveness") and the forces towards a standardised approach, leading to global efficiency by a worldwide integrated behaviour ("global integration"), are the basis of this typology (Doz 1980; Prahalad/Doz 1987; Bartlett/Beamish 2014):

■ *Global integration* means interconnecting the international activities of the MNC across all countries, identifying the strengths of the large company, and trying to achieve synergy effects. Thus, the different countries in which an MNC operates can be linked to each other. This could be, e.g., because economies of scale are particularly high in a specific industry, leading to the necessity of internationally standardised products. Alternatively, it could result from comparative cost advantages of a country that offer an incentive to specialise the activities of certain foreign subsidiaries, leading to interdependence between the worldwide activities. Necessity for worldwide learning, in order to exploit knowledge company-wide that has been created in a particular country or the situation in which relevant actors around the MNC (e.g. customers, competitors, and suppliers) are the same in different foreign markets, enhances the requirement and the potential to coordinate closely the different international activities. These interdependencies between countries (which vary by industry) are called "forces for global integration".

Global Integration

Local
Responsiveness

■ At the same time, an MNC operates in heterogeneous conditions in many different host countries. The local unit in each country deals with different local customers and host governments, different market and distribution structures, and different competitors. Multinational flexibility, i.e., the ability of a company to exploit the opportunities that arise from this heterogeneity, is necessary. This contingency condition for MNCs is referred to as the "forces for local responsiveness". This pressure to adapt varies by industry.

Forces for Global Integration

In a global industry, a firm's competitive position in one country is strongly affected by its position in other countries. The forces for global integration, also called *industry globalisation drivers*, can be divided into four categories (Yip 1989; Bartlett/Beamish 2014, pp. 102-105):

■ market drivers

■ cost drivers

■ governmental drivers

■ competitive drivers.

Market
Drivers

First of all, *homogenous customer needs* in the different markets may create opportunities to sell standardised products. With common customer needs, marketing becomes transferable across countries. The *culture convergence thesis* by Levitt (1983) suggests that different cultures become more similar, and lifestyles and tastes converge worldwide. However, this thesis is not without opposition. Meanwhile, more and more often, particularly in B2B markets, companies also meet *global customers*, i.e., companies (sometimes even private consumers) that are their customers in different country markets, e.g. different subsidiaries of the same MNC. Similarly, *global channels* such as large international retailers like *Walmart* and *Tesco*, or global e-commerce channels like *Amazon*, emerge in certain industries. All these aspects enhance the need for globalisation in an industry.

Cost
Drivers

From a cost perspective, different industries have different incentives to standardise. For example, *economies of scale* in a particular production plant can be increased with standardised products that are exported to different country markets. Economies of scale and scope as well as *experience curves* differ from industry to industry, though. This can be caused by different production technologies. The greater the potential economies of scale and the steeper the experience curve, the more likely an industry is to turn global. Furthermore, industries where *product development* is *expensive* and at the same time *product lifecycles* are *short* or technology is fast-changing usually try to use global scale effects. While *global sourcing efficiencies* might be given in an industry, leading to concentration of supply and manufacturing, inter-country differences in labour costs and factor endowments might make concentration of production useful. Over the last few decades, logistics costs have generally been decreasing, making globalisation easier to achieve. However, how energy prices, climate change, and also technological innovations will influence logistics and consequently location strategies remain to be seen.

Many governmental drivers also have an influence on the need for globalisation in an industry. For example, uniform *technical standards* are necessary for product standardisation, *liberal trading regulations* with low tariff and non-tariff barriers to trade, and common market regulations are drivers for globalisation, making cross-border trade easier. Inversely, high trade barriers obviously reduce the forces towards globalisation, protecting local particularities. *Governmental Drivers*

As the most important competitive driver, *global competitors* enhance the need for globalisation. Only companies that manage their worldwide operations as interdependent units can implement a coordinated strategy and use a competitive strategy sometimes called *"global chess"* (Bartlett/Beamish 2014, p. 105), i.e., responding to threats in one market by reactions in other markets. Additionally, large multinational companies offering the same products and brands around the world also promote the convergence of tastes and customer demands. International networks, e.g., in production, that also enhance the interdependence of countries and markets emerge in the presence of many MNCs. *Competitive Drivers*

The overall level of globalisation of an industry can be measured by the ratio of cross-border trade to total worldwide production, the ratio of cross-border investment to total capital investment, the percentage of sales of worldwide standardised products, or the proportion of industry revenue generated by large MNCs.

Forces for Local Responsiveness

Alternatively, depending on the industry, companies are facing another set of influence factors that make local responsiveness necessary (see, e.g., Hollensen 2014, pp. 25-26).

The predominant reason for the need for local responsiveness is a strong difference in *customer demand*. This might be caused by profound cultural differences in tastes, different environmental conditions (climate, topography, etc.), or different income levels and income distribution, among many other factors. A different *structure of the distributive sector* might make adapta- *Differences in Demand* tions to the distribution strategy necessary. A different *competitive situation* in different markets might also force a company to change its strategy, adapting it to the local market conditions. Similarly, *protectionism* by governments often leads to the need to produce locally and/or adapt products to specific markets. While the need for adaptation has occurred at the country level in the past, it now increasingly occurs at the level of regional integration areas such as the EU (see Chapter 7).

Differences in Country Conditions

Local responsiveness can also become necessary or beneficial due to either different labour conditions, e.g., labour cost or skill level, that require adaptation of production processes to optimise efficiency, or the availability or non-availability of suppliers. A low number of potential suppliers might make a higher level of vertical integration in the production steps more or less efficient due to a lack of alternatives. Different work attitudes that may be rooted in different cultures (see Chapter 9) might make different leadership styles more or less effective in different countries.

The I/R-Framework as a Matrix

While both forces are interconnected, they are not seen as opposing extremes of a continuum of possible situations but rather as two separate dimensions.

Figure 2.1 | *The Integration/Responsiveness-Framework*

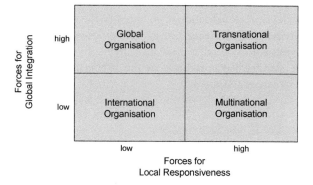

Source: Adapted from Bartlett/Ghoshal 1989, p. 438.

While the full independence of both dimensions is sometimes doubted in the literature (see, e.g., Engelhard/Dähn 2002; Morschett 2007), the advantage of the assumption is that one can try to distinguish between both sets of forces more clearly and the potential external situations that an MNC faces can be illustrated in a matrix. The typology of Bartlett/Ghoshal (1989) that builds on this two-dimensional framework is the most commonly used. In this model, MNCs are grouped according to their strategic orientation. The framework has been very influential in IB literature, in particular that regarding the transnational MNC. The four strategy types are subsequently described in more detail (see, among many other authors, Harzing 2000, and Bart-lett/Beamish 2014, for a more comprehensive description).

International Organisations

MNCs with an "international" strategic orientation tend to think of their foreign activities as *remote outposts* whose main role is to support the parent company by contributing incremental sales. This strategy type can be linked to the international life cycle model by Vernon (1966), since the focus is on exploiting knowledge, new products, or processes of the parent company by transferring them to foreign markets. Foreign countries are rather seen as a source of short-term and incremental profits. Accordingly, the company does not adapt to the specific host country, and the foreign activities are also not systematically integrated in the MNC. This strategy type is *ethnocentric* since the foreign activities only secure the company in its home territory. A strong dependence of the foreign subsidiary on the resources of the home country is a consequence.

Global Organisations

Companies with a "global" strategic orientation focus their organisation on achieving economies of scale. They are usually to be found in industries where forces for global integration are strong and forces for local respon-siveness rather low. *Price competition* in global industries is high, thus, the dominant strategic need is *global efficiency*. The most relevant resources are concentrated in the headquarters and decisions are *highly centralised*. The MNCs attempt to rationalise their production by producing *standardised products* in concentrated production plants that fulfil a worldwide demand volume. Usually, these production plants are located in the home country and the most relevant task of the foreign subsidiary is to act as a *"pipeline"* for the parent company, selling products in its local market. R&D and inno-vation are also concentrated in the home country. Information flows and product flows are *unidirectional*; the MNC follows a *centralised hub model* (see Chapter 1).

Focus on Economies of Scale

Multinational Organisations

The multinational organisation, being in the lower right corner of the matrix in Figure 2.1, focuses primarily on *national differences* to achieve its strategic objectives. Many of its characteristics are the *reverse of the global organisation*. Products, processes, strategies, even management systems, might be *flexibly modified* to each country to *adapt to local needs* and sometimes to *local governmental regulations*. This adaptation to the local markets is facilitated by *local production* and *local R&D*. While the main task of subsidiaries is to identify and fulfil local needs, the foreign subsidiary is also provided with the necessary local resources to respond to the local needs. The subsidiaries are independent of the headquarters and are also not linked to peer subsidiaries in other countries. The organisation takes the form of a *decentralised federation*.

Transnational Organisations

While global organisations and multinational organisations emphasise either global efficiency and integration or multinational flexibility and local responsiveness, the transnational organisation tries to respond *simultaneously to both strategic needs*. Thus, particularly in industries where both forces are equally strong, transnational organisations reach for the benefits of combining characteristics of both global and multinational companies.

Accordingly, a transnational strategy refers to becoming strongly responsive to local needs while still achieving the benefits of global integration. As described in Chapter 1, the underlying model is the *integrated network*, where key activities and resources are neither centralised in the headquarters nor fully decentralised to each country. Instead, resources and activities are *geographically dispersed but specialised*, leading to *scale economies and flexibility*. A certain level of product adaptation to local needs is combined with *cross-border production processes* that still concentrate production, such as that for specific common components, in single locations. This leads to *reciprocal and horizontal product flows*. Large flows of products, people, capital, and knowledge between subsidiaries are characteristic of transnational organisations. Innovation occurs in different locations and is subsequently diffused worldwide, while foreign subsidiaries can serve in strategic roles, such as for producing specific products, or as *centres of excellence*.

While this strategy type is often seen as an *ideal type* in literature, it is highly complex, costly and difficult to implement, and very ambitious. Empirical studies often show that few MNCs actually represent this type, and while many recent textbooks and management consultants invariably promote the transnational organisation as the "best" MNC type, this should be carefully analysed. The original authors recommend the complex transnational organisation only for MNCs that are confronted with a complex environment with equally high forces for integration and responsiveness. *"Organizational complexity is costly and difficult to manage, and simplicity, wherever possible, is a virtue"* (Ghoshal/Nohria 1993, p. 24). However, more and more industries are currently developing into this situation of complexity.

Comparison of the Four MNC Types

Table 2.1 summarises and compares a number of different characteristics for the four MNC types.

Selected Characteristics of the Four MNC Types

Table 2.1

	International	Global	Multinational	Transnational
Role of Subsidiary	sale of HQ products	implementation of HQ strategies	identification and exploitation of local opportunities	differentiated contribution to the worldwide competitive advantages of the MNC
Network Model	centralised hub	centralised hub	decentralised federation	integrated network
Vertical Product Flows	high, sequential	high, sequential	low	bidirectional
Inter-subsidiary Product Flows	low	low	low	high
Centralisation of Decisions	high	high	low	medium (decentralised centralisation)
Management Transfers, Visits, Joint Working Teams	low	high	low	high
Centres of Excellence	low	low	low	high
Product Modification	low	low	high	high
Local Production	low	low	high	medium
Dependency	strong dependence	strong dependence	in-dependence	inter-dependence

Source: Summarised and adapted from Macharzina 1993, p. 83, p. 102; Harzing 2000, p. 113; Bartlett/Beamish 2014, pp. 198-201.

Perlmutter's EPRG Concept

A similar typology of MNCs also prominent in International Business research has been proposed by Perlmutter (Perlmutter 1969; Wind/Douglas/Perlmutter 1973). Perlmutter developed the EPRG scheme, distinguishing between ethnocentric, polycentric, regiocentric, and geocentric attitudes. In this scheme, he recognises that managers of MNCs have different attitudes or a different *"state of mind"*, i.e., assumptions upon which key decisions in the MNC are made.

■ In the *ethnocentric* state of mind, the home country is implicitly considered to be superior. Key positions in foreign subsidiaries are staffed with expatriates from the home country and decisions are taken in the headquarters. Foreign activities are seen as less relevant than home-country activities and exports are the main entry mode. The subsidiary is highly dependent on headquarters.

■ *Polycentric* firms start with the assumption that host-country cultures are strongly different and adaptation is necessary. They acknowledge that local employees are more effective for this task and that decentralised decisions help to exploit local differences effectively.

■ While the polycentric attitude strives for optimal local solutions, this might be sub-optimal for the whole organisation. As a further development, the *geocentric* attitude emphasises interdependencies and aims for a collaborative approach between headquarters and subsidiaries as well as among subsidiaries. An optimal allocation of resources and synergy effects are aimed for.

■ The *regiocentric* approach is a mix between the polycentric and the geocentric approaches. Strategies, products, processes, etc., are closely coordinated within different regions (e.g. Europe, North America), while the regions operate relatively independently of each other.

EPRG and the I/R-Framework

While the similarity to the I/R-framework is obvious and both approaches can be linked via the three network models, with the centralised hub model being ethnocentric, a decentralised federation model being polycentric, and the integrated network being the organisational response in the case of a geocentric state of mind, there are two major differences. While the I/R-framework offers contingency conditions under which external industry forces influence an MNC strategy in a particular way, Perlmutter offers a more qualitative explanation based on the management style or on the *state of mind*. Secondly, Perlmutter's EPRG scheme is not systematically based on describing characteristics. The "regiocentric" approach, however, which is very common in modern MNCs and also very prominent in recent IB literature (see, e.g., Rugman/Verbeke 2004), was identified by Perlmutter but is not considered in the I/R-framework.

Different Levels of Integration and Responsiveness

The I/R-framework is a *contingency framework* that derives MNC strategies from a given external context. The main assumption is that an MNC in a specific industry exposed to a particular configuration of forces for global integration and local responsiveness needs to develop a strategy in accordance with the external context. However, while the original framework clearly emphasises that MNCs have complex sets of options and that not only industry characteristics determine company strategies, management literature has often applied the framework in a deterministic manner, implying that MNCs in a particular cell of the matrix *have* to use a specific strategy. Consequences were immediately drawn at the company level as a result of a categorisation of industries: "the primary use of the 'I-R grid' was to map industries, and therefore to indicate what strategy a firm should pursue" (Westney/Zaheer 2001, pp. 356-357).

Three Levels of the I/R-Framework

Figure 2.2

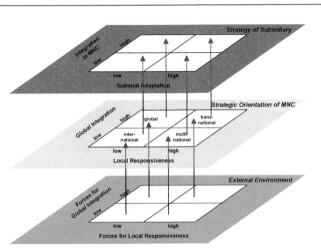

Source: Morschett 2007, p. 396.

Figure 2.2 shows an extended model for a more detailed analysis of integration and responsiveness, consisting of three levels:

- the *external environment*, where the forces for global integration and the forces for local responsiveness are at different levels, depending on the industry

- the *MNC's strategic orientation*, where some MNCs prefer to use a global strategy and others a more multinational approach, i.e., to display different levels of global integration and local responsiveness

- the *strategy of the subsidiary*, which can differ and be more or less integrated in the MNC, and which can be more or less adaptable in its behaviour to the local market, as becomes evident in the role typologies (see Chapter 3).

Strategic Orientation of the MNC

Many authors use the I/R-framework to describe different MNC *strategies* ("internationalisation strategies") or *organisational types* ("MNC organisations"). Kutschker (1999, p. 110) labels the four I/R-strategies *"archetypes of international companies"*. Here, *instead of forces*, the *degree* of integration and the *degree* of localisation of the MNC are used. In this case, as described above, the four strategy alternatives are seen as typical *bundles of strategy elements*, consisting of specific coordination mechanisms, product flows, product modifications, etc.

Externally Determined Strategy or Strategic Choice

In a contingency-oriented perspective, these strategies are often derived from the context, according to most authors. The model is based on the assumption that a match between external forces and company strategy is more efficient than a mismatch (De la Torre/Esperanca/Martínez 2003, pp. 67-69). As Yip (1989) argued, the *globalisation of the strategy* has to be aligned with the *globalisation potential of the industry*. But still, companies have a certain level of freedom in the development of a strategy, which is called *strategic choice* (Child 1972). MNCs may choose alternative strategies based on their internal resources, strategic priorities, and other considerations. Clearly, external characteristics are only one part of the factors influencing company strategy and internal forces also play an important role in the determination of strategy.

Strategy of a Specific Subsidiary

Different Subsidiary Strategies in the Same MNC

Similarly, it has to be recognised that an MNC strategy does not necessarily lead to uniformity at the level of subsidiaries. The fact that the MNC follows a global strategy or a multinational strategy alone does not fully determine the subsidiary level (Jarillo/Martinez 1990; Birkinshaw/Morrison 1995). The level of local responsiveness and the level of integration may widely differ within a particular MNC. One reason is that the forces for global integration and the forces for local responsiveness not only differ by industry but may also vary from country to country. For example, trade barriers might be low, technological standardisation high, and consumer demand similar in most countries, but the reverse might be true in others.

Contingency but Not Determination

Differentiation between subsidiaries, while most prominent in the transnational organisation, is to some degree used in all types of MNCs. Thus, in the perspective of the "differentiated network" (Nohria/Ghoshal 1997), the level of the subsidiary must be planned separately. While it is evident that multinational-oriented MNCs have a relatively high percentage of independent subsidiaries with high autonomy to exploit local market opportunities (Harzing 2000, p. 107), and most subsidiaries of an MNC with a global strategy will be dependent on the headquarters and merely implement the global strategy, heterogeneity between subsidiaries is common.

Consequently, even in globally oriented MNCs, some subsidiaries will have higher degrees of freedom and might even take over strategic roles. Particularly in transnational organisations, it is obvious that the role of each subsidiary is planned separately (see Chapter 3) and it may, in fact, for some subsidiaries mean a very low level of adaptation and a strong integration in the MNC network, usually characteristics of a global strategy.

AAA-Framework

More recently, Ghemawat (2007) from Harvard Business School proposed a three-dimensional framework to describe international strategy. It clearly builds on the integration-responsiveness tension but extends it. As Ghemawat (2007, p. 60) argues: "assuming that the principal tension in global strategy is between scale economies and local responsiveness encourages companies to ignore another functional response to the challenge of cross-border integration: arbitrage. Some companies are finding large opportunities for value creation in exploiting, rather than simply adjusting to or overcoming, the differences they encounter at the borders of their various markets." The so called AAA-triangle encompasses three dimensions of the international strategy:

- *Adaptation* intends to increase sales by optimally exploiting the local demand.

- *Aggregation* intends to reach economies of scale by creating global operations.

- *Arbitrage* intends to exploit differences between countries, often by establishing different parts of the value chain in different locations.

In fact, with this third dimension Ghemawat makes an explicit option that Bartlett and Ghoshal had already included in their description of the transnational strategy but which they had fused into one dimension with "local responsiveness".

Figure 2.3

AAA-Framework with Profiles of Two Companies

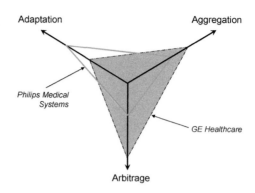

Source: Adapted from Ghemawat 2007, p. 66.

Focus on One or Two Dimensions

Ghemawat emphasises that companies could make progress in all three dimensions but that there are substantial tensions between them. Using all three dimensions effectively is therefore difficult and MNCs should instead make a strategic choice and prioritise their efforts, which would usually lead to a focus on one or two of the dimensions. In Figure 2.3, the model illustrates two companies in the diagnostic imaging industry.

Table 2.2

Selected Characteristics of the Three Dimensions of International Strategy

	Adaptation	Aggregation	Arbitrage
Competitive Advantage *Why should we globalize at all?*	to achieve local relevance through national focus while exploiting some economies of scale	to achieve scale and scope economies through international standardization	to achieve absolute economies through international specialization
Configuration *Where should we locate operations overseas?*	mainly in foreign countries that are similar to the home base, to limit the effects of cultural, administrative, geographic, and economic distance		in a more diverse set of countries, to exploit some elements of distance
Coordination *How should we connect international operations?*	by country, with emphasis on achieving local presence within borders	by business, region, or customers, with emphasis on horizontal relation-ships for cross-border economies of scale	by function, with emphasis on vertical relationships, even across organizational boundaries
Controls *What types of extremes should we watch for?*	excessive variety or complexity	excessive standardization, with emphasis on scale	narrowing spreads

Source: Ghemawat 2007, p. 61.

Detailed recommendations and considerations are made for each dimension, and examples of companies and their strategic profiles, usually focusing on two of the three dimensions, are described in Ghemawat's articles. Table 2.2 summarises a number of different characteristics for the three dimensions.

Conclusion and Outlook

The I/R-framework builds on a *tension* that is usually considered the most relevant, particularity in International Management: the *dual forces* for global integration and local responsiveness. Global efficiency on the one hand and multinational flexibility on the other hand are considered primary objectives of the MNC that are difficult to achieve simultaneously. Furthermore, worldwide learning is considered crucial for the innovation capacity of an MNC and a certain level of integration is beneficial for MNC learning.

Four MNC strategy types are proposed in the I/R-framework, each for a specific external context. While the transnational strategy is the dominant strategy recommendation in literature, most empirical studies show that few MNCs actually follow this strategy. Thus, it is an "idealized MNC model" (Birkinshaw/Morrison 1995, p. 737) rather than a common phenomenon and the exception rather than the rule.

Transnational Strategies the Exception Rather than the Rule

It should be kept in mind that all the strategy types are considered adequate – under given *circumstances* – and that the complexity of a transnational strategy is ambitious and only justified if the requirements of the external environment are complex, with simultaneously high needs for global integration and local responsiveness. Unfortunately, this situation occurs more and more often and thus the transnational strategy will likely become more common in the future.

Complexity Only if Necessary

The AAA-framework shows that it is useful to explicitly investigate a third dimension of MNC strategy, arbitrage. Companies can use differences between countries by establishing different value chain activities in the optimal location. Based on the three dimensions of the framework, a myriad of MNC strategies is possible, even though it is again recommended to avoid over-complexity. Ghemawat also recommends focussing on one or two of the three dimensions, which would result in about six generic strategies.

Multitude of Strategies in Three Dimensions

Further Reading

BARTLETT, C.A.; BEAMISH, P.W. (2014): Transnational Management: Text, Cases, and Readings in Cross-Border Management, 7th ed., Boston, McGraw-Hill.

GHEMAWAT, P. (2007): Managing Differences: The Central Challenge of Global Strategy, in: Harvard Business Review, Vol. 85, No. 3, pp. 59-68.

HARZING, A. (2000): An Empirical Analysis and Extension of the Bartlett and Goshal Typology of Multinational Companies, in: Journal of International Business Studies, Vol. 31, No. 1, pp. 101-120.

Case Study: Retailing[*]

The Retail Industry

The retail sector is being confronted with unprecedented changes. Originating from social and economic trends and a broader set of technologies, unconventional approaches, flexibility, collaboration and rapid learning strategies are becoming more and more important for retailers worldwide (Deloitte 2014, pp. 9-11). Even if retailing is one of the world's largest industries (Zentes/Morschett/Schramm-Klein 2011, p. 1), the sector faces intense competition, slow growth in major developed markets, volatile input prices and excess retail capacity in many developed markets (Deloitte 2014, p. 31).

Wave of Internationalisation

While retailing has traditionally been a very local business and internationalisation has lagged significantly behind the manufacturing sector, the last two decades have seen remarkable change. A wave of internationalisation has resulted in a high level of expansion of the largest retailers (Swoboda/Foscht/Pennemann 2009). The top ten retailers operated, on average, in 16.3 countries, in 2012 and one third of their combined retail revenue originated from foreign activities (Deloitte 2014, pp. 20-30). According to Deloitte (see Table 2.3), fashion retailers had the highest international performance followed by hardlines and leisure goods. Food retailers scored last.

---

[*] Sources used for this case study include the companies' web sites, various annual and company reports, investor-relations presentations as well as sources explicitly cited.

Level of Globalisation by Retail Sector in 2012

Table 2.3

	Retail Revenue from Foreign Operations	Average Countries	Single-Country Operators
Top 250	24.3%	10.0	36.8%
Fashion Goods	29.8%	22.2	23.8%
Hardlines & Leisure Goods	26.6%	13.1	26.9%
Fast-moving Consumer Goods	23.3%	5.1	44.5%
Diversified	22.6%	10.3	36.8%

Source: Deloitte 2014, p. 24.

Forces for Global Integration and Forces for Local Responsiveness

Over the last few decades, strong forces for global integration have been influencing the retail industry. These forces can be categorised in different ways, but can generally be divided into: buyer behaviour, costs, regulatory, competition and technology (Gillespie 2011, pp. 50-51).

- In different retail sectors, consumer needs have become more homogeneous around the world. This has been driven partly by cultural convergence. Increased travel and communication tools lead to a comparison of people's lifestyles and their standards of living with others. Cross-national TV series and music channels have been encouraging the notion of a global consumer (De Mooij 2003, p. 183). Moreover, the growing middle-class and disappearing income differences across countries support the *homogenisation of consumer behaviour*. *Converging Consumer Needs*

- Given that retailing is an increasingly complex business with high costs for infrastructure (stores, warehouses, IT-systems, etc.), economies of scale play a major role. An integration of activities – in particular of procurement activities – is necessary to gain *economies of scale* in procurement and to gain negotiation power over the supplier (Zentes/Morschett/Schramm-Klein 2011, pp. 321-332). *Costs*

- In the past, a number of multilateral *trade agreements* have accelerated global integration. Within the EU, free trade allows retailers to transport goods from central warehouses to their stores in different countries without custom duties and other obstacles. *Trade Liberalisation*

- Furthermore, since many retailers have started to internationalise, more and more often, different retailers are confronted with *global competition*. *Global Competitors*

Whether in home improvement retailing, in food retailing, in consumer electronics, more and more often the same companies meet as competitors in different foreign markets. To play such "global chess" effectively, a certain level of coordination is necessary.

ICT Technologies

■ New ICT technologies facilitate a free flow of goods and information, thus changing the retailing landscape. Information is available within seconds and enhances pricing transparency, as well as minimising cultural distance and homogenised consumer markets. Particularly store-based retailers are faced with the threat that ever more consumers will shop online in the near future, regardless of national boundaries. These *cross-border Internet sales* and delivery networks will displace more and more notorious structures (Wrigley 2010, p. 4; Deloitte 2011, pp. 3-4).

Heterogeneous Demand

On the other hand, localisation is one of the effective ways for store-based retailers to compete with e-commerce multinationals. While a trend towards convergence can be observed, consumer demand is still heterogeneous. The differences are enormous, especially concerning the new markets for retailers, like Eastern Europe, China or even India. Consequently, expenditure on clothing, electronics, appliances, etc., also differs widely. In addition, consumer tastes differ for *cultural reasons*. Whether, for instance, preferences converge concerning interior design, which influences furniture retailers and home improvement stores more and more, consumers around the world still differ.

Figure 2.4 | *Forces for Global Integration and Local Responsiveness in Different Retail Sectors*

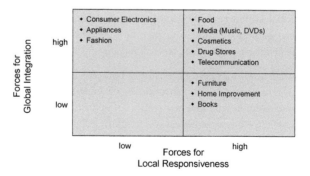

Convergence and Divergence

Figure 2.4 represents an attempt to categorise different retail sectors by the different *I/R-forces*. For example, in consumer electronics, consumer demand is rather similar worldwide and the standardisation of products and existence of only a few suppliers worldwide lead predominantly to the need for global integration. On the other hand, the supply of many product categories in home improvement is still rather local, as are consumer tastes. With "transnational" requirements, food retailing is experiencing enormous cost pressure and the emergence of global competitors, leading to the need for global integration. At the same time, disparate consumer income and consumer tastes, as well as remaining trade barriers (including the relevance of freshness, which hinders long logistics chains), lead to the necessity to adapt activities to the local markets. Similarly, when considering into drug stores and cosmetics, suppliers are more and more often the same, but consumer behaviour regarding cosmetics still differs greatly. For example, while tanning creams are sold in Western countries, whitening creams are sold in cosmetic stores in Asia. The existence of different skin types, hair colours, etc., in the human population globally, requires simultaneously high global integration and local responsiveness.

Strategic Orientation of Retail Companies

The complex and varied environmental drivers described above, influence industries, especially the retail sector, and affect strategies of global integration and local responsiveness in a variety of ways (Rugman/Collinson 2012, p. 318). Apart from the primary use to map industries, the I/R-framework indicates what strategy a firm is able to pursue in an international surrounding (Westney/Zaheer 2010, p. 348). Some chains like *Walmart* and *Best Buy* have perfected the single-minded strategy of standardisation implemented in store formats, merchandise mix, operating and marketing processes. Others, like *Kingfisher* react more flexibly to serve consumer differences (Guan 2010, p. 2).

As an example of a generally global orientation, *Hollister*, a subsidiary of *Abercrombie & Fitch*, can be used. Founded in 2000, it is designed to attract teenagers aged between 14 and 18 years. Built on a fictional background, the story of *Hollister* claims that J.M. Hollister founded the company in 1922 to bring the "Southern California Lifestyle" to the world. This vision is evident in the assortment as well as in the store layout and becomes the core of the retailer. Starting with the first store in Columbus, Ohio, the retailer operates today in many different countries with more than 580 stores worldwide. In addition to the bricks and mortar locations, the first online shop in the USA was launched in 2003. Today there are more than 60 stores across the UK, Germany, Italy, Spain and other locations within Europe.

Global Orientation

Hollister pursues a *globally centralised strategy* worldwide. All strategic processes like procurement, marketing activities and human resources are centred and managed by the headquarters in New Albany, Ohio. Both exterior and interior store layout remind the consumer of a surf atmosphere, looking like beach huts or consisting of a series of video monitors which reflect the scene of *Huntington Beach*. The interior is dimly light with spotlights, scented with the company's fragrance and equipped with a lounge area. In total, the corporate policy establishes the design, furniture, fixtures, music as well as the look of the sales associates and the merchandise presentation. Everything is carefully planned and coordinated by the company to create a consistent and unique shopping experience reflecting the *Hollister* lifestyle and conveying the principal elements as well as the personality of the brand. Apart from all that, an official manual describes the look of the employees, called store models, and instructs them which items can be worn together, and how to style them. Officially, customers should be addressed in English and the presented assortment is specified by the headquarters and changes every two months.

The two distribution centers located in New Albany, Ohio, manage the receipt, storage, sorting, packing and distribution of merchandise for the North American stores and Asian direct-to-consumer customers. *Hollister* also uses a *third-party distribution center* in the Netherlands to manage the receipt, storage, sorting, packing and distribution of merchandise delivered to stores and direct-to-consumer customers in Europe and a third-party distribution center in Hong Kong for the stores in Asia.

The global orientation enables *Hollister* to open new stores efficiently, but in addition, the strategy guarantees cost savings regarding store furniture and maximises the usage and productivity of selling space.

Transnational Orientation

As an example of a transnational orientation, *7-Eleven*, the world's largest operator, franchisor and licensor of *convenience stores*, is useful. Established in 1927 in Dallas, Texas, the company was rescued from bankruptcy in 1980 and became a subsidiary of the Japanese company *Seven & I Holding* in 2005. Today *7-Eleven* has almost 50,000 stores across the globe with the same branding and is located in more than 16 countries worldwide. Known as a convenience store where customers can buy snacks, drinks and other everyday products on the go, almost all *7-Eleven* stores are operated by franchisees. The company combines centralised processes with respect to local advantages. With regard to the product strategy, the company focuses on drinks and ready-to-eat food, but also caters for local tastes. Customers in Hong Kong can buy fresh pasta snacks or even pay their phone bills. In Taiwan they can pay traffic tickets, pump up bicycle tires and send or receive packages. The product-mix of *7-Eleven* is based on consumer analysis which the company uses in plans for products and services. The marketing team consequently searches and selects products and services which satisfy the demands of different target groups and are in line with new trends and markets changes.

One of the benefits of the transnational strategy is the (only) marginal adaption of the format – the retailer can open stores with and without gasoline, urban walkup stores or stores in strip center – another is the "retail information system", which allows the retailer to follow on trends more quickly than competitors. The typical store is located in office areas, open 24 hours and comprises a sales area of about 100 square meters with a wide variety of goods. The stores are categorised into three types: First, *corporate stores* which are owned and managed by the company. *7-Eleven* invests in retailing equipment, store decoration and inventory. Second, within the *franchise stores*, *7-Eleven* is responsible for investment in retailing equipment, store decoration and inventory. Third, the *sub-area licence store* where 7-Eleven provides only assistance and support (Ngaochay/Walsh 2011, p. 148). Data collected by the company responds to consumer needs in a timely manner, improves the line of products and develops new products accordingly, strengthens procurement power and sales forecasting, and devises targeted marketing strategies. The information system also enables store owners to learn the characteristics of the business districts in which they operate, place accurate orders and minimise inventory.

In addition, *7-Eleven* has a centralised logistics management, serving a high number of stores which are systematically opened within a certain area to enhance distribution efficiency, greater familiarity with customers and effective sales promotion. The distribution system is based on an item-by-item and temperature-separated, combined distribution center for each area.

The key to *7-Eleven's* successful model is to enact a centralised business strategy to leverage the company's buying power, marketing strategy and operative processes through an adaption to local needs based on an information system which shows changes as soon as they occur.

With total revenue of 42 billion EUR and more than 14,800 stores in different countries, the *REWE Group* is the second largest food-retailer in Germany and serves as an example of a multinational strategy. Established in 1927 and registered as a cooperative, the company nowadays operates with a variety of sales lines within their two core businesses divided into trading and travel & tourism. Due to increasing market expansion, the centralised structure with a concentration of processes in the headquarters, became more and more obsolete. In 2007, the *REWE Group* reorganised its structure to a more decentralised one. More regional autonomy, flexibility, agility and an orientation towards customers were central aspects of the *restructuring process*. Management steering roles were moved from central corporate departments to strategic business units. All decisions pertaining sales, sales-line purchasing, marketing, expansion, controlling human resources or accounting are made by those responsible for operative results. *Strategic business units* are National Full Range Stores, National Discount Stores, International Full-

Multinational Orientation

Range Stores, International Discount Stores, National Specialist Stores, Travel Sales, Package Tourism and Component Tourism. Central functions for competitive success are decentralised and centred in these units.

With different store brands in twelve countries, *REWE* serves more than 70 million customers per week. In Germany, the company maintains several formats like *REWE, toom getränkemarkt, nahkauf, TEMMA* and *PENNY*. Austria is served by the full-range stores named *Billa* (supermarket), *Merkur* (superstore), *ADEG* (supermarket), *BIPA* (drug store) and the discount format *PENNY*. By contrast, in Bulgaria, the group concentrates on the supermarket *Billa* and the discount store *PENNY MARKET*. While the expansion to East Europe is dominated by the retail formats of *Billa* and *PENNY MARKET*, indicating a standardised expansion, Romania differs from this course and underlines the partly differentiated strategy. Since 2001, the retailer represents itself with two discount formats, *PENNY MARKET XXL* (sales area up to 2,500 square meters) named *XXL Mega Discounter* since 2013, and the above mentioned *PENNY MARKET* format.

Depending on retail units and countries, the assortment differs partly within the organisation. Additionally, the working clothes of employees and the store layout of the individual formats also vary across the different units.

At the same time, strategic purchases at the group level will be continued to enhance the position of the *REWE Group* on national and international procurement markets.

International Orientation

An example of using an international strategy is *Alnatura*, a German retailer of organic and ethical products. Established in 1984, the retailer nowadays maintains about 87 stores in more than 40 cities. Almost 2,150 employees work for the company and *Alnatura* achieved an annual turnover of 593 million EUR in 2012/2013.

Standing for an organic lifestyle, *Alnatura* offers a wide range of products in its supermarket format. Known for its private label "*Alnatura*", with around 1,100 products, the retailer also provides a wide range of local products from different and regional partners. A total of 6,000 articles are offered in an ordinary *Alnatura* supermarket. As mentioned above, the company focuses on highly collaborative strategy and works together with centralised distribution centres and local partners. The stores are supplied by regional wholesalers and regional manufacturers or farmers, e.g. organic bakeries. The store area is about 600-800 square meters and the layout reflects the ecological awareness of the company with natural stone tiles on the ground, natural colouring on the walls and wooden shelves.

In 2012, *Alnatura* started its *international expansion* and has been serving the Swiss market in cooperation with the local retailer *Migros* since then. In contrast to the German branding, the brand appearance is known as *Alnatura-Migros*, a co-branding of both retailers, which implies both centralised and decentralised aspects. The association is based on the strength of *Alnatura*, which implies the wide assortment and position of *Migros* in Switzerland. The assortment range contains, as in Germany, local products from local partners. Furthermore, there are imported brands like *Rapunzel* and organic products of *Migros*. The *Alnatura* concept was partly adapted to local conditions, but also contains elements of a standardised procurement policy. The strategy is similar to that in Germany, but the assortment comprises 5,000 articles instead of 6,000. The *Alnatura-Migros* cooperation has opened two additional stores and plans to open 20-30 new stores within the country in the nearest future. Looking at the branding, *Alnatura* has the standardised look of the brand in Germany and a co-branding with *Migros* in Switzerland.

Focusing on a special target group with homogenous consumption patterns, often called as *LOHAS (Lifestyle of Health and Sustainability)*, *Alnatura* is not committed to serving specific local needs, nor any general requirements.

In Table 2.4, the findings described above are summarised. Depending on the orientation, every retailer has specific focuses and emphasises individual models of international market cultivation.

Retailers and Their Strategic Orientation   *Table 2.4*

	Hollister	7-Eleven	REWE Group	Alnatura
Brand	globally standardised	globally standardised	locally integrated	locally integrated
Marketing Strategy	globally standardised	between global standardisation and local integration	locally integrated	-
Store Layout	globally standardised	between global standardisation and local integration	locally integrated	globally standardised
Assortment	globally standardised	between global standardisation and local integration	locally integrated	between global standardisation and local integration
Distribution	Globally standardised	locally integrated	globally standardised with local Integration	between global standardisation and local integration

Summary and Outlook

This Chapter has shown that retailing is becoming increasingly international, resulting from different external and internal influences. Depending on expansion activities and organisational structures, retailers have to choose whether they follow a more global, local or combined strategy. Both the more integrated and more local approaches can bring success, depending on the sector and individual environments. As shown in the case studies, a strictly application of the theoretical model is often not feasible in practice, due to unpredictable individual factors and the complex environment. Thus, a dynamic development of the I/R-strategy on all relevant levels is necessary.

Questions

1. Describe the main critics of the I/R-framework.

2. Compare *Louis Vuitton´s* strategy with *Fressnapf´s* strategy, regarding the I/R-framework. What are the main conflicts for retailers using a strict interpretation of the characterised orientations?

3. Evaluate the strategic I/R-orientation of different multinational consumer goods' producers. To what degree are activities different to retailers?

Hints

1. See, e.g., Zentes, Morschett and Schramm-Klein 2011.

2. Examine the respective company websites: www.lvmh.com, and www.fressnapf.com.

3. See, e.g., Cavusgil, Knight and Riesenberger 2014.

References

BARTLETT, C.A.; BEAMISH, P.W. (2014): Transnational Management: Text, Cases, and Readings in Cross-Border Management, 7th ed., Boston, McGraw-Hill.

BARTLETT, C.A.; GHOSHAL, S. (1989): Managing Across Borders: The Transnational Solution, Boston, McGraw-Hill.

BIRKINSHAW, J.; MORRISON, A.J. (1995): Configurations of Strategy and Structure in Subsidiaries of Multinational Corporations, in: Journal of International Business Studies, Vol. 26, No. 4, pp. 729-753.

CAVUSGIL, S.T.; KNIGHT, G.; RIESENBERGER, J.R. (2014): International Business: The New Realities, 3rd ed., Boston, Pearson.

CHILD, J. (1972): Organizational Structure, Environment and Performance: The Role of Strategic Choice, in: Sociology, Vol. 6, No. 1, pp. 1-22.

DE LA TORRE, J.; ESPERANCA, J.P.; MARTÍNEZ, J. (2003): The Evolving Multinational: Strategy and Structure in Latin American Operations, 1990-2000, in: BIRKINSHAW, J.; GHOSHAL, S.; MARKIDES, C.; STOPFORD, J.; YIP, G. (Eds.): The Future of the Multinational Company, Chichester, Wiley&Sons, pp. 61-75.

DE MOOIJ, M. (2003): Convergence and Divergence in Consumer Behaviour: Implications for Global Advertising, in: International Journal of Advertising, Vol. 22, No. 2, pp. 183-202.

DELOITTE (2011): The Changing Face of Retail: The Store of the Future – The New Role of the Store in a Multichannel Environment, London.

DELOITTE (2014): Global Power of Retailing 2014: Retail Beyond Begins, London.

DOZ, Y.L. (1980): Strategic Management in Multinational Companies, in: Sloan Management Review, Vol. 21, No. 1, pp. 27-46.

ENGELHARD, J.; DÄHN, M. (2002): Theorien der internationalen Unternehmenstätigkeit - Darstellung, Kritik und zukünftige Anforderungen, in: MACHARZINA, K.; OESTERLE, M.-J. (Eds.): Handbuch Internationales Management: Grundlagen – Instrumente – Perspektiven, 2nd ed., Stuttgart, Gabler, pp. 23-44.

GHEMAWAT, P. (2007): Managing Differences: The Central Challenge of Global Strategy, in: Harvard Business Review, Vol. 85, No. 3, pp. 59-68.

GHOSHAL, S.; NOHRIA, N. (1993): Horses for Courses: Organizational Forms for Multinational Corporations, in: Sloan Management Review, Vol. 34, No. 2, pp. 23-35.

GILLESPIE, K. (2011): Forces Affecting Global Integration and Global Marketing, in: Wiley International Encyclopaedia of Marketing, pp. 50-51.

GUAN, W. (2010): Developments in Distribution Channels: A Case Study of a Timber Product Distribution Channel, Linköping, LiU-Tryck.

HARZING, A. (2000): An Empirical Analysis and Extension of the Bartlett and Ghoshal Typology of Multinational Companies, in: Journal of International Business Studies, Vol. 31, No. 1, pp. 101-120.

HOLLENSEN, S. (2014): Global Marketing, 6th ed., Harlow, Pearson.

JARILLO, J.; MARTINEZ, J. (1990): Different Roles for Subsidiaries: The Case of Multinational Corporations, in: Strategic Management Journal, Vol. 11, No. 7, pp. 501-512.

KUTSCHKER, M. (1999): Das internationale Unternehmen, in: KUTSCH-KER, M. (Ed.): Perspektiven der internationalen Wirtschaft, Wiesbaden, Gabler, pp. 101-126.

LEVITT, T. (1983): The Globalization of Markets, in: Harvard Business Review, Vol. 61, No. 3, pp. 92-102.

MACHARZINA, K. (1993): Steuerung von Auslandsgesellschaften bei Internationalisierungsstrategien, in: HALLER, M.; BLEICHER, K.; BRAUCHLIN, E.; PLEITNER, H.J.; WUNDERER, R.; ZÜND, A. (Eds.): Globalisierung der Wirtschaft, Bern, Haupt Verlag, pp. 77-109.

MORSCHETT, D. (2007): Institutionalisierung und Koordination von Auslandseinheiten: Analyse von Industrie- und Dienstleistungsunternehmen, Wiesbaden, Gabler.

NGAOCHAY, T.; WALSH, J.C. (2011): Success Factors 7-ELEVEN in Thailand, in: International Conference on Business and Economics Research, Vol. 1, Malaysia, pp. 147-151.

NOHRIA, N.; GHOSHAL, S. (1997): The Differentiated Network: Organizing Multinational Corporations for Value Creation, San Francisco, Jossey-Bass.

PERLMUTTER, H. (1969): The Tortuous Evolution of the Multinational Corporation, in: Columbia Journal of World Business, Vol. 4, No. 1, pp. 9-18.

PRAHALAD, C.; DOZ, Y. (Eds.) (1987): The Multinational Mission: Balancing Local Demands and Global Vision, New York, The Free Press.

RUGMAN, A.M.; COLLINSON, S. (2012): International Business, 6th ed., Harlow, Pearson.

RUGMAN, A.M.; VERBEKE, A. (2004): A Perspective on Regional and Global Strategies of Multinational Enterprises, in: Journal of International Business Studies, Vol. 35, No. 1, pp. 3-18.

SWOBODA, B.; FOSCHT, T.; PENNEMANN, K. (2009): HandelsMonitor 2009: Internationalisierung des Handels, Frankfurt, Deutscher Fachverlag.

VERNON, R. (1966): International Investment and International Trade in the Product Cycle, in: Quarterly Journal of Economics, Vol. 80, No. 2, pp. 190-207.

WESTNEY, D.E; ZAHEER, S. (2001): The Multinational Enterprise as an Organization, in: RUGMAN, A.M.; BREWER, T. (Eds.): The Oxford Handbook of International Business, Oxford, Oxford University Press, pp. 349-379.

WESTNEY, D.E.; ZAHEER, S. (2010): The Multinational Enterprise as an Organization, in: RUGMAN, A.M. (Eds.): The Oxford Handbook of International Business, 2nd ed., Oxford, Oxford University Press, pp. 341-366.

WIND, Y.; DOUGLAS, S.; PERLMUTTER, H. (1973): Guidelines for Developing International Marketing Strategies, in: Journal of Marketing, Vol. 37, No. 2, pp. 14-23.

WRIGLEY, N. (2010): The Globalization of Trade in Retail Services, Report Commissioned by the OECD Trade Policy Linkages and Services Division for the OECD Expert Meeting on Distribution Services, Paris.

YIP, G. (1989): Global Strategy: In a World of Nations?, in: Sloan Management Review, Vol. 31, No. 1, pp. 29-41.

ZENTES, J.; MORSCHETT, D.; SCHRAMM-KLEIN, H. (2011): Strategic Retail Management: Text and International Cases, 2nd ed., Wiesbaden, Gabler.

Chapter 3

Role Typologies for Foreign Subsidiaries

Differentiated networks are made up of heterogeneous organisational units in different countries. Different subsidiaries can play different roles within the MNC network and numerous classifications of generic subsidiary strategies or roles are proposed. The aim of this Chapter is to give an overview of existing role typologies and discuss the strengths and weaknesses of the various role typologies for International Management.

Heterogeneous Roles of Subsidiaries

Until the mid-1980s, as Bartlett/Ghoshal (1986) observed, many MNCs treated their foreign subsidiaries in a "remarkably uniform manner". In their critique, they labelled this the "United Nations Model", where the MNC applies its planning and control systems uniformly worldwide, involves each subsidiary's management equally (weakly) in the planning process, and evaluates them against standardised criteria. This uniformity can be partly explained by the fact that foreign subsidiaries were long (uniformly) seen as only "market access providers", without major autonomy and without their own contributions to the company strategy (see, e.g., Vernon 1966).

UN Model

However, it became increasingly obvious that this symmetrical, uniform method of International Management did all exploit all the benefits of internationalisation (Bartlett/Beamish 2014, pp. 612-618). The conceptualisation of the MNC as a differentiated network (Ghoshal/Nohria 1989), in which different subsidiaries have individual tasks to fulfil and are assigned strategically important roles, is increasingly acknowledged as a better design to exploit the capabilities of the different subsidiaries and the advantages of their locations. As shown in Chapter 1, in network firms, competitive advantages do not solely stem from headquarters in the home country but can also be created by foreign subsidiaries and then transferred and exploited throughout the network. Instead of a "centre-periphery" view, this evokes a multi-centre perspective of the MNC with distributed resources, capabilities, functions and decision powers (Schmid 2004, p. 238).

Given the premise that each subsidiary has a unique role to play in the MNC (Birkinshaw/Morrison 1995, p. 732), one major objective of role typologies is to clarify those roles. This includes: identifying the different roles for subsidiaries; distinguishing them clearly; determining various antecedents and consequences, e.g., regarding the coordination of subsidiaries in different roles, and their relations with other actors in the MNC and in the host country.

Role Definition

First the concept of a *role* must be defined. A foreign subsidiary's role is closely related to its *task* within the company network (Andersson/Forsgren 1996, p. 489): most role typologies see roles as *alternative strategies* of foreign subsidiaries (Couto/Goncalves/Fortuna 2003, p. 3). A role can be understood as a *statement of purpose*. It includes the task, the market and the customer the division is concerned with (Galunic/Eisenhardt 1996, p. 256). It can be "defined as the business – or elements of the business – in which the subsidiary participates and for which it is recognized to have responsibility within the MNC" (Birkinshaw/Hood 1998, p. 782). Thus, a role is *the specific task of a subsidiary*, e.g., "to sell the MNE's products in Australia, or to manufacture a line of products for the European market" (Birkinshaw 2001, p. 389).

Roles as Subsidiary Strategies

Some authors distinguish between a *role* (which is assigned to the subsidiary) and a *subsidiary strategy* (which is seen as suggesting some level of self-determination) (Birkinshaw 2001, p. 389). Usually, the distinction is difficult and the specific task and activity of the subsidiary is partly assigned by the headquarters, partly self-determined and partly negotiated between the two. Thus, in this book, the word "role" is used synonymously with "subsidiary strategy".

Different Role Typologies

A large number of role typologies have been proposed in the literature, with several overviews available (e.g., Schmid 2004; Morschett 2007, pp. 210-254). In most cases, the roles are described along the following dimensions (Morschett 2007, pp. 250-254):

■ the *external context* of the subsidiary, e.g. the relevance of the host country or the complexity of the environment

■ the *internal context* of the subsidiary, e.g. the strategic orientation of the MNC or the level of local resources or competences of the subsidiary

■ *coordination variables*, e.g. the level of autonomy

■ the *strategy* or task of the subsidiary, e.g. the primary motives for its establishment, share of internal or external sales, knowledge in- and outflows, markets served, products offered or value-added activities carried out.

In addition, many typologies in the literature focus on specific value-added functions, e.g. on R&D or on manufacturing activities. Some of these typologies will be discussed in Chapters 19 and 20. This Chapter explains four typical examples of role typologies on the subsidiary level.

Selected Role Typologies

Role Typology by Bartlett/Ghoshal

The most influential and best-known role typology is the one described by Bartlett/Ghoshal (1986) (Rugman/Verbeke/Yuan 2011, p. 254). They propose an organisational model with differentiated rather than homogeneous subsidiary roles and dispersed rather than concentrated responsibilities. More specifically, they suggest a role typology with the following two dimensions (Bartlett/Ghoshal 1986, p. 90):

■ The *strategic importance of the local environment* in the host country is the first dimension. Strategic importance can be assigned due to market size, but also for other reasons, for example a particularly sophisticated or technologically advanced market.

Dimensions of Bartlett/Ghoshal

■ The second dimension considers the subsidiary itself and captures the *level of internal competences* and capabilities.

Role Typology by Bartlett/Ghoshal

Figure 3.1

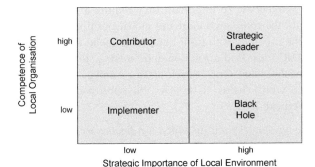

Source: Adapted from Bartlett/Ghoshal 1986, p. 90.

In a typical process for role typologies, the authors assume two dichotomous scale values for each of the dimensions (high/low), for a possible *four roles* (see also Schmid/Bäurle/Kutschker 1998; Rugman/Verbeke 2003):

Four Roles of Bartlett/Ghoshal

■ If a highly competent national subsidiary is located in a strategically important market, it can serve as a *partner* to the headquarters in developing and implementing strategy. In the role of *strategic leader*, the subsidiary can take the lead within the MNC, e.g. for a certain product or value-added function. Other authors who identify this role use labels like "world product mandate", "active", "lead-country" and "centre of excellence" for similar roles. It is particularly relevant for MNCs with a "transnational orientation" (see Chapter 2).

■ A *contributor* role can be filled by a subsidiary with distinctive capabilities that exceed those necessary in its small or generally less important market. This is particularly useful if the specialised and unique capabilities are used for (limited) projects with company-wide relevance.

Implementer as the Most Common Subsidiary Role ■ A foreign subsidiary in a strategically less important market with just sufficient competence to maintain its local operation may be assigned the role of an *implementer*, which is the most common role for subsidiaries. These subsidiaries lack the potential to contribute to overall MNC strategy beyond their local function. Thus, such a subsidiary is given the task of efficiently and effectively exploiting the local market potential and *implementing the defined strategy*. This role type is also commonly considered in role typologies, with names like "local implementer", "miniature replica", "branch plant", "receptive subsidiaries", or as a similar role, "marketing satellite". This role typically results from an MNC with a "global orientation" (see Chapter 2).

■ Some markets are so important they require a strong local presence to maintain the company's local and global position. If the local subsidiary lacks the capabilities to fulfil this requirement, this is called a *black hole*. The MNC must find a solution and "manage their way out of it" (Bartlett/Ghoshal 1986). One possible strategic move is to choose a strong local partner which helps to evolve the subsidiary's competences (Rugman/Verbeke 2003).

Roles and Coordination Often, role typologies indicate which *coordination mechanisms* are appropriate for subsidiaries with different roles (see also Part III). For example, Bartlett/Ghoshal (1986) emphasise that roles are differentiated, the MNC must also differentiate the way it manages those subsidiaries, depending on their particular roles. For example, implementers can be managed via formalisation and similar mechanisms to ensure tight control. Contributors can be centrally coordinated, but the headquarters must be careful not to discourage and frustrate local management. For subsidiaries that act as strategic leaders, however, control should be quite loose and decentralised, and the main task of the headquarters (HQ) is to support the subsidiary with the necessary resources and freedom needed to play its entrepreneurial role.

Recently, Rugman/Verbeke/Yuan (2011) extended this role typology by arguing that the model only acknowledges an aggregate role for the national subsidiary, even though foreign subsidiaries increasingly specialise in rather narrow activity sets in the value chain and may thus perform different roles in each value chain activity. As an example, they show that the subsidiaries of Japanese carmakers in the USA serve as strategic leaders in sales activities, as contributors for production function and as implementers in innovation activities. The authors argue that this extension is necessary due to changes in context (e.g. availability of ICT and better supply chains) over recent decades. "Hence, firms can now more easily fine-slice value chain activities, optimize the location of specific, narrow activity sets and coordinate these across borders" (Rugman/Verbeke/Yuan 2011, p. 255). In this argument, the "arbitrage" strategy dimension from the AAA-framework (see Chapter 2) is given more emphasis.

Different Roles for Different Value Chain Activities

Role Typology by White/Poynter

More complex is another role typology suggested by White/Poynter (1984; see also Schmid/Bäurle/Kutschker 1998, pp. 9-10). They describe the role of a subsidiary along *three dimensions*:

■ *Market scope* refers to the number of geographical markets in which the subsidiary is allowed to be active. The typology applies a dichotomy between "local" (i.e. focus on the host country) and "global".

White/Poynter's Dimensions

■ *Product scope* refers to the range of products a subsidiary manufactures or sells. Here, the distinction is between a limited scope with only single products and an unconstrained scope, where the subsidiary offers many product lines and is often even allowed to introduce product extensions autonomously.

■ *Value-added scope* describes whether the foreign subsidiary only carries out single value-added functions (often marketing, production or R&D) or whether it realises a broad value-added spectrum, up to a full value chain in the host country.

White/Poynter (1984, pp. 59-60) explain that the dimensions are influenced, *inter alia*, by local and global competitive forces and the competence level of the subsidiary. The three dimensions are combined to establish five roles (see Figure 3.2):

Figure 3.2 | Role Typology by White/Poynter

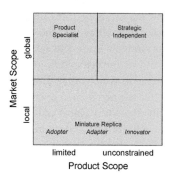 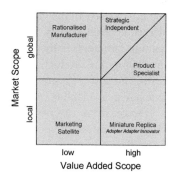

Source: Adapted from White/Poynter 1984, p. 60.

- A *miniature replica* serves the host country market via comprehensive value-added functions. The product scope can vary. Miniature replicas are, as the name suggests, *very similar* in their design *to their headquarters*. This role might be adopted due to high local demand preferences, high trade barriers, production subsidies in the host country, and/or relatively small scale effects in production in the industry which allow for distributed production. Miniature replica is considered a very common role. Depending on the product scope, its autonomy and its own creative activity, the miniature replica might *adopt, adapt* or *innovate*.

- A *marketing satellite* also exclusively serves the local market, but only focuses on a few value-added functions, mainly marketing & sales. The product scope can vary. Most frequently, products produced in the home country are imported and sold in the host country.

- *Rationalised manufacturers* are units responsible for a broad geographical area but only limited value-added functions. Often this is the manufacture of a few products (or even just product components) for the world market (or at least a larger number of countries).

World Product Mandates
- *Product specialists* have the worldwide responsibility for one product or one product line within the MNC and realise the full value-added chain for this product. The subsidiary has a so-called *world product mandate* for this product. This role is emphasised in many role typologies. It is considered to have high decision autonomy, but since there is a high interdependency with other units (who might buy and sell the products in their specific countries, or who might produce other product lines and

sell them to the product specialist), this autonomy cannot be unlimited (Roth/Morrison 1992, p. 718). The empirical relevance of this role is the subject of controversy. Some authors argue that, for strategic reasons, many headquarters hesitate to assign their foreign subsidiaries such broad responsibilities and that – with some notable exceptions – this role is still mainly filled by the headquarters itself (D'Cruz 1986, pp. 84-86).

■ *Strategic independents* also carry out many value-added activities, but they do this for a very large number of markets. The product scope is unconstrained. Here, the subsidiary is seen as only loosely coupled to headquarters, which in this situation acts more as a financial holding, giving very far-reaching autonomy to the subsidiary.

Role Typology by Gupta/Govindarajan

A very different role typology has been presented by Gupta/Govindarajan (1991). They understand the MNC as *"a network of capital, product, and knowledge transactions among units located in different countries"* (Gupta/Govindarajan 1991, p. 770), following the network perspective of authors like Bartlett/Ghoshal and others.

To reduce complexity, they focus on knowledge flows for their typology. One reason for this choice is that the modern literature on MNCs has revealed an increasing number of complex, transnationally oriented MNCs (see Chapter 2), and for *transnational MNCs* knowledge flows across subsidiaries are particularly significant. Moreover, most modern economic theories about MNCs suggest that FDI occurs predominantly because of a desire to internalise knowledge flows. Thus an analysis of knowledge flows is an investigation of the core of the MNC (Gupta/Govindarajan 1991, p. 772).

Knowledge Flows

Focusing on variations in knowledge flow patterns, the authors proposed that MNC subsidiaries can be categorised along *two dimensions*: Subsidiaries can engage in different levels of *knowledge outflow* and *knowledge inflow* from the rest of the MNC.

Gupta/Govindarajan's Dimensions

Figure 3.3   *Role Typology by Gupta/Govindarajan*

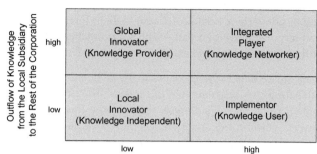

(The terminology of Randøy/Li (1998) is displayed in brackets.)

Source: Gupta/Govindarajan 1991.

Gupta/ Govindarajan's Four Roles

From these two dimensions they derive *four generic subsidiary roles* (Gupta/Govindarajan 1991, pp. 774-775). These are also used by Randøy/Li (1998), with slightly different terminology (see Figure 3.3):

- A *global innovator* (*knowledge provider*) is predominantly a source of knowledge for other subsidiaries and the headquarters. One example of such a subsidiary might be *SAP Labs US*, from which a significant portion of *SAP*'s technological innovations have originated. Located in Palo Alto, California, the subsidiary maintains strategic relationships with local organisations such as Stanford University, and its mission is to leverage the valuable assets within Silicon Valley to drive innovation (see the case study on SAP in Chapter 4).

- An *integrated player* (*knowledge networker*) is also responsible for creating knowledge that can be utilised by other subsidiaries. However, the knowledge networker must also rely on knowledge from others and thus receives and sends high levels of knowledge to and from the subsidiary. With this bi-directional integration in knowledge flows, it can be considered a "centre of excellence" that is tightly embedded in both the MNC and its local environment (Frost/Birkinshaw/Ensign 2002).

- The *implementor* (*knowledge user*) relies heavily on knowledge inflows from headquarters and from sister subsidiaries. It exploits the competitive advantages stemming from this knowledge in its host market without initiating high knowledge outflows to the rest of the corporation.

■ Finally, the *local innovator (knowledge independent)* role implies that the subsidiary is isolated from knowledge flows within the MNC and has to take local responsibility for the creation of the necessary expertise itself. In terms of network models, companies with a *multinational orientation* (Bartlett/Ghoshal 1989) consist mainly of subsidiaries that can be considered knowledge independents.

Role Typology by Andersson/Forsgren

Like Gupta/Govindarajan (1991), Andersson/Forsgren (1994) consider transactions between the subsidiaries and the rest of the MNC as relevant dimensions, but they focus on *product flows* instead of knowledge flows.

Role Typology by Andersson/Forsgren | *Figure 3.4*

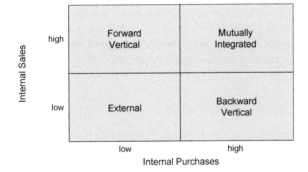

Source: Andersson/Forsgren 1994, p. 15.

Andersson/Forsgren (1994) characterise the role of the subsidiary along *two dimensions*:

Andersson/ Forsgren's Dimensions

■ *internal sales,* i.e., the share of the foreign subsidiary's output sold headquarters or peer subsidiaries rather than external customers

■ *internal purchases,* i.e., the share of inputs such as raw materials, components, semi-finished products and intangible goods delivered by headquarters and other units of the MNC rather than external suppliers.

*Andersson/
Forsgren's Four
Roles*

Using these two dimensions and the dichotomous scale values high/low, *four roles* are distinguished (see Figure 3.4) (Andersson/Forsgren 1994, pp. 14-15):

■ An *external subsidiary* receives and sends a low share of its inputs and outputs to the rest of the MNC. Thus, it produces with low integration with the MNC and sells its products to external customers. This subsidiary role is particularly common in MNCs with a *multinational orientation* (see Chapter 2).

■ Conversely, a *mutually integrated subsidiary* is very tightly integrated within the MNC, on both the sales and supply sides.

■ A *backward vertical subsidiary* receives a major part of its inputs from the MNC and sells its products to external customers. This is the traditional role for many subsidiaries acting as sales units in foreign markets (or units with a minor value-added of their own), in particular in MNCs with a *global orientation*.

■ Conversely, a *forward vertical* is a foreign unit which buys its material, products, and components from external sources in the host country and delivers its products mainly to the rest of the MNC. Here, the dominant objective is *efficiency seeking* in production or *resource seeking* in the host country rather than sales (see Chapter 4).

Weaknesses and Deficits of Role Typologies

Arbitrariness

The large number of role typologies offered in the literature can be seen as proof of their relevance, but this could also be a weakness. New role typologies frequently propose new dimensions for categorising subsidiaries, but they seldom discuss how those new dimensions are superior to those used in earlier typologies. A theoretical foundation for the dimensions is often absent and the dimensions seem to be chosen for their plausibility, rather than through thorough analysis. A certain level of *arbitrariness in the selection of role dimensions* can be observed (see Schmid 2004, pp. 246-248 with a comprehensive critique). Consequently, publications and suggestions for role typologies are frequently non-cumulative, neglect prior research results and are not connected to each other (Hoffman 1994, p. 82). It remains unclear which of the various dimensions considered for role typologies are really crucial for International Management, e.g. for the coordination of the subsidiary or for its performance.

*Over-
simplification*

Another major point of critique is the *over-simplification of subsidiary roles* that can emerge from the typologies. With mostly two dimensions and usually only two values per dimension, most typologies offer four different subsidiary roles. While the easy visualisation of four-role typologies is an advantage, nevertheless, this can obviously be seen as a defect, since four roles are unlikely to be sufficient to describe the great "heterogeneity of subsidiaries" which is the starting point of the models.

In particular, if at least some of the many typologies really have managed to describe subsidiaries along relevant dimensions, then clearly a large number of relevant subsidiary characteristics against which the role can be fixed, meaning multi-dimensional role typologies might be superior.

A more recent criticism comes from Rugman/Verbeke/Yuan (2011), who argue that subsidiary roles may differ for different value chain activities. While their argument was proposed based on the Bartlett/Ghoshal typology, it obviously holds true for all typologies presented here.

Benefits of Role Typologies

Despite their deficiencies, role typologies have shifted the focus of International Management research to the level of the subsidiary as research unit, to better understand the different strategic roles that a subsidiary can occupy. The typologies emphasise that MNCs consist of a large number of organisational units in different countries in the form of a differentiated network, all of which can take on particular roles within the MNC. Thus, role typologies have contributed to a change in perspective for International Management.

While the traditional perspective clearly saw the home country organisation as "central" and the subsidiary as "peripheral", new concepts of the MNC – and the related role typologies – emphasise that subsidiaries can take on highly relevant strategic tasks within the company network and develop into strategic decision centres. While it remains open whether the origin of these roles is still assignment from headquarters in a hierarchical manner or *subsidiary initiative* (Birkinshaw 1997), most typologies focus on the dimensions and characteristics through which subsidiaries can be distinguished. One clear benefit of typologies is to illustrate the vast array of possibilities.

Conclusion and Outlook

Role typologies are one way of analysing the heterogeneity of MNC networks. In doing so, all role typologies are based on similar assumptions (Schmid 2004, p. 244):

- Different subsidiaries can take on different roles.

- There are a limited number of roles for subsidiaries which can be used to describe the actual or intended behaviour of the subsidiary.

■ The roles can be distinguished through a limited number of role dimensions.

While these assumptions obviously run the risk of adopting a simplified attitude toward a very complex problem, typologies have contributed to a better understanding of the "differentiated network" view of MNCs. Focusing on the role of the subsidiary makes it easier to decide other central questions of International Management, e.g. the coordination of subsidiaries. More generally, it helps determine appropriate headquarters-subsidiary relations, since a uniform treatment of heterogeneous subsidiaries is clearly inadequate.

The Blind Scholars and the Elephant

The criticism that role typologies are an oversimplification is reminiscent of the Indian tale of the six blind scholars and the elephant. In this story, six blind scholars attempt to understand and describe what an elephant is. The first blind man comes from the side and feels that it is sturdy, large and straight. He says that it's like a wall. The second feels the trunk in his hand, notes that it's round and flexible, and states that the elephant is like a snake. The third feels the leg and thinks the elephant is similar to a tall tree. The other three say the elephant is like a rope (based on the tail), a sharp spear (based on the ivory tusk) and a fan (based on the ear). Mintzberg, Ahlstrand and Lampel (2005) have taken this parable about *the many-sidedness of things* to explain *the many facets of corporate strategy*. All the scholars are right, but at the same time all of them are wrong, because they each only see part of the truth. The same holds true for the investigation and analysis of a complex organisation like an MNC. It makes sense to analyse a subsidiary from very different angles and through different lenses, provided one remembers that this is not the whole picture. Role typologies should be considered as lenses through which subsidiary strategies within an MNC can be viewed. Eventually, these lenses have to be combined into a more comprehensive analysis.

Further Reading

BIRKINSHAW, J.; MORRISON, A.J. (1995): Configurations of Strategy and Structure in Subsidiaries of Multinational Corporations, in: Journal of International Business Studies, Vol. 26, No. 4, pp. 729-753.

RUGMAN, A.M.; VERBEKE, A.; YUAN, W. (2011): Re-conceptualizing Bartlett and Ghoshal's Classification of National Subsidiary Roles in the Multinational Enterprise, in: Journal of Management Studies, Vol. 48, No. 2, pp. 253-277.

SCHMID, S. (2004): The Roles of Foreign Subsidiaries in Network MNCs: A Critical Review of the Literature and Some Directions for Future Research, in: LARIMO, J. (Ed.): European Research on Foreign Direct Investment and

International Human Resource Management, Proceedings of the University of Vaasa, Vaasa, Vaasan Yliopiston Julkaisuja, pp. 237-255.

Case Study: Walmart*

Profile, History and Status Quo

Walmart, headquartered in Bentonville, Arkansas, is by far the largest retailer in the world. Figure 3.5 illustrates its dominance; it is larger than the next four competitors combined. The giant company has more than 2 million employees, making it the largest private employer in the world. It operates stores in 28 different countries. Still, approx. 70% of its sales come from the domestic USA market. A large share of domestic sales is not unusual for retailers from the USA, given the enormous size of their home market.

The Top-10 Retailers in the World by Retail Revenues 2012 (in billion USD)

Figure 3.5

Source: Deloitte 2014.

Sam Walton opened the first *Walmart* store in Rogers, Arkansas, in 1962. It was based on the principle of low prices and the company quickly expand-

---

* Sources used for this case study include corporate websites and various annual and interim reports, investor-relations presentations, information from the Lebensmittel Zeitung Internet portal and explicitly cited sources.

ed. Within less than a decade, *Walmart* reached sales of 78 million USD, had gone public and opened its first distribution centre. In 1980, *Walmart*'s sales exceeded 1 billion USD. In 1988, the first *Walmart* Supercentre was opened, combining general merchandise and a full-scale supermarket to provide one-stop shopping. From then on, the supercentre was responsible for *Walmart*'s growth.

Unlike manufacturers, internationalisation in retail started relatively late. *Walmart* took its first steps into foreign countries in the 1990s. In 1991, it entered into a joint venture with a Mexican retailer and opened its first store in Mexico. Many internationalisation steps followed, using joint ventures, greenfield investment and acquisitions. These are listed in Table 3.1. Thus, this table can also serve as a comprehensive example for the use of different foreign operation modes (see Chapter 14).

Table 3.1 | *Internationalisation of Walmart*

Entry Year	Country	Retail Units (May 2014)	Form of Entry
1991	Mexico	2,207	50:50 joint venture with local retailer Cifra; acquisition of majority stake in 1997; extension to 60% in 2000
1994	Canada	390	acquisition of 122 stores of local retailer Woolco
1995	Brazil	556	acquisition of 118 stores of local retailer Bompreco
1995	Argentina	105	opening own stores
1996	China	402	joint venture; opening of own stores; 2006 major acquisition 108 stores from foreign retailer Trust-Mart (tripling Walmart's size); 2012 acquisition of a majority stake in online supermarket Yihoadian
1997	Germany	0	acquisition of 21 stores of local retailer Wertkauf; followed by acquisition of 74 stores of Intermarché in 1999; market exit in 2006 (by selling its then 85 stores to Metro) in 2006
1998	South Korea	0	acquisition of 4 stores (and 6 undeveloped sites); market exit in 2006 (by selling its then 16 stores to Shinsegae).
1999	UK	577	acquisition of local retail company ASDA with 229 stores
2002	Japan	439	acquisition of a 6.1% stake in local retail company Seiyu with 370 stores; acquisition of majority interest in 2005; turning Seiyu in a wholly-owned subsidiary in 2008
2005	Central America	668	acquisition of 33.3% of Central American Retail Holding Company with 363 stores in Costa Rica, El Salvador, Guatemala, Honduras, Nicaragua, increased to 51% in 2006
2009	Chile	386	acquisition of local retail company D&S with 224 stores
2009	India	20	joint venture with local company Bharti Enterprises, complete take-over in 2014
2011	Africa	578	acquisition of majority stake in Massmart Holdings with 288 stores in 14 African countries (focus on South Africa)

Source: Gathered from diverse sources; Walmart 2014a; Walmart 2014b, p. 61.

Walmart does not report sales figures for individual country markets. The number of retail units can serve as a proxy for the relevance of each country, but different countries have different store sizes and strongly diverging purchasing power, leading to strongly diverging sales per store, thus making a comparison difficult.

Different Roles for Walmart's Foreign Subsidiaries

Different subsidiaries play different roles in their MNCs, as described earlier in this Chapter. These roles are usually categorised along important dimensions upon which the different role typologies build. The following section describes some of these dimensions in the context of *Walmart's* subsidiaries.

Strategic Importance of Foreign Countries and Competence of Foreign Subsidiaries

The first dimension to investigate is the strategic importance of the foreign country in which a subsidiary is located. In retailing, the size or growth rate of the market (an indicator of future market potential), are aspects of the strategic importance of a market. For example, based on current retail volume, Germany, Japan and the UK are strategically relevant countries for a global retailer. Based on the growth rate and estimated long-term market potential, China has an enormous relevance. South Korea, relative to these other countries, is less relevant.

Strategic Importance

It is difficult to evaluate the competence of the foreign subsidiary from outside of a company. However, if performance in a country is taken as the ultimate sign of competence, *Walmart's* subsidiaries in Japan, Germany and South Korea did not demonstrate a high level of competence (however this ignores the tough market conditions in some countries). On the other hand, *Walmart's* subsidiary in the UK has been successful in a very competitive market, growing in size and improving its market position to be an eye-level competitor with *Sainsbury's* for the No. 2 position.

Competence of the Subsidiary

Walmart's subsidiaries in Germany and the UK were established at roughly the same time: 1997 in Germany and 1999 in the UK. The very different performance of the *Walmart* subsidiaries in Germany and the UK is clear from the relative sales levels, sales development and the profit situation (Dawson 2006):

■ In 2005, *Asda* achieved sales of 21.6 billion EUR in the UK while *Walmart Germany* achieved only 2.04 billion EUR in Germany.

■ Between 2000 and 2005, *Walmart UK* managed to increase its sales by 36%; *Walmart Germany's* sales decreased by 27%.

■ Between 2000 and 2004, *Walmart UK* made annual profits between 400 and 880 million EUR, while *Walmart Germany* lost between 180 and 670 million EUR annually.

Black Hole

In the terminology of Bartlett/Ghoshal (see Figure 3.1), the combination of a strategically important country and a low competence subsidiary is a "black hole". This is not a role which an MNC can allow. In fact, *Walmart* has long attempted to improve the situation in Germany: It changed its management several times and tried new concepts. However, this did not improve the subsidiary's market performance; *Walmart* remained a secondary player. The market position in Germany was bad, with a market share of about 2%; the competition was superior to *Walmart* in its traditional USPs (particularly price), and there was no chance to undercut the top players in the country. So *Walmart* eventually decided to back out. *Walmart Germany*'s stated goal was an eventual store network of 500 stores, but after 9 years in the country, their original acquisition of 95 stores had fallen to 85. In autumn 2006, *Walmart* sold its stores to *Metro*. Overall, based on the buying price of *Wertkauf* and *Intermarché* in Germany and the annual losses, *Walmart* sunk between 3 and 4 billion EUR into Germany.

Implementer

Walmart South Korea can be categorised as an "implementer", displaying comparatively low competence in a market of generally low strategic importance. The stated goal in Korea was more than 100 superstores; after seven years in the country, the subsidiary had only 16. The company was No. 5 in the country without hope of achieving a better position. However, categorising this as an "implementer" illustrates how the role typologies may not be sufficiently fine-grained, a previously noted weakness. In fact, the competence (or at least performance) was so low that *Walmart* decided to leave Korea. *Walmart* sold its stores in spring 2006, making South Korea the first country the company ever excited.

Walmart UK as Strategic Leader

Along the two dimensions of Bartlett/Ghoshals role typology, *Walmart* UK may be seen as a "strategic leader". The strategic importance of the British market is high. It is a very large and highly sophisticated retail market. Many retail innovations have their origins in the UK, and it is useful to gather experience in this country. *Asda* is still *Walmart's* largest subsidiary, and it is successful in the market. They have a high competence in several fields that will be valuable throughout the *Walmart* company, e.g. in e-commerce. They are also highly competent in the private label domain, which is more sophisticated in the UK than most other countries. For example, *Asda* has a well-known and successful store clothing brand, *George*. *Asda* also has competence in direct sourcing which is still surprisingly low in the parent company. Therefore, *Walmart* intends to leverage this competence worldwide (Supply Chain Digest 2010). Thus in private label, sourcing and e-commerce,

Asda contributes to *Walmart's* global strategy and has an impact beyond the UK market.

Similarly, *Walmart's* oldest international venture, *Walmart de México*, is located in an important country with approx. 120 million inhabitants and strong long-term growth prospects. The subsidiary has been very successful in the country, becoming market leader. It has market knowledge and cultural insights into the regional markets, giving it a high competence in this field. In 2009, *Walmart de México* acquired *Walmart Centroamérica* to form *Walmart de México y Centroamérica*. The subsidiary is now responsible for operations in Mexico and five more Central American countries. It has sales of over 30 billion USD. This is a clear illustration of a "strategic leader", assuming responsibility not only in the host country but also additional markets.

Walmart Mexico as Strategic Leader

There is no clear threshold above which a country is strategically important or a subsidiary is competent. This can make categorisation difficult. For example, *Walmart Canada* has exhibited strong performance over recent decades. The retailer is the country's market leader and the store formats are constantly adjusted to the market. Sales exceed 20 billion USD. Whether the subsidiary should be labelled a "contributor" or a "strategic leader" depends on whether Canada is categorised as strategically important or not, something which only *Walmart* itself can answer.

Walmart Canada

Walmart Japan is located in one of the largest economies of the world and in the second-largest retail market. The strategic importance of the market is high. *Walmart Japan* had significant problems adapting to a different culture which has strong influences on buying behaviour (e.g. lower focus on price, less bulk purchasing, increased relevance of fresh food) and also in achieving the low-cost structure that *Walmart* has in other countries, due to the multi-level distribution system in Japan. *Walmart Japan* was unsuccessful for a long time, which, at the time, would have made it a "black hole" subsidiary. Over time, however, the situation improved and *Walmart Japan* has become more successful in catering to the needs of the Japanese. While critics argue that the company just waited for demand to change, the company itself developed competences to improve its position. For example, it created specific products to target the ageing population in Japan. It has also developed ways to circumvent the multi-level distribution system and buy a larger share of its products directly. After years of low growth, it now outpaces the market. *Carrefour* and *Tesco* have both exited Japan, while *Walmart* is starting to see success (Banjo 2012).

Walmart Japan Escaping the Black Hole

Knowledge Flows between Foreign Subsidiaries and the Rest of the MNC

Knowledge Users

Many *Walmart* subsidiaries around the world rely on the competence of their parent company in logistics, IT, the EDLP (Everyday Low Price) strategy and also its successful formats (supercentres, hypermarkets, but also wholesale clubs) and implement these in their host countries. In the terminology of Gupta/Govindarajan (1991) (see Figure 3.3), they could be labelled "implementors" or "knowledge users".

Knowledge Independents

Some subsidiaries operate in very distant markets, though, and accumulated a high level of knowledge before their acquisition by *Walmart*. *Massmart*, the subsidiary in South Africa, is an example. While, some knowledge flows from the new parent company to the subsidiary obviously occurred after the acquisition, the subsidiary had of the region which is rather location-bound; thus, it is not used by other subsidiaries. In this respect, *Massmart* could be categorised as a "knowledge independent" or "local innovator".

Knowledge Networker

Asda exchanges knowledge in both directions. It has a high level of unique knowledge due to the sophisticated retail market in the UK but it can also learn from the other *Walmart* subsidiaries and in particular from the parent company. It profited from *Walmart's* expertise in logistics and IT, for example. E-commerce provides an example of knowledge flowing from *Asda* to *Walmart USA*, because the UK is the most advanced country in this field. *Asda* is recognised within *Walmart* for its so-called "omnichannel" competence, which includes sophisticated click-and-collect techniques linking the Internet to the store network. *Walmart UK* could, thus, be labelled a "knowledge networker". This is also appreciated by *Asda's* CEO *Andy Clarke*: "I have been aggressive in building even stronger relations with *Walmart* and sharing *Asda's* experience […]. In the last three years more than the previous seven years, the way in which *Asda* is working with *Walmart* on a collaborative basis has moved forward to product, process and merchandising" (Lawson 2013).

The term "knowledge transfer" is rather abstract. As a concrete example of a knowledge transfer mechanism from *Asda* to *Walmart*, the *Asda* e-commerce director (a very high level manager at *Asda*) was promoted in May 2014 to a position in the parent company *Walmart* in the USA, as VP Operations in e-commerce. Thus, he has transferred his knowledge from the UK market to the headquarters. Similarly, Judith McKenna, who was chief operating officer (COO) of *Asda* until 2012 and gathered experience at *Asda* for more than ten years prior to that, became executive VP of strategy and international development for *Walmart International* in January 2013. In this role she leads several areas, including international strategy, mergers and acquisitions, integration, global format development and purchase leverage. Also, the president and CEO of *Walmart International, David Cheesewright*, is a Briton who worked for *Asda* for five years before being promoted to other *Walmart* subsidiaries (e.g. as CEO of *Walmart Canada*) and eventually *Walmart International*. These examples clearly illustrate some *knowledge networking* mechanisms but also the role of *Asda* as a strategic leader within the *Walmart Corporation*.

Product Scope and Market Scope

Some role typologies include the *product scope* as a relevant dimension. For a retailer, the product is its store format, i.e. a supermarket or a supercentre (Zentes/Morschett/Schramm-Klein 2011, p. 180). In the case of *Walmart's* foreign subsidiaries, the scope differs considerably:

Differing Product Scope

■ Some subsidiaries only have one or a few store formats. For example, *Walmart Canada* only operates supercentres and discount stores; *Walmart India* currently only operates the wholesale club format.

■ Other subsidiaries have a very broad product scope, i.e. many different store formats. For example, *Walmart Brazil* operates more than ten store formats, ranging from hypermarkets and supercentres to supermarkets and petrol stations.

Furthermore, the *market scope* of the subsidiaries also differs:

Differing Market Scope

■ Most *Walmart* subsidiaries only have market responsibility for their own host country. This is true even for the largest subsidiaries such as Canada or the UK.

■ However, some of the younger *Walmart* subsidiaries have a broader market scope and a mandate for several countries. *Walmart South Africa* is responsible for South Africa and 13 other countries in the region. As mentioned above, *Walmart de México y Centroamérica* has a market scope of six countries in the region.

Product Flows between Foreign Subsidiaries and the Rest of the MNC

Product flows between retailers' foreign subsidiaries are usually rather limited. Most country subsidiaries have a low level of internal sales and a low level of internal purchases.

But some subsidiaries rank higher on internal purchases. For example, as mentioned above, the Japanese market still has many levels of middlemen. This adds to the already high cost levels in the country. Recently, *Walmart*

*Global Sourcing
Office in China*

decided to use its international operations to help *Walmart Japan* buy directly through the *Walmart* network. It even added products from other subsidiaries, e.g. from the UK, to the merchandise mix in Japan.

On the other hand, *Walmart* in China is not only important as a sales market but also as a procurement location. *Walmart's Global Sourcing Office* in China was opened in 2002. For general merchandise products, China is a major import source for *Walmart USA* but and also other *Walmart* subsidiaries. More than 10,000 suppliers in China work for *Walmart*. It has often been claimed that if *Walmart* were a country, it would be among China's top 10 trading partners. This shows the enormous volume that the procurement subsidiary in China buys and sells internally to its peer subsidiaries around the world – regardless of the exact for of contract applied.

Retail operations and procurement activities in China are structurally separated – it would be reasonable to talk about two different subsidiaries in this case. But ultimately this only adds to the complexity of the analysis of MNCs, since there may also be several distinct subsidiaries in a single host country.

Summary and Outlook

Walmart is a retail giant, with sales more than four times higher than the nearest competitor, a huge number of employees, and internationalisation to almost every major world region. However *Walmart* has demonstrated that internationalisation is not a one-way street. While it is very successful in many foreign markets, it faced negative consequences in markets where the outlook was poor, and ultimately exited Germany and South Korea.

It is almost certain that *Walmart's* international expansion will continue. With more countries in its portfolio, the heterogeneity of its subsidiaries and the roles they have to take over for *Walmart* will also increase.

Questions

1. *Walmart* internationalised very quickly over the last two decades. Considering the so-called "psychic distance chain" of the internationalisation process model, would you argue that *Walmart* follows this pattern, or is the company a counter-example? Analyse each internationalisation step.

2. Considering the product inflows and product outflows of foreign subsidiaries, try to categorise some of *Walmart's* subsidiaries in this matrix. Discuss which problems arise when carrying out this categorisation.

3. This Chapter described selected role typologies and the general idea behind role typologies was explained. Which dimensions would you consider the most relevant for the categorisation of *Walmart*'s subsidiaries? Develop a role typology and use it to categorise *Walmart*'s subsidiaries.

Hints

1. See Chapter 6 for a description of the internationalisation process model.

References

ANDERSSON, U.; FORSGREN, M. (1994): Degree of Integration in Some Swedish MNCs, Working Paper, Department of Business Studies, Uppsala University, Uppsala.

ANDERSSON, U.; FORSGREN, M. (1996): Subsidiary Embeddedness and Control in the Multinational Corporation, in: International Business Review, Vol. 5, No. 5, pp. 487-508.

BANJO, S. (2012): Wal-Mart Says Time Is Right for Japan, Wall Street Journal, September 09, 2012.

BARTLETT, C.A.; BEAMISH, P.W. (2014): Transnational Management: Text, Cases, and Readings in Cross-Border Management, 7th ed., Boston, McGraw-Hill.

BARTLETT, C.A.; GHOSHAL, S. (1986): Tap Your Subsidiaries for Global Reach, in: Harvard Business Review, Vol. 64, No. 6, pp. 87-94.

BARTLETT, C.A.; GHOSHAL, S. (1989): Managing Across Borders: The Transnational Solution, Boston, McGraw-Hill.

BIRKINSHAW, J. (1997): Entrepreneurship in Multinational Corporations: The Characteristics of Subsidiary Initiatives, in: Strategic Management Journal, Vol. 18, No. 3, pp. 207-229.

BIRKINSHAW, J. (2001): Strategy and Management in MNE Subsidiaries, in: RUGMAN, A.M.; BREWER, T. (Eds.): Oxford Handbook of International Business, Oxford, Oxford University Press, pp. 380-401.

BIRKINSHAW, J.; HOOD, N. (1998): Multinational Subsidiary Evolution: Capability and Charter Change in Foreign-owned Subsidiary Companies, in: Academy of Management Review, Vol. 23, No. 4, pp. 773-795.

BIRKINSHAW, J.; MORRISON, A.J. (1995): Configurations of Strategy and Structure in Subsidiaries of Multinational Corporations, in: Journal of International Business Studies, Vol. 26, No. 4, pp. 729-753.

COUTO, J.; GONCALVES, V.; FORTUNA, M. (2003): Strategic Choice of the Subsidiaries: Contextual and Operational Factors, in: Journal of Comparative International Management, Vol. 6, No. 1, pp. 1-13.

DAWSON, M. (2006): Walmart: Auf dem Rückzug, Lebensmittel Zeitung, June 02, 2006.

D'CRUZ, J. (1986): Strategic Management of Subsidiaries, in: ETEMAD, H.; DULUDE, L. (Eds.): Managing the Multinational Subsidiary: Response to Environmental Changes and to Host Nation R&D Policies, London, Routledge, pp. 75-89.

DELOITTE (2014): Global Powers of Retailing 2014: Retail Beyond Begins, London.

FROST, T.; BIRKINSHAW, J.; ENSIGN, P. (2002): Centers of Excellence in Multinational Corporations, in: Strategic Management Journal, Vol. 23, No. 11, pp. 997-1018.

GALUNIC, C.D.; EISENHARDT, K.M. (1996): The Evolution of Intracorporate Domains: Divisional Charter Losses in High-technology, Multidivisional Corporations, in: Organization Science, Vol. 7, No. 3, pp. 255-282.

GHOSHAL, S.; NOHRIA, N. (1989): Internal Differentiation within Multinational Corporations, in: Strategic Management Journal, Vol. 10, No. 4, pp. 323-337.

GUPTA, A.; GOVINDARAJAN, V. (1991): Knowledge Flows and the Structure of Control within Multinational Corporations, in: Academy of Management Review, Vol. 16, No. 4, pp. 768-792.

HOFFMAN, R. (1994): Generic Strategies for Subsidiaries of Multinational Corporations, in: Journal of Managerial Issues, Vol. 6, No. 1, pp. 69-87.

LAWSON, A. (2013): Analysis: What Can We Learn from Walmart's AGM?, http://www.retail-week.com/analysis-what-can-we-learn-from-walmarts-agm/5049896.article, accessed on July 22, 2014.

MINTZBERG, H.; AHLSTRAND, B.; LAMPEL, J. (2005): Strategy Safari: A Guided Tour through the Wilds of Strategic Management, New York, The Free Press.

MORSCHETT, D. (2007): Institutionalisierung und Koordination von Auslandseinheiten: Analyse von Industrie- und Dienstleistungsunternehmen, Wiesbaden, Gabler.

RANDØY, T.; LI, J. (1998): Global Resource Flows and MNE Network Integration, in: BIRKINSHAW, J.; HOOD, N. (Eds.): Multinational Corporate Evolution and Subsidiary Development, Basingstoke, Palgrave Macmillan, pp. 76-101.

ROTH, K.; MORRISON, A. (1992): Implementing Global Strategy: Characteristics of Global Subsidiary Mandates, in: Journal of International Business Strategy, Vol. 23, No. 4, pp. 715-735.

RUGMAN, A.M.; VERBEKE, A. (2003): Extending the Theory of the Multinational Enterprise: Internalization and Strategic Management Perspectives, in: Journal of International Business Studies, Vol. 34, No. 2, pp. 125-137.

RUGMAN, A.M.; VERBEKE, A.; YUAN, W. (2011): Re-conceptualizing Bartlett and Ghoshal's Classification of National Subsidiary Roles in the Multinational Enterprise, in: Journal of Management Studies, Vol. 48, No. 2, pp. 253-277.

SCHMID, S. (2004): The Roles of Foreign Subsidiaries in Network MNCs: A Critical Review of the Literature and Some Directions for Future Research, in: LARIMO, J. (Ed.): European Research on Foreign Direct Investment and International Human Resource Management, Proceedings of the University of Vaasa, Vaasa, Vaasan Yliopiston Julkaisuja, pp. 237-255.

SCHMID, S.; BÄURLE, I.; KUTSCHKER, M. (1998): Tochtergesellschaften in international tätigen Unternehmungen: Ein "State-of-the-Art" unterschiedlicher Rollentypologien, Diskussionsbeiträge der Wirtschaftswissenschaftlichen Fakultät Ingolstadt, No. 104, Ingolstadt.

SUPPLY CHAIN DIGEST (2010): Walmart to Centralize Global Sourcing, http://www.scdigest.com/assets/On_Target/10-01-06-1.php, accessed on August 06, 2010.

VERNON, R. (1966): International Investment and International Trade in the Product Cycle, in: Quarterly Journal of Economics, Vol. 80, No. 2, pp. 190-207.

WALMART (2014a): Walmart, http://corporate.walmart.com/, accessed on June 05, 2014.

WALMART (2014b): 2013 Annual Report, Bentonville.

WHITE, R.; POYNTER, T. (1984): Strategies for Foreign-owned Subsidiaries in Canada, in: Business Quarterly, Summer, pp. 59-69.

ZENTES, J.; MORSCHETT, D.; SCHRAMM-KLEIN, H. (2011): Strategic Retail Management: Text and International Cases, 2nd ed., Wiesbaden, Gabler.

Chapter 4

Motives for Internationalisation

The aim of this Chapter is to clarify that internationalisation is not always driven by the desire to enhance sales, but that the motives for internationalisation can be manifold, with major consequences for market entry strategies, the coordination of international subsidiaries, country selection, organisation, etc.

Heterogeneous Strategic Objectives for Internationalisation

Internationalisation into specific foreign countries, whether it is via exporting or importing, international contracts or foreign direct investment, is always driven by certain motives of the part of an MNC. In this regard, it can be assumed that the strategic conduct of a company in a particular country is always shaped by its strategic objectives with regard to this country, as an important part of the intended strategy.

However, the literature on internationalisation often fails to differentiate between the respective objectives, assuming, often only implicitly, that sales-oriented objectives are the most relevant. The term *market entry strategy*, which is often used for the foreign operation mode, clearly indicates this assumption. Traditional concepts and studies on internationalisation (e.g. the theory of monopolistic advantage by Hymer (1978)) often assumed that companies' international activities only give them the benefit of a broader exploitation of company-specific advantages. However, very different internationalisation objective exist. As already stated in the international *product lifecycle theory* by Vernon (1966), the *production cost advantages* of a foreign market might be an important reason for relocating production to foreign countries, even if the primary sales focus is still on the home country.

Sales Objective Traditionally in the Focus

In the perspective of the MNC as a *differentiated network*, as discussed in Chapter 1, different subsidiaries are assigned different tasks and roles, and heterogeneous location advantages of the different foreign subsidiaries are exploited. This perspective clearly illustrates the *multi-faceted nature of the motives* for being active in foreign countries.

The *five motives* shown in Figure 4.1 are the most relevant objectives of internationalisation (see, e.g., Dunning 1988; Shan 1991, p. 562; Morschett 2007, pp. 310-320; Dunning/Lundan 2008, pp. 67-77).

79

Figure 4.1 | *Alternative Motives for Internationalisation*

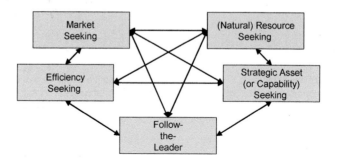

Market Seeking

The *primary motive* for starting activities in a foreign country is frequently the *access to new markets* and the sales potential offered by foreign markets. When the home market is saturated, as is increasingly the case for the industrialised countries of Western Europe, the USA or Japan, company growth can be maintained through international sales.

Orientation on the Sales Side   When market seeking is the motive, foreign countries are chosen by the sales potential they offer for the company. Country characteristics used as *selection criteria* in this case include (Grünig/Morschett 2012, pp. 97-112):

- market size

- market growth

- presence of attractive customer segments

- demand for the products or services of the company.

International market seeking objectives are not necessarily associated with foreign production; they may also be reached by home-country production that is being exported to the foreign market. While *exporting* can be used to exploit excess production capacity in the home country, and is usually less risky and can be carried out with lower initial investment, FDI in the target market can help to circumvent trade barriers, reduce logistics costs and develop a better understanding of the market. These scenarios are discussed in more detail in Chapter 19.

Given that access to a foreign market is not always easy and market knowledge of a foreign company is usually lower than that of a local company, first market entries are often achieved via *cooperative arrangements* with local companies (Erramilli/Rao 1990, p. 146). Local companies may provide the company with the necessary knowledge about the market, with access to distribution channels and with other local relations.

Cooperative Operation Modes to Improve Market Access

However, considering the significance of customer relations, in recent years companies on both a national and international level have tended to exert a *tighter control* over their foreign sales activities and are willing to use a higher level of ownership of these activities to provide the necessary coordination. *Internalisation* of these foreign marketing activities, i.e. vertical integration, and a full-ownership strategy instead of cooperative arrangements, are often the consequence. The reason is that a foreign subsidiary acts as a *gatekeeper* to the local market, which gives it a specific power versus the company in the home country, in particular when it controls distribution channels, marketing activities, etc.

Vertical Integration

The theory of this dynamic development, which is shaped by a low level of market knowledge in early phases of market entry (and, thus, often cooperative entry modes to facilitate the market entry), increasing market knowledge over time and the wish to exert a stronger control over activities (and in consequence a preference for full ownership of the subsidiary), is explained via *internationalisation stage models*, which are discussed in more detail in Chapter 6.

Dynamic Changes in Operation Modes

Follow-the-Customer

The market seeking motive focuses on sales in the foreign market. Usually, customers in the foreign country are consumers or companies resident in the host country. In business-to-business markets, however, customers in the foreign country might also be companies from the home country who have internationalised to this country. For instance, a Swiss company might sell in China to the Chinese subsidiary of another Swiss MNC.

For service companies in particular it is very common to enter a foreign market as a consequence of the internationalisation of one of their main customers (so-called *"piggybacking"*). This follow-the-customer motive is often seen as the most relevant reason for service companies to internationalise. Following a customer overseas might be necessary to protect existing sales levels (if the customer relocates parts of its home country production abroad) or it can be an opportunity to enhance sales if the customer increases its production with the new foreign facility. Existing business relationships, e.g. for professional services like business consulting, advertising

Piggybacking of Service Companies

agencies and auditing companies, are ensured and strengthened by accompanying important clients into the foreign market (Erramilli/Rao 1990, p. 141; Cardone-Riportella et al. 2003, p. 384).

Competitive Advantage through Customer Knowledge

While this motive can be seen as a *sub-dimension of market seeking*, it makes a major difference whether the customer base of the company in the host country consists mainly of local customers or customers from the company's home country. In the follow-the-customer scenario, the company has a strong advantage because the uncertainty of entering the foreign market is much lower. An important customer is already secured prior to market entry and the demand behaviour of this customer is already known to the MNC from the home country. The *liability of foreignness*, i.e. the often-stated competitive disadvantages compared with local companies due to reduced market knowledge, is reversed in this situation, because the MNC has already accumulated knowledge and information about this customer (Erramilli/Rao 1990, p. 143).

However, following the customer also leads to major *interdependencies* for international activities. Since a dominant reason for following the client is also to deepen the business relationship with this customer in the home country (Cardone-Riportella et al. 2003, p. 385), it is important that the marketing offer and the quality level of the company in the host country mirrors the offer in the home country. This strong interdependence makes centralised coordination necessary, since decisions by the MNC's headquarters must also be implemented in the foreign market. On the other hand, *centralised coordination* becomes easier, since the headquarters might have better information available on this customer and its company objectives than the specific foreign sales unit (Mößlang 1995, p. 220).

Manufacturers Following-the-Customer

While the literature assigns this objective mainly to service companies, it seems obvious that the motive can be very *relevant for manufacturing companies* as well. Industrial supplier relations are sometimes very similar and closely linked to specific customers (Ferdows 1989, p. 7; Zentes/Swoboda/Morschett 2004, p. 394). If, for instance, a large German car manufacturer establishes production facilities in Eastern Europe, this forces suppliers to consider internationalisation to these countries as well. The same phenomenon was observed when Japanese car manufacturers established their first production facilities in the USA in the 1980s and 1990s. Consequently, more than 500 automotive suppliers from Japan established production facilities in the USA in their wake (Dunning/Lundan 2008, p. 70).

Bridgehead

The activities in a specific country can also be motivated by the opportunity to establish a bridgehead for entering *adjacent foreign countries*, either immediately or at a later date. This is particularly relevant in connection with the market seeking objective.

As well as the activities in the host country, the company should identify market opportunities in other countries that are easier to enter from this bridgehead. For example, Hong Kong used to be a bridgehead for many companies to enter the attractive Chinese market, and Austria is often used by Western companies as an entry point into Eastern Europe. For example, *McDonald's*, *Aldi* and *Rewe* used their activities in Austria to enter Eastern European markets. After the establishment of activities in neighbouring countries, the bridgehead often serves as a regional headquarters.

Foreign Country as Bridgehead for Further Internationalisation

Resource Seeking

Foreign activities can also be motivated by securing the MNC access to relevant resources. These could be natural resources, but this objective can also include specific components from foreign suppliers or certain topographical sites (agricultural land, harbours, etc.) (see Rugman/Verbeke 2001, p. 158). Companies in the *primary sector* and companies that are strongly dependent on natural resources, like oil companies, tyre producers and chemical companies, often internationalised early on, with the aim of securing the necessary inputs for their companies (Bartlett/Ghoshal 2000b, p. 5).

Country characteristics that are used as the primary *selection criteria* include

- availability of important resources
- cost of resources in the country
- allocation of resources in the country, e.g. whether the resources are controlled by a few organisations or by many.

The resource seeking motive is closely linked to *cooperative operation modes* (Morschett/Schramm-Klein/Swoboda 2008). This is primarily due to local companies' *first-mover advantage* with regard to local resource access (Hennart/Larimo 1998, p. 524). Local companies have often secured access to important natural resources very early, often decades prior, and major natural resources are often at least partially controlled by the host government (e.g. in Russia). So while *acquisition* might theoretically be an option, legal restrictions often hinder this operation mode. A foreign company that wants to get resources thus often needs to partner with local companies to gain access to their networks, government relations, expertise, etc.

Partnership Strategies

It is also plausible that foreign subsidiaries which are mainly established to gain access to resources in a foreign country intend to embed themselves tightly in the local environment, tighten the relationships they have established with the help of a cooperation partner and enhance the supply security of the critical resources. The company often has to adapt to processes and routines in the host country.

Resource seeking is simultaneously linked to strong interdependence with the rest of the MNC, since the goods and resources acquired in the foreign market are either directly delivered to other organisational units of the MNC, e.g. a factory in the home country, or are further processed in the host country by the foreign subsidiary, to be subsequently delivered to foreign countries. Resource seeking thus usually leads to *one-directional, sequential flows of material* from the foreign subsidiary to the rest of the MNC.

Efficiency Seeking

Orientation on Production Efficiency

Another major motive for internationalisation is efficiency seeking, i.e. the quest for the *improvement of the overall cost efficiency* of the MNC. The foreign subsidiary in this case is often part of an *internationally configured network* of production activities. The intention is to exploit specific location advantages for specific activities and design a production network that rationalises the production processes (Rugman/Verbeke 2001, p. 159). The foreign subsidiary is then often responsible for manufacturing components or final goods that are delivered to the parent company or peer subsidiaries in cross-border production processes (Martinez/Ricks 1989, p. 469). In services, the *outsourcing and offshoring* of call centre activities to Ireland, or of IT services to India, are typical examples of efficiency seeking (see Chapter 16 for a discussion of these phenomena).

Efficiency seeking activities can either try to exploit *differences in factor costs* (i.e. between heterogeneous countries) or be designed to enhance *economies of scale* by bundling production (i.e. between broadly similar economies) (Dunning/Lundan 2008, p. 72).

Location Selection for Efficiency Seeking

Selection criteria in the case of efficiency seeking include (Grünig/Morschett 2012, pp. 167-187):

■ labour costs in the country, which differ tremendously, even within Europe (see Figure 4.2); as well as absolute wages, productivity differences also need to be considered

■ distance to relevant markets (as an influence on logistics costs)

■ possibilities to integrate the production process in the company's overall cross-border production processes

■ availability of good and efficient suppliers.

Hourly Labour Cost in Industry in Selected European Countries 2013 (in EUR)   *Figure 4.2*

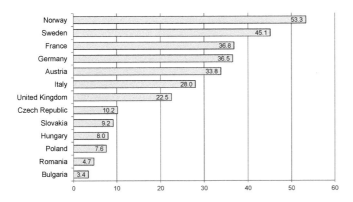

Source: Eurostat 2014.

The possibility of integrating the production processes across borders is obviously improved by reduced tariff and non-tariff barriers between countries. This is why efficiency seeking internationalisation often occurs in regionally integrated markets (Dunning/Lundan 2008, p. 72) such as the EU or NAFTA (see Chapter 7).

If the subsidiary produces components in a vertical supply relationship with other organisations within the MNC, then *tight coordination* is necessary to integrate the production processes into the MNC (e.g. Gupta/Govindarajan 1991). Thus, foreign subsidiaries that are mainly established as production sites for the MNC often have a comparatively low level of autonomy and a degree of central coordination (Young/Tavares 2004). Since their structures and processes are often similar to those of the parent company, they are sometimes called *miniature replicas* (White/Poynter 1984, p. 60; see Chapter 3). On the other hand, efficiency advantages in the host country can also be exploited by having the subsidiary carry out full value chains and assigning it a *product mandate* which gives it full (regional or worldwide) responsibility for one or several products. In this case they might be able to establish specialised resources and a high level of competence which promotes their autonomy. In any case, a certain level of coordination remains necessary for

Miniature Replicas and Product Mandates

this subsidiary due to the high interdependence with the rest of the MNC (Young/Tavares 2004, p. 221).

If the internationalisation is mainly due to efficiency motives, *cooperative arrangements* are sometimes chosen as the operation mode (Morschett 2007, p. 515). Manufacturing in the host country – at least compared with pure sales activities – is linked to very high capital costs and consequently a *risky engagement*. Sharing large investments and high risks with a local partner is a frequent motive for cooperative strategies. Local partners can also contribute to economies of scale in production (Heshmati 2003; Kutschker/Schmid 2011, p. 892).

Outsourcing Internationally

Alternatively, seeking cost efficiency might also lead to *outsourcing*. In particular, cost reasons are often seen to influence the "make-or-buy-decision". Arguments for outsourcing include flexibility, reduced investment of own company resources, specialised knowledge, economies of scale and economies of scope (Aharoni 2000, p. 17). These are discussed in more detail in Chapter 16. As an example, outsourcing production to a contract manufacturer might give a company access to a very cost-efficient international production network with high flexibility (Morschett 2005), thus giving it the opportunity to fulfil the efficiency seeking motive by using the configuration of the contract manufacturer without their own international FDI.

Strategic Asset Seeking

Besides the motive of accessing natural resources, components or other similar inputs, a company might seek *access to local knowledge*, capabilities, technological resources and innovations. The *strategic asset seeking* motive is based on the idea that an MNC's international presence gives it a major information advantage over other companies, grounded in the *scanning and learning potential* of the company network (Bartlett/Ghoshal 2000, p. 8). Research institutions, as well as suppliers, customers or competitors, can be important sources of technological knowledge (Ferdows 1989, p. 6). For example, it is often argued that access to specific knowledge and capabilities in the host country is an important reason for direct investment in the USA (see Randøy/Li 1998, p. 91). Related to the motive of strategic asset seeking is the idea that the superiority of differentiated MNC networks is due to the enhanced *innovation capability* of such networks (Ghoshal/Bartlett 1988; Bartlett/Ghoshal 1989).

Orientation on Know-how

If strategic asset seeking is a major motive for internationalisation, the country characteristics used as *selection criteria* include:

■ innovation levels

■ sophistication of demand

■ availability of related and supporting industries

■ presence of innovation clusters in the relevant industry.

While a company obviously has to consider the innovation capacity of a potential host country in its specific industry, some general evaluations can be drawn from secondary sources like the World Competitiveness Report (see Table 4.1).

Ranking of the Most Innovative Countries

Table 4.1

Country	Rank	Innovation and Sophistication Score	Country	Rank	Innovation and Sophistication Score
Switzerland	1	5.72	Denmark	11	5.14
Finland	2	5.65	Austria	12	5.14
Japan	3	5.62	Singapore	13	5.14
Germany	4	5.59	Qatar	14	5.08
Sweden	5	5.46	Belgium	15	5.07
United States	6	5.43	Norway	16	5.07
Netherlands	7	5.36	Luxembourg	17	4.84
Israel	8	5.23	France	18	4.84
Taiwan	9	5.22	Hong Kong	19	4.83
United Kingdom	10	5.15	Korea, Rep.	20	4.82

Source: World Economic Forum 2013, p. 16.

Innovation (and, related to this, an adequate location for MNCs seeking strategic assets) requires an environment that is conducive to innovative activity, supported by both the public and the private sectors. In particular, this means sufficient investment in research and development, especially by private, high-quality scientific research institutions, collaboration in research between universities and industry and protection of intellectual property (World Economic Forum 2013, pp. 8-9).

The leading countries for innovation are Switzerland, Finland, Japan, Germany and Sweden. The Competitiveness Report comments: "In the case of Switzerland, an excellent innovation ecosystem has been a significant part of making the country an attractive place to work for highly qualified people. Its well-functioning labour market and excellent educational system provide the fundamentals for innovation to prosper, instigating the close relationships among enterprises, universities, and research institutes that have made the country a top innovator. Its scientific research institutions are among the world's best, and the strong collaboration between its academic and business

Switzerland as Leading Innovative Nation

sectors, combined with high company spending on research and development, ensures that much of this research is translated into marketable products and processes reinforced by strong intellectual property protection. This robust innovative capacity is captured by its high rate of patenting per capita" (World Economic Forum 2013, p. 14). Innovation levels are often linked to the presence of *regional innovation clusters*, which are discussed in more detail in Chapter 8.

Innovation and Coordination

If the foreign activity is mainly targeted towards gaining expertise and access to strategic assets, this has clear implications for the *headquarters-subsidiary relationship*. For example, a very high level of centralisation has been shown to reduce motivation and creativity and thus to exert a negative influence on the innovation capability of a foreign subsidiary (Gates/Egelhoff 1986; Egelhoff 1988). However, there has to be a close link between the foreign subsidiary and the rest of the MNC, because internal communication flows (horizontal with other subsidiaries and vertical with the headquarters) are major determinants of the innovation capacity of an organisation (Nohria/Ghoshal 1997, p. 39). In particular, it is important that the foreign subsidiary has both the necessary capability to generate new knowledge and the necessary motivation to share this knowledge with the rest of the MNC (Nohria/Ghoshal 1997). Normative integration via a strong organisational culture has been shown to be an efficient coordination instrument which motivates and facilitates bi-directional knowledge flows (see Chapter 12).

Cooperation to Acquire Knowledge

If access to local knowledge is a primary motive for foreign activities, cooperative arrangements are often beneficial. To acquire knowledge, being strongly *embedded* in the local environment is necessary, *local relationships* are required and a close and trustworthy contact with local institutions is useful (Fisch 2001, p. 135; Morschett 2007, p. 318). Local cooperation partners, as in a *joint venture*, can support access to the necessary knowledge sources. An alternative operation mode to gain rapid access to local knowledge in foreign markets is the acquisition of a foreign competitor, including the knowledge base that is accumulated in its patents and, in particular, its employees. In both cases, *market imperfections* in the market for knowledge can be seen as reasons for the (partial) internalisation (Williamson 1985).

Since innovation potential is closely related to a company's R&D activities, this aspect is discussed in more detail in Chapter 20.

Follow-the-Leader

As early as 1973, Knickerbocker argued that companies tend to behave similarly in an oligopolistic industry situation with the objective of maintaining stability and avoiding major changes in the competitive structure. Thus, internationalisation might occur as an *oligopolistic reaction* to a competitor's move to a foreign country (Cardone-Riportella et al. 2003, p. 390). This can influence the internationalisation decision in general as well as the selection of specific foreign countries.

This strategy-based consideration becomes more relevant with increasing levels of internationalisation of the relevant competitors and with increasing competition concentration. In this situation, international activities in particular countries can also represent an *exchange of threats* between competitors (Graham 1978; Malhotra/Agarwal/Ulgado 2004, p. 4). If the same companies compete in several countries, an MNC can use its portfolio of foreign activities in a strategically coordinated manner. For example, it could use its strength in the USA to attack a competitor there who attacked it in a European market. This strategic flexibility is particularly relevant in highly globalised industries. It can be linked to any of the four motives mentioned above. For instance, it might be necessary to gain access to a specific resource, market, strategic asset or type of expertise in order to react to a competitor's action.

Exchange of Threats

Bundles of Motives

While one of the five motives above is often the dominant reason for activities in a particular country, they seldom exist in isolation. Generally, companies pursue a bundle of objectives simultaneously (Shan 1991, p. 562). As with any bundle of objectives, it must be determined whether they are concurrent or complementary. Sometimes, an MNC might have to accept a trade-off between different location characteristics that are favourable for one motive but less favourable for another.

In any case, combinations of the five motives are very common. For example, a company might be primarily market seeking, but to address the demand in a specific country it must relocate parts of its production process into this country to enhance its production efficiency with regard to this sales market. Another company might need a local presence in a country to gain access to relevant strategic assets which are necessary to develop an innovative product for this country market. Thus, the country characteristics that lead to the selection of a specific foreign country for company activities should be considered in combination.

Conclusion and Outlook

The motives of a company when entering a foreign country are not necessarily focused solely on expanding its markets. Moreover, the motivation is often not one-dimensional but multifaceted. Since the company's motives for undertaking activities in a specific country are a major part of its strategy, other major parts of its strategy, organisational behaviour, company structure, etc., have to be aligned to these motives. This shows the necessity to classify, for example, the headquarters-subsidiary relationship according to the dominant motive for internationalisation.

In the last few decades, the principal motives for entering foreign countries have shifted. For example, for many years China was seen mainly as a country for cheap production, while now it is increasingly entered by companies as an attractive market. Eastern Europe opened and simultaneously became attractive as a market and for efficiency seeking. With the perceived increasing scarcity of some natural resources, like oil and gas, some countries (e.g. Russia) have become crucial for the long-term access to the necessary supply. In tandem with the development of prices for natural resources, the same countries are also becoming more attractive as markets. Strategic assets are no longer exclusive to the USA or Europe. For example, Korea has become one of the innovation centres of the world in consumer electronics. Conversely, MNCs from emerging countries like China are increasingly internationalising to industrialised countries to gain access to expertise. Moreover, in many foreign countries, the follow-the-customer trend has accelerated over recent decades (Dunning/Lundan 2008, p. 70).

Further Reading

DUNNING, J.; LUNDAN, S. (2008): Multinational Enterprises and the Global Economy, 2nd ed., Cheltenham, Edward Elgar Publishing, pp. 67-77.

WORLD ECONOMIC FORUM (2013): The Global Competitiveness Report 2013-2014, Geneva.

Case Study: SAP*

Profile, History and Status Quo

In 1972, five former *IBM* employees had the vision of a standard piece of application software for real-time data processing. To make this vision a

---

* Sources used for this case study include the website http://www.sap.com, and various annual and interim reports, investor-relations presentations and explicitly cited sources.

reality, they founded a company called <u>S</u>ystem <u>A</u>nalysis and <u>P</u>rogram development, later known as *SAP*, in Weinheim, Germany. After only a few months
of development, the company successfully released the first version of its
software to interested clients.

Within its first year, the company built up the necessary customer base,
including the German branch of *Imperial Chemical Industries in Östringen*, to
generate over 620,000 DM (approx. 317,000 EUR) in revenues. Over the following years, *SAP* software solutions became increasingly advanced, allowing customers to handle purchasing, inventory management and invoice
verification. By the end of 1976, *SAP* and its 25 employees had generated
3.81 million DM (1.95 million EUR) in revenue.

The next decade ushered in major growth for the German-based company.
After moving their headquarters to Walldorf, *SAP GmbH* was founded and
efforts were taken to widen the capabilities of software solutions. These
developments ultimately led to the release of SAP R/2 in 1979, enabling
material management and production planning for new and existing customers. Thanks to these software enhancements and new server technology
integrated into *SAP* headquarters in 1979 and 1980 the company was able to
expand its customer base to over 200 companies by the end of 1981.

On its 10th anniversary, *SAP* reached the 100-employee milestone and had
successfully expanded its customer base to companies in Austria and Switzerland. *SAP (International) AG* was founded in Switzerland as a starting
point for *SAP's* efforts in foreign markets. In addition to this new base outside of Germany, the headquarters in Walldorf was expanded to accommo-
date further employees and provide a new base of operations for further
growth. The transition from a private, limited-liability company into the
publicly traded *SAP AG* in 1988 enabled the company to finance its further
investments.

When SAP R/3 was presented to the public in 1991, *SAP* had long outgrown
its initial borders. With over 14 subsidiaries in Canada, China, Australia and
other important markets all over the world, *SAP* had more than 2,200 customers in 31 different countries using its software. After the fall of the Iron
Curtain, *SAP* was one of the first companies to enter the Eastern European
market. They released a specialised version of SAP R/2 for the Russian market. Strengthened by fruitful cooperation with software giants like *Microsoft*
and expanding their workforce to over 3,600 employees, *SAP* reached over 1
billion DM (approx. 510 million EUR) revenue in 1993, establishing themselves as one of the most important players in the software market.

The end of the century saw *SAP* rise to become the world's leading provider
of e-business software solutions for companies. Thanks to their overall success on the stock market and further increasing revenues, *SAP* used strategi-

*Mergers &
Acquisitions*

cally suitable acquisitions to add to their product portfolio and thereby increase their employee and customer numbers. With the *mySAP.com* strategy introduced by co-CEO *Hasso Plattner* in 1999, the foundations of success in the Internet-driven days of the new millennium were built. The transformation for a simple component vendor to a full solution provider attracted numerous new customers, including the financial service provider *MLP*, *Hewlett-Packard* and later *Nestlé*, signing the biggest *SAP* contract to date.

The global financial crisis in the first decade of the new millennium forced *SAP* to make some cuts in reaction to a declining stock market. During that time, around 3,300 employees had to be dismissed in order to reduce expenses. Nowadays, *SAP* has recovered from the crisis and employees more than 66,000 employees to serve over 253,000 customers worldwide. Thanks to mostly successful acquisitions, partnerships and newly built subsidiaries, *SAP* has established offices in 130 countries and annual revenue of over 16 billion EUR.

The Software Industry

Very few industries undergo as many changes and developments as the software industry (see PWC 2014). Technological evolution and the fact that more and more businesses and people are relying on software solutions fuels the constant growth of numerous big software companies like *SAP*, *Microsoft* and *Oracle*. Furthermore, mobile devices, cloud technology and other developments are starting to reshape the way software is used and forcing software companies to rethink their strategies. *SAP* has already acted on those ongoing trends and in 2011 announced the acquisition of *Success-Factor*, a leading expert for cloud technology.

Table 4.2   *SAP Revenue Categories in 2013*

Revenue categories	%
+ Cloud subscriptions and support	4
+ Software	27
+ Support	52
Software and software-related services revenue	**83**
+ Consulting	13
+ Other services	4
Professional service and other services revenue	**17**
Total revenue	**100**
▦ one-time revenue ▦ recurring revenue	

Source: SAP 2014, p. 1.

In 2013, 4% of *SAP's* revenues (see Table 4.2) came from cloud subscriptions and over 50% from support. Based on the new product elements of their latest solutions concepts, this number is likely to increase. Overall, most of the revenues in this industry are still made via the traditional *licensing model*, but experts suggest that in 2016 almost 24% of all software related revenues will be based on cloud-related, subscription revenue (PWC 2013, p. 8). These reshaped business approaches carry some potential risks. Subscription models such as a cloud make it relatively easy and interesting for customers to switch companies after a short amount of time; therefore, product solutions must be attractive enough to ensure customers' loyalty to the given solution (PWC 2013, p. 12).

Traditionally, US companies are the leading providers of software solutions. Only a few of the biggest and most successful companies in this industry are not based in the United States (see Table 4.3). *SAP* is by far the biggest European software company. The fact that most of the biggest software companies originate in the United States also leads to a certain industry focus on this market. *SAP* has already established an office in the United States to gain access to possible cooperation partners and better access to technology that emerges from this very important market.

The US Market as the Leading Source of Innovation

Software Company Ranking in 2012

Table 4.3

Rank	Company	Country	Sales (in billion USD)	Profits (in billion USD)	Assets (in billion USD)	Market Value (in billion USD)
1	Microsoft	United States	83.3	22.8	153.5	343.8
2	Oracle	United States	37.9	11.1	86.6	185
3	SAP	Germany	22.3	4.4	37.3	97.1
4	Vmware	United States	5.2	1	12.3	48.2
5	Symantec	United States	6.8	0.9	13.3	14
6	CA	United States	4.6	1	11.8	14.1
7	Fiserv	United States	4.8	0.7	9.7	14.6
8	HCL Technologies	India	4.7	0.7	4.2	16.6
9	Intuit	United States	4.2	0.7	4.7	22.4
10	Amadeus IT Holdings	Spain	4.1	0.7	7.5	18.9

Source: PWC 2013.

Go Big – Go Global

SAP's Product Strategy

The basic product line introduced by *SAP* in the early 1970s was offered support for basic functions, such as finance, human resource management or manufacturing. Since then, *SAP* has added various functions to meet enhanced requirements. Their application suites R/2 (1981) and R/3 (1991) had a particularly large influence on their success and can be seen as industry milestones. As the Internet gained importance in the late 1990s, R/3 was rediscovered as a tool for managing globally operating businesses (Lehrer/Schlegelmilch/Behnam 2009, p. 101). Therefore, *SAP* spent the following years creating solutions suitable for different work environments and incorporating companies' major tasks.

Figure 4.3 | *SAP's Product Portfolio*

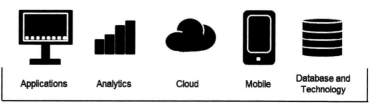

| Applications | Analytics | Cloud | Mobile | Database and Technology |

SAP HANA

Source: SAP 2012, p. 9.

Figure 4.3 shows *SAP's* product portfolio. Since the 1990s, *SAP* has added new features to its initial product line to become a *full service provider* that can cover almost every task demanded by their clients. The introduction of *SAP HANA*, a powerful database tool, in 2010 laid the foundation for the incorporation of new features, such as the support from mobile devices and cloud technology.

Differentiation of a Standardised Product to Fit Local Markets

With a global customer base in over 180 countries, *SAP* uses the internationalisation of their products as a key element to differentiate themselves from competitors. Thanks to customised packages for individual customers in line with different legal and language requirements, their widely standardised software solutions can be implemented in various companies worldwide. So far, *SAP* has delivered over 60 country versions that meet the respective legal requirements and translated products into 39 different languages.

SAP's Internationalisation Strategy

Table 4.4

Internationalisation	Localisation	Translation
technical enablement of a system to operate globally	business solutions are not viable without localisation of content	speak the language of the locals
• multilanguage support • code pages/unicodes • time zones • multiple currencies • calendars	• local best business practices • legal requirements and statutory reporting	

Source: SAP 2012, p. 10.

For *SAP*, international expansion of software solutions involves three main ideas (see Table 4.4). *Internationalisation* covers the basic possibilities for making suitable software solutions that can be implemented during the basic development of the software, enabling customers to use different languages, work in different time zones, and adjust to the given currency and other minor features. This can be regarded as highly standardised content that provides a foundation for further adjustments to suit the given environment.

Standardisation vs. Local Adaptation

By *localising* to incorporate local best business practices and meet local requirements and statutory reporting, globally active companies and their employees can easily adjust to business demands in countries different to their usual base of operation. Finally, *translation* into the local language is necessary, as language localisation is a central factor of success to reach new customers.

Global Activities of SAP

One strength of *SAP's* global operations is that they enable their customers to run a global solution to their country-specific needs. Various subsidiaries in key markets are part of *SAP's* strategy to gain *local knowledge* that can be used to differentiate of their products. With over 1,100 employees focusing on this issue, *SAP* can successfully implement business solutions in a majority of the market. *SAP* recently announced a further investment in international growth to strengthen their market position in economies such as Brazil, India and Russia. *SAPs Globalisation Services* (GS) build on the key software features discussed earlier. It is through these local service centres, that customers get the necessary support to find the best solutions to their goals in the given market.

Another very important aspect of *SAP's* success is their international research & development facilities. The *SAP Labs* and *SAP Research* organisations cooperate with partners, customers and universities to create new global solutions.

Figure 4.4 | *SAP's R&D Activities*

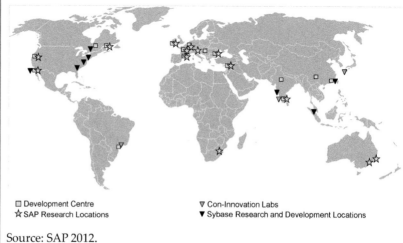

☐ Development Centre   ▽ Con-Innovation Labs
☆ SAP Research Locations   ▼ Sybase Research and Development Locations

Source: SAP 2012.

As shown in Figure 4.4, *SAP Labs* or development centres are located in major areas worldwide. The most important facilities are located in Germany, India and the USA. Global key performance indicators and development standards to ensure a certain level of quality guide the work of every station. *SAP* research centres are always co-located with a partner university or a development centre. Thanks to these facilities, *SAP* is able to react to the requirements of customers and markets alike.

Strategically Chosen Locations Ensure Competitive Advantage

These locations are chosen for numerous reasons. Being close to potential and existing customers, gives *SAP* personal contact with them – allowing *SAP* to not only present new technology and products, but also to gain knowledge about their customers' special needs. It also ensures that *SAP* is able to find new employees, new technology and new product ideas almost anywhere in the world. Being close to all the world's major technology hubs provides them with a keen advantage over other competitors.

SAP has recently begun to build up a very strong presence in India. With over 4,000 employees in their new facilities in Bangalore, it is already their second biggest branch worldwide. India is a very attractive market for several reasons. In addition to more general advantages already listed that are true for most subsidiaries, India also offers a few additional, almost unique benefits. The highly skilled workforce is a crucial factor in possible success. Well-trained college graduates are keen to work for big international companies like *SAP*. Since an entry-level worker will only earn around 7,900 EUR a year, *SAP* saves a lot of money by shifting their production and development facilities to India (Handelsblatt 2011).

Approaching New Markets – Forming a Global Brand

With the launch of their new product line *mySAP.com* in the late 1990s, *SAP* drastically changed their brand and its perception in the market. Many critics had argued that *SAP* was late in recognising e-commerce as a serious and important aspect of the overall software market. Therefore, *SAP's* management was keen to use the launch of *mySAP.com* to reinvent their brand image. By replacing the company's original brand logo with the new *mySAP.com* product line logo, the company tried to reshape their market position.

Unfortunately, this drastic step led to further confusion in the brand's perception and also had some damaging effects on brand equity. In addition, the logo appeared with different slogans all around the world, thus further confusing customers. Between 1997 and 2000, *SAP* used different slogans such as "We Can Change your Business Perspective", "A Better Return on Information", "The Time of new New Management", and "You Can. It Does." A similar approach was used for the company's online representations. With one global website, various local country sites and numerous subsidiary company sites, no clear corporate design could be identified.

This was a major obstacle that had to be overcome for future, international success. In their attempt to cater to customers' demands in numerous markets all over the world, the insufficiency of each individual offering was possibly harming their success. In order to gain the desired global market power and successfully build up a unique experience for their customers on a global basis, they had to reinvent their brand appearances. After all, the reputation they had already built was a unique resource to transfer into new markets.

At the *SAPPHIRE* conference (established by *SAP* to present new products and solutions to the media, customers and analysts) the new Global Chief Marketing Officer, Martin Homlish, announced the new vision for *SAP* mar-

Reinventing the SAP Brand

keting efforts to give the company a fresh look. One of the ideas behind the marketing concept was the transition from a German company selling worldwide to a true global player, able to compete in every market. To align with these stated goals, the team around Homlish decided to slowly transform the overall brand from *mySAP.com* back to its original. Figure 4.5 shows the newly formed brand architecture. It features a strong master brand and several sub-brands that represent individual product solutions. These changes were complemented by newly designed Internet representations that streamlined the former websites and establish one global site that, like the product itself, was able to adjust to the language of its current viewer. Thereby, the content was easily distributed in every market in a similar fashion without adding too many local influences.

Figure 4.5 | *SAP Brand Architecture*

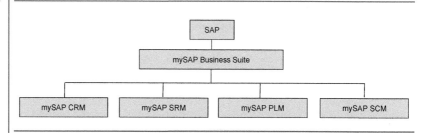

Summary and Outlook

As shown in this case study, *SAP* has made enormous efforts in the last 40 years to develop from a small 5-man start-up to one of the most important companies in the software industry. Thanks to their strategic measures to localise most of their products and solutions, *SAP* has reached customers in over 180 countries. Supported by the newest technology, enhanced R&D institutes and diversified input from different cultures and markets, the company seems able to adapt to most market requirements. Their extremely strong brand names and clear communication guidelines have strengthened their product.

New Assets for the Company through Silicon Valley

Recently, rumours have surfaced suggesting a possible relocation of *SAP's* main operation from Germany to the United States. This indicates one of its important motives in international location selection is resource seeking: Co-CEO Jim Hagemann Snabe stated that the most important industry impulses come out of Silicon Valley and a stronger presence in that area could only benefit *SAP* (Handelsblatt 2013). In 2011, *SAP* started a project in that area, already showing their interest in this location. In their new complex named *AppHaus, SAP* gathered a mix of experienced developers from their German headquarters and some new employees to design and develop new technology (Somerville 2013). Through this project, *SAP* is trying to stay ahead of possible competition and gather fresh, new impulses for the rest of the company. Innovation is an important factor in this industry, and *SAP* sees Silicon Valley as a way to access new ideas.

Questions

1. What are the main motives for internationalisation that you can identify by analysing SAP's internationalisation strategy?

2. Do you see any differences between the diverse types of activities that SAP performs in its host countries? Do motives differ by country or region?

3. How do you evaluate *SAP's* desire to move their base of operations to the United States?

Hints

1. See the company website.

2. See Handelsblatt 2013.

References

AHARONI, Y. (2000): Introduction: Setting the Scene, in: AHARONI, Y.; NACHUM, L. (Eds.): Globalization of Services: Some Implications for Theory and Practice, London, Routledge, pp. 1-21.

BARTLETT, C.A.; GHOSHAL, S. (1989): Managing Across Borders: The Transnational Solution, Boston, McGraw-Hill.

BARTLETT, C.A.; GHOSHAL, S. (2000): Transnational Management: Text, Cases, and Readings in Cross-Border Management, 3rd ed., Boston, McGraw-Hill.

CARDONE-RIPORTELLA, C.; ALVAREZ-GIL, M.; LADO-COUSTE, N.; SASI, V. (2003): The Relative Effects of Client-following and Market-seeking

Strategies in the Internationalisation Process of Financial-services Companies: A Comparison of Spanish and Finnish Entities, in: International Journal of Management, Vol. 20, No. 3, pp. 384-394.

DUNNING, J. (1988): Explaining International Production, London, HarperCollins Publishers.

DUNNING, J.; LUNDAN, S. (2008): Multinational Enterprises and the Global Economy, 2nd ed., Cheltenham, Edward Elgar Publishing.

EGELHOFF, W. (1988): Organizing the Multinational Enterprise: An Information-Processing Perspective, Cambridge, HarperBusiness.

ERRAMILLI, K.; RAO, C. (1990): Choice of Foreign Market Entry Modes by Service Firms: Role of Market Knowledge, in: Management International Review, Vol. 30, No. 2, pp. 135-150.

EUROSTAT (2014): Hourly Labour Costs Ranged from €3.7 to € 40.1 across the EU28 Member States in 2013, Newsrelease, March 27, 2014.

FERDOWS, K. (1989): Mapping International Factory Networks, in: FERDOWS, K. (Ed.): Managing International Manufacturing, Amsterdam, Elsevier Science, pp. 3-21.

FISCH, J.-H. (2001): Structure Follows Knowledge: Internationale Verteilung der Forschung & Entwicklung in multinationalen Unternehmen, Wiesbaden, Gabler.

GATES, S.; EGELHOFF, W. (1986): Centralization in Headquarters-subsidiary Relationships, in: Journal of International Business Studies, Vol. 17, No. 2, pp. 71-92.

GHOSHAL, S.; BARTLETT, C.A. (1988): Creation, Adoption and Diffusion of Innovations by Subsidiaries of Multinational Corporations, in: Journal of International Business Studies, Vol. 19, No. 3, pp. 365-388.

GRAHAM, E. (1978): Transatlantic Investments by Multinational Firms: A Rivalistic Phenomenon, in: Journal of Post-Keynesian Economics, Fall, pp. 82-99.

GRÜNIG, R.; MORSCHETT, D. (2012): Developing International Strategies: Going and Being International for Medium-sized Companies, Berlin-Heidelberg, Springer.

GUPTA, A.K.; GOVINDARAJAN, V. (1991): Knowledge Flows and the Structure of Control within Multinational Corporations, in: Academy of Management Review, Vol. 16, No. 4, pp. 768-792.

HANDELSBLATT (2011): Inside SAP, www.handelsblatt.com, accessed on August 15, 2014.

HANDELSBLATT (2013): SAP muss globaler werden, www.handelsblatt.com, August 07, 2014.

HENNART, J.-F.; LARIMO, J. (1998): The Impact of Culture on the Strategy of Multinational Enterprises: Does National Origin Affect Ownership Decisions?, in: Journal of International Business Studies, Vol. 29, No. 3, pp. 515-538.

HESHMATI, A. (2003): Productivity Growth, Efficiency and Outsourcing in Manufacturing and Service Industries, in: Journal of Economic Surveys, Vol. 17, No. 1, pp. 79-112.

HYMER, S.H. (1978): The International Operations of National Firms: A Study of Direct Foreign Investment, Cambridge, MIT Press.

KUTSCHKER, M.; SCHMID, S. (2011): Internationales Management, 7th ed., Munich, Oldenbourg.

LEHRER, M.; SCHLEGELMILCH, B.; BEHNAM, M. (2009): Competitive Advantage from Exposure to Multiple National Environments: the Induced Internationalisation of "Born-multidomestic" Firms, in: European Journal of International Management, Vol. 3, No. 1, pp. 92-110.

MALHOTRA, N.; AGARWAL, J.; ULGADO, F. (2004): Internationalization and Entry Modes: A Multitheoretical Framework and Research Propositions, in: Journal of International Marketing, Vol. 11, No. 4, pp. 1-31.

MARTINEZ, Z.; RICKS, D. (1989): Multinational Parent Companies' Influence over Human Resource Decisions of Affiliates : U.S. Firms in Mexico, in: Journal of International Business Studies, Vol. 20, No. 3, pp. 465-487.

MORSCHETT, D. (2005): Contract Manufacturing, in: ZENTES, J.; SWOBODA, B.; MORSCHETT, D. (Eds.): Kooperationen, Allianzen und Netzwerke, 2nd ed., Wiesbaden, Gabler, pp. 597-622.

MORSCHETT, D. (2007): Institutionalisierung und Koordination von Auslandseinheiten: Analyse von Industrie- und Dienstleistungsunternehmen, Wiesbaden, Gabler.

MORSCHETT, D.; SCHRAMM-KLEIN, H.; SWOBODA, B. (2008): What Do We Really Know about Foreign Market Entry Strategy Decision? A Meta-analysis on the Choice between Wholly-owned Subsidiaries and Cooperative Arrangement, Best Paper Proceedings of the Academy of International Business Annual Meeting 2008, Milan.

MÖßLANG, A. (1995): Internationalisierung von Dienstleistungsunternehmen, Wiesbaden, Gabler.

NOHRIA, N.; GHOSHAL, S. (1997): The Differentiated Network: Organizing Multinational Corporations for Value Creation, San Francisco, Jossey-Bass.

PWC (2013): PwC Global 100 Software Leaders, Frankfurt.

PWC (2014): PwC Global 100 Software Leaders, Frankfurt.

RANDØY, T.; LI, J. (1998): Global Resource Flows and MNE Network Integration, in: BIRKINSHAW, J.; HOOD, N. (Eds.): Multinational Corporate Evolution and Subsidiary Development, Basingstoke, Palgrave Macmillan, pp. 76-101.

RUGMAN, A.M.; VERBEKE, A. (2001): Location, Competitiveness, and the Multinational Enterprise, in: RUGMAN, A.M.; BREWER, T. (Eds.): Oxford Handbook of International Business, Oxford, Oxford University Press, pp. 150-177.

SAP (2012): Globalization @ SAP, http://www.sapsa.se/wp-content/ uploads/2012/05/Globalization@SAP2012_SAPSA_pdf.pdf, accessed on July 18, 2014.

SAP (2014): SAP at a Glance, The SAP Capital Market Story, http://global.sap.com/corporate-en/investors/pdf/sap-fact-sheet-en.pdf, accessed on July 18, 2014.

SHAN, W. (1991): Environmental Risks and Joint Venture Sharing Arrangements, in: Journal of International Business Studies, Vol. 22, No. 4, pp. 555-578.

SOMERVILLE, H. (2013): Software Giant SAP Innovates with an Infusion Silicon Valley Culture, http://www.mercurynews.com/ci_22962850/software-giant-sap-innovates-an-infusion-silicon-valley, accessed on July 28, 2014.

VERNON, R. (1966): International Investment and International Trade in the Product Cycle, in: Quarterly Journal of Economics, Vol. 80, No. 2, pp. 190-207.

WHITE, R.; POYNTER, T. (1984): Strategies for Foreign-owned Subsidiaries in Canada, in: Business Quarterly, Summer, pp. 59-69.

WILLIAMSON, O. (1985): The Economic Institutions of Capitalism, New York, The Free Press.

WORLD ECONOMIC FORUM (2013): The Global Competitiveness Report 2013-2014, Geneva.

YOUNG, S.; TAVARES, A. (2004): Centralization and Autonomy: Back to the Future, in: International Business Review, Vol. 13, pp. 215-237.

ZENTES, J.; SWOBODA, B.; MORSCHETT, D. (2004): Internationales Wertschöpfungsmanagement, Munich, Vahlen.

Chapter 5

Emerging Country Multinationals

In the past few decades, MNCs from emerging markets have appeared as important players in the international competitive environment. Catching up through fast growth rates, these emerging country multinationals are predicted to influence the international business environment tremendously. This Chapter presents the primary characteristics of emerging country multinationals and models of their international expansion.

Outward Foreign Direct Investment from Emerging Markets

Emerging countries are increasingly important for MNCs. Emerging countries are those markets in the transitional phase between being a developing country and a developed country. The *BRICS* (Brazil, the Russian Federation, India, China and South Africa) economies are an example of such emerging markets.

These fast growing economies nowadays account for approximately half of all economic activities. They have large populations with *increasing disposable incomes*. They are therefore prominent targets for *resource seeking, efficiency seeking* and *market seeking* foreign direct investment by MNCs. However, their role in world economic activities is changing from a passive role as a source of inputs, products, technology or value-adding capabilities, commodities, or cheap labour to a more active role as a source of new competitors on international markets (Rugman/Collinson 2012, p. 637). This changing role of emerging markets thus changes *how, where* and *who* in the world does business.

Emerging Markets

This trend is reflected in the development of global foreign direct investment (see Table 5.1). In 2012, developing countries accounted for more than half of global *FDI inflows*, exceeding the FDI inflows to developed countries. Almost half of the TOP 20 recipients of global foreign direct investment were developing countries. However, developing economies are not only recipients of global FDI; *FDI outflows* to developing economies have also grown significantly, accounting for more than 30% of global FDI outflows. Emerging markets, such as the *BRICS* countries, were among the leading sources of FDI from developing countries. In 2012, FDI from *BRICS* countries accounted for

FDI Inflows and Outflows

10% of the world total, with China as the third largest investor country in 2012, after the United States and Japan (UNCTAD 2013).

Table 5.1   *Global FDI Flows by Region (in billion USD)*

Region	FDI inflows			FDI outflows		
	2010	2011	2012	2010	2011	2012
World	**1409**	**1652**	**1351**	**1505**	**1678**	**1391**
Developed economies	696	820	561	1030	1183	909
Developing economies	637	735	703	413	422	426
Africa	44	48	50	9	5	14
Asia	401	436	407	284	311	308
East and South-East Asia	313	343	326	254	271	275
South Asia	29	44	34	16	13	9
West Asia	59	49	47	13	26	24
Latin America and the Caribbean	190	249	244	119	105	103
Oceania	3	2	2	1	1	1
Transition economies	75	96	87	62	73	55
Structurally weak, vulnerable and small economies	**45**	**56**	**60**	**12**	**10**	**10**
Least developed economies	19	21	26	3.0	3.0	5.0
Landlocked developing countries	27	34	35	9.3	5.5	3.1
Small island developing States	4.7	5.6	6.2	0.3	1.8	1.8
Memorandum: percentage share in world FDI flows						
Developed economies	49.4	49.7	41.5	68.4	70.5	65.4
Developing economies	45.2	44.5	52.0	27.5	25.2	30.6
Africa	3.1	2.9	3.7	0.6	0.3	1.0
Asia	28.4	26.4	30.1	18.9	18.5	22.2
East and South-East Asia	22.2	20.8	24.1	16.9	16.2	19.8
South Asia	2.0	2.7	2.5	1.1	0.8	0.7
West Asia	4.2	3.0	3.5	0.9	1.6	1.7
Latin America and the Caribbean	13.5	15.1	18.1	7.9	6.3	7.4
Oceania	0.2	0.1	0.2	0.0	0.1	0.0
Transition economies	5.3	5.8	6.5	4.1	4.3	4.0
Structurally weak, vulnerable and small economies	**3.2**	**3.4**	**4.4**	**0.8**	**0.6**	**0.7**
Least developed economies	1.3	1.3	1.9	0.2	0.2	0.4
Landlocked developing countries	1.9	2.1	2.6	0.6	0.3	0.2
Small island developing States	0.3	0.3	0.5	0.0	0.1	0.1

Source: UNCTAD 2013.

Role of Emerging Country Multinationals in Fortune 500

The transition of the role of *emerging markets* in international business is characterised by the rise of *emerging country multinationals*, MNCs whose origin is in emerging economies. By 2025, it is believed such companies will account for more than 45% of the *Fortune Global 500*, i.e., the top 500 world companies as measured by their revenue, rising from 5% in 1990 (see Figure 5.1). In 2009, emerging country multinationals generated approx. a quarter of all global FDI outflows; this is expected to surpass 50% in the next few years (Guillén/García-Canal 2011).

The Fortune Global 500 by Location

Figure 5.1

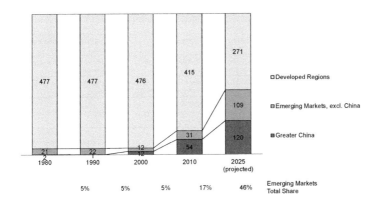

Source: McKinsey Global Institute 2013.

Characteristics of Emerging Country Multinationals

Emerging country multinationals are MNCs that are registered and based in emerging markets (Rugman/Doh 2008). MNCs with their origins in these fast growing economies have expanded around the world as key actors in global FDI and cross-border acquisitions. Several terms have been used to describe this phenomenon, such as *"emerging multinationals"*, *"emerging market firms"*, *"third world multinationals"*, *"unconventional multinationals"* or *"emerging market multinationals"* (Guillén/García-Canal 2011, p. 15). Even though these emerging country multinationals are "far from homogeneous" (Lou/Tung 2007, p. 483), they share a number of *common characteristics* that distinguishes them from their competitors which originated in developed countries (see Table 5.2).

Definition

Probably the most striking is the *pace* with which emerging country multinationals expand into international markets and close the gap between their counterparts from traditional developed economies. In many cases, they start international expansion very early in their lifecycles (Goldstein 2007, p. 149) with an *accelerated speed* of internationalisation (Dunning/Kim/Park 2008, p. 175).

Speed of International Expansion

Table 5.2 *Characteristics of Emerging Country MNCs and Traditional MNCs*

Feature		Emerging Market MNCs	Traditional MNCs
Speed of Internationalization		accelerated	gradual
Competitive Advantages		weak: upgrading of resources required	strong: required resources available in-house
Political Capabilities		strong: firms are used to unstable political environments	weak: firms are used to stable political environments
Expansion Path	In Search of Markets	dual path: simultaneous entry into developed and developing countries	single path: from less to more distant countries
	In Search of Lower Costs	into less developed countries as home country development raises production costs	into less developed countries
	In Search of Strategic Assets	into more developed countries	into similar developed countries
Preferred Entry Mode		external growth: alliances, joint ventures, acquisitions	internal growth: wholly owned subsidiaries
Organizational Adaptability		high, because of their recent and relatively limited international presence, which enables them to adapt technologies to small-scale markets, excel at projects execution and adopt new technology quickly	low, because of their ingrained structure and cultures

Source: Guillén/García-Canal 2011, p. 17.

Emerging country MNCs have shown a rapid development of comparative and competitive advantages in a wide range of industries and seem to be catching up with developed country MNCs at high rates, thus showing a parallel development across these sectors (Rugman/Collinson 2012, p. 655; see Figure 5.2).

Figure 5.2 *Development of Emerging Country Multinationals*

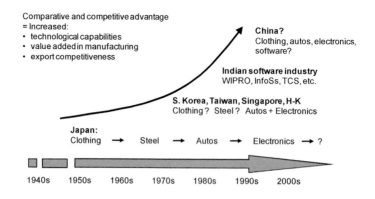

Source: Rugman/Collinson 2012, p. 654.

However, emerging country MNCs have to deal with the liability of being *latecomers* to the international markets, which is why some scholars label them as *latecomer firms* (Mathews 2006). This position represents a common *disadvantage*, one which they share in contrast to established MNCs from the advanced countries. Therefore, in many cases their marketing and technological skills and resources have to be built up from a weaker position.

To successfully grow in international markets, firms need to be able to adapt to the diverse conditions of a changing international environment. While traditional MNCs with long business track records often suffer from inertia and path dependence, emerging country multinationals enjoy higher *flexibility* and *freedom* to adapt to the requirements of internationalisation (Guillén/García-Canal 2011, p. 18).

Their origin from countries a tendency for *discretionary and unstable governments* provides emerging country multinationals with a specific skill – being able to deal with market restrictions, administrative, infrastructural and political difficulties and (in some cases heavily) regulated and rapidly changing institutional environments. This contextual embeddedness into an environment characterised by *institutional voids* has often been characterised as a liability of origin that needs to be overcome to succeed as a global player (Bartlett/Ghoshal 2000, p. 136). However, emerging country multinationals seem to have turned this liability into an asset, because it provides them with stronger *political capabilities* in contrast to traditional MNCs (Sauvant/Maschek/McAllister 2009, p. 8).

Closely connected to the institutional environment is the fact that *state influence* on emerging country multinationals is higher than for traditional MNCs (Peng 2012). State influence may take diverse forms, such as *political influence*, for example through subsidies (e.g. R&D subsidies), legislation, policies that promote internationalisation (e.g. go global policy in China, go-west policy in Russia) or prohibit internationalisation (e.g. restrictions to FDI in- and outflows).

Also, (direct or indirect) *state ownership* is quite a common phenomenon for emerging country multinationals, especially from the Russian Federation and China. Also, most companies in the oil and gas industry are state-owned. However, the internationalisation strategies of *state-owned companies* often have diverse, often non-economic motives. These motives may in some cases relate more strongly to *political objectives*, for example gaining influence over power distribution in international markets.

The relevance of state-owned companies in the global business environment is growing. For example, the number of *state-owned MNCs* that rank among the global players increased from 650 MNCs in 2010 to 845 in 2012. The majority of these state-owned MNCs originate in developing countries.

Their share of global FDI accounted for more than 10% in 2012 (UNCTAD 2013).

Trends in Emerging Country Multinationals' Internationalisation

Waves of Emerging Country Multinationals' Expansion

First Wave

Emerging market firms venturing into new markets is not a new phenomenon. In the 1970s and 1980s a first wave of MNCs from developing countries engaged in outward FDI. Back then, the internationalisation of the so-called *Third World Multinational Enterprises* was largely explained by advantages that stem from *low-cost production* using *labour-intensive* production techniques. The geographic scope of this first wave mainly focused on nearby markets, usually also developing countries. In this first wave, internationalisation was largely driven by constraints in the home country markets such as market restrictions or export difficulties (Mathews 2006, p. 7).

Second Wave

In the second wave, the phenomenon of internationalisation of developing country firms changed and was "less driven by cost factors per se, but more by a search for markets and technological innovations to compete successfully in the global economy" (Yeung 2000, p. 12). Thus, pull-factors drew emerging country multinationals into global activities (Mathews 2006, p. 7).

Industry Focus of Emerging Country Multinationals

Even though emerging country multinationals do not target homogeneous market sectors, in many cases, they (still) tend to involve *mid-tech* and *mature industries*. One of their strengths is the ability to adapt mature technologies to the specific conditions of local environments (Ramamurty/Singh 2009, pp. 415-417). In this vein, they act as imitators rather than as innovators and "have yet to achieve a distinctive global profile based on well-defined strategic competencies and differentiated brand names" (Sim/Pandia 2003, p. 38). However, some emerging country multinationals have matured from this imitator position to become leading global market players in their industries. Examples include the Brazilian firm *Embraer* in the aircraft industry, the Indian firm *Mahindra & Mahindra* for all terrain vehicles and the Chinese firm *CIMC*.

Emerging country multinationals are present across most industries. However, some core industries are of specific regional importance, in some cases with regard to specific countries (Graser 2011, p. 103):

- Major emerging country multinationals can be found in the *natural resource* sector (e.g. from Brazil, the Russian Federation or China) and in *public utilities* and *telecommunications*.

- Asian firms often focus on *high tech engineering* and *manufacturing*.

- Several major Indian MNCs focus their activities on the *pharmaceutical industry, IT* and *services* as well as the *automotive industry*.

- Because of their agricultural heritage, many emerging market players, especially from South America and Asia, operate in *food processing industries*.

Important emerging country multinationals are structured as *conglomerates*, diversified groups or business groups more frequently than their counterparts with origins in developed countries (Goldstein 2008, p. 92). These conglomerates provide advantages such as higher brand awareness and internal markets for resources such as monetary resources, as well as experts and management (Khanna/Palepu 2006).

Expansion Paths

The usual expansion path for emerging country multinationals tends to differ from that of most traditional MNCs. In terms of internationalisation direction, the main distinction is between "South-South investments" (Battat/Aykut 2005), also labelled as *"E2E investments"* (emerging market-to-emerging market), and "South-North investments":

- *South-South investments* are directed from emerging markets as home countries to other emerging markets as host countries. Usually, the motive of such internationalisation patterns is asset exploitation, thus exploiting existing competitive advantages, mainly searching for low-cost labour and market expansion.

- *South-North investments*, on the other hand, are directed from emerging markets to developed countries, mainly with asset seeking or asset-exploring motives. In addition to market seeking, emerging country multinationals strive for access to strategic assets such as technologies, brands or specific expertise.

Expansion into *developing countries* may be achieved faster, as emerging country multinationals can more easily transfer their home-grown competitive advantages to these more similar markets. This may serve as a basis to gain *operational experience*, grow in size and generate profits. However, venturing into *developed markets* provides emerging country multinationals with new competitive advantages and thus an *upgrade of capabilities* and resources (Guillén/García-Canal 2011, p. 17).

Emerging country multinationals also tend to differ with regard to the main *modes* they apply to enter new international markets. While traditional MNCs – at least in their earlier stages of international expansion – often showed a priority for *internal growth strategies* through wholly-owned subsidiaries, emerging country multinationals tend to choose entry modes based on *external growth* and cooperation. They show a preference for strategic alliances, joint ventures or mergers and acquisitions, particularly when expanding into developed countries. These foreign operation modes help them to overcome the *liability of foreignness* by gaining access to strategic assets, resources and capabilities by cooperating with partner companies in international alliances or taking over established players on the host country markets (Guillén/García-Canal 2011, pp. 17-18; see Chapters 17 and 18 for a discussion of foreign operation modes).

For *takeovers* of developing country firms, some emerging country multinationals have acted as "bargain hunters" and have taken over established firms that, however, suffered from weak business situations or even went bankrupt. For example, in March 2008, *Tata Motors* bought *Jaguar* and *Land Rover* when Ford was in financial difficulties (see the *Tata Motors* case study later in this Chapter).

Explaining Emerging Country Multinational Expansion

There are several approaches to explaining internationalisation patterns of multinational companies. One prominent approach is Dunning's eclectic paradigm, the *ownership location internalisation (OLI) framework* (see Chapter 14), which suggests that MNCs possess and leverage superior resources that enable them to successfully enter new markets. However, emerging country multinationals often do not possess a wide base of specific resources that provide them with ownership advantages. Even though they strive for lucrative international locations and internalise transactions, they typically do not possess superior expertise, technologies or management capabilities (Peng 2012).

Value-Creation Strategies in Foreign Markets

Resources, their *availability* for the firm, their *transferability* and their *substitutability* between markets play an important role in emerging country multinationals' *value-creation strategies*.

Value Creation Strategies of Emerging Country Multinationals

Table 5.3

	Transferability between Markets			
	high		**low**	
	I (Exploiters)		**II (Defenders)**	
	Resource	Firm Example	Resource	Firm Example
high	• know-how (marketing, brand & distribution)	Astrid y Gastón, Concha y Toro, Bimbo, Pollo Campero	• market share	
	• market knowledge	América Móvil, Cemex	• customer-driven	Tenaris
	• innovative capability	Tenaris	• competitor-driven	América Móvil, Cemex, Politec
	• know-how (production)	Petrobas	• market-driven	Petrobas
	IV (Others)		**III (Resource Developers)**	
			Resource	Firm example
	EMNCs use another form of access to resources lacked (e.g., imports)		• leading technology/knowledge	Bimbo, Politec, Natura
low			• financial resources	Cemex
			• know-how (marketing: brand & distribution	Bimbo
			• natural resources	Vale, Petrobas

(Left vertical axis label: Availability for the Firm)

Source: Losada Otalora/Casanova 2012, p. 9.

Based on these resource attributes, four internationalisation strategies can be distinguished (Losada Otalora/Casanova 2012, pp. 9-10; see Table 5.3):

■ *Exploiters* create value by transferring resources developed in their domestic markets to international markets. Resources of this type are mainly *knowledge-based assets* such as brands or specialised production expertise.

■ *Defenders* are companies that invest abroad to avoid loss of market share, i.e., a type of resource that is *non-transferable* between markets. The main objective is to invest abroad to defend their market position against market-driven threats such as growth constraints or market-dependence on a single or few markets.

■ *Resource developers* create value abroad by acquiring marketing, technological, financial, or natural resources. This improves their overall global capabilities; however, they are non-transferable between markets.

■ *Others:* The fourth category comprises companies that use other forms of access to resources, for example imports.

LLL-Framework: Linkage, Leverage, Learning

Firm-Specific Advantages

Despite numerous drawbacks, emerging markets are still regarded as sources of innovation. Starting from their home market conditions, emerging country multinationals have developed the capacity to innovate and continually build up sustainable *competitive advantages* that reduce their resilience on location-specific endowments (Rugman/Collinson 2012, pp. 655-656). Table 5.4 summarises the specific advantages of globally successful emerging country multinationals.

Mathews (2006) proposed the *LLL-framework*, which is closely connected to these firm-specific advantages of emerging country multinationals. In this framework, the international expansion of emerging country multinationals is driven by resource linkage, leverage and learning.

Linkage

Outward Orientation

Emerging country multinational internationalisation – as *latecomers* to the markets – start with a focus on resources, which can be acquired externally, i.e. on international markets, rather than their own advantages and capabilities. Emerging country multinationals take an *outward orientation* and seek to acquire resources and complementary assets, which can be accessed on the global market rather than in their home countries. Seeking for advantages outside their domestic markets with *resource seeking objectives* (see Chapter 4) in this vein is a prerequisite to overcoming the constraints and limitations of their domestic markets.

This outward orientation, however, is more risky than the more conservative inward focus. Therefore, forms of *collaborative strategic partnerships* in international markets such as joint ventures are important strategic choices to access external resources and – as discussed – are commonly chosen modes of foreign market entry strategies for emerging country multinationals. These forms of internationalisation are used to form *international networks* in which resources are linked up. In this way, emerging country multinationals are "drawing themselves into circuits of exchange and sources of advantage" (Mathews 2006, p. 18).

Firm-Specific Advantages of Emerging Country Multinationals

Table 5.4

Globalising...	Assets	Capabilities	Connections	Reputation
Innovation and Technology	patents, licenses, IPR. specialised tools, hardware, software, etc.	low-end (maintenance) to high-end (blue-sky R&D) expertise	strategic alliances, buyer and supplier links. R&D networks/global capability inputs	credibility, trust, track record, recognition
Marketing and Brands	own valued brands, logos, trademarks, awards, etc.	brand management protection, development of expertise	formal co-branding, supplier or buyer, distribution, and retailing affiliations	reputation for quality, price, innovation, etc., market positioning, brand recognition, market presence

Source: Rugman/Collinson 2012, p. 656.

Leverage

Establishing networks of resource exchange and exploitation can *leverage the linkages* between resources and competitive advantages. Leverage, therefore, refers to the emerging country multinationals' ability to take advantage of these unique capabilities in their *international network* of activities (Peng 2012). In this context, it is crucial to establish structures and processes that enable companies to effectively manage and utilise the resources and capabilities across the entire network. Emerging country multinationals, however, are able to leverage these resources by establishing *knowledge sharing* across the network. This may also include technology licensing contracts, imitation and reverse engineering (Mathews 2006).

Knowledge-Sharing Networks

Learning

Thanks to linkage and leverage strategies, emerging country multinationals are more adapted to the global markets that are themselves increasingly interlinked. However, it is the subsequent learning processes that accelerate expansion patterns. Companies apply repeated linkage and leverage processes that lead to organisational learning processes.

Repetition of Linkage and Leverage

The main ideas behind the LLL-framework are summarised in Table 5.5.

| *Table 5.5* | *Characteristics of the LLL-Framework* |

Criterion	LLL-Framework
Resource Utilisation	resources accessed through linkage with external firms
Geographic Scope	locations tapped as part of international network
Make or Buy?	bias towards operations created through external linkage
Learning	learning achieved through repetition of linkage and leverage
Process of Internationalisation	proceeds incrementally through linkage
Organisation	global integration sought as latecomer advantage
Driving Paradigm	capturing of latecomer advantage
Time Frame	cumulative development process

Source: Adapted from Mathews 2006, p. 21.

Models of International Expansion

The diverse directions, types and scope of emerging country multinationals' internationalisation strategies and patterns show that there is *no blueprint* for emerging country multinationals' international expansion. With particular reference industries, the phase in the companies' life cycles and the specific home country background, five models of international expansion can be differentiated (Accenture 2008, p. 10):

■ *Full-fledged global players* are more established, comparatively older and have attained international presence and relevance in terms of size and geographic scope comparable to the big Western MNCs. Examples include *Bharat Forge* and *Tata Group* from India or *CEMEX* from Mexico.

■ While global players expand their operations worldwide, the *regional players* among the emerging country multinationals limit their scope to neighbouring regional markets, usually those of higher cultural and geographic proximity. Often, these are young companies still in the early stages of internationalisation. The Polish Bank *PKO BP* or the Czech company *CEZ* are examples.

■ *Global sourcers* focus on selling on their home country markets. However, resource restraints from their domestic markets force them to source internationally. Companies from the commodities industries or energy sector often follow this strategy, for example *China National Offshore Oil Corporation (CNOOC)* or *Reliance Petroleum Limited* from India, who source oil internationally to sell it primarily to their home country markets.

■ *Global sellers*, on the other hand, seek market opportunities abroad and manufacture and source primarily on their domestic markets. The Russian energy company *SUEK* is an example.

- *Multi-regional niche players* are comparatively small companies that operate across multiple regions with a focus on specialised sectors. Innovative processes or technologies often form the basis for their expansion. *Holografika*, a Hungarian manufacturer of specialised display technology, is one such small global company, operating in a niche with a focused international scope.

Conclusion and Outlook

One of the most striking characteristics of emerging country multinationals is their *pace of international expansion* into global markets. However, this speed of internationalisation is also their most significant challenge for the future, along with a range of other challenges for future growth (Accenture 2008, pp. 45-46):

- *Input constraints*: To guarantee future growth, emerging country multinationals need sufficient inputs such as capital, energy, raw materials, qualified employees, etc.

    Challenges for Future Growth

- *Increasing competition*: MNCs, especially emerging country multinationals, are growing in number and in size, so global competition is increasing. This might limit future growth opportunities.

- *Geopolitical risk*: Emerging country multinationals operating across geographic boundaries exhibit an increasingly complex cast of regulatory and policy actors, both at the global and regional level. Regulatory practices might limit their future growth paths or direction.

- *More diverse customers*: In the global market sphere, especially when entering wealthier economies, emerging country multinationals are exposed to customer sectors with increasingly different needs and demands, which might be difficult to serve with a one-size-fits-all-approach (see the discussion of the AAA-framework in Chapter 2). This reinforces the need to continue tailoring goods and services to regional needs, one of the key strengths of emerging country multinationals.

- *Higher-value innovation*: Emerging country multinationals will need to improve their innovation capabilities and progress up the value chain to access new markets. While their earlier innovation capabilities were largely due to the need to adapt and improvise in international markets, future challenges will be to engage in high-end research.

Emerging country multinationals are clearly well positioned for future growth. The forecast is that they will gain a further share in international markets in the future, turning them into *emancipated global players*.

Further Reading

MATHEWS, J.A. (2006): Dragon Multinationals: New Players in 21st Century Globalization, in: Asia Pacific Journal of Management, Vol. 23, No. 1, pp. 5-27.

RAMAMURTI, R.; SINGH, J.V. (Eds.) (2009): Emerging Multinationals in Emerging Markets, Cambridge, Cambridge University Press.

RUGMAN, A.M.; VERBEKE, A. (2004): A Perspective on Regional and Global Strategies of Multinational Enterprises, in: Journal of International Business Studies, Vol. 35, No. 1, pp. 3-18.

Case Study: Tata Group*

Profile and Company Structure

The *Tata Group*, founded in 1868, is a global enterprise headquartered in Mumbai, India. Among other areas, the *Tata* brand received worldwide recognition through *Tata Motors*, which is part of the *Tata Group*. *Tata Motors* won renown by launching a car with a selling price of one lakh (equal to USD 2,500 or EUR 1,500), the lowest price for a car at that time, and by acquiring *Jaguar* and *Land Rover* in 2008.

Besides *Tata Motors*, the *Tata Group* consists of about 100 operating companies in seven business sectors: communications and information technology, engineering, materials, services, energy, consumer products and chemicals. Each company in the portfolio, including well-known and respected companies like *Tata Steel*, *Tata Consultancy Services (TCS)*, *Tata Power*, *Tata Chemicals*, *Tata Tea*, *Indian Hotels*, *Tata Communications*, and *Tata Motors*, operates independently and has its own board of directors and shareholders (Lala 2007). According to their own reports, the companies operate in more than 100 countries across six continents and export products and services to over 150 countries. About 63% of their revenue of 96.79 billion USD in 2012/13 was generated from business outside India. With 540,000 employees across its companies, *Tata Group* is India's largest employer.

---

* Sources used for this case study include the website www.tata.com, various company reports and explicitly cited sources.

Since 2012, Cyrus Pallonji Mistry is chairman of the *Tata Group*. He is the first chairman from outside the *Tata* family. Around two-thirds of the parent firm, *Tata Sons Ltd.*, is held by philanthropic trusts (Srivastava et al. 2012). Through these trusts, *Tata Sons Ltd.* utilises on average between 8 to 14% of its net profit every year for various social causes, such as support for academic institutions, social and community causes and programmes for underprivileged people. Figure 5.3 shows the ownership structure and revenues for each business sector within the *Tata Group*.

Ownership Structure and Business Sectors within the Tata Group

Figure 5.3

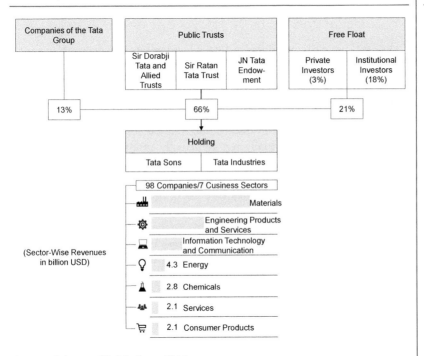

Source: Schuster/Holtbrügge 2011.

Given the *Tata Group's* origin as a family-run company, it is closely linked to its surrounding community. This is clear from a quote by *Jamsetji Nusserwanji*, the founder of the *Tata Group*: "In a free enterprise, the community is not just another stakeholder in business but is in fact the very purpose of its existence" (Srivastava et al. 2012). The company fulfils its corporate social responsibility in various ways. It feels especially committed to five core values that – by its own account – drive all of the business activities:

- *Integrity*: fair, honest, transparent in all dealings.

- *Understanding*: care, respect and compassion for customers and colleagues.

- *Excellence*: highest possible standards for goods and services.

- *Unity*: build strong relationships with partners and customers worldwide.

- *Responsibility*: What comes from the people goes back to the people many times over.

Formation and Early Development of the Tata Group

The *Tata Group* has its origins in 1868 when Jamsetji Nusserwanji Tata established a trading company in Bombay. Tata used early revenues to fund the *Tata Group's* first big industrial project in 1877: *Empress Mills*, a textiles venture set up in Nagpur in central India. Like many companies in emerging markets, *Tata* was not committed to specific products or fields. A fixed commitment would have been disadvantageous because market potentials for single products were usually not sufficiently profitable. At the same time potential customers in the emerging market had various needs that were not adequately met by existing offers. *Tata* reacted to this situation by offering a wide portfolio. In this way *Tata* made use of new market opportunities even though they had little to do with their previous business. Ravi Kant, Vice-Chairman of *Tata Motors*, describes this strategy as follows: "[We] look at opportunities in the market as they emerge. We then try to convert those opportunities into real business" (Crainer 2010, p 14). In that spirit, Tata opened up the *Taj Mahal Hotel* in Bombay in 1903. In subsequent years the *Tata Group* stuck to this strategy. In 1907 they diversified the coal and steel industry by founding the *Tata Iron and Steel Company*. In 1915, the company entered unknown territory once again by generating hydroelectric power from a site near Bombay.

From the 1930's, the *Tata Group* consolidated its business while still entering new areas, notably insurance and the production of soaps, detergents and cooking oil. The *Tata Group* continued to rely on expansions in the home market. Some prominent ventures include *Tata Chemicals* (1939); *Tata Motors* and *Tata Industries* (both 1945); *Voltas* (1954); *Tata Tea* (1962), now known as *Tata Global Beverages*; *Tata Consultancy Services* (1968) and *Titan Industries* (1984). Until the end of the 1980s this diversification was limited to the home market in India.

Development of the Tata Group since 1990

Only at the beginning of the 1990s did *Tata* become a *multinational company*. The groundwork was laid by changes in the political environment in India, leading to increasing liberalisation. At the same time, these changes were accompanied by the opening of the Indian market for foreign companies and investors. This resulted in a modified strategic orientation for the *Tata Group*: Growth was still generated through innovations in the home market. Further development of the Indian market through joint ventures with Multinational Corporations and expansion to foreign markets complemented the strategy.

Growth in the Home Market through Innovation and Joint Ventures

Liberalisation of the Indian Market in the early 1990s and innovation strategies led to new growth for many Indian companies. The goal was to harness market potential resulting from the changes in overall political conditions. The companies within the *Tata Group* also followed this approach.

One example is *Tata Motors*. The precursor of this company was founded in 1945 as a truck manufacturer. Before the liberalisation of the Indian market the company gained a leading market position in commercial vehicles in India. The new market conditions at the beginning of the 1990s made it possible for *Tata Motors* to reach new customer groups by starting production of passenger cars. The company now faced the challenge of offering products to a segment that they had hardly any experience with at that time. Their goal was to gain experience in a new market area while keeping costs and risks for the company as low as possible. They now had to decide whether to imitate competing manufacturers' existing systems or work on their own innovations (Khanna/Palepu 2006).

Tata Motors

Tata Motors decided to combine innovation and low costs: The company entered the car and utility segments with products such as the *Estate* (a station wagon), *Sierra*, and *Sumo* (a utility vehicle used in both urban and rural India for multi-passenger transportation). In 1998 and 2002, *Tata Motors* launched two very popular passenger cars, the *Indica* and the *Indigo* (Lala 2007). These innovations significantly expanded the company's customer potential and contributed to its growth (Krishnan/Jha 2011). At the same time the new products were oriented towards existing capabilities that *Tata Motors* had built in the light commercial vehicle arena. For example, the *Estate* and *Sierra* models were based on the chassis of a light truck the company had already launched. Thus *Tata Motors* were able to gain experience in a new market segment and reduce the risk associated with innovations. The locus of innovation was largely internal to the company (Krishnan/Jha 2011).

Joint Ventures

More recently, the *Tata Group* has also brought best-in-class technologies to India, mainly through joint ventures with Multinational Corporations such as automobile engines (*Cummins*), industrial controls (*Honeywell*), computer hardware (*IBM*), and telecom equipment (*Lucent Technologies*) (Basu/Maertens 2010). This strategy was another way for *Tata* to generate growth in the home market. In doing so, *Tata* offered foreign companies access and experience in a high-growth market. In return, the companies in the *Tata Group* benefit from an influx in expertise and resources.

International Growth through Mergers and Acquisitions

Diversification of Tata Tea

Since the turn of the millennium, the *Tata Group* has generated part of its growth through mergers and acquisitions outside India. The first important acquisition was that of *Tetley* by *Tata Tea* (today *Tata Global Beverages*). *Tetley* is a British beverage manufacturer, and the world's second largest manufacturer and distributor of tea with an annual turnover of 1.5 billion USD. The acquisition in 2000 was the largest overseas acquisitions by an Indian company at that time. Since 2005, *Tata Global Beverages* has been expanding strongly into Europe (*JEMCA*, Czech Republic, 2006; *Vitax* and *Flosana*, Poland, 2007; *Grand*, Russia, 2009), Africa (*Joekels Tea Packers*, South Africa, 2006) and the USA (*Good Earth Corporation* & *FMali Herb Inc.*, 2005).Nowadays, *Tata Global Beverages* makes more than 65% of its consolidated revenue in markets outside of India. The expansion not only led to an increase in revenues but also a modified orientation regarding *Tata Global Beverages'* products. The main objective was to change from an exclusive tea producer to a supplier of "good for you" beverages. Consequently, their products' sales shares changed. Before the acquisitions nearly all of their revenues came from tea interests. As a result of the diversification strategy this figure is now only 70%.

Starting in 2003, *Tata Communications* acquired three telecommunications companies: *Gemplex* (USA, 2003), *Tyco Global Network* (USA, 2004) and *Teleglobe* (UK, 2005). According to its own reports on these acquisitions, the *Tata Group* now owns and operates one of the world's largest international mobile, data and voice networks, providing 1,400 wholesale customers and 650 enterprise customers with coverage to more than 240 countries and territories.

Indian Hotels (IHCL), part of the *Tata Group*, also expanded into foreign countries very early. After *IHCL* became one of the largest and finest hotel groups in Asia, *Indian Hotels* tried to strengthen its position outside of Asia as well. In 2005 the company took over the *Starwood Group* (Australia). *Ritz Carlton* (USA) followed in 2006 and *Campton Place Hotel* (USA) in 2007.

In 2004, *Tata Motors* acquired the heavy vehicles unit of *Daewoo Motors*, South Korea. According to Ravi Kant, Vice Chairman of *Tata Motors*, the company's values and culture were an essential factor in the acquisition: "we were able to convince people in Korea that we were right for their company because we talked about our culture and values. Although in the short term it may appear that our model is not attractive because there are more roadblocks (…), in the long term, considering how important it is to have a sustainable business model" (Crainer 2010). Within a year *Tata* had purchased a 21% interest in *Hispano Carrocera S.A (HC)*, a well-known Spanish bus manufacturing company. In 2008 the acquisition of *Jaguar* and *Land Rover* (both UK) gained international attention. At the same time, *Tata Motors* was expanding into other emerging markets with its own brand. For this, the company used the experience it had gained with its own products on the home market in India. There, the company could gain customer insight on the trade-off between price and product features.

Internationalisation made it possible to launch products initially optimised for the home market into other emerging markets as well. For example, *Tata Motors* developed *Tata Nano* as a reference product for *bottom-of-the-pyramid (BOP) markets* (Holtbrügge/Schuster 2009) and contributed to the satisfaction of the increasing mobility needs of Indian households. For many Indian households the price gap between a two-wheeler and existing passenger cars was too big. The *Nano* was designed to fill this gap and give as many Indian households as possible access to passenger cars. Similar patterns of demand could be found in other emerging markets. Therefore, *Tata* was able to successfully adapt the *Nano* to other markets as well. This role can be described as local optimisation (Ramamurti 2012). For these markets, *Tata* upgraded the basic model in order to meet the safety standards. Several additional features were added, such as a more powerful engine, power steering, airbags and ABS. It was offered for a price of 6,000 USD (Grünweg 2009). *Tata Motors'* commercial and passenger vehicles are sold in several countries in Europe, Africa, the Middle East, South Asia, South East Asia, South America, CIS, and Russia.

Bottom-of-the-Pyramid Markets

Tata Steel adopted the role of a *global consolidator* by using the strength, capacities and revenues in the home market to become established in other markets (Ramamurti/Singh 2009). Unlike in developed countries, the steel industry is considered a high-growth industry in some emerging economies like India. Therefore, it was *Tata Steel's* goal to quickly expand in the Indian home market and gain both experience and capacities. This strategy made it possible for *Tata Steel* to also compete with highly developed Western firms. Although these firms were superior in terms of technologies, *Tata Steel* had modern factories and low labour costs (Ramamurti 2012). With this strategy the company became the leader in its home market. Thanks to this strong position, *Tata Steel* was able to acquire the Singapore-based *NatSteel* (2005) and *Millennium Steel* in Thailand (2006). The largest acquisition was in 2007, when *Tata Steel* acquired *Corus*, the Anglo-Dutch giant, in a landmark deal.

Branding Strategies

Tata Group chose a pragmatic approach in dealing with new acquisitions. Instead of giving all acquisitions the corporate brand name and mark, *Tata* only re-brands its acquisitions when it will clearly add value to the *Tata Group* and the acquired company (Witze 2010). For example, the *Tata Steel* brand was stronger than the relatively weak *Corus* brand, so *Corus* was re-named *Tata Steel Europe* after the acquisition by *Tata Steel* in 2010. In the case of *Tetley* the *Tata Group* decided to stick with the original name. Even though the company has been a part of *Tata* for a long time, the *Tetley* brand is independent in terms of its identity. It is possible that a tea product could benefit from an Indian brand like *Tata*, but *Tetley's* customers resolutely see it as British, and rebranding might compromise its image and reputation in their eyes (Witze 2010).

Summary and Outlook

The *Tata Group* has had a long history since its founding in 1868. During the first 60 years the company grew rapidly in the home market in various market segments. The goal was to identify as many market opportunities as possible and fill the gaps with the company's own products and services. The years between 1930 and 1990 were marked by increasing business consolidation in the home market. By 1990, many companies in the *Tata Group* were in leading positions in the Indian home market. Multinational activities hardly played a role. Only liberalisation of the Indian market and the associated political changes made it possible for the *Tata Group* to focus on expanding into different markets.

This expansion was based on mergers and acquisitions that in some cases were internationally recognised – usually due to the strong position of the respective company in the Indian home market. Thus *Tata Group* gained access to the necessary capacities and financial resources to acquire strong companies in mature markets. As well as these mergers and acquisitions, the *Tata Group* also expanded into other emerging countries with their own brand. In these cases the *Tata Group* benefitted from the experience it gained in the home market, allowing them to enter the market with low-cost products that were optimised for the needs of emerging markets.

Tata Group will probably rely on expansions in the future. This will be to either diversify the *Tata* brand, which has become a strong brand in a number of markets, or profitably invest capacities and resources from their own business into other companies in new markets: "Having said that, I hope that a hundred years from now we will spread our wings far beyond India, that we become a global group, operating in many countries, an Indian business conglomerate that is at home in the world, carrying the same sense of trust that we do today" (former group chairman Ratan Tata).

Questions

1. How has the history of the *Tata Group* up to the 1990s affected the expansions starting in 1991?

2. Why did the internationalisation of the *Tata Group* take place in the 1990s? How would you describe *Tata's* internationalisation processes? What are the advantages and disadvantages of these strategies?

3. Think of the roles played by the different *Tata Group* companies that developed in the home market until 1990. Illustrate the effect of political environment on the company's history and discuss the roles of global consolidator and local optimiser.

References

ACCENTURE (2008): The Rise of the Emerging-Market Multinational, http://www.accenture.com/SiteCollectionDocuments/PDF/MPW2.pdf, 'accessed on August 24, 2014.

BARTLETT, C.A.; GHOSHAL, S. (2000): Going Global, in: Harvard Business Review, Vol. 78, No. 2, pp. 132-142.

BASU, K.; MAERTENS, A. (2010): The Concise Oxford Companion to Economics in India, New Delhi, Oxford University Press.

BATTAT, J.; AYKUT, D. (2005): Southern Multinationals: A Growing Phenomenon, FIAS, Mumbai.

CRAINER, S. (2010): The TATA Way, in: Business Strategy Review, Vol. 21, No. 2, pp. 14-19.

DUNNING, J.; KIM, C.; PARK, D. (2008): Old Wine in New Bottles: A Comparison of Emerging-Market TNCs Today and Developed-Country TNCs Thirty Years Ago, in: SAUVANT, K. (Ed.): The Rise of Transnational Corporations From Emerging Market: Threat or Opportunity? Northampton, Edward Elgar Publishing, pp. 158-183.

GOLDSTEIN, A. (2007): Multinational Companies from Emerging Economies, Basingstoke, Palgrave Macmillan.

GOLDSTEIN, A. (2008): The Internationalization of Indian Companies: The Case of Tata, Centre for Advanced Study on India (CASI), Working Paper No. 08-02, University of Pennsylvania.

GRASER, S. (2011): Realwirtschaftliche und Finanzwirtschaftliche Internationalisierung, Wiesbaden, Gabler.

GRÜNWEG, T. (2009): Europa Version des Tata Nano: Aufgemotzter Winzling mit Platz Problemen, http://www.spiegel.de/auto/aktuell/0,1518,611259,00.html., accessed on August 12, 2014.

GUILLÉN, M.F.; GARCIA-CANAL, E. (2011): The Rise of Emerging Market Multinationals, in: IESE Insight, No. 10, pp. 13-19.

HOLTBRÜGGE, D.; SCHUSTER, T. (2009): „Bottom of the Pyramid" Märkte, in: Das Wirtschaftsstudium (WISU), Vol. 10, No. 4, pp. 1337-1342.

KHANNA, T.; PALEPU, K. (2006): Emerging Giants: Building World-Class Companies in Developing Countries, Boston, Harvard Business School Publishing.

KRISHNAN, R.T.; JHA, S.K. (2011): Innovation Strategies in Emerging Markets: What Can We Learn from Indian Market Leaders, in: ASCI Journal of Management, Vol. 41, No. 1, pp. 21-45.

LALA, R. (2007): The Creation of Wealth: The Tatas from 19th to 21st Century, London, Penguin.

LOSADA OTALORA, M.; CASANOVA, L. (2012): Resources and Internationalization Strategies: The Case of Latin American Multinationals, Working Paper 2012/82, Cornell University.

LOU, Y.; TUNG, R.L. (2007): International Expansion of Emerging Market Enterprises: A Springboard Perspective, in: Journal of International Business Studies, Vol. 38, No. 4, pp 481-498.

MATHEWS, J.A. (2006): Dragon Multinationals: New Players in 21st Century Globalization, in: Asia Pacific Journal of Management, Vol. 23, No. 1, pp. 5-27.

MCKINSEY GLOBAL INSTITUTE (2013): Urban World: The Shifting Global Business Landscape, http://www.mckinsey.com/insights/urbanization/urban_world_the_shifting_global_business_landscape, accessed on August 12, 2014.

PENG, M.W. (2012): The Global Strategy of Emerging Multinationals from China, in: Global Strategy Journal, Vol. 2, No. 2, pp. 97-107.

RAMAMURTI, R. (2012): Competing with Emerging Market Multinationals, in: Business Horizons, Vol. 55, No. 3, pp. 241-249.

RAMAMURTI, R.; SINGH, J.V. (Eds.) (2009): Emerging Multinationals in Emerging Markets, Cambridge, Cambridge University Press.

RUGMAN, A.M.; COLLINSON, S. (2012): International Business, 6th ed., Harlow, Pearson.

RUGMAN, A.M.; DOH, J.P. (2008): Multinationals and Development, New Haven, Yale University Press.

RUGMAN, A.M.; VERBEKE, A. (2004): A Perspective on Regional and Global Strategies of Multinational Enterprises, in: Journal of International Business Studies, Vol. 35, No. 1, pp. 3-18.

SAUVANT, K.P.; MASCHEK, W.A.; MCALLISTER, G. (2009): Foreign Direct Investment from Emerging Markets: The Challenges Ahead, Basingstoke, Palgrave Macmillan.

SCHUSTER, T.; HOLTBRÜGGE, D. (2011): Tata Nano: The Car for the Bottom of-the-Pyramid, in: ZENTES, J.; SWOBODA, B.; MORSCHETT, D. (Eds.) Fallstudien zum Internationalen Management, Wiesbaden, Gabler, 4th ed., pp. 83-102.

SIM, A.B.; PANDIA, J.R. (2003): Emerging Asian MNEs and Their Internationalization Strategies, in: Asia Pacific Journal of Management, Vol. 20, No. 1, pp. 27-50.

SRIVASTAVA, A.K., NEGI, G., MISHRA, V.; PANDEY, S. (2012): Corporate Social Responsibility: A Case Study of TATA Group, in: IOSR Journal of Business and Management, Vol. 3, No. 5, pp. 17-27.

UNCTAD (2013): World Investment Report 2013: Global Value Chains: Investment and Trade for Development, Geneva.

WITZE, M. (2010): Case Study: Tata, http://www.ft.com/intl/cms/s/0/8e 553742-136c-11e0-a367-00144feabdc0.html#axzz2ws1fkHc0., accessed on August 12, 2014.

YEUNG, H.W. (Ed.). (2000): The Globalization of Business Firms from Emerging Economies, Cheltenham, Edward Elgar Publishing.

Chapter 6

Important International Management Theories

International Management requires theories to explain why and how companies internationalise and how international companies carry out their activities, e.g., how they coordinate their international activities or where they locate their different subsidiaries. The same theories can also be used to predict companies' behaviour. This Chapter presents the most relevant International Management Theories.

Introduction

Until the 1960s, foreign direct investment by companies was mainly seen as movement of international capital and explained by investment theories and portfolio considerations. The main argument for international investment was that it occurs due to different rates of return between countries. This view has obvious deficiencies: It does not correctly explain the empirically observable patterns of direct investment, e.g. the two-way direct investment flows between some major countries; it does not explain why companies from the same country and even within the same industry differed in their internationalisation behaviour and it does not consider differences between the motives for international purchase of a few foreign stocks bonds (i.e. portfolio investments) and for substantial equity ownership by domestic companies in foreign companies (i.e. foreign direct investment, FDI).

International Investment as Capital Movement

During the 1960s, the perception of the multinational firm changed and the first theory of the international firm was developed. This was the work of Steven Hymer, who undertook the development of a more comprehensive theory on FDI and MNCs, emphasizing the control companies get over foreign activities by means of FDI (see Forsgren 2008, pp. 15-29, for a detailed description of Hymer's contribution). He argued that under perfect competition, all companies would have access to similar resources and technology. Since in this case local firms in a foreign market would have knowledge advantages, little foreign direct investment would occur because incumbents would have a competitive advantage over new entrants. Thus, to overcome this *liability of foreignness*, companies wanting to successfully expand abroad must have some kind of competitive advantage to compensate for their knowledge disadvantage. This competitive advantage leads to a *monopolistic advantage*, which represents a deviation from pure competition (Forsgren 2008, p. 16). Examples of such monopolistic advantages include product

Hymer's Theory of Monopolistic Advantages

differentiation, marketing skills, patents, technological expertise, economies of scale, etc. In Hymer's perspective, some level of *market imperfection* is at the root of MNCs' development. He argues (Kutschker/Schmid 2011, pp. 414-415; Forsgren 2008, pp. 20-23)

■ that it may be beneficial for a company to exploit its monopolistic advantages beyond the own domestic market and

■ that it may be beneficial for a company to do so by means of vertical integration, mainly because that gives the company higher control over foreign activities and helps to avoid competition, thus contributing to monopolistic power.

Transaction Cost Theory and Internalisation Theory

In Hymer's view, the MNC creates its benefit by maintaining a monopolistic advantage and avoiding or reducing competition. Other authors criticise this view and argue that Hymer does not sufficiently explain how company advantages are generated in the first place (i.e., that Hymer focused only on the "unfair" exploitation across borders instead of the welfare-enhancing creation of advantages) and that he ignores the fact that MNCs are potentially better at carrying out cross-border activities internally than independent companies.

Over the last decades, the dominant theories to explain internationalisation and related concepts, e.g. the choice of foreign operation mode, have been the *transaction cost approach* (TCA) (Williamson 1985) and the closely related *internalisation theory* (Buckley/Casson 1976). These approaches argue that companies internationalise in a way that minimises the cost of cross-border transactions. They point to the fact that it may be more efficient to internalise markets across borders, e.g., because a joint coordination of different activities in different countries may incur less cost ("transaction costs") than using market mechanisms between countries.

Transaction Costs

Transaction costs refer to *search and information costs*, i.e., costs incurred in determining that the required good is available on the market, who has the lowest price, etc.; *bargaining costs*, i.e., costs required to come to an acceptable agreement with the other party to the transaction, drawing up an appropriate contract, etc., and *monitoring and enforcement costs* to ensure the other party sticks to the terms of the contract, and taking appropriate action if they do not. For example, monitoring costs might include measuring output (e.g. quality control in the factory of a supplier). If conditions change, contracts might have to be adjusted which incurs *adjustment costs*.

The two basic assumptions of the transaction cost approach are:

■ *Bounded rationality*, i.e., actors intend to act rationally but are only capable of doing so in a limited way, partly because they have incomplete information and partly because they have limited processing capacity.

■ *Opportunistic behaviour*, i.e., business partners are expected to use the incompleteness of contracts and changing circumstances for their own self-interest and only adhere to the contract if they are monitored.

If markets function well, with a large number of potential business partners, competition ensures efficient results. In these cases, an MNC will favour low control modes. Business partners can be replaced easily and this threat protects the companies from opportunistic behaviour. In other cases, markets may fail. This may be the case for different types of transactions (Malhotra/Agarwal/Ulgado 2004, p. 4):

Imperfect Markets

■ *imperfect markets for goods* created by brand names, marketing capabilities, product differentiation

■ *imperfect markets for intermediate goods*, such as knowledge, whereby it is assumed that the cross-border transfer of knowledge is less efficient among separate companies than within one MNC

■ *imperfect markets for production factors* that may be created by exclusive procurement capabilities, particular management expertise or certain technologies

■ *imperfect competition through economies of scale* that lead to cost advantages for internalisation.

However, market imperfections are mainly caused by three transaction characteristics:

First, *asset specificity*, the degree to which an asset loses its value when put to an alternative use, may create a situation where an actor who has carried out specific investments runs the risk of being exploited by their partner. In this case, market transactions between independent actors might not offer sufficient protection for the business partners. Thus, the MNC might decide to carry out the transaction internally, i.e. with a wholly-owned subsidiary. Similarly, *uncertainty* may lead to market imperfections (Welch/Benito/Petersen 2007, pp. 24-25). If all future eventualities were known in advance, contract parties could plan ahead and develop comprehensive contracts. The stronger the uncertainty (e.g. changes in the external environment), the more likely it is that contracts are incomplete and have to be adjusted. These renegotiations can lead to high transaction costs. Again, the necessary flexibility to adapt to changing situations may be better granted with internalised operation modes. Third, the *frequency of transactions* plays a role. Setting up a wholly-owned foreign subsidiary is often linked to

Asset Specificity, Uncertainty, and Frequency

relatively high fixed costs, but the subsequent variable costs are usually lower than in the case of cooperative or market modes. Thus, with an increased number of transactions, the relative costs of a wholly-owned subsidiary are reduced.

Figure 6.1 | *Transaction Cost Reasoning for Different Modes of Internationalisation*

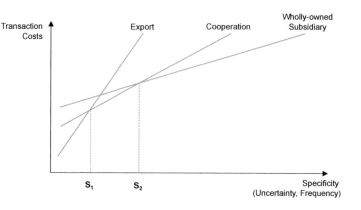

Source: Adapted from Welch/Benito/Petersen 2007, p. 26.

To summarise, the transaction cost approach compares the costs of internalisation of external markets with the costs of market transactions and cooperation (see Figure 6.1). Under certain circumstances markets are imperfect, and companies are forced to internalise transactions to compensate.

Dunning's OLI Paradigm

Because the existing approaches (e.g. the internalisation theory or the theory of monopolistic advantages) alone cannot fully explain the choice of foreign operation mode, John Dunning developed a comprehensive approach, the so-called *Eclectic Paradigm*, which aims to offer a general framework to determine which operation mode is the most appropriate.

The OLI Decision Process for Foreign Operation Modes

Figure 6.2

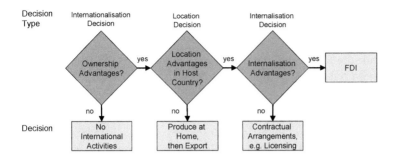

Source: Adapted from Sudarsanam 2003, p. 201; Welch/Benito/Petersen 2007, p. 31.

It specifies a set of three *conditions* that must prevail simultaneously to stimulate FDI from a company (Rugman/Collinson 2012, pp. 67-70; Dunning/Lundan 2008, pp. 96-108):

- *Ownership-specific advantages (O)*: The firm must possess some unique competitive advantages (*firm-specific advantages*, FSA) that outweigh the disadvantages of competing with local firms in their home market (*liability of foreignness*). Often, ownership-specific advantages take the form of the possession of intangible assets, which (at least temporarily) are specific to the firm. This follows the general argument by Hymer.

- *Location-specific advantages (L)*: If foreign direct investment is to take place, it must be more profitable for the company to undertake the activity in the foreign country than in the home country. Otherwise foreign markets would be served by other operation modes. Location-specific advantages (or *country-specific advantages*, CSAs) can include, for example, labour costs, an efficient and skilled labour force, tariffs, transport costs or natural resources.

- *Internalisation advantages (I)*: Companies that possess specific advantages can either exploit them themselves (*internalise* them) or sell the advantage to other companies. The internalisation choice can be explained by *internalisation theory*, as pointed out above.

Whether foreign direct investment is favourable depends on which types of advantage prevail. To undertake internationalisation via wholly-owned subsidiary, all three types of benefits, O, L and I, must be present. This case is illustrated in Figure 6.2, along with other situations that lead to different decisions about operation modes.

Resource-Based View

While the TCA focuses on transactions and analyses whether these are better carried out within the firm or between firms, the *resource-based view* (RBV) considers the firm as a *bundle of resources* (e.g. Wernerfelt 1984; Barney 1991).

Many previous approaches (e.g. the Industrial Organisation Approach) assumed that firms within an industry are generally similar in terms of strategically relevant resources and that any heterogeneity that may develop is short-lived because resources are highly mobile or even tradable. Instead, the RBV assumes (Barney 1991, p. 101):

■ Firms within an industry may be heterogeneous with respect to the strategic resources they control.

■ Resources may not be perfectly mobile across firms.

■ Therefore, heterogeneity may be long-lasting.

Physical Capital, Human Capital, and Organisational Capital

Resources are broadly defined as "those (tangible and intangible) assets which are tied semipermanently to the firm" (Wernerfelt 1984, p. 172) or, more precisely, as "all assets, capabilities, organizational processes, firm attributes, information, knowledge, etc., controlled by a firm that enable the firm to conceive of and implement strategies that improve its efficiency and effectiveness" (Barney 1991, p. 101). Barney categorises them into *physical capital resources* (such as technology, geographic location, access to raw materials), *human capital resources* (employee experience, judgement, intelligence and insight) and *organisational capital resources* (formal structures, informal relationships among groups within a firm, coordinating systems, etc.). To be the basis for a *sustained* competitive advantage, resources have to fulfil a number of criteria which have been extensively discussed over recent decades (Dierickx/Cool 1989; Barney 1991):

■ They must be *valuable*.

■ They must be *rare*.

■ They must be *imperfectly imitable* (and they must be imperfectly or not tradable).

■ There must be no strategically equivalent substitutes that are valuable but not rare or not imperfectly imitable.

Resources may be imperfect imitable or non-tradable due to *path dependency* (i.e., the availability of the resource is dependent on the unique history of the company, e.g. personal customer relationships or a strong brand), *causal ambiguity* (i.e., the link between specific resources and the performance of the company is not clear) or *social complexity* (e.g., if the resource lies in interpersonal relationships within the company). Resources may also be tied so closely into the *resource bundle* of a company and only exert their full impact in combination with these other resources that it is not possible for another company to acquire or create them separately. These are mainly intangible assets, such as knowledge or organisational capabilities, and can create long-term success.

Reasons for Imperfect Imitability

There are many strategic questions that can be analysed from the perspective of the RBV. The core question is how a company should exploit its resource base to maximise its profit, which includes the question of whether the company should exploit the resources nationally or internationally. In the latter case, one has to examine the value of the resources in a foreign country and the question of how to transfer the resources there optimally. Under the RBV, a company can also investigate the question of whether its own resources (e.g. a superior technology) must be complemented with the resources of another company in a foreign market (e.g. market knowledge or a distribution network) to optimally exploit the own resources. In this case, though, the company must consider whether its own resources are endangered by cooperation, e.g. by knowledge dissemination. Furthermore, if complementary resources in a foreign country are needed, the RBV allows the company to examine whether these are better accessed via cooperation or via the acquisition of the foreign company that controls them. Ultimately, under the RBV, internationalisation may not only be a means to exploit the given resource base but also to enhance it, e.g. by tapping into foreign knowledge.

Strategic Questions

FSA/CSA-Framework

In the terminology of another strategic concept of the international firm, the so-called *FSA/CSA-framework* (e.g. Rugman/Collinson 2012, pp. 49-52), there are two dimensions of advantages that an MNC must consider, each with a different relevance for different companies or industries:

- *Firm-specific advantages (FSA)* are strengths specific to a firm, a result of contributions that can be made by its personnel, technology, and/or equipment.

- *Country-specific advantages (CSA)* are strengths or benefits specific to a country that can result from its competitive environment, its labour force, its natural resources, its industrial clusters, etc. Porter's diamond can be used to investigate CSAs (see Chapter 8).

Combining those two dimensions in a matrix, a company can investigate several issues. If the CSAs of the home country are dominant and FSAs rather weak, economic theories argue that comparative advantages of a country (or the location within an industrial cluster) will lead to exports – regardless of the specific characteristics of the company. If FSAs are strong and CSAs are weak, the focus of the international strategy is on exploiting the company's resources, without much influence from the location. Furthermore, FSAs need to be identified as either *location-bound*, i.e., only create their full value in a specific location (e.g., due to a technology that perfectly fits a locally specific demand) or *non-location-bound*. Only *non-location-bound* FSAs can be fully used for exploitation in foreign countries. Location-boundedness can occur for firm-specific assets in the home country, but also for subsidiary-specific assets in a specific host country. In the latter case, the FSA cannot contribute to the strategy of other subsidiaries. However, FSAs and CSAs frequently both exert a strong influence, in which case a company has an incentive to operate across borders, coordinate its resources across borders and needs to *combine the FSA of the company with the CSA of the host country* (and, maybe, the CSA of the home country) to be successful (Rugman/Verbeke/Nguyen 2011, pp. 766-768). In fact, it is this combination of FSAs with CSAs in different locations that is the challenge of a true MNC.

Rugman (2010) argues that the FSA/CSA-framework can also be reconciled with Dunning's Eclectic Paradigm and that the Eclectic Paradigm can be easily transformed into the FSA/CSA-matrix, making this framework a very general analytical tool for MNC strategy.

Dynamic Theories of Internationalisation

Internationalisation is not a static phenomenon but a dynamic process. Companies change their configuration over time, enter into new countries, and/or change their operation mode. While the theories above allow an analysis at any given point in time, they do not explicitly consider changes over time. Some International Management facilitates this, however, for example the older stages models more recent born global approaches.

Stages Models of Internationalisation

The stages models of internationalisation are rooted in the *behavioural theory* of the firm. These models, of which the internationalisation process model (*IP model*, also called "*Uppsala model*") by Johanson/Vahlne (1977) is the best known, propose an association between the knowledge of the decision makers in the company and the level of resource commitment in a foreign market. The core assumption is that companies with low market knowledge about a specific foreign market prefer a low commitment in this market. Once in the market, the company accumulates experiential knowledge and this leads to the willingness to commit additional resources. In the so-called *establishment chain*, the model proposes that foreign operation modes in a specific foreign country are switched along a certain path:

Internationalisation Process Model

■ no international activities

■ export activities via agents

■ export activities via the company's own sales subsidiaries

■ establishment of production subsidiaries in the foreign country.

In addition, the IP model suggests that companies often select foreign markets based on the psychic distance to that market and that internationalisation often occurs along a *psychic distance chain*, with psychologically close markets being entered before more distant countries.

Psychic Distance Chain

In general, the common assumptions of all stages models are (Swoboda 2002, pp. 72-73):

■ Internationalisation is a slow and gradual process.

■ The process of internationalisation is not the result of long-term strategic planning, but of incremental decisions.

■ Internationalisation is an adaptive process, and with time, resource commitment in the foreign market and changes in the management of the foreign organisational unit will occur.

■ Internationalisation is a process occurring in stages, characterised by different rates of change and unsteady development.

■ During internationalisation, companies accumulate experiential knowledge which facilitates foreign activities and further internationalisation.

Overall, the stages models explain foreign operation modes mainly through the country-specific knowledge of a company that determines the perceived uncertainty and, thus, the willingness of the company to invest resources in that country.

While the stages models are highly plausible, criticism has emerged over the years. First, the models omit that management has a *strategic choice* and the operation mode decision is not only determined by a single influence factor. In particular, external influence factors (like host country conditions) are neglected. Second, the models over-simplify a complex process and certain operation modes – in particular cooperative modes – are not considered. Cooperation (and acquisitions) offers the possibility of gaining knowledge without the MNC having long-term experience of its own in the host country. Finally, MNCs often leap over certain stages in the establishment chain (*leap frogging*). Still, for many companies, the stages models of internationalisation offer a good general explanation of their observed behaviour.

Born Globals

In the last two decades, researchers have increasingly observed a "new" phenomenon, namely companies that internationalise immediately after their foundation (Oviatt/McDougall 1994; Knight/Cavusgil 1996). This, obviously, has challenged the patterns proposed by the *IP model*. Companies, mainly small companies from the IT sector, biotechnology or other high-tech-oriented industries, have been increasingly seen to take up international activities (mainly exports) very early after their creation, enter multiple countries at the same time, enter very distant markets and achieve a high percentage of their sales outside the domestic market right from their inception. This phenomenon has been labelled "International New Ventures", "International Entrepreneurs", "Innate Exporters", or "Global Start-ups", but the most frequently used term is "Born Globals"

Definitions   *Born Globals* are "business organisations that, from inception, seek to derive significant competitive advantage from the use of resources and the sale of outputs in multiple countries" (Oviatt/McDougall 1994, p. 49). More concretely, another early source defines born globals as companies that "have internationalised within 3 years of inception and have generated at least 25 per cent of their sales from export" (Knight/Cavusgil 1996, p. 12). Thus, the two main definition criteria are:

■ a short period between inception and first internationalisation

■ a high level of internationalisation.

Both definition criteria – 3 years as duration from inception to internationalisation and 25% of foreign sales – have been criticised and modified by other authors. For example, it is argued that 25% may be high from the perspective of US authors but that for many European companies from small home markets, this threshold is too low for a useful characterisation. Thus, other scholars use periods from between two and six years to characterise "from inception" and foreign sales from 25% up to 76% to characterise "high level of internationalisation". Sometimes, the geographic scope of the internationalisation is added, demanding a certain number of countries or a certain number of cultural clusters (Gabrielsson/Kirpalani 2004; Holtbrügge/Enßlinger 2004).

Several arguments have been proposed to explain why born globals can successfully adopt an internationalisation strategy that differs from the traditional models (Holtbrügge/Enßlinger 2004, pp. 374-375; Gabrielsson/Kirpalani 2004):

Explanations

- In the IP model, only the company (as an organisation) is able to gather international experience. In born global firms, however, the founder or the first management team as individuals often have international experience from previous jobs and therefore have the necessary knowledge of foreign markets and international activities.

- In the IP model, companies are considered to start with a domestic mindset and then slowly become aware of international market opportunities. Born global firms often have a global vision prior to their foundation as part of their strategy. This can be based on characteristics of the entrepreneurs or the specific industry.

- In the IP model, market knowledge can only be built from personal experience. Born global firms, however, are often integrated into formal networks, e.g. in strategic alliances with distribution partners or MNCs with subsidiaries in different countries. Such MNCs can act as system integrators and provide born globals with market access. Entrepreneurial teams can also be embedded in informal networks with former customer relationships (from previous jobs) or with private contacts that help to provide knowledge on markets around the world.

- Born globals often focus on *niche markets* where the potential in a single country is too small to survive; they therefore have to exploit the market potential in multiple countries.

- Born globals often have a unique technology and/or an innovative product or service or a superior design; thus, they follow a strategy of product differentiation. This may give them a *monopolistic advantage* which helps them to overcome the liability of foreignness in less familiar countries. Furthermore, in the industries in which born globals are most frequently observed demand in different markets is not very heterogeneous. Therefore, a product adaptation strategy is not necessary, and familiarity with the foreign country may be less relevant.

Selected Theories to Explain the Relationship between Headquarters and Subsidiaries

Information Processing Approach

The information processing approach from Egelhoff (1991) considers the *MNC* as an information processing system. Information processing refers to the gathering of data, the transformation of data into information, the communication and diffusion of information within the company and the storage of said information. Coordination requires consideration of the information processing requirements and capacities required.

Uncertainty as a Lack of Information

This approach assumes that different companies have different requirements for their information processing, partly based on the uncertainty of tasks. This *uncertainty* is defined as the difference between the amount of information necessary to perform a specific task and the information that is already available in the organisational unit. Internal and external information flows are used to reduce uncertainty (Egelhoff 1991, p. 343). Strong influences on uncertainty are the size of the MNC, the company's growth and the diversification of the company. Other external factors, like the technological dynamics of the industry, or internal factors, such as the degree of internationalisation, also affect the level of uncertainty (Wolf/Egelhoff 2001, pp. 121-122).

Different Types of Information

Different *qualities of information* to be processed stem from a distinction between *primarily strategic* or *primarily tactical* information, between routine and nonroutine information processing and between *sequential* and *reciprocal* information flows (Egelhoff 1991, pp. 350-353). These require different communication channels.

The Information Processing Approach

Figure 6.3

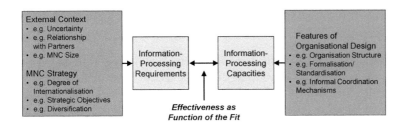

Source: Adapted from Egelhoff 1991, p. 345; Wolf/Egelhoff 2001, p. 122.

Different features of the organisational design, including coordination mechanisms, have different information processing capacities. The core argument of the information processing approach is that companies have to achieve a good *fit* or alignment between their information processing capacity and their specific information processing requirements (see Figure 6.3). Based on this approach, it can be argued that (Egelhoff 1991, p. 344; Wolf/Egelhoff 2001, p. 120):

- If information processing is routine and simple, *rules* and *programmes* (i.e. formalisation and standardisation) are sufficient to overcome the low uncertainty of the decision situation. For example, subsidiaries' reporting systems can be designed to match HQ's standards to ensure compatibility. These *standard reports* can eliminate the need for other forms of HQ-subsidiary communication.

- With increasing uncertainty, flexible and rapid decisions must be taken closer to the local host environment. *Planning*, including goal-setting, allows for more decisions to be made at lower levels in the organisation, provided they comply with the plan.

- If uncertainty increases further, the organisation's information processing capacity must be further enhanced, including coordination processes based on *vertical information systems* and *central departments*. *Informal communication* flows must be added to manage the increased uncertainty.

- With very high complexity, HQ might have problems processing all the necessary information. Thus, the use of *lateral relations* allows more information processing to be decentralised to disburden the limited information processing capacity at the higher levels of the organisation. Direct contact between executives, e.g. through project teams, linking pins, etc., enables effective information processing throughout the whole organisation (Egelhoff 1991, pp. 343-344).

Agency Theory

Agency theory (also called *principal-agent theory*) deals with *delegation relationships* in which a principal delegates certain tasks and decisions to an agent on the basis of an explicit or implicit contract. The actions taken by the agent influence the welfare of the principal. Contracts between the principal and the agent are always incomplete due to *limited information*, unpredictability of future situations and the (prohibitively) high cost of complete contracts. Furthermore, the principal-agent theory argues that usually there is *information asymmetry* in favour of the agent. Before closing a contract, the principal is not able to identify fully the capabilities and characteristics of the potential agent (*hidden characteristics*) and this might lead to a poor selection (*adverse selection*) (Richter/Furubotn 2003, pp. 218-219). More seriously (and more relevant for the case of MNCs), after the contract has been closed, the principal cannot completely observe the behaviour of his agent (*hidden action*) and the result of the delegation is also influenced by external conditions that the principal also cannot fully observe (*hidden information*) (Elschen 1991, p. 1004; Woratschek/Roth 2005, p. 152).

Risk of Opportunistic Behaviour

All this leaves room for *opportunistic behaviour* on the part of the agent. Agency theory assumes that the agent intends to maximise his individual utility and that the objectives (and the risk preferences) of principal and agent may diverge. Thus, conflicts of interest may emerge. With the assumption of *moral hazard*, it is assumed that the agent will even carry out actions that influence the welfare of the principal negatively if it enhances his own benefit.

Subsidiary as Agent of the HQ

Transferring this consideration to the HQ-subsidiary relationship, the HQ cannot make all decisions itself since it does not have the necessary information and resources. When delegating decisions and actions to the subsidiary, however, HQ must remember that the interests of the foreign subsidiary might diverge from its own. Principal-agent theory attempts to suggest mechanisms for information, incentive and control (*governance mechanisms*) that align the interests of the subsidiary with those of HQ, i.e., mechanisms that motivate the subsidiary to contribute to the overall objectives of the MNC (Nohria/Ghoshal 1994). A simple example is the possibility for a subsidiary to re-invest its profits locally instead transferring them to HQ.

Usually the HQ cannot observe and control all the actions a subsidiary carries out and the performance of the subsidiary is influenced by many aspects beyond the control of subsidiary management (*hidden information*). Thus, controlling the outcome is also not sufficient to evaluate the subsidiary management completely, and in many cases, e.g. knowledge generation or innovation in the subsidiary, performance is not readily measured. Here, *normative integration* is seen as effective for establishing close relationships between the subsidiary and the HQ to reduce the propensity to behave opportunistically and influence the subsidiary to contribute to the overall company benefit "voluntarily" without explicit *performance measurement* (Gupta/Govindarajan 2000).

Using *expatriates* as an informal coordination mechanism can make sense from an agency perspective (O'Donnell 2000). Expatriates are more likely to act on behalf of the HQ than nationals from the host country, because an expatriate's career is more strongly linked to the HQ's evaluation of his performance, and the expatriate often identifies himself more strongly with the HQ than with the local subsidiary, since he or she was socialised in the HQ.

Expatriates Sometimes Better Agents

On the other hand, the listed mechanisms all carry a cost (*agency costs*) and the costs of potentially opportunistic behaviour and the cost of control have to be balanced when deciding on the use of a coordination mechanism. Hierarchical coordination can be replaced to some extent by *market elements*. With externalisation, i.e., outsourcing activities to external partners, or "quasi externalisation", i.e., using market principles between organisational units within the company, market prices replace hierarchical authority. Considering agency theory, this is particularly appropriate when information asymmetry is strong, e.g., if the socio-cultural distance between home country and host country is high (Woratschek/Roth 2005, pp. 153-154).

Market Elements as Coordination Mechanisms

Resource Dependence Theory

Resource dependence theory (RDT) is an *environmental interaction approach* (Pfeffer/Salancik 1978; Drees/Heugens 2013). The core idea is that companies need to exchange resources with their environment and they need certain resources from external sources to survive. This creates dependencies from other organisations and thus a risk for the company. RDT highlights the situations in which resource dependency is strong and the relevance of the resources to company survival is high. It suggests strategies to minimise the risk to resource supply.

From an MNC's perspective, both relationships between different companies and relationships between different organisational units within the MNC can be considered from an RDT perspective. Subsidiaries are often strongly dependent on resources from the HQ, which facilitates coordination. However, subsidiaries may be able to obtain resources that are difficult to access for other actors, including HQ, which affects the potential for central coordi-

Subsidiaries with Access to Critical Resources

nation within the MNC and sometimes diminishes the possibility of enforcing strategy conforming behaviour at the subsidiary (Andersson/Forsgren 1996, p. 488). From this perspective, the different levels of access to resources that have different relevancies for the MNC can be a key determinant for the internal relationships within the MNC (Pfeffer 1981; Nohria/Ghoshal 1997, p. 95). A subsidiary's *internal power* increases with the relevance of its resources for the MNC's performance, as substitutability of the resource decreases and with the uniqueness of the access to the resource by this specific subsidiary.

Powerful Subsidiaries Resist Strong Centralisation

Thus, resource dependency can be a source of conflict within the MNC. With increasing dependence on resources from the subsidiary, it becomes more difficult to enforce top-down decisions (Doz/Prahalad 1981; Nohria/Ghoshal 1997, pp. 96-97). On the other hand, limiting the autonomy of the subsidiary might reduce the effectiveness of the MNC network, because this might reduce the subsidiary's access to the strategic resource. In this situation, decision centralisation has to be replaced by other mechanisms. *Normative integration* can facilitate the negotiation process between parent company and foreign subsidiary (Nohria/Ghoshal 1997, pp. 100-101).

Contingency Approach and Configurational Approach

As an overarching theoretical approach, the contingency approach emphasises that there is no universally optimal management decision (e.g., no universally valid answer to how multinational a company should be, what the best organisational structure is, what the best foreign operation mode is and no universally optimal set of coordination mechanisms), but organisational decisions should be differentiated according to the characteristics of the external environment in which the organisation acts (Lawrence/Lorsch 1967; Thompson 1967; Kieser 2002, p. 169).

"It All Depends"

For example, the optimal foreign operation mode and coordination method is situational. The argument that these decisions strongly depend on the specific context follows directly from viewing organisations as *open systems* that have to interact with their external environment (Kieser/Walgenbach 2003, p. 215). Contingencies whose influences have been investigated include, *inter alia*, company size, the dynamics of the technological and market conditions and the uncertainty of the environment.

Strategic Choice Instead of Deterministic Relationship

However, one criticism of the contingency approach is the *quasi-mechanistic relationship* between the situation and the conduct of organisations. This implies a deterministic perspective, while in practice companies have a *strategic choice* (Child 1972) about how to act within their MNC as a reaction to different external situations. However, the general assumption of the contingency approach, that the effectiveness and efficiency of coordination mechanisms (and other organisational variables) are influenced by the external environment and there is no universally best solution but rather situation-specific differences, is widely accepted. For example, it is argued that the complexity of a firm's coordination process must match the complexity of its environment (Ghoshal/Nohria 1993, p. 23).

While the contingency approach focuses mainly on the relation between context and company, the *configurational approach* adds that the internal consistency between the organisational variables also has a strong influence on the efficiency of the organisation (Khandwalla 1973, p. 493). The *gestalt* of the organisation is more than the sum of its parts, and the configurational approach argues that an organisation is effective if the *consistency* or *fit* between organisational variables (like the coordination instruments) and between internal variables and the external environment is strong (Mintzberg 1981, p. 107). The configurational approach postulates that a comparatively low number of *typical constellations* of organisational variables exist that represent the majority of all combinations of organisational characteristics existing in practice (Miller/Friesen 1984). With regard to coordination, this implies that an isolated use and analysis of each coordination instrument is insufficient, but that the combination of coordination instruments applied is crucial for success.

Internal and External Fit

Conclusion and Outlook

To understand and predict the internationalisation behaviour of companies, scholars have developed numerous theories within International Management. These theories take different perspectives on the MNC and help highlight specific characteristics that may influence company decisions. For example, transaction cost theory highlights the role of asset specificity for company decisions, while the resource-based view emphasizes resource characteristics and the optimal exploitation and creation of resources.

Depending on which company decision is analysed, different theories can be applied. Often it may be useful to combine several theories. When doing this, however, it is important to investigate the theories' assumptions to ensure they are compatible.

Further Reading

BARNEY, J. (1991): Firm Resources and Sustained Competitive Advantage, in: Journal of Management, Vol. 17, No. 1, pp. 99-120.

FORSGREN, M. (2008): Theories of the Multinational Firm: A Multidimensional Creature in the Global Economy, Cheltenham, Edward Elgar Publishing.

RUGMAN, A.M.; VERBEKE, A.; NGUYEN, Q. (2011): Fifty Years of International Business Theory and Beyond, in: Management International Review, Vol. 51, pp. 755-786.

References

ANDERSSON, U.; FORSGREN, M. (1996): Subsidiary Embeddedness and Control in the Multinational Corporation, in: International Business Review, Vol. 5, No. 5, pp. 487-508.

BARNEY, J. (1991): Firm Resources and Sustained Competitive Advantage, in: Journal of Management, Vol. 17, No. 1, pp. 99-120.

BUCKLEY, P.; CASSON, M. (1976): The Future of the Multinational Enterprise, London, Macmillan Interactive Publishing.

CHILD, J. (1972): Organizational Structure, Environment and Performance: The Role of Strategic Choice, in: Sociology, Vol. 6, pp. 1-22.

DIERICKX, I.; COOL, K. (1989): Asset Stock Accumulation and Sustainability of Competitive Advantage, in: Management Science, Vol. 35, No. 12, pp. 1504-1511.

DOZ, Y.L.; PRAHALAD, C. (1981): Headquarters' Influence and Strategic Control in MNCs, in: Sloan Management Review, Vol. 23, No. 1, pp. 15-29.

DREES, J.; HEUGENS, P. (2013): Synthesizing and Extending Resource Dependence Theory: A Meta-Analysis, in: Journal of Management, Vol. 39, No. 6, pp. 1666-1698.

DUNNING, J.; LUNDAN, S. (2008): Multinational Enterprises and the Global Economy, 2nd ed., Cheltenham, Edward Elgar Publishing.

EGELHOFF, W. (1991): Information-processing Theory and the Multinational Enterprise, in: Journal of International Business Studies, Vol. 22, No. 3, pp. 341-368.

ELSCHEN, R. (1991): Gegenstand und Anwendungsmöglichkeiten der Agency-Theorie, in: Zeitschrift für betriebswirtschaftliche Forschung, Vol. 43, No. 11, pp. 1002-1012.

FORSGREN, M. (2008): Theories of the Multinational Firm: A Multidimensional Creature in the Global Economy, Cheltenham, Edward Elgar Publishing.

GABRIELSSON, M.; KIRPALANI, V. (2004): Born Globals: How to Reach New Business Space Rapidly, in: International Business Review, Vol. 13, pp. 555-571.

GHOSHAL, S.; NOHRIA, N. (1993): Horses for Courses: Organizational Forms for Multinational Corporations, in: Sloan Management Review, Vol. 34, No. 2, pp. 23-35.

GUPTA, A.K.; GOVINDARAJAN, V. (2000): Knowledge Flows Within Multinational Corporations, in: Strategic Management Journal, Vol. 21, No. 4, pp. 473-496.

HOLTBRÜGGE, D.; ENßLINGER, B. (2004): Exportstrategien von Born Global Firms, in: ZENTES, J.; MORSCHETT, D.; SCHRAMM-KLEIN, H. (Eds.): Außenhandel: Marketingstrategien und Managementkonzepte, Wiesbaden, Gabler, pp. 369-388.

JOHANSON, J.; VAHLNE, J. (1977): The Internationalization Process of the Firm: A Model of Knowledge Development and Increasing Foreign Market Commitment, in: Journal of International Business Studies, Vol. 8, No. 1, pp. 23-32.

KHANDWALLA, P. (1973): Viable and Effective Organizational Designs of Firms, in: Academy of Management Journal, Vol. 16, No. 3, pp. 481-495.

KIESER, A. (2002): Der situative Ansatz, in: KIESER, A. (Ed.): Organisationstheorien, 3rd ed., Stuttgart, Kohlhammer, pp. 169-198.

KIESER, A.; WALGENBACH, P. (2003): Organisation, 4th ed., Stuttgart, Schäffer-Poeschel.

KNIGHT, G.; CAVUSGIL, S.T. (1996): The Born Global Firm: A Challenge to Traditional Internationalization Theory, in: Advances in International Marketing, Vol. 8, pp. 11-27.

KUTSCHKER, M.; SCHMID, S. (2011): Internationales Management, 7th ed., Munich, Oldenbourg.

LAWRENCE, P.; LORSCH, J. (1967): Organization and Environment: Managing Differentiation and Integration, Boston, R.D. Irwin.

MALHOTRA, N.; AGARWAL, J.; ULGADO, F. (2004): Internationalization and Entry Modes: A Multitheoretical Framework and Research Propositions, in: Journal of International Marketing, Vol. 11, No. 4, pp. 1-31.

MILLER, D.; FRIESEN, P. (1984): Organizations: A Quantum View, Englewood Cliffs, Longman Higher Education.

MINTZBERG, H. (1981): Organizations Design: Fashion or Fit?, in: Harvard Business Review, Vol. 59, No. 1, pp. 103-116.

NOHRIA, N.; GHOSHAL, S. (1994): Differentiated Fit and Shared Values: Alternatives for Managing Headquarters-Subsidiary Relations, in: Strategic Management Journal, Vol. 15, No. 6, pp. 491-503.

NOHRIA, N.; GHOSHAL, S. (1997): The Differentiated Network: Organizing Multinational Corporations for Value Creation, San Francisco, Jossey-Bass.

O'DONNELL, S. (2000): Managing Foreign Subsidiaries: Agents of Headquarters, or an Interdependent Network?, in: Strategic Management Journal, Vol. 21, No. 5, pp. 525-548.

OVIATT, B.; MCDOUGALL, P. (1994): Towards a Theory of International New Ventures, in: Journal of Business Studies, Vol. 25, No. 1, pp. 45-64.

PFEFFER, J. (1981): Power in Organizations, Boston, Pitman Publishing.

PFEFFER, J.; SALANCIK, G. (1978): The External Control of Organizations: A Resource Dependency Perspective, New York, Longman Higher Education.

RICHTER, R.; FURUBOTN, E. (2003): Neue Institutionenökonomik, 3rd ed., Tübingen, Mohr Siebeck.

RUGMAN, A.M. (2010): Reconciling Internalization Theory and the Eclectic Paradigm, in: Multinational Business Review, Vol. 18, No. 2, pp. 1-12.

RUGMAN, A.M.; COLLINSON, S. (2012): International Business, 6th ed., Harlow, Pearson.

RUGMAN, A.M.; VERBEKE, A.; NGUYEN, Q. (2011): Fifty Years of International Business Theory and Beyond, in: Management International Review, Vol. 51, pp. 755-786.

SUDARSANAM, S. (2003): Creating Value from Mergers and Acquisitions: The Challenges, Harlow, Prentice Hall.

SWOBODA, B. (2002): Dynamische Prozesse der Internationalisierung: Managementtheoretische und empirische Perspektiven des unternehmerischen Wandels, Wiesbaden, Gabler.

THOMPSON, J. (1967): Organizations in Action: Social Science Bases of Administrative Theory, New York, McGraw-Hill.

WELCH, L.; BENITO, G.; PETERSEN, B. (2007): Foreign Operation Methods: Theory – Analysis – Strategy, Glos, Edward Elgar Publishing.

WERNERFELT, B. (1984): A Resource-based View of the Firm, in: Strategic Management Journal, Vol. 5, No. 2, pp. 171-180.

WILLIAMSON, O. (1985): The Economic Institutions of Capitalism, New York, The Free Press.

WOLF, J.; EGELHOFF, W. (2001): Strategy and Structure: Extending the Theory and Integrating the Research on National and International Firms, in: Schmalenbach Business Review, Vol. 53, April, pp. 117-139.

WORATSCHEK, H.; ROTH, S. (2005): Kooperation: Erklärungsperspektive der Neuen Institutionenökonomik, in: ZENTES, J.; SWOBODA, B.; MORSCHETT, D. (Eds.): Kooperationen, Allianzen und Netzwerke, 2nd ed., Wiesbaden, Gabler, pp. 141-166.

Part II

The External

Environment

Chapter 7

Market Barriers, Global and Regional Integration

The international activities of companies are closely related to the liberalisation of trade and to foreign direct investment (FDI) on a global level. The most important institution concerned with the rules of liberalisation has been GATT, replaced by WTO. The remarkable level of world trade and global FDI presently has another driving force: regional economic cooperation and regional economic integration. The objective of this Chapter is to describe the different types of market barriers and the forms of regional economic cooperation.

Types of Market Barriers

The major artificial barriers to trade are classified in Figure 7.1 as tariffs and non-tariff barriers.

Categories of Market Barriers

Figure 7.1

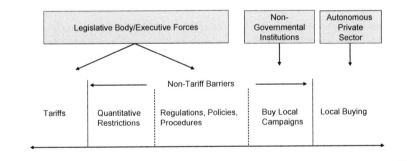

Tariffs, i.e., taxes on goods that are traded internationally, have traditionally been used to protect domestic industries by raising import prices. Because trade liberalisation has progressed over time, governments are increasingly using *non-tariff barriers* to protect some of their countries' industries: "Governments are very creative when it comes to the invention or virtuous use of non-tariff barriers to protect their countries' industries from international competition" (Mühlbacher/Leihs/Dahringer 2006, p. 147).

Trade Barriers

Non-tariff barriers can take three basic forms:

- quantitative restrictions, i.e., barriers that impose a limit on the quantity of a good that may be exported or imported

- laws, regulations, policies or procedures that impede international trade

- "buy local" campaigns.

Quotas and VER

Quotas are a popular example in the first category. These limit the quantity of a good that may be exported or imported during a certain time period, such as a year. Another example of numerical limits is the *voluntary export restraint* (VER), i.e., a promise by a country to limit its exports of a good to another country to a defined amount. This is often specifically announced to the target country in order to avoid import restrictions being imposed. Selected forms of *regulations*, *policies* and *procedures* are (Griffin/Pustay 2013, pp. 267-268):

- public-sector procurement policies

- local-purchase requirements

- product and testing standards.

Policies, Procedures, Campaigns

Public-sector procurement policies favour domestic firms in purchasing. *Local-purchase requirements* impede foreign firms by requiring domestic firms to purchase goods from local suppliers. *Product and testing standards* of a country have to be met by foreign products before the products can be sold in that country.

"Buy local" campaigns (e.g. "BuyAmerican" or "Achetez français") are sometimes conducted by non-governmental (or even governmental) institutions "to persuade their nationals to buy locally made products and services rather than those of foreign origin" (Bradley 2005, p. 130). *"Local buying"* can also be an expression of a specific behaviour of individual consumers behaviour through a desire to protect domestic producers for *patriotic* or *chauvinistic* motives.

Trade Sanctions and Trade Embargos

Besides permanent tariff and non-tariff barriers, international trade is also influenced by temporary barriers which are imposed because of reactions to specific events in intergovernmental relations: *trade sanctions*. A sanction is, generally speaking, the retaliatory reaction of a state against violations of international law by another state. Trade sanctions are also associated with the term *retorsion*, defined as *trade embargo* is an example of a sanction, and refers to governmental orders to prevent trade with a specific state. Basic variants of the trade embargo are the *export embargo*, *import embargo* and *capital embargo* (e.g. blockage of payments or prohibition of asset transfers) (Cavusgil/Knight/Riesenberger 2014, p. 212).

Restricting Foreign Direct Investment

Besides establishing actual barriers to trade (export or import), a government can deter foreign investments. Foreign direct investment (FDI) occurs when a company invests in a foreign subsidiary or joint venture with a partner firm in a foreign country, takes over a foreign company (acquisition/merger) or has a share in a foreign company. Foreign direct investment entails some degree of control, in contrast to "pure" financial investment. Besides *ownership restraints*, such as, foreign ownership being restricted to, e.g., 25%, *operation requirements* (e.g. local content) are another important instrument which influences foreign direct investment decisions. They are controls over the behaviour of the local subsidiary, such as a minimum level of local participation in top management.

Government Policy Instruments and FDI

Global Integration

Trade Liberalisation

The most important institution which has opened up new markets in almost all regions of the world has been GATT – the *General Agreement on Tariffs and Trade*. Founded in 1947, its objective was to liberalise international trade by eliminating tariffs, subsidies, import quotas, and the like. According to this multilateral agreement, the international trading system should be as follows (WTO 2014a):

GATT Rules

- *without discrimination* – a country should not discriminate between its trading partners (giving them equally "*most-favoured-nation*" or MFN status) and it should not discriminate between its own and foreign products, services or nationals (giving them "national treatment")

- *freer* – barriers coming down through negotiation

- *predictable* – foreign companies, investors and governments should be confident that trade barriers (including tariffs and non-tariff barriers) are not raised arbitrarily

- *more competitive* – discouraging "unfair" practices such as export subsidies and dumping products at below cost to gain market share

- *more beneficial for less developed countries* – giving them more time to adjust, greater flexibility, and special privileges.

Eight *rounds of trade negotiations* have led to significant reductions in tariffs and non-tariff barriers. The eighth round of negotiations, the *Uruguay Round*, created the *World Trade Organization* (WTO), which operates as an umbrella

Uruguay Round

organisation that encompasses the GATT along with new bodies, including one on services and one on intellectual property rights. Since 1 January 1995, the WTO has been responsible for monitoring the *trade policies* of member countries and arbitrating *trade disputes* among member countries.

GATS and TRIPS

The Uruguay Round led to liberalisation in both trade in services (GATS – *General Agreement on Trade in Services*) as well as agricultural goods, improvements in the protection of intellectual property rights (TRIPS – *Agreement on Trade-Related Aspects of Intellectual Property Rights*) and *anti-dumping rules,* prohibiting sales in foreign countries below cost.

Doha Development Round

The latest round, the *Doha Development Round,* which began in 2001, collapsed in July 2008. The Trade Negotiations Committee failed to agree on blueprint agreements in agriculture and industrial products. Eventually, the talks broke down over the *special safeguard mechanism* (SSM). The SSM was intended to allow developing countries to raise tariffs temporarily to deal with import surges and price falls. Most topics on the agenda had seen positions converge satisfactorily.

Bali Package

After the Ministerial Meeting in New Delhi in 2009 and the World Economic Forum in Davos in 2011, both of which failed, the first important success of the Doha Round could be reported in December 2013. At the Ninth Ministerial Conference, held in Bali, the *"Bali Package"*, a selection of issues from the broader Doha Round negotiations, was created. It focuses on trade facilitations, i.e. the simplification of customs procedures by reducing costs, improving speed and efficiency. Other important issues are for instance food security in developing countries, the reduction of export subsidies in agriculture or duty-free and quota-free market access for least-developed countries. Intellectual property aspects and trade in services were not taken into account. The "Bali Package" was planned being adopted by the General Council in July 2014. India did not adopt the protocol on the Trade Facilitation Agreement (TFA) – a part of the "Bali Package" – therefore the negotiations collapsed and the signature of the "Bali Package" was postponed indefinitely.

In any case, as a result of the activities of GATT/WTO, and also because of *regional economic cooperation*, discussed later in this Chapter, world trade increased from 2,034 billion USD in 1980 to 18,784 billion USD in 2013 (see Table 7.1).

Table 7.1

Increase in World Trade between 1980 and 2013 (in billion USD)

Year	World	Europe	Asia
1980	2,034	897	324
2013	18,784	6,636	6,285

Source: WTO World Trade Report 2014.

Investment Liberalisation

The liberalisation of trade is accompanied by a policy of the WTO members gradually allowing *foreign direct investment*, such as the establishment of subsidiaries and joint ventures or the takeover of companies. The TRIMS agreement (*Trade-Related Investment Measures Agreement*) in the Uruguay Round is an important step towards eliminating national regulations on FDI. "To this end, an illustrative list of TRIMs agreed to be inconsistent with these articles is appended to the agreement. The list includes measures which require particular levels of local procurement by an enterprise (local content requirements) or which restrict the volume or value of imports such an enterprise can purchase or use to an amount related to the level of products it exports (trade balancing requirements)" (WTO 2014b).

For example, some important steps in the timeline of relations between India and the WTO are illustrated in Table 7.2. India has become one of the most popular destinations for foreign direct investment, attracting nearly 26.6 billion USD in 2013 (Reserve Bank of India 2014).

Table 7.2 | *India's Steps to Open the Market*

Year	Event
January 1997	India allows foreign direct investments (FDI) in cash & carry (wholesale) with 100% ownership.
2001	India liberalises the insurance sector. Investment through FDI can be a maximum of 26%.
May 2001	The Indian Government opens the defence industry to the private sector. It permits 100% equity with a maximum of 26% FDI component.
March 2002	The Cabinet of India allows 100% FDI in the advertising and film industry, up from the present limit of 74%.
June 2002	The Indian Government first allows 26% FDI in news and current affairs in print media.
February 2006	The Indian Government opens up the retail sector by permitting FDI up to 51% in single-brand retail trading companies.
March 2011	Up to 100% FDI are permitted in certain agricultural activities (inter alia floriculture, horticulture, apiculture, cultivation of vegetables and mushrooms under controlled conditions, animal husbandry, pisciculture, aquaculture, tea production).
November 2011	India allows up to 51% FDI in multi-brand retail trading and 100% FDI in single-brand retail trading subject to 33% purchases from domestic sources.
September 2012	The Indian Government permits foreign airlines to make up to 49% FDI in scheduled and non-scheduled air transport services.
July 2013	The Indian Government rescinds the limit of 74% on foreign ownership in mobile services operations and allows these companies to be wholly owned by foreign investors.
August 2013	The Indian Government approved 100% FDI in the telecom sector.
January 2014	The Reserve Bank of India relaxes FDI regulations to facilitate great FDI inflows into the country.

Source: Financial Express 2002; People's World 2002; The Hindu 2011; Cedar Consulting 2012; The Economic Times 2012; The Metropolitan Corporate Counsel 2012; CIO 2013; Indian Defence Review 2013; The Economic Times 2013; India TV News 2014; The Economic Times 2014.

Regional Integration

One important exception to the *most-favoured-nation principle*, discussed in the context of the *GATT* rules, are comprehensive *trade agreements* that promote economic integration.

Trade and foreign investment liberalisation are reinforced by economic cooperation among countries, mostly within a geographical region. Economic cooperation can take the form of *bilateral agreements* or *multilateral agreements*, ranging from simple contracts on tariff reduction to political integration.

Stages of Economic Integration

A *preliminary stage* of economic integration is bilateral or multilateral agreements between countries concerning the reduction or abolition of tariffs or other barriers to trade in one or a few product groups (*free trade agreements*). The different stages of economic integration are summarised in Figure 7.2. From the least integrated level to the most integrated level they are: free trade area, customs union, common market, economic union, monetary union, and political union.

Different Levels of Economic Integration

Figure 7.2

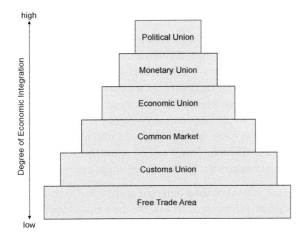

A *free trade area* is characterised by the fact that all formal barriers, especially tariffs, are abolished between the member states for a broad group of products or for all products (and services). Examples of existing free trade areas are:

Free Trade Area

■ *European Free Trade Association* (EFTA), focussing on free trade in industrial goods, including Iceland, Liechtenstein, Norway and Switzerland.

■ *North American Free Trade Agreement* (NAFTA), including Canada, Mexico and the USA, which led to 80% of all the trade of Canada and Mexico occurring within the NAFTA countries, while for the USA, its trade with NAFTA countries accounts for 33,5% (in 2012).

The *Transatlantic Trade and Investment Partnership* (TTIP) is a trade agreement that is presently being negotiated between the European Union and the United States. It aims at removing trade barriers in a wide range of economic sectors to make it easier to buy and sell goods and services between the EU and the US. The negotiations could ultimately lead to a *Trans-Atlantic Free Trade Area* (TAFTA).

Presently, there is a major discussion, initiated primarily by *nongovernmental organisations* (NGOs), but also by representatives of industrial companies, that there could be a *"race to the bottom"*, because the agreement could undermine social and ecological standards established in the EU through the need for harmonisation.

Customs Union

While the individual member countries of a free trade area maintain their independent external trade policy with regard to non-members, in a *customs union*, the member countries are committed to eliminating trade barriers corresponding to the free trade area, and adopting a common external trade policy. The most familiar and most important example of a customs union is the *European Union* (EU), although similar efforts exist in other regions too, such as MERCOSUR (*Mercado Común del Sur*) in the Southern part of Latin America. With regard to transaction costs, a customs union has a great advantage compared with free trade areas: *Certificates of origin* are not needed in intra-trade transactions. In free trade areas, there is always the possibility of realising *arbitrage effects* by importing goods into a "low tariff" country and then transferring them to "high tariff" countries within the area. To avoid these arbitrage businesses, certificates of origin are necessary.

Common Market

A common market has abolished internal tariffs and non-tariff barriers, standardised external tariffs and allows the free movement of factors of production (see Figure 7.3). The only existing common market is the *European Union* (EU), already mentioned as a customs union.

Figure 7.3 *Characteristics of a Common Market*

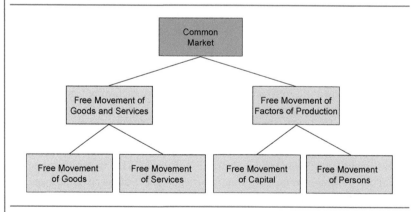

Economic Union

In an *economic union*, the next level of economic integration is that the member states harmonise their tax and subsidy policies in order to unify their fiscal policy. In this type of union, all member nations are fully integrated economically. The European Union intends to realise this stage of economic integration (*Maastricht Treaty, Amsterdam Treaty, Nice Treaty*). However, the implementation process is subject to political and economic difficulties.

Despite these difficulties, a common currency (EUR) was implemented, as of 1 January 1999. Since January 2014, 18 countries are members of the *"Euro-zone"*. The dramatic debt crisis in Greece and other countries like Spain, Portugal, Ireland and Italy, revealed deep problems in the Eurozone and it became evident that the monetary union needs to be modified to prevent future economic crises. In Figure 7.2., it is pointed out that an economic union should precede a monetary union. The current proposals from France and Germany point in this direction. A "closer economic policy coordination" as well as "binding contracts with the European Commission to implement further reforms" are required (Spiegel Online 2013).

Monetary and Political Union

The most advanced form of economic integration is a *political union*. In a political union, a body coordinates the economic, social, and foreign policy of its member states. This objective was the basic element of the *Maastricht Treaty* in 1992. In anticipation of this step, the former *European Community* agreed to rename itself the *European Union*, a truly optimistic sign.

Effects of Economic Cooperation

The effects of economic cooperation are diverse. For example, the macroeconomic effects of the implementation of a common market (within the European Community, EC) can be observed. According to the so-called *Cecchini Report* (Cecchini 1988, p. 97), the following macro-effects had been expected:

Cecchini Report

- relaunch of economic activity, adding on average 4.5% to GDP

- deflation of consumer prices by an average of 6.1%

- improving the balance of public finances by an average equivalent to 2.2% of GDP

- boosting the EC's external position by around 1% of GDP

- creating 1.8 million new jobs.

An *interim balance* (a report entitled "20 Years of the European Single Market: Together for new growth") identifies many important advantages which could be attributed to economic integration (European Commission 2012, p. 2):

Interim Balance

- The GDP of the EU-27 in 2008 was 2.13% or 133 billion EUR higher than it would have been without the Single Market. This can be equated to an average additional income of 500 EUR per EU citizen.

- During the period from 1992 to 2008, 2.77 million new jobs have been created.

■ Trade between EU countries rose from 800 billion EUR in 1992 to 2,800 billion EUR in 2011.

■ Exports to third countries (non-member) have increased from 500 billion EUR in 1992 (8% of EU GDP) to 1,500 billion EUR in 2011 (12% of EU GDP).

■ The Single Market has become much more attractive for foreign investors. The flow of foreign direct investment (FDI) between EU countries rose from 64 billion EUR in 1992 to 260 billion EUR in 2010.

Intra-EU Trade

The effects of the common market with regard to trade within the European Union *(intra-EU trade)* are shown in Table 7.3. The majority of member states of the EU-27 had an intra-EU trade share in 2013 of at least 60%.

Table 7.3

Shares of Intra-EU Trade for the EU Member States (EU-27) 2013 (in %)

State	Quote	State	Quote
Austria	69	Latvia	66
Belgium	70	Lithuania	57
Bulgaria	60	Luxembourg	81
Cyprus	58	Malta	42
Czech Republic	81	Netherlands	76
Denmark	63	Poland	75
Estonia	71	Portugal	70
Finland	55	Romania	69
France	59	Slovakia	83
Germany	57	Slovenia	69
Greece	46	Spain	63
Hungary	76	Sweden	58
Ireland	59	United Kingdom	44
Italy	53		

Source: EUROSTAT 2014.

Impact of Economic Integration on Firms

New Markets and Cross Border Value Creation

The political efforts of GATT/WTO to liberalise trade and foreign direct investment and the different regional alliances eliminating trade barriers, adopting a common external trade policy and allowing factors of production to move freely between members, have led to new markets with regard to sourcing, and selling and to new sites for production, logistics and so on (see Part V). Firms can reduce their production costs by capturing *economies of scale* when expanding their customer base within the trading bloc. The lower cost structure will also promote the firm's *international competitiveness* outside the trading blocs. "However, elimination of trade barriers also exposes a firm's home market to competition from firms located in other member countries, thus threatening less efficient firms" (Griffin/Pustay 2013, p. 288).

Conclusion and Outlook

The remarkably high level of world trade and foreign direct investment can be attributed to the political efforts of *GATT/WTO* and to the fact that regional integration has extended and intensified. This results in far-reaching liberalisation within regional cooperation, but also in discrimination vis-à-vis third countries, which is at first glance in conflict with free trade worldwide ("*most-favoured-nation status*").

In the next few years, there will be strong efforts to create new regional cooperation or to intensify the stage of integration, for example initiated by the European Union and the United States, Russia in Eurasia, or in North and South America and Asia. This offers many opportunities for companies with regard to exports and imports, for outsourcing, offshoring, strategic alliances, and greenfield and brownfield investments. If *regional agreement areas* gradually merge, regional economic cooperation will ultimately lead to far more free trade worldwide.

Trading Blocs
vs.
Free Trade

Further Reading

GRIFFIN, R.; PUSTAY, M. (2013): International Business: A Managerial Perspective, 7th ed., Upper Saddle River, New Jersey, Pearson.

HILL, C.W.L. (2013): Global Business Today, 8th ed., Boston, McGraw-Hill, pp. 249-273.

RUGMAN, A.M.; COLLINSON, S. (2012): International Business, 6th ed., Harlow, Pearson, pp. 175-187.

WOYKE, W. (2002): The European Union after Nice. A Community Facing a New Century, in: SCHOLZ, C.; ZENTES, J. (Eds.): Strategic Management: A European Approach, Wiesbaden, Gabler, pp. 3-21.

Case Study: Mazda[*]

Profile, History, and Status Quo

Since its foundation, *Mazda* has developed into an internationally known automobile brand. Its origins date back to 1920, when *Toyo Cork Kogyo Co. Ltd.* was floated by Jujiro Matsuda in Hiroshima, Japan. In 1984, the company was renamed the *Mazda Motor Corporation*, derived from its founder on the one hand and *Ahura Mazda*, the god of wisdom, intelligence and harmony of the earliest civilisations in West Asia on the other hand.

In its early stages, the company produced machine tools and three-wheel trucks. After the critical incident in Hiroshima during World War II, the headquarters was used as a military hospital. Production could be resumed in 1949 by manufacturing three-wheel trucks again which were exported to India. Due to the fact that these vehicles were tax-exempt driver's licences were not required, they were highly demanded. The first four wheel light truck was produced in 1958. In the 1960s, new product lines like the R360 Coupe, the first *Mazda* two door passenger car, were launched. In 1967, the *Mazda Cosmo Sports* (110S) was ushered in, the company's first rotary engine vehicle.

Mazda pursued an international approach very early in its history. The company started to export vehicles to China in 1932 and took up its export activities in 1949, exporting vehicles to India. The first assembly sites abroad were opened in South Korea (1962), South Africa (1963) and Malaysia (1968). This was followed by the opening of production facilities all over the world: Indonesia (1971), Philippines (1974), Thailand (1975), Colombia (1983), and the US (1985). In addition, *Mazda* established full-scale exports and sales companies in numerous regions. At the end of the 1960s, the European, Australian and Canadian markets were cultivated in this way, followed by the US in 1970. Till this day further sales companies are being opened, e.g. in Thailand (2005), Russia, Ireland (2006), and South Africa (2013).

Throughout its history, *Mazda* has shown an interest in *cooperation*. It founded the *Mazda Motor Manufacturing Corporation* in the mid-1980s. In 1992, this corporation was changed into the *AutoAlliance International, Inc.*, an equal partnership between *Mazda* and *Ford*. Three years later, the partners decided to establish the *AutoAlliance Company Ltd.* in Thailand, which produces vehicles for the Asian-Pacific and European market. In 2006, *Mazda* and *Mitsubishi Corporation* collaborated in the context of an energy supply company for Japan operations. For developing and producing sports cars, the

---

[*] Sources used for this case study include the website www.mazda.com, various company reports and explicitly cited sources.

company started a co-operative program with *Fiat* in 2012. This led to the agreement of collectively producing the new *Alfa Romeo* roadster in 2013.

Today, the company employs approximately 38,000 people, generating net sales about 2,205 billion Yen in 2013, where the largest share is apportioned to the North American region (see Table 7.4)

Consolidated Financial Statements of Mazda Motor Corporation and Consolidated Subsidiaries

Table 7.4

	2009	2010	2011	2012	2013
Net Sales (in billion Yen)	2,535.9	2,163.9	2,325.6	2,033.0	2,205.2
Net Sales - Domestic (in billion Yen)	620.3	575.0	541.5	560.2	588.0
Net Sales – North America (in billion Yen)	697.6	574.6	631.3	575.6	651.2
Net Sales - Europe (in billion Yen)	653.4	477.3	427.4	347.3	347.9
Net Sales – Other areas (in billion Yen)	564.6	537.0	725.5	549.9	618.1
Global Sales Volume (thousand of units)	1,261	1,193	1,273	1,247	1,235
Number of Employees	39,852	38,987	38,117	37,617	37,745

Source: Mazda 2014.

Trade Liberalisation in the Mexican Automotive Industry

Since 1962, regional integration between the US and Mexico has been shaped by a series of decrees. In 1990, four years before NAFTA, content requirements were reduced and imports of cars were allowed for the first time, due to the *Decree for the Development and Modernisation of the Automotive Industry*. In 1994, the *North American Free Trade Agreement* (NAFTA) came into effect, including the US, Mexico, and Canada. All states obligated themselves to remove all duties and quantitative restrictions, as scheduled in 2008 (Office of the United States Trade Representative 2014). In Article 102 Paragraph 1 of the North American Free Trade Agreement its objectives were registered as follows:

NAFTA

"a) eliminate barriers to trade in, and facilitate the cross-border movement of, goods and services between the territories of the Parties;

b) promote conditions of fair competition in the free trade area;

163

c) increase substantially investment opportunities in the territories of the Parties;

d) provide adequate and effective protection and enforcement of intellectual property rights in each Party's territory;

e) create effective procedures for the implementation and application of this Agreement, for its joint administration and for the resolution of disputes; and

f) establish a framework for further trilateral, regional and multilateral cooperation to expand and enhance the benefits of this Agreement."

Bilateral Free Trade Agreements

In addition to NAFTA, Mexico negotiated "10 FTAs [Free Trade Agreements] with 45 countries, 30 Reciprocal Investment Promotion and Protection Agreements (RIPPAs) and 9 trade agreements (…) within the framework of the Latin American Integration Association (ALADI)" (Secretariat of Economy 2013).

Mexico's Automotive Industry

Mexico has a long history of vehicle production. It began in 1925 when *Ford* established the first manufacturing plant in Mexico City. In the mid-1930s *Ford*, *GM* and *Automax* (later *Chrysler*) produced in Mexico, in 1952 *Volkswagen*, 1959 *Nissan* and 1985 *Honda* entered the Mexican market (PWC 2013, p. 9). In 1962, a decree established local content requirements, so that a 60% minimum of national inputs in auto part manufacturers was specified (Fernandez 2005). As a result, *Mercedes Benz*, *Fiat*, *Citroën*, *Peugeot*, and *Volvo* left Mexico, because they did not agree with the policy. The 1970s were characterised by several decrees which influenced exports negatively. From 1989 onwards, a more liberate approach aiming at the deregulation and economic liberalisation was pursued. In 2005, *Mazda* followed its competitors and entered the Mexican market.

Between 1985 and 2012, Mexico raised its exports of light vehicles from 600,000 to 2.4 million units. 1.1 million units of vehicles produced in Mexico are for auto producers with headquarters overseas, which equals a hundredfold increase in comparison to 1985 (Global Economic Intersection 2013). By the end of 2013, the production of light vehicles reached 2.93 million units, of which 2.42 million were exported (AMIA 2014). In 2012, 63.9% of all exported vehicles went to the US, 6.8% to Canada, 15.5% to Latin America, 1.5% to Africa, 2% to Asia, 9% to Europe, and 1.3% to other regions (PWC 2013, p. 5). Mexico developed into the *fourth largest exporter* of cars behind Germany, Japan, and South Korea and the eighth largest vehicle manufacturer worldwide (Reuters 2014) (see Table 7.5).

With the realisation of NAFTA, the inflow of FDI was increased. In Mexico, the automotive sector represented 21% of the total FDI; the auto parts sector reached a total of 1,770 million USD in 2012 (Promexico 2012). Approximately 3% of GDP, 14% of manufacturing output, 23% of all exports and about 500,000 employees can be attributed to the automotive sector (KPMG 2012, p. 4). This shows the enormous relevance of Mexico's most important industry within manufacturing.

Top 10 World Motor Vehicle Producing Countries 2008-2013 (in thousand of units)   *Table 7.5*

Top 10 (2013)	2008	2009	2010	2011	2012	2013
China	9,299	13,791	18,265	18,419	19,272	22,117
United States	8,694	5,731	7,763	8,662	10,329	11,046
Japan	11,576	7,934	9,629	8,399	9,943	9,630
Germany	6,046	5,210	5,906	6,311	5,649	5,718
South Korea	3,827	3,513	4,272	4,657	4,562	4,521
India	2,332	2,642	3,557	3,927	4,145	3,881
Brazil	3,216	3,182	3,382	3,408	3,343	3,740
Mexico	2,168	1,561	2,342	2,681	3,002	3,052
Thailand	1,394	999	1,645	1,458	2,429	2,533
Canada	2,082	1,490	2,068	2,135	2,464	2,380

Source: OICA 2014.

The main assemblers in Mexico's consolidated automotive sector are *Nissan, Volkswagen,* and the Big Three – *Ford, General Motors* and *Chrysler,* which covered over 93% of total production and 94% of internal sales between January and May 2014. In the same period, *Nissan* was the market leader with almost 50%, followed by *General Motors* with approximately 24% and *Volkswagen* with about 13% of internal sales, while *Mazda* was responsible for only approximately 1%, which can be ascribed to the circumstance that the production plant had just been opened (AMIA 2014). As shown in Table 7.6, *Mazda* was ranked No. 8 in units sold in Mexico.

Table 7.6 | *Top 10 Manufacturers in Mexico Based on Units Sold in 2013*

Rank	Manufacturer	Sold Units
1.	Nissan	263,477
2.	General Motors	201,604
3.	Volkswagen	156,313
4.	Ford	85,721
5.	Chrysler	78,974
6.	Toyota	60,740
7.	Honda	58,381
8.	Mazda	33,348
9.	Seat	21,189
10.	Renault	21,187

Source: Autoblog 2014.

Mexico has a tight net of car production plants. Especially the centre and Northern regions of the country reveal a concentrated manufacturing presence. The activities of manufacturers are not only confined to assembly. In fact, some companies also maintain design and engineering centres.

Due to the positive situation in Mexico, car manufacturers are still investing large amounts of money (see Table 7.7). Besides new automakers which are planning to build factories, established manufacturers want to expand their investments in favour of higher capacity.

Table 7.7 | *Selection of Projects of Automobile Manufacturers in Mexico in 2014*

Manufacturer	Project
Audi	1.3 billion USD: new production plant for Q5 model
Chrysler	164 million USD: expansion for Tigershark engines
Daimler	19 million USD: bus-assembly plant expansion
General Motors	349 million USD: new transmission plant
Honda	7 million USD: CR-V vehicles plant expansion
Mazda	770 million USD: new production plant
Mercedes-Benz	20 million USD: new assembly line expansion
Nissan	14 million USD: diesel engines
Volkswagen	118 million USD: new engine configuration

Source: Mexiconow 2014.

Entry and Operating Strategy of Mazda in Mexico

In December 2004, *Mazda Motor de Mexico* was established. This was followed by *Mazda*'s market entry in 2005. Since then, the company could sell approximately 180,000 vehicles in Mexico, and about 33,000 units only in 2013 alone. In this period of time, the brand's image in Mexico was improved so, that today it is highly regarded.

The next step in the Mexican history of *Mazda* took place in 2011. The company had to face different difficulties in its home country. Besides an earthquake, consequences on the supply chain and the catastrophe in Fukushima, even the global economic crisis forced the company to reflect on the possibility of relocating production. In addition, the development of the strong Yen endangered the company's success, because of the carmaker's reliance on exports from Japan. While, in 2008, a record profit of 162.1 billion Yen was generated, *Mazda* experienced a large profit decline in the following years. Consequently, the company was forced to take extensive steps. In January 2011, *Mazda* announced that it planned to produce automobiles in Mexico.

One of the most important reasons for establishing production plants in Mexico can be seen in numerous *free trade agreements*. Substantial FTAs in the automotive sector are the NAFTA, MEFTA, ACE-55, and the AAE. FTAs eliminate barriers like tariffs or quotas and allow duty-free trade within the member states, what can lead to demand-side effects, especially in the often high-priced automotive sector. In this context, local content requirements often constitute important conditions. They fix a certain share of local production of vehicles or auto parts. Within NAFTA, a local content of 62.5% is required to be covered from the exemption from customs duties. For duty-free export to Japan, a local content share of 65% is postulated (see Table 7.8).

Overcoming Market Barriers

In comparison to the European Union, which is a customs union, NAFTA does not restrict its member states concerning the negotiation of FTAs with other countries. The member states keep their degrees of freedom in reference to its trade policy. Consequently, none of the member states of NAFTA needs permission if it wants to conclude a new bilateral free trade agreement with another country. In contrast, customs unions have common tariffs on external countries.

Mazda's major sales markets are, among others, the US, Japan, China, Europe, Australia, the ASEAN member states, Canada and Mexico. Compared to Mexico's existing FTAs, almost all relevant markets are covered. Mazda had to introduce a production plant in Mexico to fulfil the local content requirements that were anchored in the FTAs, on order to participate in duty-free sales. As a result, the production plant in Salamanca, Mexico was

Production Plant in Mexico

established, that serves as a hub for exports. In February 2014, the official opening of the engine and vehicle assembly plant took place.

Table 7.8

Selected Free Trade Agreements of Mexico

Agreement	Member States	Duty-free Trade in the Automotive Sector	Local Content Requirement
North American Free Trade Agreement (NAFTA)	Mexico, USA, Canada	since 01.01.2004	62.5%
Middle East Free Trade Area (MEFTA)	Mexico, European Union	since 01.01.2007	50%
Mercosur/ACE-55	Mexico, Argentina, Brazil	since 01.01.2007/ 19.03.2012	60% Argentina and Brazil, 35% Mexico
Economic Partnership Agreement (AAE, by its initials in Spanish)	Mexico, Japan	since 01.04.2011	65%

Source: AHK Mexiko 2012, p. 25.

The facility is a joint venture by *Mazda* and the Japanese trading company *Sumitomo Corporation*. It was the first time that *Mazda* went overseas without another automotive partner (Entrada Group 2013). While *Sumitomo* owns 30%, *Mazda* is a 70% shareholder of the 770 million USD plant (Automotive News 2014b). In Salamanca, *Mazda* employs 4,500 people. Besides the production of *Mazda* 2 and *Mazda* 3, the facility will be producing engines from October 2014. Thus, the number of locally produced parts will increase and local content requirements will be adhered more easily. At the end of 2016, the plant is supposed to have an annually capacity of 230,000 units. Additionally, from 2015 on 50,000 *Toyota*-branded cars should be produced there.

Vehicles produced in Salamanca are sold to Canada, Mexico, Central and South America, as well as Europe; even other regions in the world are not excluded. In its first months of operation until May 2014, 18,700 vehicles were produced in total. While only a fraction was sold in the Mexican market, over 75% went to the US (AMIA 2014).

Structural Reform Plan

In February 2012, the *Structural Reform Plan* was established. This plan was formulated in order to achieve the company's mid- to long-term objectives and to strengthen business in emerging markets. The aim was to reach an operating income of 150 billion Yen by 2016. Another target is to increase the share of vehicles produced outside Japan from 30% in 2012 to 50% in 2016. The establishment of the Mexican plant is one step to achieve these targets. Yamanouchi, the CEO of *Mazda* Motor Corporation, made clear that "Mazda's Structural Reform Plan, upon which the very future of the company hinges, positions this plant as [the] most important global strategic base" (Automotive News 2014a).

For achieving objectives of the Structural Reform Plan, *Mazda* follows the approach of producing abroad to circumvent market barriers like customs regulations. Besides Mexico, the company also established a production plant in Thailand, which is an ASEAN member state. Within ASEAN, companies that fulfil the requirement of 40% local content are eligible to benefit from the 0-5% preferential tariff rate. *Mazda* operates in all ten ASEAN member states, even Myanmar, which was under international economic sanctions until recently. Only in 2011, were import restrictions imposed by the military government loosened (Reuters 2013).

Questions

1. *Mazda* and other carmakers use Mexico as a production country. Summarise the advantages that accrued for the Mexican automotive industry through the country's access to the NAFTA. Except the evasion of market barriers, which benefits are there in the context of producing vehicles in Mexico?

2. Compare the possibility of relocating a production facility to Mexico with the advantages and disadvantages an automotive manufacturer could have shifting its production to the ASEAN region.

3. Define different types of market barriers and show their effect on the market entry mode. Explain different strategies a company can use to deal with entry barriers in the context of the internationalisation of its business. Give some examples.

Hints

1. See Gachúz Maya 2011.

2. See Ball et al. 2012, pp. 63-93, as well as Kotabe and Helsen 2014, pp. 30-59.

References

AHK MEXIKO (2012): Zielmarktanalyse im Rahmen der Geschäftsanbahnung Automobilzulieferer Mexiko, Mexico.

AMIA (Asociación Mexicana de la Industria Automotríz) (2014): Producción total, http://www.amia.com.mx/prodtot.html., accessed on August 24, 2014.

AUTOBLOG (2014): Ventas enero-diciembre 2013: México, http://es.autoblog.com, accessed on August 24, 2014.

AUTOMOTIVE NEWS (2014a): Honda's Celaya Plant Boosts Mexico Factory Presence, http://www.autonews.com/article/20140221, accessed on August 24, 2014.

AUTOMOTIVE NEWS (2014b): Mazda's Mexico Plant "Most Important" Base, Chairman Says, http://www.autonews.com/article/20140227/OEM 01/ 140229879/mazdas-mexico-plant-most-important-base-chairman-says, accessed on August 24, 2014.

BALL, D.A.; GERINGER, M.; MCNETT, J.M.; MINOR, M.S. (2012): International Business: The Challenge of Global Competition, 13th ed., New York, McGraw-Hill.

BRADLEY, F. (2005): International Marketing Strategy, 5th ed., Harlow, Pearson.

CAVUSGIL, S.T.; KNIGHT, G.; RIESENBERGER, J.R. (2014): International Business: The New Realities, 3rd ed., Boston, Pearson.

CECCHINI, P. (1988): Europa '92: Der Vorteil des Binnenmarktes, Baden-Baden, Nomos.

CEDAR CONSULTING (2012): India Foreign Direct Investment Trends, http://www.cedar-consulting.com/pdf/Cedar_USIBC_%20Report.pdf, accessed on May 12, 2014.

CIO (2013): India Allows Wholly Foreign-owned Mobile Operators, http://www.cio.de/news/cio_worldnews/2013/2922938/, accessed on August 24, 2014.

ENTRADA GROUP (2013): Mazda to Increase Production Capacity in Mexico, http://www.entradagroup.com/mazda-to-increase-production-capacity-in-mexico/, accessed on August 24, 2014.

EUROPEAN COMMISSION (2012): 20 Years of the European Single Market: Together for new growth, Directorate-General for the Internal Market and Services, Brussels.

EUROSTAT (2014): Eurostat Statistics in Focus, http://epp.eurostat.ec. europa.eu, accessed on August 18, 2014.

FERNANDEZ, O. (2005): Historia de la Industria Automotriz en México, http://catarina.udlap.mx/u_dl_a/tales/documentos/mec/fernandez_d_ao/capitulo_1.html, accessed on August 24, 2014.

FINANCIAL EXPRESS (2002): Cabinet Clears 100% FDI in Films and Advertising, http://www.financialexpress.com/news/cabinet-clears-100-fdi-in-films-and-advertising/39476, accessed on August 13, 2014.

GACHÚZ MAYA, J.C. (2008): The Impact of NAFTA on the Automotive Industry in Mexico: An Analysis in Political Economy, Saarbrücken.

GLOBAL ECONOMIC INTERSECTION (2013): Mexico Growing Importance in North American Auto Production, http://econintersect.com/b2evolution/blog1.php/2013/04/11/mexico-growing-importance-in-north-american-auto-production, accessed on August 24, 2014.

GRIFFIN, R.; PUSTAY, M. (2013): International Business: A Managerial Perspective, 7th ed., Upper Saddle River, New Jersey, Pearson.

HILL, C.W.L. (2013): Global Business Today, 8th ed., Boston, McGraw-Hill.

INDIA TV NEWS (2014): Foreign Direct Investment in Multi-brand Retail: A Hope in Abeyance, http://www.indiatvnews.com/business/india/breaking-news-foreign-direct-investment-in-multi-brand-retail-9565.html, accessed on August 24, 2014.

INDIAN DEFENCE REVIEW (2013): FDI in Defence: Dispelling the Myths, http://www.indiandefencereview.com/news/fdi-in-defence-dispelling-the-myths/, accessed on August 24, 2014.

JOHNSON, J.R. (1999): NAFTA and the Trade in Automotive Goods, http://oldfraser.lexi.net/publications/books/assess_nafta/auto_goods.html, accessed on August 22, 2014.

KOTABE, M.; HELSEN, K. (2014): Global Marketing Management, 6th ed., New York, Wiley & Sons.

KPMG (2012): Assessing an Investment in the Mexican Automotive Industry, Global Strategy Group (GSG) KPMG Mexico.

MAZDA (2014): Annual Report 2013, Hiroshima.

MEXICO TODAY (2012): Ford Invests in Hermosillo, Mexico Plant, http://mexicotoday.org/article/ford-invests-hermosillo-mexico-plant, accessed on August 24, 2014.

MEXICONOW (2014): Mexico's Automotive Industry Main Projects 2014, https://www.mexico-now.com/online/data/files/images/online/069_MAIN_4.jpg, accessed on August 24, 2014.

MÜHLBACHER, H.; LEIHS, H.; DAHRINGER, L.; (2006): International Marketing, 3rd ed., London, Thomson Learning.

NISSAN (2013): Nissan Inaugurates All-New Aguascalientes, Mexico Plant, Building on a Reputation for Quality and Efficiency, http://www.nissan-global.com, accessed on August 24, 2014.

OFFICE OF THE UNITED STATES TRADE REPRESENTATIVE (2014): North American Free Trade Agreement (Nafta), http://www.ustr.gov/trade-agreements/free-trade-agreements/north-american-free-trade-agreement-nafta, accessed on August 24, 2014.

OICA (2014): 2013 Production Statistics, http://www.oica.net/category/production-statistics/, accessed on August 24, 2014.

PEOPLE'S WORLD (2002): Foreign Direct Investment Threatens Indian Media, http://www.peoplesworld.org/foreign-direct-investment-threatens-indian-media/, accessed on August 24, 2014.

PWC (2013): Doing Business in Mexico: Automotive Industry, http://www.pwc.de/de/internationalemaerkte/assets/doing-business-mexico-mining.pdf, accessed on July 12, 2014.

PROMEXICO (2012): The Automotive Sector 2012, http://mim.promeco.gob.mx/work/sites/mim/resources/LocalContent/319/2/Automotive_Industry.PDF, accessed on August 24, 2014.

PROMEXICO (2013): The Auto Parts Industry, Mexico City.

PROMEXICO (2014): Uncorking Logistics Bottlenecks in the Automotive Industry, http://negocios.promexico.gob.mx/english/12-2013/guest-opinion/, accessed on August 24, 2014.

RESERVE BANK OF INDIA (2014): Foreign Investment Inflows: Monthly, http://dbie.rbi.org.in/DBIE/dbie.rbi?site=statistics, accessed on August 24, 2014.

REUTERS (2013): Mazda to Start Selling New Cars in Myanmar, http://in.reuters.com/article/2013/09/16/mazda-myanmar-idINL3N0HC1L320130916, accessed on August 24, 2014.

REUTERS (2014): Mexico 2013 Auto Output, Exports Hit Records for 4th year, http://www.reuters.com/article/2014/01/08/mexico-autos, accessed on August 24, 2014.

RUGMAN, A.M.; COLLINSON, S. (2012): International Business, 6th ed., Harlow, Pearson.

SECRETARIAT OF ECONOMY (2013): International Trade Negotiations, http://www.economia.gob.mx/trade-and-investment/foreign-trade/international-trade-negotiations, accessed on August 24, 2014.

SICE (2014): Information on Mexico, http://www.sice.oas.org/ctyindex/MEX/MEXagreements_e.asp, accessed on August 24, 2014.

SPIEGEL ONLINE (2013): Merkel Speech: Chancellor Urges Reforms to Preserve Euro, http://www.spiegel.de/international/europe/merkel-calls-on-eu-members-to-agree-binding-reforms-a-939813.html, accessed on August 24, 2014.

THE ECONOMIC TIMES (2012): Review of Policy on Foreign Direct Investment in Civil Aviation Sector, http://articles.economic-times.indiatimes.com, accessed on August 24, 2014.

THE ECONOMIC TIMES (2013): Cabinet Approves 100% FDI in Telecom, http://articles.economictimes.indiatimes.com/2013-08-01/news/40962900_1_telecom-sector-cent-fdi-100-fdi, accessed on August 24, 2014.

THE ECONOMIC TIMES (2014): RBI Eases Rules to Boost Foreign Direct Investment, http://articles.economictimes.indiatimes.com, accessed on August 24, 2014.

THE ECONOMIST (2013): Mexico's Car Industry: Steaming Hot, http://www.economist.com/blogs/schumpeter/2013/11/mexico-s-car-industry#sthash.CASjR0L8.dpbs, accessed on August 24, 2014.

THE FINANCIAL EXPRESS (2002): Cabinet Clears 100% FDI in Films and Advertising, http://www.financialexpress.com/news/cabinetclears100fdiin-filmsandadvertising/39476, accessed on August 24, 2014.

THE HINDU (2011): 100% FDI Allowed in Some Areas of Farm Sector, http://www.thehindu.com, accessed on August 24, 2014.

THE METROPOLITAN CORPORATE COUNSEL (2012): India's Foreign Direct Investment Policy Opens the Door to Multi-Brand Retail, http://www.metrocorpcounsel.com, accessed on August 24, 2014.

VILLARREAL, M.A. (2012): Mexico's Free Trade Agreements, https://www.fas.org/sgp/crs/row/R40784.pdf, accessed on August 24, 2014.

WALL STREET JOURNAL (2014): BMW Considers First Plant in Mexico, http://online.wsj.com, accessed on August 24, 2014.

WOYKE, W. (2002): The European Union after Nice: A Community Facing a New Century, in: SCHOLZ, C.; ZENTES, J. (Eds.): Strategic Management: A European Approach, Wiesbaden, Gabler, pp. 3-21.

WTO (2014a): Understanding the WTO: Principles of the trading system, http://www.wto.org, accessed on August 24, 2014.

WTO (2014b): Legal Texts: the WTO Agreements, http://www.wto.org, accessed on August 24, 2014.

Chapter 8

Competitive Advantage of Nations and Regional Clusters

This Chapter gives an overview of the main sources of national competitive advantages, based on Porter's diamond model, and discusses the role of regional clusters of industries. In this context, it is explained, how MNCs can benefit from locating their operations in country markets with a high level of national competitive advantage or in regional industry clusters.

National Competitive Advantage

Multinational corporations can benefit from favourable environmental conditions by locating their operations in countries with certain market conditions. As the globalisation of international markets increases and the liberalisation of markets simplifies cross-border transactions, MNCs have a broad selection of potential locations from which to select. Most attractive for MNCs are locations with a high level of national (or regional) competitive advantage. The level of a *country's competitiveness* reflects the extent to which it is able to provide rising prosperity to its citizens. A nation's prosperity is intimately linked to the productivity of the economy. If a nation is able to improve its productivity, it can improve prosperity.

In this context, Porter (1990b, p. 73) argues that: "National prosperity is created, not inherited". Thus, not only firms compete internationally, but, as global competition increases, countries also need to position themselves as attractive places to invest and do business. Following this view, each country needs to explore its potential *sources of competitive advantage* to achieve the sustainable growth, which is the basis for long-term economic wealth and prosperity of the nation.

Each year, the *World Economic Forum* publishes a Global Competitiveness Report in which countries are ranked according to their competitiveness (see Table 8.1). The ranking builds on the *Global Competitiveness Index (GCI)* which is developed from the "12 pillars of competitiveness" that are regarded as sources of national competitive advantage. In this regard, factors such as the institutional environment in a country, its macroeconomic stability, the educational system or infrastructure are analysed, as well as a country's market size or its level of (technical) innovation (World Economic Forum 2013, pp. 4-

Global Competitiveness Index

9). Thus, the determinants of competitiveness are manifold and countries need to explore which dimensions are important for to building on in order to improve national competitiveness.

Table 8.1

Global Competitiveness Index Ranking 2013-2014

Country/ Economy	Rank	Score	Country/ Economy	Rank	Score
Switzerland	1	5.67	Austria	16	5.15
Singapore	2	5.61	Belgium	17	5.13
Finland	3	5.54	New Zealand	18	5.11
Germany	4	5.51	U. Arab Emirates	19	5.11
United States	5	5.48	Saudi Arabia	20	5.10
Sweden	6	5.48	Australia	21	5.09
Hong Kong SAR	7	5.47	Luxembourg	22	5.09
Netherlands	8	5.42	France	23	5.05
Japan	9	5.40	Malaysia	24	5.03
United Kingdom	10	5.37	Korea, Rep.	25	5.01
Norway	11	5.33	Brunei	26	4.95
Taiwan	12	5.29	Israel	27	4.94
Qatar	13	5.24	Ireland	28	4.92
Canada	14	5.20	China	29	4.84
Denmark	15	5.18	Puerto Rico	30	4.67

Source: World Economic Forum 2013, p. 15.

Porter's Diamond Model

While the underlying understanding of competitiveness in the GCI relates to the economy as a whole, there are differences in the patterns of competitiveness relating to each particular industry. No nation will be competitive in all or even most industries.

At the *industry level*, Porter (1990a; 1990b) attempted to explain why a nation achieves international success in a particular industry. Based on an intensive investigation of 100 industries in ten nations, he identified four attributes that promote or impede the creation of competitive advantage: (1) factor conditions, (2) demand conditions, (3) related and supporting industries, and (4) firm strategy, structure, and rivalry.

These four attributes shape the environment in which local firms compete and determine the success of nations in international competition. They constitute the *diamond* (see Figure 8.1), a mutually reinforcing system in which the effect of one attribute is contingent on the state of the other attributes. Each of the four determinants of national competitive advantage is briefly discussed below.

Determinants of National Competitive Advantage: Porter's Diamond Model

Figure 8.1

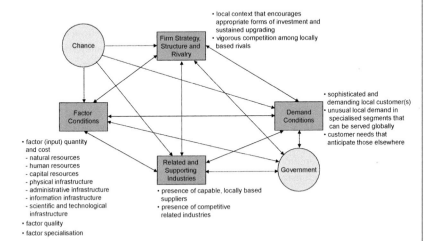

Source: Porter 1990a, p. 127.

Factor Conditions

The first element of the diamond is the nation's possession of factors of production. Consistent with the *factor proportions theory* (Heckscher-Ohlin), every country has a relative abundance of certain factor endowments. In his diamond model, Porter distinguishes between basic and advanced factors.

Basic factors are those such as land, climate, natural resources or demographics, while *advanced factors* relate to more sophisticated ones, including the nation's stock of knowledge resources (e.g. scientific, technical or market knowledge), the transportation and communication infrastructure or a sophisticated and skilled labour force (Rugman/Collinson 2012, p. 303).

Basic Factors and Advanced Factors

In the diamond model, the *advanced factors* are regarded as being most significant for competitive advantage. These factors can be created through training, research and innovation and thus are a product of investment by individuals, companies or the government. The basic assumption is that a nation must continually *upgrade* or adjust its factor conditions. The basic factors provide the country with an initial advantage that can subsequently be reinforced by investing in *advanced factors*. On the other hand, disadvantages in

177

basic factors mean that countries need to invest in advanced factors (Porter 1990b). Thus, upgrading a nation's advanced factors, such as the educational system or infrastructure, is regarded as a means to improve a nation's competitive advantages.

Demand Conditions

Home Market Demand

Demand conditions refer to the nature and size of the *domestic demand* for an industry's products and services. Here, the main characteristics are the *strength* and *sophistication* of domestic customer demand. Porter (1990b, pp. 79-80) argues that companies are most sensitive to the needs of their closest customers. Thus, home market demand is of particular importance in shaping the attributes of the companies' products. The more sophisticated and demanding their local customers, the more pressure is created for innovation, efficiency and upgrading product quality. Therefore, it is assumed that with increasing consumer sophistication in their home markets and, consequently, with increasing pressure on local sellers, their competitive advantage will escalate (Hill 2013, pp. 198-199).

Size of Home Market

While the nature of home market demand mainly relates to pressure to improve local companies' performance, the *size* of the home market is important, as it enables companies to achieve economies of scale and experience curve advantages. This is even more important when scale economies limit the number of production locations. In this case, the size of its market is an important determinant of the country's attractiveness as a potential location. Additionally, empirical evidence shows that efficient firms are often forced to look for international opportunities at stages when their early (large) home market becomes saturated. Their home markets provide these companies with scale advantages that can be used in the global marketplace (Hollensen 2014, pp. 103-104).

Related and Supporting Industries

Industrial Cluster

The presence of a business environment comprising related suppliers, competitors and complementary firms is regarded as highly supportive for an industry to build competitive advantages. Such a (geographical) concentration of companies, suppliers and supporting firms at a particular location is labelled an *industrial cluster* (Porter 2000, p. 254).

Firm Strategy, Structure, and Rivalry

This element of the diamond relates to the firm-based theories of internationalisation that focus on the actions of individual firms. National context and national circumstances strongly influence how companies are created, organised and managed and the nature of domestic rivalry (Porter 1990b, p. 81).

Domestic competition affects companies' ability to compete in the global marketplace. Not only does the presence of *local competitors* automatically cancel out advantages that come from a nation's factor endowment or characteristics of home market demand, but the higher the level of domestic competition, and the stronger the rivals in the home market, the more companies are forced to become more efficient and to adopt new technologies. High pressure in a competitive home market leads to *selection processes* and leaves only the most efficient firms as survivors. At the same time, this is associated with continuous pressure on companies to innovate and to improve (Griffin/Pustay 2013, pp. 184-187).

Domestic Competition

Not only does competitive pressure vary between countries, but managerial practices, organisational modes, company goals and individual achievement goals also differ significantly between countries. These differences lead to *dissimilar international strategies* of the firms. Additionally, Porter argues that specific managerial systems are needed to be successful in each of the diverse industries. Thus, if a nation's firms follow a specific managerial system this only can be successful in selective industries. Thus, such differences also play an important role in the diamond model, because different management ideologies influence the ability to build national competitive advantage (Porter 1990b, pp. 81-82).

Managerial Systems

The Role of Chance and Government

As already mentioned, the basic underlying view of the diamond model is that competitive advantage can be created. Therefore, nations can influence competitive advantage by systematically improving each of the elements of the diamond. In this connection, it is important to note that *government interventions* must be considered in terms of their impact on domestic company activities, because the underlying view in the diamond model is that "firms, not nations, compete in international markets" (Porter 1990a, p. 33).

Government Interventions

Governments can, for example, cultivate new and superior *factor endowments*, influence the nature of *local competition, home market demand* or *clustering of firms* by using measures such as subsidies, investing in the educational system, monetary and fiscal policy (e.g. tax incentives or low interest loans), the development and maintenance of a strong infrastructure (e.g. IT, communication systems, transportation), antitrust regulations or enforcing product and safety standards. However, one must not forget that such well-intentioned government actions can also *backfire* and lead to the creation of a "sheltered" domestic industry that is unable to compete in the global marketplace (Rugman/Collinson 2012, p. 304).

Role of Chance

Additionally, the role of *chance* in building competitive advantage is recognised in the diamond model. However, this influence of chance is by its very danger not predictable. For example, chance influences the creation of new ideas or new inventions. Also wars, significant shifts in world financial markets, discontinuities in input costs (e.g. oil price shocks) or major technological breakthroughs can have a significant impact on a nation's competitive advantage.

Evaluation of the Diamond Model

Each of the four elements of the diamond model has an influence on the nation's competitive advantage in a specific industry, with all of these attributes depending on the state of the others. Usually, the presence of all four components is required to increase competitive advantage, with weaknesses in any one determinant constraining an industry's potential for advancement and upgrading. While the diamond is regarded as a *self-reinforcing system*, the role of two additional forces is also important: government and chance.

Role of Multinational Companies

A controversial debate centres on the role of MNCs in the diamond model. Several researchers (e.g. Dunning 1993; Moon/Rugman/Verbeke 1998) have argued that *multinational activity* should be included as a third outside variable, because MNCs are influenced in their competitiveness by the configuration of the diamond in other than their home countries and this in turn influences the competitiveness of the home country. "Therefore, Porter's original diamond model has been extended to the generalized double diamond model whereby multinational activity is formally incorporated into the model" (Moon/Rugman/Verbeke 1998, p. 137; see also Moon/Rugman/Verbeke 1995).

The Generalised Double Diamond

Figure 8.2

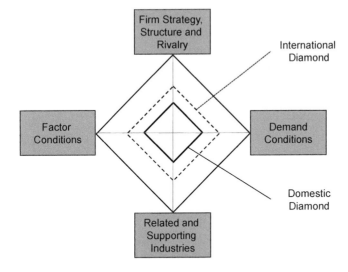

Source: Adapted from Moon/Rugman/Verbeke 1998, p. 138.

Figure 8.2 shows the *generalised double diamond*. "The size of the global diamond is fixed within a foreseeable period, but the size of the domestic diamond varies according to the country size and its competiveness. The diamond of dotted lines, between these two diamonds, is an *international diamond* which represents the nation's competitiveness as determined by both domestic and international parameters. The difference between the international diamond and the *domestic diamond* thus represents international or multinational activities. The multinational activities include both outbound and inbound foreign direct investment (FDI)" (Moon/Rugman/Verbeke 1998, p. 138).

Stages in National Development

The diamond model can be used to distinguish between three *growth stages* of national competitive development (Porter 1990a, pp. 555-565):

- *Factor-driven stage*: This first stage relates to industries that draw their advantages solely from the nation's factor endowments, mainly from basic factors of production such as natural resources (e.g. mineral deposits). These industries can be successful internationally but they compete primarily on price.

■ *Investment-driven stage*: This stage implies efforts of upgrading of the nation's industry as companies invest in modern technology and more efficient facilities.

■ *Innovation-driven stage*: While in the second stage investment in modern, but already existing technology dominates, the third stage is characterised by the creation of new technology or (production) methods. These improvements are yielded by internal innovation as well as by innovation in cooperation with, or with assistance from, suppliers and companies in related industries.

This model mainly relates to the stages of a nation's industries. Usually, countries span two or more stages in this model, because there are likely to be industries (or companies) in all countries that are operating at each stage.

Competitive Advantages of Emerging Countries

The ongoing integration of *emerging countries* into the global economy has further strengthened the importance of these ambitious countries within the business strategies of most multinational companies (Rugman/Collinson 2012, p. 637). According to recently published projections, the combined economic output of Brazil, China and India – the three biggest economies among the *newly industrialised countries* – will surpass the aggregate output of Canada, France, Germany, Italy, the United Kingdom and the United States by the year 2020 (United Nations Development Programme 2013, p. IV) (see also Chapter 5).

As early as 1926, John Maynard Keynes summed up – although in a different context – what can still be considered the foundation of many competitive advantages emerging countries have compared to highly developed nations: "The political problem of mankind is to combine three things: Economic Efficiency, Social Justice and Individual Liberty" (Keynes 2009, p. 187). Since the process of industrialisation started in the 19th century, the now so-called *developed economies* have achieved remarkable success in terms of labour conditions, environmental protection, human rights and animal protection or social insurance. On the one hand, these accomplishments have contributed to social justice and individual liberty. On the other hand, they have slowed down these countries' efforts towards maximising economic efficiency.

Most emerging countries, especially the so-called BRICs, have managed to turn this shortfall regarding social and political development into a huge competitive advantage in the first stage by offering low labour costs, an almost inexhaustible quantity of nonunionised workers (e.g. China, India) or almost unrestricted access to energy (e.g. Russia) and precious raw materials such as rare earth elements (e.g. Brazil) (Sheth 2011, p. 170). At the same time, these countries demand only insignificant environmental or health and safety at work regulations, negligible taxes and only a loose commitment to corporate social responsibility (Deng/Li 2012, p. 157; Humphries 2013, p. 9; Meulen Rodgers/Menon 2013, p. 934). These competitive advantages are boosted even further by constant infrastructural improvements and decreasing costs of transportation and logistics.

In a second step, they are now improving the social and ecological standards, training and educating the personnel, which finally leads to substantial progress in research and development: They presently combine cost advantages with skills, as can be seen in China (largest export country, see Chapter 5) or India (global IT competence centre).

Because of this economic development, emerging countries do not just play a major role in MNC's sourcing or production strategies, but also in their distribution strategy. While highly developed countries are increasingly marked by saturated markets in many product categories, the ascending wealth in emerging countries enables more and more customers in these countries to consume Western products from powerful brand manufacturers such as *BMW*, *Mercedes Benz* or *Apple* (Jansson 2007, p. 14). Another important effect of the competitive advantages of emerging countries is the growing appearance of *emerging country multinationals* in the global arena (see Chapter 5).

Regional Clusters

In the diamond model, the regional clusters play a prominent role: "We define a cluster as a geographically proximate group of interconnected companies, suppliers, service providers and associated institutions in a particular field, linked by externalities of various types" (Porter 2003, p. 562). Therefore, clusters are closely linked with the dimensions "related and supporting industries" and "firm strategy, structure, and rivalry" of Porter's diamond model.

Figure 8.3 | *Actors in Regional Clusters*

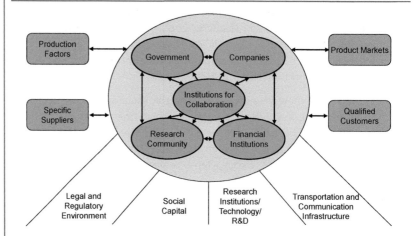

Source: Adapted from Sölvell/Lindqvist/Ketels 2003, p. 18; Andersson et al. 2004, p. 31.

Competition and Cooperation

Clusters can include *suppliers* of specialised inputs (e.g. components, machinery, and services) or providers of specialised *infrastructure* (see Figure 8.3). They are usually extended downstream to customers and laterally to complementary industries and companies in industries through by technologies, common inputs or skills. Often, clusters also encompass governmental and other institutions (e.g. universities, think tanks, or standard-setting agencies) that provide specialised research, education, training, and technical support (Porter 1998, p. 78).

The nature of clusters thus leads to an internal constellation that promotes both competition and cooperation *("co-opetition")*. *Competition* occurs between the rival companies located in geographical proximity, while *cooperation* mainly relates to vertical channel relationships with related companies, related industries or local institutions.

Advantages of Regional Industry Clusters

The advantages from such a clustering of firms mainly stem from the presence of a specialised *infrastructure*, industry-sector-specific *factors of production* and *skilled labour* in the specific professional field, from *information and knowledge synergies*, and access to appropriate or *superior inputs*.

If an industry is located close to its suppliers, it will enjoy better *communication* and the exchange of cost-saving ideas and inventions with those suppliers. This is mainly a result of *geographical proximity*, which enables close working relationships. This yield advantages from short lines of communication and a quick and constant flow of information with companies having the opportunity to influence their suppliers' technical efforts, which can help to accelerate the pace of innovation (Cavusgil/Knight/Riesenberger 2014, p. 182).

The nation's industry benefits most from clustering, if the suppliers or the complementary firms themselves are internationally competitive (Porter 1990b, p. 81).

Cluster Lifecycle

One of the main results of Bergman's (2008, pp. 114-132) extensive analysis of cluster lifecycle concepts is the finding that "at present there is no single best metric of cluster activity, nor is there an agreed-upon aggregation principle by which to create one" (Bergman 2008, p. 127). There is no doubt that internal factors of a cluster – such as industry classification, pace of innovation or flows of tacit knowledge – as well as external factors – such as national legal systems, regional geographic characteristics or global resource markets – influence cluster characteristics and growth in a way that leads to very different paces of cluster evolution and highly divergent *cluster life spans* (Sonderegger/Täube 2010, p. 384). Nevertheless, in most cases, cluster development can be explained as an ongoing process with clusters passing through a number of stages, although not all clusters go through the lifecycle in full and not all companies within a cluster necessarily experience the lifecycle synchronously. Therefore, Bergman (2008, pp. 126-127) proposes considering relevant lifecycle concepts "as leading to a better understanding of detailed phases and stages, using the conventional life-cycle as a discussion template", which basically consists of the following three phases, supplemented by several sub-phases: existence/emergence, expansion and exhaustion.

Analysis of Concepts

Based on these findings, it is logical to propose an ideal type of lifecycle cluster development in six phases (see Figure 8.4) (Schramm-Klein 2005; Aziz/Norhashim 2008, pp. 366-367; Sölvell 2008, pp. 39-44):

1. *Emergence of pioneers*: Cluster development is usually stimulated by several causes, including a combination of basic or advanced factors in a region, such as natural resources, specific knowledge (e.g. in universities or research institutions), specific customer demand or technological innovation. According to the *diamond model*, these diverse drivers can be regarded as sources of competitive advantage. Primary companies emerge that

185

focus on the deployment of these advantages. In the initial stage of cluster development, more and more companies emerge that focus on these specific competitive advantages, and they are often *spin-offs* of these primary companies. Thus, an agglomeration of companies with similar production structures evolves. This increases local competition which in turn drives improvement and innovation among the local competitors.

Outsourcing and Specialisation

2. *Development of specialised suppliers*: In the second stage of the lifecycle, specialised suppliers and service companies locate close to the core companies. This may partly be a result of (local) *outsourcing* activities. Additionally, at this stage of cluster development, the development of a specialised employment market occurs. The *specialisation* of companies and suppliers, which is associated with lower *transaction costs*, access to lower-cost and more *specialised inputs* (e.g. components, machinery, or business services), as well as access to highly *specialised personnel*, lead to quality improvements and increased efficiency in the industry. These advantages are not available to competitors located in less agglomerate regions and are an important source of competitive advantage stemming from the external effects of firm clustering.

Local Cooperation

3. *Emergence of related institutions*: In the next stage, institutions such as *universities, research institutes* or *governmental institutions* locate in the cluster. These institutions foster local cooperation, mutual learning processes, and the local diffusion of technological developments. Thus, a cluster-specific knowledge base is established.

Informal Cooperation

4. *Attraction of related companies and specialised workforce*: The cluster externalities attract related firms and specialised personnel to locate in the cluster region. This in turn leads to an additional enhancement of cluster attractiveness and of cluster externalities.

5. *Development and upgrading of informal and personal relationship quality*: This stage is characterised by the development of relationships between cluster members at an informal and personal level. Such relationships foster informal cooperation and knowledge transfer between companies and institutions in the cluster. In this context, the transmission of *tacit knowledge* is of fundamental importance.

Inertia and Inflexibility

6. *Decline or transformation of the cluster*: After a period of positive development, most regional clusters enter the *decline stage*. Often, the further advance of clusters is inhibited by technological, institutional or sociocultural factors that initially fostered positive development, but in the long term, can cause *inflexibility* or even *inertia*. In such cases, clusters are trapped in their specialisation and further innovation is impeded. On the other hand, if such stages of inflexibility can be avoided, clusters at some stage of their development will need to adapt to changes in the market,

processes or technology. This leads to a *transformation* of the clusters into new forms, such as through focusing on new or diverse activities.

Cluster Lifecycle

Figure 8.4

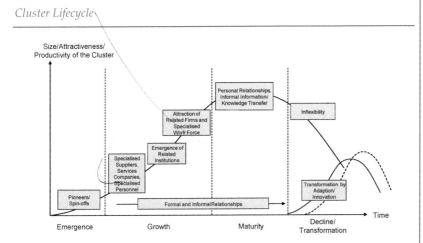

Source: Adapted from Schramm-Klein 2005, p. 542; Menzel/Fornahl 2010, p. 218.

Cluster Initiatives

Clusters can emerge and develop without any governmental influence, simply as a result of specific beneficial constellations of a region (e.g. factor endowment or specific technology). On the other hand, the diamond model implies that governments can try to influence cluster development and to initiate clusters by providing specific benefits in a region, so as to improve the competitive advantage of the nation (or of specific regions).

Cluster initiatives are organised efforts to enhance the growth and competitiveness of a cluster. They involve private industry, public authorities and/or academic institutions (Sölvell/Lindqvist/Ketels 2013, p. 1). Public authorities can make use of different means to enhance and improve cluster development, such as described by Sölvell (2008, pp. 53-54; see also Boja 2011):

- *Human resources upgrading*: enhancement of the available skills pool, e.g. through vocational training or management education

- *Cluster expansion*: measures to increase the number of firms, e.g. through incubators designed to promote new business formation or by promoting inward investment within the region

- ◼ *Internationalisation*: promotion of firm internationalisation, e.g. export promotion

- ◼ *Promotion of commercial cooperation*: encouraging firms to communicate and interact with each other

- ◼ *Promotion of innovation*: promotion of product, services and process innovation, e.g. through enhanced cooperation and networking between firms or through cooperation between firms and research institutions (e.g. university spin-offs)

- ◼ *Enhancement of environmental conditions*: enhancement of conditions for business, e.g. through improving the legal and institutional setting or the physical infrastructure.

These instruments are mainly meant to create a favourable environment that promotes the conditions for operating in the cluster, so as to improve competition, growth and innovation. In this connection, the enhancement of the attractiveness of a cluster for all in the cluster is one of the main motives of public authorities.

Conclusion and Outlook

Nations as well as companies strive to build competitive advantage, in order to expand their role in the global marketplace. An important model for explaining competitive advantage for specific industries of a country is *Porter's diamond model*, expanded into the *generalised double diamond*.

National Circumstances and Company Strategy

The main idea behind this diamond model is that the *characteristics of the home country* play a central role in a company's international success. A firm's competitive advantage results from an effective combination of national circumstances and company strategy. The specific conditions in the home base can create an environment in which firms can attain international competitive advantage, but it is important to note that it is up to each company to seize the opportunity (Hollensen 2014, p. 101).

Cluster Externalities

In this connection, the role of regional clusters is stressed. Competitive advantage in regional clusters can be explained basically by three forms of *cluster externalities* (Porter 1998, p. 80):

- ◼ *Enhancement of productivity and efficiency*: The sophisticated nature of competition forces companies to improve productivity continually. Additionally, synergies resulting from specialised inputs, personnel, infrastructure and information transfer between cluster companies reinforce such improvement.

- *Facilitation of innovation processes and pace of innovation*: Potential areas for innovation are often detected earlier and proceed faster in regional clusters because of access to specialised resources, information sharing, close communication and cooperation between cluster members.

- *Stimulating the foundation of new businesses*: The foundation of new businesses is fostered because of favourable site-related factors in regional clusters, such as specialised suppliers, infrastructure or customers. Additionally, outsourcing and specialisation lead to new business cluster actors realising new business opportunities earlier and therefore, for example, spin-offs are brought forward.

Further Reading

KETELS, C. (2013): Recent Research on Competitiveness and Clusters: What Are the Implications for Regional Policy?, in: Cambridge Journal of Regions, Economy and Society, Vol. 6, No. 2, pp. 269-284.

PORTER, M.E. (2008): On Competition, Boston, Harvard Business School Press, pp. 171-305.

SHETH, J.N. (2011): Impact of Emerging Markets on Marketing: Rethinking Existing Perspectives and Practices, in: Journal of Marketing, Vol. 75, No. 4, pp. 166-182.

Case Study: London Financial Cluster[*]

History

"A consistent theme throughout the history of international banking has been the importance of international financial centres. Since the 19th century, internationally active banks have sought a London branch" (Committee on the Global Financial System 2010, p. 12).

---

[*] Sources used for this case study include the web sites www.isc.hbs.edu, www.cityoflondon.gov.uk, www.londonstockexchange.com and www.thecityuk .com as well as explicitly cited sources.

Emergence

Located right by the River Thames, London has profited throughout its history from the river's role as an important trade route, making London an inland sea-port. "This placed London at the heart of trade within the British Isles, and also established its status as an international entrepôt" (Mollan/Michie 2012, p. 544). With Britain as the world's first modern economy, commerce as the dominant economic activity developed strong needs for trade finance. Over the centuries, London became the world's largest centre in terms of wealth, population, trade and communications by the end of the 19th century. Comprising a geographically proximate group of interconnected merchants, commodity brokers, and markets, all of them served by numerous support services, the City of London was the largest cluster of commercial firms in the world at that time (Mollan/Michie 2012, p. 539). Accordingly, the groundwork for the development of a supporting collection of financial institutions, nowadays referred to as the *London Financial Cluster*, had been laid.

Financialisation

In the 20th century, the City of London's role underwent a fundamental transformation. While London's commercial cluster suffered from a continuing decline, the process of financialisation, which means "the growing importance of financial markets as a source of profits in the economy" (Krippner 2011, p. 27), gained even further strength. In contrast to most of London's commercial sectors, the financial cluster demonstrated an outstanding ability to adapt, innovate and change over the years, eventually emancipating itself from its supporting role for the commercial cluster by focussing on domestic and international finance and related activities (Mollan/Michie 2012, p. 575).

Despite the ongoing success of London's financial cluster in the second half of the 20th century, the UK government had to acknowledge more and more, that when other countries act without restriction, a single country can no longer afford a strict control of capital flows without putting its domestic financial institutions at a severe comparative disadvantage. There is no doubt, that over the decades, strengthening competition between New York, London, and Tokyo to become the world's most important financial centre, was responsible for the rapid reduction of capital controls in the UK, the USA and Japan, starting after the collapse of *Bretton Woods* (Rajan/Zingales 2003, p. 25). As a result, in October of 1986, the *London Stock Exchange* became the first major European market to be deregulated.

Deregulation

A series of measures aiming at further deregulation of financial markets made this development possible. This dramatic *financial liberalisation*, which has been known since then as the "Big Bang", dismantled most barriers, increased London's competitiveness as a global financial centre and attracted large American banks such as *Citibank, Chase Manhattan*, and *Shearson Lehman*.

Nowadays, the *London Financial Cluster* can still be considered as one of the most important financial centres in the world. The most impressive aspect about this fact is the "remarkable consistency in the attractions of the City of London for international banking, despite repeated global financial crises and ongoing financial innovation" (Shenk 2010, p. 240) and despite two World Wars.

Profile

The importance of London as a global financial centre to the UK economy is fundamental: In 2011, London based financial and related professional services (accounting, management consulting, legal services) contributed 79,979 billion GBP to the UK economy, accounting for 5.95% of total economic output.

London Financial Cluster

The cluster's global importance can be demonstrated by its market share in several key areas. For example, the *London Financial Cluster* has a share of 46% of the "over the counter" (OTC) derivatives market; 70% of global *Eurobond* turnover is traded in London; there is a foreign exchange turnover of 1.9 trillion USD per day in London, representing 37% of the global share; London is responsible for a share of 96% of the EU emissions trading scheme; and London obtains more than 80% of hedge fund assets under management in Europe. There are more head offices of banks in London than in any other city in the world. At the same time, London is home to 251 foreign banks and to the European headquarters of over a third of all "Fortune 500" firms.

To sum it up, the London financial centre placed second in the *Global Financial Centres Index* 2015 with an overall rating of 784 index points, positioned between New York with 786 points and Hong Kong with a rating of 761. Drawing on two separate sources of data – instrumental factors (third party measures and indices) and responses to an online questionnaire – the "*Global Financial Centres Index*" (GFCI) provides profiles, ratings and rankings for 80 financial centres in the world.

Table 8.2 | *GFCI 15 Industry Sector Sub-Indices Top 10*

Rank	Investment Management	Banking	Government & Regulatory	Insurance	Professional Services
1	New York (-)	New York (-)	London (-)	New York (+2)	London (-)
2	London (-)	Hong Kong (-)	New York (-)	London (-1)	New York (-)
3	Hong Kong (+1)	London (-)	Hong Kong (-)	Singapore (-)	Hong Kong (-)
4	Singapore (-1)	Singapore (-)	Zurich (-)	Hong Kong (-2)	Singapore (-)
5	Tokyo (-)	Seoul (-)	Singapore (+1)	Seoul (+23)	Zurich (-)
6	Boston (-)	Zurich (+2)	Geneva (-1)	Zurich (-1)	Tokyo (+3)
7	Zurich (-)	Tokyo (-1)	Tokyo (-)	Chicago (+4)	Geneva (-1)
8	Toronto (-)	Shanghai (+5)	Seoul (+6)	Boston (-2)	Chicago (+6)
9	Geneva (+1)	San Francisco (+1)	Frankfurt (-1)	Geneva (-1)	Toronto (+1)
10	Chicago (+1)	Geneva (-1)	Toronto (-)	Tokyo (+5)	Washington DC (+20)

(The range from previous years is displayed in brackets.)

Source: Z/YEN LTD. 2014, p. 31.

Achieving these impressive figures requires a highly trained, mostly *multilingual workforce*. After hitting a low of 635,900 employees in 2010, employment has more than only recovered from the huge impact of the financial crisis. Since 2010, a constant rise in employment has led to a new record. In 2013, 688,800 people worked in the financial and related professional services sector in London, spread over the following sub-sectors.

Table 8.3 | *Financial and Related Professional Services: Employment in London at End 2013*

Rank	Sector	Employment	Change from previous year
1	Accounting & Management Consultancy	215,500	1.4%
2	Banking	147,100	2.4%
3	Auxiliary & Other	126,400	2.1%
4	Legal Services	106,000	2.8%
5	Insurance	70,700	0.5%
6	Fund Management	23,100	3.6%

Source: TheCityUK 2014.

According to a recent forecast, this record will even topped in 2014, with a new high of 707,500 employees.

The co-location of various entities that form the *London Financial Cluster* has been essential to its strong performance. Its securities exchanges and OTC markets form the heart of the *London Financial Cluster*. On one hand, these include more familiar exchanges such as the *London Stock Exchange (LSE) Group*, which operates a broad range of international equity, bond and derivatives markets, including: *Financial Markets: Exchange and OTC*

- the *Main Market* as London's flagship market for larger and more established companies

- the *Alternative Investment Market* (AIM) as *LSE*'s international market for smaller growing companies

- the *Professional Securities Market* as an enabler for companies to raise capital through the listing of specialist securities, including debt and depositary receipts, and extending to professional investors.

The *London Stock Exchange Group* also operates the Milan-based exchange *Borsa Italia*, which is Italy's leading stock exchange and was acquired in 2007 for a price of 1.6 billion EUR, the *Italian Derivatives Exchange Market* (IDEM), *MTS* as the premier facilitator for the electronic fixed income trading market and the *Turqouise* platform that trades derivatives. Furthermore, the *LSE Group* performs post trade and custody services, sells real-time market information and reference data, and offers trading technology to capital markets clients through Sri Lanka-based *MilleniumIT*, which was acquired in 2009.

On the other hand, the *London Financial Cluster* also consists of numerous lesser-known, but undoubtedly fundamentally important commodities markets such as the *London Metal Exchange*, the world centre for industrial metals trading and price-risk management, *APX Power Spot Exchange* or the *London Bullion Market* (LBMA), a wholesale OTC market for the trading of gold and silver.

Since its emergence, the cluster has been exposed to many of external factors and developments that implied potentially dramatic changes to the *cluster's business model*. The advent of electronic trading can be seen as one of the most fundamental parameters in determining the future direction of the cluster, as it led to a paradigm shift with massive consequences for all major securities markets in the world. Prior to the introduction of the *automated trading system* in 1997, London's financial services sector relied on securities specialists to act in person on the exchanges' trading floors, making the co-location of all discussed entities essential. This applied to both transaction-related services and intermediaries that bring companies to and place capital *Paradigm Shift* from custodian, commercial and investment banks at the markets. The conversion to electronic trading has reduced this need for a co-location of financial services. In addition, it has accelerated the consolidation process of securities exchanges, finding expression, for example, in several acquisitions that the *London Stock Exchange Group* finalised within the last few years.

Driving Forces of the Cluster Formation

Based on *Porter's Diamond Model*, the main attributes that promote or impede the creation of competitive advantage can be divided into: (1) factor conditions, (2) demand conditions, (3) related and supporting industries, (4) structure of firms and rivalry, and (5) other advantages.

Based on work at the *Institute for Strategy and Competitiveness* of the *Harvard Business School*, these assumptions can be transferred to the *London Financial Cluster* and are presented below. Advantageous factor conditions, especially the availability of skilled personnel, can be declared as the primary reason behind the cluster's competitiveness. The government's role should be seen as the second most crucial component of competitiveness, mainly because of the vital high importance of a competent, trustworthy and reliable regulator. Nevertheless, there are still numerous other factors influencing a financial clusters regional and global competitiveness (see Figure 8.5 for an assessment of the competitiveness of *London Financial Cluster*).

London Financial Cluster in Porter's Diamond Model

Figure 8.5

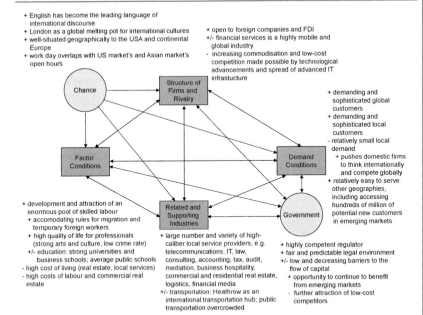

+ English has become the leading language of international discourse
+ London as a global melting pot for international cultures
+ well-situated geographically to the USA and continental Europe
+ work day overlaps with US market's and Asian market's open hours

+ open to foreign companies and FDI
+/- financial services is a highly mobile and global industry
- increasing commodisation and low-cost competition made possible by technological advancements and spread of advanced IT infrastucture

Chance

Structure of Firms and Rivalry

+ demanding and sophisticated global customers
+ demanding and sophisticated local customers
- relatively small local demand
    + pushes domestic firms to think internationally and compete globally
+ relatively easy to serve other geographies, including accessing hundreds of million of potential new customers in emerging markets

Factor Conditions

Demand Conditions

+ development and attraction of an enormous pool of skilled labour
+ accomodating rules for migration and temporary foreign workers
+ high quality of life for professionals (strong arts and culture, low crime rate)
+/- education: strong universities and business schools; average public schools
- high cost of living (real estate, local services)
- high costs of labour and commercial real estate

Related and Supporting Industries

Government

+ large number and variety of high-caliber local service providers, e.g. telecommunications, IT, law, consulting, accounting, tax, audit, mediation, business hospitality, commercial and residential real estate, logistics, financial media
+/- transportation: Heathrow as an international transportation hub; public transportation overcrowded

+ highly competent regulator
+ fair and predictable legal environment
+/- low and decreasing barriers to the flow of capital
+ opportunity to continue to benefit from emerging markets
- further attraction of low-cost competitors

Source: Adapted from Porter 1990a, p. 127.

Factor Conditions

The factor conditions in general are advantageous for the financial cluster of London. In addition, the cluster benefits from existing specialised tangible and intangible factors:

■ *Cluster-specific human resources* are being financially educated in institutions that belong to the best around the globe. Greater London offers one of the largest concentrations of universities and higher education institutions in the world, including elite institutions such as the *London School of Economics*. Furthermore, the famous world-class universities of *Oxford* and *Cambridge* are situated only about 60 miles from London. In addition, programmes offered by private and industry sponsored course providers are available both online and offline and are customised to the specific needs of the following sectors: banking, investment banking, asset/fund management, insurance and capital markets.

Cluster-Specific Factor Conditions

■ The *government* provides a high standard of regulation by regulators with deep industry knowledge and technical skills appropriate for complex financial business, reinforced through strong cooperative relationships between the financial and related professional services sector and the government. Also, stable, transparent and consistent immigration rules that do not constrain international mobility and that do not prevent highly skilled international students from becoming local professionals are crucial to the success of the *London Financial Cluster*. The same goes for local employment laws: The sector benefits from a flexible recruiting process that makes hiring simple and downscaling in a harsh business environment relatively expensive.

■ The *cluster-specific infrastructure* is designed to ensure high connectivity and openness to other financial centres and international market infrastructures through electronic trading systems, allowing fast and reliable data links coupled with remote access to financial markets around the globe.

Local and Demand Conditions

Local and Global Demand, Size and Qualities

The demand conditions can be subdivided into two relevant factors. On the one hand, the level of local demand is important for a cluster, on the other hand, the nature of local demand qualities play a decisive role. Although not as relevant to *London Financial Cluster's* competitiveness as the factor conditions, demand conditions still display another solid advantage:

■ The magnitude of local demand is an advantage in a paradoxical way. Since local demand is no more than average in the London area, the financial and related professional services sector is forced to think internationally and compete globally. Broad openness and high connectivity to the world's leading financial and commercial centres, as well as gaining access to the huge potential of new customers in the aspiring emerging economies, contribute to the overall very satisfactory demand conditions.

■ Regarding the nature of local and global demand, the *London Financial Cluster* is still very attractive to demanding and sophisticated global customers. Nevertheless, these customers will not tolerate any uncertainty about the regulatory framework. Thus, British and international business leaders are gradually raising the pressure on the UK government to end the debate on Britain's EU membership.

Related and Supporting Industries

As described in the "Profile" section, the *London Financial Cluster* is not solely composed of the financial services sector, but related professional services, such as accounting, management consulting and legal services. Considering the specific needs of these institutions, a strong supporting infrastructure related to IT, telecommunications and commercial real estate has emerged. Furthermore, the cluster is aided by *London Heathrow Airport* that provides reliable international transport. With more than 72 million passengers in 2013, *London Heathrow* is by far the busiest airport in Europe and the third busiest airport worldwide in total passenger traffic, transporting more international passengers than any other airport in the world. Additionally, the emergence of a modern and flexible business hospitality industry should be mentioned in this context, which conforms well to the requirements of London's financial services sector by offering suitable hotels, conference centres or restaurants. In conclusion, London is home for two of the world's most influential financial services publications, *The Financial Times* and *The Economist*.

Structure of Firms and Rivalry

The "Structure of Firms and Rivalry" attribute includes several conditions that result in both further advantages of the *London Financial Cluster* as well as selected disadvantages.

The vigorous competition among local firms and individuals is a very important driver of innovation. Global players are attracted by the city's openness to foreign companies, and they especially appreciate a just and predictable regulatory environment with few constraints and minimal political pressure. Nevertheless, low and decreasing barriers to the flow of capital also have a downside; they increase commodisation and low-cost competition. This high level of competition puts a lot of pressure on all competitors to innovate, improve and optimise efficiency.

Another aspect that should be mentioned in this context is the concept of "co-opetition", which refers to cooperation between essentially competing companies. On the one hand, this creates further advantages, such as participating companies learn from each other or conduct joint research or education projects. On the other hand, very close *collaboration* can encourage participating companies to ignore legal barriers. The latter resulted in a series of fraudulent actions connected to the *London Interbank Offered Rate* (Libor). Since 2012, the involved banks such as *Barclays, Deutsche Bank, HSBC, Société Générale, Royal Bank of Scotland, UBS* or *JP Morgan* were fined for manipulation, altogether amounting to several billion EUR.

Co-opetition

Summary and Outlook

Despite the decreasing need for co-location and the related consolidation process, *mutual trust* is still the basis of most financial transactions. Even with modern technology, in most cases, the principal parties to a financial transaction prefer to meet in person and establish a *personal relationship* before proceeding. The information and knowledge exchanged within the *London Financial Cluster* can be considered a potent driver of ideas and market innovation. The result is that a distinguishing feature of financial centres is the concentration of people, firms and activities in one place. These include intermediaries, such as banks and brokers, investors such as hedge funds and other asset managers, major corporations, and related professions such as legal, accounting, IT and PR firms.

In summary, the *London Financial Cluster* as one of the top financial centres in the world is not in danger. Nevertheless, risk factors, such as ongoing uncertainty over Britain's EU membership, could strain the cluster's global competitiveness.

Questions

1. What are the conditions for cluster formation in general? Elaborate in this context on the diamond model of Porter. Analyse the proposal of several researchers (e.g. Dunning 1993; Moon/Rugman/Verbeke 1998) to include multinational activity as a third external variable in Porter's diamond model within the scope of *London Financial Cluster*.

2. Describe the influence of clusters on innovation with regard to the different types of organisation and cooperation of clusters.

3. Discuss the advantages and disadvantages of cluster location for the participating companies. Reflect on the consequences of a London location for the resident businesses.

Hints

1. See Z/Yen Ltd. 2005.

2. See OECD 2009.

References

ANDERSSON, T.; SCHWAAG SERGER, S.; SÖRVIG, J.; WISE HANSSON, E. (2004): The Cluster Policies Whitebook, Malmö, IKED.

AZIZ, K.A.; NORHASHIM, M. (2008): Cluster-based Policy Making: Assessing Performance and Sustaining Competitiveness, in: Review of Policy Research, Vol. 25, No. 4, pp. 349-375.

BERGMAN, E.M. (2008): Cluster Life-cycles: An Emerging Synthesis, in: Karlsson C. (Ed.): Handbook of Research on Cluster Theory, Cheltenham/Northampton, Edward Elgar Publishing, pp. 114-132.

BOJA, C. (2011): Clusters Models, Factors and Characteristics, in: International Journal of Economic Practices and Theories, Vol. 1, No. 1, pp. 34-43.

CAVUSGIL, S.T.; KNIGHT, G.; RIESENBERGER, J.R. (2014): International Business: The New Realities, 3rd ed., Boston, Pearson.

COMMITTEE ON THE GLOBAL FINANCIAL SYSTEM (2010): Long-term Issues in International Banking, in: CGFS Papers, No. 41, pp. 1-37.

DENG, Q.; LI, S. (2012): Low-paid Workers in Urban China, in: International Labour Review, Vol. 151, No. 3, pp. 157-171.

DUNNING, J. (1993): Multinational Enterprise and the Global Economy, New York, Addison-Wesley.

GRIFFIN, R.; PUSTAY, M. (2013): International Business: A Managerial Perspective, 7th ed., Upper Saddle River, New Jersey, Pearson.

HILL, C.W.L. (2013): International Business: Competing in the Global Marketplace, 9th ed., New York, McGraw-Hill.

HOLLENSEN, S. (2014): Global Marketing, 6th ed., Harlow, Pearson.

HUMPHRIES, M. (2013): Rare Earth Elements: The Global Supply Chain, http://www.fas.org/sgp/crs/natsec/R41347.pdf, accessed on August 18, 2014.

JANSSON, H. (2007): International Business Strategy in Emerging Country Markets: The Institutional Network Approach, Cheltenham/Northampton, Edward Elgar Publishing.

KETELS, C. (2013): Recent Research on Competitiveness and Clusters: What Are the Implications for Regional Policy?, in: Cambridge Journal of Regions, Economy and Society, Vol. 6, No. 2, pp. 269-284.

KEYNES, J.M. (2009): Essays in Persuasion, New York, W.W. Norton & Company.

KRIPPNER, G.R. (2011): Capitalizing on Crisis: The Political Origins of the Rise of Finance, Cambridge, Harvard University Press.

MENZEL, M.-P.; FORNAHL, D. (2010): Cluster Life Cycles: Dimensions and Rationales of Cluster Evolution, in: Industrial and Corporate Change, Vol. 19, No. 1, pp. 205-238.

MEULEN RODGERS, Y. van der; MENON, N. (2013): Labor Regulations and Job Quality: Evidence from India, in: Industrial & Labor Relations Review, Vol. 66, No. 4, pp. 933-957.

MOLLAN, S.; MICHIE, R. (2012): The City of London as an International Commercial and Financial Center since 1900, in: Enterprise and Society, Vol. 13, No. 3, pp. 538-587.

MOON, H.C.; RUGMAN, A.M.; VERBEKE, A. (1995): The Generalized Double Diamond Approach to International Competitiveness, in: RUGMAN, A.M.; VAN DEN BROECK, J.; VERBEKE, A. (Eds.): Research in Global Strategic Management: Vol. 5: Beyond the Diamond, Greenwich, CT:JAI Press, pp. 97-114.

MOON, H.C.; RUGMAN, A.M.; VERBEKE, A. (1998): A Generalized Double Diamond Approach to the Global Competitiveness of Korea and Singapore, in: International Business Review, Vol. 7, No. 2, pp. 135-150.

OECD (2009): Local Economic and Employment Development Programme: Clusters, Innovation and Entrepreneurship, Paris.

PORTER, M.E. (1990a): The Competitive Advantage of Nations, New York, The Free Press.

PORTER, M.E. (1990b): The Competitive Advantage of Nations, in: Harvard Business Review, Vol. 68, No. 2, pp. 73-93.

PORTER, M.E. (1998): Clusters and the New Economics of Competition, in: Harvard Business Review, Vol. 76, No. 6, pp. 77-90.

PORTER, M.E. (2000): Corporate Structure, Strategy, and Location: Competition, Location, and Strategy, in: CLARK, G.; FELDMAN, M.; GERTLER, M. (Eds.): Oxford Handbook of Economic Geography, Oxford, Oxford University Press, pp. 253-274.

PORTER, M.E. (2003): The Economic Performance of Regions, in: Regional Studies, Vol. 37, No. 6-7, pp. 549-578.

PORTER, M.E. (2008): On Competition, Boston, Harvard Business School Press.

RAJAN, R.G.; ZINGALES, L. (2003): The Great Reversals: The Politics of Financial Development in the Twentieth Century, in: Journal of Financial Economics, Vol. 69, No. 1, pp. 5-50.

RUGMAN, A.M.; COLLINSON, S. (2012): International Business, 6th ed., Harlow, Pearson.

SCHRAMM-KLEIN, H. (2005): Wettbewerb und Kooperation in regionalen Branchenclustern, in: ZENTES, J.; SWOBODA, B.; MORSCHETT, D. (Eds.): Kooperationen, Allianzen und Netzwerke, 2nd ed., Wiesbaden, Gabler, pp. 531-556.

SHENK, C.R. (2010): The Decline of Sterling: Managing the Retreat of an International Currency, 1945-1992, Cambridge, University Press.

SHETH, J.N. (2011): Impact of Emerging Markets on Marketing: Rethinking Existing Perspectives and Practices, in: Journal of Marketing, Vol. 75, No. 4, pp. 166-182.

SÖLVELL, Ö. (2008): Clusters: Balancing Evolutionary and Constructive Forces, Stockholm, Ivory Tower Publishers.

SÖLVELL, Ö.; LINDQVIST, G.; KETELS, C. (2003): The Cluster Initiative Greenbook, Stockholm, Ivory Tower Publishers.

SONDEREGGER, P; TÄUBE, F. (2010): Cluster Life Cycle and Diaspora Effects: Evidence from the Indian IT Cluster in Bangalore, in: Journal of International Management, Vol. 16, No. 4, pp. 383-397.

THECITYUK (2014): London Employment Survey: February 2014, http://www.thecityuk.com/research/our-work/reports-list/london-employment-survey/, accessed on August 22, 2014.

UNITED NATIONS DEVELOPMENT PROGRAMME (2013): Human Development Report: The Rise of the South, New York.

WORLD ECONOMIC FORUM (2013): The Global Competitiveness Report 2013-2014, Geneva.

Z/YEN LTD. (2005): The Competitive Position of London as a Global Financial Centre, London.

Z/YEN LTD. (2014): The Global Financial Centres Index 15, London.

Chapter 9

The Role of Country Culture in International Management

Cultural differences within and between countries affect the way business is practised. The consideration of these cultural differences and sensitivity are crucial factors in cross-cultural management. This Chapter provides an overview on the core characteristics that differentiate cultures and their meaning for international business.

The Concept of (Country) Culture

Human thought processes vary between different parts of the world. There is a general understanding that *culture* (and cultural differences) is one of the main reasons for such variation. However, culture as a concept is difficult to define, and many different definitions have been given in the past. Perhaps the best-known definition in International Management is that by *Hofstede* (1980, p. 21): "Culture is the collective programming of the mind which distinguishes the members of one human group from another. [...] Culture, in this sense, includes systems of values; and values are among the building blocks of culture."

Culture, then, is regarded as multidimensional, consisting of several elements. In this connection, it is important to notice that culture includes both *conscious and unconscious* values, ideas, attitudes and symbols that shape human behaviour (Terpstra/David 1991). Additionally, culture can be thought of as consisting of both *visible and invisible* elements, much like an iceberg: you can easily see the tip; however, most of it is hidden beneath the water (Dlablay/Scott 2011, p. 58; see Figure 9.1) (Schein 1992, pp. 15-20):

- *Artefacts and creations*: The most external level is the tangible aspects of culture, i.e. visible and audible behaviour and the constructed physical and social environment. In this context, the important expressions of culture are symbols, i.e., objects, words or pictures that carry a specific meaning to those who share a culture, heroes, i.e., (real or imaginary) persons that serve as role models to a culture, and rituals, i.e. specific, socially essential collective activities (De Mooij 2014, pp. 62-63).

- *Values and ideologies*: A deeper level is that of values that reflect convictions about the nature of reality and what should be done to successfully cope with reality.

Levels of Culture

203

■ *Basic assumptions and premises*: The deepest – and least visible – layer of culture consists of the basic assumptions and beliefs about human nature and relationships with the environment.

Figure 9.1 | *Levels of Culture*

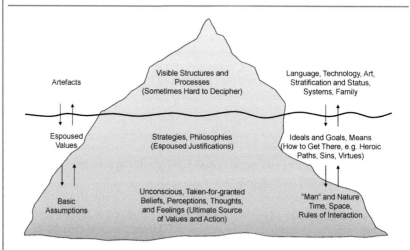

Source: Adapted from Schein 1992, pp. 15-20.

Layers and Characteristics of Culture

Main Levels

The individual decision-making process is influenced by different layers of culture. These levels are nested within each other, constituting a system of interrelated cultural aspects of different cultural layers (see Figure 9.2). In international business negotiation settings between companies with origins in different countries, the behaviour of the individual actors is influenced by cultural elements of diverse, interrelated and nested levels. The main levels of this nesting are: *national culture*, which constitutes the overall framework of cultural concepts and legislation for business activities; *industry culture*, which is characterised by specific norms and ethics that in some cases may be similar across borders and *company culture* (organisational culture), which is expressed through the shared values, beliefs, or meaning of the members of an organisation (Hollensen 2014, pp. 245-246).

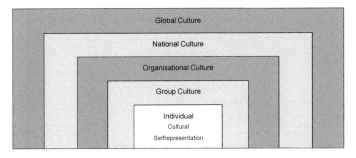

Source: Adapted from Erez/Gati 2004, p. 288.

These different cultural layers affect *individual behaviour*, because the individual interacts with the other actors in his or her cultural surroundings. Culture is an outcome of past (and present) actions of a group or its members, and is simultaneously the result and origin of a group's actions. Members of a group *share* cultural values and they are transmitted from one generation to another through *social learning processes* of modelling and observation or through the effects of individual actions (e.g. eliciting rewards or avoiding punishments) (Bandura 1986). Cultural elements such as daily behaviours, religion or fairy tales are interdependent, i.e. *connected* to each other.

Individual Behaviour

Summing up, a culture is defined as a group of people that share a common set of values and norms. Culture is the ways in which a society understands, decides and communicates, and it is characterised as being *learned*, *shared* and *interrelated* (Hollensen 2014, p. 244). Culture thus serves as an anchoring point to the members of a society and offers a set of *codes of conduct* (Czinkota/Ronkainen 2013, p. 61).

Culture is reinforced by its components such as language, behaviour and often the "nation". However, it can be below or above the *nation level* because there is not a strict correspondence between a society and a nation-state. Nation-states are political creations that can contain a single culture or several (Hill 2013, p. 102). Thus, national borders may define cultures, especially when natural barriers isolate countries, but a nation also may contain *subcultures* that have little in common.

Culture vs. Nation

Influence of Culture in Different Business Contexts

A range of business contexts, both within individual firms and between two or more firms, are influenced by the different cultural backgrounds of the individuals involved (see Figure 9.3).

Figure 9.3 | *Environmental Influences on International Management Functions*

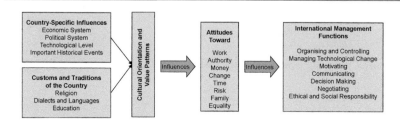

Source: Adapted from Phatak/Bhagat/Kashlak 2009, p. 115.

Cross-Cultural
Business
Encounters

In International Management encounters, a wide array of business contexts raise cross-cultural issues that evolve both within individual companies, e.g. managers and employees from different countries, and between different firms or between the company and its customers, such as in international buyer-seller relationships or cross-border alliances (see Figure 9.4).

Cross-cultural proficiency, therefore, is important in many international business managerial tasks, including (Cavusgil/Knight/Riesenberger 2013, p. 135):

- communicating and interacting with *foreign business partners*

- screening and selecting *foreign distributors* and other *partners*

- negotiating and structuring *international business ventures* or *international alliances*

- interacting with *customers* from abroad

- dealing with *national institutions* in host countries

- developing *products* and *services*

- preparing *advertising* and *promotional materials*.

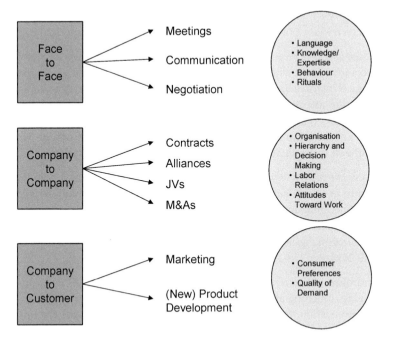

Source: Rugman/Collinson 2012, p. 136.

Cross-cultural differences may complicate *communication* within the individual firm, for example when managers from a foreign parent company communicate with local employees. In *cross-border partnerships*, alliances or ventures, there needs to be an understanding of the *organisational and cultural differences*. Often, *cultural compromise* is required to establish successful partnerships (Rugman/Collinson 2012, p. 136).

Elements of Culture

There are many components that can be considered integral elements of culture. These components are *interrelated*. The elements of culture most likely to matter in International Management are: language, social structure, religion, values and attitudes.

Language

Language is considered a *primary discriminant* of cultural groups as – in an obvious way – countries differ in the languages used within them. Both spoken and unspoken languages are important means of communication.

Spoken Language

Spoken language refers to the vocal sounds or written symbols that people use to communicate with one another (Kotabe/Helsen 2014, p. 98). Spoken language structures the way the members of a society perceive the world. It can direct the attention of its members to certain features of the world rather than others (Hill 2013, p. 118) by *filtering* observations and perceptions and thus affecting the messages sent when individuals communicate with one another (Griffin/Pustay 2013, p. 114).

Multiple Language Groups

If one *language group* dominates a country, it tends to have a homogeneous culture in which nationhood is important. Conversely, countries with more than one language tend to be heterogeneous. For example, Canada has an English-speaking culture and a French-speaking culture. In Switzerland, three main languages are spoken, along with other (sub-)cultural differences (Hill 2013, pp. 118-119).

Silent Cues

Unspoken or *nonverbal communication* includes gestures, facial expressions, moving, touching and other forms of *body language* that supplement spoken communication. Forms of nonverbal communication include (Griffin/Pustay 2013, p. 118):

- dress styles, e.g. fashionable, conservative

- hand gestures

- facial expressions, e.g. smiles, frowns, nods, eye contact (or lack of it)

- greetings, e.g. hugs, kisses, bows, hand shakes

- physical contact, e.g. hand holding, pats on the back

- time-related aspects, e.g. promptness, early or late arrival

- walking styles, e.g. fast, slow, in a group or single file.

Many of these *silent cues* are culturally bound and can lead to misunderstandings in cross-cultural communication.

Social Structure

The social structure determines individuals' roles within a society. Cultures differ in the way they define *groups* and the relative importance they place on the *individual's role* within a group. While human life is generally viewed as social, cultures differ according to the degree to which they regard groups as the primary means of social organisation (Hill 2013, p. 104). Cultural value systems, for example, differ in terms of their emphasis on *individual performance*. In many Western societies, the social standing of individuals is mainly a function of their individual performance rather than which group they belong to. In many other cultures, *social status* is determined by the standing of the group to which an individual belongs, and commitment and attachment to *group membership* is much more important.

Additionally, cultures differ in their degree of *social stratification*. In all cultures, people are categorised into *hierarchies* to a certain extent on the basis of elements such as income, occupation, family background, educational achievement or other attributes. However, the importance of these categories in defining how individuals interact with each other within and between groups differs between cultures. Also *social mobility*, i.e., the extent to which individuals can between strata and change hierarchical status, is distinct between cultures (Griffin/Pustay 2013, p. 112).

Social Stratification

Religion, Values and Attitudes

Most of the world's ethical systems, i.e., set of moral principles or values that guide and shape individuals' behaviour, are a product of religion. *Religion* shapes attitudes toward a huge variety of things such as work, consumption, or individual responsibility (Hill 2013, p. 109). Religion plays an important role in many societies, with its impact differing from country to country. The impact of religion depends on the country's legal system, the *homogeneity* of religious beliefs and the *toleration* of other religious viewpoints (Griffin/Pustay 2013, p. 122).

However, religion does not always contribute to divergence between cultures. It can also provide the basis for *trans-cultural similarities*. Approximately 75% of the world's population adhere to one of the four dominant *religions*: Christianity (2.3 billion adherents), Islam (1.6 billion adherents), Hinduism (943 million adherents), and Buddhism (463 million adherents).

World Religions

In addition to religious value systems, all cultures are characterised by secular value systems and attitudes. *Values* are understood as principles and standards that are accepted by the members of a culture. *Attitudes* relate to actions, feelings and thoughts as a result of those values (Griffin/Pustay 2013, p. 122).

Value systems are deeply rooted and intrinsic to an individual's identity. They influence people's *attitudes* towards factors such as time, age, status or education. The underlying *norms*, i.e. accepted rules, standards and models of behaviour, direct the individual's behaviour. Thus, values determine what actions are regarded as appropriate, important or desirable in a culture.

Value Systems

Dimensions of Culture

Several conceptualisations exist to classify cultures according to the underlying values. The most prominent *cultural frameworks* are the work of *Hall*, *Hofstede* and the *GLOBE* project (Global Leadership and Organisational Behaviour Effectiveness).

Hall's Low Context and High Context

In this conceptualisation, cultures are classified according to how *context laden* their communication is. The extent to which communication partners rely on the context for determining the meaning of what is said is relevant for both direct (e.g. face-to-face) communication and indirect communication (Usunier/Lee 2013, pp. 69-70).

High Context – Low Context

"A high context communication or message is one in which most of the information is already in the person, while very little is in the coded, explicit, transmitted part of the message. A low context communication is just the opposite, i.e., the mass of the information is vested in the explicit code" (Hall/Hall 1990, p. 6).

Table 9.1   *Comparative Characteristics of High Context and Low Context Cultures*

Characteristic	Low Context/Individualistic (e.g. Western Europe, US)	High Context/Collectivistic (e.g. Japan, China, Saudi Arabia)
Communication and Language	• explicit, direct	• implicit, indirect
Sense of Self and Space	• informal handshakes	• formal hugs, bows and handshakes
Dress and Appearance	• dress for individual success, wide variety	• indication of position in society, religious rule
Food and Eating Habits	• eating is a necessity, fast food	• eating is social event
Time Consciousness	• linear, exact, promptness is valued, time = money	• elastic, relative, time spent on enjoyment, time=relationships
Family and Friends	• nuclear family, self-oriented, value youth	• extended family, other oriented, loyalty and responsibility, respect for old age
Values and Norms	• independence, confrontation of conflict	• group conformity, harmony
Beliefs and Attitudes	• egalitarian, challenge authority, individuals control destiny, gender equity	• hierarchical, respect for authority, individuals accept destiny, gender roles
Mental Process and Learning	• linear, logical sequential, problem solving	• lateral, holistic, simultaneous, accepting life's difficulties
Business/Work Habits	• deal oriented ("quickly getting down to business"), rewards based in achievement, work has value	• relationship oriented ("first you make a friend, then you make a deal"), rewards based on seniority, work is a necessity

Source: Hollensen 2014, p. 248.

Thus, the interpretation of messages in *high context cultures* rests heavily on the context. It is important to use and interpret the elements surrounding the message to be able to understand it. In *low context cultures*, on the other hand, clear communication modes dominate. These cultures rely on spoken and written language for meaning (Hollensen 2014, pp. 247-248).

Table 9.1, summaries some areas in which high and low context cultures.

Hofstede's Five Dimensions

One of the most influential schemes of cultural classification is the work of *Geert Hofstede*. *Hofstede's* findings are based on a study of 116,000 people working for *IBM* in about 40 countries carried out in the late 1960s and early 1970s. Although this work has been criticised for several methodological weaknesses and cultural biases resulting from the fact that only one company with a strong organisational culture was analysed, it remains the largest and most comprehensive work of its kind. Hofstede identified five important *dimensions* along which people differ across cultures (Griffin/Pustay 2013, p. 126).

The first dimension is labelled *power distance*. It refers to the extent and acceptance of unequal distributions of power. *Power respect* means that people in a culture tend to accept power and authority on the basis of positions in the hierarchy. Thus, societies that are high in *power distance* believe that everyone has a rightful place in society and they tolerate relatively high social inequalities (Kotabe/Helsen 2014, p. 113). Conversely, cultures with low power distance are characterised by *power tolerance*. They attach less significance to a person's position in the hierarchy and tend to question decisions or mandates from someone at a higher level (Griffin/Pustay 2013, pp. 129-130). These cultures tend to be more egalitarian.

Power Distance

The second dimension is the *social orientation* in a culture. This relates to the beliefs about the relative importance of the individual and the groups to which an individual belongs. *Individualism* describes the degree to which individuals view themselves as independent of groups and are motivated by their own preferences, needs or rights (Phatak/Bhagat/Kashlak 2009, p. 120). *Individual independence* plays an important role. The opposite of individualism is *collectivism*. Collectivistic cultures are characterised by people prioritising the goals of the group to which they belong over their own personal goals. Identity is based in the *group* to which the individual belongs and he or she shows long-term loyalty to that group (Hollensen 2014, p. 257).

Individualism vs. Collectivism

A third dimension is *uncertainty avoidance,* which refers to the *risk-taking attitude* in a culture. It thus relates to the feelings people have regarding uncertain and ambiguous situations. In a culture which is characterised by

Uncertainty Avoidance

uncertainty avoidance, people dislike change and ambiguity and try to avoid it. On the other hand, in cultures with high levels of *uncertainty acceptance*, people are stimulated by change (Griffin/Pustay 2013, pp. 131-133).

Masculinity vs. Femininity

Masculinity and *femininity* relate to the degree to which "masculine" values or "feminine" values dominate. In *masculine cultures*, masculine values such as achievement, performance, competition, success and money are important (Hollensen 2014, p. 257). Additionally, in these cultures, social gender roles are clearly distinct. In *feminine societies*, gender roles tend to overlap. Thus, both men and women are supposed to follow feminine values, such as caring for others, valuing quality of life, maintaining personal relationships and service (Hofstede 1991, pp. 82-83).

Long-Termism

The fifth dimension, *long-termism*, was identified in a follow-up study to Hofstede's original work. It refers to the distinction between cultures with a long-term orientation and those with a short-term focus (Kotabe/Helsen 2014, p. 114). Cultures with a *long-term orientation* are characterised by values such as perseverance and thrift. In *short-term oriented* cultures, personal steadiness and stability are important (Hollensen 2014, p. 258).

Table 9.2 gives an overview of how countries differ in terms of these five Hofstede dimensions.

Table 9.2 — *Hofstede's Culture Dimensions in Selected Countries*

Country	Power Distance	Individualism	Masculinity	Uncertainty Avoidance	Long-Term Orientation
France	68	71	43	86	-
Germany	35	67	66	65	31
Hong Kong	68	25	57	29	96
India	77	48	56	40	61
Japan	54	46	95	92	80
Malaysia	104	26	50	36	-
Netherlands	38	80	14	53	44
Singapore	74	20	48	8	48
South Korea	60	18	39	85	75
Sweden	31	71	5	29	33
Switzerland	34	68	70	58	-
United Kingdom	35	89	66	35	25
United States	40	91	62	46	29

Source: Hofstede 1991, pp. 312-313.

As an enhancement of these cultural dimensions, *indulgence vs. restraint* was developed by Minkov (2007) and added to Hofstede's framework as a sixth dimension. *Indulgence* relates to the degree to which a society allows relatively free gratification of basic and natural human drives related to enjoying life and having fun. *Restraint*, on the other hand, implies that a society tends to suppress gratification of needs and regulates this by means of strict social norms (De Mooij 2014, p. 102).

Indulgence vs. Restraint

GLOBE - Global Leadership and Organizational Behaviour Effectiveness

Global Leadership and Organizational Behaviour Effectiveness (GLOBE) is a large-scale research programme which comprised a network of 170 social scientists and management scholars. The study is based on a survey of 17,000 managers from three industries (banking, food processing and tele-communications) across 62 cultures. The GLOBE researchers identified nine dimensions of culture (House et al. 2002; Magnussen et al. 2008, p. 186):

1. *Uncertainty avoidance*: The extent to which a society tries to avoid the unpredictability of future events, e.g. by relying on rituals or bureaucratic practices.

   GLOBE Dimensions

2. *Power Distance*: The degree to which members of a culture expect and accept power to be distributed unequally.

3. *Collectivism I (Societal Collectivism)*: The degree to which organisational and societal institutional practices encourage collective distribution of resources and collective action.

4. *Collectivism II (In-Group Collectivism)*: The degree to which individuals express loyalty and cohesiveness in their organisations or families.

5. *Gender Egalitarianism*: The extent to which a society minimises gender role differences and discrimination.

6. *Assertiveness:* The degree to which individuals are assertive, confrontational and aggressive in social relationships.

7. *Future Orientation*: The degree to which individuals engage in future-oriented behaviours such as delaying gratification, planning and investing in the future.

8. *Performance Orientation*: The extent to which a society encourages and rewards group members for performance improvement and excellence.

9. *Humane Orientation*: The degree to which individuals encourage and reward individuals for being fair, altruistic, friendly, generous, caring or kind.

Figure 9.4 | *Latin Europe Cluster's Societal Culture Scores*

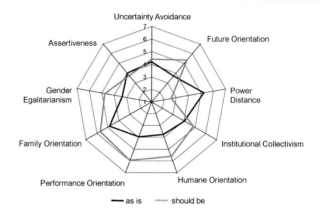

Source: Jesuino 2002, p. 85.

The purpose of the project was to find out which *leadership behaviours* are universally accepted and which are culturally contingent. While there is some overlap between the Hofstede and GLOBE dimensions, the GLOBE study goes beyond Hofstede's approach, assessing culture from two angles: *cultural practices* (culture "as is") and *cultural values* ("what should be").

Figure 9.4 displays the societal culture scores of the "Latin Europe cluster", which comprises Italy, Spain, France, Portugal, the French speaking part of Switzerland and Israel.

Cultural Sensitivity

Cultural sensitivity refers to the state of *awareness* of the values and frames of reference of host country cultures. In this context, the extent of a manager's cultural parochialism, ethnocentrism, polycentrism or geocentrism is crucial (Phatak/Bhagat/Kashlak 2009, pp. 116):

■ *Cultural parochialism*: The belief that there is no alternative to doing things the way they are done in one's own culture.

- *Cultural ethnocentrism*: Ethnocentrism is related to parochialism, but it reflects a sense of superiority. Thus, ethnocentricity involves the attitude that one's own way of doing things is the best, no matter the cultural environment.

- *Cultural polycentrism*: Polycentric managers tend to adapt to local cultural norms. They accept the need for differentiation, for example, in terms of procedural norms, reward systems, and organisation design. Thus, polycentrism involves adaptation to each local cultural context.

- *Cultural geocentrism*: Geocentrism reflects the belief that responsiveness to local cultures is necessary but that there is the need to develop courses of action that can be employed in most (or all) cultural environments.

This understanding of cultural sensitivity is related to the emic and etic views of culture. The *etic perspective* assumes that business practices can be applied universally and thus are relevant in all cultures and not specific to the context in which they were developed. Conversely, the *emic perspective* argues that each culture has specific requirements (Sue/Sue 2007). Therefore, business practices need to be adapted to each cultural context. Typically, the etic approach to international business is anchored in the domestic market context and thus reflects either *cultural parochialism* or *ethnocentrism*.

Emic vs. Etic

Based on these diverse *cultural predispositions*, firms can respond with diverse organisation types (see Table 9.3).

Organisation Types Reflecting Cultural Predispositions

Table 9.3

	Imperialist	Interventionist	Interactive	Independent
Organisation	ethnocentric	ethnocentric	geocentric	polycentric
Structure	steep hierarchy	flat hierarchy	network	federation
Strategy	dictated	centrally decided	jointly specified	locally specified
Decision Making	centralised	distributed	shared	devolved

Source: Rugman/Collinson 2012, p. 151.

An *imperialist firm* employs cultural parochialism and involves a common organisational culture wherever the company is present. The *independent company* is associated with the polycentric orientation. In this structure, each national subsidiary bases its own culture on local norms and values, thus creating a *federalist structure*. Both of these extremes have associated problems, resulting from either an etic cultural perspective that involves unsuita-

Organisation Types

ble standardisation across all subsidiaries or the complexity of differentiated, polycentric systems. Therefore, firms often try to strike a balance between *standardisation* and *differentiation*. Some elements are centralised across the whole organisation while others are adapted to the local cultural context (Rugman/Collinson 2012, pp. 147-151).

Conclusion and Outlook

Cultural
Convergence

While culture is considered to be *relatively stable* and cultural differences are important in International Management, there is an ongoing debate on the question of whether *cultural convergence* is occurring or not. The starting point of this debate was Levitt's *Globalisation Thesis* (Levitt 1983), which argued that factors such as increased and better communications worldwide, including international media consumption, consumer travel patterns and the spread of multinational companies lead to cultural convergence. However, even though the cross-border operations of multinational companies integrate the world's economies, there are many counterarguments against there being a homogenisation of cultures. Even within most countries, a great *diversity* of behaviours and tastes co-exists. The internationalisation of companies widens the options available to local people. *Cultural homogeneity* and *heterogeneity* do not seem to be mutually exclusive alternatives or substitutes; instead they can co-exist simultaneously in a semi-globalised context (Ghemawat 2007; Cavusgil/Knight/Riesenberger 2013, p. 134).

Cultural Clash

Cross-cultural management involves cultural differences between groups of people in different business situations, both inside a single firm and between several firms, e.g. suppliers, partners in strategic alliances or M&As, or with customers. Such cultural differences are not necessarily a problem. However, they can create *difficulties* in terms of communication, motivation, coordination or teamwork. They can lead to a *cultural clash*, which is where differences in values, beliefs and styles of communication or behaviour lead to miscommunications and misunderstandings, antagonism or other problems (Rugman/Collinson 2012, pp. 147-151).

Acculturation

Companies need to respond to these challenges of managing across cultural boundaries. In this context, *acculturation* plays an important role. Acculturation is the process of understanding foreign cultures and modifying and adapting the company or the manager's behaviour to make it compatible with other cultures (Cavusgil/Knight/Riesenberger 2013, p. 120).

Further Reading

CHANEY, L.; MARTIN, J. (Eds.) (2014): Intercultural Business Communication, Harlow, Pearson.

DE MOOIJ, M. (2014): Global Marketing and Advertising: Understanding Cultural Paradoxes, 4th ed., Thousand Oaks, Sage Publications.

HOFSTEDE, G. (2001): Culture's Consequences: Comparing Values, Behaviors, Institutions and Organizations Across Nations, Thousand Oaks, Sage Publications, pp. 1-36.

HOFSTEDE, G.; HOFSTEDE, G.J.; MINKOV, M. (2010): Cultures and Organizations: Software of the Mind, 3rd ed., New York, McGraw-Hill.

Case Study: Russia

History and political system

To understand Russian culture, it is important to take into account Russian history. From the Kievan Rus, the Tsarist Empire and the Soviet Union to today's Russian Federation, Russian history has significant impacted global developments and the history of two continents.

Consequences of the *First World War*, economic weakness and the lack of societal provision, among other reasons, fomented the February Revolution of 1917. The prevailing *tsardom* was an absolutist and centralised state based on the French model and was replaced by a parliament (*Duma*) and workers' and soldiers' councils (*Russian Soviet*). However, the proposed election of a *Constituent Assembly*, which would decide on Russia future form of government, did not take place and the *Bolsheviks*, a faction of the Russian Social Democratic Labour Party, came violently into power in the October Revolution under the leadership of Lenin. The new regime, the socialist *Soviet Union*, controlled the people of the Russian Empire and led them on a path to modernity which differed in many respects from that of countries in Western and Central Europe.

First World War

Stardom

Lenin and Stalin

The *Bolsheviks* defended their position of power and implemented a sustenance dictatorship. Industrial production fell to a minimum, the black market flourished and they lost their entire social base. After Lenin's death, fierce leadership battles started that were ultimately won by Stalin. He knew how to exploit the emotional reaction to the death of Lenin, by organising a *"cult of Lenin"* which was accompanied by the development of a bureaucratic organisation. Like Lenin, Stalin became the object of cultic worship, and was thus able to gain great power.

Second World War

In 1941, during the Second World War, German forces attacked without declaring war on the USSR. This was the outbreak of the "Great Patriotic War" between the Soviet Union and Nazi Germany and its allies, which lasted until the 9th of May 1945 when the USSR prevailed over *Hitlerite fascism*.

With the death of Stalin his cult of personality collapsed and the democratisation and liberalisation of the judiciary began. Based on the break with the People's Republic of China (1960) due to ideological disputes, Russia started the industrialisation and development of the Siberian region. Over the following years, various authorities took the helm and tried to reform the country. Thus, Gorbachev managed to introduce the democratic freedoms. Despite popular vote for the continued existence of the USSR, the Soviet Union was dissolved in 1991. However, many of the former Soviet republics soon founded the *Commonwealth of Independent States* (CIS). In the same year, Yeltsin became Russia's first democratically elected president. He implemented the system of *free market economy* and *presidential democracy*. His presidential term was characterised by liberalisation, institutional development, privatisation and stabilisation.

Putin

Since 2000, Putin has held an important position in Russian politics, first as president, then as prime minister and finally again as president. Since 2008, he has worked in tandem with Medvedev. The security of one's power is a core point of Putin's policies.

Russia at a Glance

Russia is the world's largest country, approximately 1.8 times the size of the United States, with an area of 17.1 million km². This is about 11% of the whole land area of the world. But it is only the ninth largest country by population, with 144 million inhabitants in 2012. The country's capital is Moscow (11.6 million inhabitants in 2012) and Saint Petersburg (4.9 million inhabitants in 2012) is another important centre (The World Bank 2014; UN Data 2014).

Geographic Profile

Russian *business culture* differs from that of most members of the European Union. Russia has risen from a decade of post-Soviet disorder and disintegration to reassert itself as a major player on the world stage, both politically and economically. The Russians missed the three great cultural revolutions: the Reformation, the Renaissance and the Enlightenment. These revolutions characterise much of modern Western European behaviour, while in Russia the *totalitarian party rule* lasted until 1989. Doing business in Russia therefore involves many challenges and barriers caused by political chaos, crime and corruption, but it is of great importance, since Russia is now one of the most important economic regions of the world due to its size and population. Nowadays, the Russian Government has the ambitious goal of improving in the World Bank's Doing Business ranking from position 120 in 2011 to 20 by 2018. This is why the Russian authorities consider the improvement of the *investment climate* a top priority (PWC 2008).

Russian Business Culture

Russia is therefore one of the largest and fastest growing *emerging markets* in the world. It is an influential great power with *strong national interests*. In 2013, the Russian Federation was the eighth largest economy with a GDP of 2.015 trillion USD (see Figure 9.5) (The World Bank 2014; UN Data 2014). With the fall of the Soviet Union, Russia has gone through a remarkable transformation from a globally isolated, centrally planned economy to a more market-based and globally integrated economy.

Compared to the other countries of the CIS, Russia is characterised by the strongest *reformation* in recent years and has both high growth rates and the highest level of investment. However, it should be noted that Russia has lost its wide industrial production base. Today, Russia is labelled as an emerging economy and its economic strength is based on its wealth of *natural resources*. Russia's oil and gas resources are particularly significant for the global economy. In recent years there has been steady increase of exports of oil due to rising oil prices. In 2011, Russia became the world's leading oil producer, surpassing Saudi Arabia. Russia is also the second-largest producer of natural gas and it holds the world's largest natural gas reserves, the second-largest coal reserves and the eighth-largest crude oil reserves. Russia is also a top exporter of metals such as steel and primary aluminium.

Figure 9.5   *Development of GDP from 2005 to 2012 (in billion USD)*

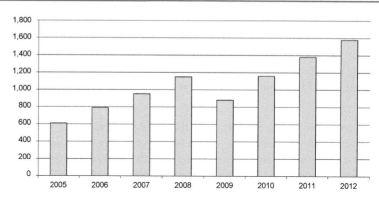

Source: The World Bank 2014, p. 4.

Employment and Workforce

Workers fared rather poorly during Russia's transition from a planned economy to a market economy. Surveys have shown that the average unemployment rate is 8.07% (1993-2014) (The World Bank 2014; UN Data 2014). 33% of the unemployed were not able to find a new job within one year or longer. The Russians work on a daily basis, characterised by *networking* and using contacts, especially when hiring people. Entrepreneurs recruit a person rather than someone to fulfil a specific function. This typical Russian behaviour is especially noticeable in small and medium sized enterprises (Welter/Slonimski/Smallboune 2006, pp. 33-50). In general, Russia has highly qualified workers, but pays comparatively low wages. However, Russians people believed to be happier to have a job than to be in love or respected by the state. These low wages lead to a high susceptibility to bribery and corruption. Often, it is "normal" to pay bribes in the form of presents, for example to speed up processes. To understand this typical Russian behaviour, it is necessary to take a closer look at Russian culture and its characteristics.

Russian Culture According to GLOBE

Russian governance is influence by the time of the Tatar-Mongol rule tribute, the period of the Tsars, the time of Communist Party rule until the current presidency's autocratic leader. A *strong hierarchical thinking* still prevails in economy and politics, but the Russian populace has adjusted to live a life independent from the state. The state is something abstract for the people, formal and far away from the daily problems which influence their lives.

Parameter-Values for the Culture-Dimensions of Russia

Figure 9.6

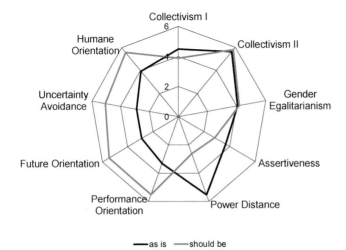

Source: House/Javidan 2004.

The rulers enjoy a privileged life and do not need to follow general legal rules and regulations. The findings for the different culture dimensions by the GLOBE study are presented in Figure 9.6.

Collectivism had a great importance in the Soviet Union and was taught everywhere. The tradition of collectivistic thought and action was made into a societal ideology by the government during Soviet times (Löwe 2002, p. 99). In Soviet times, the state expropriated, divided private property and became a *classless society* where everyone was equal. The idea of *equality* for everyone reinforced the tendency of today's Russian society toward collectivism. People who satisfied the rules of collectivism were accepted. Those that acted

Collectivism

differently and had different opinions from the ruling Communist Party were labelled public enemies in the Stalin era, and many of them lost their freedom or lives. For this reason, it was important to integrate well into group life and to join the majority just to avoid being different. This way of thinking had such a strong influence on the Russian mentality that it is perceptible even today (Yoosefi/Thomas 2003, p. 46). The establishment of a small or medium-sized private enterprise is not the pragmatism of a more or less dominated capitalist company crucial to success, but primarily about giving the impression of active social responsibility.

Accordingly, the collectivism (collectivism I) and family collectivism (collectivism II) dimensions are highly distinctive.

Gender Egalitarianism

Gender equality (gender egalitarianism) was common and taught even before *Perestroika*. The relationship and gender roles of Russian men and women are incomprehensible to many Western people. In the Soviet Union, women took part in building a socialist society. They were often forced to work more than men, as they had to be mothers and maintain their households at the same time, often without their husbands' support. Women were also responsible for earning their family's living, to a certain extent. Therefore the traditional role of women in Russia is strong (Yoosefi/Thomas 2003, p. 128). Men still have a dominant role in political and economic life. Nevertheless, this gender equality must be considered carefully, because an equal distribution of jobs is not enough to make an assertion about the actual equality. There are also, depending on the social level, quite *patriarchal* and *matriarchal* tendencies.

Masculinity

In terms of work ethic and style, Russia has a slight tendency to a *"masculine" society*. Russians pursue success in their professional lives, but at the same time they try not to lose quality of life. In Russia it is necessary to focus on maintaining friendly relations. Colleagues regard each other as a big family or community. They often spend their leisure time together. Supervisors and staff avoid confrontations and direct criticism, as good relationships and a harmonious atmosphere are important to the collective (Yoosefi/Thomas 2003, p. 70).

Assertiveness

In the Soviet Union, comrades had to bend to the politics of totalitarianism. Equality and collectivism were propagated. Accordingly, *self-enforcement* (assertiveness) was less pronounced. Today, many people need to fight with certainty for their goals, whether in society or a company.

Power Distance

Power distance was highly distinct in the days of the Soviet Union, and today the distance between a manager and their staff is still high. But in the GLOBE study there is a huge gap between "what is" and "what should be". Managers strive for a lower power distance. The consequences of a high power distance structure are passivity, little initiative and low acceptance of responsibility. Russian employees try to get "protection" from the top. Hence, before performing any task, they ask their line manager for the right approach.

Under communism, efficiency in the working world was of little importance, because there were no rewards for achieving high results that did not fit into the state-designed economic plans. There was thus limited *performance orientation*. Today, however, these ethical principles have been lost and people often work for a wage that is just enough to live on. The average monthly salary per capita in 2011 was 580 EUR (24,000 RUB). Quite often results are achieved by ignoring ethical standards and morality, making the performance orientation a contradictory weapon in competition (Grachev/Rogovsky/Rakitski 2001, p. 8). The findings show that a decrease in this orientation is demanded overall.

Before Perestroika, during decades of strong beliefs in better life through communism and national long-term planning systems, there were no negative comments about the *future orientation* (Grachev/Rogovsky/Rakitski 2001, p. 9). The Soviet Union produced propaganda to make the population feel content. Since Perestroika, the future is more uncertain than ever. People and businesses in the mid-1990s did not rely on savings, quickly transferring inflated roubles into hard currencies and/or spending money beyond any sensible limits (Grachev/Rogovsky/Rakitski 2001, p. 9). The economy, managers and employees are all focused on the short term. While managers are beginning to aim for a more secure future; the *short-term orientation* still seems strongly anchored in the general Russian population.

Uncertainty avoidance, which indicates a moderate level of tolerance for uncertainty and ambiguity, for example unstructured situations, is low within Russian society. In Russian history, there have been many global changes in society, state-transformations and political turbulences. People are confronted by the uncertainty of life nearly every day. Life in Russia is full of risks, as demonstrated by the popular saying: "He who does not risk anything, does not drink champagne" (Yoosefi/Thomas 2003, p. 128). In recent years, life has become more stable.

Russian business partners sometimes need a long time for decision-making processes. Employees do not like to take responsibility and they divert decisions to their supervisors. However, some things are changing: "Younger managers apparently perceive much higher level of uncertainty avoidance in perestroika days than their older counter-parts [...] Clearly, the business climate under communism made uncertainty avoidance a cornerstone of living in general and particularly in managing Soviet enterprises" (Veiga/Ynouzas/Buchholz 1995, p. 23).

Humane
Orientation

The humane orientation plays little role in Russia. Ethical principles are not respected and morality is questionable. In Russia competition is often unfair and beyond the law. This is aggravated by violence and a growing *shadow economy* (illegal sector or legal business by illegal means) (Grachev/Rogovsky/Rakitski 2001, p. 10). The struggle for survival is increasingly important. This is reflected in high and even growing corruption. Interestingly, family life shows the opposite of this "outside-ignorance" as evidenced by high collectivism. In addition, the Russian hospitality should not be underestimated.

Paternalism

Russia has a social system based on high power distance, which leads people to believe in *paternalism*, especially for those who have lived a significant portion of their lives in a society where paternalism is particularly widespread. During a crisis, weak and incapacitated people often defer to powerful and stronger stakeholders, such as the state, an institution or a work superior. Centuries of near-continuous social and economic crises brought about by a succession of Russian governments have given the state practically unlimited power over the whole of society in the industrial, agricultural and social spheres. This happened during the early years when Russia's city states were ruled by princes, then in Tsarist times, during the time of the Russian empire and finally under communism (Bollinger 1994; Veiga/Ynouzas/Buchholz 1995; Naumov/Puffer 2002, p. 716).

The Impact of Russian Culture on Human Resource Management and Marketing

Human Resource Management

Recruitment activities in Russia are comparable to those in Western countries. The most frequently used *recruitment* methods are employment advertisements in mass media, e.g. newspapers and magazines. Most businesses and organisations recruit employees through direct recruitment and recruitment agencies. Genuine recruitment agencies began working in Russia comparatively recently, at the beginning of the 1990s. Foreign recruitment agencies which came to Russia at this time in order to find personnel for their customers opening affiliates in Russia were the pioneers in this sphere. These recruitment agencies can be divided into three main types: traditional recruitment agencies, executive search companies, colloquially known as headhunters, and state employment centres. Russia is an important developing global market, one that is seen as key to global development over the next years. Therefore some large agencies united and formed the Association of Recruitment Consultants to build a collective *think tank* and share their knowledge. The most popular globally active companies provide recruitment and human resources services, e.g. *Hays*. But there is another recruitment method which epitomises the Soviet way of life: the tried and tested *"Soviet Method"*, which always begins with the phrase "on my friend's recommendation" (Grachev/Rogovsky/Rakitski 2007, pp. 803).

Marketing and Sales

Russian Special Economic Areas

The last few years have seen much investment in key projects in the fields of infrastructure, communication technology, power efficiency, medical engineering, nano and nuclear technology and space technologies. Russia's aim is to improve its competitiveness and diversification. Therefore, Russia established several special economic areas: (1) *industrial* special economic areas like Jelabuga and Lipezk, (2) *technological* special economic areas like Moscow, St. Petersburg, Dubna and Tomsk, (3) special economic areas for *tourism and recreation*, e.g. Kaliningrad, Stavropol, and (4) special economic areas for *innovation* like Skolkowo.

The Luxury Goods Sector in Russia

The Russian *luxury goods sector* is rapidly expanding thanks to sophisticated and mature consumers, growing faster than any other luxury market in the world. Small leather goods, timepieces and jewellery are showing particularly strong growth rates, while designer clothes, beauty and personal care products are gradually returning to their pre-crisis growth rates. Despite the fact that the Russian luxury market is considered to be relatively mature, the potential for further growth and the adoption of new brands are expected. With an improving economic situation, middle class consumers will reconsider their expenditure and pay more attention to luxuries (PWC 2008).

Russian consumers want to enjoy and experience their wealth, and especially show it to the rest of the world. Being in Moscow, it is essential to go to "Rublijowka", the "it place to be" when there is luxury to show. "Rublijowka" is a symbol for success, wealth, satisfaction and the elite when you are wealthy and able to afford luxury. For everybody else, it is just a shopping street: nice to visit and window-shop. The recently increase in the number of high net worth individuals in Russia, the wide presence of global brands and Russians' strong aspirations to luxury will ensure healthy performance.

Conspicuous Consumption

From the outset, the luxury goods market in Russia was driven by several local companies, which owned exclusive distribution rights to globally known fashion brands. Within a few years, the portfolios of *Bosco di Ciliegi*, *Mercury*, *JamilCo* and *Crocus Group* became impressive enough to represent a full range of global luxury brands (Euromonitor International 2013). Popular luxury brands (*Gucci, Prada, Hermès*, etc.) established their representative offices in Russia to strengthen their positions and improve their sales results.

Summary and Outlook

Russia is one of the largest and fastest growing emerging markets, not least because it is the world's leading oil producer, the second-largest producer of natural gas and it holds the world's largest natural gas reserves, the second-largest coal reserves, the eighth-largest crude oil reserves as well as considerable metal reserves. It is also one of the fastest growing consumer markets, especially in the luxury sector. The Russian *way of life* differs from the European one, although they are slowly beginning to converge. The competitive environment is hard to penetrate if foreign companies and specialists are not familiar with the typical Russian features and specifics. Hence, it is mandatory for Western companies to not only be aware of these characteristics, but to also adjust their management systems and procedures accordingly.

Questions

1. Imagine that the import tariff and ban of imports may lead to a compartmentalisation of the Russian economy, even though Russia is a member of the World Trade Organization. What consequences may be seen in the relationship between Russia and the other countries of the WTO?

2. Surveys show that foreign companies identify corruption and costs of bureaucracy as the main barriers for business in Russia. How do the Russian culture and mentality influence these barriers and how can this problem be solved?

3. Although the Russian political system has undergone a lot of changes, especially in the balance of power, the Russian population is satisfied as never before with their social, political and financial situation. Why is it so important for the Russian population to show their wealth and experience luxury? What consequences are there foreign brands and companies trying to satisfy this demand?

References

BANDURA, A. (1986): Social Foundations of Thought and Action: A Social Cognitive Theory, Englewood Cliffs, Prentice Hall.

BOLLINGER, D. (1994): The Four Cornerstones and Three Pillars of the "House of Russia" Management System, in: Journal of Management Development, Vol. 13, No. 2, pp. 49-54.

CAVUSGIL, S.T.; KNIGHT, G.; RIESENBERGER, J.R. (2014): International Business: The New Realities, 3rd ed., Boston, Pearson.

CHANEY, L.; MARTIN, J. (Eds.) (2014): Intercultural Business Communication, Harlow, Pearson.

CZINKOTA, M.; RONKAINEN, I. (2013): International Marketing, 10th ed., Hampshire, Cengage Learning.

DE MOOIJ, M. (2014): Global Marketing and Advertising: Understanding Cultural Paradoxes, 4th ed., Thousand Oaks, Sage Publications.

DLABLAY, L.R.; SCOTT, J.C. (2011): International Business, 4th Edition, Nashville, South-Western Cengage Learning.

EREZ, M.; GATI, E. (2004): A Dynamic, Multi-Level Model of Culture: From the Micro Level of the Individual to the Macro Level of a Global Culture, in: Applied Psychology: An International Review, Vol. 53, No. 4, pp. 583-598.

EUROMONITOR INTERNATIONAL (2013): Market Research for the Luxury Goods Industry: Country Report: Luxury Goods in Russia, http://www.euromonitor.com/luxury-goods-in-russia/report, accessed in May 20, 2014.

GHEMAWAT, P. (2007): Redefining Global Strategy: Crossing Borders in a World Where Differences Still Matter, 1st ed., Watertown, Harvard Business Review Press.

GRACHEV, M.; ROGOVSKY, N.; RAKITSKI, B. (2001): Leadership and Culture in Russia: The Case of Transitional Economy, in: Business Review, Vol. 10, No. 1, pp. 615-643.

GRIFFIN, R.; PUSTAY, M. (2013): International Business: A Managerial Perspective, 7th ed., Upper Saddle River, New Jersey, Pearson.

HALL, E.; HALL, M. (1990): Understanding Cultural Differences, Yarmouth, Intercultural Press.

HILL, C.W.L. (2013): International Business: Competing in the Global Marketplace, 9th ed., New York, McGraw-Hill.

HOFSTEDE, G. (1980): Culture's Consequences: International Differences in Work-related Values, Thousand Oaks, Sage Publications.

HOFSTEDE, G. (1991): Cultures and Organizations, New York, McGraw-Hill.

HOFSTEDE, G. (2001): Culture's Consequences: Comparing Values, Behaviors, Institutions and Organizations across Nations, Thousand Oaks, Sage Publications.

HOFSTEDE, G.; HOFSTEDE, G.J.; MINKOV, M. (2010): Cultures and Organizations: Software of the Mind, 3rd ed., New York, McGraw-Hill.

HOLLENSEN, S. (2014): Global Marketing, 6th ed., Harlow, Pearson.

HOUSE, R.; JAVIDAN, M. (2004): Overview of GLOBE, in: HOUSE, R.; HANGES, P.; JAVIDAN, M.; DORFMAN, P.; GUPTA, V. (Eds.): Leadership and Organisations: The GLOBE Study of 62 Societies, London, SAGE, pp. 9-28.

HOUSE, R.; HANGES, P.; JAVIDAN, M.; DORFMAN, P.; GUPTA, V. (2002): Culture, Leadership, and Organizations: The GLOBE Study of 62 Societies, Thousand Oaks, Sage Publications.

JESUINO, J. (2002): Latin Europe Cluster: From South to North, in: Journal of World Business, Vol. 37, No. 1, pp. 81-89.

KOTABE, M.; HELSEN, K. (2014): Global Marketing Management, 6th ed., New York, Wiley & Sons.

LEVITT, T. (1983): The Globalization of Markets, in: Harvard Business Review, Vol. 61, No. 3, pp. 92-102.

LÖWE, B. (2002): Kulturschock Russland, 3rd ed., Bielefeld, Reise Know-How Verlag.

MAGNUSSEN, P.; WILSON, R.; ZDRAVKOVIC, S.; ZHOU, J.; WESTJOHN, S. (2008): Breaking Through the Cultural Clutter: A Comparative Assessment of Multiple Cultural and Intuitional Frameworks, in: International Marketing Review, Vol. 25, No. 2, pp. 183-201.

MINKOV, M. (2007): What Makes Us Different and Similar: A New Interpretation of the World Values Survey and Other Cross-cultural Data, in: Journal of Cross-Cultural Psychology, Vol. 39, No. 5, pp. 654-658.

NAUMOV, I.; PUFFER, S. (2002): Measuring Russian Culture Using Hofstede's Dimensions, in: Applied Psychology: an International Review, Vol. 49, No. 4, pp. 709-718.

PHATAK, A.; BHAGAT, R., KASHLAK, R. (2009): International Management, 2nd ed., Boston, McGraw-Hill.

PWC (2008): Shopping for the Future: Russian Retail Market Survey, Frankfurt.

RUGMAN, A.M.; COLLINSON, S. (2012): International Business, 6th ed., Harlow, Pearson.

SCHEIN, E. (1992): Organizational Culture and Leadership, San Francisco, Jossey-Bass.

SUE, D.W.; SUE, D. (2007): Counseling the Culturally Diverse: Theory and Practice, 5th ed., Hoboken, Wiley & Sons.

TERPSTRA, V.; DAVID, K. (1991): The Cultural Environment of International Business, 3rd ed., Cincinnati, South-Western.

THE WORLD BANK (2014): Doing Business 2014, http://www.doing-business.org/~/media/GIAWB/Doing%20Business/Documents/Annual-reports/English/DB14-Full-Report.pdf, accessed on April 11, 2014.

UN DATA (2014): Country Profile: Russian Federation, https://data.un.Org/CountryProfile.aspx?crName=Russian%20Federation, accessed on May 12, 2014.

USUNIER, J.-C.; LEE, J. (2013): Marketing Across Cultures, 6th ed., Upper Saddle River, New Jersey, Prentice Hall.

VEIGA, J.; YNOUZAS, J.; BUCHHOLZ, K. (1995): Emerging Cultural Values Among Russian Managers: What Will Tomorrow Bring, in: Business Horizonts, Vol. 38, No. 4, pp. 20-27.

WELTER, F.; SLONIMSKI, A.; SMALLBONE, D. (2006): Internationalisation of Entrepreneurship in Belarus: National and Regional Aspects, in: Economic Bulletin, Vol. 6, No. 1, pp. 33-50.

YOOSEFI, T.; THOMAS, A. (2003): Beruflich in Russland: Trainingsprogramm für Manager, Fach- und Führungskräfte, Göttingen, Vandenhoeck & Ruprecht.

Part III

International

Coordination

Chapter 10

Formal and Informal Coordination Mechanisms

As has been shown in the preceding Chapters, MNCs are characterised by internationally dispersed activities. To integrate all of an MNC's activities and organisational units under a common strategy, coordination is necessary. This Chapter is an overview of different coordination mechanisms, including the strengths and shortcomings of each mechanism.

Introduction

The successful implementation of international strategies strongly depends on adequate coordination of the dispersed activities by the MNC (e.g., Andersson/Forsgren 1996, p. 487), mostly by the MNC's headquarters. Solving the problem of coordinating *heterogeneous and geographically distant subsidiaries* is an essential part of International Management.

Coordination can be defined as the process of integrating activities that remain dispersed across subsidiaries (Martinez/Jarillo 1991, p. 431). "A mechanism of coordination is any administrative tool for achieving integration among different units within an organisation, i.e. to align a number of dispersed and yet interdependent international activities" (Martinez/Jarillo 1989, p. 490).

The core coordination task for an MNC is to ensure that all subsidiaries strive towards *common organisational goals* and the actions and behaviour of the subsidiaries conform to the MNC's overall strategy. At the same time, coordination must support the necessary capabilities, *motivation* and entrepreneurship of the subsidiary management in adapting to the local environment of their host countries (Macharzina 1990, p. 372). This should be achieved with minimum management costs (or *agency costs*). So-called *administrative rationality* (Thompson 1967) argues that the most efficient type of coordination should be chosen in each situation.

Usually, many coordination mechanisms are used simultaneously. Bartlett/Beamish (2014, pp. 287-289) suggest an illuminating analogy between the MNC and the human body. They argue that three different types of mechanisms are necessary to coordinate the MNC:

■ The *anatomy* of the organisation, i.e., the formal organisational structure, which is necessary but not sufficient.

Coordination and Coordination Mechanisms

■ This must be accompanied by the *physiology*, i.e. a company's systems and decision processes.

■ The final (crucial) component is *psychology*, i.e. the organisation's culture.

A broader categorisation groups the coordination mechanisms into two sets of mechanisms: formal and informal. Informal mechanisms are more subtle. Table 10.1 gives an overview of the most common coordination mechanisms.

Table 10.1   *The Most Relevant Sets of Coordination Mechanisms*

Formal Mechanisms	Informal Mechanisms
organisational structure: departmentalisation or grouping of organisational units	**lateral or cross-departmental relations**: direct managerial contact, temporary or permanent teams, task forces, committees, integrators, and integrative departments
centralisation: centralisation or decentralisation of decision making through the hierarchy of formal authority	**informal communication**: personal contacts among managers, management trips, meetings, conferences, transfer of managers, etc.
formalisation and standardisation: written policies, rules, job descriptions, and standard procedures, through instruments such as manuals, charts, etc.	**normative integration**: building an organisational culture of known and shares strategic objectives and values by training, transfer of managers, career path management, reward systems, etc.
planning: strategic planning, budgeting, functional plans, scheduling, etc.	

Source: Adapted from Martinez/Jarillo 1989, p. 491.

Formal Coordination Mechanisms

Structural Coordination Mechanisms

The formal organisational structure is concerned with how the company decides to *divide itself into subunits* (Hill 2013, pp. 452-453). This has far-reaching consequences for information flow within the organisation, decision processes and the allocation of resources. The formal organisational structure is discussed in detail in Chapter 11.

However, the *macro structure* of integrating subsidiaries into the organisational structure of an MNC is a "very crude" instrument for controlling activities (Birkinshaw/Morrison 1995, p. 737). The basic organisational types describe the general structure of the organisation at the highest organisational level. Given that subsidiaries act in diverse external contexts with unique constellations of characteristics and resources and different tasks, a uniform organisational structure is hardly sufficient to consider this heterogeneity (Nohria/Ghoshal 1997, p. 4). Structural coordination mechanisms are generally symmetrical and not tailored to the needs of a specific subsidiary. Hence, they are chosen based on the overall requirements of the MNC.

Centralisation/Decentralisation

Centralisation refers to *the locus of decision power*. It determines the degree to which decision-making authority is concentrated in the higher hierarchy levels of the organisation (e.g. Lawrence/Lorsch 1967a). For international business, it indicates the degree to which decisions are taken by the corporate HQ in the home country or by the subsidiary itself. It also determines the strength of the subsidiary's influence on these decisions (Morrison/Roth 1993, p. 802).

Obviously, strongly integrated behaviour of different organisational units can be achieved if all decisions are taken by the HQ and the subsidiaries only implement those strategies without any autonomy. Decisions taken centrally are based on a good overview of all the different parts of the MNC and fully reflect the requirements of the HQ. Centralisation is particularly suitable for enforcing *global strategies*.

Advantages of Centralisation

However, strong centralisation has various drawbacks. First, centralisation has negative effects on the motivation of subsidiary managers. Resistance against a high degree of centralisation is common. Also, centralised decisions are taken based solely on HQ's. While HQ has a total picture of all parts of the MNC, its knowledge of each specific host country is limited. If a subsidiary's situation is complex and the environment and requirements are very different from those in the home country, the knowledge of the HQ is unlikely to be sufficient to make adequate decisions. Since centralisation also needs *intensive information flows* across hierarchies, such decisions are often slow, and decentralisation is better suited to quick and flexible reactions to changes in the local environment and to exploit local market opportunities (Nohria/Ghoshal 1997, pp. 97-98). MNCs with a *multinational orientation* are more likely to use decentralisation.

Disadvantages of Centralisation

Centralisation or decentralisation of MNCs is influenced by many factors (see the overviews by Welge 1987, c. 1539; Young/Tavares 2004; Rugman/Collinson 2012, p. 289). Decision centralisation tends to be higher if a subsidiary

■ belongs to a large MNC that is active in many countries

■ is relatively important to the MNC

■ is responsible for more than the local host market

■ is interdependent with the MNC with intensive product flows between the different subsidiaries

■ is located in a host country with low cultural distance to the home country

■ is located in a host country with relatively stable political conditions.

On the other hand, subsidiaries are usually granted a high level of autonomy if

■ they belong to an MNC with a high growth strategy

■ they are oriented towards the local host market

■ they are tightly embedded in a local cluster within the host country

■ local investors hold a substantial capital share

■ the products and services that the subsidiary offers are not related to the products and services offered by the parent company

■ the geographical distance between home country and host country is large and/or

■ the local environment of the subsidiary, in particular market and competitive conditions, is very dissimilar from that of the home country.

Different Levels of Centralisation of Different Functions

The level of centralisation might also differ across the functional areas of the MNC. While financial management and R&D decisions are often highly centralised, human resource management is usually the least centralised. Manufacturing and marketing fall in between (Young/Tavares 2004, p. 218).

Strategic Decisions Stronger Centralised

Strategic decisions are more likely to be centralised, while operational decisions are often decentralised. The different availability of information needed for these decisions is an important factor. While the knowledge necessary for long-term and strategic decisions is often more available at the HQ, subsidiaries are granted more autonomy for operational decisions in which they have better access to information and which need quick decisions, especially if they have few far-reaching consequences for the overall MNC (Young/Tavares 2004, p. 218).

Centralisation AND Decentralisation

More recent literature does not view centralisation and decentralisation as purely opposing mechanisms. In particular, *transnational strategies* might require "avoiding the simplistic centralization-decentralization dichotomy" (Martinez/Jarillo 1989, p. 500). As explained in Chapter 1, networks can be coordinated via so-called *decentralised centralisation*, where activities are globally integrated and aligned; however, in some cases and for some products, a foreign subsidiary rather than HQ acts as a strategic leader for worldwide activities (Birkinshaw/Morrison 1995, p. 734).

Formalisation and Standardisation

Formalisation and standardisation refer to the extent to which *written policies*, rules, job descriptions, standard procedures, etc., are established and written down in manuals and other documents. Procedures are established through *standard routines*. The intention is to provide clear and formal behavioural guidelines to subsidiaries (Lawrence/Lorsch 1967a; Martinez/Jarillo 1989, p. 491). Formalisation, as a bureaucratic mechanism, can be seen as the *routinisation* of decision behaviour (Hedlund 1981). It defines impersonal rules and standard processes, independent of specific persons or situations. Standardisation refers to binding rules for uniform procedures and programmes that lead to homogeneous task completion.

In management practice, standardisation and formalisation have become considerably more important due to *quality management* procedures (e.g. ISO 9000), environmental management (e.g. ISO 14000), compliance rules for corporate governance and *codes of conduct* for corporate social responsibility (see Chapter 13). Most of these management systems require a formalised written set of standards and conducts that are applied throughout the company.

Formalisation as Part of Quality Management and of CSR

A high level of product flows and cross-border production usually requires higher levels of standardisation and formalisation for production processes to facilitate an optimal workflow and the integration of products and product components into a single worldwide supply chain.

The basic advantage of formalisation and standardisation as a coordination mechanism is that they identify certain routine situations that occur repeatedly and establish generalised decision rules before those situations occur. Their coordination effect is particularly strong if they group potential decisions and activities into categories. Thus, they help to replace direct, centralised coordination with an indirect form and reduce coordination costs (Morrison/Roth 1993, pp. 802-803). Compared with decision centralisation, formalisation and standardisation provoke less resistance since they refer to a generally valid set of rules instead of potentially "unfair" decisions (Nohria/Ghoshal 1997, pp. 99-100).

Advantages of Formalisation/ Standardisation

However, since formalisation and standardisation have to solve problems *ex ante* (i.e., before the decision is taken), they are best suited to static problems and rarely suitable for highly dynamic tasks in complex environments. They lead to standardised solutions which might be a *barrier to flexibility* and new and innovative solutions. They also reduce the ability to adapt to local con-

Adequate in Stable Task Environments

237

ditions and might thus reduce the motivation of local management.

On the other hand, formalisation and standardisation might help to establish a stable context for bilateral communication and coordination between subsidiaries. Even in inter-company cooperation (e.g. in supply chain management), *common standards* (for data and processes) are increasingly seen as necessary *enabling technologies* for true cooperation (see Zentes/Morschett/Schramm-Klein 2011, pp. 371-372). In the MNC context, formalisation and standardisation are certainly insufficient for complex situations, but they can provide fertile ground for the use of other coordination mechanisms (Morschett 2007, pp. 507-511). Lateral agreements, horizontal cooperation, etc., are facilitated if formalisation and standardisation provide standards that help to exchange products, data and information and facilitate cross-border production processes, marketing strategies, etc. For MNC control, a common definition of key performance indicators, etc., is necessary for *internal benchmarking*.

Planning

Planning, understood as the *periodically repeated establishment of goals* and objectives by HQ for subsidiaries, is a process of *ex ante coordination*, in which higher-ranking organisation objectives broken down into lower hierarchy goals and specified stepwise. It refers to systems and processes like strategic planning, budgeting, establishment of schedules and goal setting (Martinez/Jarillo 1989, p. 491). Qualitative strategic objectives are transformed into quantitative objectives, and those objectives are linked to specific resources and organisational units and given a specific time frame. Thus, subsidiaries receive concrete objectives from the HQ that are established to guide and channel the activities and actions of independent units.

Informal Coordination Mechanisms

Lateral Relations and Informal Communication

Lateral relations are established *across the formal hierarchical structure*. They directly link people in the organisation who share common problems and might develop joint solutions together, without relying on clear vertical lines of authority. The top management's decision and information task is reduced by these *direct horizontal relations*. They include direct contact among managers of different organisational units, temporary or permanent task forces, teams, cross-national committees, integrating roles, integrative departments, etc. (Martinez/Jarillo 1989, p. 492). These lateral relations establish common procedures, internal discussion, knowledge sharing, etc., in the organisation.

Lateral relations also enhance informal communication by creating a *network of informal and personal contacts* among managers across different company units (Martinez/Jarillo 1989, p. 492). Such *informal communication* can be stimulated by corporate meetings, management trips, personal visits, manager transfers, intensive use of expatriates, etc. They are associated with intensive direct communication, whether in person or via electronic media (e.g. video-conferencing). Frequent meetings and visits by representatives of the HQ to the subsidiary or vice versa are commonly employed (Kieser/Walgenbach 2003, pp. 109-110).

Normative Integration

Normative integration (also called *socialisation*) refers to building a strong *organisational culture* of known and shared strategic objectives, perspectives and values. This is often achieved through a *socialisation process*, openly communicating the method of doing things and the decision-making style, training, management transfers, career path management, measurement and reward systems, etc., to generate identification with the organisation, developing incentive systems, etc. (Egelhoff 1984).

Organisational Culture

One tremendous advantage of this subtle and indirect mechanism is that the subsidiary can conduct its daily operations autonomously without direct orders from HQ. The subsidiary will have very *high flexibility* and the opportunity to adapt to the local context, and its conduct will still be aligned with company goals (Birkinshaw/Morrison 1995, p. 738). Normative integration as a coordination mechanism is discussed in detail in Chapter 12.

Evolution from Formal to Informal Mechanisms

Simple strategies need little coordination and are easily implemented by using structural and other formal mechanisms. More *complex strategies* need a much higher coordination effort, and are therefore implemented through a more complex set of coordination mechanisms. In particular, network oriented, transnational strategies are more complex since they focus on the dual need of achieving global synergy effects and exploiting local market differences. Thus, in addition to structural, formal and relatively simple tools, informal, more subtle and sophisticated instruments are used. However, since these instruments are very costly and rather slow to implement, an MNC usually only applies these informal instruments if they are really necessary to implement a strategy (Martinez/Jarillo 1989, p. 492).

From Simple to Complex Strategies

Formal and Informal Coordination Mechanisms

In an early study by Hamel/Prahalad (1983), it was argued that in a situation with relatively stable and clear external conditions, structural coordination instruments have the highest effectiveness. In situations which are ambiguous, complex or involve dynamic environments, however, normative integration and other personal coordination instruments, like informal communication, are the most effective (see Figure 10.1).

Figure 10.1 | *Effectiveness of Different Coordination Mechanisms*

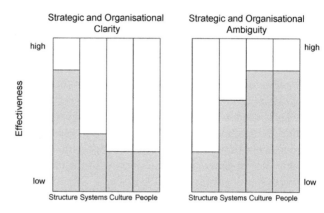

Source: Hamel/Prahalad 1983, p. 349.

Patterns of Evolution

Over time, a *pattern of evolution* can be observed. More and more MNCs are beginning to focus on subtler and more informal mechanisms, abandoning their unidimensional focus on structural issues (Martinez/Jarillo 1989, p. 489). This is often the result of a change in external environment and a move towards more complex strategies, which shifts the relative effectiveness of the different coordination mechanisms.

Adaptation of Coordination to the Subsidiary

Given that coordination mechanisms have different strengths and weaknesses and the effectiveness and efficiency of certain coordination mechanisms are at least partly dependent on the role of the subsidiary (see Chapter 3), then it follows that the use of coordination mechanisms should vary between different subsidiaries (Young/Tavares 2004, pp. 220-221). Since the organisational structure cannot be adapted to the specific subsidiary roles, informal mechanisms are necessary to adapt coordination. However, formal mechanisms like the level of centralisation or autonomy are still necessary.

Selection of Coordination Mechanisms

The economic perspective, based on so-called *administrative rationality* (Thompson 1967), argues the most efficient type of coordination must be selected in each situation. This entails considering the cost and effectiveness of each instrument.

Normative integration is a powerful instrument but costly to implement, since comprehensive administrative resources (e.g. visits by managers) require investment, for initial socialisation as well as maintaining the relationships. Formalisation and standardisation, on the other hand, are usually inexpensive to implement. Centralisation is also comparatively inexpensive to establish, since it is based on the hierarchical authority of the HQ. On the other hand, centralisation might require comprehensive resources within the HQ to be able to make decisions adequately (Nohria/Ghoshal 1997, pp. 102-103). These and other cost aspects must be balanced with the differing effectiveness in different situations to decide on optimal coordination.

Normative Integration More Costly Than Formalisation

From a theoretical perspective, the *contingency approach* (which is explained in more detail in Chapter 6) convincingly argues that there is no universally optimal way of coordinating an MNC. Instead, organisational coordination should be differentiated by the characteristics of the external environment in which the organisation acts (Lawrence/Lorsch 1967b; Thompson 1967) and other contingencies. Furthermore, *configurational perspective* suggests that a company should not focus on coordination instruments separately; instead a *holistic perspective* is necessary. The interplay between coordination instruments, and the resulting requirement for internal consistency between the coordination instruments applied which has a strong influence on the efficiency of the organisation (Khandwalla 1973, p. 493).

Contingency Approach - "It All Depends"

Conclusion and Outlook

Coordination mechanisms are administrative tools for achieving integration among different units within an MNC, i.e., to align a number of disparate yet interdependent international activities. They are used to ensure that all subsidiaries strive towards common organisational goals (Martinez/Jarillo 1989).

With the increasing complexity of MNC strategy and heterogeneous environmental contexts, managerial practice has evolved from the use of simple instruments like organisational structure to more complex instruments like normative integration. These informal mechanisms supplement the formal mechanisms rather than replace them. Thus, MNCs increasingly apply multi-dimensional combinations of coordination mechanisms instead of the unidimensional focus on company structure seen in the past. Following the configurational approach, it is important to consider MNC coordination as being realised through a combination of coordination mechanisms. These specific use patterns of coordination instruments build on an optimal bundle of instruments that supplement each other's strengths and weaknesses.

Network-
Oriented
Perspective

The modern network-oriented perspectives of MNCs strongly favour informal and more subtle mechanisms. In this context, Bartlett/Beamish (2014, p. 386) argue that a process of change within a modern MNC is better initiated through corporate culture rather than using the formal structure. They argue that using the formal structure as a coordination instrument is a blunt and slow mechanism which might take years to fully implement. To instigate change, instead of installing a new structure, HQ should employ other instruments. Following their analogy of the human body, they recommend starting a process of change by altering the company's "psychology", i.e. the corporate culture. After changing beliefs, norms and attitudes, changing the "physiology", e.g. communication and decision processes, can reinforce this *cultural change*. Later, companies might consolidate and confirm their progress by realigning organisational anatomy through a change in the formal structure.

However it must be remembered that more complex coordination systems are only suitable when the situation requires them. "Simplicity, wherever possible, is a virtue" (Ghoshal/Nohria 1993, p. 24).

Further Reading

MARTINEZ, J.; JARILLO, C. (1989): The Evolution of Research on Coordination Mechanisms in Multinational Corporations, in: Journal of International Business Studies, Vol. 20, No. 3, pp. 489-514.

Case Study: McKinsey*

Profile and History

McKinsey & Company, Inc. is a global management consulting firm, headquartered in New York City, USA. The company belongs to its 1,200 partners, 400 of which are directors. Every three years, the directors elect a man-

---

* Sources used for this case study include the website http://www.mckinsey.com, various company reports and company presentations, as well as explicitly cited sources.

aging director to represent the company globally. Once a partner retires, the company withdraws his shares.

As of 2014, *McKinsey* has more than 100 local offices with equal rights in more than 50 countries. Between them, these offices speak over 120 languages and represent more than 100 nationalities. The firm serves as an adviser to businesses, governments and institutions and claims that over 80% of *Fortune's list of the Most Admired Companies* are among their clients. Between 2002 and 2014, *McKinsey* was ranked first on the "The Best Consulting Firms: Prestige" list on the *Vault.com* career intelligence website and was cited as the "most prestigious consulting firm of all" in a 2011 *New York Times* article. Being a private entity, the company does not publish many business figures. *Forbes* estimated their overall annual revenues at 7.8 billion USD in 2013 (Forbes 2014).

Multinational Company

McKinsey is professionally organised into industry and functional practices. The practices are centres of competence that concentrate on one field. They are organised as a network and share their expertise with colleagues worldwide. In this way, *McKinsey* hopes to maintain a global and closely interlinked web of functional expertise and industry knowledge.

In order to understand *McKinsey & Co*.'s coordination mechanisms and development, it is worth looking at their company history: The precursor of *McKinsey & Co* as it exists today was *James O. McKinsey & Company*, founded in Chicago in 1926 and named after its founder (see Bhidé 1996 for the company history and a comprehensive portrait). James O. McKinsey was a certified public accountant and professor of accounting at the University of Chicago. His company specialised in accounting and advising managers, which was called "managing engineering" at that time.

Origin and Precursor

The entry of Marvin Bower into the company in 1933 was a milestone in the company's development. After graduating from Harvard Law School in 1928, he had already gained experience at the prestigious law firm *Jones, Day*. Bower remembers his close cooperation with the company's senior partner: "I made it an immediate objective to learn why it [*Jones, Day*] had been so successful. From observation and analysis during my *Jones, Day* years began the formulation of the program that I later brought with me to *McKinsey*." The firm's professional approach, recruiting standards and the prominence of its partners in charitable, social and cultural organisations left their mark on Bower. Therefore, he established all these elements years later at *McKinsey & Co* when he was in charge (Bhidé 1996, p. 8).

Entry of Marvin Bower

After James O. McKinsey's sudden death at the end of 1937, the firm nearly disintegrated (Hill 2011). Extensive reorganisations and changes to the company structure in 1939 facilitated a prompt recovery. An essential contribution to the successful reorganisation of the company is attributed to Bower, who was deputy manager of *McKinsey's* New York Office at that time. One central element was the focus on management consulting which had been moved to a single, central location in New York. Accounting was abandoned. The primary emphasis was now on solving major management problems. The services were based on high standards of integrity, professional ethics and technical intelligence. Bower's impact and his experience from his time at *Jones, Day* was also visible in the focus on human resources: The stated aim was to select, train and advance personnel so that the firm would be self-perpetuating (Bhidé 1996).

Growth and Internationalisation

McKinsey & Co used the subsequent years to build the company's economic base. In the 1940s the company grew rapidly in the US home market in terms of both clients and offices. In 1944, *McKinsey & Co* opened their first office outside of New York, in San Francisco, and between 1947 and 1951 offices followed in Chicago, Los Angeles and Washington, DC. The first office outside of the US was opened in 1959 in London. In the following years the company transformed into an increasingly global consultancy, expanding into more than 50 countries. There was also enormous growth in the number of employees: *McKinsey* had only 15 consultants worldwide in 1933 and 80 in 1950, but they had 700 employees at the beginning of the 1980s. During the dotcom boom of the late 1990s, *McKinsey* grew significantly: Between 1994 and 2001, the number of consultants doubled from 3,300 to 7,700. This growth placed high demands on the management principles and the coordination mechanisms of the company, a demand which continues today.

Management Principles and the One Firm Principle

Management Principles

Even today, *McKinsey's* management principles are based on the goals that Bower and his partners set for the firm in 1939. The main goal was to build a firm that would continue in perpetuity. Foundation was the next principle, encouraging "every individual to protect and build the firm's future and reputation so that each generation of partners would pass the firm along to the next generation stronger than they had found it" (Bhidé 1996).

McKinsey states that the company's work is based in values that oblige them to meet the highest professional standards. "Client first" is the *primary principle of consulting*. This idea is followed to such an extent that *McKinsey* only accepts orders when the consultants are convinced they can usefully contribute to the solution of a major problem. Likewise, if a client is no longer satisfied and is not benefitting from the consultation as hoped, the cooperation can be terminated at any time.

A prerequisite for objective consulting is professional independence: the partners own *McKinsey*'s working capital. Once a partner leaves the company, *McKinsey* takes back his shares. This is to ensure that only active partners in the company who are bound by the company's objectives have a vital interest in the business activity.

Professional Independence

Strict secrecy of customer information is essential for trustworthy cooperation. The security of this trust in the long run is part of the *code of conduct* that every partner accepts when joining the company. There has, however, been one violation of the code of conduct: In 2011, Anil Kumar, a former *McKinsey* partner, admitted leaking information learnt from *McKinsey* clients while working for the firm (Hill 2011).

McKinsey views entrepreneurial challenges as an independent outsider and always from the perspective of the top management. Solution and implementation strategies are individually coordinated with the client's different needs, goals and company cultures – always in close cooperation with the client's top-level management.

Joining *McKinsey* as a consultant should provide individual development and be great career path if the consultant performs well. *McKinsey* has an integrated working atmosphere, free from any hierarchy. The company provides mentors, who assist the individual in his personal development, span his individual network and help him benefit from his colleagues' expertise. All consultants are expected to uphold the obligation to dissent, meaning that constructive criticism is explicitly encouraged and should be expressed.

McKinsey's global business activity is a daunting management challenge. The "client first" principle requires that every regional entity internalises the characteristics of the local market. At the same time, every local office and every consultant should share the same global company values.

"The One-Firm"- Principle

McKinsey tries to balance these by using a strategy that Maister (1985) labelled the *"one firm principle"*. Despite being embedded into the cultural characteristics of every region, the individual *McKinsey* offices form one common firm that shares its principles and values worldwide. This means the company is strongly decentralised. Every region acts independently as far as possible and makes independent decisions. In this way, the company can take regional markets and their characteristics into consideration. On the other hand, every consultant knows the values they must live by and the code of behaviour they must follow. Everyone is equally and intensively trained in these values and protocols. Everyone also knows that if an individual is in trouble, the group will expend every effort to help (Maister/Walker 2006).

Warlord Model

The opposite of the one-firm approach is what Maister/Walker (2006) call the *warlord model*. It encourages internal competition, individual entrepreneurship, distinct profit centres, decentralized decision making and the strength that comes from stimulating many diverse initiatives driven by relatively autonomous operators. In contrast, *McKinsey* expect each office to put the overall organisation's best interest before that of the office itself – a principle that is not compatible with warlord firms.

Coordination Mechanisms

The one firm strategy at *McKinsey* is implemented via a number of coordination mechanisms. The following paragraphs used examples to list important formal and informal coordination mechanisms used by *McKinsey & Co.*

Formal Coordination Mechanisms

Decentralisation of Decision Making

McKinsey is a decentralised organisation. To a great extent, management remains in the hands of the active partners, who are also *McKinsey's* shareholders and manage the company in a *consensus building* style. The individual regions, represented by the respective managing partners, act mostly independently; however, they are bound by the goals and values of the company. In this way, *McKinsey* can reduce the confusion that often accompanies growth by applying formal policies instead of *ad hoc* decisions.

Partnership Committees

The partners also preside over general affairs and the central control of the company. In order for these processes to be efficient, *McKinsey & Co.* established three committees in the 1950s: The *executive committee* was established to act for all of the partners on matters requiring more than a small group of people. The *planning committee* was formed to discuss important management questions and make recommendations to all the partners. Finally, the *profit-sharing committee* was formed to expedite the allocation to profits to the partners (Bhidé 1996). In practice, these committees have proven efficient even when many partners are involved. The decision making process takes longer but decisions are more likely to be accepted by firm members than if the leadership had acted unilaterally. This is another characteristic of the one-firm strategy.

Recruitment Process

Other important formal coordination mechanisms characterise the one-firm strategy. One central element is recruiting. As a one-firm company, *McKinsey* invests a significant amount of senior professional time in its recruitment process and tends to be much more selective than its competitors. As a *McKinsey* partner noted in the 1980s: "It's not just brains, not just present ability: you have to try and detect the potentially fully developed professional in the person, and not just look at what they are now. Some firms hire in a superficial way, relying on the up-or-out system to screen out the losers. We do have an up-or-out system, but we don't use it as a substitute for good recruiting practices" (Maister 1985, p. 8). This strategy is still applied today. Thus, to ensure that all entities follow the same values and goals despite the decentralised organisation, the company tends to "grow their own" professionals, rather than making significant use of lateral hiring of senior professionals. The young graduates are socialised during their time at *McKinsey* and internalise these values quicker than experienced consultants who only join *McKinsey* later in their careers.

McKinsey also adjusts financial incentives to the employee's coordination. Compensation systems (particularly for partners) are designed to encourage intrafirm cooperation and are based mostly on *group performance*, not individual performance. Promotions into a leading position require an associate to prove his long-term contribution to the firm and his impact to the team.

Compensation Mostly on Group Performance

Informal Coordination Mechanisms

McKinsey uses a number of mechanisms to coordinate the decentralised regional offices. The foundation of these mechanisms is the existence of shared values (see Table 10.2), which underpins sustained management effectiveness. The central goal is to establish extensive *intrafirm communication*, with broad use of consensus-building approaches.

Shared Values

Table 10.2 | *Shared Values at McKinsey & Co.*

Put the client's interest ahead of our own This means we deliver more value than expected. It doesn't mean doing whatever the client asks.
Behave as professionals Uphold absolute integrity. Show respect to local custom and culture, as long as we don't compromise our integrity.
Keep our client information confidential We don't reveal sensitive information. We don't promote our own good work. We focus on making our clients successful.
Tell the truth as we see it We stay independent and able to disagree, regardless of the popularity of our views or their effect on our fees. We have the courage to invent and champion unconventional solutions to problems. We do this to help build internal support, get to real issues, and reach practical recommendations.
Deliver the best of our firm to every client as cost effectively as we can We expect our people to spend clients' and our firm's resources as if their own resources were at stake

Source: McKinsey 2014.

Training

To achieve these goals, *McKinsey* invests in firm-wide training, both as a way to increase juniors' substantive skills and as an important group socialisation function. Part of this process is *McKinsey*'s two-week training program for new professionals. The program is run by one or more of the firm's senior professionals, who spend a significant amount of time inculcating the firm's values by telling Marvin Bower stories. The program is specifically designed as a global training program that rotates between the countries where *McKinsey* has offices. This not only supports the one-firm approach but also has a dramatic effect on the young professionals' view of the firm.

Part of these informal mechanisms is imparting *company history*. All young professionals are given a copy of Marvin Bower's history of the firm, *Perspectives on McKinsey*, which unlike many professional firm histories, is full of philosophy and advice and low on historical facts (Maister 1985). The goal is that *McKinsey* employees internalise the company values and work together for the well-being of the company (in contrast to companies that emphasise individual entrepreneurialism, autonomous profit centres, internal competition and highly independent activities).

The criteria according to which new team members are chosen already fulfils this demand: *McKinsey* is looking for graduates that are not only smart, hardworking and ambitious but have also proven agreeable and able to work in a team. The goal is to prevent stardom. *McKinsey* members see themselves as belonging to an institution that has an identity and existence of its own, above and beyond the individuals who happen currently to belong to it.

The principles that guide *employee behaviour* at *McKinsey & Company* are summarised in Table 10.3.

Guiding Principles at McKinsey & Company   *Table 10.3*

We operate as one firm. We maintain consistently high standards for service and people so that we can always bring the best team of minds from around the world—with the broadest range of industry and functional experience—to bear on every engagement.
We come to better answers in teams than as individuals. So we do not compete against each other. Instead, we share a structured problem-solving approach, where all opinions and options are considered, researched, and analysed carefully before recommendations are made.
We give each other tireless support. We are fiercely dedicated to developing and coaching one another and our clients. Ours is a firm of leaders who want the freedom to do what they think is right.

Source: McKinsey 2014.

Summary and Outlook

McKinsey & Co is a consulting firm that wants to keep the balance between a global perspective and local activities. An essential part of coordinating the independent regional entities is the one-firm strategy. This is based on the idea that the company's partners should take essential decisions together and by consensus, that the company's values are more important than short-term success and that the team is more important than individual success.

Maister/Walker (2006, p. 2) summarise the elements of the one-firm approach as follows:

■ highly selective recruitment

■ a "grow your own" people strategy as opposed to heavy use of laterals, growing only as fast as people can be developed and assimilated

■ intensive use of training as a socialisation process

■ rejection of a "star system" and related individualistic behaviour

■ avoidance of mergers, in order to sustain the collaborative culture

■ selective choice of services and markets, winning significant investments in focused areas rather than many small initiatives

■ active outplacement and alumni management, so those who leave remain loyal to the firm

■ compensation based mostly on group performance, not individual performance

■ high investments in research and development

■ extensive intrafirm communication, with broad use of consensus-building approaches.

This approach is supported by *organic growth* of these values in the company history. This leads to a strong culture and clear principles. Because all employees at *McKinsey* follow the same values and strive toward the same goals, every regional entity can act autonomously without fragmenting the global *McKinsey* network.

Nevertheless, a decentralised organisation depends on individual decision-makers. The formal and informal coordination mechanisms have not always been able to keep up, particularly during the dotcom boom and the associated company growth. Therefore, even at *McKinsey* individual executives have taken advantage of their decision making powers and acted in their personal interests instead the company's (e.g. the case of Anil Kumar, mentioned above). Paul Friga, who worked at *McKinsey* in the late 1990s and now lectures on consulting at the University of North Carolina's Kenan-Flagler business school, asks one key question that *McKinsey* needs to answer in the future: "How do you maintain quality with growth?"

Questions

1. What is the one-firm principle? What are the advantages and disadvantages of this strategy? (Discuss the company's owner structure and the role of decentralisation in the organisation of the *McKinsey* entities.)

2. What role do partners play in coordinating the regional entities of the company?

3. Why do recruiting and personnel management play such a central role in the McKinsey's management? What is the employee's role in implementing the formal and informal coordination mechanisms.

References

ANDERSSON, U.; FORSGREN, M. (1996): Subsidiary Embeddedness and Control in the Multinational Corporation, in: International Business Review, Vol. 5, No. 5, pp. 487-508.

BARTLETT, C.A.; BEAMISH, P.W. (2014): Transnational Management: Text, Cases, and Readings in Cross-Border Management, 7th ed., Boston, McGraw-Hill.

BHIDÉ, A.V. (1996): Building the Professional Firm: McKinsey & Co.: 1939-1968, Working Paper, Tufts University.

BIRKINSHAW, J.; MORRISON, A.J. (1995): Configurations of Strategy and Structure in Subsidiaries of Multinational Corporations, in: Journal of International Business Studies, Vol. 26, No. 4, pp. 729-753.

EGELHOFF, W. (1984): Patterns of Control in U.S., U.K., and European Multinational Corporations, in: Journal of International Business Studies, Vol. 15, No. 2, pp. 73-83.

FORBES (2014): America's Largest Private Companies, http://www.forbes.com /companies/mckinsey-company, accessed on August 22, 2014.

GHOSHAL, S.; NOHRIA, N. (1993): Horses for Courses: Organizational Forms for Multinational Corporations, in: Sloan Management Review, Vol. 34, No. 2, pp. 23-35.

HAMEL, G.; PRAHALAD, C. (1983): Managing Strategic Responsibility in the MNC, in: Strategic Management Journal, Vol. 4, No. 4, pp. 341-351.

HEDLUND, G. (1981): Autonomy of Subsidiaries and Formalization of Headquarters Subsidiary Relationships in Swedish MNCs, in: OTTERBECK, L. (Ed.): The Management of Headquarters-Subsidiary Relationships in Multinational Corporations, New York, Gower Publishing, pp. 25-78.

HILL, A. (2011): Inside McKinsey, http://www.ft.com/intl/cms/s/2 /0d506e0e-1583-11e1-b9b8-00144feabdc0.html#axzz33rvBO16g, accessed on August 22, 2014.

HILL, C.W.L. (2013): International Business: Competing in the Global Marketplace, 9th ed., New York, McGraw-Hill.

KHANDWALLA, P. (1973): Viable and Effective Organizational Designs of Firms, in: Academy of Management Journal, Vol. 16, No. 3, pp. 481-495.

KIESER, A.; WALGENBACH, P. (2003): Organisation, 4th ed., Stuttgart, Schäffer-Poeschel.

LAWRENCE, P.; LORSCH, J. (1967a): Differentiation and Integration in Complex Organizations, in: Administrative Science Quarterly, Vol. 12, No. 1, pp. 1-47.

LAWRENCE, P.; LORSCH, J. (1967b): Organization and Environment: Managing Differentiation and Integration, Boston, R.D. Irwin.

MACHARZINA, K. (1990): Führungsstruktur der Unternehmung bei Weltmarktstrategien, in: FEUCHTE, P.; ROMMEL, M.; RUDEL, O. (Eds.): Initiative und Partnerschaft, Baden-Baden, Nomos, pp. 371-383.

MAISTER, D. (1985): The One-firm Firm: What Makes It Successful, in: Sloan Management Review, Vol. 27, No. 1, pp. 3-13.

MAISTER, D.; WALKER, J. (2006): The One-Firm Firm Revisited, http://davidmaister.com/articles/the-one-firm-firm-revisited, accessed on August 22, 2014.

MARTINEZ, J.; JARILLO, J. (1989): The Evolution of Research on Coordination Mechanisms in Multinational Corporations, in: Journal of International Business Studies, Vol. 20, No. 3, pp. 489-514.

MARTINEZ, J.; JARILLO, J. (1991): Coordination Demands of International Strategies, in: Journal of International Business Studies, Vol. 22, No. 3, pp. 429-444.

MCKINSEY (2014): McKinsey, http://www.McKinsey.com, accessed on August 14, 2014.

MORRISON, A.; ROTH, K. (1993): Relating Porter's Configuration/Coordination Framework to Competitive Strategy and Structural Mechanisms: Analysis and Implications, in: Journal of Management, Vol. 19, No. 4, pp. 797-818.

MORSCHETT, D. (2007): Institutionalisierung und Koordination von Auslandseinheiten: Analyse von Industrie- und Dienstleistungsunternehmen, Wiesbaden, Gabler.

NOHRIA, N.; GHOSHAL, S. (1997): The Differentiated Network: Organizing Multinational Corporations for Value Creation, San Francisco, Jossey-Bass.

RUGMAN, A.M.; COLLINSON, S. (2012): International Business, 6th ed., Harlow, Pearson.

THOMPSON, J. (1967): Organizations in Action: Social Science Bases of Administrative Theory, New York, McGraw-Hill.

WELGE, M. (1987): Multinationale Unternehmen, Führung in, in: KIESER, A.; REBER, G.; WUNDERER, R. (Eds.): Handwörterbuch der Führung, Stuttgart, Schäffer-Poeschel, col. 1532-1542.

YOUNG, S.; TAVARES, A. (2004): Centralization and Autonomy: Back to the Future, in: International Business Review, Vol. 13, pp. 215-237.

ZENTES, J.; MORSCHETT, D.; SCHRAMM-KLEIN, H. (2011): Strategic Retail Management: Text and International Cases, 2nd ed., Wiesbaden, Gabler.

Chapter 11

International Organisational Structures as Coordination Mechanism

Organisational structures can be understood to represent the "anatomy" of the organisation. They describe the formal design of the resources and responsibilities. Different organisational structures lead to different behaviours of employees, because the structure and subordination in hierarchies define the focus of work as well as the official channels of knowledge transfer. The aim of this Chapter is to give an overview of organisational structures and to discuss the strengths and weaknesses of each.

Introduction

The *formal organisational structure* is concerned with how the company decides to divide itself into subunits (Hill 2013, pp. 452-453). The structure is the result of a departmentalisation or grouping of activities within organisational units, following the principle of *labour division* as a mechanism of organisational influence (Martinez/Jarillo 1989, p. 489). A fundamental consideration concerning the organisational structure of companies can be based on an argument by Thompson (1967, p. 70), who argued that – under *administrative rationality* – companies that are active in heterogeneous task environments attempt to identify more homogeneous subsegments in those tasks and create organisational units that have responsibility for one of those more homogeneous tasks. Compared with a purely national organisation, MNCs face an *additional heterogeneity*, namely the different conditions in different host countries (Nohria/Ghoshal 1997).

Organisational design can be seen as the *anatomy* of the organisation which describes the formal structure of its resources, assets and responsibilities (Bartlett/Beamish 2014, p. 287). The organisational structure of a company has a number of functions (see, e.g., Griffin/Pustay 2013, pp. 394-395):

- ■ It defines the *activities* that are grouped together and assigns *tasks* to employees.

- ■ It defines the *hierarchical structure*, including lines of authority, subordination and responsibilities within the organisation.

- ■ It designs the *allocation* of organisational resources.

■ It establishes official *lines of communication* to transfer information necessary for problem solving, *decision making* and effective organisational
control.

*Balance
Responsiveness
and Integration*

In particular, for an MNC, the organisational structure helps to influence the
balance between responsiveness and integration. The need for responsiveness stems from diverse requirements that exist due to heterogeneity between countries, but also between product lines and organisational functions. The need for integration comes from the need to coordinate the activities of the MNC in order to ensure effective strategy implementation, to
exploit synergies and to optimise resource allocation (Shenkar/Luo 2008,
p. 314). This *integration* may also, inter alia, be across countries, product
lines, and/or functions. In selecting a specific organisational structure, companies influence the level of differentiation and integration. As with International Management in general, it is the goal of the company to find a structure that balances the needs for (external) *effectiveness* and (internal) *efficiency*.

*Types of
Organisational
Structures*

The most relevant *organisational structures* for internationally active companies are (Griffin/Pustay 2013, pp. 394-404; Deresky 2014, p. 244):

■ domestic structure with export department

■ international division

■ global functional structure

■ global product structure

■ global area structure

■ global matrix structure

■ hybrid global structure.

Structures at Early Stages of Internationalisation

In the early stages of internationalisation, an organisation is often split into
functions reflecting the company's most relevant value chain activities (e.g.
production, marketing & sales, finance, HRM). When companies commence
their international involvement with their first exports, this does not usually
change the organisational structure. Instead, these *exports* are often realised
as part of the activities of the *marketing & sales department*.

*Export
Department*

In the next stage, with increasing exports, the domestic structure may be
expanded by adding a specific *export unit* or *export department* (Deresky 2014,

p. 244). Such a structure is often realised via a *direct reporting structure,* since the export manager reports directly to the top management of the company.

International Division

With further international expansion, *operation modes* often change (see Chapter 14). Sales subsidiaries are common and exporting is often supplemented by foreign production. Thus, the complexity and relevance of international activities lead to a need for internal specialists in those activities. The company may then decide to bundle all foreign activities within an international division which is largely independent. In this structure, the various foreign subsidiaries and activities, from sales offices to production plants, are organised in the *international division* and the subsidiary managers report to its head. This manager, in turn, often has a *direct reporting relationship* to the CEO of the company. The *internal organisation* of the international division may be based on function, product, or geography.

Characteristics of the International Division

The international division allows the MNC to allocate and coordinate resources and it accumulates all knowledge for foreign activities in one organisational unit, facilitating flexible responses to changes in the international environment, such as the emergence of new market opportunities. The division leads to *clear responsibilities.* On the other hand, the separation of all international activities might lead to *conflicts* over additional resources and it runs the risk of reducing the knowledge flow and synergy effects between the international and domestic business. *Redundant efforts* might also pose a problem (Zentes/Swoboda/Morschett 2004, pp. 757-761; Shenkar/Luo 2008, p. 315; Deresky 2014, pp. 244-245).

Integrated Structures

When the relevance of foreign activities grows further, that is, the percentage of foreign revenues increases and the complexity of foreign activities raise due to different types of value-added activities abroad, the deficits of structures in which international and domestic operations are separated become more evident. In such cases, a company may choose to develop an *integrated global structure* in which *domestic and foreign operations* are combined in the same organisational units and are led by the same top managers (Deresky 2014, pp. 244-245). This structure can be organised in various ways, including along functional, product or geographical lines.

Global Functional Structure

In a global functional structure, the activities of the MNC are organised around specific functions of production, marketing, finance, etc. (for an example of such a structure, see Figure 11.1). Departments are created that have *worldwide responsibility* for the specific function.

Figure 11.1

Global Functional Structure at STIHL AG

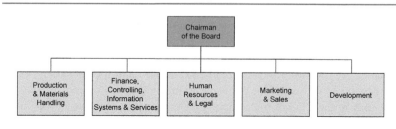

Source: STIHL 2014.

*Advantages
of the
Functional
Structure*

Foreign operations are integrated into the activities and responsibilities of each department, so as to gain *functional specialisation* and accumulate *functional expertise*. Furthermore, function-related *know-how transfer* is facilitated. Usually, functional structures lead to *centralised decision making* and companies that intend to impose *uniform standards* on all their worldwide activities can do that via a functional structure. Thus, this organisational form is sometimes called a *"U-form organisation"*, where the "U" stands for "unitary". For subordinates, a clear line of responsibility and authority is given and duplication of effort can mostly be avoided. Further advantages are presented in Table 11.1.

Table 11.1

Strengths and Weaknesses of a Global Functional Structure

Strengths	Weaknesses
• intensive knowledge transfer concerning the function • focus on key functions • functional expertise • centralisation/standardisation • helps to "unify" the corporation • one line of responsibility • avoidance of double work	• knowledge transfer concerning other fields rather low (specific requirements of certain product groups, regions, customer groups often neglected) • potentially low motivation due to centralisation • slow reaction to changes in certain countries due to standardisation and formalisation • high requirements for information processing by top management • potentially lack of market orientation • difficult for subsidiaries with whole value-added chains

Source: Adapted from Zentes/Swoboda/Morschett 2004, p. 765.

Disadvantages of the Functional Structure

However, the *specific requirements* of certain product groups and regions might be neglected in this structure. There is the risk of a *lack of market orientation* in the organisation and high requirements for information processing at the top, where all major decisions for a function are made.

The structure is mainly appropriate if the company has rather *homogeneous product lines*, i.e. a low level of diversification, and if markets for its products are not strongly heterogeneous. For example, a *global strategy* which intends to exploit economies of scale and international synergies by integrating activities around the world can be implemented through a functional structure.

Global Product Structure

In a global product structure, the activities of the MNC are organised around specific products or product groups (see Figure 11.2). Departments or divisions are created that have worldwide responsibility for all functions concerning the specific product or product group. This structure is frequently used by MNCs. It is often called an "*M-form*" organisation, where "M" stands for "multi-divisional".

Figure 11.2

Global Product Structure at Liebherr

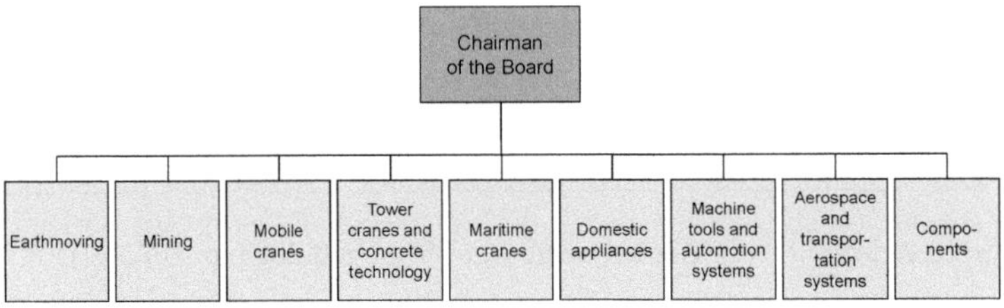

Source: Liebherr 2014.

Advantages of the Product Structure

The product structure allows managers to accumulate knowledge on their specific product or product group and develop substantial expertise. *Knowledge transfer* concerning the product is high. The structure aids *efficiencies in production*, e.g., to achieve economies of scale, and to exploit synergy effects fully. Similarities in needs across different markets are usually emphasised. Managers have the responsibility for all value chain activities for the product, i.e. production, marketing, development, which strongly increases cross-functional collaboration. This facilitates the establishment of *cross-border value chains* for a product, where development might take place in highly developed countries, the manufacturing of most components is located in low-cost countries and other, more sophisticated production steps in industrialised countries (Shenkar/Luo 2008, p. 320). Furthermore, a rapid and flexible response to changes in market conditions is facilitated by this structure.

Disadvantages of the Product Structure

On the other hand, all *functions* (e.g. marketing, sales, and production) are duplicated in this organisational structure. Each product group needs to develop functional skills and often even its own physical facilities for operations. Economies of scope, e.g. knowledge concerning certain production processes or cross-use of new technological economies, are not fully considered. Regional knowledge needs to be developed in each product unit on its own and *divisional egoism* is a common source of conflict. A more detailed list of advantages and disadvantages is shown in Table 11.2.

Table 11.2 | *Strengths and Weaknesses of a Global Product Structure*

Strengths	Weaknesses
• intensive knowledge transfer concerning the product/product groups • focus on differences between products • expertise for specific products • usually high market orientation of product divisions • coordination in companies with heterogeneous products facilitated • holistic view of the value chain • promotion of entrepreneurial behaviour • economies of scale easily exploited • flexible response to changes in product requirements	• duplication of functions • knowledge transfer concerning other fields (e.g. functions, regions) rather low • coordination and cooperation between different product divisions more complicated • risk of divisional egoism • difficult for foreign subsidiaries with more than one product line • lack of economies of scope

Source: Adapted from Zentes/Swoboda/Morschett 2004, p. 767.

Usually, a global product structure is appropriate for companies with very heterogeneous product lines and technological requirements for those product lines, because common expertise for all product lines would be too complex. In particular, the structure can be applied when knowledge exchange and coordination between different product lines are not very important. Furthermore, the product structure is also appropriate for implementing a *global strategy* in which product-specific decisions are standardised worldwide.

Global Area Structure

In a global area structure (also called *global geographic structure* or *regional structure*), the activities of the MNC are organised around specific areas (or regions). An area may be a country or a group of countries. Departments or divisions are created that have responsibility for all functions and all products concerning the specific region (see Figure 11.3).

Global Area Structure at Mondelez International   *Figure 11.3*

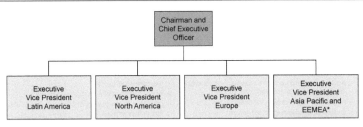

*Eastern Europe, Middle East, Africa

Source: Mondelez International 2014.

Geographic divisions may be based on country borders, but also on cultural similarities (for example the D-A-CH region (Germany (D)-Austria (A)-Switzerland (CH)), regional integration agreements (like the EU), or logistical requirements (Shenkar/Luo 2008, p. 316). Following a trend from globalisation to regionalisation (Rugman/Verbeke 2003), a trend *to geographic organisational structures* seems likely to re-emerge (Shenkar/Luo 2008, p. 316).

Divisions with responsibility for one region facilitate a flexible and rapid response to changes in the local environment and help to exploit *local market opportunities* by enhancing responsiveness. *Coordination* is easier, not least due to geographical proximity. *Lines of authority* are very clear and they are local, providing easy channels for communication. The structure provides a holistic view on all business activities in the region, thereby also helping to develop a uniform image in the region. Market and marketing-oriented companies often use this structure. Regional knowledge is accumulated and regional particularities fully acknowledged in the organisation, which each area tending to be self-contained.

Advantages of the Area Structure

However, integration across the other organisational dimensions is weaker and often, the complexity of heterogeneous product offers is not fully considered. Functions are duplicated in the different regions and due to a *lack of worldwide synergy effects*, resources are often also accumulated and estab-

Disadvantages of the Area Structure

lished in each region. The risk of *regional egoism* emerges and it might be difficult to transfer knowledge across regions. Thus, the diffusion of techno- logical innovations in the organisation may be slow and the "not invented here syndrome" could form a barrier to knowledge transfer. Synergy effects, as well as economies of scale, are often not fully exploited in this structure (Zentes/Swoboda/Morschett 2004, pp. 769-771; Shenkar/Luo 2008, p. 318). A list of strengths and weaknesses is displayed in Table 11.3.

| *Table 11.3* | *Strengths and Weaknesses of a Global Area Structure* |

Strengths	Weaknesses
• intensive knowledge transfer concerning the region • focus on differences between regions • regional expertise • communication and coordination advantages: personal communication as coordination instrument easy to use, due to geographic proximity • holistic view on business in the region • uniform company image in the region • flexible response to changes in local environment (local responsiveness easy)	• duplication of functions • duplication of resources • coordination and knowledge transfer across regions might be difficult and slow • risk of regional egoism • risk of overemphasis on regional differences • risk of low cost efficiency and low economies of scale due to local adaptation • diffusion of technology might be slowed down • "not invented here" syndrome • problems in technologically dynamic environments

Source: Adapted from Zentes/Swoboda/Morschett 2004, p. 770.

Thus, this structure is most appropriate for companies that intend to adapt to foreign markets (such as in the consumer goods sector) and that accept low information flows between different regions. In the I/R-framework (see Chapter 2), a *multinational strategy* seems to correspond closely to the strengths of a global geographic structure.

Other Dimensions of Structures: Customers or Projects

Besides functions, products or areas, other dimensions for global structures are possible. The question for a company is which object of its business is so relevant and at the same time so heterogeneous that it demands specific attention, expertise and treatment. This may be, for construction companies, specific projects.

More and more often, this object is the customer. If a company has very heterogeneous customer groups (such as commercial customers and private customers) or just a few very powerful customers (for example, some auto- motive suppliers or companies that sell their products via independent re- tailers), a company organises around these customers, with specific departments being responsible for a customer group or even a specific customer on a worldwide basis. In the latter case, the *global customer structure* is equivalent to *key account management*.

Global Matrix Structure

While the organisational structures that have been discussed above are *uni-dimensional*, i.e., they structure the top level of the organisation, based on one single dimension (e.g. functions, products, or areas), the matrix design is *multi-dimensional*. A global matrix structure is the result of applying two structural dimensions simultaneously at the highest level of hierarchy.

Global Matrix Structure at Procter & Gamble   *Figure 11.4*

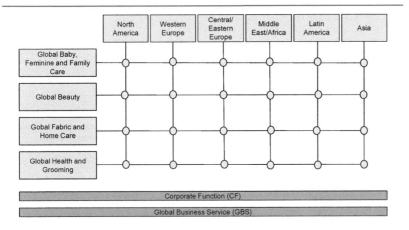

Source: Procter & Gamble 2014.

For example, a global area structure and a global product structure could be used at the same time (see Figure 11.4), but any other combination of areas, functions, regions, customers, etc., is also possible. The managers in the matrix cells (nodes in the grid above) which represent, for example, managing directors of specific foreign subsidiaries, are simultaneously responsible to two executives in the two specified lines of authority.

The main advantage of this structure can be seen in the access to all advantages of the two underlying dimensions, without combining all the caveats. For example, the MNC can build on both the product and the regional expertise of the two different lines of authority. *Knowledge transfer* is inten-   *Advantages and Disadvantages of the Matrix*

sive, and the simultaneous consideration of specific requirements of at least two dimensions makes decision processes complex, but often very balanced between the different needs. This forced consideration of two aspects of the business should lead to an efficient allocation of resources. *Conflicts* in the organisation (which result from the two-dimensional lines of authority) are intended, but are assumed to enhance efficiency. Usually, this structure is *flexible* and easily adapted to changing external conditions. The structure is intended to promote coordination among the different structural dimensions. At the intersection of two lines of authority, a subsidiary manager has to report to two different supervisors. This enhances the information flow and the consideration of different aspects of a decision. However, this can also lead to *ambiguity*, slow decision processes and conflicts which, in this situation, result in pressure on the subsidiary manager. Often, to overcome this problem, a matrix structure is accompanied by decentralisation of decision power to lower levels in the hierarchy. Advantages and disadvantages of the matrix are listed in Table 11.4.

Table 11.4 | *Strengths and Weaknesses of a Global Matrix Structure*

Strengths	Weaknesses
• provides access to advantages of the other organisational structures	• complex and costly
• combination of two or more areas of expertise	• high requirements for information and communication
• good knowledge transfer throughout the organisation	• high requirements for cooperative behaviour
• simultaneous consideration of product, region and/or function	• potential ambiguity of orders
• better allocation of resources due to forced consideration of multiple aspects simultaneously	• decisions may take longer, often extensive meeting culture
• good opportunity to decentralise the decision process	• risk of power struggles
	• appropriate for firms with many products and unstable environments

Source: Adapted from Zentes/Swoboda/Morschett 2004, p. 783; Griffin/
            Pustay 2013, pp. 401-402.

Internal and External Complexity

In particular, in dynamic and heterogeneous industries, a multi-dimensional organisation might be well suited to respond to the *external complexity* (Bartlett/Beamish 2014, p. 368). On the other hand, problems of internal complexity are not worth tackling in the case of relatively stable markets and homogeneous products (Griffin/Pustay 2013, pp. 401-402).

Hybrid Global Structures

Mix of Other Structural Types

Companies with hybrid global structures do not apply the "ideal types", or pure structures that have been described above, but mix elements of different types. For example, a company might decide to organise around products, but one specific product might be so important that the company divides the responsibility for this product among three regional managers. Another example is given in Figure 11.5.

Hybrid Global Structure at Coca-Cola

Figure 11.5

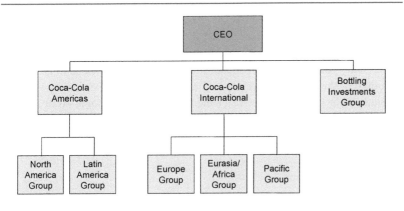

Source: Coca-Cola 2014.

Most MNCs are likely to use – to some degree – hybrid structures and blend elements of all types (Griffin/Pustay 2013, pp. 402-404). The advantages of such mixes are that companies can differentiate between those elements of their business that need *differentiation*, while they can combine and integrate the dimensions that are better suited for *common leadership*. Since these dimensions are often not uniform across all products, functions and/or regions (or customers), a differentiated, hybrid approach might be more suitable. Taking the example of the *Coca-Cola Group*, different geographic areas should obviously be treated differently (and unified within) for most business activities. However, in addition, the organisational unit "bottling investments" manages all of the company's consolidated bottling investments, so as to drive growth and improve operating performance in this field across all markets in which *Coca-Cola* owns the bottling operations fully or partly. This, these operations should be treated uniformly across the world – with the worldwide responsibility given to one division of the *Coca-Cola Group*.

Wide Use of Hybrid Structures

Structure Follows Strategy

As the descriptions of the various organisational structure types have shown, different structures are more or less suitable for specific MNCs. Based on studies by Chandler (1962), it has been proposed that *structure follows strategy*. In this perspective, organisational structure is seen as a mechanism for implementing a certain strategy. Furthermore, since each strategy has specific requirements, the choice of an organisational structure must be adapted to these requirements in order to maximise the success of the respective strategy.

Well known studies on organisational structure, many of them from the late 1960s and early 1970s, investigated the *structure-strategy relationship*. The best known of these studies, by Stopford and Wells (1972), empirically showed a relationship between different elements of the international strategy of the MNC (the degree of international diversification and the percentage of foreign sales) and the likelihood of certain organisational structures (see Figure 11.6).

Figure 11.6	*The Stages Model of Stopford and Wells*

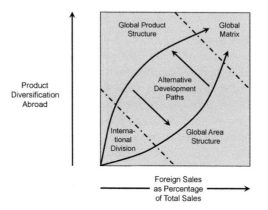

Source: Adapted from Stopford/Wells 1972, p. 65.

Strategic Choice However, the statement that "structure follows strategy" has been criticised as too simplistic. Indeed, it does to be too deterministic. In reality, companies have some *degree of choice* regarding which organisational structure they want to implement, and the strategy does not force the MNC to choose one particular structure. Furthermore, a certain organisational structure also influences resource allocation within the company, as well as company objectives and decision processes. Thus, the strategy process is also influenced by the organisational structure, and sometimes, therefore, "*strategy follows structure*".

In a *contingency perspective*, companies have to align their strategies to the external environment, such as the industry requirements, and, discussed above, differences in the external environment (e.g. between regions) might imply certain organisational structures. Thus, some recent literature argues that there is no unidirectional influence of strategy on structure or vice versa, but that rather corporate strategy and corporate structure have to be aligned to each other with existing degrees of freedom, and *corporate strategy* and *corporate structure* both have to conform to the *external environment*.

Fit between Structure, Strategy and External Environment

Furthermore, different organisational structures have different information processing capacities, and since different MNC strategies result in different information processing requirements, different organisational structures might also be proposed from the information perspective (the *information processing approach* is explained in Chapter 10).

Dynamic of Structures

Studies on organisational structure often identify *patterns of development* (see, e.g., Figure 11.6). In an *evolutionary perspective*, companies may change their structure over time, for instance, as a consequence of learning. As MNCs develop and grow, they may have to change their structure. As has been shown in this Chapter, early internationalisation is often implemented with an international division, while the growing importance of international activities might lead to globally integrated structures.

Even a mature MNC must make structural changes from time to time, such as to facilitate changes in strategy. For example, if the company changes its strategy from global standardisation to regionalisation, an appropriate organisational structure (e.g. a global area structure) strongly supports the implementation of the new strategy. Thus, following the *structure-follows-strategy thesis*, MNCs might adapt their structure when they change their strategy.

Changing Structure when Changing Strategy

However, the simple patterns proposed by Stopford and Wells are often regarded as too simplistic and deterministic, and more recent studies have identified *development paths* from "simpler" types of organisations to more complex ones and vice versa (Buckley 1996, p. 43; Wolf/Egelhoff 2001, p. 136; 2013, pp. 598-600). Changes in the external environment might be another reason for structure switches.

Conclusion and Outlook

Organisational structures are an important *mechanism* for coordinating the international activities of a company. While it has been mentioned that the *"anatomy"* of the organisation is not sufficient as a coordination mechanism, it is undoubtedly a necessary component.

The suitability of certain organisational structures for certain MNC strategies and particular businesses has been discussed in this Chapter. In a dynamic perspective, it becomes evident that the choice of a structure is complex, and deterministic selection models tend to oversimplify. Generally, however, a *fit between strategy, context and structure* is seen as necessary in order to fully exploit the potential of a strategy.

While switches between organisational structures are a very common element of strategic change in organisations, a uniform trend cannot be identified. Some authors observe a trend away from *globalisation to regionalisation*. As a consequence of this trend, global area structures seem to emerge more often, but within regions, and differences often seem rather small. Thus, companies with regional structures tend to integrate their activities across a larger group of countries. For example, consumer goods manufacturers like *Unilever* or *Procter & Gamble* nowadays often combine all their activities in the German-speaking countries – Germany, Austria and Switzerland – into one organisational unit. Similarly, operations in a number of Asian regions or in Latin America are more and more often bundled into one organisational unit.

Further Reading

WESTNEY, D.E.; ZAHEER, S. (2010): The Multinational Enterprise as an Organization, in: RUGMAN, A.M. (Ed.): The Oxford Handbook of International Business, 2nd ed., Oxford, Oxford University Press, pp. 341-366.

WOLF, J.; EGELHOFF, W. (2001): Strategy and Structure: Extending the Theory and Integrating the Research on National and International Firms, in: Schmalenbach Business Review, Vol. 53, April, pp. 117-139.

WOLF, J.; EGELHOFF, W. (2013): An Empirical Evaluation of Conflict in MNC Matrix Structure Firms, in: International Business Review, Vol. 22, June, pp. 591-601.

Case Study: Microsoft[*]

Profile, History, and Status Quo

Founded as a two-man business in a garage in 1975, *Microsoft Corporation* has become one of the largest software companies in the world with more than 100,000 employees in over 100 countries (see Figure 11.7). In addition to developing, licensing and supporting a wide range of software products, *Microsoft Corporation* also designs and sells hardware devices, such as consumer electronics. Besides the world's most widely used operating system, *Microsoft Windows*, and the productivity application *Microsoft Office*, the Multinational Corporation is also known for *Internet Explorer*, the *Xbox* game console, as well as the *Microsoft Surface Series* of tablets.

Development of Total Number of Employees (in thousands)

Figure 11.7

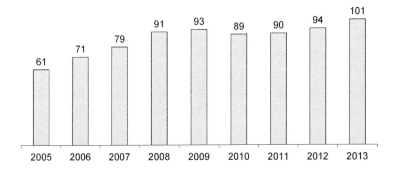

Source: Microsoft 2013a.

The company's success story began with the idea of developing an implementation of the programming language *BASIC* for the recently demonstrated *MITS* (Micro Instrumentation and Telemetry System) product *Altair 8800*. Already in 1978, three years after the foundation, *Microsoft* opened its first international office in Japan. After the initial success with several BASIC-Interpreters (even for one of the first *Apple* computers, the mass-produced *Apple II* microcomputer), a major *milestone* in the company's history was the development of the operating system *MS-DOS* in 1981 for the first *IBM Personal Computer*. In the following years, *Microsoft* released one of the first

---

[*] Sources used for this case study include the website http://www.microsoft.com, various company reports and company presentations, as well as explicitly cited sources.

operating systems (OS) with a *graphical user interface* (GUI). The company named it *"Windows"*, because it best described the boxes that were fundamental to the new OS. Meanwhile, *Microsoft* began introducing its popular office product *Microsoft Office*, a bundle of different applications, such as *Microsoft Word* and *Microsoft Excel*. In 1986, *Microsoft* moved from Bellevue, Washington, to Redmond, Washington, where the company is still located. In the same year, the company went public with an *initial public offering* (IPO), raising 61 million USD at 21.00 USD per share. With the development of *Windows 3.0, Microsoft Windows* had become the most widely used *OS* in the world and broadened its business from then on to different soft- and hardware products.

Focus on Online Services

With the beginning of the *Internet age* and Bill Gates' internal "Internet Tidal Wave memo" in 1995, *Microsoft* started to focus on "computer networking and the World Wide Web". The popular *Windows 95* was the company's first OS including an online service like *MSN* as well as a web browser called *"Internet Explorer"*. Over the years, the *Windows OS* was continuously developed (*Win98, WinNT, Win2000, WinXP, Windows Vista, Windows 7, Windows 8*) and is still the world's most widely used system on personal computers.

Development of New Segments

Besides the software segment, *Microsoft* entered the game console market in 2001 with the first version of the *Xbox* to compete with the main players *Sony* and *Nintendo*.

Starting with revenue of 16,005 USD in 1976, *Microsoft Corporation* doubled its revenues from 2005 to 2013 to 77.9 billion USD (see Figure 11.8).

Figure 11.8 | *Development of Revenue (in billion USD)*

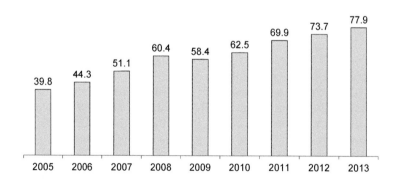

Source: Microsoft 2013a.

Organisational Development over the Years

Since its foundation in 1975, *Microsoft*'s organisational structure has changed several times, although not all changes were visible and openly communicated. Starting as a private company with eleven employees and a *flat organisational structure*, *Microsoft*'s progressive development led to a need to adapt the organisational environment.

Already in 2005, *Microsoft* recognised the upcoming danger of new competitors such as *Google Inc.* and *Yahoo Inc.* and therefore adapted its own structure. These changes were intended to help *Microsoft* "move toward more Internet-based service offerings" (The New York Times 2005). Within this change, the former seven operative business units *"Client"*, *"Server and Tools"*, *"Information Worker"*, *"Microsoft Business Solutions"*, *"MSN"*, *"Mobile and Embedded Devices"* and *"Home and Entertainment"* were aggregated into five new business units:

Organisational Change in 2005

■ The *"Client"* division had the overall responsibility for the technical architecture, engineering, and product delivery of the *Windows* product family. This division was also responsible for the relations between *Microsoft* and computer manufacturers or OEMs, as well as for the marketing, sales and product development expenses.

■ The *"Server and Tools"* division dealt with the development and marketing of software service products, services and solutions.

■ Besides the management of third party alliances, such as *expedia.com* or *MSNBC.com*, the *"Online Services Business"* division was responsible for e-mail and instant messaging. Furthermore, the division was in charge of the *MSN* and live search portals.

■ The *"Microsoft Business Division"* offered the famous *Microsoft Office* products and the *Microsoft Dynamics* business solutions.

■ *Microsoft*'s video game system *Xbox*, as well as the accessories and games, were managed by the *"Entertainment and Devices Division"*.

All these divisions are responsible for engineering as well as for marketing and sales. Through this company structure, *Microsoft* had a classic *divisional organisation structure*. The teams were organised around individual products and not around different functions. Figure 11.9 shows the organisational structure of *Microsoft* as of 2006, including the corporate affairs groups, such as *"Human Resources"* and *"Finance"*. The divisions *Client, Server and Tools* as well as *Online Services Business* report directly to the President of the *"Platforms & Services Division"*.

Figure 11.9 | Microsoft's Organisational Structure as of 2006

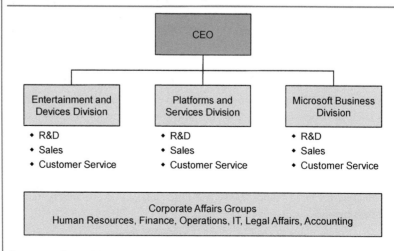

Source: Adapted from Microsoft 2006.

Strategic Change 2013: "One Microsoft"

Mobile Internet as a Driver of Change

Due to the tremendous growth of *broadband and mobile Internet,* as well as changes in consumer experiences with innovative devices such as *tablets and smartphones,* former CEO Steve Ballmer realised the need for change. "We have entered an always-on, always-connected era that holds new promise for what technology can bring people's lives and to businesses everywhere on the planet. And this gives us an opportunity to help people lean in and do more in every part of their lives".

In a memo that was sent to all employees on July 11, 2013, former *Microsoft* CEO Steve Ballmer announced a "far-reaching realignment" of the company in order to position *Microsoft* for the future. This repositioning should help "to innovate with greater speed, efficiency and capability in a fast changing world (...). Today's announcement will enable us to execute even better on our strategy to deliver a family of devices and services that best empower people for the activities they value most and the enterprise extensions and services that are most valuable to business", explained the CEO.

Even in 2012, the strategic change of *Microsoft* commenced with a complete working-over and a fundamental change of the *business model.* Starting predominantly as a software company, *Microsoft* now has to deal with all new competitors on the market. Competing companies like *Apple, Google* and

Facebook already focus on their products, whereas *Microsoft* until now has concentrated on its different divisions, which hindered the company in its efforts to innovate faster and in a more market-oriented manner. A worldwide downturn, in 2012, in PC buying was distinguishable and *Microsoft* also struggled to establish itself in mobile devices and services. Therefore, *Microsoft* developed a single strategy as one company, instead of several different divisional strategies with the overall goal of having *"One Microsoft"*. The idea behind this is to collaborate and allocate resources even more efficiently.

Strategic change had already become apparent from the acquisitions of voice-over-IP service (VoIP) *Skype* in 2011, enabling Microsoft to emerge as a provider of innovative services and devices. Due to this acquisition, *Microsoft* retired its *Windows Live Messenger* instant messaging service. Some further major acquisitions are summarised in Table 11.5.

List of Major Microsoft Corporation Acquisitions   *Table 11.5*

Year	Company
1987	Forethought (computer software)
1997	Hotmail (web-based email service)
2000	Visio (drawing software)
2002	Navision (software programming)
2007	aQuantitave (digital marketing)
2008	Fast Search & Transfer (data search technologies)
2011	Skype (telecommunications)
2012	Yammer (social networking)
2013	Nokia mobile phones unit
2014	Parature (customer service software)

Source: Microsoft 2014.

In the end, *Microsoft* managed to develop from a software provider to a company that focusses on "creating a family of devices and services for individuals and businesses", a typical structure for competitors such as *Apple* and *Google*. As a logical consequence, *Microsoft* acquired the mobile phones unit of the Finnish information technology company *Nokia*, a supplement to the *existing cooperation* between the companies.

Provider of Devices and Services

273

The Impact of "One Microsoft" on the Organisational Structure since 2013

Structure Follows Strategy

In conformity with the *"structure follows strategy"* thesis of Chandler (1962), *Microsoft's* new strategy necessitated some major adjustments to the organisational structure. The former divisional structure was phased out and replaced by a *functional organisational* structure. The five divisions *"Business Division"*, *"Server and Tools"*, *"Windows"*, *"Online Services"*, as well as *"Entertainment and Devices"*, which were renamed continuously since the last major reorganisation disappeared and were substituted by four engineering groups (including supply chain activities and datacentres):

■ The *"Operating Systems Engineering Group"* is responsible for the development of the *OS* for the *Xbox* console, as well as for mobile devices, personal computers and back-end-systems. *Windows* embedded systems that focus mainly on appliances and cars are also included in this group.

■ The *"Devices and Studios Engineering Group"* is responsible for the development of *Microsoft's* hardware products as well as for the studio experiences. In this group, the game console *Xbox* will be advanced to compete with *Sony* and *Nintendo*, as well as the *Microsoft Surface* tablet and other hardware devices, such as mice, keyboards, joysticks and gamepads.

■ The *"Applications and Services Engineering Group"* is taking care of broad application and core services technologies in communication, productivity, search, and other information categories. They produce *Microsoft's* online services *Skype*, *Bing*, *SkyDrive*, *MSN* and *Outlook.com*, as well as the enterprise applications *Exchange* and *SharePoint*. Furthermore, the office software *Microsoft Office* is integrated into this group.

■ The *"Cloud and Enterprise Engineering Group"* deals with the development of back-end technologies, like datacentre, database, and other enterprise IT-related technologies, cloud computing platforms, like *Windows Azure*, and other server-related products.

As a special case, the *"Microsoft Dynamics Team"* was left as it was. No far-reaching changes are planned other than "matrixing in the marketing and some of the other functions" (PCWorld 2014). Besides the engineering groups, the realignment resulted in different *centralised groups*:

■ The *"Advanced Strategy and Research Group"* focusses on the intersection of technology and policy.

■ The *"Marketing Group"* is mainly responsible for centralised advertising and media functions as well as for marketing strategy.

■ The *"Business Development and Evangelism Group"* centralises management with the key partners, especially the innovation partners, such as OEMs and key developers.

■ The *"Finance Group"* takes responsibility for and centralises all product group finance organisations.

■ The *"Legal and Corporate Affairs Group"* including the *General Counsel* deals with the company's legal and corporate affairs.

■ The *"HR Group"* takes care of all staffing issues.

■ The *"COO"* continues leading worldwide sales, field marketing, services, support, as well as IT, licensing and commercial operations.

Figure 11.10 summarises the new organisational structure of *Microsoft* in 2013.

Microsoft's Organisational Structure as of 2013   *Figure 11.10*

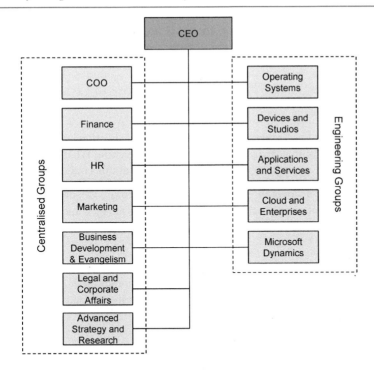

Source: Adapted from Microsoft 2013b.

11

Process Change

To gain from the new strategy and the organisational change, the way staff works together is the key success factor. It is necessary to move on from recent procedures into innovative ways of thinking and acting. *Microsoft* defined *new processes* of working in teams and runs various *initiatives*. Each initiative is handled by a cross-company team, consisting of members from the different groups and will be led by a so-called *"champion"*. The groups have a *core*, which delivers key technology or services. Through this project-like structure, involving the engineering and centralised groups, *Microsoft* wishes to enhance the innovation process in order to be more competitive against the main rival companies.

Summary and Outlook

Founded as a small software enterprise in 1975, *Microsoft* has developed from a software company to a provider of a wide range of IT-related devices and services. Due to this development, organisational changes were the logical consequence, in order to remain competitive in the closely contested technology market. Tremendous organisational change like this needs time to work effectively. However, the odds are that these changes will boost *Microsoft's* endeavour to capture a higher share, especially of the smartphone and tablet markets.

Questions

1. *Microsoft Corporation* fundamentally changed its organisational structure in 2013, from a divisional to a functional structure. What potential problems can accompany organisational changes of this kind?

2. *Microsoft's* overall organisational structure is described as a functional one. What are the important advantages and disadvantages for the *Microsoft Corporation* that result from this shift in organisational structure?

3. As a listed, Multinational Corporation in the IT sector, *Microsoft* is continuously striving to grow. Accordingly, numerous other companies were acquired during the last three decades. Describe the potential impacts of M&As on a company's organisational structure.

Hints

1. See, e.g., Folger and Skarlicki 1999, pp. 35-50.

2. See, e.g., Griffin and Pustay 2013, pp. 398-400.

References

BARTLETT, C.A.; BEAMISH, P.W. (2014): Transnational Management: Text, Cases, and Readings in Cross-Border Management, 7th ed., Boston, McGraw-Hill.

BUCKLEY, P. (1996): The Role of Management in International Business Theory: A Meta-analysis and Integration of the Literature on International Business and International Management, in: Management International Review, Vol. 35, No. 1 Special Issue, pp. 7-54.

CHANDLER, A. (1962): Strategy and Structure: Chapters in the History of the American Industrial Enterprise, Cambridge, MIT Press.

COCA-COLA (2014): 2013 Annual Review, Atlanta.

DERESKY, H. (2014): International Management: Managing Across Borders and Cultures, 8th ed., Boston, Pearson.

FOLGER, R.; SKARLIKI, D. (1999): Unfairness and Resistance to Change: Hardship as Mistreatment, in: Journal of Organizational Change Management, Vol. 12, No. 1, pp. 35-50.

GRIFFIN, R.; PUSTAY, M. (2013): International Business: A Managerial Perspective, 7th ed., Upper Saddle River, New Jersey, Pearson.

HILL, C.W.L. (2013): International Business: Competing in the Global Marketplace, 9th ed., New York, McGraw-Hill.

LIEBHERR (2014): The Organizational Structure of the Group, http://www.liebherr.com/en/deu/about-liebherr, accessed on July 18, 2014.

MARTINEZ, J.; JARILLO, J. (1989): The Evolution of Research on Coordination Mechanisms in Multinational Corporations, in: Journal of International Business Studies, Vol. 20, No. 3, pp. 489-514.

MICROSOFT (2006): Annual Report 2006, Seattle.

MICROSOFT (2013a): Annual Report 2013, Seattle.

MICROSOFT (2013b): One Microsoft, http://www.microsoft.com/en-us/, accessed on June 22, 2014.

MICROSOFT (2014): Acquisition History, http://www.microsoft.com/investor/, accessed on July 14, 2014.

MONDELEZ INTERNATIONAL (2014): Annual Report 2013, Deerfield.

NOHRIA, N.; GHOSHAL, S. (1997): The Differentiated Network: Organizing Multinational Corporations for Value Creation, San Francisco, Jossey-Bass.

PCWORLD (2014): Ballmer: Three-layered Plan Will Lead to "One Microsoft", http://www.pcworld.com/article/2049102/ballmer-threelayered-plan-will-lead-to-one-microsoft.html, accessed on July 22, 2014.

PROCTER & GAMBLE (2014): Corporate Structure, http://www.pg.com/en_US/company/global_structure_operations/corporate_structure.shtml, accessed on July 11, 2014.

RUGMAN, A.M.; VERBEKE, A. (2003): Regional Multinationals: The Location-bound Drivers of Global Strategy, in: BIRKINSHAW, J.M.; GHOSHAL, S.; MARKIDES, C.; STOPFORD, J.; YIP, G. (Eds.): The Future of the Multinational Company, Chichester, Wiley&Sons, pp. 45-57.

SHENKAR, O.; LUO, Y. (2008): International Business, 2nd ed., Thousand Oaks, Sage Publications.

STIHL (2014): Unternehmensstruktur, http://www.stihl.de/unternehmens-struktur.aspx, accessed on July 17, 2014.

STOPFORD, J.; WELLS, L. (1972): Managing the Multinational Enterprise, London, Longmans.

THE NEW YORK TIMES (2005): Microsoft Announces Major Reorganization, http://www.nytimes.com/2005/09/20/technology/20wire-msft.html, accessed on June 22, 2014.

THOMPSON, J. (1967): Organizations in Action: Social Science Bases of Administrative Theory, New York, McGraw-Hill.

WESTNEY, D.E.; ZAHEER, S. (2010): The Multinational Enterprise as an Organization, in: RUGMAN, A.M. (Ed.): The Oxford Handbook of International Business, 2nd ed., Oxford, Oxford University Press, pp. 341-366.

WOLF, J.; EGELHOFF, W. (2001): Strategy and Structure: Extending the Theory and Integrating the Research on National and International Firms, in: Schmalenbach Business Review, Vol. 53, April, pp. 117-139.

WOLF, J.; EGELHOFF, W. (2013): An Empirical Evaluation of Conflict in MNC Matrix Structure Firms, in: International Business Review, Vol. 22, June, pp. 591-601.

ZENTES, J.; SWOBODA, B.; MORSCHETT, D. (2004): Internationales Wertschöpfungsmanagement, Munich, Vahlen.

Chapter 12

Corporate Culture as Coordination Mechanism

The concept of corporate culture has gained attention in International Management practice and research since the late 1970s. In particular, the success of Japanese companies with their different management style raised awareness of the so-called "soft factors" that strongly contributed to those companies' success. This Chapter explains the phenomenon and development of corporate culture and describes its contribution to the coordination of an MNC.

Introduction

While the traditional model of the MNC primarily focuses on coordination via formal (or so-called bureaucratic) mechanisms, where the performance and the behaviour of managers of foreign subsidiaries is tightly controlled and supervised, modern network-oriented models of the MNC propose the use of *normative integration* as the dominant coordination mechanism. Here, coordination is mainly provided through an organisation-wide culture. The employees and managers of the MNC accept and adopt the values and objectives of the company and act in accordance with them (Birkinshaw/Morrison 1995, p. 738).

Normative integration (also called *socialisation*) refers to building a strong *organisational culture* or *corporate culture* of known and shared strategic objectives and values (Egelhoff 1984). Corporate culture can be defined as "a pattern of shared basic assumptions that was learned by a group as it solved its problems of external adaptation and internal integration, that has worked well enough to be considered valid and, therefore, to be taught to new members as the correct way to perceive, think, and feel in relation to those problems" (Schein 2004, p. 17).

Corporate Culture

When considering corporate culture as a coordination mechanism, the focus is on the power of culture to shape behaviour and on the active and conscious socialisation of members of the organisation, in particular managers at HQ and the foreign subsidiaries, in a system of joint values, objectives and perspectives (Birkinshaw/Morrison 1995, p. 738). Coordination through *normative integration* means functional behaviours and rules for determining them have been learned and internalised by individuals, thereby obviating the need for procedures, hierarchical orders and surveillance. These formal mechanisms may be partially replaced by social integration, as individuals choose to do what the hierarchy would have ordered or what is prescribed by the procedures (Edström/Galbraith 1977, p. 251).

Corporate culture is a particularly important organisational attribute for companies operating in an international environment (Bartlett/Beamish 2014, pp. 288-289). First, employees come from a variety of different national and cultural backgrounds. Thus, management cannot assume that they will all automatically share common values and relate to common norms. Second, since subsidiaries and HQ management are separated by large distances, formal coordination mechanisms are often limited in their effectiveness. Therefore, shared values might be a more powerful coordination tool.

Levels of Corporate Culture

As with all cultural phenomena (see also Chapter 9 on country culture), most scholars emphasise that corporate culture has different levels. While Schein's well-known model includes three levels of culture (see Figure 7.1), most authors distinguish only two (Sackmann 2006, pp. 26-27; Kutschker/Schmid 2011, p. 675):

Percepta Level

■ On the surface there is the level of visible *artefacts*, which includes all cultural phenomena that are easily perceived and can be empirically observed. This is also called the *percepta level*. The main *manifestations* of culture are the *behaviour* of the organisation's members and *symbols*. *Material symbols* include the company's buildings and architecture, the interior design, the work places, the dress code, etc. *Interactional symbols* include traditions, customs, rites and rituals as well as taboos, etc. *Verbal symbols* include the company's specific language, stories, myths, slogans, etc. (Schmid 1996, pp. 145-151).

Concepta Level

■ The underlying foundation of corporate culture – its real cultural core – operates on a deeper level. This *concepta* level includes the basic assumptions, values, norms and attitudes that prevail in the organisation.

Several components of this cultural core can be identified (Muijen 1998, pp. 113-132; Kutschker/Schmid 2011, pp. 688-690).

Basic Assumptions

Basic assumptions are the deepest level of a corporate culture. They refer to general and abstract basic beliefs about reality, humans, society, etc. Usually, these basic assumptions are unconscious and become taken for granted. "In fact, if a basic assumption comes to be strongly held in a group, members will find behaviour based on any other premise inconceivable" (Schein 2004, p. 31).

Values express essential consequences of basic assumptions. They define a set of normative and moral anchors that guide the behaviour of organisation members and provide a sense of common direction for all employees (Deal/Kennedy 1982, p. 21). Values reflect assumptions about what is right or wrong. The current shift of company practices and visions to include corporate social responsibility (see Chapter 13) can be seen as an enhanced relevance of certain values.

Norms are informal principles about what actions are expected in a particular situation. They are embedded in values and provide group members with standardised behavioural rules of a binding nature. Compared to values, norms are less abstract and more instrumental. They link basic assumptions and values to actual behaviour and offer guidelines for specific situations.

Frequently, the levels of culture are compared to an *iceberg*. The artefacts form the visible part of the iceberg that sticks out of the water. However, only the "tip of the iceberg" is visible and this tip rests upon a much larger and hidden basis – the assumptions, values, norms, etc. (Kutschker/Schmid 2011, p. 675). This makes it very difficult for researchers – and also company management – to capture completely understand a corporate culture. This is particularly true since many cultural phenomena are subconscious; even the members of the organisation itself are not fully aware of them.

Values

Norms

Types of Corporate Cultures

Given the complexity of corporate cultures, there are naturally many categorisations to be found in the literature. A well-known categorisation by Deal and Kennedy (1982) describes cultures from a contingency perspective. It is argued that external factors are responsible for the success or failure of certain corporate cultures. The model includes four types of culture (see Figure 12.1):

Corporate Culture in a Contingency Perspective

■ A *tough-guy, macho culture* fits in industries in which success and failure occur very quickly. The risk attached to individual decisions is very high and feedback from the market comes very rapidly. Examples include venture capital companies, the media or management consulting. The focus is mainly on speed, not endurance.

■ A *bet-your-company culture* fits where managers have to take very big decisions but years can pass before they pay off (or not). This high-risk, slow-feedback environment is present in the oil industry, in mining companies, in capital-goods companies, etc. These companies must invest vast sums in projects that take years to come to fruition.

■ *Work hard/play hard cultures* are often found in sales-oriented organisations, e.g. automotive distribution or retail, as well as in fast-moving consumer goods. The employees of these companies live in a world of comparatively low risk, since no single sale, product or even new store is likely to be a huge success or dramatic failure for the MNC. Feedback is very rapid, often on a daily basis. Activity and dynamic change is highly important; more than other corporate cultures, this culture relies on competition and internal contests, including motivational events, company parties, etc.

■ Finally, companies in industries where the market provides little or no feedback on employee performance and risks are small tend to develop a *process culture*. Public administration is a typical example of a sector in which this occurs. The financial stakes for each decision are generally low, but unlike in the *work hard/play hard* culture, employees obtain virtually no feedback. As a result, they have no idea how effective they are until someone complains. This lack of feedback forces employees to focus on *how* they do something, not *what* they do. The values in this culture focus on technical perfection, i.e., getting the process and the details right.

Figure 12.1 | *Generic Corporate Cultures*

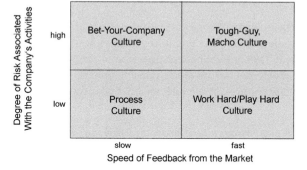

Source: Adapted from Deal/Kennedy 1982, pp. 107-108.

Effects of Corporate Culture as Coordination Mechanism

Organisational culture greatly influences the way the MNC operates. "Normative integration is the glue that holds differentiated networks together as entities called firms" (Nohria/Ghoshal 1997, p. 6). More practically, normative integration and shared values that are accepted and understood by the different members of an organisation guarantee that "the actors want what they should want and act as they should act" (Nohria/Ghoshal 1997, p. 118).

A tremendous advantage of normative integration – a subtle, indirect and implicit mechanism – is that the subsidiary can act autonomously without direct orders from the HQ in daily operations, in a *highly flexible* manner and with the opportunity to adapt to the local context, and yet its conduct is still aligned with company goals. Instilling shared values and beliefs across subsidiary managers and HQ makes it more likely that subsidiaries will use their specific local knowledge and resources to pursue the interests of the MNC as a whole and not just their own partisan interests, even in the absence of formal control by HQ. It provides common rules for encoding, decoding and interpreting information and for achieving mutual understanding. In contrast with formal coordination methods, the direction provided to organisation members is aggregate rather than specific. Overall, normative integration allows for a more decentralised decision-making process (Baliga/Jaeger 1984, p. 27; Martinez/Jarillo 1989, p. 498; Birkinshaw/Morrison 1995, p. 738).

Decentralisation and Integration

Monitoring for normative integration occurs through interpersonal interactions. Since all members of the culture are familiar with and share its expectations, performance and compliance with the culture are observed by many members of the organisation and feedback is given verbally, often in informal conversations (Jaeger 1983, p. 94).

Monitoring through Interpersonal Interactions

The positive effect can also be explained from the perspective of the *principal-agent theory* (see Chapter 6). Here, common values can be seen as a tool to reduce the risk of an agent's *opportunistic behaviour* since normative integration enhances the alignment between the objectives of the principal and the agent (Ouchi 1980, p. 138). Similarly, corporate culture should influence the negative assumption of opportunism in *transaction cost theory* (see Chapter 6). From the perspective of behavioural theory, a positive disposition toward the organisation created through normative integration may reduce opportunism (Ghoshal/Moran 1996, p. 21).

More concretely, corporate culture serves a number of functions within a company (Sackmann 2006, pp. 29-31; Kutschker/Schmid 2011, pp. 676-677):

■ *Reduction of complexity*: Culture facilitates the daily business of the MNC. It serves as a perception filter, and the collective thought patterns provide situation-specific guidelines that link to established and proven behaviour patterns. It also supports the cooperation of individuals in an organisation by offering guidelines for behaviour and help in understanding and interpreting the actions of others.

■ *Providing a source of meaning and motivation*: The specific content of the basic assumptions will influence the extent to which employees derive meaning from their work. Thus, the MNC's culture affects the motivation of employees and their willingness to put effort into the business, since it provides a legitimate basis and deeper purpose for actions.

■ *Ensuring continuity*: The stability of a strong corporate culture protects the organisation from sudden, unplanned changes.

Commitment to the MNC

A further objective of normative integration is to create *commitment* to the MNC as a whole. In this context, "commitment" can be defined as comprising three elements (Edström/Galbraith 1977, pp. 255-256): *Identification*, i.e. adopting the values and objectives of the MNC as one's own; *involvement*, i.e. psychological immersion or absorption in one's work; and *loyalty*, i.e. a feeling of affection for and attachment to the organisation.

Developing a Strong Corporate Culture

A culture's primary characteristic is that it concerns aspects and thoughts that are shared or held in common by the members of a group (Schein 2004, p. 12). Therefore the main aim of a company intending to coordinate through normative integration is to create a strong corporate culture by inducing individuals to internalise the values and objectives of the organisation (Ghoshal/Moran 1996, p. 25). The following paragraphs present tools that are considered to be particularly important to affect normative integration in an MNC (Bartlett/Beamish 2014, pp. 288-289, 368-372).

Building a Shared Vision

The first instrument to achieve effective normative integration within an MNC is a clear, shared understanding of the MNC's vision and objectives. In a complex organisation like an MNC, every manager's frame of reference may be limited to their specific responsibilities. The only way to integrate specific responsibilities within a broader framework and give every individual's roles and responsibilities a context is by developing a clear sense of *corporate purpose*, shared and understood by every manager and employee.

Such a shared vision for the MNC should fulfil three criteria: clarity, continuity and consistency.

■ For a corporation's vision to achieve *clarity*, it has to be *simple*. *ABB* corporate vision can serve as an example: "As one of the world's leading engineering companies, we help our customers to use electrical power efficiently, to increase industrial productivity and to lower environmental impact in a sustainable way" (ABB 2014). The vision has to be *relevant* and important to the people concerned. The vision should not be too abstract; the broad objectives of the vision have to be linked to concrete agendas and actions. Finally, it has to be constantly *reinforced*, for example by always referring to the vision when developing annual plans or budgets. *Clarity*

■ *Continuity* of purpose underscores the enduring relevance of the organisation. Despite changes in the company's management and short-term adjustments, the broad sweep of strategic objectives and organisational values must remain constant over a longer period of time. Managers and employees in different parts of the world will only develop a shared understanding of the company's vision over time. *Continuity*

■ Finally, to be effective, *consistency* has to be ensured, i.e., that everyone within the MNC shares the same vision. Inconsistency, or strong subcultures, carries with it the risk of confusion and might even lead to chaos, with different units of the organisation pursuing policies and behaviours that are mutually conflicting. *Inconsistency* may involve differences between what managers of different organisational units consider to be the MNC's primary objectives. *Consistency*

Role Models

The second tool for creating a strong company culture is the visible behaviour and public actions of senior management. They represent the clearest role models for behaviour and provide a signal of the company's strategic and organisational priorities. A well-known example is Akio Morita, the CEO and founder of *Sony Corporation*, who moved to New York for several years to establish *Sony's* US operations, clearly emphasising the relevance of this overseas business. Another example is Richard Branson, founder of the *Virgin Group*.

Many strong corporate cultures are shaped by company founders or long-term managers. Often this is done through *charisma*, which is a particular ability to capture subordinates' attention and to communicate major assumptions and values in a clear and vivid manner (Schein 2004, p. 245). However, there are also more systematic ways for leaders to embed the organisation's culture in individuals. The following are the primary embedding mechanisms (Schein 2004, p. 246):

- What leaders pay attention to, measure and control on a regular basis.

- How leaders react to critical incidents and organisational crises.

- How leaders allocate resources.

- How leaders deliberately act as role models, teach and coach their subordinates.

- How leaders allocate rewards and status.

Heroes Role models can be *founders, managers* or any other important person in the MNC's past or present. Sometimes these are seen as "heroes" that personify the culture's values (Deal/Kennedy 1982, p. 14). Jack Welch at *General Electric*, Gottlieb Duttweiler at *Migros*, Jeff Bezos of *Amazon* and many others are all role models whose behaviours and principles are known to almost every employee in the company.

Initial Socialisation

The development of an organisational culture through a process of socialisation includes communicating the way of doing things, the decision-making styles in the MNC, etc. (Martinez/Jarillo 1989, p. 492). Thus, an organisation has to pass on elements of its culture to new members of the organisation. Initial socialisation is particularly relevant since it provides the individual with a clear view of the work context, guides experience, and orders and shapes personal relationships. It educates new members of the organisation about the range of appropriate solutions to problems they may encounter during work, the rules for choosing particular solutions and the goals and values of the organisation (Maanen/Schein 1979, p. 212; Nohria/Ghoshal 1997, pp. 158-159).

Compared with organisations in which formal coordination instruments are dominant, MNCs with predominantly cultural coordination attach a higher relevance to *training* and *socialisation*. A new member of the organisation must not only learn a set of explicit, codified rules and regulations, but he or she must also learn and become a part of a subtle and complex coordination system which consists of a broad range of values and norms. Thus, the orientation programme for new employees is usually intensive, and new employees of foreign subsidiaries are more frequently sent to HQ or other subsidiaries for training (Jaeger 1983, pp. 94-96).

Human Resource Policies

To build common norms and values, a strong emphasis is placed on human resource (HR) policies such as the selection, promotion and rotation of managers (Edström/Galbraith 1977).

Members of an organisation that attempts to build a strong corporate culture must be integrated into the organisational culture in order to be functional and effective actors in the organisation. Therefore, *selection* of members is of prime importance. In addition to having the necessary hard skills for the job, a candidate must be sympathetic to the organisational culture and willing to learn and to accept its norms, values and behavioural prescriptions (Jaeger 1983, p. 94). *Promotion* policies can emphasise the relevance of technical skills or focus on the relevance of interpersonal skills and personal flexibility. *Measurement* and *reward systems* (see Chapters 22 and 23) can be built around different performance indicators, thus indicating their importance.

Continued international transfer throughout an employee's career is seen as a key tool for achieving normative integration, and is simultaneously a powerful means of facilitating the necessary information flow within the MNC (Martinez/Jarillo 1989, p. 498). These *job transfers* also help individual managers to understand how the MNC network functions, increase knowledge of the network, develop multiple contacts within it and increase the likelihood that these contacts will be used to support the overall strategy (Edström/Galbraith 1977, p. 251). This is automatically linked to a high proportion of expatriates in upper and middle management positions in foreign subsidiaries (Baliga/Jaeger 1984, p. 26).

Intensive Employee Transfers

Another element of the HR strategy that facilitates the establishment of a strong corporate culture is *long-term employment*. It is generally emphasised that stability of membership in a group is necessary for the existence and continuity of a culture. Thus, a "hire and fire" strategy weakens the corporate culture, since MNCs cannot invest in an employee's socialisation if it is expected they will leave soon (Baliga/Jaeger 1984, p. 27).

Long-Term Employment

Other Measures and Tools

In addition to the ones mentioned above, additional tools can be used to strengthen the corporate culture. These are essentially all instruments that are also used to promote formal and informal *lateral communication* between managers and employees in different organisational units, including:

- direct managerial contact through regular visits from HQ management to the subsidiaries and vice versa

- regular meetings and conferences

■ permanent or temporary cross-country teams (like committees or task forces)

■ integrated roles (e.g. managers serving as linchpins between different organisational units).

Together with the substantial use of *expatriates*, these activities can create informal and interpersonal communication networks between dispersed organisational units, contributing to the creation of a strong corporate culture and leading to normative integration (Edström/Galbraith 1977, p. 258; Nohria/Ghoshal 1997, p. 6).

Caveats of Normative Integration

Compared with bureaucratic control, the explicit *costs* for normative integration tend to be greater, involving greater use of expatriates and frequent visits between headquarters and subsidiaries, meetings, international task forces, etc.. In addition, intensive initial socialisation requires long and expensive training sessions (Baliga/Jaeger 1984, pp. 29-31).

Another concern is the limited ability of MNCs that are dominantly based on cultural coordination to handle employee turnover. This is a particular problem in industries with very volatile demand. If such a company needs to adapt its workforce accordingly, this would limit its potential to establish a strong corporate culture (Baliga/Jaeger 1984, p. 36).

Culture is also a stabilising factor. While this is often valuable, it can cause difficulties when adjusting to major environmental changes. Most changes in a corporate culture must be incremental, because people's beliefs cannot be changed quickly (Baliga/Jaeger 1984, p. 36).

Three Culture Transfer Strategies

Finally, a major question for an MNC is whether it is possible and effective to transfer a corporate culture into a host country which may be strongly divergent from the home country culture. Organisational culture is very often embedded in the national culture of the home country (see Chapter 9). In the case of an MNC, however, the organisational culture has to spread across different national cultures. Generally, an MNC has three options for its culture strategy (Scholz 2014, pp. 469-471):

■ a *monoculture strategy* in which the corporate culture of the parent company is transferred to all foreign subsidiaries

■ a *multiculture strategy* where all foreign subsidiaries are allowed to develop their own organisational cultures which can then be closely aligned to the host country cultures

■ a *mixed culture strategy* where a homogeneous or at least harmonised corporate culture develops as a *synthesis* between the parent company culture and the cultures of the different foreign subsidiaries.

In the case of a multicultural strategy, the MNC consciously avoids using cross-national normative integration as a coordination mechanism. Only the monoculture strategy and the mixed culture strategy actively use corporate culture as a unifying mechanism. In the case of cultural coordination, the internal values and behaviour patterns of the subsidiary must be similar to those of the headquarters and those of other subsidiaries, and a largely *homogeneous culture* must exist throughout the MNC (Jaeger 1983, p. 96). However, differences between subsidiaries need not be completely avoided. To a certain degree, these might even help exploit the advantages of being an MNC. But, a minimum level of harmonisation has to be ensured to avoid intercultural communication barriers and diverging sets of values within the MNC.

Conclusion and Outlook

Every company has a specific corporate culture – whether intentionally or not (Sackmann 2006, p. 26). If actively used, the coherence in values and objectives created by a strong corporate culture can be a powerful coordination mechanism, giving all managers and employees a common direction for their decisions and actions.

Corporate culture is a particularly important coordination mechanism in *transnational organisations*. Sufficient flexibility for each subsidiary to remain responsive to local differences while retaining enough consistency to benefit from global opportunities and synergies cannot be achieved through formal coordination alone (Martinez/Jarillo 1989, p. 500). With effective normative integration, foreign subsidiaries can be granted a high level of autonomy and the MNC can still be assured that their conduct is aligned with the company's objectives and strategies.

Further Reading

MUIJEN, J. van (1998): Organizational Culture, in: DRENTH, P.; THIERRY, H.; DE WOLFF, C. (Eds.): Organizational Psychology: Handbook of Work and Organizational Psychology, 2nd ed., London, Psychology Press, pp. 113-132.

SCHEIN, E. (2004): Organizational Culture and Leadership, 3rd ed., San Francisco, Jossey-Bass.

12

Case Study: Apple[*]

Profile, History and Status Quo

In 2013, *Apple Inc.* declared worldwide revenues of 170 billion USD, while maintaining over 400 retail stores in 13 different countries, employing approximately 80,000 full time professionals. The company's product line consists of personal computers, portable media devices and digital music players. They also sell and deliver digital content, such as music, movies, books and games through their in-house online distribution channels: the iTunes Store, the App Store and the iBookStore.

Steve Jobs, Steve Wozniak and *Ron Wayne* founded *Apple Inc.* in the US state of California in 1977. Their first product – a micro-computer board called *Apple I* – was sold to small businesses. Their second model – the *Apple II* with an additional floppy disk drive and colour graphic interface – became the first globally successful *personal computer*.

Macintosh   In 1984, *Steve Jobs* was in charge of the *Macintosh* project at *Apple Inc.* With its highly innovative graphical user interface, the *Macintosh* became the first computer which could be utilised by ordinary consumers without any background knowledge or specific computer skills. Although the *Macintosh* was easy to use, the computer itself was a commercial failure and *Apple's* net income fell a daunting 17% in 1985. As a consequence of this mismanagement, the executive board ordered Steve Jobs to leave the company, shortly followed by *Steve Wozniak*.

From 1985 to 1993, *John Sculley*, a former *PepsiCo* CEO and marketing expert, was *Apple's* chief executive officer. He was hired by *Steve Jobs* in 1983, who reportedly asked him: "Do you want to sell sugared water all your life?" He and *Apple* faced massive competition from *IBM* computers, as well as rapid changes in technology. They also had to deal with the expanding field of venture capital-driven investments that created new competitors, combined with the uncertainty of which markets to aim for.

Sculley was unable to solve these problems, so *Michael Spindler* (engineer and *Apple's* former president) succeeded him, becoming CEO from 1993 to 1996. *Gilbert Amelio*, a PhD physicist and former CEO of *National Semiconductor*, was Apple's CEO from 1996 to 1997.

These rapid shifts in higher management positions inevitably resulted in a lack of consistency in the corporate strategy and culture. Furthermore, the

---

[*] Sources used for this case study include the website http://www.apple.com, and various annual and interim reports, investor-relations presentations and explicitly cited sources.

290

business market was almost entirely dominated by the cooperation between *Windows* operating systems and *Intel* processors. The lack of a consistent strategy resulted in a huge variety of products and projects, which were either never completed or completely failed.

Despite the huge success of the *PowerBook* laptop computer in the 1990s, various attempts to create a set-top box for TVs and infamous *Newton* personal digital assistant completely failed. *Don Norman*, a well-known design expert who worked as the vice president of an advanced technology company from 1993 to 1997, noted that more than 70 *Macintosh* computer models were released between 1992 and 1997. Critics identified that the rapid proliferation of models confused customers and increased complexity at *Apple*.

Meanwhile, *Steve Jobs* founded *NeXT Incorporation* and the first computer animation film studio *Pixar*. In 1997, *Apple Inc.* bought *NeXT* for 427 million USD and *Steve Jobs* returned to the company as CEO. Immediately after his return, *Steve Jobs* drastically reduced the product portfolio, changed the distribution system, established the *www.apple.com* website for direct sales, and reintegrated himself into the process of innovation.

Steve Jobs and Tim Cook

In 1998, *Tim Cook*, a former employee of *IBM*, became *Apple's* new chief operating officer. As time moved on, Jobs and Cook drastically pushed the development of extremely original, creative, innovative and very successful products, like the *iMac*, the portable laptop *MacBook*, the music player *iPod*, the *iPhone* and the tablet PC *iPad*.

Thanks to this enormous progress, *Apple Inc.* became the world's most valuable brand in 2013, according to the *Omnicom Group's* "Best Global Brands" report. Since August 24, 2011, *Tim Cook* has been the CEO, succeeding *Steve Jobs* who passed away the same year.

The most important brand values of *Apple Inc.* spring from the creative dynamic source of *Steve Jobs* and *Tim Cook*. Both placed particular value on *innovation, communication, high quality,* and *user experience*. They believed that *Apple* should not only be innovative in the technical sense of the word, but also in the sense that their products should fulfil and satisfy the needs of the customer, with clear advantages over competing products. Table 12.1 outlines these principles.

Table 12.1   *Apple's Brand Values*

Brand Values	Characteristics
Innovative	frequent hardware and software updates
Customer Support	highly trained and skilled retail staff; on-site ability for the customer to get their hands on the product
High Quality Products	high build quality; low error count in both hardware and software, therefore a low amount of customer complaints
Great Design	high attention to detail; an overall consistent brand image, reflected by design, form and function
Easy to Use	no previous background knowledge required

Source: Adapted from Apple 2014.

Corporate Structure

Apple Inc.'s headquarters are located in California. They also have office facilities in Cork in the South of Ireland. *Apple's* products are all designed in the headquarters in California and produced by *Foxconn*, a Taiwanese electronics manufacturing company. *Apple's* international activities are primarily focused on their retail stores. *Apple Inc.* run over 400 retail stores in 13 countries with highly standardised furnishings and a minimalist design, mostly located in hot-spot locations such as shopping malls and other highly frequented places. The company has cultivated a monoculture strategy and assigns its predefined brand values and norms to all international stores. There are no local adjustments to the products or services. On location, the highly trained staff provides product information, services and training for the operating systems and hardware to ensure a satisfying customer shopping experience. *Apple* sees offering a high quality sales and after-sales experience as the key to retaining existing customers and gaining new clients. The company currently sells and resells their own and third-party products directly to consumers in most major markets. For this reason, *Apple* could be seen as a work-hard/play-hard culture company. It's a sales oriented organisation, which currently generates 30% of total net sales through these direct distribution channels.

Passion   These high product and service quality standards became the underlying principle not only for the retail stores, but for every department at *Apple*. Steve Jobs always insisted that all members of the executive board be fully integrated and full of *passion* for the products they developed. He believed that, as long as all managers or leaders involve themselves in the development process, employees would follow. They have to contribute and become an important part of the products' success. *Jobs* always emphasised that strong leadership, appealing product characteristics and an outstanding user experience are far more important than simple economic rationality.

Steve Jobs would often say that *Apple Inc.* was the biggest start-up business worldwide, because it was a gathering of teams, consisting of a leader with his fellow players, where each team was always responsible for a specific assignment. These tasks always varied depending on the given business processes, e.g. marketing, retail, design and engineering. *Apple* is split into ten departments as shown in Figure 12.2. The company's structure is characterised by minimal management layers, high levels of teamwork and overall confidence that every department will be able to accomplish its tasks in the most efficient manner without being constantly supervised. Therefore interpersonal meetings and verbal proposals became the most important management control tool.

Biggest Start-Up
Business
Worldwide

Apple´s Departments

Figure 12.2

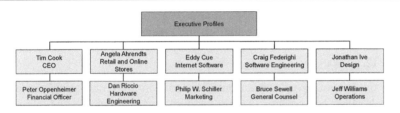

Source: Adapted from Apple 2014.

Working as an efficient "digital hub" is the primary vision, once espoused by *Steve Jobs* himself. Hence, all employees are urged to work as a team, raising industry standards and making the *Macintosh* into the workstation of choice for customers around the world. In addition, the software package *iLife* (including *iPhoto*, *iMovie*, *iTunes*, *Keynote*, *Numbers* and *Pages*) allows *Macs* to control mobile devices, cameras, music players, smartphones and all other office applications – a huge competitive advantage (Yoffiie/Rossano 2012, pp. 7-8).

Corporate Culture

Most prominently, *Apple* enjoys an unusually deep *brand loyalty* from their customers. Known for their highly innovative products and outstanding quality, their creativity arises from their organisational, employee and product value characteristics. The following analysis focuses on these different aspects of *Apple's* corporate culture.

The first factor involves *internal communication* at *Apple*. *Apple* is not a company with strict processes and rules. Instead, they encourage an open and honest communication culture. Where other companies may not show much interest, *Apple* highly values the opinions and perspective of all its employees. The higher management always strives to include any internal feedback to improve the overall process. The goal is an atmosphere where *honesty* is the most valued characteristic and the key factor for product success.

This kind of commitment automatically ensures that the best ideas or best problem solutions will be communicated to the top managers as soon as possible. Furthermore, valuing employees' contributions and opinions lets them know how important they are to success factors and productivity, resulting in increased loyalty and passion for the company.

The multitude of different ideas creates a rapidly evolving process, influencing designs, products, services, processes and solutions, which are always being improved and refined through interpersonal communication. *Steve Jobs* focused exclusively on product improvement and success, not cost reduction or efficiency management, always striving for perfection (Lin et al. 2012, p. 2300).

A fundamental part of this mentality is to recruit the right people for every task. *Apple* has crafted a highly complex and selective process to acquire only the best. Taking every possible dimension into consideration, they focus on the candidate's *vision, passion* and *personality*. *Steve Jobs* always had an eye for innovation and creativity, which were also a part of his character.

Jobs encouraged interdisciplinary collaboration across all departments. Even though every team worked on their own tasks, *Jobs* considered them as all being in the same boat simultaneously rowing towards the same product. An overall understanding of other parts of the company is a vital part of steady progress, because it enables sophisticated interdisciplinary problem solving. This coordinated approach also insures that the solutions reached can be integrated with the rest of the company. An organic approach ensures that these problems are recognised long before they would have been in a classical, linear approach (Lin et al. 2012, p. 2301).

In the 1970s, *Steve Jobs* proclaimed the advantages of personal computers for the individual customer – a revolutionary mindset in those days. Based on the idea that people should be able to use this technology without any background knowledge, he expected they would ultimately "fall in love" with computers. As time went by, this approach became the guiding principle for every development process, completely skipping any market research techniques. They relied solely on the idea that the leadership was able to anticipate the needs of people in the future and that the most elegant solution would most likely survive the selection process. This was supported by the cultural typology *Apple* established, which has strongly influenced the external perception of this brand worldwide (Thomke/Feinberg 2010, p. 2).

Summary and Outlook

Apple Inc. is committed to bring the best user experience to its customers through innovative hardware, software and services. The company's business strategy exposes its unique ability to design and develop its own operating systems, hardware, application software and services to provide outstanding products and solutions which are easy to use, seamlessly integrated and innovatively designed. Continued investment in research and development, marketing and advertising are critical to the development and sale of innovative technologies, which is a key factor of the brand value.

Summarising the corporate culture elements, the following factors are of upmost importance to *Apple*:

- Increase internal communication.

- The best ideas are obliged to be implemented, irrespective of their origin in the hierarchy.

- Inspire the employees and encourage them to voice their own thoughts.

- Focus on any detail which could increase value to the user.

- Pay attention to customer feedback.

- Define a vision for the company.

All these elements symbolise the company's philosophy on an abstract level. These elements of the corporate culture act as coordination mechanisms and engage the employees with the company's vision.

Questions

1. Explain and illustrate *Steve Jobs'* "digital hub" strategy.

2. How important was *Steve Jobs* to *Apple's* success, and how different is the vision of the company under CEO *Tim Cook*?

3. Due to the unbearable working conditions at *Apple's* supplier *Foxconn*, several *Foxconn* employees died in 2010. Evaluate the possible image damage Apple may face because of this incident.

Hints

1. Visit the company website and the annual report for further information.

2. See, e.g., Lin et al. 2012, p. 2298.

3. See Yoffiie and Rossano 2012.

References

ABB (2014): Our Strategy, http://new.abb.com, accessed on July 12, 2014.

APPLE (2013): Annual Report, http://investor.apple.com/secfiling. cfm?filingID=320193-95-16&CIK=320193, accessed on August 21, 2014.

APPLE (2014): Apple, http://www.apple.com, accessed on August 14, 2014.

BALIGA, B.; JAEGER, A. (1984): Multinational Corporations: Control Systems and Delegation Issues, in: Journal of International Business Studies, Vol. 15, No. 2, pp. 25-38.

BARTLETT, C.A.; BEAMISH, P.W. (2014): Transnational Management: Text, Cases, and Readings in Cross-Border Management, 7th ed., Boston, McGraw-Hill.

BIRKINSHAW, J.; MORRISON, A.J. (1995): Configurations of Strategy and Structure in Subsidiaries of Multinational Corporations, in: Journal of International Business Studies, Vol. 26, No. 4, pp. 729-753.

DEAL, T.; KENNEDY, A. (1982): Corporate Cultures: The Rites and Rituals of Corporate Life, Reading, Basic Books.

EDSTRÖM, A.; GALBRAITH, J. (1977): Transfer of Managers as a Coordination and Control Strategy in Multinational Organizations, in: Administrative Science Quarterly, Vol. 22, pp. 248-263.

EGELHOFF, W. (1984): Patterns of control in U.S., U.K., and European Multinational Corporations, in: Journal of International Business Studies, Vol. 15, No. 2, pp. 73-83.

GHOSHAL, S.; MORAN, P. (1996): Bad for Practice: A Critique of the Transaction Cost Theory, in: Academy of Management Review, Vol. 21, No. 1, pp. 13-47.

JAEGER, A. (1983): The Transfer of Organizational Culture Overseas: An Approach to Control in the Multinational Corporation, in: Journal of International Business Studies, Vol. 14, No. 1, pp. 91-114.

KUTSCHKER, M.; SCHMID, S. (2011): Internationales Management, 7th ed., Munich, Oldenbourg.

LIN, S.-P.; HUANG, J.-L.; CHANG, J.; KAO, F.-C. (2012): How to Start Continuously Improving Innovation in Organizational Knowledge, in: Technology Management for Emerging Technologies (PICMET), 2012 Proceedings of PICMET '12, Vancouver, pp. 2290-2309.

MAANEN, J. van; SCHEIN, E. (1979): Toward a Theory of Organizational Socialization, in: STAW, B. (Ed.): Research in Organizational Behavior, Greenwich, CT, JAI Press, pp. 209-269.

MARTINEZ, J.; JARILLO, J. (1989): The Evolution of Research on Coordination Mechanisms in Multinational Corporations, in: Journal of International Business Studies, Vol. 20, No. 3, pp. 489-514.

MUIJEN, J. van (1998): Organizational Culture, in: DRENTH, P.; THIERRY, H.; DE WOLFF, C. Eds.): Organizational Psychology: Handbook of Work and Organizational Psychology, 2nd ed., East Sussex, Psychology Press, pp. 113-132.

NOHRIA, N.; GHOSHAL, S. (1997): The Differentiated Network: Organizing Multinational Corporations for Value Creation, San Francisco, Jossey-Bass.

OUCHI, W. (1980): Markets, Bureaucracies, and Clans, in: Administrative Science Quarterly, Vol. 25, pp. 129-141.

SACKMANN, S. (2006): Success Factor: Corporate Culture, Gütersloh, Bertelsmann Foundation.

SCHEIN, E. (2004): Organizational Culture and Leadership, 3rd ed., San Francisco, Jossey-Bass.

SCHMID, S. (1996): Multikulturalität in der internationalen Unternehmung, Wiesbaden, Gabler.

SCHOLZ, C. (2014): Personalmanagement: Informationsorientierte und verhaltenstheoretische Grundlagen, 6th ed., Munich, Vahlen.

THOMKE, S.; FEINBERG, B. (2010): Design Thinking and Innovation at Apple, Boston, Harvard Business School Publishing.

YOFFIIE, D.; ROSSANO, P. (2012): Apple Inc. in 2012, Boston, Harvard Business School Publishing.

Chapter 13

MNCs' Corporate Social Responsibility

The interface between business and society is changing in a world in which new environmental and social risks are emerging and the challenge of sustainability is ever more apparent. The roles, responsibilities and functions of business, especially with regard to MNCs in the context of globalisation, have to be redefined. This discussion has led to the development of the concept of corporate social responsibility (CSR) over the past few years. This Chapter presents models and instruments to explore and organise CSR within MNCs.

Loss of Confidence, the Challenge of Responsibility and Sustainability

Global companies and even large local companies are suffering a crisis of confidence. Figure 13.1 shows several incidents that have stimulated the evolution and development of Corporate Social Responsibility (CSR).

Events in the Evolution and Development of CSR

Figure 13.1

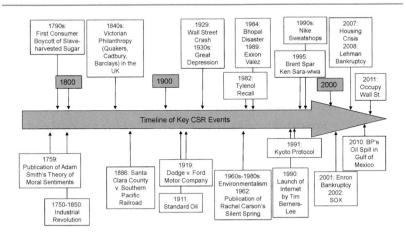

Source: Adapted from Chandler/Werther 2014, p. 15.

Contemporary society expects sustainability and responsibility from its companies, which means that the traditional role of companies ("the only business of business is to do business," ascribed to *Milton Friedman*) has to be rewritten.

Companies are required to act "sustainably", i.e., to act responsibly in a wider context that goes beyond the predominantly economic view (Jonker/De Witte 2006, p. 2). Sustainability in this context refers to the (external) environment and demands care in using resources, such as water, raw materials, energy, etc. Companies are not the only entities held responsible for the environment. The new normative perspective includes topics such as human rights, child labour, etc. Organisations have to meet the needs of a wide range of internal and external *stakeholders*. A stakeholder can be defined, according to Freeman (1984, p. 46), as "any group or individual who can effect or is affected by the achievement of the organization's objectives". Stakeholders include customers, suppliers, stockholders, employees, banks, non-governmental organisations (NGOs) and society in general.

Corporate Social Responsibility and the Stakeholder View

Historical Roots

The concept of corporate social responsibility has gained importance over the past few years. In academic discussion, however, it is by no means a new idea: The concept itself and the debate about CSR date back to the 1930s. For example, Dodd (1932, p. 1149) argues that managers are not only responsible to their shareholders but they are also responsible to the public as a whole because a company is "permitted and encouraged by the law primarily because it is a service to the community rather than because it is a source of profit to its owners". The concept has developed since then, and many more facets of responsiveness have been added to the understanding of CSR.

Schuler and Cording (2006, p. 544) point out that CSR is "a voluntary (i.e. not directly mandated by government regulation) business action that produces social (third-party) effects". Therefore, the general concept includes three main domains:

■ social outcomes

■ market and social behaviour

■ voluntary behaviour.

Triple Bottom Line Concept

Under this approach, firms are responsible for their social and environmental effects on society, in addition to generating profits. On the most basic level, the *triple bottom line concept* (TBL) claims that companies should not only measure their success through financial performance (e.g. profits or return on investment) but need to take into account their impact on the broader economy, the environment and general society (Savitz/Weber 2014, p. 4; see Elkington 1997).

Profit, People, Planet

Measures to Capture the Triple Bottom Line

Table 13.1

Economic	Environmental	Social
sales, profits, ROI	pollutants emitted	health and safety record
taxes paid	carbon footprint	community impacts
monetary flows	recycling and reuse	human rights, privacy
jobs created	water and energy use	product responsibility
supplier relations	product impacts	employee relations

Source: Adapted from Savitz/Weber 2014, p. 5.

Company success, in this view, has to be measured in a multidimensional way, capturing mainly these three areas (see Table 13.1). In a helpful mnemonic, the triple bottom line concept refers to "profit, people, planet", and hence can be seen as the "PPP-approach".

Corporate Social Responsibility Pyramid

Carroll (1979; 1991) developed the widely used *"corporate social responsibility pyramid"* (see Figure 13.2).

According to this concept, corporate social responsibility is conceptualised as four expectations that society has of organisations:

- ◼ the economic domain ("being profitable")
- ◼ the legal domain ("obeying the law")
- ◼ the ethical domain ("being ethical")
- ◼ the philanthropic domain ("being a good citizen").

Figure 13.2 | *Corporate Social Responsibility Pyramid*

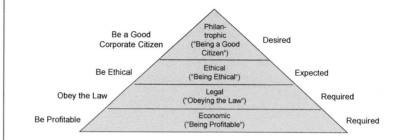

Source: Carroll 1991.

Stakeholder Map for an MNC

Stakeholders and Shareholders

The concept of CSR is seen within the *stakeholder approach*. According to this view, a firm should not only maximise profit for *shareholders*, but should satisfy the aspirations of all stakeholders (Mellahi/Frynas/Finlay 2005, p. 107).

Figure 13.3 | *MNC Stakeholders*

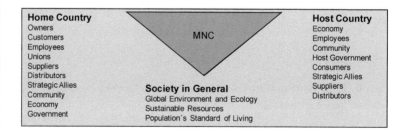

Source: Adapted from Deresky 2014, p. 62.

Figure 13.3 shows the wide variety of stakeholders, all of which have different issues and concerns. Multinational firms have to pay attention not only to the stakeholders in their *home country* but also to those in a multitude of *host countries*.

CSR Management Model

Companies' CSR activities or practices can be classified in different ways (see, e.g., Schramm-Klein et al. 2014). According to Sen and Bhattacharya (2001), CSR activities can be categorised into six broad fields:

- community support (e.g. health programmes, educational initiatives)

- diversity (e.g. family, gender or disability-based initiatives)

- employee support (e.g. job security, safety concerns)

- environment (e.g. waste management, pollution control, animal testing)

- non-domestic operations (e.g. overseas labour practice, operations in countries with human rights violations)

- product (e.g. product safety, antitrust disputes).

The CSR activities or practices of a corporation have to be embedded in the organisation, i.e., linked to the business proposition and every added value in the value chain (Jonker/De Witte 2006, p. 4). Based on this approach, an *integrated management model* can be developed (see Figure 13.4).

The CSR Management Model   Figure 13.4

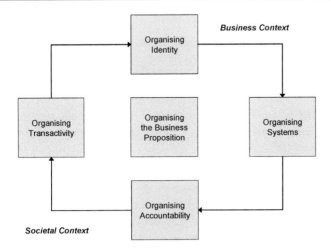

Source: Jonker/De Witte 2006, p. 5.

The starting point of the CSR model is a company's *business proposition*, comprising vision, mission and overall competitive strategy. Four interlinked domains have to be defined under the umbrella of the business proposition in either a business or competition context and societal context (Jonker/De Witte 2006, p. 6):

■ *Organising identity*: This covers issues such as core values, branding, image and corporate identity.

■ *Organising systems*: This refers to internal and external communication and the design of primary and supporting processes.

■ *Organising accountability*: This includes auditing, reporting, monitoring performance and standards.

■ *Organising transactivity*: This includes developing partnerships, organising dialogues, etc.

International Codes of Conduct

For *organising accountability*, a considerable number of organisations have developed codes of conduct which provide consistent *guidelines* for Multinational Corporations, for instance in production and sourcing.

Business Social Compliance Initiative

BSCI As an example, the *Business Social Compliance Initiative* (BSCI) of the European *Foreign Trade Association* (FTA) can be used to demonstrate how retail and wholesale companies follow codes of conduct, implement and run audits and react through corrective actions in global purchasing:

■ The BSCI Code of Conduct is built on internationally recognised labour standards to protect workers' rights, in particular the *ILO Core Labour Conventions.*

■ The practical implementation of the code is controlled by independent auditing companies accredited by the international organisation *Social Accountability International (SAI)*, which issues the *SA8000* standard. To control the BSCI process, the members share the results of their audits in a common database. This also avoids multiple audits, thus reducing *audit fatigue.*

■ The BSCI is based on a *development approach* and does not rely solely on audits. It aims to continuously improve the social performance of suppliers, encouraging them to apply for SA8000 certification. The BSCI develops follow-up measures such as implementation controls and training measures in order to support suppliers.

■ The whole BSCI process is accompanied by local and European stake-holder networks, which bring their expertise to the initiative and help to ensure the long-term local ownership of the process. Cooperation with governmental authorities, trade unions, NGOs and associations also fa-cilitates social acceptance and independence of the system.

Social Accountability 8000 (SA8000)

The Social Accountability Standard 8000 (SA8000), published in late 1997 and revised in 2008 and 2014, is a credible, comprehensive and efficient tool for assuring human rights in the workplace. The SA8000 system includes (Social Accountability International 2014):

■ *factory-level management system requirements* for ongoing compliance and continual improvement

■ independent, expert *verification of compliance* by certification bodies ac-credited by Social Accountability Accreditation Services (SAAS)

■ *involvement from stakeholders* including participation from all key sectors in the SA8000 system, workers, trade unions, companies, socially respon-sible investors, non-governmental organisations and government

■ *public reporting* on SA8000 certified facilities and Corporate Involvement Programme (CIP), annual progress reports through posts on the SAAS and SAI websites

■ *harnessing of consumer and investor concern* through the SA8000 Certifica-tion and Corporate Involvement Programme by helping to identify and support companies that are committed to assuring human rights in the workplace

■ *training partnerships* for workers, managers, auditors and other interested parties in the effective use of SA8000

■ *research and publication* of guidance in the effective use of SA8000

■ *complaints, appeals and surveillance processes* to support the system's quali-ty.

Overview

The SA8000 Standard is based on the *international workplace norms* of the *International Labour Organisation* (ILO) *conventions*, the *Universal Declaration of Human Rights* and the UN *Convention on the Rights of the Child*. The main elements of the SA8000 standard are (Social Accountability International 2014):

SA8000 Elements

- *Child Labour*: No workers under the age of 15; minimum age lowered to 14 for countries operating under the ILO Convention 138 developing country exception; remediation of any child found to be working.

- *Forced or Compulsory Labour*: No forced labour, including prison or debt bondage labour; no holding of deposits or workers' identity papers by employers or outside recruiters.

- *Health and Safety*: Provide a safe and healthy work environment; take steps to prevent injuries; regular training of workers in health and safety; system to detect threats to health and safety; access to bathrooms and potable water.

- *Freedom of Association and Right to Collective Bargaining*: Respect the right to form and join trade unions and bargain collectively; where law prohibits these freedoms, facilitate parallel means of association and bargaining.

- *Discrimination*: No discrimination based on race, caste, national or social origin, religion, disability, gender, sexual orientation, family responsibilities, union or political affiliation or age; no sexual harassment.

- *Disciplinary Practices*: No corporal punishment, mental or physical coercion or verbal abuse.

- *Working Hours*: Comply with the applicable law but, in any event, no more than 48 hours per week with at least one day off for every seven-day period; voluntary overtime paid at a premium rate and not to exceed 12 hours per week on a regular basis; overtime may be mandatory if part of a collective bargaining agreement.

- *Remuneration*: Wages paid for a standard work week must meet legal and industry standards and be sufficient to meet the basic needs of workers and their families; no disciplinary deductions.

- *Management Systems*: Facilities seeking to gain and maintain certification must go beyond simple compliance to integrate the standard into their management systems and practices.

CSR and Profitability

Conflicting Results

Many studies have addressed the impact of CSR activities on companies' performance, focusing, among other things, on companies' market value or corporate financial performance. Despite the number of studies into this relationship, there is still limited understanding of whether and how CSR actions have a positive impact on firms' performance. This is mainly due to the *conflicting results* of these empirical studies. Several scholars show that the returns on CSR activities are positive in some studies but insignificant or negative in others (see Schramm-Klein et al. 2014 and Aguinis/Glava 2012). Peloza (2009) argues that these differing results are mainly due to the lack of consistency regarding the conceptualisation of the CSR construct and the variability in measures used to capture financial performance across different studies.

For example, Figure 13.5 illustrates a comparison between the development of the Morgan Stanley Capital International Index (MSCI World), which includes 1,500 stocks in 23 developed countries worldwide with no expressed commitment to sustainability, and the Dow Jones Sustainability Index (DJSI World). This index includes more than 330 global companies that are committed to sustainable development. This comparison shows a (modest) advantage in total return for the second group. "Companies that balance the interests of multiple stakeholders do as well or better than their peers when it comes to financial performance" (Gossen 2007, p. 17; see also Scholz/Zentes 2006, pp. 288-300).

DJSI World
vs.
MSCI World

Development of DJSI World and MSCI World

Figure 13.5

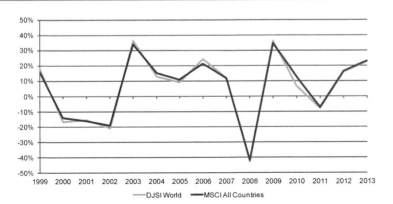

Source: Robecosam 2014.

Environmental responsibility is a measure increasingly used in *public rankings* of companies. For example, Table 13.2 shows the *"Newsweek* Green Ranking" that ranks world's biggest companies according to their sustainability. These rankings underline the growing public interest in companies' environmental and social activities.

Sustainability Ranking and Reporting

Table 13.2 | *Newsweek Green Ranking: World's Greenest Companies*

Rank	Company Name	Industry Group	Energy Productivity	Carbon Productivity	Water productivity	Waste Productivity	Reputation	Newsweek Green Score
1	Vivendi	Telecommunication Services	73.3%	67.8%	97.6%	82.9%	87.7%	85.3%
2	Allergan	Pharmaceuticals, Biotechnilogy	72.2%	85.2%	61.1%	82.0%	100.0%	85.1%
3	Adobe Systems	Software & Services	82.7%	87.1%	99.2%	91.9%	51.4%	84.4%
4	Kering	Consumer Durables & Apparel	67.7%	70.2%	81.5%	82.2%	90.1%	83.6%
5	NTT DOCOMO	Telecommunication Services	81.7%	57.7%	90.5%	90.6%	100.0%	83.1%
6	Ecolab	Materials	73.2%	80.1%	84.3%	59.6%	90.1%	82.6%
7	Atlas Copco	Capital Goods	78.0%	89.4%	81.9%	87.4%	58.7%	77.2%
8	Biogen Idee	Pharmaceuticals, Biotechnilogy	69.2%	82.7%	84.5%	97.0%	53.4%	75.7%
9	Compass Group	Consumer Service	74.3%	69.3%	91.3%	83.9%	87.4%	75.3%
10	Schneider Electric	Capital Goods	73.0%	71.9%	79.5%	68.0%	57.0%	75.3%
11	Centrica	Utilities	57.4%	82.2%	58.5%	82.6%	65.6%	75.2%
12	Kone	Capital Goods	73.6%	63.9%	69.5%	59.4%	72.2%	74.4%
13	Hyundai Mobis	Automobiles & Components	85.7%	94.9%	72.2%	53.6%	81.7%	72.3%
14	Skandinaviska Enskilda Banken	Banks	66.6%	92.3%	66.6%	53.3%	51.7%	72.1%
15	Christian Dior	Consumer Durables & Apparel	58.5%	67.6%	36.3%	50.5%	100.0%	71.9%
16	Bayerische Motoren Werke	Automobiles & Components	75.0%	87.5%	83.6%	82.2%	11.0%	71.4%
17	Adidas	Consumer Durables & Apparel	81.8%	90.0%	84.3%	81.7%	3.6%	71.4%
18	Cardinal Health	Health Care Equipment & Services	75.5%	70.1%	81.9%	64.6%	61.0%	71.0%
19	Itau Unibanco Holding	Banks	59.6%	90.6%	49.4%	56.9%	62.1%	70.9%
20	Baker Hughes	Energy	75.4%	74.9%	60.8%	14.1%	85.3%	70.8%

Source: Newsweek 2014.

CSR and Corporate Governance

Corporate social responsibility is an important part of *business ethics*. Besides the responsibility towards the environment and the observance of human rights, other ethical issues include the appropriate moral behaviour with regard to *bribery* (corruption), especially in the international arena of competition (see, e.g., Deresky 2014, pp. 71-74), and good and responsible *governance*.

Corporate governance rules clarify the rights of shareholders with regard to the general meeting (of stockholders), the supervisory board, and the management board, they establish guidelines for *transparency* and the treatment of *conflicts of interest* in order to promote the *trust* of investors, customers, employees and the general public in the company's management and supervision.

For example, the "German Corporate Governance Codex" comprises the following rules concerning these conflicts with regard to the supervisory board:

German Corporate Governance Codex

- ■ Each member of the Supervisory Board shall inform the Supervisory Board of any conflicts of interest which may result from a consultant or directorship function with clients, suppliers, lenders or other business partners (Article 5.5.2).

- ■ Advisory and other service agreements and contracts for work between a member of the Supervisory Board and the company require the Supervisory Board's approval (Article 5.5.4).

Conclusion and Outlook

Under a variety of headings, such as corporate social responsibility, corporate citizenship, stakeholder engagement or corporate governance, lively debates have emerged worldwide about the roles, functions and balance of and between institutions in contemporary society. In this context, the acceptable *social behaviour* of companies is being redefined in order to achieve a new *societal balance*.

New Societal Balance

This is of great importance for MNCs, which operate not only in their developed home country, but also in a multitude of host countries, frequently in less developed (transition) countries with low wages and low standards of environmental and labour conditions.

Ethical behaviour of MNCs, in the sense of corporate social responsibility, raises the problem of potential competitive disadvantages due to the *opportunistic behaviour* of competitors. *Non-compliance* with social and environmental standards can lead to advantages in costs and therefore better competitive positions in the global arena.

Opportunistic Behaviour

This opportunistic behaviour is probably a short-term approach, because corporate social responsibility is an investment in the competitiveness of companies, true to the motto "What is good for society, is also good for business" (Jack Welch, the former CEO of *General Electric*).

Further Reading

CHANDLER, D.; WERTHER, W. (2014): Strategic Corporate Social Responsibility: Stakeholders, Globalization and Sustainable Value Creation, 3rd ed., Thousand Oaks, SAGE Publications.

PORTER, M.E.; KRAMER, M.R. (2006): Strategy & Society: The Link between Competitive Advantage and Corporate Social Responsibility, in: Harvard Business Review, Vol. 84, No. 12, pp. 78-92.

SCHOLZ, C.; ZENTES, J. (Eds.) (2014): Beyond Sustainability, Baden-Baden, Nomos.

Case Study: Coop/Remei[*]

Overview

This case study provides an example of a cooperation in the context of corporate social responsibility (CSR) and sustainability, including ethical sourcing, sustainable production, support for the local community in developing countries and the success of such initiatives in the international market from the companies *Coop* and *Remei*, both based in Switzerland.

Coop is the second largest retail company in Switzerland. Its turnover was 17.3 billion CHF in 2013 (i.e. 14.3 billion EUR).

Store Brands   The consumer cooperative *Coop* has more than 2.5 million members. *Coop* has a network of more than 1,400 outlets in Switzerland including convenience stores, small and large supermarkets and hypermarkets. In its stores the company offers a broad assortment of food and non-food products. Besides well-known manufacturer brands, they stock a large variety of socially responsible and sustainable *Coop* store brands – which account for more than half of sales – focussing on organic and fair-trade products in several categories. These are crucial to the company's overall success (see Figure 13.6). This shows the remarkable relevance of social, ethical and environmental factors for successfully conducting business. These are also reflected in the company's *code of conduct*, which is mainly based on transparency, solidarity, fairness and extraordinary environmental and social efforts.

---

[*] Sources used for this case study include the websites http://www.coop.ch and http://www.remei.ch, along with information, press releases, annual reports and sustainability reports from Coop and Remei.

Figure 13.6

naturaplan	**Coop Naturaplan** Organically produced food bearing the Bio Suisse bud label, including regional organic specialties. Uncompromisingly organic, uncompromisingly tasty.
naturafarm	**Coop Naturafarm** Swiss meat and eggs from animals and poultry reared subject to very rigorous animal husbandry standards, with stalls designed to meet animals' needs and feed that is free of genetically modified plants.
oecoplan	**Coop Oecoplan** Environmentally friendly products for home and garden, flowers and plants with Bio Suisse bud logo, timber products with the FSC label, products made from recycled materials, energy-efficient appliances and ecological services.
naturaline BIO COTTON	**Coop Naturaline** Textiles made from organically grown cotton and produced according to socially and environmentally responsible methods, and plant-based cosmetic products.
Pro Montagna	**Pro Montagna** Products produced and processed in the Swiss mountain areas – with a donation tot he Coop Aid for Mountain Regions scheme.
Presidio Slow Food	**Slow Food** Traditional, sustainably manufactured specialities for rediscovering the pleasure of real food.

Source: Coop 2013a.

One of *Coop's* most successful store brands is *Naturaline,* introduced in 1993, which focuses on textiles and fashion products sourced from organic cultivation and fair trade, and cosmetics produced from natural raw materials.

In cooperation with the Swiss trading company *Remei,* a supplier of high quality fashionable textiles from fair trade organic cotton – the foundation *bioRe*® was established. The aim of the foundation and of this alliance is to help people in developing countries to help themselves. The foundation invests to improve the quality of work and life for farmers and their families in India and Tanzania. The efforts include support for the cultivation of organic cotton as well as social projects to ensure a long-term secure existence within a healthy environment. In doing so, the vision of *bioRe*® was to manufacture high quality fashion products in a controlled and transparent way, from organic farming through to the processing of finished products, always satisfying ecological and social requirements based on five principles:

- *Organic*: Promotion of, and conversion to, controlled organic farming and crop rotation.

■ *Fairness*: Dignified conditions of work for farmer families and textile workers.

■ *Ecology*: No use of toxic chemicals.

■ *Transparency*: Full product traceability and control over all stages of the production process.

■ *Innovation*: Long-term thinking and environmentally conscious use of resources involving reduction and offsetting of CO_2 emissions.

From the beginning, adherence to these principles has led to a successful partnership in which *Coop* and *Remei* have reached several milestones over the past twenty years (see Figure 13.7). Overall, sustainability in several areas of corporate social responsibility is an integral part of the cooperation and a cornerstone for its long-term success. The sustainable characteristics of *Naturaline's* labelled textiles and fashion products include CSR initiatives throughout the entire supply chain, including organic farming, processing of organic cotton, and the monitoring of these processes. They have also established training centres for local farmers, hospitals and village schools and invested in the social infrastructure.

Figure 13.7 | *Milestones in the Cooperation between Coop and Remei*

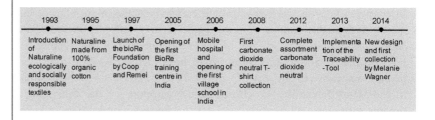

Sustainable and Social Responsible Sourcing of Merchandise

BSCI | In 2005, *Coop* committed to the *BSCI Code of Conduct* (Business Social Compliance Initiative). The company has committed itself to auditing its suppliers of non-food products on a regular basis. To meet the high CSR standards of the BSCI as well as the company's high standards for its *Naturaline* products, *Coop* had to cooperate with a strong partner, whose core competence was the sourcing of high-quality textiles and fashion products. Furthermore, this business partner had to fulfil the same high standards with regard to sustainability and socially responsible corporate behaviour as *Coop* had defined for their own business, especially with regard to the sourcing of merchandise. The use of raw materials associated with destruction of the tropical forests or loss of bio-diversity is prohibited. Packaging must use as little material as possible and should only generate a minimum of waste.

In this context, both *Coop* and *Remei* try social, ethical and environmental aspects for their overall business success into account, without compromising their economic goals. The *bioRe®* foundation promises to pay its farmers *fair wages* and provide good working conditions. Farmers have the opportunity to organise themselves into worker unions and they have the right to enjoy equality of opportunity, regardless of race, colour or other characteristics.

Organic Farming

The cultivation of organic cotton is one of the key elements of *Naturaline* and therefore the cooperation between *Coop* and *Remei*. Cultivation of organic cotton has had a positive impact not only on the environment but also the farmers' social and economic well-being. Traditional cultivation of cotton requires a huge amount of pesticides and fertilisers and genetically modified seeds were often used. In *developing countries* farmers often cannot afford these expensive means of production. Therefore, they have to take out a loan and pay high interest rates (up to 36%). In years with a poor harvest, farmers are often pushed into a spiral of debt.

In *organic farming*, the situation is completely different. Farmers in the *bioRe®* foundation cannot use such expensive chemicals. The *bioRe®* foundation offers interest-free loans for the acquisition of seeds and agricultural equipment. The stabilisation of the ecosystem and renouncing monocropping has mitigated the negative impact of poor harvests in years with drought or pest infestation. Additionally, the farmers receive a monetary bonus for the organic cotton (up to 15% of the average market price), creating added value. The ban on pesticides not only has a positive impact on the farmers' financial situation; it is also good for their health. Accidents or chronic diseases as a consequence of the use of pesticides and fertilisers will be avoided.

The farmers from the *bioRe®* foundation obtain considerable logistic support, and it is further guaranteed that the foundation will purchase their organic cotton. The cultivation of (organic) cotton also requires a huge amount of water. This causes serious problems in regions which are often affected by drought, as water is mainly used for the cultivation of cotton and not as drinking water. To deal with periods of drought, the *bioRe®* foundation invests in the construction of drip irrigation systems, which considerably reduce water use for the cultivation of organic cotton. In summary, the principles and high standards of *Coop* and the *bioRe*® foundation for the cultivation of organic cotton offers the farmers the following additional benefits:

■ Training and support in organic farming by experts in training centres funded by *Coop*.

■ Purchase guarantee for the (organic) cotton harvest.

■ An additional bonus of 15% for the (organic) cotton harvest (based on the average market price of the last five years).

■ Investments and re-investments of assets in the local infrastructure.

Processing

Sustainability is also crucial for the processing of organic cotton in the production of *Naturaline* labelled products. The aim of *Coop Naturaline* is to reach the ecologic optimum regarding all parts of the production process. More precisely, this means minimising the impact of the production on the biosphere, to avoid negatively impacting the health of the textile workers as well as consumers.

At the same time, *Naturaline* products must fulfil and exceed consumers' quality expectations. Conventional finishing processes for textiles use a considerable amount of water and chemicals, which causes serious problems for the health of the textile workers and has a strong negative impact on the environment. There are considerable differences in the finishing of *Naturaline* products compared with conventional textile and fashion products. Only selected companies which have committed to *Coop's* high standards of sustainability and socially responsible corporate behaviour can be a part of the *Naturaline* supply chain. To become a part of the *Naturaline* supply chain, these companies have to fulfil several criteria:

■ Bleaching solely with oxygen.

■ No use of colours containing heavy metals and dyes, and no allergenic dyes used in the finishing of *Naturaline* products.

■ Formaldehyde-free processing of *Naturaline* products.

■ Double-stage wastewater treatment.

The relevance of reaching the ecologic optimum for *Coop* in the production of *Naturaline* products is also reflected in the company's commitment to the Detox campaign from *Greenpeace*. The Detox campaign focuses on combating water and soil pollution, together with the effects on employee health in production countries. *Coop* is the first Swiss company to sign a declaration of intent with *Greenpeace* with the aim of reducing hazardous chemicals in textile production by 2020. By signing the declaration of intent, *Coop* has demonstrated its commitment to sustainability in the area of fair, environmentally friendly textile production and has implemented a number of different measures to reduce chemicals, e.g. passing a textiles and leather guideline to regulate social, environmental and toxicological requirements for farming and processing; requiring business partners to maintain transparent supply chains and to switch to non-hazardous chemicals; establishment of a chemicals specialist team within *Coop* and implementation of controls in supply chains and testing of random samples.

As well as the previously mentioned initiatives, in 2004 *Coop* entered into a commitment with the Swiss Government with the aim of improving its energy efficiency and lowering carbon dioxide (CO_2) emissions. It became the first retail group in Switzerland to reach concrete CO_2 target agreements with the Swiss Government. In 2008, *Coop* took the pioneering decision to reach CO_2 neutrality by 2023, in all areas in which it could influence these emissions directly as a retail company. Above all, this commitment includes every technically possible and financially justifiable measure to steadily reduce CO_2 emissions for which *Coop* is responsible. Saving energy is a particularly effective way to reduce CO_2 emissions. Hence, *Coop* has also set itself the target of lowering its overall energy consumption wherever possible. CO_2 emissions that can be only avoided at disproportionately high cost or cannot be avoided at all will be offset by funding high-quality projects.

This commitment has also affected *Naturaline* labelled products. For example, 100,000 CO_2 neutral *Naturaline* T-shirts have been produced in India and Tanzania. The CO_2 initiatives of *Coop* and *Remei* are mostly pioneering projects and show what might be possible if both partners include the principles of sustainability and corporate social responsibility as an integral part of their overall business strategy. *Naturaline's* CO_2 neutrality target should be achieved, thanks to efforts to minimise carbon dioxide emissions during the production process. The main aim of this initiative is to sustainably improve working and living conditions for the *bioRe*® farmers and their families in India and Tanzania.

Overall, the *Naturaline* labelled products show the potential positive impact of sustainable and socially responsible corporate behaviour. This is not only reflected in the improvements to working and living conditions for the organic cotton farmers and their families and the long-term positive impact on the environment in developing countries, but also in the economic success of *Naturaline* labelled products (see Figure 13.8). However, since 2009 the net sales of *Naturaline* textiles have slightly decreased. One possible explanation is that competing companies have also become aware of consumers' demand for organic fashion products, resulting in higher competition in this segment of the international textile market.

| Figure 13.8 | Net Sales of Naturaline Textiles (in billion CHF) |

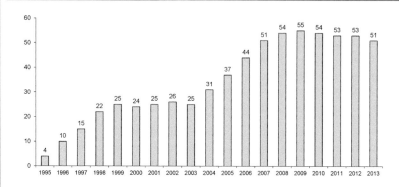

Source: Coop 2013b.

Summary and Outlook

Naturaline, Coop's own-label sustainability brand, stands for fair and environmentally friendly textile production and has proven a huge success over the past 20 years. Its supply chains are transparent, the use of chemicals is very tightly regulated, and hazardous chemicals are prohibited in all stages of production. Independent monitoring institutions inspect the various processes regularly.

Through this brand, *Coop* is the world's largest supplier of textiles made from organically grown fair-trade cotton, with sales of more than 50 million CHF in 2013. Today, the *Coop Naturaline* consists out of more than 500 articles.

As well as their economic success, *Coop* and *Remei* have received several awards for their joint *bioRe*® initiative. In June 2011, the independent rating agency *oekom research AG* in Munich declared *Coop* the "most sustainable retailer" in the world. This put *Coop* well ahead of its competitors, including the four largest retail chains in the world: *Walmart* (USA), *Carrefour* (France), *Metro* (Germany) and *Tesco* (UK). Such awards support the successful implementation of the companies CSR principles and also affect consumers' perception of the company, positively influencing corporate image and shopping behaviour.

Questions

1. How can companies generate competitive advantages in international markets by implementing a business strategy which focuses on sustainability and responsibility? Provide reasons for your answer.

2. Take a closer look at Coop's various international CSR initiatives. What are the success factors?

3. How is "Performance based on Sustainability" implemented at the international level by Coop? Provide and explain three examples.

Hints

1. See Porter and Kramer (2005), Smith (2007), and Schramm-Klein et al. (2014) for further information.

2. See the company's website and the sustainability reports for further information.

3. Again, see the company's website and the sustainability reports for further information.

References

AGUINIS, H.; GLAVAS, A. (2012): What We Know and Don't Know About Corporate Social Responsibility: A Review and Research Agenda, in: Journal of Management, Vol. 38, No. 4, pp. 932-968.

CARROLL, A. (1979): A Three-dimensional Conceptual Model of Corporate Performance, in: Academy of Management Review, Vol. 34, No. 4, pp. 497-505.

CARROLL, A. (1991): The Pyramid of Corporate Social Responsibility: Toward the Moral Management of Organizational Stakeholders, in: Business Horizons, Vol. 34, No. 4, pp. 39-48.

CHANDLER, D.; WERTHER, W. (2014): Strategic Corporate Social Responsibility: Stakeholders, Globalization and Sustainable Value Creation, 3rd ed., Thousand Oaks, SAGE Publications.

COOP (2013a): Annual Report 2013, http://www.coop.ch/pb /site /common/get/documents/coop_main/elements/ueber/geschaeftsbericht/ 2014/_pdf/COOP_GB_2013_e/COOP_GB_2013_e_low.pdf, accessed on September 01, 2014.

COOP (2013b): Sustainability Report 2013, http://www.coop.ch/pb/site /common/get/documents/coop_main/elements/ueber/geschaeftsbericht/ 2014/_pdf/COOP_NHB_2013_e/COOP_NHB_2013_e_low.pdf, accessed on September 01, 2014.

DERESKY, H. (2014): International Management, Managing Across Borders and Cultures, 8th ed., Boston, Pearson.

DODD, E.M. (1932): For Whom Are Corporate Managers Trustees?, in: Harvard Law Review. Vol. 45, No. 7, pp. 1145-1163.

ELKINGTON, J. (1997): Cannibals with Forks: The Triple Bottom Line of 21st Century Business, Oxford, Capstone Publishing.

FREEMANN, R. (1984): Strategic Management: A Stakeholder Approach, Boston, Prentice Hall.

GOSSEN, R. (2007): Walking the Talk, in: Corporate Social Responsibility Review, Autumn 2007, pp. 16-22.

JONKER, J.; DE WITTE, M. (2006): Finally in Business: Organising Corporate Social Responsibility in Five, in JONKER, J.; DE WITTE, M. (Eds.): Management Models for Corporate Social Responsibility, Berlin, Springer, pp. 1-7.

MELLAHI, K.; FRYNAS, J.; FINLAY, P. (2005): Global Strategic Management, Oxford, Oxford University Press.

NEWSWEEK (2014): World´s Greenest Companies 2014, http://www.newsweek.com/green/worlds-greenest-companies-2014, accessed on August 11, 2014.

PELOZA, J. (2009): The Challenge of Measuring Financial Impacts From Investments in Corporate Social Performance, in: Journal of Management, Vol. 35, No. 6, pp. 1518-1541.

PORTER, M.E.; KRAMER, M.R. (2006): Strategy & Society: The Link between Competitive Advantage and Corporate Social Responsibility, in: Harvard Business Review, Vol. 84, No. 12, pp. 78-92.

ROBECOSAM (2014): Sustainability Investing, http://www.robecosam.com /de/sustainability-insights/uber-sustainability/sustainability-investing.jsp, accessed on August 18, 2014.

SAVITZ, A.; WEBER, K. (2014): The Triple Bottom Line, How Today's Best-Run Companies Are Achieving Economic, Social, and Environmental Success – and How You Can Too, 6th ed., Jossey-Bass, Wiley & Sons.

SCHOLZ, C.; ZENTES, J. (2006): A Strategy Map for Germany: From Passive Self-Pity to Offensive Self-Renewal, in: SCHOLZ, C.; ZENTES, J. (Eds.): Strategic Management: New Rules for Old Europe, Wiesbaden, Gabler, pp. 531-556.

SCHOLZ, C.; ZENTES, J. (Eds.) (2014): Beyond Sustainability, Baden-Baden, Nomos.

SCHRAMM-KLEIN, H.; ZENTES, J.; STEINMANN, S.; SWOBODA, B.; MORSCHETT, D. (2014): Retailer Corporate Social Responsibility Is Relevant to Consumer Behavior, in: Business & Society, pp. 1-26.

SCHULER, D.A.; CORDING, M. (2006): A Corporate Social Performance: Corporate Financial Performance Behavioral Model for Consumers, in: Academy of Management Review, Vol. 31, No. 3, pp. 540-558.

SEN, S.; BHATTACHARYA, C. (2001): Does Doing Good Always Lead to Doing Better? Consumer Reactions to Corporate Social Responsibility, in: Journal of Marketing Research, Vol. 38, No. 2, pp. 225-243.

SMITH, A.D. (2007): Making the Case for the Competitive Advantage of Corporate Social Responsibility, in: Business Strategy Series, Vol. 8, No. 3, pp. 186-195.

SOCIAL ACCOUNTABILITY INTERNATIONAL (2014): SA8000, http://www.sa-intl.org, accessed on August 18, 2014.

THE CO-OPERATIVE GROUP LIMITED (2013): Sustainability Report 2013, Manchester http://www.co-operative.coop/Corporate/CSR/sustainability-report-2013/downloads/54684%20CO-OP-2013_FULL_LINKED_v3.pdf, accessed on August 22, 2014.

Part IV

Foreign Operation

Modes

Chapter 14

Basic Types of Foreign Operation Modes

The choice of foreign operation mode is one of the most important components of an internationalisation strategy, since the operation mode determines the type and intensity of control over foreign market activity, necessary resource transfers and the associated risks. This Chapter provides an overview of different operation modes and highlights their various characteristics.

Introduction

A company planning to conduct business activities in a foreign market must choose an appropriate operation mode. Most tasks can be performed in various ways, including via vertically integrated organisational units in the foreign country (wholly-owned subsidiaries), via external organisational units (e.g. distributors in the foreign market), or jointly (cooperative arrangements).

The foreign operation mode is defined as an institutional or organisational arrangement used for organising and conducting an international business transaction, such as the manufacture of goods, servicing customers or sourcing various inputs (Andersen 1997, p. 29; Welch/Benito/Petersen 2007, p. 18). The choice of foreign operation mode is strategically important. It is a core component of the internationalisation strategy and exerts a strong and lasting influence on many of the company's other activities and options. It is seen as a crucial success factor, because it is not easily reversible in the short- and mid-term.

Definition

Many textbooks discuss the issue of foreign operation modes under the heading of *market entry modes*. For two reasons, the term "foreign operation mode" is used throughout this book instead:

Market Entry Modes vs. Foreign Operation Modes

■ First, the issue is still relevant even when the entry context no longer applies (Welch/Benito/Petersen 2007, p. 10). In recent decades, the focus has shifted from "going international" to "being international" (Bäurle 1996, p. 123). Thus, for an MNC, the initial market entry mode is often less important than the operation mode chosen at any given point in time.

■ Second, the term "market entry" suggests that the international activities are sales-related. Even though this Chapter mainly focuses on this dimension, foreign operation modes are broader, and also apply to procurement, production, R&D, services, etc.

The Basic Types of Foreign Operation Mode

Different schemas for classifying foreign operation modes can be found in the literature. A distinction is frequently made between

- export modes (indirect export, direct export via agents, etc.)

- contractual modes (e.g. licensing, franchising, contract manufacturing)

- investment equity entry modes (e.g. joint ventures, wholly-owned subsidiaries).

An increasing level of *vertical integration* can generally be seen here. Export modes – at least when intermediaries in the host country are used – are market modes (see Chapter 15). Contractual and equity alliances are cooperative modes (see Chapters 16 and 17). Wholly-owned subsidiaries constitute the highest level of vertical integration (i.e. "hierarchy") (see Chapter 18). It should be noted, however, that export modes can differ significantly. If, e.g., an MNC exports to a foreign customer through a direct customer relationship, this affords the MNC a very high level of control over this transaction.

Figure 14.1	*Classification of Selected Foreign Operation Modes*

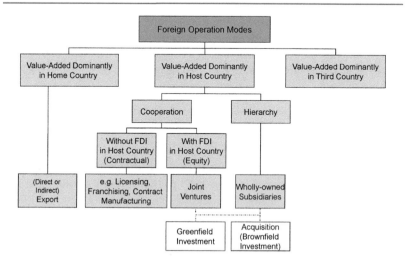

Source: Adapted and expanded from Zentes 1993, p. 67.

More concretely, the choice of foreign operation mode involves several different dimensions (see Figure 14.1): *Where* to locate production, whether to *cooperate* and whether the MNC should *invest* abroad. During the *establishment process*, joint ventures and wholly-owned subsidiaries can be established through a greenfield investment, i.e., by building a new facility in the host country, or through acquisition of existing facilities.

Location of Value-Added

There are three main options when deciding on *location*: producing in the home country and then exporting to the target market; having the value added mainly in the target market (through internal production or via a partnership); or producing in a third country (with internal production or via a partnership) and then exporting to the target market. Different determinants for this decision have been investigated in the literature. In the early economic approaches, international trade (and, thus, the location of value-added) was explained through *comparative cost advantages* or, building on these, via *relative factor endowments* in a country.

Later, dynamic approaches were developed. In the *international product lifecycle theory* of international trade, Vernon (1966) argued that *new product innovations* are usually developed and produced in a company's home country, even if factory costs are high. In the early stage, cost is of secondary importance due to the innovating company's monopoly. Also, demand is difficult to predict. Foreign demand emerges during the later stages of a *maturing product*, but new competitors also bring cost pressures. Production is partly shifted to foreign countries, closer to the new sales markets. Finally, in the third stage (*standardised product*), industrialised countries may still be the most important markets, but they have become too expensive for production. Thus, production is shifted to emerging countries. From there, the MNC (or competitors) exports the product to the relevant markets.

Generally, location theories of internationalisation assume that the decision for value-added in a specific country is determined by location characteristics. The relevant characteristics include *market factors* (e.g. market size, market potential) and *cost-related factors* (e.g. differences in labour costs, input goods, taxes). Another relevant location factor is the *country risk*. In cases of high risk, exporting or contractual arrangements reduce the risk exposure of the MNC compared with a wholly-owned subsidiary where the commitment of the MNC's own resources is substantial.

The *configuration decision* will be discussed in more detail for the different value chain activities, i.e. production (see Chapter 19) and R&D (see Chapter 20).

Cooperation vs. Hierarchy

The decision whether to establish foreign value-added via cooperation (e.g. a joint-venture or via contract manufacturing) or in a hierarchical operation mode (e.g. a wholly-owned subsidiary) depends on many influence factors. A comprehensive study by Morschett, Schramm-Klein and Swoboda (2008; 2010) has shown that a number of factors have a strong influence on this decision. The likelihood that an MNC uses a wholly-owned subsidiary instead of a cooperative arrangement increases with:

■ the *number of employees*: because larger MNCs can more easily afford to establish a subsidiary on their own and have the necessary management capacity to coordinate their subsidiaries

■ *experience* in the host country: because increased knowledge about the country decreases the uncertainty in the market and makes a partner less necessary

■ *advertising intensity*: since a partner in a foreign country may "free-ride" on an MNC's high reputation. This can best be avoided by exploiting the good reputation of the MNC through a wholly-owned subsidiary (advertising intensity is usually seen to indicate high specificity)

■ *export intensity*: because a higher percentage of foreign sales indicate that the MNC has substantial knowledge of foreign markets, and thus is less dependent on a partner.

Conversely, MNCs seem to prefer cooperation over a wholly-owned subsidiary, if

■ *country risk* is high

■ *legal restrictions* in the host country are tight

■ the *market size* of the foreign market is large (which might be explained by the high investments necessary in large markets)

■ the *resource intensity* of the foreign activity is high, since host-country companies often have a first-mover advantage over local resources which can only be tapped through a partnership

■ the subsidiary is active in a business field that is not closely related to the business of the parent company, requiring *external (partner) knowledge* for this subsidiary.

Additional arguments for cooperative and hierarchical operation modes are discussed in Chapters 16 and 17.

Part IV

Characteristics of Foreign Operation Modes

To make a rational decision about a foreign operation mode, several partly interconnected characteristics have to be considered. Table 14.1 lists and evaluates these for selected operation modes.

Characteristics of Selected Foreign Operation Modes

Table 14.1

	Export	Contractual Cooperation	Equity Cooperation	Wholly-owned Subsidiary
Control	low/medium/high	low	medium	high
Resource Commitment	low	low	medium	high
Flexibility	high	medium	medium-low	low
Knowledge Dissemination Risk	low	high	medium	low

Source: Adapted from Driscoll/Paliwoda 1997, p. 60.

The ability to exert tight control over foreign operations is seen as the main advantage of the stronger internalised operation modes. Control refers to the authority over strategic and operational decisions during foreign operations. Compared with cooperative operation modes, "maintaining decision-making control allows the MNC to determine its own destiny" (Driscoll/Paliwoda 1997, p. 64), and control is "the single most important determinant of both risk and return" (Anderson/Gatignon 1986, p. 3). As Table 14.1 illustrates, different operation modes imply different levels of control. While wholly-owned subsidiaries allow for tight coordination (*full control modes*), most cooperative modes lead to limited or joint control (*shared control modes*). In the case of contractual agreements (like licensing), the control over foreign markets is largely shifted to the licensee in exchange for payment.

Control

Often, the trade-off between control (*benefits of integration*) and the necessary *resource commitment* (*cost of integration*) is highlighted as the main decision for an MNC. Resource commitment refers to the assets that an MNC needs to dedicate to the foreign market operations. Obviously, a high resource commitment by an MNC enhances its risk exposure. In the case of export and contractual cooperation, this is comparatively low. In the case of wholly-owned subsidiaries, the resources have to be invested by the company alone. Equity cooperation falls between these two extremes. Sharing equity investment with a cooperation partner allows for a reduction in personal risk.

Resource Commitment

Flexibility is closely linked to resource commitment. It refers to a company's ability to switch the chosen operation mode rapidly and at comparatively low cost or even to withdraw from a foreign market when external condi-

Flexibility

tions change (Anderson/Gatignon 1986). High resource commitment acts as market exit barrier and thus reduces the strategic flexibility of the MNC.

Dissemination Risk

A fourth characteristic of foreign operation modes is the so-called *"dissemination risk"*, i.e., the risk that knowledge is absorbed by another company which then uses this knowledge against the MNC's interests (Agarwal/Ramaswami 1992). Since technological and marketing expertise are crucial competitive advantages, it is important to secure the company against uncontrolled knowledge outflows, since this may reduce the income a company can generate from its knowledge. Protection against knowledge dissemination is therefore a major criterion for the choice of operation mode (Driscoll/Paliwoda 1997, p. 66). In particular, cooperative operation modes, where a partner company (e.g. a licensee) is actively provided with the company's knowledge, are characterised by a high risk of knowledge dissemination. The lowest risk exists in the case of wholly-owned subsidiaries (or through direct exports to a foreign customer).

Cost and Profit Potential

Different foreign operation modes lead to different *costs of serving* the selected markets (Grünig/Morschett 2012, p. 143). Producing in the host country may reduce production costs due to lower labour costs and reduced costs of distribution logistics. It may help to overcome substantial custom tariffs. But decentralised production also leads to reduced economies of scale and therefore higher unit costs. With partner strategies, the profit has to be shared with partners but it may be higher due to better market knowledge. With licensing, a company gets its income from royalties, not directly from sales. All of these aspects have to be considered when evaluating different market entry modes.

Choice of Foreign Operation Mode

The literature provides a number of theories to explain the choice of international market entry mode. These theories are covered in more detail in Chapter 6:

■ The dominant theory to explain the choice of foreign operation mode in recent decades has been the *transaction cost approach* (Williamson 1985) and the closely related *internalisation theory* (Buckley/Casson 1976). These approaches argue that companies choose operation modes that minimise the cost of cross-border transactions.

■ Internalisation logic alone is not sufficient to explain location choice, i.e., it does not fully explain why a company might locate its production in the host country instead of merely exporting from the home base. Dunning's *eclectic paradigm* offers a general framework to determine which operation mode is the most appropriate. It is also known as *OLI paradigm* because it argues that three conditions must prevail simultaneously to stimulate FDI by a company (Dunning/Lundan 2008, pp. 96-108): ownership-specific advantages (O), location-specific advantages (L) and internalisation advantages (I).

◼ With a dynamic perspective, the *internationalisation process model* (IP model) proposes that companies follow a specific sequence of foreign operation modes in a foreign country, based on increasing experiential knowledge: no international activities, export activities via agents, export activities via the company's own sales subsidiaries or establishment of production subsidiaries in the foreign country (Johanson/Vahlne 1977).

Corporate Strategy as Determinant

One influence factor on the choice of foreign operation mode that is largely neglected by the approaches described above is *corporate strategy*. For example, the MNC's concrete motive for entering the host country (see Chapter 4) is likely to have an effect on the chosen operation mode.

The corporate strategy approach focuses on the competition and required characteristics of the operation mode that stem from the corporate strategy and the specific role of the foreign subsidiary in its host country. Following the general idea that *structure and strategy* should be aligned, this approach investigates strategy variables and their influence on the operation mode choice. More particularly, "the strategy approach regards the issue of ownership structure primarily as a question of the level of control that is needed in order to coordinate global strategic action" (Benito 1996, p. 164). There are many influential strategy variables here (Kim/Hwang 1992; Malhotra/Agarwal/Ulgado 2004, p. 19):

Structure and Strategy

◼ *Synergy effects* emerge if companies can use certain resources and processes like R&D, production or marketing to achieve economies of scale and scope across different host countries. Usually, tight control and the corresponding operation modes are considered favourable for achieving synergy effects.

◼ *Global strategic motives* refer to whether the MNC follows a global or multinational orientation (see Chapter 2). A multinational orientation allows for low-control operation modes and, e.g., partnerships in the host countries, while a global strategy implies wholly-owned and tightly controlled subsidiaries.

◼ *Market concentration* is a relevant external factor since it leads to a worldwide oligopoly. Following Knickerbocker's theory of *oligopolistic reactions*

(Knickerbocker 1973), it is argued that the interdependency of different countries in this case is high, and a tight coordination of the foreign subsidiaries is necessary to react flexibly to a competitor's actions. From this perspective, direct investment in a foreign country can also be seen as an "exchange of threats" between competitors.

Foreign Operation Mode Combinations and Foreign Operation Mode Changes

In recent years, there has been substantial and relevant criticism concerning previous foreign operation mode research. Welch, Benito and Petersen (2007) point out that most research assumes that an MNC applies one specific foreign operation mode in a specific host country while "observation of business practice reveals a 'messier' reality" (Benito/Welch/Petersen 2009, p. 1455). They put forward three main arguments in their bid for a more realistic   conceptualisation   of   foreign   operation   modes (Welch/Benito/Petersen 2007; Benito/Peterson/Welch 2009).

■ *Mode combinations* (or "mode packages") in a specific country whereby companies use different modes for different value chain activities are not the exception but the rule. Companies may, for example, use a wholly-owned subsidiary for production activity and a joint-venture for distribution activity. Even within the same type of activity (e.g. sales), companies may use their own sales force for one group of customers (e.g. large industrial companies) while selling via independent distributors to another group of customers (e.g. smaller commercial customers). Or they may combine operation modes, e.g. by creating a joint venture to which they grant a production licence. This is logical when considering the different influence factors. From a transaction cost perspective, some of the activities carried out in the host country may be characterised by high asset specificity while others have low asset specificity. This, together with the increased unbundling of different value chain activities leads to a separate optimisation for both the location and operation of these activities, even within the same country.

As a consequence, it is not sufficient to recommend one specific foreign operation mode. A specific foreign operation mode for each value chain activity and the links between them must be considered to create a specific combination.

■ Switches are not confined to foreign operation modes; in fact, *within-mode changes* are very common as well. For example, within exporting, one distributor could be exchanged with another, or within licensing, the number or extent of technologies and brands that are licenced to a foreign partner can be increased or reduced. In equity-based modes, the share in a joint venture may be increased or reduced, etc.

■ *Mode switches* are also very common, and not necessarily in the systematic sequence of a few stages that the IP model would imply. In terms of explanatory models for the mode choice, there is no reason to assume that there is always an increase towards "more commitment"; changes in the context or the strategy can also justify switches to "lower" foreign operation modes. However, switching costs must also be considered.

It must be remembered that these aspects act together, increasing complexity. Thus, instead of investigating one foreign operation mode for each county in a static manner, the dynamic changes from one combination of foreign operation modes in one country to another combination provides a more realistic conceptualisation of the managerial problem. These dynamic changes may include within-switches, between-switches, and reductions or increases in the number of different operation modes, which clearly points to a very complex managerial decision process.

Conclusion and Outlook

The choice of a foreign operation mode is one of the most important internationalisation strategy decisions. This Chapter has presented the basic types. For each of the three basic options – market, cooperation and hierarchy – the following Chapters will provide a more detailed discussion.

It must be stressed, however, that a choice of foreign operation mode has to be made for each value chain activity. Thus, an MNC might – for a specific foreign country – decide to outsource its R&D, internalise its sales and marketing activities, offer its after-sales service in a joint venture with a local partner and have major production steps carried out by a contract manufacturer. In addition, the interdependence between these activities has to be considered, since inter-functional coordination is also affected by the chosen operation modes.

Considering the theoretical explanations and the complex influences on the choice of operation mode, most recent texts argue that the different perspectives should be seen as complementary.

Further Reading

ANDERSEN, O. (1997): Internationalization and Market Entry Mode: A Review of Theories and Conceptual Framework, in: Management International Review, Vol. 27, No. 2, pp. 27-42.

WELCH, L.; BENITO, G.; PETERSEN, B. (2007): Foreign Operation Methods: Theory – Analysis – Strategy, Glos, Edward Elgar Publishing.

Case Study: AB InBev[*]

Profile, History and Status Quo

AB InBev is a leading global brewer and one of the world's top five consumer product companies. Based in Leuven, Belgium, the company sells in more than 100 countries and has geographically diversified operations in 25 countries on four continents. With a portfolio of over 200 beer brands and a beer volume of 400 million hectolitres, *AB InBev* realised a turnover of 43.2 billion USD in 2013. With the vision of being the "best beer company in a better world", the brewer focuses on a consumer-centric, sales driven growth approach, aiming to occupy the No. 1 or 2 position in leading markets.

Figure 14.2	*The Creation of AB InBev*

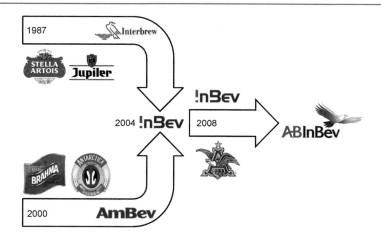

Source: AB InBev 2014.

---

[*] Sources used for this case study include the corporate websites (mainly http://www.ab-inbev.com) and various annual and interim reports, investor-relations presentations and explicitly cited sources.

The *AB InBev* group looks back on more than 600 years of experience in beer brewing. Today's structure is the result of four huge mergers or acquisitions, characterised by a strong international orientation. The first merger took place in 1987, between the two largest breweries in Belgium: *Artois*, located in Leuven, and *Piedboeuf*, located in Jupille, signalling the formation of *Interbrew*. *Interbrew* operated as a family-owned business, before joining the stock market at the end of 2000. The second merger took place in 1999, when the Brazilian breweries *Brahma* and *Antarctica* created *AmBev*. The two breweries were founded in the 1880s belonging to the first breweries in the country. *AmBev* is seen as the nucleus of the group, controlled by the Swiss-Brazilian dual citizen Jorge Paulo Lemann and his investment fund *GP Investimentos* (Barmettler 2014, p. 7). A decisive event in the formation of *AB InBev* was the merger between *Interbrew* and *AmBev* to create *InBev* in 2004. Then, in November 2008, *InBev* took over *Anheuser-Busch*, a brewery multinational from the United States to become today's MNC, *AB InBev*, a strong global player (see Figure 14.3).

Establishment Process of AB InBev

AB InBev's Global Presence

Figure 14.3

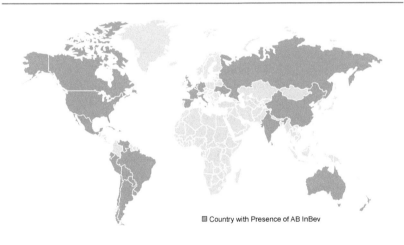

☐ Country with Presence of AB InBev

Source: AB InBev 2014.

AB InBev's Business Development

As the history of *AB InBev* has already shown, the company has a strong focus on global markets. Different foreign operation modes play a role in the company's market development; a number of foreign operation modes de-

Brand Strategy and Outlook on Focus Markets

scribed in this Chapter can be identified. *AB InBev's* business development and market selection is closely linked to their brand strategy. They distribute more than 200 brands of which 17 individually have estimated retail sales values of more than 1 billion USD. Six of them ranked among the global top 10 most valuable beer brands (AB InBev 2014). To achieve this, the brands are structured into three categories:

◼ global brands: *Budweiser, Corona Extra, Stella Artois*

◼ international brands: *Beck's, Leffe, Hoegaarden*

◼ local champions: e.g. *Bud Light, Skol, Antarctica, Jupiler, Sibirskaya Korona, Modelo Especial, Harbin.*

For its operations, *AB InBev* focuses on a balanced mix of both developed and fast-growing regions, with zone operations covering North America, Mexico, Latin America North, Latin America South, Europe and the Asia-Pacific region. In North America, the focus is on strong innovations and the extension of the brand portfolio, whereas in Mexico the goal is the creation of strong brands. In the Latin America North key region including Brazil, *AB InBev* has bet on its key commercial strategies of innovation, premiumisation, expansion in the Northern and North-Eastern regions and packaging, like redesigning or the use of returnable bottles. Latin America South is characterised by a growing market share, a focus on trade programmes and the strengthening of key brands' digital profiles. To gain a stable market share in Europe, *AB InBev* defines its key goals as driving the premiumisation of products and increasing the profitability of the brands sold in a shrinking market. The Asia-Pacific region provides a strong consumer market, and a solid execution of a growth strategy with brand focus is possible.

AB InBev has defined four focus markets (USA, Brazil, China, Mexico); these markets provide nearly half of the beer industry's worldwide volume and are expected to generate the industry's strongest growth opportunities in the near future (see Figure 14.4). To strengthen its global presence, *AB InBev* used different operation modes with different levels of commitment to enter new markets, reflecting the importance of a market to *AB InBev's* strategy. A selection of these is described below.

Characteristics of AB InBev's Focus Markets

Figure 14.4

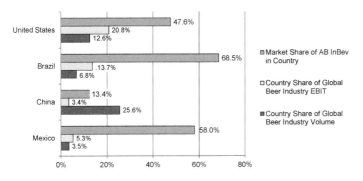

Source: AB InBev 2014.

Mergers

As already shown with the foundation process of *AB InBev*, mergers have been used to form new, larger entities and gain access to specific foreign markets. The most important merger in the company's history was that with American brewer *Anheuser-Busch* in 2008 to create a new global leader in the beer industry. 40% of the merged company's revenues are now generated in the US market and the former *Anheuser-Busch* headquarters is the new North America headquarters to profit from the existing knowledge in this important market. Thanks to the merger, the newly shaped company is geographically diversified, with leading positions in the world's top beer markets of China, USA, Russia, Brazil and Germany and balanced exposure to developed and developing markets with huge potential for future growth.

Wholly-Owned Subsidiaries and Acquisitions

AB InBev has a market presence in about 140 countries and has employees in about 25 countries. In total, 452 companies belong to *AB InBev's* widespread network. For example, brewing subsidiaries have been established in Belgium, China, France, Germany, Mexico, The Netherlands, United Kingdom and the United States.

The company buys many existing assets in foreign countries to establish wholly-owned subsidiaries with the aim of growing and gaining market share. In 2000, *AB InBev* bought the second and the third largest brewers in the United Kingdom, *Whitbread Brewing* and *Bass Brewers*, with a combined turnover of 2.9 million GDP and a combined UK market share of 32%. The two brewers are focus brewers committed to UK beer heritage and offering a rich portfolio of typical UK ales and lagers, from which UK consumers can benefit. Therefore, the two breweries remain independent, however they both can benefit from international network synergies with *AB InBev*. Furthermore, *AB InBev* was able to take advantage of the rapid consolidation of the UK beer market and regain full control over its *Stella Artois* brand in UK, which has been brewed under licence by *Whitbread* since 1976.

Further noteworthy acquisitions include the acquisition of the Canadian brewer *Labatt* in 1995, which allowed *AB InBev* to double its size overnight and move from 17th place to 2nd position in the world's brewing industry five years later, as well as the acquisition of the breweries *Beck's* and *Diebel's* in Germany in 2001. These two acquisitions created a solid platform in the German beer market and further progressed *AB InBev's* strategy of being a leading operator in the world's major beer markets.

A huge acquisition occurred in 2013, when the Mexican brewer *Grupo Modelo* with its flagship brand Corona was acquired for 20 billion USD and integrated into the portfolio. The combination of the two companies was logical, given their long-standing partnership of more than 20 years and *AB InBev's* 50% stake in *Grupo Modelo*. This integration created a new global leader in the world's beer industry with an annual beer volume of 460 million hectolitres, as well as enhancing revenues and saving costs due to scale effects.

At the beginning of 2014, *AB InBev* announced their re-acquisition of the largest brewer in South Korea, *Oriental Brewery*, to strengthen their position in the Asia-Pacific region. *Oriental Brewery* was sold in 2009 to reach deleveraging targets after the merger with *Anheuser-Busch*. The repurchase from the investment group *KKR* had already been arranged as part of the 2009 deal.

Export

For those markets in which the company has no operations, export is the preferred option for generating sales. To centralise part of their export functions, a European shared service centre was established in the Czech Republic in 2006 to bundle orders and provide export services for Belgium, Bulgaria, Croatia, the Czech Republic, Germany, Hungary, Ireland, the Netherlands, Romania, Russia, the UK and Ukraine.

Furthermore, *AB InBev* has contracts with independent distributors to import, distribute and market brands in specific regions. As an example, a distribution agreement was signed in 2004 with *Carlton & United Breweries* to import and market the brands *Leffe* and *Hoegaarden* in Australia, to take advantage of the success of Belgian beer in the Australian market, which falls outside the traditional Australian mainstream beer territory. A further distribution agreement for these two brands was signed with the brewery *Lion Nathan* in 2005 to serve the New Zealand market, in order to benefit from the strong growth in Belgian beer consumption in the country.

Before the merger between *Anheuser-Busch* and *InBev* took place, *InBev* had used *Anheuser-Busch* since 2007 as their exclusive US importer. *Anheuser-Busch* was also responsible for the distribution, promotion and sale of *InBev's* premium European brands. An additional example of an *AB InBev* export brand is *Corona*, exclusively brewed in Mexico and exported in more than 180 countries.

In the beer industry, export can have the advantage of positive country-of-origin image. This sometimes becomes apparent when production location is changed. For example, *Beck's* beer has long been exported to the US market from Germany. When the company changed its production location to St. Louis (where it is now brewed alongside with *Budweiser*), many US customers complained, arguing that it would no longer taste "German". This discussion can be found on Internet forums and social networks.

Loss of Country-of-Origin Image

Licensing

Shipping beer to foreign countries is relatively expensive for such a low value product, and the transport takes time. Thus, brewing in the target country can help reduce costs and improve delivery and service levels. To achieve this without using its own resources, *AB InBev* makes use of licensing agreements in several countries. The relevance of this operation mode becomes apparent in *AB InBev's* claim on its website: "With operations and licence agreements around the globe, *AB InBev* is a truly global brewer" (AB InBev 2014).

In Australia, an exclusive long-term agreement was concluded in 2004 with the brewer *Lion Nathan* to brew, distribute and market the international brand *Beck's* (which *Lion Nathan* had already been distributing and marketing since 2001). For *Lion Nathan*, which also acts as an importer for other *AB InBev* Brands, *Beck's* is a key brand in the growing premium segment. In 2004 *Beck's* had a market share of 9% in the country; this agreement was an opportunity to secure the future and further growth of the brand in the Australian market.

Another brewing licence for the *Stella Artois* brand was held by the *Foster's Group*. This licence was originally granted in 1997 and later renewed in 2002 for ten years. The renewal was based on the brand's outstanding Australian growth results under the stewardship of *Foster's* since the first licence was awarded and an ongoing growth of approximately 15% per year in the premium beer premium segment. However, in 2012 *Foster's* lost the licence to *Lion Nathan*. It is noteworthy that *Foster's* had at that point been acquired by *SABMiller*, the No. 2 brewing company in the world, and a fierce competitor of *AB InBev*, while *Lion Nathan* was acquired in 2009 by *Kirin*, the Japanese brewing group. *Lion Nathan* is now *AB InBev*'s partner for all company brands in Australia and in New Zealand, distributing and marketing all of them and producing many of them under licence agreements. This illustrates how MNCs may have the choice between several competent licence partners in a country. It also shows, from *Lion Nathan's* perspective, how a successful licence partnership may be the basis for further contracts in the future.

In the Thai market, *AB InBev* has operated with brewing licences since 1975. In 2003, the licence for the *Kloster* brand was transferred from *Thai Amarit* to *Boon Rawd*, Thailand's oldest brewing company and owner of the country's most internationally recognised brands, *Singha* and *Leo*. This agreement between the two companies reflects the importance of Thailand in the company's Asian strategy. *Boon Rawd's* vast knowledge of the local beer market has provided a solid base for increasing the brand's market share.

Another interesting example of licensing as a substitute for internal production operations can be observed in Central Europe. *AB InBev* sold its operations in this region in 2009 to an investment fund. The newly formed company took over *AB InBev*'s operations in Central Europe (e.g. Czech Republic, Hungary, Romania, Bulgaria, Bosnia-Herzegovina, Croatia). In 2012, this company was acquired by the Canadian brewer *Molson Coors*. *Molson Coors Central Europe* now acts as a distributor for *Hoegaarden* and *Leffe* in Central Europe and brews *Beck's* and *Stella Artois* for these countries under a licence agreement.

Joint Ventures and Buying Stakes in Foreign Companies

AB InBev also employs the operation mode of joint ventures in some countries. Reasons include governmental regulations, risk reduction, the partner's assets or the need to gain market knowledge. In 2001, a strategic partnership with *Union Breweries*, the second largest brewer in Slovenia, was signed. *AB InBev* took over a minority participation of 20% in *Union Breweries* with the aim of strengthening its presence in the growing Central European markets. Furthermore, *AB InBev* promotes the *Union* brand outside the Slovenian borders and strengthens the brand in the South-East European region by using its existing distribution capabilities.

In 2002, a joint venture with the Chinese *Zhujiang Brewery* was signed, taking over 24% of the shares in *Zhujiang* and actively participating in the management of the brewery. While entering this strategic partnership, *Zhujiang's* beers were available in more than 30 provinces or autonomous regions in China and the brewer was the largest in terms of hectolitres sold in China. The brewery had a market share of 50% in Guangdong province and above 80% in Guangzhou province.

In 2007, another strategic and long-term joint venture was entered into with the *RKJ Group*, a leading beverage group in India, to invest in this promising beer market. While this partnership will not have a material impact on *AB InBev's* global business in the short- to medium-term, the company expects, that its 49% stock will provide access to a strong distribution network and that it is possible to build a meaningful presence over time.

Foreign Operation Modes as Complex Cross-Country Activities

These examples have clearly shown that the practice for MNCs often goes far beyond the simple single-country perspective. For example, export and wholly-owned subsidiaries with internal production operations are not mutually exclusive. In fact, *AB InBev* exports are frequently done from countries other than the MNC's home country of Belgium, and it may also occur from countries other than the country-of-origin of the specific beer brand. Once a production location in a foreign country is established, it may serve neighbouring countries as well. For example, *Beck's* beer is brewed locally in the USA and the plan is to export from this production site to neighbouring countries, e.g. Canada.

This becomes even more evident when analysing the acquisitions that *AB InBev* has undertaken. Acquiring *Grupo Modelo* not only gave *AB InBev* a much stronger position in the focus market Mexico (in which *AB InBev* had already been present before the acquisition) it gave them ownership of *Corona*, a global brand that is the leading import beer in 38 countries worldwide, and of production facilities in different countries.

Thus, if an MNC acquires another MNC or merges with it, this usually influences operations in many different countries. Instead of just looking at the home country and one host country, the overall portfolio of production locations (owned or in partnerships) and the overall portfolio of sales markets has to be considered.

Summary and Outlook

In summary, the example of *AB InBev* illustrates the wide range of possible options a company has for operating in foreign countries. With its chosen strategy, *AB InBev* is able to adapt its needs to match the conditions of particular countries. Thanks to its market diversification strategy, *AB InBev* is able to profit from both mature and developing markets. In future, the world's largest brewing company expects further growth and the creation of long-term value, especially in its key markets of the USA, Mexico, Brazil and China.

Questions

1. Explain the basic types of foreign operation modes that a brewer can choose when pursuing the international expansion of its business operations.

2. *AB InBev* enters foreign markets with different operation modes. Try to explain the choice of a specific operation mode based on market conditions and the importance of the market in *AB InBev's* strategy. Provide an explanation and examples for each operation mode addressed in the previous question.

3. Within its business development and brand strategy, *AB InBev* structures its brands in three categories. Explain the chosen structure and speculate why the selected brands are in these categories.

Hints

1. See, e.g., http://www.ab-inbev.com for an overview of *AB InBev's* company structure and strategy.

References

AB INBEV (2014): Annual Report 2013, Leuwen.

AGARWAL, S.; RAMASWAMI, S. (1992): Choice of Foreign Market Entry Mode: Impact of Ownership, Location and Internalization Factors, in: Journal of International Business Studies, Vol. 23, No. 1, pp. 517-551.

ANDERSEN, O. (1997): Internationalization and Market Entry Mode: A Review of Theories and Conceptual Framework, in: Management International Review, Vol. 27, No. 2, pp. 27-42.

ANDERSON, E.; GATIGNON, H. (1986): Modes of Foreign Entry: A Transaction Cost Analysis and Proposition, in: Journal of International Business Studies, Vol. 29, No. 1, pp. 1-26.

BARMETTLER, S. (2014): Der Brauer vom Zürichsee, in: Handelzeitung, No. 19, May 10, 2014.

BÄURLE, I. (1996): Internationalisierung als Prozeßphänomen: Konzepte – Besonderheiten – Handhabung, Wiesbaden, Gabler.

BENITO, G. (1996): Ownership Structures of Norwegian Foreign Subsidiaries in Manufacturing, in: The International Trade Journal, Vol. 10, No. 2, pp. 157-198.

BENITO, G.; PETERSEN, B.; WELCH, L. (2009): Towards More Realistic Conceptualisations of Foreign Operation Modes, in: Journal of International Business Studies, Vol. 40, No. 9, pp. 1455-1470.

BUCKLEY, P.; CASSON, M. (1976): The Future of the Multinational Enterprise, London, Macmillan Interactive Publishing.

DRISCOLL, A.; PALIWODA, S. (1997): Dimensionalizing International Market Entry Mode Choice, in: Journal of Marketing Management, Vol. 13, No. 1, pp. 57-87.

DUNNING, J.; LUNDAN, S. (2008): Multinational Enterprises and the Global Economy, 2nd ed., Cheltenham, Edward Elgar Publishing.

GRÜNIG, R.; MORSCHETT, D. (2012): Developing International Strategies: Going and Being International for Medium-sized Companies, Berlin-Heidelberg, Springer.

JOHANSON, J.; VAHLNE, J. (1977): The Internationalization Process of the Firm: A Model of Knowledge Development and Increasing Foreign Market Commitment, in: Journal of International Business Studies, Vol. 8, No. 1, pp. 23-32.

KIM, W.; HWANG, P. (1992): Global Strategy and Multinationals' Entry Mode Choice, in: Journal of International Business Studies, Vol. 23, No. 1, pp. 29-53.

KNICKERBOCKER, F. (1973): Oligopolistic Reaction and Multinational Enterprise, Boston, Harvard Business School Publications.

MALHOTRA, N.; AGARWAL, J.; ULGADO, F. (2004): Internationalization and Entry Modes: A Multitheoretical Framework and Research Propositions, in: Journal of International Marketing, Vol. 11, No. 4, pp. 1-31.

MORSCHETT, D.; SCHRAMM-KLEIN, H.; SWOBODA, B. (2008): What Do We Really Know About the Foreign Market Entry Strategy Decision? A Meta-analysis on the Choice between Wholly-owned Subsidiaries and Cooperative Arrangement, Best Paper Proceedings of the Academy of International Business Annual Meeting 2008, Milan.

MORSCHETT, D.; SCHRAMM-KLEIN, H.; SWOBODA, B. (2010): Decades of Research on Market Entry Modes: What Do We Really Know About External Antecedents of Entry Mode Choice?, in: Journal of International Management, Vol. 16, No. 1, pp. 60-77.

VERNON, R. (1966): International Investment and International Trade in the Product Cycle, in: Quarterly Journal of Economics, Vol. 80, No. 2, pp. 190-207.

WELCH, L.; BENITO, G.; PETERSEN, B. (2007): Foreign Operation Methods: Theory – Analysis – Strategy, Glos, Edward Elgar Publishing.

WILLIAMSON, O. (1985): The Economic Institutions of Capitalism, New York, The Free Press.

ZENTES, J. (1993): Eintritts- und Bearbeitungsstrategien für osteuropäische Konsumgütermärkte, in: TIETZ, B.; ZENTES, J. (Eds.): Ost-Marketing, Düsseldorf, Econ, pp. 63-101.

Chapter 15

Export Modes

International trade, e.g. the exchange of goods and services across national boundaries through exporting or importing, is the most traditional form of international business activity and still plays a major role in the world economy. Exporting can be organised in a variety of ways. This Chapter discusses export channels, practices and
procedures.

Historical and Empirical Relevance of Exporting

Looking briefly at the history of international trade, three periods can be
identified (Seyoum 2014, pp. 1-3): the ancient period, the colonial period and
the present (post-1900).

International trade started around 2500 BC (*ancient period*). The *colonial period* *Ancient and*
(1500-1900) can be divided into two sub-periods. The first phase (until 1750) *Colonial*
was characterised by national monopolies controlling commerce between *Period*
colonies and the mother country and granting private companies, such as
the *English East India Company* or the *Dutch East India Company*, a monopoly
trade in the colonies. The second phase is characterised by more commercial
considerations, initiated by the *Industrial Revolution*.

From 1900 until the outbreak of World War I, there was a further develop- *Period 1900*
ment in international trade, followed by the disrupted trading links, state *to the Present*
intervention and restrictive economic policies in the post-World War I period. To avoid a repeat of this situation, the allied countries established the
International Monetary Fund (IMF) and the *International Bank for Reconstruction*
and Development (IBRD) before the end of World War II, followed by the
General Agreement on Tariffs and Trade (GATT) in 1947 to enable the free flow
of goods among countries (see Chapter 7).

The economic importance of international trade is shown in Figure 15.1: the *Economic*
development of global merchandise exports from 1980 to 2013. *Importance*

Figure 15.1 | *Global Merchandise Exports from 1980 to 2013 (in billion USD)*

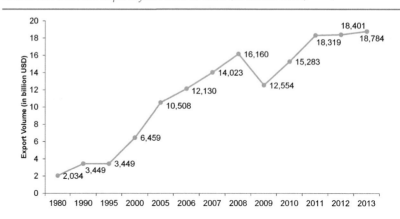

Source: WTO World Trade Report 2014.

The leading export countries in terms of merchandise trade are presented in Figure 15.2. Since 2009 China has been No. 1 in global merchandise exports.

Figure 15.2 | *Leading Export Countries (Merchandise Trade): Share of World Trade 2013 (in %)*

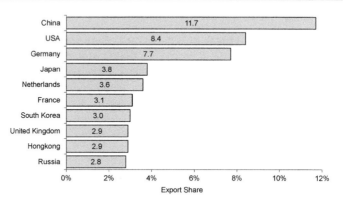

Source: WTO World Trade Report 2014.

Exporting is usually a company's first type of foreign business operation because it involves the least commitment of resources and the least degree of

risk (see also Chapter 14). In the *process of internationalising* business operations, a second dimension, of exports can be identified. *Cross-border value
creation* combined with foreign direct investment (FDI) leads to integrated
networks (see Chapter 1), in which different subsidiaries are interlinked:
Parts and components are produced in country A, exported to country B, in
which they are assembled together with components coming from country C
and the final products are sold to countries D, E, F, etc.. The economic effect
of this *new global structure* of value creation processes is shown in Figure
15.3. Except during the financial crises of 2009, the growth in world trade
has been higher than the growth of world production.

*World Trade
and World
Production*

Growth of World Trade and World Production (in %)   *Figure 15.3*

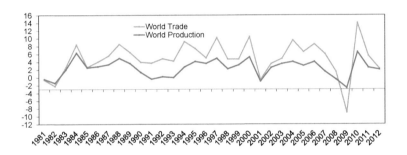

Source: WTO World Trade Report 2013.

Channels of Distribution

Exporting can be realised through two principal channels of distribution:
indirect or direct channels. In *indirect export modes* a firm uses independent
export organisations located in its own country. "In indirect exporting the
sale is like a domestic sale; in fact the firm is not really engaging in global
marketing, because its products are carried abroad by others. Such an approach to exporting is most likely to be appropriate for a firm with limited
international expansion objectives" (Hollensen 2014, p. 349). *Direct exporting*
means that a firm sells directly to foreign distributors, trading companies or
final customers (buyers). Direct export could also be achieved through
agents located in a foreign country. "Indirect exporting is associated with
poor control, inadequate feedback, and shorter time to market than does
direct exporting. Direct exporting requires a higher level of investment in

*Indirect and
Direct Chan-
nels*

financial, technical, and other resources than indirect exporting" (Seyoum 2014, p. 86).

Indirect Channels

Types of Intermediaries

For indirect channels, several types of *intermediaries* can be differentiated:

- exporters that sell on behalf of a manufacturer, e.g. *manufacturer's exports agents* or *export management companies*

- exporters that buy for their foreign/overseas customers, e.g. *export commission agents*, representing foreign buyers such as large industrial users

- exporters that buy and sell for their own accounts, e.g. *export merchants* or *international trading companies (ITCs)*.

Besides these basic types there is a further indirect channel: cooperative exporters. These are firms, predominantly manufacturers, which sell other companies' products in foreign markets together with their own (Ball et al. 2013).

International Trading Companies

Sogo Shosha and Chaebol

International trading companies are firms that not only buy products or act as an export intermediary but also import, invest, manufacture or engage in *countertrading* (the trading of goods for other goods, instead of money). They usually operate across many national markets and handle a variety of products (Mühlbacher/Leihs/Dahringer 2006, p. 416). Traditional trading companies include the Japanese *Sogo Shosha*, e.g. *Mitsubishi* and *Mitsui*, or the *Chaebol* from South Korea, such as *Daewoo*, *Hyundai* and *Samsung*. In European countries their origins can be traced back to the colonial period, such as the *English East India Company*, the *Dutch East India Company* and the *French East India Company* .

Market Expansion Services

In the context of globalisation and outsourcing (see Chapter 16) new players have emerged: *market expansion services* (MES) *providers*. This new industry offers specialised services that help companies expand efficiently and effectively into new markets, especially in Asia: "MES providers help companies increase their market share, improve market coverage and deepen market penetration – while naturally also freeing up resources, lowering the fixed cost base and reducing operational complexity. In effect, market expansion services have emerged as the high end of the outsourcing landscape." (DKSH/Roland Berger 2013, p. 9).

A leading market expansion services provider is *DKSH*, with a focus on Asia. *DKSH* has a nearly 150-year-long tradition of doing business in and with Asia, and is deeply rooted in communities and business across Asia-Pacific.

Direct Channels

A manufacturer has different options for selling its products directly to foreign countries:

- ◼ direct selling from the home country
- ◼ selling through agents and distributors
- ◼ selling through resident sales representatives, foreign sales branches and foreign sales subsidiaries.

Cooperative direct export modes also exist, e.g. export marketing groups. They are frequently found among small and medium-sized enterprises (SMEs) to support initial foreign market entry, because many such firms do not have adequate management and marketing resources available.

Direct Selling from the Home Country

A firm may sell directly to a foreign manufacturer, retailer or consumer through catalogue sales/telephone or domestic-based sales representatives, i.e., domestic employees of the exporting firm traveling abroad to perform the sales function.

This export mode often leads to the establishment of an *export department* (see also Chapter 11). "This is not actually a form of market entry; rather, it is an internal response to the need or desire to move into new country-markets or regions. Located within the home organisation, the export department is responsible for international sales and possibly shipping, advertising, credit evaluation, and other activities related to operating in foreign markets" (Mühlbacher/Leihs/Dahringer 2006, p. 418).

Export Departments

The growing importance or use of the Internet (*E-Business* or *E-Commerce*) is dramatically increasing the direct sale of products and/or services to private or commercial customers (*B2C* and *B2B*).

Direct Selling through Agents and Distributors

Agents are independent companies that sell to customers on behalf of the manufacturer. The agents are not employees of the home organisation; they work on a *commission basis*. Usually they do not stock the products; the manufacturer (exporter) ships the merchandise directly to the customers.

An *exclusive agent* has exclusive rights to specified territories; *non-exclusive agents* handle a variety of goods. Distributors are *independent merchants*. They buy on their own accounts, stock the products and are free to select their own customers and run their own marketing programmes.

Resident Sales Representatives, Foreign Sales Branch and Foreign Sales Subsidiaries

Export Modes and Customer Commitment

The common feature of these modes is that the sales function is transferred to the foreign market. *Resident sales representatives* display a greater market or customer commitment than using domestic-based sales representatives. A *foreign sales branch* or *formal branch office* is an institutional extension of this export mode. The resident salespersons are assigned to this sales office, which is a legal part of the exporting company. Usually, taxation of profits takes place in the manufacturer's country.

A *wholly-owned sales subsidiary* often results from the positive development of the firm. The sales office will be transferred to a local company owned and operated by a foreign company under the laws and taxation of the host country (Hollensen 2014, p. 401).

The simplest form of market presence is a *representation office*. The task of the representation office is to make contact with potential customers, form a network of important stakeholders and gather market information. The office does not make direct sales and has no individual legal status. Usually it is not taxed.

The advantages and disadvantages of these different export modes (indirect vs. direct exporting) are shown in Table 15.1.

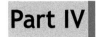

Export Mode	Advantages	Disadvantages
Indirect Exporting	◆ limited commitment and investment required ◆ minimal risk (market, political) ◆ little or no involvement or export experience needed ◆ suitable for firms with limited resources ◆ good way to test-market products, develop goodwill, and allow clients to become familiar with firm's tradename	◆ no control over marketing mix elements other than the product ◆ an additional domestic member in the distribution chain may add costs ◆ lack of contact with the market ◆ lower profit margin due to commissions and other payment to intermediaries ◆ limited contact/feedback from end users ◆ limited/no opportunity to learn international business know-how and develop marketing contacts ◆ difficulties in taking over the business after the relationship has ended.
Direct exporting - Domestic-Based Sales Representatives	◆ better control of sales activities compared to independent intermediaries	◆ high travel expenses
- Agents/Distributors	◆ access to market experience ◆ shorter distribution chain (compared to indirect exporting) ◆ acquisation of market knowledge ◆ more control over marketing mix (especially with agents) ◆ local service support available	◆ little control over market price and lack of distribution control (especially with distributors) ◆ some investment in sales organisation required (contact with distributors or agents) ◆ cultural differences, providing communication problems
- Resident Sales Representatives/Foreign Sales Branches/Foreign Sales Subsidiaries	◆ full control of operation ◆ direct acquisation of market knowledge	◆ initial capital investment required (subsidiary) ◆ less flexibility (subsidiary) ◆ high risk (market, political) ◆ taxation problems

Source: Adapted from Hollensen 2014, p. 362, p. 398; Seyoum 2014, p. 94.

Export Performance Analysis

There is a broad literature analysing the performance of exporting in comparison with other foreign entry or operation modes along with the performance of the different sub-modes, e.g. direct or indirect exports (see, e.g., Morschett 2007, pp. 102-103; Zentes/Swoboda/Schramm-Klein 2013, pp. 285-287). Several *literature reviews* (see, e.g., Leonidou/Katsikeas/Coudounaris 2010, p. 86) and *meta analyses* (see, e.g., Morschett 2007; Morschett/Schramm-Klein/Swoboda 2010) discuss the partly contradictory findings of empirical studies.

15

Countertrade

Countertrade describes a variety of *commercial agreements* in which a seller or exporter delivers products (goods, services, technology) and agrees to a *reciprocal purchasing obligation* with the buyer or importer in terms of full or partial percentage of the sales value.

Barter

"The origins of countertrade can be traced to ancient times, when international trade was based on the free exchange of goods. Barter flourished in Northern Mesopotamia as early as 3000 BC, when inhabitants traded in textiles and metals" (Seyoum 2014, p. 259). Even today, in a *money economy*, countertrade still continues as a medium of exchange. Present-day countertrade is more than the use of simple *barter*. Countertrade includes the exchange of currency or goods and services between two or more countries, including *third parties*, e.g. international trading companies, which operate as an intermediary. They acquire the purchasing obligation from the exporter and sell the countertrade products for their own accounts.

Benefits

The most important benefits of countertrade are (Seyoum 2014, pp. 260-261):

■ for buyers or importers: access to modern technology as well as diminishing balance-of-payments difficulties

■ for seller or exporters: increase in sales opportunities as well as access to sources of supply (e.g. natural resources or raw materials).

Figure 15.4 shows a classification of countertrade transactions.

Forms of Countertrade

Figure 15.4

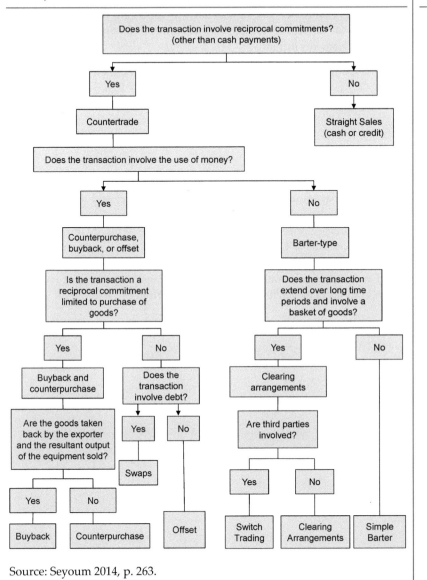

Source: Seyoum 2014, p. 263.

Procedures and Techniques

Executing *cross-border transactions*, such as exporting or importing, means handling a variety of complex legal, contractual and financial factors. Essential elements include:

■ the fixing of prices, currencies, delivery terms and methods of payment

■ the fixing of tasks, costs and risks associated with transportation and delivery of goods.

Trade Terms

Incoterms

Trade terms define the *method of delivery* of goods sold and the responsibilities of the parties involved, i.e. the seller or exporter and the buyer or importer. They also help in the *calculation* of the sales prices and/or the comparison of purchase prices. The most important trade terms are those developed by the *International Chamber of Commerce (ICC)*, the *Incoterms (International Commercial Terms)*. Incoterms have existed since 1936, with seven revisions, and are a set of rules rather than laws. *Incoterms 2010*, the most recent revision, consists of eleven terms, briefly characterised in Table 15.2.

Term	Transport	Transport Insurance	Clearance	Taxes	Export license	Import license	Transfer of risk
EXW (Ex-Works)	buyer	buyer (although not obligated to insure)	buyer	buyer	buyer	buyer	when goods are placed at the disposal of the buyer
FCA (Free Carrier)	buyer	buyer (although not obligated to insure	buyer	buyer	seller	buyer	upon seller's delivery to the carrier at the named place
FAS (Free Alongside Ship)	buyer	buyer (although not obligated to insure	buyer	buyer	seller	buyer	when goods are placed alongside the ship
FOB (Free on Board)	buyer	buyer	buyer	buyer	seller	buyer	when goods are placed on board the vessel at the port of departure
CFR (Cost and Freight)	seller	buyer (although not obligated to insure	buyer	buyer	seller	buyer	when goods are placed on board the vessel at the port of departure
CIF (Cost, Insurance and Freight)	seller	seller	buyer	buyer	seller	buyer	when goods are placed on board the vessel at the port of departure
CPT (Carriage Paid To)	seller	buyer	buyer	buyer	seller	buyer	upon seller's delivery to the main carrier at the place of departure
CIP (Carriage and Insurance Paid To)	seller	seller	buyer	buyer	seller	buyer	upon seller's delivery to the main carrier at the place of departure
DAT (Delivered At Terminal)	seller	seller	buyer	buyer	seller	buyer	when the goods are unloaded from the arriving vehicle (not cleared) and are at the buyer's disposal at the agreed place of destination
DAP (Delivered At Place)	seller	seller (although not obligated to insure)	buyer	buyer	seller	buyer	when the goods are placed at the buyer's disposal at the agreed destination (not unloaded and not cleared)
DDP (Delivered Duty Paid)	seller	seller (although not obligated to insure)	seller	seller	seller	seller	when goods cleared and duty paid (not unloaded) are placed at the buyer's disposal at the agreed destination

Source: ICC Germany 2013.

Conclusion and Outlook

Exporting and importing, i.e. the exchange of goods and services across national boundaries, is the most traditional form of international business activity. International trade has played a major role in both *economic history* and *world history*. International trade is still of great and growing importance to the global economy. Global merchandise and service exports will continue to grow.

Over the past few decades a shift in the *direction of trade* can be observed. Trade among industrial market economies has been the dominant pattern. The dynamic growth of developing countries, especially the so-called *emerging countries*, has led to an enormous increase in trade with and among these developing nations.

New Directions of Trade

Exporting is also the first type of foreign business operation undertaken by most companies from emerging countries developing into *emerging market multinationals*. Exporting will continue to play an important role in industrial market economies. It is the first step toward entering new markets, such as emerging countries.

Further Reading

ALBAUM, G.; DUERR, E. (2011): International Marketing & Export Management, 7th ed., Harlow, Pearson.

JOHNSON, T.E.; DONNA, L.B. (2010): Export/Import Procedures and Documentation, Osborne, McGraw-Hill Professional.

SEYOUM, B. (2014): Export-Import Theory, Practices and Procedures, 3rd ed., New York, Routledge.

Case Study: Herrenknecht[*]

Profile, History and Status Quo

Herrenknecht is a German manufacturer of tunnel-drilling machines, headquartered in Allmannsweier near Schwanau, Germany. The professionally managed family enterprise is the *global market leader* in mechanised tunnelling for tunnel infrastructures, as well as for underground energy sources and raw material extractions. As of 2013, it is the only company in its respective field that delivers cutting-edge tunnel-drilling machines for all ground conditions and in all diameters, ranging from 0.10 to 19 meters.

The company's origins date back to 1975 when *Martin Herrenknecht* established the eponymous engineering company in a small office in Lahr, Germany. Over the next two years, *Herrenknecht* and its six employees developed the MH1 to MH3 machine models for pipe jacking in loose soils, and in 1977 *Herrenknecht GmbH* (i.e. a limited liability company) was founded. In 1980, the company relocated its office to Schwanau, where its first assembly plant was opened. During the 1980s, *Herrenknecht* launched various devel-

---

[*] Sources used for this case study include the website http://www.herrenknecht.com, various company reports, investor-relations presentations as well as explicitly cited sources.

opments, e.g. micro machines for non-accessible tunnel diameters or the so-called "mixshield generation" for larger tunnel diameters. In 1984, the company opened its first subsidiary abroad in Sunderland, England. The manufacturer continued its growth by acquiring the shares of *Maschinen- und Stahlbau GmbH* in Dresden, Germany in 1991. In 1998, *Herrenknecht GmbH* was converted into a non-listed joint stock company (*Herrenknecht AG*). This conversion was followed by the founding of diverse subsidiaries around the world. In the meantime, *Herrenknecht* has become market leader in mechanised tunnelling technology. In 2005, the company reached record sales, surpassing 500 million EUR. Two years later, the tunnel manufacturer received inflow orders passing the one billion EUR mark for the first time. As of 2010, the company holds the world record for the construction of the largest tunnel-drilling machine. 2011 was another year of new records: Order inflow increased by 25% to 1,143 million EUR and sales increased by 9% to 1,017 million EUR.

In 2013, with some 4,800 employees (including trainees and temporary workers) the enterprise enjoys a stable position with sales of 1,051 million EUR and an order inflow of 1,082 EUR. All aforementioned data is shown in Table 15.3.

Selected Data of Herrenknecht (2008 to 2013)   *Table 15.3*

	2008	2009	2010	2011	2012	2013
Sales (in million EUR)	926	866	935	1,017	1,147	1,051
Order inflow (in million EUR)	939	908	916	1,143	1,051	1,082
Number of staff*	3,831	3,960	4,154	5,635	5,079	4,777

*including trainees and temporary workers

Source: Herrenknecht 2014.

Thanks to their positive business development, *Herrenknecht* has gained considerable significance in the German industry sector.

According to a 2013 brand study commissioned by the German business magazine *WirtschaftsWoche*, *Herrenknecht* occupies the top position among German world market leaders in the mid-sized business sector. Compared to 2011, when *Herrenknecht* was also in first place, the company has further increased its performance, and is the most valuable business-to-business brand among these German companies.

No. 1 in Brand Ranking

Figure 15.5 provides a summary of the *milestones* in *Herrenknecht's history*, from its foundation up to 2013.

Figure 15.5 | *Milestones in Herrenknecht's History (1975 to 2013)*

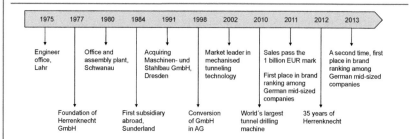

Source: Herrenknecht 2014.

Core Markets and Brands

The *Herrenknecht Group*, which operationally consists of *Herrenknecht AG*, numerous subsidiaries and associated companies working in related fields, offers full range solutions in three core markets:

- *Herrenknecht Tunnelling* can be divided into traffic tunnelling and utility tunnelling. *Traffic tunnelling* refers to all technical solutions for modern infrastructure. It includes the construction of efficient road tunnels, transregional and transnational railway networks and efficient metro networks. *Utility tunnelling* comprises all technologies for efficient underground supply tunnelling systems, e.g. construction and installation of water and sewage systems, pipelines, conduits for power, Internet and telephone lines as well as headrace tunnels for hydropower plants.

- *Herrenknecht Mining* concerns the company's mechanised tunnelling operations for constructing cutting-edge underground mining infrastructures. In light of the growing world demand for ore, extracting underground raw material deposits at great depths is gaining in importance. *Herrenknecht* supplies an entire range of innovative solutions based on proven technology to serve this field.

- *Herrenknecht Exploration* comprises the company's technical innovations to explore and develop new energy deposits, which are mostly located in difficult to access areas. It encompasses the optimisation of drilling ecology for geothermal energy, as well as the exploration and development of new raw material reservoirs with advanced technologies.

As illustrated in Figure 15.6, the *Herrenknecht's* tunnelling and mining market o is dominated by the core brand called *Herrenknecht Tunnelling Systems*, while exploration is dominated by the *Herrenknecht Vertical* brand, which exclusively develops and manufactures deep drilling systems to explore energy resources at extreme depths. *Herrenknecht Vertical*, which was founded in 2005, is one of the company's most impressive innovations. Instead of the horizontal tunnelling usually employed in tunnelling processes, *Herrenknecht* seized the opportunity to transfer its competencies to vertical drilling, especially for geothermal purposes, which show extremely strong promise. Thus, *Herrenknecht* added a complete new growth market to its portfolio.

Core Brands

Core Markets and Brands

Figure 15.6

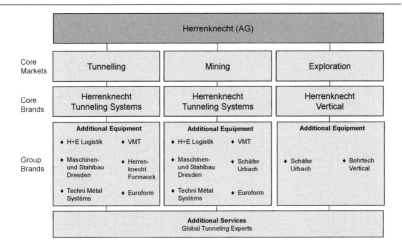

Source: Herrenknecht 2014.

Worldwide Operations

Herrenknecht is currently working on 850 infrastructure projects for supply and disposal tunnels worldwide. As of 2013, exports account for 95% of *Herrenknecht's* global business. In doing so, the manufacturer uses various subsidiaries and sales representatives in Germany and abroad. At time of writing, the enterprise group owns 78 subsidiaries – including the Netherlands, Australia, New Zealand, China, France, Great Britain, India, Iran, Italy, Malaysia, Russia, Singapore, Spain, Switzerland, Thailand, Ukraine, the United Arab Emirates, the United States and Venezuela.

Subsidiaries and Representatives

15

Worldwide Partnerships

Along with these subsidiaries, *Herrenknecht* maintains partnerships with a dozen companies, including *Anakon, Bohrtec* (Germany), *Hodapp Hispanica* (Spain), *HS Tunnel-Engineering* (Switzerland) and *Commodore Cement Industries* (United Arab Emirates). With a presence in 38 countries, *Herrenknecht* holds a world market share of over 70%.

Numerous distribution and service locations on all continents support the company in providing a comprehensive range of services close to the project site and the customer.

Table 15.4 shows *Herrenknecht´s worldwide operations*, divided into distribution, service and production locations. It clearly shows that, despite its international business, the German headquarters is still of paramount importance. The main production locations are still based in Germany – not least because the quality label *"Made in Germany"* is applied to all *Herrenknecht technology.*

Table 15.4 | *Worldwide Operations (2014)*

Region	Country	Number of distribution locations	Number of service locations	Number of production locations	Region	Country	Number of distribution locations	Number of service locations	Number of production locations
Africa & Middle East	Egypt	1				Italy	3	2	1
	Qatar	1	1			Netherlands	2	2	
	Saudi Arabia	1	1			Portugal	1		
	South Africa	1				Romania	1		
	United Arab Emirates	2	2	1		Russia	2	2	
Asia	China	2	7	4	Europe	Spain	1	1	
	India	1	1	1		Sweden	1		
	Indonesia	2				Switzerland	3	2	1
	Malaysia	1				Turkey	1		
	Singapore	1	1			Ukraine	1	1	
	South Korea	1				United Kingdom	1	1	
	Thailand	1	1		Northern America	Canada	1		
Australia & Oceania	Australia	2	1			United States	1	1	1
Central America	Mexico	2	1			Argentina	2	1	
	Panama	1	1			Brazil	1	1	
Europe	Azerbaijan	1			South America	Chile	1	1	
	Bulgaria	1				Colombia	1	1	
	France	2	1	1		Peru	1		
	Germany	9	8	8		Venezuela	1	1	

Source: Herrenknecht 2014.

Herrenknecht's Position in the German Export Market

With its eight production plants in the German cities of Schwanau (3 plants), Alsdorf, Bochum, Dresden, Ratingen and Bruchsal, *Herrenknecht* offers and supplies integrated tunnelling solutions, including project-specific equipment, as well as service packages to customers from all over the world. Continuous process innovations, which are mainly driven by the R&D department in Schwanau, as well as consistent knowledge transfer to local markets, have supported the company in the internationalisation of its business.

With this strong track record for innovation, *Herrenknecht*, as previously mentioned, leads the list of the German mid-sized companies. This elite tier known as *"hidden champions"* was identified by *Simon* (1996; 2009; 2012) as the driver of Germany's export success (for reference: Germany was market leader in world exports from 2003 to 2008, and is still one of the main export countries).

Herrenknecht as a Hidden Champion

Herrenknecht belongs to this elite tier because it meets many of the criteria suggested for a typical hidden champion (Simon 2012, p. 83). These criteria are: belonging to the top three in their global market, or No. 1 on their continent (determined by market share), having revenues below 5 billion USD and being little known to the general public.

Characteristics of Hidden Champions

Like *Herrenknecht*, most of these exceptionally successful mid-sized companies are family-owned businesses with headquarters based in small towns. The extraordinary relevance of these hidden champions lies in their export strength, as they account for about 25% of German exports and have created over a million new jobs in the last ten years. With their high export ratios, they contribute significantly to their country's balance sheet and are often more successful than average. *Herrenknecht*'s impressive track records in innovation over the last 35 years, as well as its customer loyalty due to its global presence are further examples. With its increasingly global market share, *Herrenknecht* has also created a massive wave of new innovations. Compared to China and the United States, where exports are dominated by highly visible traditional internationalisers, German exports are determined by a huge number of hidden champions like *Herrenknecht*.

From Export to Offshore Production

Despite the aforementioned relevance of Germany as *Herrenknecht's* main production location, the company has expanded its production geographically in recent years.

Herrenknecht's selective production expansion is shown in Figure 15.7. While in its first twenty years *Herrenknecht* grew through domestic production and exporting, the opening of the US production facility in 1997, and more importantly the opening of further production facilities beginning in 2005 in China, Switzerland, India, the United Arab Emirates and France are testament to a new wave of *production expansion.*

Figure 15.7 | *Selective Production Expansion*

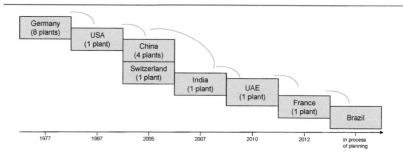

Source: Adapted from Herrenknecht 2014.

The Asian market is of paramount importance. Both China and India are "among the key markets in the Asia-Pacific region, due to its enormous demand" (Herrenknecht 2014). In order to provide projects and customers with high quality and reliable tunnelling technology according to schedules, the company has established several production facilities in China and India.

China | The first manufacturing location for the assembly of tunnelling equipment in China was opened in Guangzhou in 2005. This was followed by a new assembly plant opened in Nansha in 2006. In 2007, and later in 2011, *Herrenknecht* opened production facilities in Chengdu, which is one of the world's fastest growing cities (Forbes 2010). Compared to Germany, where almost 95% of *Herrenknecht's* products are exported, most of the products and machines manufactured in China remain in the Chinese market. Manufacturing in China offers great advantages to *Herrenknecht* and its customers. Among other things, Asian contacts are more familiar with local conditions in the Asia-Pacific region, costs are reduced through shorter transportation times and the availability of equipment can be optimised. Even though *Herrenknecht* "still produces electronic and hydraulic equipment at its main plant in Schwanau, but domestic sales would not have been sufficient to keep the operation running at full capacity" (Spiegel Online 2010). To ensure that all assembly plants fulfil the same quality standards used in Schwanau, a team of experts is regularly sent to offshore production facilities to locally monitor the production and train staff on site.

Herrenknecht is building up production facilities in India for the same reasons as in China. In 2007, *Herrenknecht* opened an assembly plant in Chennai, the biggest industrial centre in South India. Within the 3,000 square metre plant, the company assembled the EPB (Earth Pressure Balance) shields that were delivered to the Delhi Metro for construction of their new metro tunnel system (The Economic Times 2012). Furthermore, India is developing an expanding horizontal drilling rigs market, which is used for trenchless laying of oil and gas pipelines. Thus more and more construction companies are turning to horizontal drilling rig equipment made by *Herrenknecht*, whereby products are partly imported from *Herrenknecht* in Germany and partly produced on site.

Besides China and India, Brazil is also increasingly important as a production site for *Herrenknecht*. The company has announced plans to establish an assembly plant in Brazil to export its equipment to the rest of Latin America and Africa.

Summary and Outlook

With experience from more than 2,300 global projects, *Herrenknecht* is the leading provider of holistic technical solutions in mechanised tunnelling. Exporting plays a major role in *Herrenknecht's* story of success, but at the same time their "Made in Germany" label is still of paramount importance. However, *Herrenknecht* is also expanding its production geographically as markets like China or India become more important. The overall goal, laid down in the company's vision statement, is to maintain their position as "the leading premium supplier worldwide for all-round technology solutions in mechanized tunnelling for tunnel infrastructures of all kinds, as well as for underground energy sources and raw materials extraction" (Herrenknecht 2014). In line with this vision, the combination of its technology-based product leadership with close customer relationships provides the basis for a further positive development of this family enterprise.

Questions

1. *Herrenknecht* uses different methods to sell its products to foreign countries. Describe the different distribution channels and discuss why the specific channels are applied. What are the main advantages and disadvantages of other direct and indirect distribution channels?

2. Although the *hidden champion* concept is attracting increasing attention all over the world, its prevalence in Germany suggests it as a German phenomenon. Describe the hidden champion concept, discuss why

Germany has so many of them, and elaborate some lessons other companies can learn from hidden champions.

3. Exporting is usually the first step for foreign operations, and *Herrenknecht* was no exception. Analyse and describe why nowadays the company not only exports its products from its headquarters in Schwanau to China or India, but also produces there on site.

Hints

1. See, e.g., Hollensen 2014 or Seyoum 2014.

2. See, e.g., Simon 2009; 2012.

References

ALBAUM, G.; DUERR, E. (2011): International Marketing & Export Management, 7th ed., Harlow, Pearson.

BALL, D.A.; GERINGER, I.M.; MINOR, M.S.; MCNETT, J.M. (2013): International Business, Irwin, McGraw-Hill.

CHETTY, S.; CAMPBELL-HUNT, C. (2004): A Strategic Approach to Internationalization: A Traditional Versus a "Born-Global" Approach, in: Journal of International Marketing, Vol. 12, Nr. 1, pp. 57-81.

COOK, G.; JOHNS, J. (Eds.) (2013): The Changing Geography of International Business, New York, Palgrave Macmillan.

DKSH; ROLAND BERGER (2013): Roland Berger Strategy Consultant Confirms Promising Prospects of MES Industry in Asia, http://www.dksh.com/data /docs/download/101465/en/RBSC-Market-Study-DKSH-Press-Release-ENG.pdf, accessed on August, 2014.

FORBES (2010): The World's Fastest-growing Cities, http://www.forbes.com /2010/10/07/cities-china-chicago-opinions-columnists-joel-kotkin.html, accessed on August 13, 2014.

HERRENKNECHT (2014): Herrenknecht, www.herrenknecht.com, accessed on August 12, 2014.

HOLLENSEN, S. (2014): Global Marketing, 6th ed., Harlow, Pearson.

ICC GERMANY (2013): ICC Incoterms®-Regeln, http://www.icc-deutsch-land.de/icc-regeln-und-richtlinien/icc-incotermsR.html, accessed on September 01, 2014.

JOHNSON, T.E.; DONNA, L.B. (2010): Export/Import Procedures and Documentation, Osborne, McGraw-Hill Professional.

LEONIDOU, L.; KATSIKEAS, C.; COUDOUNARIS, D. (2010): Five Decades of Business Research Into Exporting: A Bibliographic Analysis, in: Journal of International Management, Vol. 16, No. 1, pp. 78-91.

MORSCHETT, D. (2007): Institutionalisierung und Koordination von Auslandseinheiten: Analyse von Industrie- und Dienstleistungsunternehmen, Wiesbaden, Gabler.

MORSCHETT, D.; SCHRAMM-KLEIN, H.; SWOBODA, B. (2008): Decades of Research on Market Entry Modes: What Do We Really Know About External Antecedents of Entry Mode Choice?, in: Journal of International Management, Vol. 16, No. 1, pp. 60-77.

MÜHLBACHER, H.; LEIHS, H.; DAHRINGER, L.; (2006): International Marketing, 3rd ed., London, Thomson Learning.

SEYOUM, B. (2014): Export-Import Theory, Practices, and Procedures, 3rd ed., New York, Routledge.

SIMON, H. (1996): Lessons from 500 of the World's Best Unknown Companies, Boston, Harvard University Press.

SIMON, H. (2009): Hidden Champions of the 21st Century, Dordrecht et al., Springer.

SIMON, H. (2012): Hidden Champions: Aufbruch nach Globalia, Frankfurt, Campus.

SPIEGEL ONLINE (2010): Beijing's High-Tech Ambitions: The Danger of Germany's Dependence on China, http://ml.spiegel.de/article.do?id=7 13478&p=1, accessed on August 13, 2014.

THE ECONOMIC TIMES (2012): Delhi Metro Completes First Tunnelling of Phase-III Project, http://articles.economictimes.indiatimes.com/2012-07-26/news/32869791_1_metre-long-tunnel-first-tunnel-herrenknecht, accessed on August 13, 2014.

ZENTES, J.; SWOBODA, B.; SCHRAMM-KLEIN, H. (2013): Internationales Marketing, 3rd ed., Munich, Vahlen.

Chapter 16

Outsourcing and Offshoring

A key strategic decision for an MNC is the choice between internalisation and externalisation for every activity in the value chain. This strategic choice raises the question of what is the appropriate value chain architecture of a firm. In the context of internationalisation or even globalisation new options such as offshoring have emerged. The purpose of this Chapter is to highlight the importance of corporate boundary and location decisions and to describe the variety of alternatives.

Internalisation vs. Externalisation

In *new institutional economics* (for theoretical explanations, see Chapter 14) there are two opposing choices for realising activities. A value chain activity can be performed internally, i.e. controlled or coordinated via hierarchy/integration, or externally, i.e. by other firms. Externalisation always means *buying* or *sourcing* goods or services. In this case, the *market mechanism* assumes the role of coordination (see Figure 16.1). In more practitioner-oriented terminology these two basic alternatives are also called *make or buy* (see Zentes/Swoboda/Morschett 2004, pp. 243-250).

Market vs. Hierarchy

If an activity currently being realised internally is transferred to an external firm, this process is called *outsourcing*, i.e. the use of outside resources. In contrast, if an activity is integrated into the internal value chain (intra-firm transaction), this process is called *insourcing*.

Transaction Modes

Figure 16.1

Market	Cooperation	Hierarchy/ Integration

Internalisation →

← Externalisation

Between these two polar alternatives there are a wide range of *cooperative agreements* (see Chapter 17) with only vague delimitations between externalisation and internalisation, such as *contract buying, contract manufacturing, licensing, franchising* or *equity joint ventures*.

Advantages and Disadvantages of Outsourcing

The strategic choice between internalisation (insourcing) or externalisation (outsourcing) affects all activities in a firm's value chain.

Motives

In a *meta study* of the scientific literature, Matiaske and Mellewigt (2002, pp. 646-647) identified four main *motives* for outsourcing:

- *Cost advantages:* A major motive for outsourcing is cost reduction. The logic behind this argument is that an external firm can realise the function in question more efficiently than the outsourcing firm, because the firm is specialised in this field, i.e., the activity belongs to its core competences. The assumption is that the external firm is willing to transfer this cost advantage completely or partly to the outsourcing firm.

- *Concentration on core business:* From a strategic point of view, a strong concentration on core business is another important motive for outsourcing. By outsourcing minor/peripheral or supporting activities, a firm can focus its resources on the core activities of the value chain.

- *Improvement of efficiency and performance:* Bringing in external service providers can lead to performance improvements. Specialists are likely to have better expertise, better qualified personnel and be more technologically up-to-date than the outsourcing firm.

- *Advantages in financing and risk transfer:* Outsourcing activities related to high financial investment, reduces the amount of capital tied up and the firm's funding requirements. At the same time, the financing of reserve capacities in order to meet peaks in demand can be dropped. Finally, fixed costs are "converted" to variable costs.

A recent *Ernst & Young* (2013) study across eight European countries identified the most important reasons for outsourcing business processes and IT services. Improvements in *cost levels* is still the most frequently cited reason for outsourcing. "Efficiency improvements and a greater focus on core business are the second and third reasons for outsourcing within Europe" (Ernst & Young 2013, p. 14) (see also Figure 16.2).

Most Important Reasons for Outsourcing

Figure 16.2

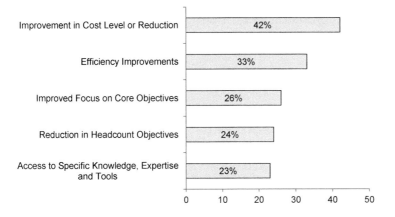

Source: Ernst & Young 2013, p.15.

Matiaske and Mellewigt (2002, p. 651) identify the following *risks* of outsourcing:

■ *higher total costs* than alternatives due to *transaction costs* (costs of negotiating, control, etc.)

■ *opportunistic behaviour* by the firm (supplier) to which an activity has been transferred

■ *loss of expertise*

■ *transfer of core competences.*

This last risk describes a situation where core competences are not recognised as such and transferred externally.

As shown in Figure 16.3, *dependence on the external service provider* is perceived as the most important risk when organisations outsource, following the recent *Ernst & Young* study (2013). These results largely correspond to the findings in the meta-study by Matiaske and Mellewigt (2002).

Figure 16.3 | *Most Important Risks for Outsourcing*

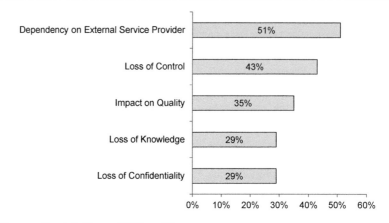

Source: Ernst & Young 2013, p. 15.

Strategic Relevance/ Competence- Matrix

Outsourcing can also be positioned in the so-called *"strategic relevance/competence-matrix"*, developed by Krüger and Homp (1997) (see Figure 16.4). Following this model, outsourcing is useful if the strategic relevance or importance and the firm's competence with regard to an activity or process are low ("outsource"). This situation is typical for support activities, such as facility management, legal services or payroll services. If the strategic relevance is high but the firm's competence in this field is low, the firm has to invest in order to narrow the gap ("develop"). The competence can be transferred, i.e. sold, to other companies, even competitors, if the firm's capabilities are high and this asset is not crucial to market success ("transfer"). The combination of high competence and high strategic relevance forms the basis of *competitive advantages*. Activities or processes in this field are realised internally, rather than outsourced or transferred ("use").

When the right outsourcing decisions are made, the resulting benefits serve to strengthen the company's internal resources (Nordin 2008). So outsourcing allows the company to concentrate on the business activities that create greater competitive advantages for them.

Figure 16.4

Strategic Relevance/Competence-Matrix

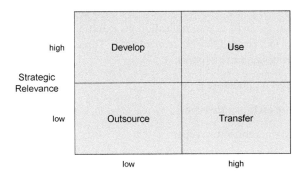

Source: Adapted from Krüger/Homp 1997, p. 105.

There is not one single outsourcing model. The *"A.T. Kearney* Strategic Outsourcing Framework" (Martin 2010) shows different *strategic choices* (see Figure 16.5):

■ *outsource*: Services are provided by a third party.

■ *co-source*: Services are provided by one or more providers.

■ *contest*: Services are contracted to multiple suppliers at the same time.

Figure 16.5

A.T. Kearney's Strategic Outsourcing Framework

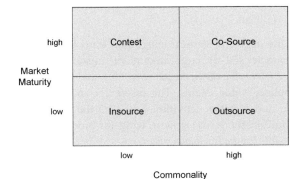

Source: Martin 2010, p. 165.

New Forms of Value Chain Architecture through Outsourcing

Decisions in the field of internalisation vs. externalisation lead to fundamental changes in a firm's *value chain architecture*. Three typical architecture types for core processes can be found:

- *traditional* architecture type

- *assembler* architecture type

- *coordinator* architecture type.

Traditional Architecture Type

The traditional model, characterised by supply chain processes and the market-oriented processes which are realised internally, is still common in specific industries, such as the chemical and pharmaceutical industries. At first glance this type operates in most industries, but the degree of *vertical integration* has been dramatically reduced.

Assembler Architecture Type

In the automotive industry, the average degree of vertical integration is between 20 and 30%. The production of parts or components has been transferred or outsourced to suppliers. For example, a typical car contains more than 10,000 components. In this industry manufacturers constantly face make-or-buy decisions: "*Toyota* produces less than 30% of the value of cars that roll off its assembly lines. The remaining 70%, mainly accounted for by component parts and complex subassemblies, comes from independent suppliers" (Hill 2013, p. 424).

Reducing the degree of vertical integration leads to the *assembler* type. This type is characterised by large amount of outsourcing, but the assembler controls the *total value chain*, i.e. its own value chain as well as the basic parts of its suppliers' value chains. The assembler coordinates R&D, sourcing, production and logistics activities. For R&D the (outsourcing) firm is responsible for *innovation management*, while for production and sourcing they are responsible for *quality management*.

Supplier Pyramid   Due to the division of labour between a manufacturer and its suppliers, *supplier pyramids* are characterised by several layers of contractors or subcontractors. The *tier structure* of this supplier network is illustrated in Figure 16.6.

Figure 16.6

Supplier Pyramid

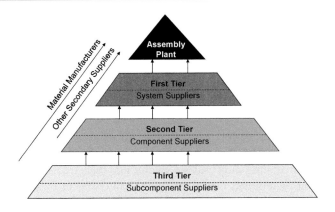

The *assembler* type of value chain architecture shows the fuzzy delimitation between externalisation and cooperative agreements. Two sub-types can be distinguished:

■ contract buying

■ contract manufacturing.

Contract buying is characterised by suppliers offering products and/or services developed and designed on their own and delivering these goods on the basis of mid-term or even long-term agreements *(contracts)*. Sourcing of raw materials and energy is typical for this type of agreement. *Contract manufacturers* produce parts or components which are developed and designed by the outsourcing firm (see Morschett 2005; see also Chapter 17). In some cases, they have no R&D activities of their own.

Coordinator Architecture Type

The farthest-reaching type of outsourcing is typical for the value chain architecture of a *coordinator* or "*orchestrator*". This architecture occurs when a manufacturer undertakes no production activities at all, i.e., all production has been outsourced. The *coordinator* type is becoming more prominent, especially in the consumer goods industries. Companies such as *Ralph Lauren, Nike, Adidas* and *Puma* concentrate on product development, design and the control of the supply chain. Their production activities are totally transferred to suppliers operating on a *contractual basis*. The same tendency can be observed in the electronic industries (see the case study in this Chapter).

Manufacturers without Production

The value chain architecture of a coordinator is not only relevant to manufacturers. A growing number of retail and wholesale companies are adopting this form, migrating from the traditional architecture (buyer) to that of a coordinator. The development and design of *store brands* produced by contract manufacturers is an example (see, e.g., Zentes/Morschett/Schramm-Klein 2011, pp. 232-237).

Insourcing through Verticalisation

Marketing, especially selling/distribution, displays a completely different trend, especially in the consumer goods industries. Manufacturers are increasingly integrating direct sales activities into their value chains by establishing their own outlets *(equity stores)* or retail chains or by selling directly to consumers via the Internet *(E-Commerce)* (Zentes/Swoboda/Morschett 2005; Zentes/Neidhart/Scheer 2006). As well as this form of *secured distribution*, there is a wide range of *contractual agreements* with legally independent retailers or dealers *(controlled distribution)*, for example, franchise agreements or shop-in-shop agreements (see Zentes/Morschett/Schramm-Klein 2011, pp. 98-104).

Insourcing market-oriented activities, such as selling to final consumers *(B2C-distribution)*, are frequently combined with the supply chain oriented architecture of a coordinator. The companies mentioned above *(Ralph Lauren, Nike,* etc.) are pioneers in this field. In the extreme case, a manufacturer has no production of its own and a pure controlled distribution network. It "only" coordinates the supply chain and market-oriented processes.

Offshoring

While outsourcing involves the decision of whether to make or buy *(corporate boundary decision)*, neglecting cooperative transactional modes regardless of where the activity takes place, the location decision *(configuration decision)* refers to where the activity takes place regardless of whether it is inside or outside the corporate boundary (see Figure 16.7).

Offshoring refers to relocating activities to foreign countries, mostly low-cost countries, e.g. *newly industrialised countries* (NICs) that are emerging as production sites, sourcing and/or selling markets. This offers the opportunity for international production and international sourcing to make use of comparative advantages, such as low wages (see Chapter 19). The literature sometimes draws a distinction between *offshoring* and *nearshoring*. Offshoring refers to remote, lower cost locations, nearshoring to nearer lower cost countries.

Transactional Modes and Configuration

Figure 16.7

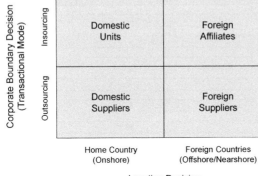

Source: Adapted from Abramovsky/Griffith 2006, p. 595.

The previously mentioned *Ernst & Young* study (2013, p. 13) identified three options for *locations of outsourced activities* (see Figure 16.8):

Locations of Outsourced Activities

■ *onshore*: provided from the same location or country

■ *nearshore*: provided from another country in the same continent

■ *offshore*: provided from an offshore location, usually located in Asia, the Middle East, Africa or Latin America.

Denmark has the highest percentages provided from offshore (16%) and nearshore (26%), followed by Germany with 14% and 21% respectively.

Figure 16.8 | *Location of Outsourced Business Processes and Services by Country*

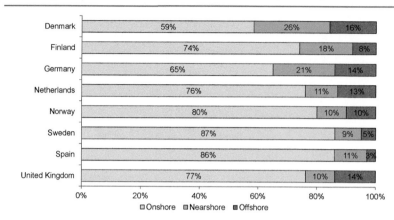

Source: Ernst & Young 2013, p. 13.

Emerging countries are mostly interested in attracting foreign capital and expertise by establishing plants or R&D units in order to accelerate the economic transformation and development process or to produce and deliver to foreign countries in order to create values and reinforce their home labour markets. Therefore they support or even sponsor such activities or processes through tax reductions or temporary tax concessions which increase the *comparative advantages* of these countries. Sometimes they establish special *tax free areas*: territories with exemption from duties, often geographically connected with ports, to attract foreign production sites (see also Chapter 8).

Offshoring/Outsourcing of Management and Support Activities

In recent years, the outsourcing decision has gone beyond the production of physical products. Outsourcing also refers to support and service activities as well as management process activities, such as human resource management, information management, etc. ("moving *white collar jobs* offshore"). This field of *management and support activities*, also combines the corporate boundary decision to outsource with the location decision of offshoring, e.g. to prefer suppliers in low-cost countries. "For example, many US-based companies from credit card issuers to computer companies have outsourced their call centres to India. They are 'buying' the customer call centre function, while making other parts of the product in house. Similarly, many information technology companies have been outsourcing some parts of the software development process, such as testing computer code written in the

USA, to independent providers based in India. Such companies are 'making' (writing) most of the code in-house but "buying", or outsourcing, part of the production process (testing) to independent companies"(Hill 2013, pp. 424-425).

As an example, Figure 16.9 shows the degree of outsourcing of IT services per industry. IT services are outsourced most in the automotive industry, followed by the telecommunication and consumer product industries.

Outsourcing of IT Services per Industry   *Figure 16.9*

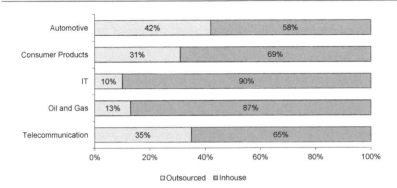

Source: Ernst & Young 2013, p. 12.

Vertical Integration and Re-Location as Counter-Trends

"Every trend engenders a counter-trend." When it comes to outsourcing and offshoring, some important strategic developments can be observed. Due to the dramatic expansion of the world population and the consequent growing demand for agricultural and industrial raw materials, *supply security* is increasingly important, leading to long-term contracts with suppliers, e.g. farmers (*contract farming*), or even acquisitions of suppliers in this field (Zentes 2011).

This tendency towards insourcing is triggered by a quite different factor. Pursuing the aim of being a *sustainable player*, i.e. operating in a socially and ecologically responsible manner, ultimately requires total control of all value chain activities, including preliminary stages of the production process. This can be achieved through complex and costly control mechanisms or by in-sourcing (Bastian/Zentes 2011).

Sometimes these requirements lead to re-location of production or sourcing activities to countries which guarantee or enable compliance with social and ecological standards (nearshore), or even back to the home country.

Conclusion and Outlook

Outsourcing and Insourcing

An asymmetrical tendency can be seen in value chain architecture. On the one hand, outsourcing or externalisation is the strategic mainstream for the supply chain process, which results in new value chain models such as *assembler* or *coordinator*. On the other hand, companies are interested in controlling or even securing the distribution in order to have *direct relations* with private and/or commercial customers. This strategic approach leads to new marketing and sales structures – insourcing or internalisation is the consequence.

The political and legal developments in the context of globalisation reinforce the tendency of offshoring, i.e. shifting production and/or sourcing to foreign countries. Companies in high-cost countries are increasingly concentrating on *intellectual value creation*, i.e., innovation management, quality management and brand management, which increasingly includes *channel management*.

Some triggers of insourcing and re-locating can be observed: securing supplies of agricultural and industrial raw materials and ensuring social and ecological standards in the value chain process.

Outsourcing Dilemma

Offshore production or *offshore sourcing* sometimes results in one of the biggest challenges facing international business or managers of international companies: defining ethical standards and operating in a socially and ecologically responsible manner (Griffin/Pustay 2013, pp. 143-149, see Chapter 13). Companies are often faced with real *ethical dilemmas* where the appropriate action is not clear: "They are situations in which none of the available alternatives seems ethically acceptable" (Hill 2013, p. 132). "For example, at a first glance, it is uncritical for a company to outsource production to a factory in a low-cost country with unsafe working conditions". But people in that country might argue that as unattractive as they might seem to outsiders, those jobs are superior to the ones that would otherwise be available" (Griffin/Pustay 2013, pp. 142-143).

Part IV

Further Reading

DOZ, Y.; SANTOS, J.; WILLIAMSON, P.J. (2003): The New Global Game: How Your Company Can Win in the Knowledge Economy, in: BARTLETT, C.A.; GHOSHAL, S.; BIRKINSHAW, J. (Eds.): Transnational Management, 4th ed., Boston, McGraw-Hill, pp. 832-839.

HILL, C.W.L. (2013): Global Business Today, 8th ed., Boston, McGraw-Hill, pp. 411-436.

KOTABE, M.; HELSEN, K. (2014): Global Marketing Management, 6th ed., New York, Wiley & Sons.

MILBERG, W.; WINKLER, D. (2013): Outsourcing Economies: Global Value Chains in Capitalist Development, New York, Cambridge University Press.

Case Study: Foxconn[*]

Profile, History and Status Quo

Hon Hai/Foxconn Technology Group, better known by its trading name *Foxconn*, is a multinational electronics contract manufacturer headquartered in Tucheng, New Taipei, Taiwan. The enterprise group (hereinafter collectively called *Foxconn*) is the world's largest and fastest-growing company in the field of manufacturing services providers for the so-called 3Cs: computers, communication, and consumer electronics. *Foxconn* is the manufacturer of some of America's most popular consumer electronic devices for companies like *Apple* or *Microsoft*, and has widespread manufacturing facilities worldwide, but most of all in China. Thus, it is "a symbol of US outsourcing" (EPS 2014).

The company's origin dates back to 1974, when *Terry (Tai-min) Gou* founded *Hon Hai Precision Industry Company Ltd.*, the parent company of *Foxconn*, "guided by the belief that electronic products would be an integral part of everyday life in every business and every home" (Foxconn 2014). Convinced by the idea of providing the lowest cost solutions and thus making electronic products affordable for the entire market, the founder established *Foxconn* with only 7,500 USD, borrowed from his mother. At the end of the 1980s, *Foxconn* opened its main manufacturing plant in Shenzhen, China. In 1991,

---

[*] Sources used for this case study include the websites http://foxconn.com, annual and company reports, as well as explicitly cited sources.

the company was listed on the Taiwan Stock Exchange Corporation (TSEC), and is currently worth about 1.1 trillion TWD (37 billion USD).

Since its foundation, *Foxconn* has been awarded and nominated several times. Among other examples, *Foxconn* was selected as the "Best Management Company in Taiwan" by Asian Money in 1999. In 2001, according to Taiwanese surveys, the company became the largest private manufacturing enterprise in Taiwan, and in 2002 it became the largest exporter in China. According to *IR Magazine,* it has been nominated as the "Best Investor Relation Company in Taiwan" three times, in 2003, 2006 and 2007. In 2011, *Foxconn* was ranked 60th among the "Fortune Global 500" by *Fortune magazine* and 9th in "IFI CLAIMS® 2011 Top 50 United States Patent Assignees" as a leader in innovation and technical expertise. The contract manufacturer was responsible for 5.9% of exports in China in 2011, and was ranked as the largest exporter in the country for ten consecutive years (2002-2012).

Foxconn had been granted more than 55,000 patents up to 2012 – with about 92,000 patents already registered. This made *Foxconn* a recognised leader of innovation and technical expertise in further rankings such as *MIT's* or *IPIQ's* patent scorecard. In 2012, *Foxconn* was ranked 30th among the world's biggest companies by "Fortune Global 500".

Figure 16.10 shows a summary of the *milestones* in *Foxconn´s* history, from its founding until 2012.

Figure 16.10 | *Milestones in Company History (from 1974 to 2012)*

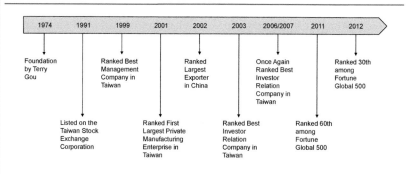

Today, *Foxconn* employs some 1.6 million people globally and has production facilities in Asia, Europe, Mexico and South America that together assembled some 40% of the consumer electronics products sold in 2013. The company´s revenue of 132 billion USD for 2013 is estimated to double within the next 10 years.

The long-lasting success of *Foxconn* is based on the following three visions, which have guided the company since its foundation:

- making electronic product usage an attainable reality for all of mankind through the most efficient *"total cost advantages"*

- revolutionising the conventional inefficient electronics outsourcing model through the proprietary one-stop shopping vertically integrated *eCMMS model*

- achieving a *win-win model* for all stakeholders including shareholders, employees, community and management through a devotion to greater social harmony and higher ethical standards.

Guided by these visions, *Foxconn's* competitive advantages lie in the aforementioned *eCMMS business model* and its unique *"Foxconnian culture"*. *Foxconn's eCMMS*, which stands for e-enabled components, modules, moves and services, is the vertically integrated business model formed by integrating mechanical, electrical and optical capabilities. This process means quicker speed to market, higher quality, better engineering services, greater flexibility and cost savings. Moreover, it allows the company to generate solutions ranging from moulding, tooling, mechanical parts, components, modules, and system assembly to design, manufacturing, maintenance and to logistics. On the strength of the *eCMMS model*, *Foxconn's* Shenzhen Campus in Southern China is both the world's largest 3C manufacturing base and shortest supply chain.

Manufacturing Services and Major Customers

Aided by its business model, *Foxconn* provides four different manufacturing services, including *CEM, EMS, ODM* and *CMMS*. These manufacturing services are shown in Figure 16.11.

The Company's Manufacturing Services

Figure 16.11

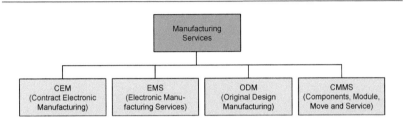

16

Foxconn provides services for the biggest companies in the field of electronics and information technology. Its clients include American, European and Japanese companies which outsource the manufacturing of hardware or other components in order to lower production costs and withstand competitive pressures. One of *Foxconn's* most important contract partners is *Apple*, as *Foxconn* draws an estimated 40 to 50% of its revenue from assembling their products and other work. It further manufactures components for *Amazon, Dell, Blackberry, Intel, HP, Microsoft*, and many others. A selection of *Foxconn's* major customers is presented in Table 16.1.

Table 16.1

Major Customers and Devices Produced by Foxconn

Customer	Manufacturing Product
Amazon	Kindle
Apple	iPad, iPod, iPhone, Mac mini, Macbook pro
Cisco	Video and Telecommunication Equipment
Dell	Laptops
Hewlett-Packard	Personal Computer, Laptops, Printer
Intel	Mainboards
Microsoft	X-Box, X-Box 360
Nintendo	DS, Wii
Nokia	Components of Mobile Phones
Blackberry	Smartphones
Sony	Playstation
Huawei	Smartphones
Acer	Smartphones

Figure 16.12 shows shares of the company's revenue by geographic area, based on the location of customers. The vast majority of customers come from the USA and Ireland, which represent more than half of *Foxconn's* revenues.

Figure 16.12

Revenue by Geographic Area Based on the Location of Customers (in 2012)

Source: Foxconn 2014.

Offshoring to China

After the communist economy opened up, many companies from highly developed countries began offshoring their production to the Far East, and mostly to China, by taking advantage of lower wages and operating costs.

Foxconn, today China's largest employer, benefited greatly from China's embracing of Western economic policies by receiving outsourcing contracts from *Apple* and other companies. It quickly dwarfed competitors like *Flextronics International Ltd.*, *Jabil* and *Sanmina*, and has become the No. 1 global EMS provider (EPS 2014).

Development in the IT Market of China

Anchoring and assuring *Foxconn's* swift growth, the Chinese IT market is of extraordinary importance to its business activities. *Foxconn* owns 13 factories in 9 Chinese cities and currently employs 1.4 million people in China alone. Along with fast growing companies like *Foxconn*, China has become the leading global business location for remote functions, including IT services, support contact centres and back-office support. Since 2010, the IT industry has gained strong momentum, riding a new wave of IT investment.

Software as Growing Service Industry

Based on a new development within China, companies are increasingly seeking improved efficiencies by using software to lower costs and improve productivity. Software is one of China's fastest growing service industries. Since software development creates more manufacturing processes, the Chinese software industry is gaining in importance. With the global economy predicted to expand faster this year, China is expected to further narrow the gap with the industry leaders, the United States and Japan, in the 2 trillion USD global information technology market, shown in Figure 16.13. Total government and business spending in IT on the Chinese mainland is estimated to increase by 10.5% to 124.5 billion USD in 2014. Multinational companies continue to invest in key IT products sourced from China. US computer giant *Dell*, for example, spends more than 25 billion USD a year on the mainland on manufacturing and sourcing of IT components and related products. Before today, companies focused on China's emergence as an important and successful outsourcing market. In spite of this, making strategic decisions to identify the optimal location can be challenging as every country has its own unique offerings.

Figure 16.13

Markets for IT Goods and Services 2014 (in billion USD)

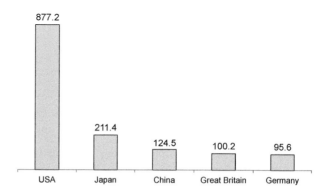

Source: SCMP 2014.

Overall, offshoring covers such a wide variety of nations, products and practices that it is difficult to estimate market size. A significant share of offshoring revenue is created by contract manufacturing of electronics, laptop computers, tablet computers, cellular telephones and items such as *iPods*. Another major sector in offshoring is contract manufacturing of shoes, apparel and accessories. Contract electronics manufacturing is estimated at 404.5 billion USD for 2013, growing to 451.9 billion USD by 2016. Products manufactured offshore for corporations headquartered in the United States, Canada, Japan and other developed nations are frequently intended for sale in offshore markets. For example, offshore electronics contract manufacturing firms such as *Foxconn* produce *Apple's* extremely popular smartphones. While *Apple's* products are sold in North America and Europe, a growing portion of their sales takes place in Asia itself where the products are made. There are definite advantages to conducting manufacturing close to the rapidly growing business and consumer markets of Asia.

Reversing the Offshoring Trend

Despite the extraordinary relevance of China, *Foxconn* has manufacturing operations outside of China. Today, it owns factories and has operating units in more than 10 countries or regions, and plans to further increase production in locations outside of China (see Figure 16.14).

Operating Units (in 2013)

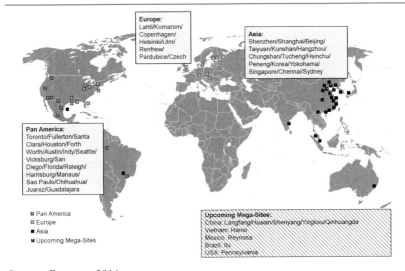

Source: Foxconn 2014.

Figure 16.14

Foxconn is facing changing economic conditions as manufacturing costs in former low-cost countries like China are rising quickly. For example, in recent years *Foxconn* has been involved in numerous scandals related to manufacturing activities, such as safety issues, bad working conditions and labour disputes in China. The aforementioned *Foxconn* scandals also impacted its contract partners, such as *Apple*. This was particularly apparent in May 2010, when the media reported on the series of worker suicides at a *Foxconn Apple* factory. As a consequence, *Foxconn* started to increase salaries in many of its Chinese manufacturing locations and set stricter limits on workers' overtime.

Increasing costs, growing numbers of natural and man-made disasters and the long tail of logistics have forced *Foxconn* to rethink manufacturing in China. There is now an alternate plan to get *Foxconn's* products to its customers without any interruptions, as lower production costs can quickly be nullified by other problems, if products do not make it to market on time at

Changing Market Conditions

an optimum price.

According to *McKinsey's* analysis, locating manufacturing out of China closer to demand makes it easier to identify and meet local needs (EPS 2014). Thus, the development in manufacturing is towards being closer to the customer as it emphasises both proximity to demand and to innovation (McKinsey 2014). *Foxconn's* plan to increase factories in the US also emerged from the reality that customers want greater guarantees than they are currently offered. It represents an opportunity to retain current contracts and gain new ones. Terry Gou, Chairman of *Foxconn,* is seeking to resettle capital-intensive and high-tech manufacturing in the USA. Specifically, *Foxconn* intends to build a display-manufacturing facility, and is further convinced that automation, software and technology innovation will be the priority of US production in the forthcoming years. As well as planning to expand in the US, *Foxconn* intends to make Indonesia a key partner for production: *Foxconn* and *Blackberry* recently entered into a deal to design and market phones in Indonesia. In addition, *Foxconn* is investing 10 million USD into a venture with *Carnegie Mellon University* for research into robotics and manufacturing. Furthermore, *Foxconn* is collaborating with *Google* on a new vision of robotised factories, with *Google* extending its robot technology in general. By getting closer to their customers, *Foxconn* aims to better serve them and to position the company for further growth.

Summary and Outlook

The case study illustrates the relevance of *Foxconn's* major role as an electronics manufacturer. Since its beginnings in 1974, *Foxconn* has become one of the world's leading exporters of electronics, with major clients including *Apple, Cisco, Hewlett-Packard, Microsoft, Dell, Nintendo* and *Sony.* In the coming years, automation, software and technology innovation will be the key focus in the United States. The trend towards greater proximity to the customer, and thus getting closer to demand and innovation, includes different factors such as varied and crucial sets of production locations. Efficient partnerships are vital, as well as the availability of technical skills. The transfer of *Foxconn's* production out of China into the United States implies that the offshoring era has reached a peak. Amongst other reasons, this is because recent offshoring strategies have resulted in increasing unemployment rates, making local production a political factor for Western companies. Furthermore, *Foxconn's* customers like *Google* and *Apple* have announced that they want to produce more of their products in the United States. This could put collaborations with pro-China companies such as *Foxconn* at risk.

Part IV

Questions

1. *Foxconn* is the main contract manufacturing firm for many huge companies in the field of consumer electronics. Discuss the advantages and disadvantages outsourcing brings to outsourcing companies, as well as to *Foxconn*.

2. *Foxconn* wants to set up plants in the United States, reversing the offshoring trend of the last 20 years. Does this shift make sense, and what will it mean for *Foxconn*, its competitors and the entire electronics industry? What opportunities and challenges will *Foxconn* face by extending its activities into the US? What possibilities, opportunities and risks does manufacturing outside of China bring?

3. Discuss the advantages and disadvantages of the collaboration between *Google* and *Foxconn*.

Hints

1. See, e.g., Schniederjans and Schniederjans 2005, pp. 21-35.

References

A.T. KEARNEY (2007): Offshoring for Long-Term Advantage: The 2007 A.T. Kearney Global Services Location Index, Chicago.

ABRAMOVSKY, L.; GRIFFITH, R. (2006): Outsourcing and Offshoring of Business Services: How Important Is ICT?, in: Journal of the European Economic Association, April-May, pp. 594-601.

AINAVOLU, S. (2007): Leveraging the Outsourcing Wave: Performance of the Indian IT Industry, in: IIMB Management Review, Vol. 19, No. 3, pp. 251-261.

AMBASTHA, A.; MOMAYA, K. (2004): Challenges for Indian Software Firms to Sustain Their Global Competitiveness, in: Singapore Management Review, Vol. 26, No. 2, pp. 65-77.

AMIT, R.; SCHOEMAKER, P.J.H. (1993): Strategic Assets and Organizational Rent, in: Strategic Management Journal, Vol. 14, No. 1, pp. 33-46.

ARORA, A.; ATHREYE, S. (2002): The Software Industry and India's Economic Development, in: Information Economics and Policy, Vol. 14, No. 2, pp. 253-273.

BANERJEE, A.V.; DUFLO, E. (2000): Reputation Effects and the Limits of Contracting: A Study of the Indian Software Industry, in: The Quarterly Journal of Economics, Vol. 105, No. 3, pp. 989-1017.

BASTIAN, J.; ZENTES, J. (2011): Ethical Sourcing: Choice of Sourcing Strategies and Impact on Performance of the Firm in German Retailing, in: European Retail Research, Vol. 25, No. 1, pp. 85-105.

DOZ, Y.; SANTOS, J.; WILLIAMSON, P.J. (2003): The New Global Game: How Your Company Can Win in the Knowledge Economy, in: BARTLETT, C.A.; GHOSHAL, S.; BIRKINSHAW, J. (Eds.): Transnational Management, 4th ed., Boston, McGraw-Hill, pp. 832-839.

EPS (2014): Foxconn Weighs Plan for U.S. Plant, http://electronicspurchasingstrategies.com/2014/01/28/foxconn-coming-america-offshoring-peaked/, accessed on August 12, 2014.

ERNST & YOUNG (2013): Outsourcing in Europe: An In-depth Review of Drivers, Risks and Trends in the European Outsourcing Market, http://www.ey.com/Publication/vwLUAssets/Outsourcing_in_Europe_2013/$FILE/EY-outsourcing-survey.pdf, accessed on July 17, 2014.

ETHIRAJ, S.; KALE, P.; KRISHNAN, M.; SINGH, J. (2005): Where do Capabilities Come From and How do They Matter? A Study in the Software Services Industry, in: Strategic Management Journal, Vol. 26, No. 1, pp. 25-45.

FOXCONN (2014): Annual Report 2013, New Taipei.

GRIFFIN, R.; PUSTAY, M. (2013): International Business: A Managerial Perspective, 7th ed., Upper Saddle River, New Jersey, Pearson.

HENLEY, J. (2007): Outsourcing the Provision of Software and IT-enabled Services to India, in: International Studies of Management & Organization, Vol. 36, No. 4, pp. 111-131.

HILL, C.W.L. (2013): Global Business Today, 8th ed., Boston, McGraw-Hill.

IBEF (2009): IT & ITeS: September 2009, http://www.ibef.org/download/IT_and_ITes_171109.pdf, accessed on July 12, 2014.

KAPUR, D.; RAMAMURTI, R. (2001): India's Emerging Competitive Advantage in Services, in: Academy of Management Journal, Vol. 15, No. 2, pp. 20-31.

KOTABE, M.; HELSEN, K. (2014): Global Marketing Management, 6th ed., New York, Wiley & Sons.

KPMG (2008): The Indian ICT Industry: Enabling Global Competitiveness and Driving Innovation with Equitably Growth, Chennai.

KRÜGER, W.; HOMP, C. (1997): Kernkompetenzmanagement: Steigerung von Flexibilität und Schlagkraft im Wettbewerb, Wiesbaden, Gabler.

MARTIN, A. (2010): Mercy for Those Realizing Global Opportunities Through Offshoring and Outsourcing Effectively, in: IJIOUI, R.; EMMERICH, H.; CEYP, M.; HAGEN, J. (2010): Globalization 2.0, Heidelberg, Springer.

MATIASKE, W.; MELLEWIGT, T. (2002): Motive, Erfolge und Risiken des Outsourcings: Befunde und Defizite der empirischen Outsourcing-Forschung, in: Zeitschrift für Betriebswirtschaft, Vol. 72, pp. 641-659.

MCKINSEY (2014): Next-shoring: A CEO's Guide, http://www.mckinsey.com/insights/manufacturing/nextshoring_a_ceos_guide, accessed on August 11, 2014.

MILBERG, W.; WINKLER, D. (2013): Outsourcing Economies: Global Value Chains in Capitalist Development, New York, Cambridge University Press.

MORSCHETT, D. (2005): Contract Manufacturing, in: ZENTES, J.; SWOBODA, B.; MORSCHETT, D. (Eds.): Kooperationen, Allianzen und Netzwerke, 2nd ed., Wiesbaden, Gabler, pp. 597-622.

NASSCOM (2009): Indian IT-BPO Industry 2009, Mumbai.

NORDIN, F. (2008): Linkages between Service Sourcing Decisions and Competitive Advantage: A Review, Propositions, and Illustrating Cases, in: International Journal of Production Economics, Vol. 114, No. 1, pp. 40-55.

PANKAJ, M. (2009): Indian IT Needs to Raise Revenue per Employee, http://economictimes.indiatimes.com, accessed on May 12, 2014.

PORTER, M.E. (2004): Competitive Advantage: Creating and Sustaining Superior Performance, New York, The Free Press.

POWER, M.; BONIFAZI, C.; DESOUZA, K.C. (2004): The Ten Outsourcing Traps to Avoid, in: Journal of Business Strategy, Vol. 25, No. 2, pp. 37-42.

SCHNIEDERJANS, M.J.; SCHNIEDERJANS, D.G. (2005): Outsourcing and Insourcing in an International Context, New York, M.E. Sharpe.

SCMP (2014): China's Enterprise IT Market Set for Stable Growth in 2014, http://www.scmp.com/business/china-business/article/1396953/chinas-enterprise-it-market-set-stable-growth-2014, accessed on May 12, 2014.

STRAUBE, F.; KROKOWSKI, W.; BECKMANN, T, GOH, M. (2007): International Procurement in Emerging Markets: Discovering the Drivers of Sourcing Success, Bremen, Deutscher Verkehrs-Verlag.

WIPRO (2009): Annual Report 2008-09, Bangalore.

WORLD ECONOMIC FORUM (2010): Stimulating Economies through Fostering Talent Mobility, Cologne.

ZENTES, J. (2011): Sustainability – Supply Security – Distributive Justice: A Global Area of Conflict, in: Annals of the University of Craiova, Economic Sciences Series, Vol. 2, No. 39, pp. 201-218.

ZENTES, J.; HILT, C.; DOMMA, P. (2007): HandelsMonitor Spezial: Global Sourcing im Einzelhandel, Frankfurt, Deutscher Fachverlag.

ZENTES, J.; MORSCHETT, D.; SCHRAMM-KLEIN, H. (2011): Strategic Retail Management: Text and International Cases, 2nd ed., Wiesbaden, Gabler.

ZENTES, J.; NEIDHART, M.; SCHEER, L. (2006): HandelsMonitor Spezial: Vertikalisierung: Die Industrie als Händler, Frankfurt, Deutscher Fachverlag.

ZENTES, J.; SWOBODA, B.; MORSCHETT, D. (2004): Internationales Wertschöpfungsmanagement, Munich, Vahlen.

ZENTES, J.; SWOBODA, B.; MORSCHETT, D. (2005): Markt, Kooperation, Integration: Asymmetrische Entwicklungen in der Gestaltung der Wertschöpfungsprozesse am Beispiel der Konsumgüterindustrie, in: ZENTES, J.; SWOBODA, B.; MORSCHETT, D. (Eds.): Kooperationen, Allianzen und Netzwerke, 2nd ed., Wiesbaden, Gabler, pp. 675-700.

Chapter 17

International Alliances

International alliances using cooperative relationships come in all shapes and sizes, often under the rubric of strategic alliances. This Chapter discusses the different types of international alliances and the motives and logic behind them.

Basic Types of International Alliances

In general, *strategic alliances* or *strategic partnerships* can be defined as "a coalition of two or more organizations to achieve strategically significant goals that are mutually beneficial" (Kotabe/Helsen 2014, p. 282). International alliances or *cross-border alliances* are partnerships of organisations/companies from different countries. By setting up a partnership, the companies strive for a *joint competitive advantage*. This joint competitive advantage is based on combining strengths or mitigating weaknesses (see Figure 17.1). From the point of view of *new institutional economics*, strategic alliances are positioned between the transactional options market and integration/hierarchy (see Chapters 15 and 18), or on a scale between externalisation and internalisation.

Joint Competitive Advantage

Strategic Advantages of Alliances

Figure 17.1

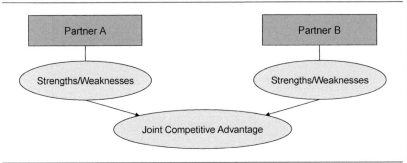

Strategic alliances result in a new economic phenomenon: *co-opetition*. Cooperation and *competition* are no longer considered direct opposites. Rivalry, a basic feature of dynamic competition, is compatible with cooperation in order to achieve a common aim. This tendency also leads to a new perspec-

Co-opetition

tive or even a new *paradigm* in competition theory and competition strategy. From the perspective of legislation, strategic alliances are not only more tolerated than before but are even actively being encouraged. However, any cooperation that could lead to *collusion*, such as price fixing, is still considered a highly sensitive subject.

Critical Mass Alliances and Closing Gap Alliances

Y-Alliances

Critical mass alliances or *Y-Alliances* (Porter/Fuller 1986) achieve a joint competitive advantage by compensating for individual weaknesses. Companies in this case tend have similar strengths and weaknesses in their value chain activities. Critical mass can be achieved through cooperation in upstream- or downstream-based collaboration in the value chain (see Figure 17.2), for example, by bundling the partners' purchasing volume in a *buying group* or through joint R&D in creating an important innovation, such as in the field of semi-conductors, biotechnology or gene technology. The logic of this type of alliance is based on *economies of scale.*

X-Alliances

Closing gap alliances or *X-Alliances* (Porter/Fuller 1986) are based on combining asymmetric but complementary strengths in value chain activities (see Figure 17.2). They therefore rely on mutual access to resources and potentials, such as local resources and capital, expertise, technologies, image, etc.

Figure 17.2 | *International Y-Alliances and X-Alliance: Examples*

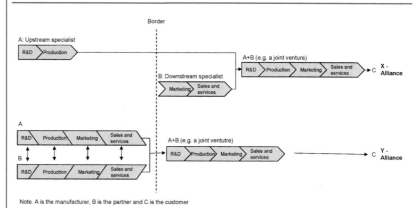

Note. A is the manufacturer, B is the partner and C is the customer

Source: Adapted from Hollensen 2014, p. 370.

One example is entering a foreign market by establishing a firm (equity joint venture) with a domestic partner in the target country. The domestic partner knows the local market and has access to distribution channels, while the "entering" partner has, for example, a strong brand and marketing expertise. Figure 17.2 illustrates the differences between Y-Alliances and X-Alliances.

Non-contractual Alliances, Contractual Alliances and Equity Alliances

A further distinction involves the formal structure of *cooperative arrangements:*

- non-contractual alliances
- contractual alliances
- equity alliances.

Non-contractual alliances are usually formed *ad hoc*, even if they are planned to continue in the long term. This informal cooperative relationship is used, for example, in joint-buying activities, such as in electronic *reverse auctions* on Internet platforms (see, e.g., Zentes/Morschett/Schramm-Klein 2011, p. 77).

Non-Contractual Alliances

There are numerous forms of contractual alliances, also known as *contractual joint ventures*. The most well-known, described in this Chapter, are:

Contractual Alliances

- licensing
- franchising
- management contracting.

Equity alliances are characterised by the capital investment made by the alliance partners or parental partners. This can be structured in a number of ways. The first is a form of *cross shareholding*, an instrument predominantly chosen to stabilise an alliance.

Equity Alliances

In *equity joint ventures* the alliance is institutionalised in a new legally independent unit, in which the alliance partners each hold an interest, jointly assuming the risk as well as the responsibility for the management. Equity joint ventures are not necessarily characterised by *equal ownership* (50-50 ownerships). Equity joint ventures will also be described in this Chapter.

Comprehensive and Functional Alliances

Comprehensive alliances and functional alliances can be distinguished by their *scope*. *Functional alliances* are narrow in scope: Only a single function of the business area is involved. Functional alliances include procurement

Scope of Strategic Alliances

alliances, R&D alliances, production alliances, marketing alliances or financial alliances.

Comprehensive alliances are characterised by a high degree of collaboration. The participating firms perform all or at least the main activities of the value chain together. The airline alliances *oneworld*, *Star Alliance* and *SkyTeam* are examples of this type.

Selected Forms of International Alliances

International Licensing

Licensing Agreement In licensing agreements the *licensor* grants the rights to intellectual property to the *licensee* for a defined period. The licensee pays *royalty fees* in return. The nature of licensing agreements varies depending on the value chain activity, e.g. production or distribution/marketing (see e.g. Hill 2013, pp. 274-276) (see Figure 17.3).

Figure 17.3 | *Types of Licence Agreements*

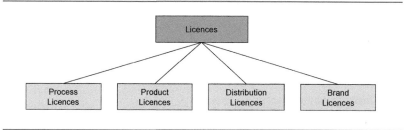

In *process licences*, the licensor grants the licensee the right to use a specific production technology, often based on a patent, e.g. in the chemical or pharmaceutical industries. In the case of a *product licence*, the licensor grants the right to manufacture a product or certain products in accordance with specific procedures, processes or formulas. *Contract manufacturing*, a contractual agreement between a company and a foreign producer under which the foreign producer manufactures the company's product (see, e.g., Hollensen 2014, p. 369), is often combined with this type of licensing. In this case the licensee produces on behalf of the licensor and sells the products to him; the licensee has no *distribution licence*.

If a *distribution licence* has been granted, the licensee has the right to market the products in a specific territory. In the case of a "simple" distribution licence or a "pure" distribution licence, the licensor remains the manufacturer and therefore the supplier. These kinds of licensing are a *foreign entry choice*.

Brand licences are very important for marketing as they entitle a licensee to use a brand name. A specific kind of brand licensing is to grant a licensee the right to use a *trademark* for products other than those the licensor produces. An example of this kind of licensing of intellectual property rights is the American *Coty Group*, which sells world-famous perfume brands like *Calvin Klein, Cerruti, Vera Wang, Chloé* and *Davidoff* on the basis of brand licences. *Coty* bought the division of luxury perfumes from the Dutch-British *Unilever Group*. Advantages and disadvantages of licensing in international markets are listed in Table 17.1.

Advantages and Disadvantages of Licensing

Table 17.1

Advantages	Disadvantages
• Increases income on products already developed as a result of expensive research. • Permits entry into markets that are otherwise closed on account of high rates of duty, import quotas and so on. • A viable option where manufacture is near the customer's base. • Requires little capital investment and should provide a higher rate of return on capital employed. • There may be valuable spin-offs if the licensor can sell other products or components to the licensee. If these parts are for products being manufactured locally or machinery, there may also be some tariff concessions on their import. • The licensor is not exposed to the danger of nationalization or expropriation of assets. • Because of the limited capital requirements, new products can be exploited rapidly, on a worldwide basis, before competition develops. • The licensor can take immediate advantage of the licensee's local marketing and distribution organization and of existing customer contacts. • Protects patents, especially in countries that give weak protection for products not produced locally. • Local manufacture may also be an advantage in securing government contracts.	• The licensee may prove less competent than expected at marketing or other management activities. Costs may even grow faster than income. • The licensee, even if it reaches an agreed minimum turnover, may not fully exploit the market, leaving it open to the entry of competitors, so that the licensor loses control of the marketing operation. • Danger of the licensee running short of funds, especially if considerable plant expansion is involved or an injection of capital is required to sustain the project. This danger can be turned to advantage if the licensor has funds available by a general expansion of the business through a partnership. • Licence fees are normally a small percentage of turnover, about 5 per cent, and will often compare unfavourably with what might be obtained from a company's own manufacturing operation. • Lack of control over licensee operations. • Quality control of the product is difficult - and the product will often be sold under the licensor's brand name. • Negotiations with the licensee, and sometimes with local government, are costly. • Governments often impose conditions on transferral of royalties or on component supply.

Source: Hollensen 2014, p. 390.

International Franchising

Franchising is defined as a contractual agreement between two legally and financially separate companies, the *franchisor* and the *franchisee*.

Figure 17.4 | *Types of International Franchise Agreements*

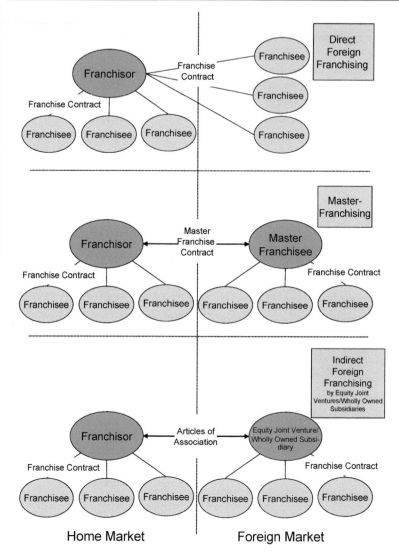

Source: Adapted from Zentes/Swoboda/Schramm-Klein 2013, p. 250.

In franchise agreements the *franchisor* not only grants intangible properties, e.g. a trademark, to the *franchisee*, but it also includes advice and help in the management of their business. In addition, the franchisees can profit from the experience of all other franchise partners, (see Zentes/Morschett/ Schramm-Klein 2011, pp. 99-100).

There are different options for *international franchising* (see Zentes/Swoboda/Schramm-Klein 2013, pp. 247-250) (see Figure 17.4). In *direct foreign franchising* the franchisor signs individual contracts with partners in the different countries. In *master franchising*, the franchisor signs a *single contract* with the *master* or *general franchisee* in a country-market or in a region, which is then allowed to grant franchises (sub-franchise relationships) in that market.

Direct Franchising

An *indirect franchise structure* is characterised by a wholly owned subsidiary or an equity joint venture created in a foreign country-market, which operates as a franchisor in that market. In this case, franchising is a mixture between a contractual alliance and an equity alliance or ownership strategy in the foreign market.

Indirect Franchising

From the franchisor's perspective, franchising in international markets offers a higher degree of control and is associated with lower risks and lower overhead costs. It also lets companies expand more quickly over a wider area. This is especially the case with new and distant international markets that may be accessed relatively quickly and on a larger scale. The franchisees are usually highly motivated business partners. They act as entrepreneurs that invest their own monetary resources, offer local market knowledge and (often) experience in their field of business. Also, the franchisor can avoid being confronted with day-to-day business details and instead rely on the skills of people with local knowledge and regional experience (Hollensen 2014, p. 390).

Franchisor's Perspective

However, franchising can also have several disadvantages for the franchisor. To guarantee the reputation and (often global) image of the franchise system, they need to monitor the franchisees' business operations, despite lacking a full level of control. Additionally, if single franchisees underperform, the franchise system's brand and (international) reputation are at risk. Thus, costs for protecting the brand name and the franchise system's reputation result. Because the main business activities and customer contact are handled by the franchisees, the company is only passively involved with the international markets. It also opens up its internal business expertise to its franchisees, thus possibly creating future competitors.

The advantages from the franchisee's perspective include retaining entrepreneurial independence due to the relation based on *partnership*, the great variety of support activities and frequently the guarantee of *"territorial sovereignty"* in the local market. Therefore, franchising can be a very attractive option for SMEs.

Franchisee's Perspective

International Management Contracting

Management Service Contracts

Using international management contracts or *management service contracts* a company is allowed to be involved in the management of a firm in a foreign market of which the managing company has no shares (see, e.g., Hollensen 2014, p. 389). Through such agreements a firm provides managerial expertise and operates the daily business of the second firm for a specified period in return for monetary compensation. The managing firm gets a commission based on the revenues or profits of the managed firm and/or yearly (minimum) lump-sum payments.

In the case of international management contracts there is a clear distinction between the investors or shareholders and the company which manages the operations, sometimes simultaneously training national managers until they are able to take over. Recent examples of management contracts can be found in industries like hotels (e.g. *Accor* or *Marriott*), hospitals, airports, seaports and public utilities.

Managed Firm and Managing Firm's Perspectives

International management contracts are a way for managed firms to attain expertise and/or experience in a new field (Czinkota/Ronkainen 2013, pp. 303-304). For the managing firm, such a contract serves as a *source of income* as well as an opportunity to scout a new market and establish the company or its brand there. This occurs when the managed firms appear externally as part of a *global chain*, usually under an internationally recognised name.

Figure 17.5 illustrates the structure of the management contract system used by German Fraport AG in managing Cairo International Airport.

Figure 17.5 | *Structure of a Management Contract System in the Airport Industry*

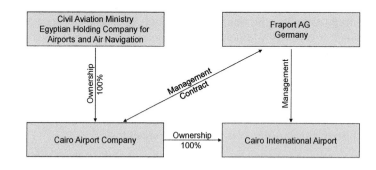

Source: Fraport AG 2014.

International Equity Joint Ventures

The reasons for establishing an equity joint venture with foreign partners, i.e., a firm that is jointly owned by two or more otherwise independent firms, are legislation or the need for the other partner's skills, competences or assets. Some governments, mainly in less developed countries, insist on joint ventures with local partners. This policy restricts the *ownership strategy alternatives*. Access to the local partner's assets, such as capital, is another reason for entering into an equity partnership.

Equity joint ventures may provide access to *complementary resources*, e.g. technology, market knowledge, property rights or well-known international brands. Local partners may even accept such assets as a substitute for monetary resources as a payment for shares of the subsidiary's equity (Robock/Simmonds 1989, p. 216).

Access to Complementary Resources

The main disadvantages of equity joint ventures are potential conflicts in managing the business and transaction costs in coordinating the foreign operations. This situation is typical for equal ownership rather than acquiring a majority stake. The advantages and disadvantages of international equity joint ventures are summarised in Table 17.2.

Advantages and Disadvantages of Equity Joint Ventures

Table 17.2

Advantages	Disadvantages
• access to expertise and contacts in local markets • typically, international partner contributes financial resources, technological know-how or products, the local partner provides local skills and knowledge • reduced market and political risk • shared knowledge and resources, shared risk of failures • overcomes host government restrictions • may avoid local tariffs or non-tariff barriers • possibly better relations with local governments through having a local partner (meets host country pressure for local participation)	• objectives of respective partners may be imcompatible, resulting in conflicts • contribution to joint venture can become disproportionate • loss of control over foreign operations • partners may become locked into long-term incvetments from which it is difficult to withdraw • transfer pricing problems as goods pass between partners • importance of venture to each partner may change over time • loss of flexibility and confidentiality • problems of management structures and dual parent staffing of equity joint ventures

Source: Adapted from Hollensen 2014, p. 391.

Organisational Structure of Strategic Alliances

A fundamentally different distinction can be made regarding the strategic alliance is organised. Looking at *network management*, one can differentiate between the following organisational models (see Figure 17.6; see also Chapter 1):

- centralised hub

- decentralised federation

- integrated network model.

Network Topology

The *centralised hub* is characterised by a star formation, with the centre as the hub. This is the case in traditional franchising systems, with the franchisor operating as the centralised hub. A *federation* is characterised by a decentralised structure. A federation of largely independent players is coordinated by one organisational unit, which possesses only limited decision-making power. This is the case, for example, in buying and marketing alliances (functional alliances) of several very large retail companies. The *integrated network model* is characterised by a marked organisational and performance-oriented interdependence.

Figure 17.6 | *Organisational Modes of Alliances*

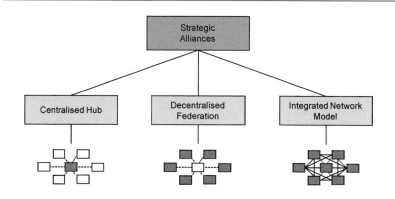

Source: Adapted from Bartlett/Ghoshal/Beamish 2008, pp. 338, 342.

Stability of Strategic Alliances

Fits and Stability

The chances of the establishment of a strategic alliance and the stability of such alliances are dependent to a great extent on the *fits* between the partners (Zentes/Swoboda/Schramm-Klein 2013, pp. 259) (see Figure 17.7). These fits can also be used as *guidelines in assessing* potential partners.

Figure 17.7

Fits in Cooperative Agreements

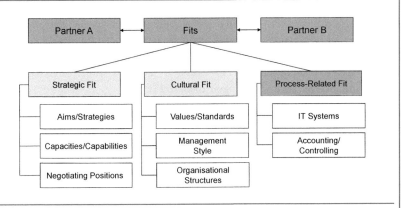

A *strategic fit* is based on partners' aims and strategies, capacities/capabilities and negotiating positions. For example, if one partner does not fully commit to the alliance because the partners do not have similar strategic goals, this lack of commitment may affect the attainment of the alliance's objectives. Another *relational risk* or reason for the failure of partnerships is cultural divergence. This means that the values and standards, management styles and organisational structures must be compatible (*cultural fit* or *cultural proximity*). The process/infrastructure fit (*process-related fit*) refers to correspondence, or at least compatibility, between the organisation's technical systems, such as the IT systems, the accounting/controlling system, etc.

Relational Risks

Conclusion and Outlook

In both national and international contexts, *networks of value creation* emerge. They represent a new organisational model for complex processes of value creation. A broad and growing variety of forms can be distinguished. Important manifestations of alliances have been discussed in this Chapter.

Networks of Value Creation

Besides the multitude of variants that are frequently implemented in a combined manner in companies, another phenomenon can be seen: Strategic alliances have spread to all industries and even to other social sectors. As seen, management contract systems, which are of great importance in the hotel industry, are increasingly being transferred to other industries, such as airports, seaports and other infrastructure entities or public utilities.

Social Franchising

Another example is *social franchising*. In social franchising, the techniques from commercial franchising are adapted to the context of projects which benefit the social aims of a non-profit organisation such as *Healthstore Kenya*, which operates a franchised network of health stores, or *De Kringwinkel*, a franchise system that operates shops selling used goods. The rise in the number of non-profit initiatives using franchising can be attributed "to the increased openness of the third sector to using commercial tools and to acting more entrepreneurially in order to become more effective" (Bundesverband Deutscher Stiftungen 2008, p. 25).

Further Reading

HAMEL, G.; DOZ, Y.L.; PRAHALAD, C. (2008): Collaborate with Your Competitors – and Win, in: BARTLETT, C.A.; GHOSHAL, S.; BEAMISH, P.W. (Eds.): Transnational Management: Text, Cases, and Readings in Cross-Border Management, 5th ed., Boston, McGraw-Hill; pp. 640-647.

OHMAE, K. (1993): The Global Logic and Strategic Alliances, in: Harvard Business Review, Vol. 67, No. 2, pp. 143-154.

Case Study: Danone[*]

Profile History and Status quo

Danone, established in 1919, is one of the top companies in the worldwide food processing industry after competitors such as *Nestlé* and *Coca-Cola*. The French company focuses on four businesses: fresh dairy products, waters, baby nutrition and medical nutrition. In 2013, *Danone* was the world leader in fresh dairy products and had around 100,000 employees in 57 countries on five continents, achieving solid growth by generating about 21.3 billion EUR in sales revenues. The emerging markets of Mexico, Indonesia, China, Russia, the United States and Brazil accounted for 54% of group sales in the same year.

In 1966 Danone merged with the glass bottle manufacturer *BSN – Boussois Souchon Neuvesel*. Four years later, in 1970, *BSN* decided to diversify into the

---

[*] Sources used for this case study includes various annual reports, press releases, the website http//www.danone.com, as well as explicitly cited sources.

food and beverage industry by acquiring *Brasseries Kronenbourg, Société Européenne de Brasseries* and *Société Anonyme des Eaux Minérales d'Evian*, which were all major customers of *BSN*. Finally, in 1972, *Danone Group* was founded after *BSN's* merger with Spanish yogurt producer *Danone*.

After the foundation, the group primarily concentrated on further expansion in Western Europe. In the 1990s, the company prepared for its international development by completing numerous acquisitions and joint ventures outside of Western Europe, focusing on Asia-Pacific, Latin America and Eastern Europe, as well as in selected markets such as South Africa and the Middle East. In 2007, the Group sold nearly all of its biscuits and cereal products business to *Kraft Foods* in order to focus on health food as the new core business sector. It was then that *Danone* defined its mission as "bringing health through food to as many people as possible" which is consistent with the company's overall strategy.

International Expansion

Principal Markets and Major Alliances

Danone's principal markets are Europe, including Turkey, North America and the CIS zone (Commonwealth of Independent States), including Russia and the ALMA zone (Asia-Pacific, Latin America, the Middle East and Africa). In 2013, Europe and the ALMA zone represented 39% each of group sales, while North America with the CIS zone accounted for 22% of group sales.

Group Sales by Geographic Region (in billion EUR)

Figure 17.8

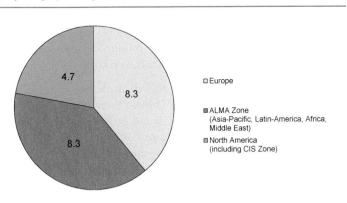

□ Europe

▣ ALMA Zone
(Asia-Pacific, Latin-America, Africa, Middle East)

▣ North America
(including CIS Zone)

Source: Adapted from Danone 2014.

Since the reframing of the core business as described above, *Danone* accelerated its international development by acquiring Dutch baby food nutrition
and medical nutrition producer *Numico*, as well as the *Unimilk Group* companies in Russia and the CIS, the *Wockhardt Group* nutrition activities in
India, *Centrale Laitière* in Morocco and *Fan Milk* in West Africa.

These acquisitions are characterised by the combination of *Danone's* expertise and investment experience, as well as insights into local presence at the
target market. The company aims to accelerate the growth and penetration
of the local alliance partner's portfolio of leading consumer beverage and
food brands in the principal markets.

Strategic Benefits and Risks of Alliance Membership

In 2004, an important co-operational agreement evolved with Japanese *Yakult Honsha Co. Ltd.* Given that their probiotic and fermented milk drinks are
similar, the companies initially cooperated on product research and promotion, with options to extend collaboration into more operational areas. *Danone* is a major shareholder in *Yakult Honsha Co., Ltd.*, with a 20% share.

However, since the differences in areas such as corporate culture and marketing techniques could not be eliminated, the companies decided to replace
their strategic alliance with a looser cooperation framework. Without being
interested in a takeover, *Danone* intended instead to strengthen their
„"friendship", as the Japanese milk drinks producer described their business
relationship, and continued collaboration in markets such as India and Vietnam on probiotics and other products (Cruz/Yamaguchi 2013).

Strategic alliances often lead to benefits for both sides, such as support
through sharing expertise and capabilities of major international groups, or
strong complementaries in terms of product ranges, R&D, brand positioning, geographical presence, and distribution channels.

Frictions Nevertheless, alliances do not always work out as initially intended, as
shown in the case of *Danone* and Chinese *Wahaha Group Co. Ltd.* The strategic
partnership with *Danone*, which ended in 1996, enabled *Wahaha* to become
the dominant player in the Chinese bottled water and other nonalcoholic
beverage market, but broke up only about a decade later. However, in 2007,
Wahaha blamed the French food giant for setting up competing joint ventures with other local companies, such as *Mengniu Dairy* or *Bright Dairy &
Food*, whereas *Danone* accused *Wahaha* of using the brand outside the scope
of their joint ventures. This contention finally made the French company
abandon the alliance, which had accounted for about 10% of *Danone's* total
worldwide sales.

Clearly, *Danone* initially aimed to gain access to *Wahaha's* distribution networks in China, one of the fastest-growing regions in the world, with the most lucrative markets, whereas *Wahaha* was looking for capital, management experience, branding and high technology from the foreign MNC.

This particular case, however, shows explicitly that there might be incompatible managerial, cultural and legal discrepancies inherent in a strategic alliance between global foreign companies and that these are potentially hazardous for international business relationships. Potential foreign investors must therefore make a serious effort toward genuine integration compatibly if they aim to enter different national or geographical markets.

Eventually, in 2013 *Danone* joined forces with Chinese state-owned *COFCO* and China's leading dairy company *Mengniu* to accelerate the development of fresh dairy products in China. One year later, *Danone* has already announced its intention to increase its share in *Mengniu* to approve as a shareholder (Melewar 2006, p. 410).

Another strategic alliance which led to unsatisfactory outcomes and was therefore subsequently cancelled was the joint venture called *CCDA*, which was formed by *Danone* and the American multinational nonalcoholic beverage corporation *Coca-Cola Company*. In 2002, the companies decided to collaborate in producing and distributing *Danone's* luxury brand mineral water *Evian* to offset declines in sales of its flagship *Evian* water in the rapidly growing US beverage industry.

This joint venture was unique, because the miscellaneous opponents in the non-alcoholic beverages markets chose to participate in a so called "co-opetition" meaning that they placed themselves in the paradoxical situation of being both partners and competitors simultaneously. The alliance was designed to enhance the *Evian* brand in the US by offering a better-organised distribution network and greater marketing backup to compete with lower priced brands of mineral water, including *Coca-Cola's* own *Dasani* brand. The idea of building this joint venture was appealing, because *Coca-Cola* already distributed Evian in 60% of the US market and the French luxury water brand was considered a good complement to *Coca-Cola's Dasani* brand.

However, in 2005, after a minimal amount of co-operation time, the alliance was suddenly dissolved. This was surprising given the huge investments the companies had made in the alliance, totalling hundreds of millions of dollars. In effect, *Coca-Cola* bought out *Danone's* stake of 49% in CCDA (Bierly/Scott 2007, pp. 137-138).

In the end, the joint venture between *Coca-Cola* and *Danone* was a huge misunderstanding of strategic fit. The companies failed in evaluating consumers' willingness to pay for basically the same product which was just positioned differently through branding. In this case, the managers lacked an accurate understanding of the synergetic benefits of the integration of the two firms' resources. This could have been prevented by:

- installing an effective IT system to collect, integrate and disseminate information

- ensuring decision makers used the IT systems and other resources available to them

- involving all key organisational members in the decision-making process

- creating a knowledge-sharing culture

- challenging overly optimistic assumptions about the alliance.

Branding and Identity

Danone's social commitment to focus on product categories recognised for their positive contribution to nutrition and therefore health inspired the group to found *Grameen Danone Foods Ltd.* together with *Bengal Grameen Bank* in 2006. *Grameen Danone* is a cross-sector alliance. It can be characterised as an inter-organisational venture and a combination of for-profit and non-profit partners, with a combination of social and economic goals.

Social Responsibility

Grameen Danone combines competencies and resources in a process of systematic learning with the goal of creating social value through a new business model. As *Danone* had limited experience in markets where malnutrition is widespread, a relationship with an organisation like *Grameen* was a perfect match, considering the latter's great experience in developing business models in subsistence marketplaces. The social venture is *Grameen Bank* CEO *Muhammad Yunus'* first concerted social business joint venture in Bangladesh. *Yunus* originally started the *Grameen Bank Project* to provide banking services targeted at the rural poor and in 2006 was awarded the *Nobel Peace Prize* for the bank's efforts to create economic and social development from below.

Within this context of social development in the most densely populated territorial state in the world, *Grameen Danone* is understood as a social business that aims to alleviate malnutrition among children by selling fortified yogurt at an affordable price. The founders agreed on the following criteria for their products:

- product appropriateness

- affordability

■ accessibility

■ availability

■ awareness.

The venture also aims to leverage local resources, create employment throughout the value chain and to emphasise co-creation and co-innovation. According to *Yunus'* social business concept, the company's success should not be judged by the amount of revenue in the long run, but by the number of children who avoid malnutrition each year. As a social business this joint venture is designed to meet social goals without paying any dividends, and also sells products at prices that make *Grameen Danone* self-sustaining.

The advantage for *Danone* mainly lies within the learning effects that came with developing this new business model: acquiring new approaches and skills, including handling new business contacts, and creating new relationships with consumers in a comparatively unexploited market. The main benefits for *Grameen* are the extension of their portfolio of for-profit and non-profit enterprises helping the poor in Bangladesh, as well as the enhancement of *Grameen's* extensive reach and high credibility in rural communities (Danone Communities 2012).

Another alliance *Danone* joined to prove their sense of responsibility is the *Bioplastic Feedstock Alliance (BFA)*. The cross-sector alliance including *Coca-Cola, Danone, Ford, H.J. Heinz Company, Nestlé, Nike, Procter&Gamble* and *Unilever* was founded in collaboration with wildlife charity organisation the *WWF* in 2013. The initiative aims to make packaging more sustainable and find alternatives to fossil energies in their production process.

Cross-Sector Alliance

An essential part of this task is gathering knowledge on available bioplastic supply chains, evaluating the related challenges and guiding responsible packaging upstream of raw material choices. Looking for sustainable alternatives to petroleum-based products, the *BFA* wants to bring together experts from industry, academia and civil society to develop and support informed science, collaboration, education and innovation for the development of materials that can be made into bioplastics. *Danone Nutricia Research* in particular chose to be part of the *BFA* due to their commitment to creating new packaging solutions to ensure the best possible impact on people and the environment (Nestlé 2013).

Summary and Outlook

Danone's identity is closely associated with the pursuit of a dual mission combining economic and social objectives, which the company considers inseparable. In the sense of strategic philanthropy, in which a company like *Danone* makes a contribution in collaboration with competitors to a social cause related to its core business, like in the case of *BFA*, it alters the context by producing a positive impact on its business. This effect can be seen in many alliances *Danone* has joined all over the world.

Of course there is always the risk of partnerships being accumulated haphazardly. But complementary features (e.g. in geographical presence, product ranges or distribution networks) can actually strengthen a company and therefore its brands. In order to strengthen its activities around the world, *Danone* continues to develop the consumption of its product categories through innovation in Mexico, Indonesia, China, Russia, the United States and Brazil, pursuing a targeted acquisition strategy to strengthen its positions in these countries and looking for expansion opportunities in new countries in order to develop new sources of growth.

Questions

1. The decision-making process behind the selection of alliances and partners can be complex and challenging. Describe the major risks and opportunities of international alliances using an example from *Danone Group's* history.

2. Ultimately the alliance between *Danone* and *Coca-Cola* can be seen as a strategic misfit. Illustrate the importance of trust, strategy and cultural fit for such international cooperation.

Hints

1. See the company's website for further information.

2. See, e.g., Bierly and Gallagher (2007) for the selection process of alliance partners.

References

BARTLETT, C.A.; GHOSHAL, S.; BEAMISH, P.W. (2008): Transnational Management: Text, Cases, and Readings in Cross-Border Management, 5th ed., Boston, McGraw-Hill.

BIERLY, P.; GALLAGHER, S. (2007): Explaining Alliance Partner Selection: Fit, Trust and Strategic Expediency, in: Long Range Planning, Vol. 40, No. 2, pp. 134-153.

BUNDESVERBAND DEUTSCHER STIFTUNGEN (Ed.) (2008): Social Franchising: A Way of Systematic Replication to Increase Social Impact, Berlin.

CRUZ, J.; YAMAGUCHI, Y. (2013): Danone Agrees to Renewed Alliance with Yakult on Yogurt, http://www.bloomberg.com/news/2013-04-26/yakult-pares-loss-on-report-danone-to-raise-stake-tokyo-mover.html, accessed on August 17, 2014.

CZINKOTA, M.; RONKAINEN, I. (2013): International Marketing, 10th ed., Hampshire, Cengage Learning.

DANONE (2014): Danone, http://www.danone.com, accessed on September 01, 2014.

DANONE COMMUNITIES (2012): Grameen Danone Foods Ltd, http://www.danonecommunities.com, accessed on May 12, 2014.

FRAPORT AG (2014): Fraport, http: www.fraport.com, accessed on September 01, 2014.

HAMEL, G.; DOZ, Y.L.; PRAHALAD, C. (2008): Collaborate with Your Competitors – and Win, in: BARTLETT, C.A.; GHOSHAL, S.; BEAMISH, P.W. (Eds.): Transnational Management: Text, Cases, and Readings in Cross-Border Management, 5th ed., Boston, McGraw-Hill; pp. 640-647.

HILL, C.W.L. (2013): Global Business Today, 8th ed., Boston, McGraw-Hill.

HOLLENSEN, S. (2014): Global Marketing, 6th ed., Harlow, Pearson.

KOTABE, M.; HELSEN, K. (2014): Global Marketing Management, 6th ed., New York, Wiley & Sons.

MELEWAR, T.C. (2006): Danone Branding Strategy in China, in: Brand Management, Vol. 13, No. 6, pp. 407-417.

NESTLÉ (2013): Nestlé Joins Alliance for Responsible Plant-based Plastics, http://nestle.com, accessed on August 21, 2014.

OHMAE, K. (1993): The Global Logic and Strategic Alliances, in: Harvard Business Review, Vol. 67, No. 2, pp. 143-154.

PORTER, M.E.; FULLER, M. (1986): Coalitions and Global Strategy, in: PORTER, M.E. (Ed.): Competition in Global Industries, Boston, Harvard Business School Press.

ROBOCK, S.; SIMMONDS, K. (1989): International Business and Multinational Enterprises, 4th ed., Homewood, Irwin Professional Publishing.

ZENTES, J.; MORSCHETT, D.; SCHRAMM-KLEIN, H. (2011): Strategic Retail Management: Text and International Cases, 2nd ed., Wiesbaden, Gabler.

ZENTES, J.; SWOBODA, B.; SCHRAMM-KLEIN, H. (2013): Internationales Marketing, 3rd ed., Munich, Vahlen.

Chapter 18

Wholly-Owned Subsidiaries, Greenfield Investments and Mergers & Acquisitions

Wholly-owned subsidiaries afford an MNC increased control over its international business operations. This Chapter discusses the advantages and disadvantages of the main methods for acquiring wholly-owned subsidiaries, building new facilities (greenfield investments) and buying existing assets (acquisitions).

Foreign Direct Investment and Wholly-Owned Subsidiaries

FDI is an *internationalisation strategy* involving the transfer of equity funds to other nations to gain (whole or partial) ownership and control of foreign assets. *Partial ownership* relates to international collaborative ventures, i.e. international joint ventures or international strategic alliances (see Chapter 17). *Wholly-owned subsidiaries*, in contrast, represent full ownership (100%) and full control over foreign business entities. By establishing wholly-owned subsidiaries, companies can achieve ownership, location and internalisation advantages, as proposed in the OLI Paradigm (see Chapter 6).

In contrast to FDI, *international portfolio investment* involves passive ownership of foreign securities such as bonds or stocks. The main purpose of portfolio investment is to generate *financial returns*. In contrast, FDI seeks control of business units abroad and represents a long-term commitment (Cavusgil/Knight/Riesenberger 2014, p. 423). In order to qualify as FDI, the investment must afford the parent enterprise control over its foreign affiliate. To define *control*, the United Nations uses a benchmark of 10% or more of the ordinary shares or voting power of an incorporated firm or its equivalent for an unincorporated firm (UNCTAD 2013).

International Portfolio Investment

Foreign direct investment inflows are very important for the world economy. They have continued to rise over recent years (see Figure 18.1), thus highlighting the importance of this internationalisation strategy. However, roles have changed between developed and developing countries with regard to FDI. In 2012, for the first time ever, developing countries accounted for more than 50% of global FDI inflows, and thus absorbed more FDI than developed countries. Developing countries have emerged as an important source of FDI flows and account for almost one third of global FDI outflows (UNCTAD 2013).

Figure 18.1 | *Global FDI Inflows (in billion USD)*

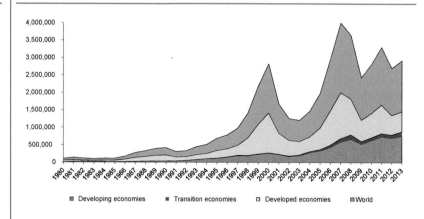

Source: UNCTAD 2014.

Characteristics of Wholly-Owned Subsidiaries

This Chapter focuses on wholly-owned subsidiaries as a specific form of FDI. They are characterised by several key features (Cavusgil/Knight/Riesenberger 2014, pp. 423-425):

■ *Greater resource commitment*: Establishing wholly-owned subsidiaries involves the highest commitment in terms of a firm's resources and capabilities.

■ *Local presence and operations*: By establishing subsidiaries in the host countries, the MNC chooses to have a local presence and establish direct contact with local actors such as customers, intermediaries, suppliers or governmental institutions.

■ *Global scale efficiencies*: By launching wholly-owned subsidiaries in different countries, MNCs can enhance their global performance if each location is chosen on the basis of competitive advantages. For example, R&D activities can be located in the most knowledge-intensive countries, or production facilities can be built at locations that provide the best ratio of productivity to labour cost.

■ *Substantial risk and uncertainty*: Wholly-owned subsidiaries represent the highest level of risk because this strategy involves substantial local investment in the form of a permanent and fixed presence in the host country and thus exposes the MNC to local risk such as government inventions or inflation. It also reduces the company's flexibility.

■ *Greater importance of cultural or social variables of the host markets*: Because of the high commitment to the host country markets, MNCs must deal more closely with particular social and cultural variables in order to minimise potential problems.

Table 18.1 shows the main advantages and disadvantages of wholly-owned subsidiaries.

Advantages and Disadvantages of Wholly-owned Subsidiaries

Table 18.1

Advantages	Disadvantages
♦ direct and independent presence	♦ investment requirements and barriers
♦ independent marketing activities	♦ high risks especially in insecure countries
♦ pushing of own strategies, easy alignment of own structures	♦ build up of considerably resources
♦ uniformity of market appearance	♦ cost intensive acquisitions and time consuming start up
♦ influence- and supervision options	♦ decision for investment much less reversible than other transaction forms
♦ bundling and deployment of company know-how (supervision of inflow and outflow)	▪ disadvantages in terms of flexibility because of capital commitment but advantages through decision superiority
♦ increasing market power towards buyers, suppliers and competitors	
♦ frequent settlement sponsorships by host countries	

Source: Adapted from Kutschker/Schmid 2011, pp. 908-909.

Types of Wholly-Owned Subsidiaries

Establishing wholly-owned subsidiaries can be done in several ways. The main routes are *greenfield ventures* and *M&As*. *Greenfield investments* involve the establishment of new facilities in foreign markets, as opposed to *acquisition strategies*, i.e., purchasing existing facilities or existing companies in the host country.

Greenfield Investment

The *greenfield strategy* involves starting operations in the host country "from scratch" (Griffin/Pustay 2013, p. 363). As the term "greenfield" implies, companies typically invest in empty plots of land and build new facilities such as production plants, logistics subsidiaries, or other facilities for their own use (Cavusgil/Knight/Riesenberger 2014, p. 428).

This strategy gives the firm a much greater ability to build the kind of subsidiary company needed to efficiently pursue its *international strategy*. Firms can, for example, select the site that best meets their needs and construct modern or contemporary facilities (Griffin/Pustay 2013, p. 363). Unlike acquisitions, firms that follow the *greenfield strategy* start their activities in the host country with a clean record and do not need to deal with existing debts or problems resulting from the past activities of existing firms.

Government Incentives

Host countries often prefer MNCs to undertake greenfield investments because in many cases they create new jobs, new production capacity, and contribute to enhanced transfer of expertise to locals. Many governments therefore offer *incentives* such as flat tax or construction subsidies to encourage greenfield investments (Cavusgil/Knight/Riesenberger 2014, p. 428).

Tacit Knowledge

Greenfield investments may be also favoured by companies that operate in businesses where transferring competencies, skills, and expertise is difficult; *tacit knowledge* often plays an important role. By establishing new ventures, companies can build an organisation culture from scratch, which is much easier than changing the existing culture of an acquired unit. Also, it is easier to establish processes and procedural methods in a new venture than to convert existing operating routines of acquired units (Hill 2013, p. 498).

However, greenfield ventures are slower to establish. They are often riskier because of a higher degree of uncertainty, both in terms of future revenue and profit prospects (Hill 2013, p. 499).

Other *drawbacks* can be associated with specific types of subsidiaries. For example, when firms establish new production plants, it is important that land in the desired location is available. Additionally, firms must comply with various local regulations, recruit staff from the local workforce and train them to meet the MNC's performance standards (Griffin/Pustay 2013, p. 364). This can be a very *time consuming* process.

Mergers & Acquisitions

Brownfield Strategy

The second strategy to establish wholly-owned subsidiaries is the acquisition of existing facilities or existing firms in the host country. This strategy is also called the *"brownfield strategy"* of international expansion.

Merger

In a *merger,* two (or more) firms join to form a new, larger entity. The corporations combine and share their resources and often the shareholders of the combining firms remain as joint owners of the combined company. In an *acquisition,* the acquired firm becomes a part of the acquirer. In a merger a new entity is formed, subsuming the merging firms (Sudarsanam 2010, p. 3).

Cross-border M&As can be accomplished across different types of industries. In *horizontal M&As*, firms that operate in the same business, i.e. firms selling the same products or a similar range of products, are acquired or come together in a merger. These firms share certain commonalities such as inputs, technology, knowledge base, marketing or sales and distribution. In a horizontal M&A, the firms operate on the same level of the value chain.

Horizontal Vertical and Conglomerate M&As

In contrast, a *vertical M&A* is a combination of firms that produce goods or services that represent the output of successive stages of the same vertical chain, i.e. downstream or upstream activities in the flow of the production and distribution process. These forms of M&As represent a specific type of *vertical integration* (Barney/Hesterly 2012, pp. 164-166).

In horizontal and vertical M&As, firms that operate in the same industry are combined. *Conglomerate M&As* differ, because the firms that come together operate in unrelated businesses. Conglomerate M&As thus represent the *diversification* of business activities for the acquiring firm or the merging firms.

M&As may take many forms. Table 18.2 gives an overview of a selection of M&A strategies.

Types of M&A Strategies

Table 18.2

Strategy	Method
Merger of Equals	Companies of equal size come together. Often, one of the merging companies is considered the "primus inter pares" once the merger has taken place.
Friendly Takeover	The management of the takeover target has a positive attitude towards the takeover.
Tender Offer	Public, open offer by an acquirer to all shareholders. The bidder contacts the shareholders directly, inviting them to sell their shares to the offer price.
Unfriendly/Hostile Takeover	The takeover target is unwilling to be acquired or the target's management has no prior knowledge of the offer.
Proxy Contest	Specific type of a hostile takeover in which the acquiring company attempts to convince the existing shareholders to use their proxy votes to install a new management that is open for the takeover.
Builder Acquisition	The objective of the acquisition is to integrate the takeover target into the network of the MNC, e.g. to realise synergies, economies of scale, etc.
Raider Acquisition	Acquisitions that are conducted with the purpose of post-acquisition asset stripping.
Leveraged Buyout (LBO)	Acquisition of a company with cash that is raised with a preponderance of debt raised by the acquirer. Several different types of LBO exist, depending on the acquiring party, for example investor buyout, management buyout, or employee buyout can be distinguished.

Empirically, cross-border M&As are the most relevant strategy. Table 18.3 gives an overview of worldwide cross-border M&A activity by home country of both selling and purchasing companies.

Table 18.3   *Cross-border M&As by Region of Purchaser and Seller in 2012*

Value of cross-border M&As by region/economy of seller, 2012 (in million of USD)		Value of cross-border M&As by region/economy of purchaser, 2012 (in million of USD)	
United States	66,113	United States	79,885
United Kingdom	35,852	Canada	39,474
Canada	29,325	China	37,111
Australia	23,087	Japan	35,666
Netherlands	17,051	Switzerland	16,254
Brazil	16,359	Germany	15,453
Ireland	12,096	Chile	9,764
France	11,985	Malaysia	9,292
China	9,995	Hong Kong/China	8,016
Switzerland	8,635	Russian Federation	7,807

Source: UNCTAD 2013.

Motives and Barriers of Cross-border M&As

M&As often take place in industries that are in the mature or declining stages of the product life cycle. These industries are characterised by low overall growth, excess capacity and a small number of large competitors. The main *motives* for cross-border M&As are revenue enhancement and cost savings (see Sudarsanam 2010, pp. 123-140):

- *Revenue enhancement*: (Horizontal) M&As lead to an increase in the market share of the merging firms, conferring enhanced market power. Additionally, the merging firms may be able to exploit each other's marketing resources, such as brands or general marketing expertise. The distribution channels established by each firm in the diverse countries may be used to sell the joint firm's products and thus the global presence of the new entity can be created expeditiously.

- *Cost savings*: A consolidating M&A is associated with opportunities for economies of scale, scope and learning in various functional activities such as production, marketing, distribution, logistics or R&D. However, the merging firms or the acquirer may also rationalise production and remove excess capacity from the new entity or the MNC's network. Additionally, redundancies in other functions such as marketing or distribution may be reduced, thereby reducing the fixed costs of the joint entity.

Nevertheless, cross-border M&As face a variety of *obstacles*. In the diverse economic and legal frameworks of different countries, there are barriers that can complicate M&As and hinder the attainment of objectives. The main *barriers* to M&As in different countries are described in Table 18.4.

Barriers to Cross-border M&As

Table 18.4

Structural Barriers	
Statutory	• strong powers for supervisory boards to block mergers; unions and workers' councils have say on takeovers and strong redundancy rights
	• issue of bearer shares, double voting or non-voting shares; absence of one share, one vote (OSOV) principle
	• discriminatory tax laws against foreign acquirers, e.g. withholding taxes on dividends
Regulatory	• antitrust regulation, foreign investment review, rules of stock exchange and professional self-regulatory bodies
	• absence of statutory or voluntary bodies to regulate takeovers
Infrastructure	• absence of M&A services, e.g. legal, accounting, investment banking services
Technical Barriers	
Management	• two-tier boards which cannot be removed or changed quickly
	• families dominate shareholding
	• powers to issue shares with differential voting rights or to friendly persons
	• powers to limit maximum voting rights; powers to override shareholders in company's interest
Information Barriers	
Accounting	• accounting statements not available, quality of information poor
	• low compliance with international generally accepted accounting principles; accounting practice biased to avoid tax liability, or conservative, hence accounting statements opaque
Shareholders	• due to issue of bearer shares, shareholding structure not known
Regulation	• regulatory procedures not known or unpredictable
Culture and Tradition	
Attitude	• "to sell is to admit failure" syndrome; dislike of hostile bids; dislike of institutional constraints on dividends or short-term profits
	• unwillingness to disclose information
Value system	• high premium on trust and confidence in negotiations rather than formal contracts

Source: Adapted from Sudarsanam 2010, p. 231.

Advantages and Disadvantages of M&As

The high relevance of cross-border M&As is a result of the major advantages associated with this strategy. By acquiring existing ventures or merging with partner firms, a company can obtain *quick access* to new markets and rapidly build their presence in the host country. In acquisitions, for example, the acquiring firm can use this strategy to rapidly build a sizable presence in the target market, because it gains control over the acquired firm's facilities, employees, technology, brands or distribution networks. It is important to notice that M&As add no new capacity to the industry. This is an obvious benefit in mature markets or if markets are characterised by *overcapacity* (Griffin/Pustay 2013, p. 364).

Entering foreign markets via M&A can also be a strategy to *pre-empt* an MNC's *competitors*. This is of major importance in highly globalised industries with intense competition (Cavusgil/Knight/Riesenberger 2014, p. 429). Cross-border M&As in this context can be used to rapidly obtain global scale and improve *competitive strength* compared with the MNC's global competitors (Hill 2013, p. 501).

Even though *acquisition strategies* are associated with large sums that have to be paid to acquire the takeover candidate, usually shortly after the deal is closed, acquisition strategies are often regarded as less risky than *greenfield investments*. The main argument is that the acquisition provides the MNC with an immediate stream of revenue and profits. Additionally, the firm acquires a set of tangible assets (e.g. factories, logistics systems) and intangible assets (e.g. local brands, local management expertise) that can reduce the risk of *mistakes* or *failure* in foreign markets (Hill 2013, pp. 501-503).

In *mergers*, the companies pool tangible and intangible resources and capabilities of the partner firms in the new entity. This is associated with economies of scale and scope. If these resources are complementary, the competitive advantage of the new venture may be enhanced.

Hidden Liabilities

However, cross-border M&As are associated with several disadvantages and often produce disappointing results. One of the main reasons for failures or problems in international acquisitions is that as well as purchasing all the valuable assets of the acquisition candidate, the acquiring firm is also confronted with all its *liabilities* (e.g. managerial or financial liabilities).

Often, the MNC cannot anticipate all the liabilities and buys "a pig in a poke". The acquired firm may, for example, reveal *hidden liabilities* such as poor labour relations or unfunded financial obligations once the acquisition process is finished (Griffin/Pustay 2013, p. 364).

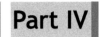

Table 18.5

Advantages and Disadvantages of Cross-border M&As

Advantages	Disadvantages

• access to customers, distribution channels, materials, HR
• rapid market development
  ▪ time savings/synergy effects
  ▪ if applicable fast market entry in numerous geographic regions
  ▪ positive cash-flow
• scale effects
• gain of know-how
  ▪ complementary effects
• gain of market position/image
• fastest mode of diversification
• no increasing competition intensity in host
• country
  ▪ little danger of overcapacity
	• massive risk
	• huge capital availability as requirement
	  ▪ best case scenario: financial markets as balancing instrument
	  ▪ in reality: limited range of alternatives for SME
	• high information and search costs
	  ▪ adequate target company as basic requirement
	  ▪ negotiation problem (Information asymmetries)
	• necessity of coordination and integration of heterogeneous structures, systems, cultures
	• adaptation of market appearance required
	• provisos/resistances of local management
	  ▪ possibly brain drain
	• provisos/resistances of host country government (foreign infiltration)
	• growing management complexity

Source: Adapted from Zentes/Swoboda/Morschett 2004, p. 658.

In this connection, another problem in acquisition strategies relates to the calculation of an adequate price for the takeover candidate. It is difficult for acquiring firms to estimate the appropriate takeover sum and they often *overpay* for the assets of the firm acquired. This is often the case if more than one firm bids for the target firm (Hill 2013, p. 503). The main general advantages and disadvantages associated with cross-border M&As are summarised in Table 18.5.

Table 18.6

Causes of Failure and Success in Cross-border M&As

Cause of Failure	Cause of Success
• target management attitudes • cultural differences • no post-acquisition integration planning • lack of knowledge of industry or target • poor management of target • no prior acquisition experience	• detailed post-acquisition integration plans • speed of implementation • clarity of acquisition purpose • good cultural fit • high degree of target management cooperation • knowledge of target and its industry

Source: Adapted from Sudarsanam 2010, p. 726.

The disadvantages of M&As frequently lead to *integration failures*. Particularly in cross-border M&As, empirical evidence shows that in many M&A transactions the companies are not able to achieve the expected outcomes, e.g. in terms of economies of scale, market performance or synergy effects (see Table 18.6).

Conclusion and Outlook

Foreign direct investment is a hierarchical mode of international market entry. The establishment of wholly-owned subsidiaries, either by greenfield operations or by cross-border M&As, represents an *internalisation* strategy.

Despite high investment costs and a time-consuming process of entry into new markets, the main advantage of *greenfield investments* is that companies are able to establish *"optimal" facilities* that fit with the interests of the firm. Greenfield strategies offer the possibility to integrate *state-of-the art* technology (e.g. production facilities) and thus can result in increased operation efficiency.

Post-Merger Integration

Cross-border M&As also represent entry strategies that are usually associated with high investment costs. Additionally, they are characterised by high *costs of integration* of the diverse companies with diverse organisational (and national) cultures. While M&As provide opportunities for *rapid entry* into new markets and quick access to distribution channels, existing management experience, local knowledge, contacts with local markets, suppliers and governments and established brand names or company reputation, there also are high risks. For example, taking over companies that are regarded as a *country's heritage* can raise national resentments in the host country. Also, a lack of integration with the acquiring company's existing operations, between the merging firms or *communication* problems between the companies can produce unfavourable outcomes (Hollensen 2014, p. 413).

Further Reading

DUNNING, J.; LUNDAN, S. (2008): Multinational Enterprises and the Global Economy, 2nd ed., Cheltenham, Edward Elgar Publishing, pp. 116-144.

GHEMAWAT, P.; GHADAR, F. (2000): The Dubious Logic of Global Megamergers, in: Harvard Business Review, Vol. 78, No. 4, pp. 65-72.

HARZING, A. (2002): Acquisitions versus Greenfield Investments: International Strategy and Management of Entry Modes, in: Strategic Management Journal, Vol. 23, No. 3, pp. 211-227.

Case Study: ThyssenKrupp[*]

Profile History and Status Quo

This case study concerns the German company *ThyssenKrupp* and several of its business operations in international markets. More precisely, this case study provides insights into the company's activities with regard to wholly-owned subsidiaries, especially greenfield investments and mergers & acquisitions.

Today, *ThyssenKrupp* is the largest steel producer in Germany and one of the largest steel producing companies in the world. The multinational conglomerate is based in Germany and consists of 630 companies in 77 countries and has about 160,000 employees worldwide. As well as steel production, the company also provides components and systems for the automotive industry, elevators, escalators and industrial services.

The company is the result of the merger between *Thyssen AG* and *Krupp*, and now has its operational headquarters in Essen. The negotiations for the merger started in the early 1980s. The two companies then cooperated closely in several business areas and the proposed alliance was finalised in 1983. In 1997, the two companies combined their activities in the flat steel business and formed *Thyssen Krupp Stahl AG*. In the same year, *Krupp* and *Thyssen* further negotiated on expanding their cooperation into other business areas. During these talks, both companies identified a great potential for strategic development and operating synergies through a full merger, which took place in 1999.

In 2009, the company was reorganised into eight business areas, which fall under the Materials and Technology divisions. After a further reorganisation, the Technology division was divided into Plant and Mechanical divisions. Today, the Mechanical division designs and manufactures high-quality components for the automotive, machinery, energy and construction industries. Furthermore, as a part of this division, the company also produces innovative technological goods such as modern elevator systems.

The Plant division extends from the engineering and construction of complete industrial complexes to a global service network and advanced naval technology. Last but not least, the Material division includes custom material solution, efficient materials manufacturing and processing with a focus on stainless steel and carbon steel, and materials services. The portfolio is fur-

---

[*] Sources used for this case study include the website http://www.thyssenkrupp.com as well as information from press releases and annual reports from ThyssenKrupp.

ther supplemented by *ThyssenKrupp Business Services* and *ThyssenKrupp IT Services* (see Figure 18.2).

Figure 18.2 | *ThyssenKrupp Group Structure*

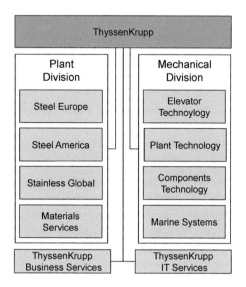

Source: ThyssenKrupp AG 2010.

The company's strategy focuses on the development of innovative products, high quality materials and intelligent industrial processes and services for a sustainable infrastructure and resource efficiency, providing several challenges and business opportunities (see Figure 18.3).

To achieve these strategic aims, *ThyssenKrupp* has to combine its traditional competitive advantage in materials with its engineering expertise and broad technology expertise to deal with a worldwide demographic change, the globalisation of goods flows and the rapid growth of mega cities, meaning that global demand still will continue to rise.

Figure 18.3

Business Opportunities for ThyssenKrupp

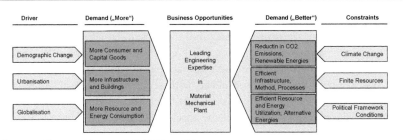

Source: ThyssenKrupp AG 2013, p. 31.

ThyssenKrupp has made several investments and previous attempts to deal with the aforementioned challenges and to realise future business opportunities in international markets. Throughout the company's history, an integral part of the company's business strategy for expansion and international growth has involved wholly-owned subsidiaries and mergers and acquisitions in emerging markets and international markets with a suitable infrastructure and a stable demand for the company's products. After a brief overview of activities in the company's early history, the following provides some detailed examples of greenfield investments and mergers and acquisitions made by *ThyssenKrupp*.

The Company's International Expansion

In the early 1970s, *Thyssen* was already considering ideas to strengthen the group's international focus. Plans to produce steel in different locations around the world and process it in Duisburg were abandoned after the 1973 oil crisis. To expand their business base and to reduce the company's dependency on steel demand, the *Budd Company* (USA) was acquired in 1978. With the acquisition of *Budd's* automotive operations in 1978, *ThyssenKrupp* entered the North American automotive industry. *Budd Company* became the automotive division of *Thyssen* and was operated in North America as *Budd Thyssen*, later *ThyssenKrupp Budd Co.* In October 2006, *ThyssenKrupp* sold *ThyssenKrupp Budd's* North American body and chassis operations to *Martinrea International Inc.*

During the 1990s, further international expansion was based on a concentration on selected fields of business with good market and earnings potential. In this context, it is worth highlighting the acquisitions of the machine tool manufacturer *Giddings & Lewis Inc.* (USA) and *Copper and Brass Sales Inc.*

Mergers and Acquisitions

421

(USA), a leading trading and service centre for nonferrous metals in North America, in 1997, and of *Dover Elevators* (USA), market leader in hydraulic elevators in North America, in 1998.

Four years later, *ThyssenKrupp* acquired the Korean-based *Dongyang Elevator*. These latter acquisitions can be considered the starting point of the company's tremendous success in the international elevator market. After that, *ThyssenKrupp Elevator* pressed ahead with acquisitions of established small and medium-size elevator companies in the USA in the following years. In 2013, *ThyssenKrupp* acquired all the assets of Ohio-based *Edmonds Elevator, Inc.* With this acquisition, *ThyssenKrupp* continued its international growth strategy and strengthened the company's service business in the North American market.

Investment in North America

In 2007, as a part of their forward strategies for profitable and sustainable growth, *ThyssenKrupp* started to plan a new plant in the USA at a cost of 2.3 billion EUR. After a phase of extensive preliminary investigations, the site selection process focussed on Alabama and Louisiana. The investigations revealed several positive factors in these states in terms of energy costs, logistical advantages and geological conditions.

This greenfield venture was mainly intended to considerably strengthen *ThyssenKrupp's* position in North America. The NAFTA (North American Free Trade Agreement) is one of the biggest volume markets for high-quality flat carbon steel, and *ThyssenKrupp* thought that the company would be able to leverage the strengths of its broad range of high-quality products in this sector. Another reason for setting up a new production facility was that at this point in time *ThyssenKrupp* was already an established producer on the NAFTA market thanks to its cold rolling mill in Mexico and sales/distribution bases in the USA. Hence, the new plant was intended to produce for the fast-growing US market, while the production facility in Mexico focused more on the Mexican market. The central element of the new plant was a hot strip mill, which would be used primarily to process slabs from the new *ThyssenKrupp* steel mill in Brazil. In addition, the plans for the new plant included cold rolling and hot-dip coating capacities for high-quality flat carbon steel end products.

Overall, the estimated annual capacity of the new production facility was about 4.5 million metric tons of end products and the planned costs of the investment were about 1.8 billion EUR. The new plant opened in December 2010. It was ultimately one of the largest foreign investments in the history of *ThyssenKrupp*. Contrary to expectations, the overall costs of the new production facility were about 3.7 billion EUR.

*Greenfield
Investment in
Brazil*

In 2005, *ThyssenKrupp* started planning the construction of a new facility to produce steel in Brazil for the global market. The initial estimated costs for the establishment of the new production facility were about 1.3 billion EUR. But, when construction was finished in 2010, the final costs for this greenfield investment proved to be much higher (about 5.3 billion EUR). The reasons for this tremendous increase in costs were the strict constraints put in place by the Brazilian government regarding environmental protection, especially concerning prevention of atmospheric pollution. The new plant was intended to produce five billion tons of steel, which would be refined in Germany and in North America for the automotive industry in Europe, North America and China.

In 2014, *ThyssenKrupp* started the construction of a new automotive supply plant for the production of assembled cylinder-head modules in Brazil (Pocos de Caldas, Minas Gerais). The company has invested about 40 million EUR in the construction of the plant, which is expected to be completed by the end of 2014 and will create about 170 jobs. The production is planned to start in early 2015. With this greenfield investment, *ThyssenKrupp* will be able to produce more than one million modules a year. The finished products will mainly be supplied to car producers in Brazil.

The new Brazilian plant is the fourth such plant being built or put into operation around the world by *ThyssenKrupp* since 2013, and it is an important part of the company's global growth strategy as a supplier of high-performance components for the automotive industry. As a result of extraordinary efforts in the development of innovative and high-quality components for the automotive industry, *ThyssenKrupp* now has a substantial competitive advantage compared to its competitors in the global market. For example, *ThyssenKrupp's* products allow car producers to reduce weight by up to 30%. This will considerably lower fuel consumption and hence reduce carbonate dioxide emissions.

But ultimately the greenfield investments in the North and South American market strategy were not a success. With the beginning of the worldwide recession starting in 2008 and the associated cutbacks, *ThyssenKrupp* lost about 8 billion EUR on its two new plants in North America and Brazil, which sold steel below the cost of production. Hence, the two steel production facilities were offered for sale as a consequence of continuous losses. *ThyssenKrupp's* stainless steel division, including the stainless portion of the US plant, was sold to Finnish stainless steel company *Outokumpu* in 2012. In 2013, *ThyssenKrupp* offered the remaining portion of the plant for sale at less than 4 billion USD. Finally, *ThyssenKrupp's* Clavert carbon steel production facility was sold to *ArcelorMittal* and *NipponSteel* in 2014.

Overall, the greenfield investments of *ThyssenKrupp* in North America and

Brazil and the related losses have caused serious problems for the whole company. While this strategy has allowed *ThyssenKrupp* to protect their tacit knowledge from competitors in the new market to a certain degree, these investments show the associated high risks of this kind of internationalisation strategy for the overall business success of a company, due to the high investments and long time required to establish new production facilities and create a business in a foreign country.

*International
Expansion into
the Chinese
Market*

For *ThyssenKrupp*, China is the world's most important growth market. In the last two fiscal years the company has invested about 250 million EUR in new supply plants for the Chinese automotive industry and now has seven Chinese production facilities in this technology sector.

In 2013, *ThyssenKrupp* opened a new automotive supply plant in China (Chengdu, Sichuan Province). Thanks to the opening of this new production facility, the company now produces springs and stabilisers for the Chinese automotive market. Springs and stabilisers are important comfort and safety related components in cars. They ensure even grip, while absorbing and cushioning shocks from the road surface and centrifugal forces during cornering. *ThyssenKrupp* has invested around 20 million EUR in the new plant and has created about 200 new jobs. The strategic expansion of automotive supply plants in one of the world's fastest growing regions is a key component of *ThyssenKrupp's* transformation into a diversified technology group.

Overall, since 2010 the company has invested around one billion EUR in the global expansion of its auto components business. Another production facility for cylinder head modules is currently under construction. The components produced there support the company in its ability to meet the still rising demand for greater personal mobility in the Asian market, by meeting the need for lighter, more comfortable, more economical and safer vehicles.

A new production line for cylinder-head modules in Dalian and a new crankshaft plant in Nanjing were opened in 2013. In Shanghai, a new production line for steering systems also started operation. The company has invested around 350 million EUR in these projects.

Overall, *ThyssenKrupp's* range of automotive products in China now ranges from crankshafts, camshafts, cylinder head modules and steering systems to springs and stabilisers. In total, *ThyssenKrupp* employs around 3,800 people at ten production facilities in the components sector for the Chinese auto, truck and building machinery and wind power industries. In the 2012/2013 fiscal year, the company generated sales of around 750 million EUR in this segment in China, with the automotive sector accounting for about two thirds of this result.

Summary and Outlook

The company's strategy of global growth through greenfield investments and mergers and acquisitions is an integral part of *ThyssenKrupp's* business strategy and has considerably strengthened the company's position in the international markets. Today, *ThyssenKrupp* generates about 69% of its consolidated sales in international markets, while customers in the German domestic market account for the remaining 31%. Overall, the member countries of the European Union (24%) and North America (21%) are the key foreign markets for the company's business activities.

ThyssenKrupp companies hold leading positions with their products in numerous international markets and the degree of internationalisation of the whole group is still rising. *ThyssenKrupp* is already the world market leader in assembled camshafts and is continuously optimising this established technology in line with the latest findings and requirements. The company is able to meet car manufacturers' demands for lightweight components and the associated reduction in fuel consumption. Furthermore, *ThyssenKrupp* is one of the world's leading elevator manufacturers (sales: 5.7 billion EUR in the 2011/2012 fiscal year). Their portfolio consists of passenger boarding bridges, stair and platform lifts, as well as tailored services for all components.

Questions

1. List the potential advantages and disadvantages of greenfield investments and M&As and evaluate *ThyssenKrupp's* current situation.

2. Does the sequence of *ThyssenKrupp's* strategy of international expansion follow the theoretical concept of psychic distance?

3. Which processes and organisational structures are important for creating new subsidiaries in foreign countries?

Hints

1. See Gaughan 2002.

2. See Chapter 14 as well as Sousa/Bradley 2004 for an explanation of the concept of psychic distance.

3. See Collis 2014.

References

BARNEY, J.; HESTERLY, W. (2012): Strategic Management and Competitive Advantage: Concepts, 4th ed., Upper Saddle River, New Jersey, Pearson.

CAVUSGIL, S.T.; KNIGHT, G.; RIESENBERGER, J.R. (2013): International Business: The New Realities, 3rd ed., Boston, Pearson.

COLLIS, D. (2014): International Strategy and Competition, New York, Wiley & Sons.

DUNNING, J.; LUNDAN, S. (2008): Multinational Enterprises and the Global Economy, 2nd ed., Cheltenham, Edward Elgar Publishing.

GAUGHAN, P. (2002): Mergers, Acquisitions, and Corporate Restructurings, 3rd ed., New York, Wiley & Sons.

GHEMAWAT, P.; GHADAR, F. (2000): The Dubious Logic of Global Megamergers, in: Harvard Business Review, Vol. 78, No. 4, pp. 65-72.

GRIFFIN, R.; PUSTAY, M. (2013): International Business: A Managerial Perspective, 7th ed., Upper Saddle River, New Jersey, Pearson.

HARZING, A. (2002): Acquisitions versus Greenfield Investments: International Strategy and Management of Entry Modes, in: Strategic Management Journal, Vol. 23, No. 3, pp. 211-227.

HILL, C.W.L. (2013): Global Business Today, 8th ed., Boston, McGraw-Hill.

HOLLENSEN, S. (2014): Global Marketing, 6th ed., Harlow, Pearson, pp. 471-648.

KUTSCHKER, M.; SCHMID, S. (2011): Internationales Management, 7th ed., Munich, Oldenbourg.

SOUSA, C.M.; BRADLEY, F. (2006): Cultural Distance and Psychic Distance: Two Peas in a Pod?, in: Journal of International Marketing, Vol. 14, No. 1, pp. 49-70.

SUDARSANAM, S. (2010): Creating Value from Mergers and Acquisitions: The Challenges, 2nd ed., Harlow, Financial Times Prentice Hall.

THYSSENKRUPP AG (2010): 11th General Stockholders' Meeting ThyssenKrupp AG, Bochum.

THYSSENKRUPP AG (2013): Annual Report 2012/2013, Essen.

UNCTAD (2013): World Investment Report 2013: Global Value Chains: Investment and Trade for Development, Geneva.

UNCTAD (2014): World Investment Report 2014: Investing in the SDGs: An Action Plan, Geneva.

ZENTES, J.; SWOBODA, B.; MORSCHETT, D. (2004): Internationales Wertschöpfungsmanagement, Munich, Vahlen.

Part V

Selected

Value Chain

Activities

Chapter 19

International Production and Sourcing

MNCs are complex phenomena, but their ultimate objective is to sell their products to customers. While other value-chain activities (like R&D and marketing) are certainly highly relevant, the MNC must ultimately provide the goods and services it wants to offer. Sourcing the necessary inputs and producing the right outputs is a complex task that is at the core of an MNC's strategy. This Chapter briefly explains the basic decision between sourcing and production, discusses the configuration of production and sourcing activities and highlights basic production processes. In addition, different types of foreign production plants are described and the main developments in international sourcing explained.

Introduction

The term *"production"* refers to the value-generating activities that transform inputs into outputs and eventually create products. While this term includes manufacturing and service activities, this Chapter will focus mainly on manufacturing activities, i.e. the production of physical products. *"Sourcing"* includes all activities that organise the supply of the company with input goods and services that are needed but not produced within the company itself. *Sourcing* usually involves the identification of the required goods and services, supplier selection, price negotiations, etc. Generally, ensuring security of supply of products of an adequate quality and at an adequate price is the main objective of sourcing managers.

Given that in some industries more than 50% of the value of the final product stems from externally procured inputs, the relevance of sourcing for the MNC's success is enormous. However, both production and sourcing can be understood as *different operation modes* for the same activity. An early decision is providing an answer to the "make-or-buy" question (see Chapter 16). For example, if a car company needs a lighting component as an input for its final product, the company has to decide whether it wants to manufacture this component itself or procure the component from an external supplier. From the perspective of transaction cost theory, this decision merely fixes the level of *vertical integration* in a production chain, i.e., it just determines "who" is carrying out a certain activity. For international production strategies, many authors also use the term "sourcing" when referring to *"internal suppliers"*, i.e. other production units within the same MNC. In this Chapter,

Relationship between Production and Sourcing

however, the term "sourcing" is used for procurement from external suppliers.

Configuration of Production Activities

Definition | The first issue that needs to be decided is configuration. Configuration determines where in the world each value chain activity is performed, including the number of locations (Porter 1986, p. 17).

Concentration vs. Decentralisation of Production Sites

An MNC has to decide whether it wants to carry out production activities in one factory in a centralised location or whether it prefers to decentralise the activities across different countries. For example, Swiss manufacturers of luxury watches, like *IWC*, often locate all their production activities in Switzerland and serve the world market from there. Conversely, Japanese car manufacturers started to relocate their production facilities to their target markets in the 1980s and often serve regional markets from regional production sites (see the case study on *Mazda* in Chapter 7).

Advantages of Production Decentralisation | Advantages of decentralising production activities into different countries include:

■ *Circumvention of trade barriers*: MNCs can save custom tariffs and overcome non-tariff barriers by locating production in the target market.

■ *Acceptance by local governments*: Host country governments prefer local production which has benefits for their labour market, trade balance, etc. Often, they are willing to give incentives for locating production in their countries.

■ *Easier adaptation to local markets*: Locating production facilities in the target market leads to increased sensitivity to local market needs.

■ *Advantages in distribution logistics*: By locating production closer to the markets, MNCs reduce delivery costs to their foreign customers and shorten delivery times. This shortens their *time-to-market* (which is important for clothing companies like *Zara* or consumer electronics like the *Sony PlayStation*) and to deliver to their commercial customers *just-in-time*.

■ *Increased flexibility*: By having production capacity in different countries rather than a single location, MNCs can reduce their risk exposure and shift production more flexibly, e.g. in the case of changes to cost structures or foreign currency exchange rates. In addition, they can exploit arbitrage advantages and market imperfections, e.g. by using cheap labour in one country, better resource access in another country, differences in tax systems or interest rates, etc.

- *Better access to local inputs and better relations with local suppliers*: Local production not only facilitates access to customers but also to local inputs. This can be natural resources (oil, ores, etc.), agricultural products (coffee, rubber, etc.) or other input goods. Relations with suppliers in a foreign market are also improved by locating facilities in their proximity.

- *Potentially lower production costs*: Particularly for MNCs from high-income countries, relocating production to different foreign countries gives them access to lower input prices, most notably a labour force with a lower wage-level.

- On the other hand, concentrating production in one location (in this case, still very often the home country of the MNC) also has some major benefits, including: *Economies of scale and experience curve effects*: Having one large production plant instead of several smaller ones enhances the output volume of the factory, which results in economies of scale and positive effects on unit costs thanks to the experience gained in the production process.

Advantages of Production Concentration

- *Ease of coordination*: While the dispersion of production processes might reduce production costs, it usually drastically increases coordination costs (e.g. between factories in different countries that work in the same production chain). Concentrating production activities in one location reduces the challenge of coordinating dispersed production processes.

- *Better bundling of procurement volume*: Similarly, concentrated production usually leads to better integration of the necessary inputs. Prices for input goods that are centrally negotiated for a large volume delivered to one location are often substantially lower. The coordination effort to bundle procurement of factories in different countries is high (even with modern IT systems) and even in the case of perfect coordination, suppliers will demand higher prices for decentralised deliveries.

- *Better availability of capabilities in some home countries*: For MNCs in industrialised countries like Switzerland, the availability of skilled labour offers quality advantages that are often not available in foreign host countries.

- *Country-of-origin effect*: For many MNCs, the home country is still a major source of its image advantage. Thus, e.g., producing Swiss watches in Switzerland or a *Porsche* car in Germany provides the companies with a competitive advantage.

In some cases, concentration in the home country is a consequence of *path dependency* and *inertia*. If the existing production facilities are concentrated in the home country, the *cost of relocation* is substantial. *Sunk costs* in existing facilities, existing labour contracts and supplier relations may make a switch to a foreign location – which might be better in a static comparison – too expensive. Closing a factory in the home country is usually met with great opposition by the home-country government and local trade unions. The expected negative image effects of plant closure also lead to inertia.

Fragmentation and Regional Concentration

As a general trend in recent decades, production processes have become increasingly fragmented (i.e., split into different production stages which are located in different countries, an issue that will be discussed later in this Chapter). At the same time, each stage in the production process has become proportionately more concentrated, to avoid inefficient duplication. *Lower logistics costs* (in the last few decades) and *reduced trade barriers* are responsible for this trend. For instance, in areas of regional integration like the European Union, many companies no longer have dedicated factories for each country, instead centralising production to one or a few factories that deliver throughout the region. This trend can be observed clearly in the consumer goods industry (e.g. companies like *Unilever* or *Procter & Gamble*) where in previous decades national factories were created, but where companies are now increasingly concentrating their production. Increased logistics costs – caused by rising oil prices and climate control regulation – may change this trend in the future.

Influence Factors on the Configuration Decision

Given the opposing forces towards concentration and decentralisation, specific influence factors on this decision must be considered (Zentes/Swoboda/Morschett 2004, pp. 390-402; Griffin/Pustay 2013, pp. 486-490). Ultimately, these influence factors help the MNC manager to decide on the optimal production configuration and explain why the optimal decision differs strongly among MNCs.

Product and Production Technology Related Issues

An initial set of influence factors is provided by product and production technology related factors. These include:

- *Product-specific trade barriers*: While some products no longer face major trade barriers, encouraging centralisation, others are still exposed to high custom tariffs, pulling production to the target markets.

- *International standardisation of product*: If there are few national differences in consumer taste and preference for products, the need for local responsiveness is reduced, facilitating centralised manufacturing.

■ *Value-to-weight ratio*: Logistics costs are strongly driven by the weight (and volume) of products. If value-to-weight is low (as in the case of beer as illustrated by the case study on *AB InBev* in Chapter 14), there is greater pressure to manufacture the product in multiple locations; if it is high (as in the case of luxury goods), logistics costs do not pose a barrier to producing the product in a single location and exporting it to other parts of the world.

■ *Product-specific country image*: Country-of-origin image advantages are usually only present for certain industries, like high-tech products from Japan or the USA, highly reliable products from Germany or Switzerland, or design-oriented products from Italy.

■ *Characteristics of the manufacturing technology:* In some industries, *fixed costs* (e.g. for setting up a manufacturing plant) are very high and *minimum efficient scale* (at which most economies of scale are exploited) is also high. In these cases, a company is more likely to centralise its production in one or a few plants (and vice versa). As another characteristic of the manufacturing technology, it has to be considered whether the production process can be separated into different stages or not. If yes, this may influence the location choice for each stage separately, while one continuous and inseparable process often leads to concentrated production in the home country.

In addition, country-related issues have to be considered. Obviously, the MNC's *home country* plays a major role for location decisions, since in most cases *relative advantages* are considered. MNCs from industrialised countries already have access to a skilled but relatively expensive labour force. In addition, the home country's inclusion in regional trade agreements (like ASEAN or the EU) or free trade agreements influences the relevance of trade barriers. Besides home country factors, a plethora of characteristics of the potential *host countries* play a role in location decisions. These include competitiveness, country risk, host government influences, corruption, trade barriers, regional integration agreements, national culture and many more.

Country-Related Issues

Configurational decisions also depend on the MNC, its characteristics and its *strategy*. For example, the competitive strategy (cost leadership vs. quality leadership), the production and inventory strategy (e.g. just-in-time), the international orientation (e.g. global strategy vs. multinational strategy), the configuration of the other value-added activities (like marketing, R&D, etc.) will all have an impact on the configuration of production facilities.

MNC-Related Issues

Additionally, customer- and marketing-oriented factors will influence the optimal configuration decision. For example, if the company is attempting to *standardise* its products worldwide, the centralisation option is more viable than in the case of multinational marketing with adaptation of the products

Customer- and Marketing-Related Issues

to each country. The necessity of flexibility in production and the importance of *delivery times* (like in the high-fashion industry) will shift production closer to the target markets, and the exploitation of the country-of-origin image differs with the marketing strategy. Also, customers' production strategies (in the case of business-to-business transactions) will influence the necessity of locating the MNC's production facility close to the customer.

Location Choice

Countries differ and so does their attractiveness as potential locations for foreign production. The varied characteristics of these different countries (and, linked to this, the customer-related factors) have been discussed above.

Table 19.1 | *Example of a Scoring Model for the Selection of a Production Location*

Location Characteristic	Importance of Criterion in Percent (w_i)	Evaluation of Country (e_i) (from 1 - very bad to 10 - excellent)	Combined Score ($w_i \times e_i$)
Attractiveness of Local Market	20%	8	1.6
Logistics Costs	5%	4	0.2
Wage Level	15%	2	0.3
Availability of Skilled Labour	15%	9	1.35
Innovativeness of Country	10%	8	0.8
Availability of Suppliers	20%	8	1.6
Stability of Local Currency	5%	9	0.45
Political Risk	10%	4	0.4
SUM (Overall Score)	**100%**	-	**6.7**

The selection of a certain location is – as becomes evident when looking at the different reasons for concentration vs. decentralisation – important because it influences production costs, logistics costs (procurement logistics, production logistics and distribution logistics), access to resources and customers but also the development of capabilities, e.g. the ability to adapt products to a certain market. Given the various reasons for establishing international production sites, the weight that companies attach to these individual factors naturally differs. Thus, a *scoring model* is usually a pragmatic instrument for selecting a location for a production facility, since it integrates location characteristics and considers the differing requirements of each company. An example is given in Table 19.1. Here, a single location is evaluated. The overall score of different locations has to be compared for the final selection.

Given the effort required to evaluate many locations using this procedure and in particular to gather the necessary data, *multi-stage selection procedures* are often applied. Here, many countries are initially screened based on very few, often macroeconomic, criteria. This greatly reduces the set of feasible alternatives. In a second stage, more criteria are included for the reduced country set and all countries below a certain threshold are eliminated. In the third stage, specific locations within countries are compared using a more detailed set of criteria that are customised to the MNC's specific objectives.

Re-Relocation

The last few decades have seen major shifts in global production. Often, companies have relocated their production to foreign countries. However, many studies also reveal that relocation is not a one-way street. Instead, *divestment* from foreign countries is also a very common phenomenon, where companies close down (or sell) foreign production plants and relocate their production back to their home countries. The most frequently cited reasons for "re-relocation" or "reshoring" are the low flexibility of foreign production sites (in particular with regard to the integration of foreign production processes into production chains with home-country factories), logistics costs, transport times, lower delivery reliability, product quality problems in many low-wage countries and the increased cost of coordination. Specifically, foreign production sites require intensive travelling by production managers, frequent meetings, etc., which are too expensive for many SMEs. For the US, where many manufacturing MNCs are currently reconsidering the location of their production activities, further aspects are relevant: a weak dollar, rising wages in developing countries and falling energy prices (due to shale gas exploitation in the US) (UNCTAD 2013, p. 26).

Divestment and Reshoring

Split Production Processes

The case implicitly considered in the preceding sections is a rather simple one: a one-stage production process and a company that only produces one product. Reality, however, is much more complex. Here, production processes are usually fragmented into *multi-stage production processes* where the different stages have to be linked to form complex production chains.

As a typical example of such multi-stage production processes, a process from the clothing and textiles industry can be illustrated: the manufacture of a pair of jeans. For a pair of jeans that is eventually sold in France, the cotton may be grown and picked in Uzbekistan, then spun into thread and woven into cloth in India. From there, the parts are transported to Bangladesh.

Multi-Stage Production Processes

Buttons that have been produced in South Korea and labels that are manufactured in Mexico also arrive in Bangladesh where the cloth is cut and made into a pair of jeans. From Bangladesh, the finished jeans are transported via ship to the destination port in Le Havre (for a negligible transport cost of approximately 0.20 EUR per garment).

To give an overview of the basic options for a company in such a case, a (still simple) three-stage production process will be investigated in the subsequent section. A company produces some parts from input goods and raw materials in stage 1, then manufactures components out of those parts in stage 2 and finally assembles finished products in stage 3.

Figure 19.1	*Basic Types of Production Configurations*

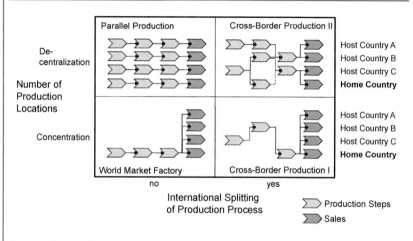

Source: Grünig/Morschett 2012, p. 301.

World Market Factories and Parallel Production

Figure 19.1 illustrates four basic solutions for the configuration of such multi-stage processes based on two dimensions: Is the production process split across different countries and are there one or several production locations for each production step? In the case of a *world market factory*, a product is completely produced in one factory (often in the home country) and transported from there to the different international markets. This is the highest possible level of concentration and it takes advantage of all concentration benefits. It also suffers from all the disadvantages of concentration. In the case of *parallel production*, full production chains are replicated in different country markets and each factory serves its local market. Frequently, high trade barriers are the motivation for this production strategy. This strategy is also employed in cases where different or highly adapted products are produced for the different markets.

Nowadays, multi-stage production processes are very often designed as *split cross-border production processes*. These are characterised by geographically dispersed production stages that are in a vertical flow relationship and by the international flow of goods between the MNC's different production units (given the interrelatedness of production and sourcing, some of those production units might not even belong to the MNC but to suppliers, outsourcing partners, etc.). For each production step, it is still possible to determine whether one country is chosen as location or whether each (or at least one) production step is carried out in several countries.

This fragmentation and separate configuration of the production process has major advantages. In the case of a non-separated production chain, all production stages are exposed to the same country conditions. However, different production stages might have different requirements (e.g. different intensity of capital or labour) which logically results in suboptimal locations for most of the stages in the case of a combined location. This disadvantage can be overcome by splitting production stages and selecting optimal locations for each specific production stage. For instance, labour intensive manufacturing steps can be located in low-wage countries while knowledge and capital intensive stages can be located in countries where skilled labour and the necessary infrastructure are available. However, even in the case of fragmentation, the interrelatedness of the production stages must be considered, i.e. the coordination effort and the logistics costs that result from the overall production chain.

Fragmentation of Processes

The majority of MNCs are *multi-product companies*. Thus, in addition to being split into different production stages, the production may or may not be split by product type. The *specialisation* of factories to single products (or product groups) has advantages but reduces economies of scope that might emerge from efficiency advantages when several products are produced jointly.

Product Split

In practice, companies do both simultaneously. For example, *Mercedes-Benz* produces only engines and other components at its factories in Berlin, Hamburg and Stuttgart-Untertürkheim (thus, single production stages), while it undertakes many production stages for its M-class in Tuscaloosa (USA) and the S-class in Sindelfingen (a type of world market factory). For the C-class, as of 2014 the company has started to produce it at four production sites on four continents: Germany, South Africa, China and the USA. Thus, this is a type of parallel production.

19

Types of International Production Plants

Foreign production plants are frequently categorised using a model developed by Ferdows (Ferdows 1989; 1997). It is accepted that foreign production plants are often established with one dominant motive. This can be either *access to low cost production factors, proximity to attractive sales markets* or the use of superior *local technological resources*. But the competence of the site or, more concretely, the *extent of technical activities* carried out at foreign production plants also varies widely. Six groups of foreign production plants can be identified based on those two dimensions (see Figure 19.2).

Figure 19.2 | *Types of Foreign Production Plants*

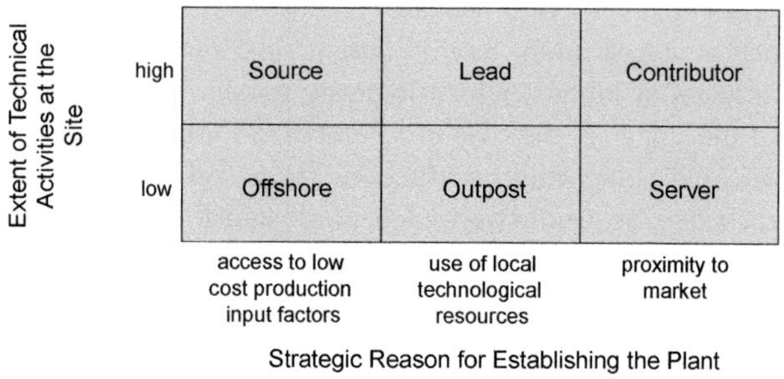

Source: Ferdows 1989, p. 8; 1997, p. 77.

For example, an *offshore factory* is mainly established to exploit low labour costs in a foreign country. Certain simple parts or components are produced there and usually delivered to the MNC's main production site in the home country or a third country. *Job processing,* where only certain labour intensive production stages are carried out in a nearby foreign country, is a typical example of this factory type (the *maquiladoras* on the Mexican-US border are an extreme example). Technical competence at the site can be very limited and it merely implements production processes that are decided centrally at the HQ or in other factories. A *server factory* often assembles final products from components that are delivered from the home country. Server factories are established to circumvent trade barriers or to adapt the last production stages to the local market needs. With a similar objective but a more complete value-added chain, a *contributor factory* serves local markets (often in the form of parallel production). As a final example, the *lead factories* strategically contribute to the success of the MNC by realising full value-chains and developing products and production processes based on local technical competence.

International Sourcing

Production involves the transformation of inputs into outputs. It is a question of vertical integration whether the company produces necessary inputs by itself or sources them from external suppliers. A detailed discussion of this decision was presented in Part IV.

Over the past few decades there has been a general trend towards reducing companies' own value-adding and replacing companies' internal production activities with those of external suppliers. The global car industry has demonstrated the benefits of this strategy, with Japanese manufacturers leading the way. As has been pointed out in Chapter 16, this reduction in companies' own value-added has been combined with a development from traditional sourcing to modular sourcing. In *traditional sourcing*, a "one-tier" model was used where numerous suppliers delivered single parts or raw materials to a company. This company then carried out the complex assembly and production task. In *modular sourcing*, a few module suppliers deliver a few complex and pre-assembled modules to a company that only does the final assembly and few of its own production steps.

From Traditional to Modular Sourcing

However, these advantages of single sourcing for strategic components and systems must be balanced with the disadvantages. For certain goods, it might be better to focus supply on a few suppliers rather than just one, e.g. in the case of so-called *dual sourcing*. While the procurement volume from each supplier is lower, with the attendant disadvantages for the negotiation of procurement prices, dual (or more generally multiple) sourcing enhances the *security of supply*. If one supplier cannot deliver, e.g. due to a strike or a political disruption, the other supplier can often replace this volume.

Single Sourcing and Multiple Sourcing

Configuration of Sourcing Activities

For sourcing, the optimal configuration of these activities must also be decided. Given the close association of production and sourcing, many of the arguments mentioned above for and against concentration and decentralisation and activities in foreign countries also hold true for sourcing. The trend towards *global sourcing* has a number of causes (Zentes/Swoboda/Morschett 2004, pp. 313-315):

Global Sourcing

- ■ unavailability of certain products in the home market

■ cost reduction by using international sourcing markets, e.g. due to lower wages, prices for raw materials, taxes, etc.

■ improving the quality of inputs due to a wider selection of suppliers

■ improving innovation by monitoring different procurement markets

■ securing and stabilising supply by spreading the procurement volume across different countries

■ stabilising procurement prices by avoiding sudden volatility in specific regions (e.g. with regard to foreign currencies).

Furthermore, the opening of procurement markets in Eastern Europe and China, which were previously very difficult to access, drastically increased *international procurement*. The increasing competition and strong cost pressure on MNCs resulted in efforts to reduce input prices and, in the last few decades, global sourcing has often been seen as the response to this pressure.

Counter-Trend towards Regional Sourcing

However, the trend towards international or even global sourcing is opposed by a counter-trend towards national or even *regional procurement*. The reasons for bringing back sourcing to the home country or at least home region are manifold. First, the trend towards reduction of inventories and *just-in-time production* as well as towards close supplier relationships promotes local relationships and nearby suppliers than can reliably deliver goods on time. Tight business relationships in *regional clusters* (see Chapter 8) are based on similar arguments. In the motor vehicle industry, *supplier parks* have been developed that gather all relevant suppliers in a geographic location near the manufacturing plant to be able to realise those strategies. *Security of supply* is demonstrably higher in the case of domestic sourcing. Furthermore, consumers increasingly value *regional products* in a globalised world; a trend which has been strengthened in recent years by concern about environmental problems resulting from global transport chains. In the near future, *climate problems* and the scarcity of oil are likely to result in rising logistics costs that may make regional sourcing more efficient.

Objectives and Trade-Offs for International Sourcing

To summarise, international sourcing has to follow four main objectives simultaneously:

■ reduction of *costs* of input goods

■ *security* of supply

■ improvement of *quality* of input goods

■ *speed* of delivery.

An international sourcing strategy must balance these four objectives since they are partly complementary but also partly conflicting. For example, sourcing from China is usually substantially cheaper than sourcing from Western Europe, but products take several weeks to transport by container ship or are very costly to transport by plane. The quality level is – as some recent cases have highlighted – not always guaranteed and, given the long transport routes, the security of supply is at risk throughout the logistics chain. On the other hand, from the perspective of a Western European MNC, sourcing in the home country might secure supply and guarantee the quality with very short delivery times, but the cost level might be prohibitive. In this case, Eastern Europe might be a good sourcing location when considering the four objectives simultaneously.

Overall, it is important to note that sourcing decisions should not be solely based on cost considerations but on a bundle of objectives. Also, cost considerations have to include not only the purchasing price of the goods but also logistics costs, risk premiums, etc., which often makes more proximate solutions optimal. Studies have shown that, in the case of German companies, approximately 15% of the total costs of procurement in China are logistics costs.

Operation Modes for Production and Sourcing

As mentioned above, from the perspective of transaction cost theory, production and sourcing merely fix the level of vertical integration in a production chain, i.e., it just answers determines "who" is carrying out a certain activity. In a more detailed view, the available operation modes, illustrated in Figure 19.3, can be broadly categorised into four groups, with different options within each (Grünig/Morschett 2012, p. 187):

- A company can buy products from foreign manufacturers *via trading companies*. These can be located in the home country or in the host country. Foreign manufacturers often establish sales subsidiaries in different markets that act as pure trading houses for their products.

- In the second group of operation modes the domestic company buys directly from an *independent manufacturer abroad*. In this case, the company usually buys products from the foreign supplier's standard product programme. The product technology is usually owned by the foreign manufacturer.

Figure 19.3 | *Alternative Modes for Producing and Sourcing from Abroad*

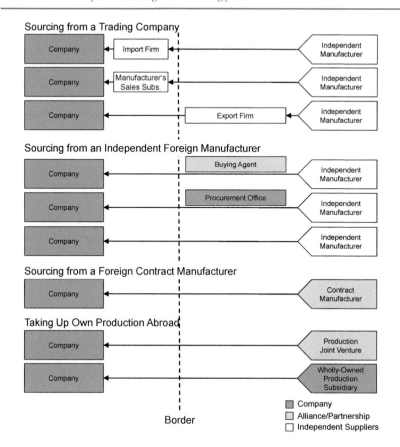

Source: Grünig/Morschett 2012, p. 188.

■ In the third category, a foreign manufacturer produces on behalf of the domestic company. The product specifications are determined by the domestic company, which also owns the product technology. The manufacturer abroad is independent but bound by a *manufacturing contract* (see Chapter 17).

■ The last group comprises *companies' own production abroad*. In this case, the domestic company uses foreign direct investment in the selected production market to own or co-own (in the case of a joint-venture) the production facilities. These modes are also referred to as *internal sourcing*, since the supplier is a foreign affiliate.

Conclusion and Outlook

Production and sourcing are core activities for an MNC. Recent decades have seen a dramatic increase in internationalisation of these activities. New locations like Eastern Europe, China and India have emerged as potential locations for production and sourcing. Cost pressures in industrialised countries force companies to internationalise production and reduce sourcing costs. New technologies (in information technology and logistics) act as enablers, reducing transaction costs for cross-border transactions.

Cross-border production processes are the rule, not the exception, as confirmed by the fact that about one-third of world trade today occurs as intra-company trade. However, decentralisation, cross-border production and international sourcing are not only beneficial. There are risks and costs for companies as well as externalities, and it is by no means clear whether this trend will remain or might even be reversed in the coming decades. In any case, optimal management of operations is necessary to achieve the MNC's objectives efficiently and effectively.

Further Reading

FERDOWS, K. (1997): Making the Most of Foreign Factories, in: Harvard Business Review, Vol. 75, No. 2, pp. 73-88.

GRÜNIG, R.; MORSCHETT, D. (2012): Developing International Strategies: Going and Being International for Medium-sized Companies, Berlin-Heidelberg, Springer, pp. 187-211.

UNCTAD (1993): World Investment Report 1993: Transnational Corporations and Integrated International Production, Geneva, pp. 111-178.

Case Study: Audi[*]

Profile, History and Status Quo

In 1910, the first *Audi* car was produced in Zwickau, Saxony. In 1932, *Audi* merged with three other *Saxony* car manufacturers (*DKW*, *Horch* and *Wanderer*) to form the *Auto Union AG*. The four rings in *Audi*'s logo have their origin in this merger. The company produced cars under the four original

---

[*] Sources used for this case study include the corporate websites and various annual and interim reports, investor-relations presentations and explicitly cited sources.

brands but production under the *Audi* brand was stopped in 1940. After World War II, the former production sites of *Auto Union* were in the Soviet occupation zone and the company was expropriated.

Creation of the Company in Ingolstadt

In 1949, the former managers of *Auto Union* recreated the company in Ingolstadt in Bavaria in West Germany. Production began again with the four ring logo but under the brand *DKW*. In 1958/1959, *Daimler-Benz* acquired 100 per cent of *Auto Union*, which in 1965 was sold to the *Volkswagen Group* to which it still belongs today. In 1965, the company also switched from two-stroke engines to the modern four-stroke engines, a move that was accompanied by a brand change. From 1965, the *Audi* brand was used again.

Merger with NSU in Neckarsulm

A further merger, in 1969, with car manufacturer *NSU* is also noteworthy. *NSU* was located in Neckarsulm, were the headquarters of the new company was located from 1969 until 1985 when it moved to Ingolstadt. The merger also brought the production site in Neckarsulm into the company.

Two other acquisitions brought new brands to the company that are still used and very popular today. Since 1998, the Italian luxury sports car manufacturer *Lamborghini* belongs to *Audi*; in 2012, *Audi* acquired *Ducati Motors*, the Italian manufacturer of high-performance motorcycles.

Surpassing Mercedes

The *Audi* brand has developed very well since its rebirth in 1965. It slowly moved into the premium segment of the passenger car market, i.e. against its main competitors *BMW* and *Mercedes*. Sales grew steadily. In the last ten years, sales have more than doubled (see Figure 19.4). In 2011, *Audi* surpassed *Mercedes-Benz* to become the No. 2 premium car manufacturer in the world. The strategic target for 2020 is to sell more than 2 million cars.

Underperforming in the USA

Audi's largest single market is China, where it achieves more than 30 per cent of its sales and where it is the leader ahead of *BMW* and *Mercedes* (see Figure 19.4). From the perspective of the current production strategy it is notable that the USA only makes up 10% of *Audi's* sales. In this market, *Audi* is much less successful than its main rivals *BMW* and *Mercedes*.

Deliveries (Sales) of Audi – Development and Geographical Distribution

Figure 19.4

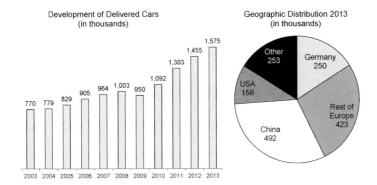

Source: Audi 2014a and several annual reports.

Production of Audi Vehicles around the World

Audi operates under the slogan "Vorsprung durch Technik". With a work-force of 73,000 people, *Audi* currently produces cars with the *Audi* brand in the two traditional German production sites in Ingolstadt and in Neckarsulm and in eight more countries in Europe (Hungary, Belgium, Spain, Russia, Slovakia) and Asia (China, India, Indonesia). Two further production countries are planned for the near future: Mexico, where production should start in 2016, and Brazil, where production will start in 2015 (see Figure 19.5). The different factories produce different car models or components and they serve different purposes which will be explained below. One challenge is to guarantee consistent quality. In light of this, *Audi* has the same motto for every factory: *"one name, one standard, everywhere".*

2014 marks the first year when *Audi* will produce more cars outside Germany than in its two factories in Germany.

Figure 19.5 Audi Production Sites around the World

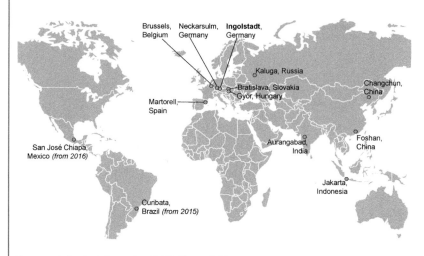

Source: Adapted from Audi 2014b, p. 145.

Production Sites in Germany as the Traditional Core of the Production Network

Home Country as Largest Production Country

Ingolstadt is *Audi's* most important location. It is where the company was founded in 1949, it is the location of the headquarters and it is also *Audi's* biggest manufacturing site. More than one third of all *Audi* cars are produced in Ingolstadt (577,000 cars in 2013). It has all the major parts of the car manufacturing production process: a body shop, a paint shop, an assembly line and even a press shop.

The factory builds some of the company's most important car models (A3, A4, A5 and Q5). For many of the models, Ingolstadt serves almost as a world market factory, supplying most countries with their respective models, and having a high level of value added for these models.

The Ingolstadt factory even has an in-house tool making department which develops and builds meta-forming tools and assembly-line systems for the factory but also for other factories in the *Audi* and the *Volkswagen Group*.

Audi's second German location is in Neckarsulm, about 250 km away from Ingolstadt. It is another major production site with a production of about 275,000 cars. It is characterised by a broad product diversity, building the *Audi* A4 sedan, *Audi* A5/S5 cabriolet, *Audi* A6 (sedan, Avant, S6, allroad

Quattro, hybrid), *Audi* A7/S7, *Audi* A8 and *Audi* A8, and *Audi* R8 models (in its different versions) as well as the high end models for different *Audi* ranges (RS).

Production in other European Countries

Audi had established its first foreign production site in 1993 in Győr, Hungary. Its main task is to be the global production centre for engines, with an output of almost 2 million engines per year (compared to 1.6 million *Audis* sold last year), supplying the other *Audi* factories and some other customers. The site has also been responsible for the assembly of various models of *Audi* TT since 1998, with the body being built and painted in Ingolstadt. The factories in Ingolstadt and Győr are linked by rail to transport the components between them. In an extension of the factory, *Audi Hungary* has recently taken up series production of the *Audi* A3 (sedan and cabriolet). These two models are the first to be built entirely in Győr. In 2013, about 40,000 cars were produced in Győr.

Engine Production in Hungary

In 2005, *Audi* started to assemble its SUV Q7 in Bratislava, the capital of Slovakia. From there, the Q7 is exported globally (there are two more assembly sites for the Q7, Russia and India, but these merely assemble, have low value-added and serve only their local markets). It is the final stage in a cross-border production process in which many body components are produced in Ingolstadt and Neckarsulm and the engines are produced in Hungary before being assembled in Bratislava. Győr and Bratislava are only 80 km apart. The factory produced 63,500 Q7s in 2013.

Assembling the Audi Q7 in Slovakia

Since 2007, *Audi* also has a factory in Brussels, Belgium. It took over this factory from *Volkswagen*. *Audi* Brussels focuses on the production of the A1 series (A1, sportback, S1, S1 sportback) and it is the only *Audi* site to produce these models. Its output in 2013 was 121,000 cars. An "Automotive Park" helps to link the *Audi* factory to its suppliers. The logistics and supply centre is adjacent to the *Audi* plant and has a direct link to the production site via a bridge.

Producing the Audi A1 in Belgium

In Spain, *Audi* recently started to use a production site owned by *SEAT* (another division of the Volkswagen Group). *SEAT* and *Audi* invested a combined 330 million EUR in the now joint production site, helping both divisions to achieve larger economies of scale in their production and creating synergies within the *Volkswagen Group*. Since 2011, the SUV *Audi* Q3 has been produced in a factory in Martorell, with an output of 107,000 cars in 2013. Martorell is the world market factory for the Q3, from which it is exported globally. One exception is the Chinese market, where the Q3 is locally produced.

Producing the Audi A3 in Spain

Audi has experienced strong growth rates in Russia over recent years, with sales of 36,000 cars in 2013. Even though the economy is currently weak, Russia is considered one of the strategic growth markets for *Audi* in Europe. To begin production in the country, *Audi* established a production site in Kaluga in 2013. This is an SKD production site for the *Audi* A6, A7 and A8L sedans and the Q5 and Q7 SUVs. *Audi* has not reported their planned production figures for the Kaluga plant. Kaluga has developed into an automotive cluster within Russia (see Chapter 8). The *Volkswagen Group* has been in the city since 2007, with full production processes for *Volkswagen* and *Skoda*. Other companies have also come to the city: *PSA Peugeot Citroën* for passenger vehicles and *Volvo* and *Renault* for trucks. Further, automotive suppliers such as *Magna International, Continental, Benteler, Severstal-Gonvarri* have followed their customers and built plants in the region (Russian-German Chamber of Commerce 2014).

Production in China, Audi's Most Important Market

China is Audi's most important market, with sales of 492,000 vehicles in 2013. This is way ahead of *BMW* and more than twice as many cars as *Mercedes* sold in this country. *Audi's* long relationship with the market and local production spanning more than two decades have certainly played a role in this success.

*Production in a
Joint Venture*

Audi produces in a production site in Changchun, a complete production facility owned by *FAW-Volkswagen Automotive Company*. This joint venture was created between *First Automotive Works* (FAW), a state-owned Chinese company and one of China's largest automotive companies, and *Volkswagen* in 1991. In 1995, *Audi* became the third joint venture partner, with an equity holding of 10%. At that time, it was not possible for a foreign company to wholly-own a production plant in China. Currently, the plant in Changchun produces the *Audi* A4L and *Audi* A6L, in particular the long-wheelbase versions, which are very popular in the Chinese market. In fact, the *Audi* A6L is *Audi's* bestselling car in China; the *Audi* A4L is the second highest selling model. The *Audi* Q3 and *Audi* Q5 SUVs are produced mainly for the local market for a total output of 420,000 cars in 2013.

*Establishment of
a Second
Production Site*

Given that the compact market in China is fast-growing, it is also important to produce cars in this segment in the country. In 2013, the *FAW-Volkswagen-Audi* joint venture established a second production plant, also a complete production facility, in Foshan in Southern China. The *Audi* A3 sedan and the A3 sportback are produced at this site, and production in the first year is expected to reach 150,000-200,000 cars.

Local production in China has a number of advantages. Among other things, it helps *Audi* to avoid the 25% import tax in China (Team 2014).

Production in India and Indonesia

In India, *Audi* has had a small-scale production in a contract manufacturing agreement with *Skoda*, another *Volkswagen* division, since 2007. *Škoda Auto India Private Ltd.* assembles about 9,000 *Audis* for the Indian market, of different models (A4 sedan, A6 sedan, Q3, Q5, and Q7).

In fact, the value-added in India is very low; the cars are assembled from parts produced in Europe. For example, the *Audi* A6 is assembled from ca. 2,500 parts that are shipped in containers from Hamburg and Bremerhaven in Germany. Car bodies are already painted, the engines completed and many components (like the front seats) are preassembled. From these parts and components, the workers in India assemble the final cars. *Assembling in India*

Indonesia has a very strong growth rate, and with 240 million inhabitants and a growing middle class it is likely to soon become the largest car market of South-East Asia. However, import tariffs are very high, at 40% for vehicles. This makes local production or at least assembly favourable. The tariff duties in Indonesia for CKD kits (completely-knocked-down kits of cars that are then assembled) are substantially lower, approx. 10% (DB Research 2011, p. 9).

Audi has some of its models for the Indonesian market assembled in the country. In 2011, it began a cooperation with *PT National Assembler*, a local vehicle assembly company (and a subsidiary of *Indomobil*), which also assembled some *Volkswagen* models. This partner assembles the A4 and A6 models for the Indonesian market in an SKD (semi-knocked-down) process. In this process, the cars are first completely produced and assembled at other *Audi* plants (mainly in Germany). They are then disassembled again and packaged as assembly kits which are shipped to Indonesia. *PT National Assembler* completes the car and employees specially trained by *Audi* carry out the final quality inspection. The capacity and long-term plan is for several thousand cars per year (the original target was set at 2,700 cars by 2015) but the current development is very weak. In 2013, only 186 *Audis* were produced in Indonesia, following a weak demand due to devaluation of the local currency. *SKD Assembly in Indonesia*

Establishing a New Major Factory in Mexico

Audi is strong in Asia but it is weaker than its rivals in the US. *BMW* and *Mercedes* have both established production plants in the USA which gives them advantages in the country. In January 2012, *Audi* stated that strong growth in the USA would be crucial for the company's strategy and that an *Audi* production plant in the region would be important to achieve this objective (Handelsblatt 2012). In a series of press releases, *Audi* revealed more details about this plan.

Location Choice for North America

In mid-2012, the company announced that its North American plant would be located in Mexico. The location close to the US market, competitive cost structures, good infrastructure and the over 40 existing free trade agreements between Mexico and other countries (including integration in the NAFTA) were cited as reasons (see the case study in Chapter 7). Later, it was announced that a detailed location evaluation process, with more than a dozen locations analysed, had chosen San José Chiapa, State of Puebla (less than 100 km from an existing *Volkswagen* plant in Puebla City) and *Audi* would invest about 900 million EUR in this production site. A number of criteria were mentioned for this location choice – site conditions, logistics link, infrastructure, well-qualified employees and quality of life. Highly reputable universities and colleges of advanced technology as well as internationally recognised schools help to find qualified employees but are also important to *Audi* for international assignments. As HR director T. Sigi explained: "When deciding on a new site, it is important that we can find well-qualified employees there. Internationally recognised schools for the children of employees sent on assignment to Mexico are also crucial" (Volkswagen AG 2012).

World Market Factory for Q5

Production in Mexico is planned to start in 2016; *Audi* will produce its SUV Q5 in the plant and supply the world market for this model from Mexico. The expected volume is about 150,000 cars per year. Some additional features are noteworthy in the case of *Audi* in Mexico (Stadler 2013):

Very Strong Local Sourcing

■ *Audi* declared that it intends to have a local content of 65% in the medium term; thus, 65% of all sourced parts for the Q5 will come from North America, increasing to 90% in the long-term.

■ Thus, global suppliers are encouraged to relocate their production for the Q5 to Mexico as well. The *Volkswagen Group* will build a just-in-sequence suppliers' park halfway between San José Chiapa and Puebla City, from where suppliers will be able to quickly supply both the *Volkswagen* plant and the *Audi* plant.

■ The plant brings enormous benefits for the local economy. *Audi* expects that for each job at *Audi*, another five jobs will be created in the vicinity, at suppliers and in the rest of the economy. In total, they expect up to 20,000 new jobs to be created as a result of the new production site.

Made by Audi in Mexico

The new plant in Mexico also illustrates the standardisation of production at *Audi*. As the Chairman of the *Audi* board pointed out in a speech when laying the foundation stone to the factory: "The 3D animation of the factory's layout shows: Each machine here will have the same position as all over the world, thanks to our modular production toolbox. Our *Audi* Production System ensures that our customers all over the world can rely on the seal of quality *'made by Audi'"* (Stadler 2013).

Establishing Production in Brazil

As a further step to increase its international production footprint, *Audi* also announced that it would begin production in Brazil from 2015. The *Audi* A3 sedan and the *Audi* Q3 will be produced in Curitiba in Southern Brazil. The car market in Brazil is booming and the premium segment is growing particularly strongly. With production in Brazil, *Audi* wants to have a basis for further growth in the region. Starting in 2014, *Audi's* competitor *BMW* is produces in its own plant in Brazil. These moves are certainly to circumvent the high tariffs on imported cars and take advantage of the tax incentives given by Brazil for such investments.

Production will take place in a *Volkswagen* brand production plant but *Audi* will invest in a specific production line for its models. *Audi* also intends to buy locally. Up to 35% of the sourced parts for the A3 should come from Brazil. To achieve this objective, *Audi* has started to build up relationships with Brazilian suppliers.

Production Together with Volkswagen

Production of other Brands of the Audi Group

The production configuration of the *Audi Group's* two other brands is rather simple. *Lamborghini* manufactures its sports cars at its headquarters in Sant'Agata Bolognese in Italy.

Centralised Production for Lamborghini

Ducati has until recently only manufactured its products in its site in Bologna in Italy. But in 2011 *Ducati* opened an assembly factory in Thailand in order to better penetrate emerging countries. It has shifted the final assembly of some models for Southeast Asian markets to this plant in order to avoid the extremely high import tariffs on foreign-made motorcycles. Furthermore, *Ducati* now lets a contract manufacturer (*DAFRA*) assemble its motorcycles in a CKD process in Manaus in Brazil from parts produced in the Italian factory. This is to improve its position in the emerging markets of South America and particularly Brazil, which is the third biggest motorcycle market in the world for medium- to high-capacity bikes.

Some Foreign Assembly for Ducati

Summary and Outlook

Audi uses a sophisticated production strategy in which different configuration strategies are used for different models and components. The increasing shift of market growth away from Western Europe to Asia and the Americas requires a shift in production locations. The new production locations do not replace the existing ones but complement them in meeting the new demand in other parts of the world.

Similarly, *Audi* does not apply the same operation mode in every production country. In some cases, *Audi* establishes wholly-owned subsidiaries; in others, it partners with other divisions of the *Volkswagen Group*; and in other countries, alliances with local companies, on different levels and with different strategic relevance, are considered the optimal choice.

With different partners and different production countries, it is a challenge to guarantee a uniformly high quality. *Audi* follows a standard production system everywhere, which is intended to ensure that *"made by Audi"* entails the same quality no matter where the product comes from.

Questions

1. *BMW, Audi's* main rival, has announced a strategic principle of "production follows the market". Analyse whether *Audi* also follows this principle.

2. In China, *Audi* cars are produced in a joint venture with *Volkswagen* and a local, state-owned automotive company. Discuss the benefits and risks of this approach.

3. For the North American market, *Audi* has decided to locate its production in Mexico. Just a few years before, *Volkswagen* decided to establish a production site in the USA in order to conquer this market. Compare both strategies.

References

AUDI (2014a): Welcome to the World of Audi, http://www.Audi.com/about-us/, accessed on June 25, 2014.

AUDI (2014b): Annual Report 2013, Ingolstadt.

DB RESEARCH (2011): ASEAN Auto Market, Frankfurt.

FERDOWS, K. (1989): Mapping International Factory Networks, in: FERDOWS, K. (Ed.): Managing International Manufacturing, Amsterdam, Elsevier Science, pp. 3-21.

FERDOWS, K. (1997): Making the Most of Foreign Factories, in: Harvard Business Review, Vol. 75, No. 2, pp. 73-88.

GRIFFIN, R.; PUSTAY, M. (2013): International Business: A Managerial Perspective, 7th ed., Upper Saddle River, New Jersey, Pearson.

GRÜNIG, R.; MORSCHETT, D. (2012): Developing International Strategies: Going and Being International for Medium-sized Companies, Berlin-Heidelberg, Springer.

HANDELSBLATT (2012): Audi will auf dem US-Markt groß angreifen, http://www.handelsblatt.com, accessed on September 01, 2014.

PORTER, M.E. (1986): Changing Patterns of International Competition, in: California Management Review, Vol. 28, No. 2, pp. 9-40.

RUSSIAN-GERMAN CHAMBER OF COMMERCE (2014): Fallbeispiel: Die Region Kaluga, http://www.regionen-russland.de/regionen-auf-einen-blick/zentral/kaluga/, accessed on June 25, 2014.

STADLER, R. (2013): Speech on the Occasion of Laying the Foundation Stone for the Audi Production Site Mexico, San José Chiapa, April 20, 2013.

TEAM, T. (2014): Mercedes Faces the Audi Challenge in China's Compact Luxury Car Market, in: Forbes Online, May 20, 2014.

UNCTAD (1993): World Investment Report 1993: Transnational Corporations and Integrated International Production, Geneva.

UNCTAD (2013): World Investment Report 2013: Global Value Chains: Investment and Trade for Development, Geneva.

VOLKSWAGEN AG (2012): News: New Audi plant in Mexico: San José Chiapa the chosen location, http://www.volkswagenag.com/content, accessed on September 01, 2014.

ZENTES, J.; SWOBODA, B.; MORSCHETT, D. (2004): Internationales Wertschöpfungsmanagement, Munich, Vahlen.

Chapter 20

International Research & Development

International R&D is ever more important. But as well as the many advantages of R&D internationalisation for MNCs, it also poses a major challenge. This Chapter discusses the benefits and caveats of international R&D. Different roles of foreign R&D units are highlighted, the coordination of international R&D investigated and different organisational models for MNC's international R&D described.

Introduction

Given the high relevance of innovation for the competitiveness of MNCs, R&D is a core value chain activity. The internationalisation of R&D is not a new phenomenon. A certain level of international R&D to adapt products and technologies to local markets has always been necessary. However, basic and applied research was traditionally reserved for MNCs' home countries. In recent decades, however, some new trends have emerged (UNCTAD 2005; Shenkar/Luo 2008, p. 356), and MNCs' R&D is increasingly conducted abroad.

Empirical Relevance of International R&D

For example, the European Commission shows in their scoreboard (containing economic and financial data for the world top 2,000 companies) that, together with the US and Japan, the EU plays a major role in international investment. Between 2003 and 2012, the EU attracted 22% of FDI projects in R&D from the set of non-EU-companies, while 26% of FDI projects in R&D invested from the EU are based in non-EU-countries. In comparison, for the same period the US obtained only 8% of FDI projects and contracted 52% to non-US-countries. Looking at the geographical distribution of the BRIC countries, the figures confirm the increasing role of these regions. Despite these countries playing a limited role in R&D outflows (3%), they play a major role in R&D inflows (41%) (European Commission 2013a, p. 72).

In some developing countries, MNCs' R&D is increasingly targeting global markets and is integrated into the companies' core innovation efforts. The opening of the new *Audi R&D Center Asia* in Beijing (2013) or the new *Bosch* research centre in Bangalore (2014) are just two examples of the strategic importance of the internationalisation of innovation. In addition, MNCs from newly industrialised nations like Singapore, South Korea or Taiwan have begun to relocate R&D activities to other countries as well (see Chapter 5).

However, the magnitude of foreign R&D differs substantially between in-dustries. Most foreign investments in R&D (60%) during the period 2003-2012 were concentrated in information and communication technology (production and services), pharmaceuticals, biotechnology, automobiles and parts. In contrast, industries such as traditional/alternative energy and transport showed little interest in R&D internationalisation. This differing degree of R&D internationalisation can be partly explained through the different levels of R&D intensity in those industries; those industries with a very high R&D intensity display above average levels of R&D internationali-sation. A classification of industries by *R&D intensity*, i.e. R&D expenditure as a percentage of net sales, is provided by the European Commission (see Table 20.1).

Table 20.1 | *Grouping of Industrial Sectors According to R&D Intensity*

Industry Category	R&D Intensity	Examples of Industries
High R&D Intensity	>5%	pharmaceuticals and biotechnology; health care equipment and services; technology hardware and equipment; software and computer services; aerospace and defence
Medium-high R&D Intensity	2-5%	electronics and electrical equipment; automobiles and parts; industrial engineering and machinery; chemicals; personal goods; household goods; general industrials; support services
Medium-low R&D Intensity	1-2%	food products; beverages; travel and leisure; media; oil equipment; electricity; fixed line telecommunications
Low R&D Intensity	<1%	oil and gas; industrial metals; construction and materials; food and drug retailers; transportation; mining; tobacco; multi-utilities

Source: European Commission 2013a, p. 27.

Types of R&D | While R&D is often considered a homogeneous task, it is important to dis-tinguish different types (UNCTAD 2005, p. 103). The objective of basic re-search is to gain a more comprehensive knowledge or understanding of the subject under study without targeting specific applications. In industry, basic research refers to research that advances scientific knowledge but does not have specific immediate commercial objectives. The objective of applied research is to gain the necessary knowledge or understanding to meet a specific, recognised need. In industry, applied research includes investiga-tions to discover new scientific knowledge that has specific commercial objectives, e.g. with respect to products. At last, development is the system-atic use of the knowledge or understanding gained from research directed towards the production of useful materials, devices, systems or methods, including the design and development of prototypes and processes.

Configuration of R&D

As with all value chain activities, the first basic decision focuses on the choice of location(s). Before concrete location(s) are selected, it must be decided whether R&D should be concentrated in one country (commonly the MNC's home country) or geographically dispersed across a number of R&D units.

The *forces models* of R&D internationalisation emphasise that there are positive and negative influence factors on the internationalisation of R&D which act as *opposing forces*. Centrifugal forces pull R&D away from the centre, i.e., the MNC's home country, while *centripetal forces* act to keep R&D in the centre (Pearce 1989, p. 38; Fisch 2001, p. 20; 2003, p. 1382). These opposing forces explain a tension over the degree of internationalisation; having the forces in equilibrium is considered to be optimal.

Centrifugal-Centripetal Forces Model

Motives for the Internationalisation of R&D

The general trend towards internationalisation of R&D is based on a number of different motives (Schmid 2000, pp. 2-3; Zentes/Swoboda/Morschett 2004, pp. 537-540; Shenkar/Luo 2008, pp. 356-360; OECD 2008, p. 39; Schmiele 2012, pp. 101-106; European Commission 2012, pp. 3-7):

- *access to scarce production factors*, in particular qualified research personnel

- exploitation of *cost advantages* in the host country, e.g. lower wages

- enhanced *speed* of R&D, e.g. through international division of labour

- *tapping local knowledge* in host countries and establishing links to local information and communication networks, e.g. by establishing "listening posts" in lead markets or in regional innovation clusters (see Chapter 8), and *proximity to scientific institutions*, e.g. universities or private research institutes, to gather knowledge and capabilities

- enhanced *innovation power* by creating competition between R&D units

- development and exploitation of *complementary resources* and *competences* in different locations

- *circumvention of legal restrictions* in the home country or better acceptance of certain technologies in different host countries

- securing *market access* and fulfilling *legal requirements* (e.g. local content)

- better *identification of local market needs* and easy *adaptation* of technologies to local markets by the presence of R&D in the host country

■ *avoiding not-invented-here syndrome* at the foreign subsidiaries

■ *enhancing the innovation capacity* of the MNC by leveraging the knowledge of different R&D units to identify a diversity of ideas and local needs and developing a truly transnational R&D process in which these diverse stimuli are systematically combined.

R&D Internationalisation as By-Product

Frequently, R&D internationalisation is a *by-product* and not the result of planned internationalisation. In the case of M&As, which are not usually targeted at the R&D units of the acquired companies, the dispersion of R&D may be the result of "administrative heritage" and is often retained to avoid a brain drain (Schmid 2000, pp. 6-7).

Motives for a Regional Concentration of R&D

There are a number of arguments against the internationalisation of R&D. These *centripetal forces* are mainly based on the dispersion of R&D activities and not necessarily against internationalisation. Given that concentrated R&D activities are usually located in the MNC's home country, i.e. in the headquarters, the effect is the same. Advantages of R&D concentration include (Schmid 2000, pp. 5-6; Zentes/Swoboda/Morschett 2004, pp. 541-542; Shenkar/Luo 2008, p. 359; European Commission 2012, p. 6):

■ achieving *economies of scale* and reaching a *critical mass* for R&D activities

■ *economies of scope*, since carrying out various R&D projects in one location can produce spill-over effects

■ easier *coordination and control* of the activities which might help to avoid dissipation of efforts and to reach a better alignment between R&D activities and corporate goals

■ *better communication* due to the presence of all researchers in a single location and personal *face-to-face contact*, which is particularly important in the case of tacit knowledge (since R&D requires dense knowledge exchange)

■ establishment of *informal networks* among the different researchers

■ *simplified organisation*, since complex cross-border structures and processes can be avoided

■ *avoidance of unintended duplication* of research work, since local researchers are usually better informed about their colleagues' projects

■ *avoidance of conflicts* between researchers at different locations

■ relevance of *country-of-origin effects* that are usually rooted in the MNC's home country

■ higher likelihood of establishing a *uniform R&D culture*

■ better chance of avoiding a *proprietary knowledge leak* when research results and innovations only have to be communicated within a single R&D centre.

Overall, these aspects lead to R&D being traditionally highly concentrated in the MNC's home country and being the least fragmented of an MNC's economic activities (UNCTAD 2005, p. xxiv).

Internationalisation of Different Types of R&D

When it comes to the different advantages and disadvantages of R&D internationalisation, the mentioned forces affect different types to different extents. Thus, R&D is often not undertaken in the same location (Kuemmerle 1997; Boutellier/Gassmann/Zedtwitz 2008, p. 189). Development is often collocated at manufacturing sites while basic research frequently either remains at the corporate headquarters or is located in *regional innovation clusters*. Both development and applied research serve to support local marketing while basic research helps in scanning and evaluating external sources, e.g. by establishing listening posts or tapping the knowledge of university spin-offs. Finally, development and applied research are pulled towards attractive markets since their purpose is adaptation of technology to particular market needs, while basic research is pulled towards the quality of scientific input.

Roles of International R&D Units

For subsidiaries in general (see Chapter 3), international R&D units can be categorised into different roles. Based on the type of R&D undertaken and the primary motives for the establishment of the R&D unit, UNCTAD (2005, pp. 138-139) suggests the following typology (see also Pearce 1989, pp. 111-112; Nobel/Birkinshaw 1998, pp. 481-483; Fisch 2004, p. 148; Zedtwitz 2005, pp. 1-4; Shenkar/Luo 2008, p. 361):

UNCTAD Typology

■ Local adapters are *"market seeking"* R&D units. Their purpose is to facilitate exploiting HQ technologies by adapting them to local context.

■ Locally integrated laboratories (also called "indigenous technology units" or "international independent laboratories") are more advanced than local adapters and are capable of *independent innovation* aimed primarily at local (and perhaps regional) markets. The units remain linked to local production and are usually a natural evolution from local adapters.

■ The most advanced type of innovative activity conducted by foreign affiliates is the international technology creator (also called "internationally interdependent laboratory" or "global technology unit"). This unit serves the same purpose as core innovating centres in the home country. These facilities can do both research and development, and their output is typically aimed at *global exploitation* by the parent company.

■ The fourth role for a R&D unit is the *technology scanning* or *monitoring unit*. This is typically a "business intelligence" function undertaken to identify and generate new ideas. With the same purpose, but in the absence of a separate R&D facility, scanning can also be done by another department of the MNC.

These four roles are closely linked to the necessary *communication flows* in the R&D network. More explicitly, a model proposed by Bartlett/Beamish (2014, pp. 374-385) describes different innovation models that explain the direction of knowledge flows (see also Gassmann/Zedtwitz 1996, p. 10). In the *"centre-for-global"* model, R&D is carried out in one concentrated location and the new technology is then exploited globally. This follows the traditional *"centralised hub"* model for MNCs (see Chapter 1). *"Local-for-local"* R&D is undertaken in different country subsidiaries and relies on subsidiary-based knowledge used to identify local market needs and create innovations targeting the local market. Cross-border communication is low in this case. In *"local-for-global"* processes, a foreign R&D unit takes a leading role as an *international technology creator* and creates innovations that are subsequently used by the whole MNC. This case of a specialised task is a clear expression of a *transnational organisation*. Another transnational innovation model leads to *"global-for-global"* processes, where R&D units work together to create an innovation. Globally linked but widely dispersed capabilities and resources are used to enhance the MNC's R&D capacity and the results are exploited by all organisational units within the MNC.

International R&D Alliances

Besides the configuration and role of international R&D, the MNC must also consider its operation mode (see Chapter 14 for the basic options). As well as conducting R&D on their own, in wholly-owned R&D units, MNCs can also choose cooperative operation modes for their R&D activities, e.g. by establishing a joint venture or through a contractual arrangement like (active or passive) licensing. As with other value-added activities, the market option is available, i.e. purchasing new technologies from independent external sources.

R&D alliances have a number of benefits (Rotering 1990, pp. 80-81; Zentes/Swoboda/Morschett 2004, pp. 552-553; Dunning/Lundan 2008, p. 379):

■ *synergy effects* through the exploitation of complementary technological knowledge

■ *expansion of internal expertise* by tapping the partner's tacit and explicit knowledge

■ *sharing of costs* of R&D projects

■ *enhanced flexibility* to react to changes in the technological environment, e.g. by enabling a higher number of simultaneous research projects

■ *reduced risk* by spreading technological and financial risk, given the high uncertainty in the field of R&D

■ *shorter innovation cycles*

■ concentration of resources on *core competences*

■ joint *establishment of norms and standards* for new technologies

■ *better exploitation of research findings*, e.g. due to complementary marketing potentials (e.g. sales regions or products).

Benefits of R&D Alliances

Unfortunately, R&D alliances also have many substantial disadvantages. Theoretically, these can often be explained with the *transaction cost approach* (via the low efficiency of inter-company knowledge transfer) or the *knowledge-based view* (via the better effectiveness of intra-company knowledge transfer). Caveats include (see, e.g., Rotering 1990, p. 85; Zentes/Swoboda/Morschett 2004, pp. 553-554; Oesterle 2005, pp. 776-778):

Disadvantages of R&D Alliances

■ *technological dependence* on external partners and potential *erosion of core competences*

■ *problems* in the course of the *knowledge transfer* between partners due to low absorptive capacity for proprietary knowledge and a lack of effective knowledge transfer mechanisms in alliances

■ danger of *knowledge dissemination* to the partner or others

■ risk of losing a competitive advantage (alliances as *learning races*)

■ high *coordination effort* and high negotiation costs

■ *reduction in internal decision power* and company-individual flexibility

- ■ *difficulties in assigning profits* from an innovation to each partner

- ■ *potentially enhanced time requirements* due to coordination and communication efforts.

Strong Growth in R&D Alliances

Overall, as a basic trend, strategic R&D alliances are strongly on the increase. The relevance of cooperative R&D has been increasing for the last 50 years (UNCTAD 2005, p. 126; OECD 2008, p. 59). Rising international competition and ubiquitous knowledge lead to collaboration to reach strategic goals. The data from the Cooperative Agreements and Technology Indicators shows the steady growth between 1980 and 2006 of worldwide business technology partnerships (National Science Foundation 2010, pp. 52-53). Although collaborative activity in R&D is not new, it has evolved towards direct strategic uses (Narula 2003, p. 110). Companies increasingly set up collaborations with other enterprises, suppliers, commercial laboratories, universities or other external parties. In the EU-27 over one in four enterprises (25.5%) were engaged in such a cooperation for product and/or process innovation (Eurostat 2013). In addition to the importance of collaboration, MNCs still seem to prefer R&D partners that are geographically close (Belderbos/Gilsing/Jacob 2011, p. 10). Since 2005, the number of well-chosen collaborations has increased in the health and biotechnology sector. The growing demand for new medicines, the "patent cliff" of expiring blockbuster patents and new opportunities in therapeutic biotech have shown that no single company can develop excellence in all the areas of research required to develop a new drug. Moreover, there are strong pressures on pharmaceutical companies to reduce drug development costs and share the risks involved (UNCTAD 2005, p. 126; European Commission 2013a, p. 57).

Open Innovation

A new type of R&D cooperation is gaining importance, regardless of national or international/global perspective. Firms are increasingly open to *outside innovation* (open innovation, open R&D) (Gassmann/Enkel/Chesbrough 2010). Open innovation can be defined as "the use of purposive inflows and outflows of knowledge to accelerate internal innovation, and expand the markets for external use of innovation, respectively" (Chesbrough/Vanhaverbeke/West 2006, p. 1). Companies investing in *open innovation activities* have reported considerable success, but they also face risks and barriers. "*Procter & Gamble* announced that they were able to increase their product success rate by 50% and the efficiency of their R&D by 60% by introducing the open innovation concept to the organization. *Philips* has a well-established open innovation environment, while *Siemens* started a huge corporate open innovation program in 2009." (Enkel/Gassmann/Chesbrough 2009, p. 312).

Organisational Model for International R&D

Boutellier, Gassmann and Zedtwitz (2008, pp. 77-95) have proposed an organisational model for international R&D that is frequently applied in literature. This model, which is based on the concepts of Bartlett/Ghoshal and Perlmutter (see Chapter 2), involves the simultaneous configuration and coordination of international R&D. It distinguishes R&D concepts based on the *geographical dispersion* of internal competencies and knowledge bases and the *degree of cooperation* between R&D sites, which reflects the level of global integration of R&D activities.

Ethnocentric Centralised R&D

Figure 20.1

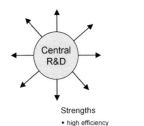

Behavioural Orientation
* ethnocentric inward orientation
* think tank as national treasure in home country
* protection of core technology against competitors
* homogeneous R&D culture

Configuration
* central R&D in home country
* central and tight coordination and control of R&D programme

Strengths
* high efficiency
* low R&D costs (scale effects)
* short cycle times
* protected core technologies

Weaknesses
* lack of sensitivity for local markets
* danger or missing external technology
* not-invented-here syndrome
* tendency towards rigid organisation

Source: Boutellier/Gassmann/Zedtwitz 2008, p. 80.

In the *ethnocentric centralised R&D organisation*, all R&D is concentrated in the home country. Examples include *Toyota* or *IBM*. The MNC assumes that the HQ is technologically superior to its subsidiaries. Central R&D creates new products and technologies which are then distributed worldwide. Physical colocation of R&D employees and a common understanding of the R&D strategy facilitate the control of R&D activities and enhance efficiency. Other advantages and disadvantages are shown in Figure 20.1.

The more dependent the company is on foreign markets, the more inappropriate the ethnocentric approach becomes. In the *geocentric centralised* model (see Figure 20.2), a multicultural and multinational work force is hired but the efficiency of centralisation is maintained by concentrating the activities at a central R&D site. Examples include *Beiersdorf* and *P&G*. Geocentric centralised R&D combines the advantages of internationalisation with the advantages of a physically centralised R&D.

Figure 20.2 | *Geocentric Centralised R&D*

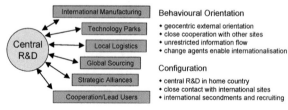

Source: Boutellier/Gassmann/Zedtwitz 2008, p. 82.

Centralisation often limits the potential adaptation to local markets. In the *polycentric decentralised R&D model* (see Figure 20.3), differences between markets are emphasised by giving autonomy to dispersed R&D units who have the task of developing technologies and products that fulfil the requirements of their host country. The units in the different countries are *independent* from each other and there is no strong corporate R&D to supervise the dispersed activities. This model was frequently used by European MNCs in the 1970s and 1980s.

Figure 20.3 | *Polycentric Decentralised R&D*

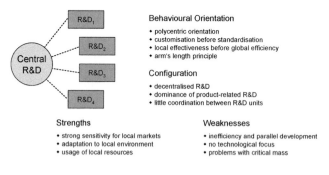

Source: Boutellier/Gassmann/Zedtwitz 2008, p. 84

In the *R&D hub model* (see Figure 20.4), strategic R&D is concentrated in the home country where the main research centre is located. This research centre is responsible for all basic research activities and takes a global lead in most technologies.

R&D Hub Model

Figure 20.4

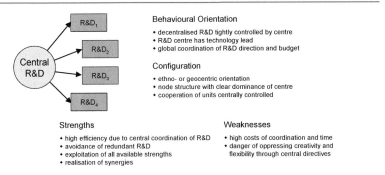

Behavioural Orientation

- decentralised R&D tightly controlled by centre
- R&D centre has technology lead
- global coordination of R&D direction and budget

Configuration

- ethno- or geocentric orientation
- node structure with clear dominance of centre
- cooperation of units centrally controlled

Strengths	Weaknesses
• high efficiency due to central coordination of R&D • avoidance of redundant R&D • exploitation of all available strengths • realisation of synergies	• high costs of coordination and time • danger of oppressing creativity and flexibility through central directives

Source: Boutellier/Gassmann/Zedtwitz 2008, p. 86.

Frequently, the foreign units start as *listening posts* to tap into local knowledge which they then transfer to the HQ. The common R&D strategy is developed in the HQ and duplication of work avoided via tight control. An example of a hub model is *Volkswagen*: its group research at *Volkswagen* HQ in Wolfsburg, responsible for all of *Volkswagen AG's* brands, is supplemented by research satellites in Palo Alto, a research lab in China and another in Tokyo.

Integrated R&D Network

Figure 20.5

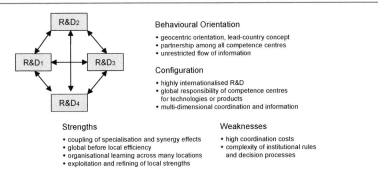

Behavioural Orientation

- geocentric orientation, lead-country concept
- partnership among all competence centres
- unrestricted flow of information

Configuration

- highly internationalised R&D
- global responsibility of competence centres for technologies or products
- multi-dimensional coordination and information

Strengths	Weaknesses
• coupling of specialisation and synergy effects • global before local efficiency • organisational learning across many locations • exploitation and refining of local strengths	• high coordination costs • complexity of institutional rules and decision processes

Source: Boutellier/Gassmann/Zedtwitz 2008, p. 88.

Finally, an *integrated R&D network* (see Figure 20.5) contains a number of interdependent R&D units in which specialisation is common and units take over the role of a *centre of excellence* in close interaction with their peer units. As described in the role typologies (see Chapter 3), units hold a "world product mandate" which is often achieved through their own initiative.

Trends within the Organisational Model

Most MNCs have realised that ethnocentric models are not adequate for meeting heterogeneous market needs and exploiting the diverse competencies in their units around the world. This leads to the establishment of *listening posts* (i.e. increased dispersion of R&D units) and to an increasing geocentric orientation which requires coordination of R&D activities. Given the complexity of R&D, the time lag between effort and result and the creativity required, foreign R&D units are increasingly empowered and given a certain level of autonomy to increase their own initiative. MNCs which have applied polycentric R&D models in the past are increasingly realising that excessive levels of autonomy can lead to inefficiency, redundant work, under-exploitation of synergy effects and insufficient exchange of knowledge, which limits innovation capacity. Thus, the result of current trends is some form of *integrated R&D network*. Once MNCs have established these, however, they realise the complexity in a widely dispersed network is high and that lateral coordination between R&D units is expensive and sometimes slow. As a consequence, the number of main research centres in an MNC is reduced and decisions re-centralised in a smaller number of research centres that take a leading role as *competence centres* for a certain technology, product or process. This consolidation process is an attempt to achieve economies of scale and improve coordination while maintaining the advantages of internationalisation (Boutellier/Gassmann/Zedwitz 2008, pp. 92-93).

Conclusion and Outlook

Effective and efficient international R&D is a prerequisite for the maintenance of an MNC's sustainable competitive advantage. Diverse market needs and growing competences all around the world mean the advantages of R&D internationalisation increasingly outweigh the disadvantages. Empirical studies – such as those by UNCTAD (2005) or the European Commission (2013b) – clearly reveal increasing levels of internationalisation. This is particularly true for development, but also increasingly for basic and applied research. Linked to this internationalisation is the trend towards R&D alliances where complementary skills are exploited by joining forces with another company.

However, a network of foreign R&D subsidiaries poses the challenge of coordinating these activities in order to align all units to the corporate goals and to reach a level of integration that optimises the opposing needs of efficiency and effectiveness. Different organisational concepts for R&D can be observed in practice, and the integrated R&D network currently seems to offer the optimal trade-off between dispersion, autonomy and integration.

The alignment of R&D with a company's other activities, which might also be dispersed worldwide, poses an additional challenge. International marketing has the task of identifying current and future customer needs (see Chapter 21). This is one root of successful R&D, besides basic research. R&D has to find solutions to customer needs which then have to be marketed by the marketing & sales department. Thus, a close link between R&D and marketing is necessary because both activities are aimed at creating *customer demand*. Furthermore, newly developed products have to be manufactured cost-efficiently and time to market has to be minimised. This requires close *collaboration* between R&D and manufacturing to acknowledge the necessities of manufacturing at the R&D stage. Conversely, manufacturing can also provide input for R&D, since it experiences suboptimal production design or unnecessary components in its daily work. Thus, tight *cross-functional integration* between R&D, manufacturing and marketing is necessary for long-term success, but it increases the complexity of finding the optimal configuration and coordination for the three activities simultaneously (Zentes/Swoboda/Morschett 2004, pp. 532, 701-705; Hill 2013, pp. 605-606).

Besides this cross-functional integration, *institutional openness* is becoming increasingly popular, both in practice and academia. "The field of open innovation is still at an early stage; it offers a wide field in which academics, practitioners and policy makers can be active" (Gassmann/Enkel/Chesbrough 2010, p. 219).

Integration of Dispersed R&D Networks

Cross-Functional Integration

Further Reading

BOUTELLIER, R.; GASSMANN, O.; ZEDTWITZ, M. von (2008): Managing Global Innovation: Uncovering the Secrets of Future Competitiveness, 3rd ed., Berlin, Springer.

EUROPEAN COMMISSION (2013a): EU R&D Scoreboard: The 2013 EU Industrial R&D Investment Scoreboard, Luxembourg.

GASSMANN, O.; ENKEL, E.; CHESBROUGH, H. (2010): The Future of Open Innovation, in: R&D Management, Vol. 40, No. 3, pp. 213-221.

UNCTAD (2005): World Investment Report 2005: Transnational Corporations and the Internationalization of R&D, Geneva.

20

Case Study: Sanofi[*]

Profile, Business Areas and History

Sanofi is an internationally active pharmaceutical (pharma) company head-quartered in Paris, France. The company offers prescription and over-the-counter medicines, vaccines, various medical supplies and other therapeutic solutions. *Sanofi* operates in more than 100 countries and runs 112 industrial sites in 41 countries, with more than 110,000 employees worldwide.

Business Areas and Financial Figures

As a result of different future opportunities and challenges, *Sanofi* adapted its business structure in 2009 and divides its activities into seven different business areas, also called *growth platforms* (see Table 20.2).

Table 20.2

Growth Platforms and Economic Importance

Growth Platform	Function	Sales in billion EUR (in 2013)
Emerging Markets	Offers a broad product portfolio adapted to local needs of emerging markets.	10.96
Diabetes	Offers patients integrated and personalised solutions (treatments, services and technologies) to simplify the management of diabetes.	6.57
Vaccines	Deals with the task of human immunization and prevention of epidemics around the world.	3.7
Consumer Healthcare	Includes for example pain killers and treatments for coughs and colds.	3.0
New Genzyme	Therapeutic solutions for rare diseases provided and developed by *Genzyme*, a subsidiary of *Sanofi*.	2.1
Animal Health	Launches innovative products for pets and production animals and is executed by *Merial*, the animal health subsidiary of *Sanofi*.	2.0
Innovative Products	Includes products launched since 2009, and do not belong to other growth platforms with a focus on the development of biologic medicines.	0.7

Source: Sanofi 2014.

Recent History

Sanofi's net sales totalled 33.0 billion EUR in 2013, while their net income was 6.7 billion EUR. In pharmaceuticals alone, *Sanofi* had revenue of 27.3 billion EUR in 2013. However, they lost sales of 1.3 billion EUR to new *generic competition*. *Sanofi's* net sales decreased by 0.5% in 2013 compared to the previous year, while industry average was a growth of 1.9% (European Commission 2013b, p. 47).

---

[*] Sources used for this case study include the websites www.sanofi.com, various annual and interim reports, investor-relations presentations and explicitly cited sources.

Sanofi in its current state was formed in 2004 by a merger between *Sanofi-Synthélabo* and *Aventis*. Initially named *Sanofi-Aventis*, the company's name was simplified to *Sanofi* in 2011. *Sanofi-Synthélabo* came into existence in 1999 as the result of a merger between *Sanofi*, at the time a subsidiary of French oil company *Elf Aquitaine*, and *Synthélabo*, a French biopharma company. *Aventis* was a Franco-German pharmaceutical company, which emerged from the merger between the two pharmaceutical and chemical companies *Rhône-Poulenc* and *Hoechst Marion Roussel*. While an initial hostile takeover attempt by *Sanofi-Synthélabo* was prevented by *Aventis*, the French government intervened after *Aventis* sought a merger with Swiss pharmaceutical giant *Novartis*. With the goal of keeping jobs in France, the French government managed to convince the *Aventis* shareholders to accept a takeover bid of 54 billion EUR.

Significance of R&D in the Pharmaceutical Industry

Internal R&D efforts are one of the most important factors in a company's ability to develop and introduce innovative or significantly improved products and services. However, many European countries still see outsourcing R&D efforts to external companies as only moderately important for a company's innovative capacity (European Commission 2013a, pp. 29-30). Pharmaceutical R&D in general is crucial for the development of new innovative drugs and treatments, which are defined as new medications or modes of action to take care of diseases which previously could not be adequately treated (Nusser/Tischendorf 2006, p. 8).

Sanofi itself describes the importance of extensive R&D activities as follows: "To be successful in the highly competitive pharmaceutical industry, we must commit substantial resources each year to research and development in order to develop new products to take the place of products facing expiration of patent and regulatory data exclusivity or competition from new products that are perceived as being superior" (Sanofi 2012, p. 6). According to *PhRMA*, an association representing the research and manufacturing pharmaceutical companies of the United States, "a vibrant pharmaceutical research industry requires a business environment that inspires and rewards investment in research and development (…), a thriving and collaborative scientific ecosystem that advances knowledge and innovation [and] a modern, transparent regulatory system (…)" (PhRMA 2014).

The significance of R&D for the pharma industry becomes further apparent when looking at the top 50 companies worldwide in terms of investment in R&D. In 2013, 15 out of those 50 were pharma or biotech enterprises – *Sanofi* ranks 15th out of 50. With a share of roughly 18% of all R&D investments combined, the pharma and biotech sector is the most R&D intensive across

Investments in R&D

471

all industry sectors, with the majority of activities carried out in the United States (European Commission 2013a, pp. 40-41). Pharmaceutical R&D however is a costly, lengthy and risky process. The average time to develop a new drug is approximately 12 years. During this time, a pharma company has to invest huge amounts of capital which will be tied up in the development project. This means high opportunity costs for the company because the invested capital cannot be put to other uses (CBO 2006, p. 2). Additionally, only one in 10,000 initially examined substances will actually pass clinical trials in later stages and gain the approval of regulation authorities, leading to an effective drug reaching the market (Nusser/Tischendorf 2006, p. 36). These clinical trials can take more time than the actual research and development activities (CBO 2006, p. 19).

The high cost of drug development is evident when comparing a company's investment in R&D to the number of new drugs brought to market. *Sanofi*, for example, has spent an average of 10.1 billion EUR per new drug in the last ten years (Forbes 2013). In 2013, *Sanofi* spent a total of 4.8 billion EUR on R&D, a ratio to net sales of 14.5%. This ratio is called *R&D intensity*. It is usually much higher for pharma companies than other industries (CBO 2006, p. 9). *Sanofi's* R&D intensity is close to the industry average of 14.4% (European Commission 2013a, p. 45).

R&D Decentralisation

Due to challenges arising from less and less efficient R&D efforts and the growing competition from generic products, *Sanofi* started efforts in 2009 to radically overhaul its R&D structure. The people in charge aim to create the best R&D organisation among drug makers by 2015. Their goal is to significantly increase the capacity to translate scientific discoveries into new drugs, replacing those with expiring patents and replenishing revenues (Bloomberg 2012).

Research Hubs   One cornerstone of *Sanofi's* approach towards a streamlined and more efficient R&D structure is its decentralisation. This means that R&D activities are not exclusively carried out in a single research facility attached to the company's headquarters but instead at various local sites. *Sanofi* has divided its R&D into four different areas which are called "hubs" and described as "geographically-focused integrated research innovation centers" (Sanofi 2012, p. 47). These hubs in France, Germany, Asia and the United States – specifically the Boston area – serve to facilitate communications between different research teams and are supposed to open up R&D structures for external input. As a consequence, *Sanofi's* research is expected to be more integrated into the respective local environments, making it easier to leverage local expertise and resources and to cater to country-specific conditions and needs (FierceBiotech 2013).

Sanofi's Geographically Focused Research Hubs

Figure 20.6

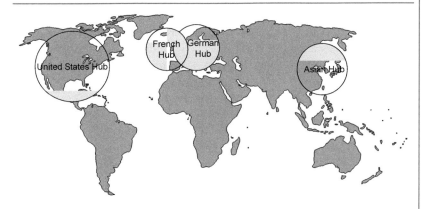

Source: Sanofi 2014.

This form of organisation allows *Sanofi* to settle into *local areas of excellence* where expert knowledge and innovative forces congregate. The Boston area, for example, is a place where many world class research institutes (e.g. *Harvard University* and *Massachusetts Institute of Technology*) and highly innovative *start-up companies* get together. By regrouping its R&D structure in consideration of such factors, *Sanofi* is able to actively benefit from the concentrated expertise and talent in the area. Thereby, specific core strengths and unique skills can be developed inside a particular hub, which are indispensable for handling and advancing the development of high potency drugs (CPhI 2014, p. 4).

Areas of Excellence

Sanofi's strategy of decentralisation is consistent with an overall trend in the industry to "move away from investing in single large scale R&D sites to diversifying interest across geographic regions, technologies and partnering firms" (CPhI 2014, p. 2). Besides an improved leverage of local expertise and talent, such an R&D structure increases the company's ability to react quickly and flexibly to changing market conditions or a competitor's breakthrough in one of the company's own fields of research. Switching between different innovative targets is easier and generally smoother (CPhI 2014, p. 2). The idea behind a hub is the combination of a core of strong internal competences and the advantages of a large, global company, along with the establishment of channels for external communication and collaboration. Thus, *Sanofi* aims to establish a form of organisation known as a *global R&D*

Benefits

network. Such a structure is characterised by a combination of global and local action. More specifically, it means active engagement with innovative local research ecosystems while at the same time maintaining large scale global development capabilities. This idea is consistent with empirical evidence that new innovative products are generally more successful when "internal research capability and external network resources are combined" (Kim/Park 2010, p. 43). A global R&D network is open to external opportunities and allows a company to "effectively capitalize on innovation from a wide range of sources" (Sanofi 2012, p. 47). Furthermore, this R&D organisation is characterised by a core/periphery structure, in which a few significant countries represent the core of the network and a variety of less important countries its periphery. The core countries each form the centre of a hub with a number of particular periphery countries at its outskirts. The respective hubs hold a strong position within the network (European Commission 2013b, pp. 22-39).

With the shift from relying mainly on internal R&D projects to a more open approach, *Sanofi* is partaking in a general industry trend to increase *collaborations* with external partners, with the expectation of increasing the innovative potential in research and ensuring better development practices (CPhI 2014, pp. 4-5).

R&D Collaborations

According to a survey by the consulting company *McKinsey*, the pharmaceuticals industry has become more fragmented than ever before. The number of significant players has more than doubled since 1989. Additionally, companies specialising in certain parts of the value chain show growth rates far above industry average, while big pharmaceutical companies, which traditionally cover the whole value chain of developing, producing and marketing a drug, have grown at below average rates. As a result, they have begun to focus on sales and marketing while engaging in research partnerships or even outsourcing parts of their R&D. This development has led to a significantly disaggregated pharmaceutical value chain (Hunt/Manson/Morgan 2011, pp. 3-5).

Sanofi has recognised the signs of the times and begun to acquire forward-thinking biotech companies or begun engaging in selected *project-related collaborations* with them. Since 2009, the company has already invested 24 billion EUR in external growth. Biotechs are said to be generally more innovative than big pharmaceutical companies because they are more flexible, dynamic and specified. Accordingly, they are important for replenishing the major player's drug pipelines. By 2018, 50% of new drugs are expected to come from biotechs (European Commission 2013a, pp. 57-58). While biotechs and start-ups are able to deliver an input of new creative ideas and approaches, big pharmaceutical companies have the necessary financial resources and expertise in lengthy clinical trials at their disposal and are capable of translating innovative ideas into marketable products. In this way, both parties profit from the collaboration. Half of *Sanofi's* current research portfolio already originates from external sources. *Sanofi* acknowledges that they have to go the *extra mile* – especially in biotechnology – to remain competitive. Because of rapid technology changes, a plethora of companies working toward the same targets simultaneously and the possibility of a promising product being outperformed by a competitor, *Sanofi's* business activities are exposed to constant risk. By engaging in collaborative R&D activities, these risks can at least be partially shared and thereby effectively countered.

As mentioned above, research pharma companies operate under significant risk of failure and have to bear high costs for drug development. In response to these challenges, *Sanofi* has partnered with nine other leading pharma companies, including for example *Johnson & Johnson, GlaxoSmithKline* and *Pfizer*, to form the non-profit organisation *TransCelerate BioPharma*. The association's agenda includes combining financial and personnel resources from all founding partners to collaboratively solve industry-wide challenges, the establishment of guidelines for knowledge sharing and the development of clinical data standards.

Exemplary Partnerships

Types and Characteristics of Sanofi's Collaborations

Figure 20.7

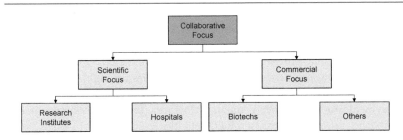

Source: Adapted from Sanofi 2014.

The second feature of *Sanofi* opening up its R&D process to an *inflow of knowledge* and ideas from outside is an enforced collaboration with research institutes and universities at a more fundamental level of research or with hospitals during biological and clinical trials. These partnerships may also be the source of new medical devices to improve therapies. The approach during joint research activities is to form combined, project-related teams composed of *Sanofi's* own research staff and scientists from institutes and universities. Instead of having two separate teams working on the same project and barely communicating with each other, as was the case in the past, this new approach facilitates communications between the involved parties and increases personal identification with the project. Company researchers visit the institute for a defined amount time and members of the institute work in *Sanofi's* laboratories for a while. For certain projects, there are even *common laboratories* being established.

One example is the foundation of a *centre of excellence* for natural products with *Fraunhofer-Gesellschaft*, Europe's biggest research institute for applied science. *Sanofi* and *Fraunhofer's* molecular biology division are going to work together on researching naturally occurring chemical and biological substances which can be transformed into antibiotics for treating infectious diseases. Within the partnership, a combined team of scientists is formed under shared leadership. They will conduct the research together, in the hope that the collaboration will lead to significant findings.

Summary and Outlook

The current prevailing trend in pharma is the encouraged and facilitated inflow of external knowledge, innovative ideas and novel compounds into a company's own R&D processes. *Sanofi* relies heavily on acquisitions to achieve external growth and receives additional input and risk- and resource-sharing partnerships in which they secure the rights to the product under development in exchange for carrying out milestones and royalty payments to the partner company. However, there are several other approaches towards externalised R&D activities.

Questions

1. Collaboration is increasingly important for the pharma industry. Describe the advantages and disadvantages of collaboration across the pharma industry.

2. Explain the concept of "open innovation" and envisage how it could be applied by *Sanofi*.

3. Compare the R&D structure of *Sanofi* with that of *Novartis* and *Pfizer*. Analyse the main differences.

Hints

1. See, e.g., Bartlett and Beamish 2014.

2. See, e.g., Chesbrough, Vanhverbeke and West 2006.

3. Examine the respective company websites www.sanofi.com, www.novartis.com, and www.pfizer.com.

References

BARTLETT, C.A.; BEAMISH, P.W. (2014): Transnational Management: Text, Cases, and Readings in Cross-Border Management, 7th ed., Boston, McGraw-Hill.

BELDERBOS, R.; GILSING, V.; JACOB, J. (2011): Technology Alliances in Emerging Economies: Persistence and Interrelation in European Firms' Alliance Formation, Working Paper, UNU-MERIT, United Nations University, United Nations.

BLOOMBERG (2012): Sanofi Aims to Be Pharma's Top R&D Organization, Zerhouni Says, http://www.bloomberg.com/news/2012-05-31/sanofi-aims-to-be-pharma-s-top-r-d-organization-zerhouni-says.html, accessed on March 24, 2014.

BOUTELLIER, R.; GASSMANN, O.; ZEDTWITZ, M. von (2008): Managing Global Innovation: Uncovering the Secrets of Future Competitiveness, 3rd ed., Berlin, Springer.

CBO (2006): Research and Development in the Pharmaceutical Industry: A Study by the Congress of the United States' Congressional Budget Office, Washington.

CHESBROUGH, H.; VANHAVERBEKE, W.; WEST, J. (2006): Open Innovation: Research a New Paradigm, New York, Oxford University Press.

CPHI (2014): Pharma Insights Research & Development Report, http://www.cphi.com/documents/129623/1317492/CPhI+WW+R%26D+Report+March+2014/27d4ec7d-52bd-4390-ac14-737a375b6df5, accessed on July 21, 2014.

DUNNING, J.; LUNDAN, S. (2008): Multinational Enterprises and the Global Economy, 2nd ed., Cheltenham, Edward Elgar Publishing.

ENKEL, E.; GASSMANN, O.; CHESBROUGH, H. (2009): Open R&D and Open Innovation: Exploring the Phenomenon, in: R&D Management, Vol. 39, No. 4, pp. 311-316.

EUROPEAN COMMISSION (2012): Internationalisation of Business Investments in R&D, Brussels.

EUROPEAN COMMISSION (2013a): EU R&D Scoreboard: The 2013 EU Industrial R&D Investment Scoreboard, Luxembourg.

EUROPEAN COMMISSION (2013b): The Global R&D Network: A Network Analysis of International R&D Centers, Working Paper by the European Commission's Institute for Prospective Technological Studies, Seville.

EUROSTAT (2013): Innovation Statistic, Luxembourg, European Commission.

FIERCEBIOTECH (2013): Sanofi Rebuilds Early Stage R&D Strategy in Thriving Boston/Cambridge Hub, http://www.fiercebiotech.com/story, accessed on March 24, 2014.

FISCH, J.-H. (2001): Structure Follows Knowledge: Internationale Verteilung der Forschung & Entwicklung in multinationalen Unternehmen, Wiesbaden, Gabler.

FISCH, J.-H. (2003): Optimal Dispersion of R&D Activities in Multinational Corporations with a Genetic Algorithm, in: Research Policy, Vol. 32, No. 8, pp. 1381-1396.

FISCH, J.-H. (2004): Allocating Innovative Activities in International R&D with Fuzzy Logic, in: Management International Review, Vol. 44, No. 3 Special Issue, pp. 147-166.

FORBES (2013): How Much Does Pharmaceutical Innovation Cost? A Look at 100 Companies, http://www.forbes.com/sites/matthewherper/2013/08/11, accessed on July 22, 2014.

GASSMANN, O.; ZEDTWITZ, M. von (1996): Internationales Innovationsmanagement: Ein Referenzrahmen, in: GASSMANN, O.; ZEDTWITZ, M. von (Eds.): Internationales Innovationsmanagement, Munich, Vahlen, pp. 3-16.

GASSMANN, O.; ENKEL, E.; CHESBROUGH, H. (2010): The Future of Open Innovation, in: R&D Management, Vol. 40, No. 3, pp. 213-221.

HILL, C.W.L. (2013): International Business: Competing in the Global Marketplace, 9th ed., New York, McGraw-Hill.

HUNT, N.; MANSON, N.; MORGAN, P. (2011): A Wake-up Call for Big Pharma: Lower Profit Margins Suggest a Need for New Business Models, McKinsey Quarterly, December 2012.

KIM, C.; PARK, J. (2010): The Global Research-and-Development Network and Its Effects on Innovation, in: Journal of International Marketing, Vol. 18, No. 4, pp. 43-57.

KUEMMERLE, W. (1997): Building Effective R&D Capabilities Abroad, in: Harvard Business Review, Vol. 75, No. 2, pp. 61-70.

NARULA, R. (2003): Globalization & Technology: Interdependence, Innovation Systems and Industrial Policy, Oxford, Blackwell Publishing.

NATIONAL SCIENCE FOUNDATION (2010): Science and Engineering Indicators 2010, Arlington.

NOBEL, R.; BIRKINSHAW, J. (1998): Innovation in Multinational Corporations: Control and Communication Patterns in International R&D Operations, in: Strategic Management Journal, Vol. 19, No. 5, pp. 479-496.

NUSSER, M.; TISCHENDORF, A. (2006): The Research-based Pharmaceutical Industry as a Chance for the Business Location Germany: A Study on Behalf of PhARMA and the German LAWG, Karlsruhe.

OECD (2008): The Internationalisation of Business R&D: Evidence, Impacts and Implications, Paris.

OESTERLE, M.-J. (2005): Kooperation in Forschung und Entwicklung, in: ZENTES, J.; SWOBODA, B.; MORSCHETT, D. (Eds.): Kooperationen, Allianzen und Netzwerke, 2nd ed., Wiesbaden, Gabler, pp. 769-795.

PEARCE, R. (1989): The Internationalization of Research and Development by Multinational Enterprises, Basingstoke, Palgrave Macmillan.

PHRMA (2014): About, http://www.phrma.org/about, accessed on March 24, 2014.

ROTERING, C. (1990): Forschungs- und Entwicklungskooperationen zwischen Unternehmen: Eine empirische Analyse, Stuttgart, Schäffer-Poeschel.

SANOFI (2012): Annual Report, Paris.

SANOFI (2014): Sanofi, http://www.sanofi.com., accessed on September 01, 2014.

SCHMID, S. (2000): Dezentralisierung von Forschung & Entwicklung in internationalen Unternehmungen, Diskussionsbeiträge der Wirtschaftswissenschaftlichen Fakultät Ingolstadt, No. 139, Ingolstadt.

SCHMIELE, A. (2012): Drivers for International Innovation Activities in Developed and Emerging Countries, in: The Journal of Technology Transfer, Vol. 37, No. 1, pp. 98-123.

SHENKAR, O.; LUO, Y. (2008): International Business, 2nd ed., Thousand Oaks, Sage Publications.

UNCTAD (2005): World Investment Report 2005: Transnational Corporations and the Internationalization of R&D, Geneva.

ZEDTWITZ, M. von (2005): International R&D Strategies in Companies from Developing Countries: The Case of China, Paper Presented at the UNCTAD Expert Meeting on the Impact of FDI on Development, Geneva, January 24-26, 2005.

ZENTES, J.; SWOBODA, B.; MORSCHETT, D. (2004): Internationales Wert-schöpfungsmanagement, Munich, Vahlen.

Chapter 21

International Marketing

This Chapter discusses the diverse options of standardising versus adapting the marketing strategy in the context of the international marketing mix. International marketing mix strategies are presented in relation to their component strategies, i.e. international product strategy, international pricing strategy, international communication strategy and international sales and distribution strategy.

International Marketing Strategy

One of the most frequent motives for internationalisation is the search for new markets (see Chapter 4). An international marketing strategy brings *customer focus* to the firm's international strategy. International marketing, in general, is concerned with identifying, measuring and pursuing *market opportunities* abroad. It implies "the application of marketing orientation and marketing techniques to international business" (Mühlbacher/Leihs/Dahringer 2006, p. 38) and alludes to the *positioning* of the MNC itself and its products and services in foreign markets (Cavusgil/Knight/Riesenberger 2014, pp. 499-500).

The basic types of international marketing strategies can be classified according to the integration/responsiveness-framework (see Chapter 2):

Basic Strategy Types

- *International marketing strategy*: This type of marketing strategy can be considered an *ethnocentric* marketing strategy, and is characterised by the application of the marketing strategy of the home country to all foreign markets without adaptation to the local environment. It represents a standardised approach to marketing that is referred to as *"transference"*, i.e., the marketing strategy that has been developed for the home market is transferred to (all) other markets (Shoham/Rose/Albaum 1995, p. 15).

- *Global marketing strategy*: The global marketing strategy is associated with a firm's commitment to coordinate its marketing activities across national boundaries in order to satisfy global customer needs (Hollensen 2014, p. 7). Global marketing is associated with a *standardised* approach, i.e., a marketing strategy being applied in multiple markets at the same time (Shoham/Rose/Albaum 1995, p. 15) with the objective of achieving global efficiency and economies of scale.

■ *Multinational marketing strategy*: Multinational marketing strategies focus on the diversity of international marketing and imply a strong adaptation to the needs of each market. Thus, *individual marketing programmes* are developed for each individual market, with a multitude of diverse marketing programmes being applied simultaneously.

■ *Transnational marketing strategy*: The transnational marketing strategy implies the combination of global efficiency and multinational diversity with a strategy that strives to satisfy the mantra "think globally, act locally". This strategy is sometimes referred to as *"glocalisation"*.

This classification of marketing strategies (see Figure 21.1) centres on the basic decision between *standardising* and *adapting* the marketing strategy, marketing processes or marketing programme to local needs.

Figure 21.1 | *Classification of Marketing Strategies*

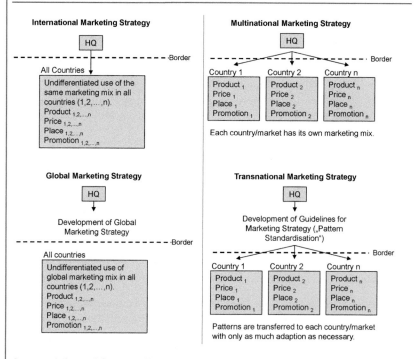

Source: Adapted from Hollensen 2014, p. 474.

Standardisation vs. Differentiation

The two sides of the market globalisation debate started by Levitt (1983; see Chapter 2) are local marketing versus global marketing and focus on the central question of whether a *standardised* (global) or a *differentiated*, country-specific marketing approach is better. The main factors that favour standardisation versus local adaptation (differentiation, customisation) of marketing strategies are summarised in Table 21.1.

Selected Factors Favouring Standardisation vs. Differentiation

Table 21.1

Factors Favouring Standardisation	Factors Favouring Differentiation
• economies of scale, e.g. in R&D, production and marketing (experience curve effects)	• local environment-induced adaptation, e.g. government and regulatory influences, legal issues, differences in technical standards (no experience curve effects)
• global competition	
• convergence of tastes and consumer needs (consumer preferences are homogeneous)	• local competition
• centralised management of international operations (possible to transfer experience across borders)	• variation in consumer needs (consumer needs are heterogeneous, e.g. because of cultural differences)
• a standardised concept is used by competitors	• fragmented and decentralised management with independent country subsidiaries
• high degree of transferability of competitive advantages from market to market	• an adapted concept is used by competitors
• easier communication, planning and control (e.g. through Internet and mobile technology)	• low degree of transferability of competitive advantages from market to market
• stock cost reduction	

Source: Adapted from Hollensen 2014, p. 477.

Standardisation might be beneficial for international operations because it offers the potential to standardise global operations: "The global corporation operates with resolute constancy – at low relative cost – as if the entire world (or major regions of it) were a single entity; it sells the same things in the same way everywhere" (Levitt 1983, pp. 92-93). With *standardisation*, producers obtain global economies of scale and experience curve benefits in production, distribution, marketing and management. Also there are *cross-border segments* of consumers. These are consumers with homogeneous consumption patterns across cultures. Typically, these cross-border segments are younger, richer and more urban than the rest of the population (Quelch 1999, p. 2).

Standardisation and adaptation of the marketing strategy are two extremes of a continuum, i.e., as adaptation increases standardisation decreases and *vice versa*. The discussion of standardisation versus local adaptation on a strategic level can affect diverse aspects of the marketing strategy (Hollensen 2014, pp. 474-476):

Perspectives on Standardisation/ Differentiation

■ *Regional perspective*: Full standardisation in this context relates to a *global marketing strategy*, in which the same marketing strategy is applied to all markets served by the company. In contrast, in a *multinational marketing strategy*, individual marketing strategies are developed for each local market; thus, each country market is considered separately. A mixture of standardisation and adaptation is represented by the *multi-regional marketing strategy*. This strategy distinguishes several homogeneous regions and develops specific marketing strategies for each one (e.g. European Marketing, North American Marketing).

■ *Marketing process perspective*: A standardisation of marketing processes relates to standardised *decision-making processes* for cross-country or multi-regional marketing planning. Standardisation in this context relates to, for example, the standardised launch of new products or standardised marketing controlling activities, and seeks to rationalise the general marketing process.

■ *Marketing components/marketing mix perspective*: From the marketing components perspective, standardisation or differentiation affect the degree to which the individual elements of the *marketing mix* are unified into a common approach. A fully standardised approach consists of standardisation across all marketing components. On the other hand, a fully differentiated approach implies the adaptation of all marketing mix elements to local requirements. A mixed strategy implies that some components are standardised or adapted to one degree, others to a different degree.

The International Marketing Mix

"4 Ps" of International Marketing

The key elements of the *international marketing programme* that constitute the international marketing mix are international product strategy, international pricing strategy, international marketing communication and international distribution strategy. These elements are also referred to as the *"4 Ps"* (product, price, placement and promotion).

International Product Strategies

Core of International Marketing Mix

An international product strategy encompasses all decisions that relate to the firm's product and services offerings in the international marketplace. It comprises decisions on which products (or product lines) will be offered in each country market, decisions on product (and product line) standardisation or customisation and new product development. The *international product strategy* is often regarded as the core of the international marketing mix strategy. The product and its core benefits must ultimately fulfil the customers' desires; the other elements of the marketing mix usually cannot compensate for product deficiencies. The product strategy is often the starting point for further marketing mix decisions. For example, decisions on standardisation or customisation of the communication strategy often depend on whether the *product* is standardised or locally adapted.

Products are complex combinations of tangible and intangible elements. They not only consist of the *core physical properties* but also comprise additional elements such as packaging, branding or other *augmented features,* e.g. support services (Czinkota/Ronkainen 2013, pp. 357).

Product Elements

Several types of international product strategy can be distinguished. Depending on their general marketing strategy, companies have *four alternatives* for approaching international markets (Czinkota/Ronkainen 2013, pp. 358-359; Kotabe/Helsen 2014, pp. 332-334):

Product Strategy Alternatives

■ *extension* of the home-grown product strategy to foreign markets and selling the same product abroad

■ *modification* of products for each local market according to local requirements

■ an *invention* strategy involving designing new products for the global market

■ incorporating all differences into one flexible product design and introducing a *standardised product*.

In this context, the major question is which *product features* should be tailored to market conditions. The possibilities and pressures for standardising product elements in the international context differ, with adaptation being most necessary for *augmented product features* and standardisation of the *core product* (i.e. functional features, performance) being the easiest (Doole/Lowe 2012, p. 253).

To minimise the *cost of customisation*, companies can use product design policies that allow them to modify products to meet local requirements with few operating expenses. For example, *modular design* approaches allow the firm to assemble individual products for each country market using a selection from a range of standardised product components that can be used worldwide. *Common platform approaches* start with the design of a mostly uniform core-product or platform to which customised attachments can be added for each local market (Kotabe/Helsen 2014, pp. 338-339). A specific strategy that allows a standardised product to be sold in each country mar-

Customisation Strategies

ket even though there are specific local requirements is a strategy known as *"built-in flexibility"*. The products incorporate all local differences in one product and adapt flexibly to the local requirements (e.g. mobile phones that adapt to differences in voltage or different network frequencies).

*International
Product Range
Strategy*

As most MNCs do not offer a single product but a range of products, companies also need to specify their *international product range strategy*. For each country market, it is necessary to decide on the *breadth* of the product range, i.e., the number of product lines to be offered, and on the *depth* of the product range, i.e., the number of products or product variants to be offered per product line. In this context, decisions have to be taken on standardisation versus adaptation of the product range to local requirements.

International Pricing Strategies

International pricing is often considered the most critical and complex issue in international marketing. When talking about the price of a product, it is important to notice that it is a sum of all monetary and non-monetary assets the customer has to spend in order to obtain the benefits it provides. The main *pricing decisions* in international marketing comprise the following (Mühlbacher/Leihs/Dahringer 2006, pp. 661-662):

*International
Pricing Decisions*

- ◼ The *overall international pricing strategy* determines general rules for setting (basic) prices and using price reductions, the selection of terms of payment, and the potential use of countertrade.

- ◼ The *price setting strategy* determines the basic price of a product, the price structure of the product line, and the system of rebates, discounts or refunds the firm offers.

- ◼ The *terms of payment* are contractual statements fixing, for example, the point in time and the circumstances of payment for the products to be delivered.

A company's *pricing strategy* is a highly cross-functional process that is based on inputs from finance, accounting, manufacturing, tax and legal issues (Kotabe/Helsen 2014, pp. 358-360), which can be diverse in an international context.

It thus is not sufficient to place sole emphasis on ensuring that *sales revenue* at least covers the *cost* incurred (e.g. cost of production, marketing or distribution); it is important to take many other factors into consideration that may differ internationally (Doole/Lowe 2012, pp. 361-362). The most important factors that influence international pricing strategy are summarised in Table 21.2.

Factors Influencing International Pricing Strategy   *Table 21.2*

Company and Product-specific Factors	Market Factors	Environmental Factors
• corporate and marketing objectives • firm and product positioning • degree of international product standardisation or adaptation • product range, cross subsidisation, life cycle, substitutes, product differentiation and unique selling proposition • cost structures, manufacturing, experience effects, economies of scale • marketing, product development • available resources • inventory • shipping cost	• consumers' perceptions, expectations and ability to pay • need for product and promotional adaptation, market servicing, extra packaging requirements • market structure, distribution channels, discounting pressures • market growth, demand elasticities • need for credit • competition objectives, strategies and strength	• government influences and constraints • tax, tariffs • currency fluctuations • business cycle stage, level of inflation • use of non-money payment and leasing

Source: Adapted from Doole/Lowe 2012, pp. 358-359.

There are several options in terms of general price determination. They represent different levels of adaptation to local requirements.

A *standard pricing strategy* is based on setting a uniform price for a product, irrespective of the country where it is sold. This strategy is very simple and guarantees a fixed return. However, no response is made to local conditions (Doole/Lowe 2012, p. 368).

Standard Price

With *standard formula pricing*, the company standardises by using the same formula to calculate prices for the product in all country markets. There are different ways to establish such a formula. For example, *full-cost pricing* consists of taking all cost elements (e.g. production plus marketing, etc.) in the domestic market and adding additional costs from international transportation, taxes, tariffs, etc. A *direct cost plus contribution margin formula* implies that additional costs due to the non-domestic marketing process and a desired profit margin are added to the basic production cost. The most useful approach in standard formula pricing is the *differential formula*. It includes all incremental costs resulting from a non-domestic business opportunity that would not be incurred otherwise and adds these costs to the production cost (Mühlbacher/Leihs/Dahringer 2006, p. 664).

Standard Formula Pricing

Price Adaptation

While these strategies accentuate elements of international standardisation in pricing, in *price adaptation strategies* prices are typically set in a decentralised way (e.g. by the local subsidiary or local partner). Prices can be established to match local conditions. While this ability to comply with *local requirements* constitutes a clear advantage, there can be difficulties in developing a global strategic position.

Parallel Markets/ Grey Markets

Additionally, the potential for price adaptation is limited by *interconnections* between the diverse international markets. Therefore it is necessary to coordinate the pricing strategy across different countries because otherwise *re-imports, parallel market* or *grey market* situations can emerge. In these situations, products are sold outside of their authorised channels of distribution. As a specific form of arbitrage, *grey markets* develop when there are price differences between the different markets in which products are sold. If these differences emerge, products are shipped from low-price to high-price markets with the price differences between these markets allowing the goods to be resold in the high-price market with a profit. *Parallel markets*, while legal, are unofficial and unauthorised and can result in the cannibalisation of sales in countries with relatively high prices, damaging relationships with authorised distributors.

Geocentric Pricing

To avoid these drawbacks in totally standardised or differentiated approaches, *geocentric pricing approaches* can be chosen. There is no single fixed price, but local subsidiaries are not given total freedom over setting prices. For example, firms can set *price lines* that set the company's prices relative to competitors' prices (i.e. standardised price positioning) or they can centrally coordinate pricing decisions in the MNC (Doole/Lowe 2012, pp. 368-369).

In this context, it is important to notice that international pricing decisions also depend on the degree of industry globalisation. *Global industries* are dominated by a few, large competitors that dominate the world markets (Solberg/Stöttinger/Yaprak 2006). Which international pricing strategy is appropriate depends on the firm's ability to respond to the diverse external, market-related complexities of international markets (see Figure 21.2).

Taxonomy of International Pricing Practices | *Figure 21.2*

Source: Adapted from Solberg/Stöttinger/Yaprak 2006, p. 31.

International Marketing Communication

International marketing communication includes all methods companies use to provide information to and communicate with existing and potential customers and other stakeholders. The *international communication process* is affected by many factors that complicate communication in an international (cross-country or cross-cultural) setting (see Chapter 9). In this context, aspects such as language differences, economic differences, socio-cultural differences, legal and regulatory differences or competitive differences are crucial.

The *international communication mix* consists of a diverse set of communication tools such as advertising, personal selling, sales promotions, public relations or direct marketing (see Table 21.3).

The most viable form of communication is *advertising*, which often constitutes the most important part of the communication mix in the consumer goods industry. However, in *business-to-business markets*, advertising is often less important than personal selling.

Table 21.3   *Communication Tools in International Marketing*

Advertising	Public Relations	Sales Promotion	Direct Marketing	Personal Selling
• newspapers • magazines • journals • directories • television • radio • cinema • outdoor • Internet	• annual reports • house magazines • press relations • events • lobbying • sponsorships	• rebates and price discounts • catalogues and brochures • samples, coupons, gifts • competitions	• direct mail • database marketing • Internet marketing • mobile marketing (SMS, MMS) • social media marketing • viral marketing • location-based marketing • advertising games	• sales presentations • sales force management • trade fairs • exhibitions

Source: Adapted from Zentes/Swoboda/Schramm-Klein 2013, p. 389.

The main decisions for international communication strategy relate to the *choice of communication modes* for each country market and to the *choice of communication themes* in the international context. Both aspects can be standardised or differentiated internationally.

Communication Mode

Similar to price strategies, *standardisation* of *communication tools* or communication *media selection* can be performed either through a totally standardised approach that implies the use of the same tools (or same media) in all countries, or by setting uniform selection methods (e.g. relating to media reach, contact situation or modality) for communication tools and media that are employed in all markets. Usually, a more *differentiated approach* is necessary because of international differences in culture, media use or media availability.

Communication Themes

For *communication themes* or the content of communication *messages*, the optimal degree of standardisation depends on the intended positioning in each country market. The main options for companies are internationally standardised campaigns, locally adapted (differentiated) campaigns or mixed campaigns that use the same communication theme (*"umbrella campaign"*) but adapt the execution to local requirements, for example by adapting media, language, tonality or colours or by adapting testimonials. This strategy is also referred to as *"pattern standardisation"* (Kotabe/Helsen 2014, pp. 435-436).

There are several advantages in *standardised campaigns*. For example, economies of scale are also relevant in marketing communication. They can result from reduced planning and development costs for marketing campaigns. Additionally, standardised campaigns can help to establish a *uniform* product and company *image* in all markets. This is particularly important with international customers, cross-national sectors or if there is a media overlap between country markets (or globally). Standardised campaigns can be co-ordinated internationally more easily and allow good ideas and creative talents to be used better. By running global campaigns, it is also possible to benefit from high-quality, creative campaigns for small markets or countries with low subsidiary resources (Kotabe/Helsen 2014, pp. 434-435).

Nevertheless, it is not possible or beneficial to use standardised campaigns in all cases. For example, *cultural barriers*, especially language, are often stronger than expected. Customers do not always understand foreign languages well and problems such as mistakes, misinterpretations or changed meanings can arise when translating standardised messages. Other problems might result,

- if products or the use of products are culture bound (e.g. in the case of food)

- if the communication topic is culture bound (e.g. hygiene products)

- if the communication design is culture bound (e.g. the use of colours or background music)

- if the communication content is culture bound (e.g. gender issues, eroticism).

Additional difficulties might emerge if products are in *different stages of their product lifecycle* in different countries, because different life cycle stages require different communication content (Hollensen 2014, pp. 487-489). Also *legal differences* might restrict certain types of communication or certain communication messages in the diverse countries. Examples include the advertising of pharmaceuticals or "vice products" such as alcohol or cigarettes, the application of comparative advertising or advertising targeting children.

International Branding Strategies

Closely linked to product positioning and communication issues in international marketing are decisions on *international branding strategies*. The main purpose of branding is to differentiate the company's offerings and to create brand identification and awareness. Branding strategies can be distinguished according to the *brand architecture* into single brand strategies or family (or umbrella) brand strategies (for a number of products). Companies may also choose to market several brands in a single market.

Geographic Branding Strategies

The company needs to decide which general branding strategy, in terms of the brand architecture, is to be applied for each country market. The main problem in international branding strategies is whether to choose an integrated, *global branding* approach, which employs a uniform branding approach for all markets, or to use differentiated, regional or *local branding* strategies. In this context, decisions about the geographic extension of brands are necessary.

The basic strategies are *global brands*, i.e. establishing a single brand for all markets ("*universal brand*") and *local brands*, implying the use of individual brands on each country market. Mixed strategies are also possible, for example by establishing several *regional brands* with a focus on several country markets.

Advantages of Global Brands

Many companies strive for *global brands* because of the advantages associated with this strategy. Global brands offer the highest possibility of achieving a *consistent image* across the world and are also a necessary requirement for global advertising campaigns. Global brands have much higher *visibility* than local brands and their global nature often adds to the image of a brand, and global brands reach the highest (overall) *brand equity* (Kotabe/Helsen 2014, p. 367). Also, *economies of scale* are associated with global branding. For example, the cost of creating and strengthening the brand can be spread over large sales volumes.

Advantages of Local Brands

However, there are limitations to global branding. For example, if companies offer a diverse product range in international markets, the product offer in the host country does not always fit the global brand's image, thus limiting its applicability. *Local brand names* might also be easier to understand, and not all global brand names are suitable for internationalisation. Also, if other elements of the international marketing mix are adapted to local conditions, local branding might be more appropriate. For example, if advertising messages are adapted to each market or if products are changed through customisation, product design or recipes to meet local requirements, these strategies are easier to implement under different *local brand names*.

This also applies to price differentiation, which is easier with different brand names. Thus, brand differentiation can be used as a strategy to limit parallel or grey markets. In this context, companies can also implement *mixed strategies*, in which a global corporate brand is used in all markets but product brand names are adapted to the local requirements.

International Distribution Strategies

The international distribution strategy is closely connected to the foreign operation modes the MNC applies in the diverse markets. It mainly relates to decisions on the structure of the marketing channels and to marketing logistics:

- *International channel structure and channel design*: e.g. types of intermediaries (alternative distribution channels), coverage (intensive, selective, exclusive), length (number of levels), control resources and degree of integration

- *International marketing logistics*: physical movement of goods through the international channel systems, e.g. order handling, transportation, inventory, storage, warehousing.

International *channel configuration* is highly dependent on the availability of marketing channels on each country market and on customer characteristics and culture that determine channel use. Additionally, factors relating to channel costs, channel control or continuity of channel relationships are important.

International Channel Configuration

Channels can vary from direct channels to multilevel channels, employing many types of intermediaries that each serve a particular purpose (Doole/Lowe 2012, p. 327). *International channel relationships* are complicated by many factors such as those relating to product ownership, geographic, cultural and economic distance and different rules of law.

Conclusion and Outlook

The *key decisions* in international marketing strategy relate to the standardisation or the adaptation of the marketing mix to local conditions. In practice, few marketing mixes are totally standardised or totally differentiated, and mixed strategies are usually applied.

Also, the degree of standardisation and adaptation differs between the diverse instruments of the marketing mix. Figure 21.3 shows the *general standardisation level* for different elements of the international marketing mix.

Figure 21.3 | *General Standardisation Level for Different Elements of the Marketing Mix*

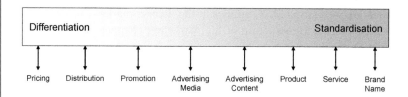

Source: Adapted from Zentes/Swoboda/Schramm-Klein 2013, p. 449.

Interrelatedness in the Marketing Mix

In this context, it is important to note that the decisions relating to each element of the international marketing mix cannot be taken separately. The efficiency and effectiveness of sub-strategies such as international product strategy, international pricing strategy or branding decisions, depend on their fit with all elements in the marketing mix. Thus, it is important to take into account the *interrelationship* between all elements in the marketing mix. Additionally, the *coordination* between the diverse country markets in which the company is present is important.

Further Reading

CZINKOTA, M.; RONKAINEN, I. (2003): An International Marketing Manifesto, in: Journal of International Marketing, Vol. 11, No. 1, pp. 13-27.

HOLLENSEN, S. (2014): Global Marketing, 6th ed., Harlow, Pearson, pp. 471-648.

SOLBERG, C.A. (2002): The Perennial Issue of Adaptation or Standardization of International Marketing Communication: Organizational Contingencies and Performance, in: Journal of International Marketing, Vol. 10, No. 3, pp. 1-21.

Part V

Case Study: Nestlé[*]

Profile, History, and Status Quo

In 1867 the pharmacist *Henri Nestlé* invented a formula for baby and infant food that ultimately led to the foundation of *Nestlé S.A.* The world's largest food and beverage company has been based in Vevey, Switzerland ever since. Through further investments in the last years of the 19th century, nutrition became the cornerstone of *Nestlé*. An immigrant from Germany, *Henri Nestlé* immediately sought to expand onto international markets. After merging with one of the biggest competitors in the Swiss market in 1905, further growth was initiated.

The First World War led to severe disruptions to *Nestlé*'s production process but ultimately helped the company as demand for dairy products started to rise thanks to the establishment of governmental contracts. After the necessary adjustments (operations were streamlined) to survive the financial crisis in the 1920s, the company acquired the *Peter, Cailler, Kohler Swiss Chocolate Company* and made chocolate an important part of their business. As a direct result of this, several new products were introduced, the most important of which was released in 1938: *Nescafé*. The brand's initial launch suffered greatly on the outbreak of the Second World War, but was eventually strengthened when it became an official staple beverage of the United States Servicemen stationed in Europe and Asia. *The Influences of the First World War*

After the Second World War came to an end, *Nestlé* entered a phase of rapid growth and expansion. Within only a few years numerous new factories were established and acquisitions enhanced the product variety. The merger with *Alimentana S.A.* in 1947 that made the *Maggi* products part of *Nestlé* and the introduction of *Nesquik* both had big impacts on the company.

With investments in *L'Oréal*, a global leading producer of cosmetics, *Nestlé* started to diversify its product range. After this first move outside of its traditional product line they added numerous other industries, such as pharmaceutical and ophthalmic products, in the following years. Further additions were also made to the original branches of the company. With the 3 billion USD acquisition of the American Food Supplier *Carnation*, they further strengthened their presence in international markets. New brands like *Nespresso* and *Buitoni* were also added to their product portfolio. *Gaining Market Power through Diversity*

---

[*] Sources used for this case study include the websites www.nestle.com, ww.nestle.de, www.nestle-waters.com, as well as explicitly cited sources.

495

When the 1990s emerged and the fall of the iron curtain opened up Eastern European markets, *Nestlé* immediately began to invest in those regions. Through more recent acquisitions within and outside of their original branches they have grown to a worldwide cooperation with more than 330,000 employees and over 75 billion EUR in annual revenue. Although only 2% of their overall sales are made in Switzerland, *Nestlé* still considers itself a Swiss company.

"Good Food, Good Life"

One of *Nestlé's* major concerns, which is also raised in many campaigns and statements, is their focus on customers' needs. *Nestlé* and their product range cater to people of every age group and they therefore try to incorporate a strict vision for themselves that reflects their companies' goals to the public. Parts of this so-called "Good Food, Good Life" approach incorporate *sustainability* as well as creating shared value (see Figure 21.4).

Figure 21.4 | *The Vision of Nestlé*

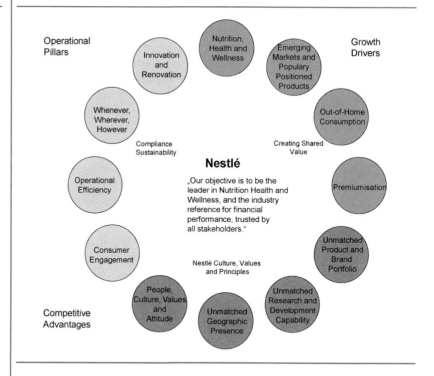

Ethical Challenges

Although *Nestlé* claims to work according to the same ethical standards and norms worldwide, large environmental organisations (NGOs) such as *Greenpeace* accuse *Nestlé* of using the lack of governmental regulations in developing countries to run production facilities that definitely do not implement normal European business and safety standards (Onkvisit/Shaw 2004, p. 82). A feature documentary by Swiss filmmaker Urs Schnell and journalist Res Gehriger showed, for example, how *Nestlé Waters* took advantage of lower productions costs. To produce the popular water brand *"Pure Life"*, the company exploited the water supply of several small villages. As well as leaving insufficient water to meet the villages' needs, it also had a bad influence on the water quality, especially affecting younger children and seniors (Regenass 2012).

International Marketing Strategy

Peter Brabeck-Letmathe, Chairman of *Nestlé*, stated that the founder's key attitudes like "pragmatism, flexibility, the willingness to learn, an open mind and respect for other people and cultures" are still very much alive in the company's corporate culture. Since its beginnings in the 19th century, *Nestlé* has grown to be one of the world's biggest companies. *Nestlé* products are sold in every country, even in North Korea (Onkvisit/Shaw 2004, p. 2).

To achieve this goal, *Nestlé* managed to build up a single *global identity* that is able to incorporate various products, brands and production strategies. For obvious reasons, *Nestlé* is constantly trying to refine and optimise its line of production to achieve higher revenues and gain larger shares in different markets. One large obstacle to overcome is cultural borders, even more than country borders. *Nestlé* tries to carefully serve various cultural preferences while simultaneously creating economies of scale (Onkvisit/Shaw 2004, p. 2). Examples of this strategy will be given later in this case study.

Global Identity as Key

To provide a more detailed insight to *Nestlé's* marketing strategies, the following part of this case study will describe the "four P s" (product, price, promotion and place) in the context of *Nestlé*.

Product

Nestlé sells over 1.2 billion products worldwide every day. Very important to this figure is the fact that *Nestlé* is home to over 8,000 different brands, which are organised and marketed in very different fashions (see Figure 21.5). In some cases, brands are only offered in one local market and therefore adjusted to the given circumstances. These local brands are designed to perfectly meet the demand in that particular market and are distributed solely in this one region.

Other, global brands are distributed worldwide or at least in several markets at the same time and advertised almost identically in most of those markets. Well-known brands such as *Nespresso*, *Nescafé* or *KitKat* are typical examples. Logos and other basic features may be slightly different from country to country, but the overall look remains similar in most cases.

Figure 21.5 | The Nestlé Brand Tree

	Examples:		
Around 8,300 Local Brands Responsibility of local markets	• Savory • Sahne-Nuss • McKay • Buxton	• Haoji • Totole • La Vie • Erikli	• Levissima • Minéré • Theodora
140 Regional Strategic Brands Responsibility of strategic business unit and regional management	• Herta • Findus • Alpo • Vittel	• Stouffer's • Arrowhead • Calistoga • Deer Park	• Ice Mountain • Ozarka • Zephyrhills
Around 55 Worldwide Strategic Brands Responsibility of general management at strategic business unit level	• Kit Kat • Polo • Cerelac • Baci	• Mighty Dog • Smarties • After Eight • Coffee-Mate	
10 Worldwide Corporate Brands	• Nestle • Maggi • Perrier	• L'Oreal • Buitoni • Carnatio	

Source: Adapted from Zentes/Swoboda/Schramm-Klein 2013, p. 450.

Supplying products in a single brand to numerous markets is always a challenge. For example, *Nestlé* had problems with communicating and selling its popular powdered infant formula in several developing countries. The marketing campaign was focused on selling breast-milk substitutes to women that were unable to afford those products and often incapable of using them properly. Consumers and several other organisations identified this issue and confronted *Nestlé* in a harmful process (Onkvisit/Shaw 2004, p. 424).

Adapting Products to Local Markets

Despite this example, *Nestlé* generally understands how to adapt their global and local brands to the given markets and find a suitable niche to place its products. Through an intense process of research and development in local affiliates, *Nestlé* is able to find certain product variations that are suitable for a given market. For example, their global brands *KitKat* and *Maggi* are very well adjusted to different markets. In Japan, for example, *KitKat* is sold in numerous flavours that cannot be found elsewhere. Even within the country itself, *Nestlé* implemented some variations for only a small part of it. These variations range from yubari melon and baked corn from Hokkaido Island to cherry and bean flavoured chocolate bars in the Tokyo region (Madden 2010). A similar tactic is also used for the *Maggi* brand, where different types of soup are designed to fit individual market preferences.

Examples of Various KitKat Flavours Figure 21.6

Source: Alimenta 2014.

By adjusting so well to the given market while keeping the brand on a global level, *Nestlé* successfully gains customers' trust all over the world. This "glocal" (think globally – act locally) approach has proven to be very successful and is the basis for *Nestlé*'s international strategy.

Think Global – Act Local

Due to the high number of in-house brands and brands added to the company through acquisitions, *Nestlé* often consolidates them under one unified brand. Doing so is a very long and costly process, which generally takes up to 5 years. Adding the *Nestlé* brand name to the given package design alongside the local brand and slowly enlarging it until it finally replaces the local brand altogether is a process that *Nestlé* has executed numerous times.

Price

Another important instrument in the marketing mix can be seen in price strategies. Since *Nestlé* is home to a vast range of different brands, it is hard to identify one overall strategy for all products. *Nestlé's* brands are positioned in both lower and higher price segments.

Popularly Positioned Products

As mentioned earlier, *Nestlé* is very keen on providing affordable nutrition solutions on a global basis. Their Popularly Positioned Products (PPP) strategy is the direct result of that. The key aspect of this strategy is meeting the specific needs of 3 billion lower-income consumers worldwide and providing affordable brands/products to cater to those needs. Almost 4,000 different products are offered within this strategy, and even global brands like *Nescafé* and *Maggi* are represented. In this case the price is intentionally lowered to meet the demand of the market and reach as many customers as possible.

Nespresso

A very different approach is used for *Nespresso*. This brand is positioned in a very high price segment. Being sold exclusively in special stores and online, this product clearly stands out from most other *Nestlé* brands. Based on a relatively high profit margin of every portion of coffee sold, this price strategy clearly differs from their PPP strategy (Matzler et al. 2013, p. 36). To maintain this advantage *Nestlé* even spread false rumours that their coffee machines could only be used with the original coffee capsules sold by licenced partners (Datamonitor 2007, p. 3). *Nespresso* may not sell as much coffee as most competitors, but by staying within the premium sector it remains one of *Nestlé's* most profitable brands.

Promotion

Promotion, the next marketing mix instrument, focuses on the different ways a company communicates with its audience. *Nestlé*, in this case, uses different methods to do so. As mentioned before, the basic brand layout for internationally sold brands usually remains identical for the different markets, but the package design and some advertising ideas are unique to smaller regions. A combination of globally run campaigns and regional advertisements is therefore used in most markets.

In this vein, *Nestlé* has also engaged in new forms of advertising. One of the more recent campaigns was based on cooperation between *KitKat* and *Google*. To promote both the new version of *Google's* operating system "*Android*" and *Nestlé's* chocolate bar, they joined forces on a global scale. By naming the newest *Android* version "*KitKat*" and thus generating a worldwide media buzz, both companies generated enormous attention for their brands (Marketo 2014).

Nestlé was particularly able to boost their appearances in social media platforms such as *Facebook* and *Google+*. With over one billion *Android* activations worldwide and an *Android*-shaped *KitKat* chocolate bar, both companies invested heavily in the campaign's success. As part of this global campaign, *KitKat* also released a special version of their bars in the shape of the world famous *Android* logo. Furthermore, *Google* implemented logos of *KitKat* in their software. Therefore, users all over the world were targeted through this campaign.

Global Campaign with Android

A very different marketing approach was applied in Japan, where a local campaign was also quite successful. In Japanese, "*KitKat*" can be translated to "surely win", a fact that *Nestlé* very cleverly used in their promotion strategy. In cooperation with the local postal service they prepared "*Kit Kat Mail*", a chocolate bar looking like a postcard that customers could send as a good-luck charm (Madden 2010). To launch this idea, *Nestlé* also decorated several post offices in a special *KitKat* design. Similar combinations of local and global promotion strategies can be found in numerous cases across very different *Nestlé* brands.

Local Campaigns for Selected Markets

Nespresso Magazine

Figure 21.7

Source: Nespresso 2014.

Another global example is *Nespresso*. An exclusive *Nespresso Club* with over seven million members is an important part of this brand's communication success (Matzler et al. 2013, p. 36). A lot of communication is done via TV spots, which are only translated into the requested language. Furthermore, *nespresso.com* is available in over 10 different languages to cover over 60 different countries. Therefore, the same look and feel of this product can be experienced in all those markets.

In addition to the TV spots and the website, a regularly issued magazine is sent out to the members of *Nespresso Club* and can be downloaded to tablets and smartphones. Through these magazines the reader gets additional information about new products. Stories that feature lifestyle ideas surrounding the *Nespresso* look and feel are used to further enhance the exclusivity of the product itself.

Place

Being one of the biggest suppliers of nutrition worldwide and thereby selling products consumed by customers on a daily basis, most *Nestlé* brands can be found all over the world in grocery stores, food markets and other similar places. This is a typical approach for global brands like *KitKat, Maggi* and similar brands and products.

As part of their PPP strategy, which tries to reach only lower income customers, *Nestlé* implemented a unique distribution network. By using street markets, vendors and door-to-door distribution, they are able to reach these additional customers.

Exclusive Products at Exclusive Places

A rather atypical example for *Nestlé* can be found in *Nespresso*. *Nespresso* boutiques are being built all over the world. Combined with the numerous languages covered by the official *Nespresso* website, almost every major market has already been entered. The key to the brand's success lies in *Nestlé's* exclusive distribution channels. By selling coffee capsules almost exclusively through their own stores, *Nestlé* has absolute control. To attract new customers they do, however, allow their coffee machines to be sold in other locations (Datamonitor 2007).

Summary and Outlook

Building on its already overwhelming worldwide success, *Nestlé* is further planning on expanding its business. In this vein, with a huge 1 billion USD investment in new infant nutrition factories in Mexico, they are underlining their efforts to further push their original product lines all over the world (WSJ 2014).

Nestlé relies on strong brands and a perfect strategy to remain flexible enough to cater to any customer's demands. With their combination of globally thinking brands and locally acting products they are already very successful, with both a respectable market share and high profits.

A further approach that *Nestlé* focuses on is its attempts to gain additional market power in premium sectors. Being a company that usually focuses on economies of scale and high market shares, they are yet to widely succeed with truly high-class products. However, they have tested potential in that area that is less sensitive to the economic decline of recent years through customised treats from their Swiss brand *"Cailler"* (Bloomberg 2012b).

Questions

1. Identify the strengths of *Nestlé's* "glocal" marketing approach.

2. Discuss the advantages of *Nestlé's* combination of local and global brands in its international brand portfolio.

3. Which pricing strategies are best suited to *Nestlé's* global brands? Which are most suitable for their local brands?

4. Nestlé has been subject to several negative campaigns (so-called *"shitstorms"*) that highlighted unethical behaviour by the company. What strategy did the company apply to deal with these campaigns? Do you think the brand was harmed?

Hints

1. See the company's websites.

2. See Onkvist/Shaw 2004.

3. See WSJ 2014.

References

ALIMENTA (2014): Nestlé eröffnet erste KitKat Boutique, http://www.alimentaonline.ch/News/NewsDetail/tabid/124/Article/133189/Default.aspx., accessed on May 12, 2014.

BLOOMBERG (2012): Nestlé Bites into Chocolate's $8 Billion Premium Market: Retail, http://www.bloomberg.com/news/2012-02-12/nestle-bites-into-chocolate-s-8-billion-premium-market-retail.html, accessed on May 13, 2014.

CAVUSGIL, S.T.; KNIGHT, G.; RIESENBERGER, J.R. (2014): International Business: The New Realities, 3rd ed., Boston, Pearson.

CZINKOTA, M.; RONKAINEN, I. (2003): An International Marketing Manifesto, in: Journal of International Marketing, Vol. 11, No. 1, pp. 13-27.

CZINKOTA, M.; RONKAINEN, I. (2013): International Marketing, 10th ed., Hampshire, Cengage Learning.

DATAMONITOR (2007): Nespresso Case Study, Lifestyle Branding in Coffee, http://www.datamonitor.com, accessed on June 10, 2014.

DOOLE, I.; LOWE, R. (2012): International Marketing Strategy, 6th ed., Hampshire, Cengage Learning.

HOLLENSEN, S. (2014): Global Marketing, 6th ed., Harlow, Pearson.

KOTABE, M.; HELSEN, K. (2014): Global Marketing Management, 6th ed., New York, Wiley & Sons.

LEVITT, T. (1983): The Globalization of Markets, in: Harvard Business Review, Vol. 61, No. 3, pp. 92-102.

MADDEN, N. (2010): Soy-Sauce-Flavored Kit Kats? In Japan, They're No. 1, http://adage.com/print/142461, accessed on June 10, 2014.

MARKETO (2014): Google Android and Nestle KitKat: The Ultimate Co-Branding Marketing Takeaways, http://blog.marketo.com/2013/11/ google-android-and-nestle-kitkat-the-ultimate-co-branding-marketing-take-aways.html., accessed on August 29, 2014.

MATZLER, K.; BAILOM, F.; VON DEN EICHEN, S.F.; KOHLER, T. (2013): Business model innovation: coffee triumphs for Nespresso, in: Journal of Business Strategy, Vol. 34, No. 2, pp. 30-37.

MÜHLBACHER; LEIHS; DAHRINGER (2006): International Marketing: A Global Perspective, 3rd ed., London, Thomson Learning.

NESPRESSO (2014): Your Free Digital Nespresso Magazine, http://www.nespresso.com, accessed on August 29, 2014.

ONKVISIT, S.; SHAW, J. (2004): International Marketing: Analysis and Strategy, 4th ed., London, Routledge.

QUELCH, J. (1999): Global Brands: Taking Stock, in: Business Strategy Review, Vol. 10, No.1, pp. 1-14.

REGENASS, R. (2012): Dok-Film übt massiv Kritik an Nestlé, http://www.tagesanzeiger.ch/wirtschaft/unternehmen-und-konjunktur/ Dokufilm-uebt-massiv-Kritik-an-Nestle/story/31103319, accessed on August 29, 2014.

SHOHAM, A.; ROSE, G.; ALBAUM, G. (1995): Export Motives, Psychologic Distance, and the EPRG Framework, in: Journal of Global Marketing, Vol. 8, No. 3-4, pp. 9-37.

SOLBERG, C.A. (2002): The Perennial Issue of Adaptation or Standardization of International Marketing Communication: Organizational Contingencies and Performance, in: Journal of International Marketing, Vol. 10, No. 3, pp. 1-21.

SOLBERG, C.A.; STÖTTINGER, B.; YAPRAK, A. (2006): A Taxonomy of the Pricing Practices of Exporting Firms: Evidence from Austria, Norway, and the United States, in: Journal of International Marketing, Vol. 14, No. 1, pp. 23-48.

WSJ (2014): PepsiCo, Nestlé to Invest in Mexico, http://online.wsj.com/news/articles 0, accessed on August 29, 2014.

ZENTES, J.; SWOBODA, B.; SCHRAMM-KLEIN, H. (2013): Internationales Marketing, 3rd ed., Munich, Vahlen.

Part VI

Selected

International

Business Functions

Chapter 22

International Human Resource Management

Human resources are among the most critical success factors of International Management. Human Resource Management (HRM) for MNCs involves challenges that go far beyond those of purely domestic operations. For example, MNCs are faced with intercultural issues and needs to manage expatriate assignments. This Chapter explains the basic activities, models and particularities of international HRM.

Introduction

Human Resource Management (HRM) refers to those activities undertaken by a company to effectively acquire and utilise its personnel to achieve a firm's objectives. More specifically, it encompasses the process of recruiting, selecting, training, appraising and compensating employees (Dowling/Festing/Engle 2013, p. 2).

While in principle the tasks of international HRM (IHRM) are the same as in purely domestic companies, managing human resources in MNCs is much more *complex*. For instance, different cultural environments influence the effectiveness of management techniques in different countries. Furthermore, employees from one country, e.g. the MNC's home country, might be allocated to operations in another country, or *vice versa*. To analyse the complexity of IHRM, the model illustrated in Figure 22.1 considers three dimensions (Morgan 1986; Zentes/Swoboda/Morschett 2004, p. 857):

- The first dimension considers the *different activities* of IHRM (e.g. recruitment and selection).

- The second dimension considers the *regional aspect*, i.e., for which country the HRM is carried out. The usual distinction is between the home country, the host country and other countries, where the host country is the location of the specific foreign subsidiary that is focused on in a specific analysis (e.g. Spain when discussing the recruitment of employees for a Spanish subsidiary).

- The third dimension considers different *employee groups*. Here, the usual categorisation distinguishes employees from the home country (often called *parent-country nationals*), employees from the host country and employees from other countries (*third-country nationals*).

Dimensions of IHRM

Figure 22.1	*Dimensions of International Human Resource Management*

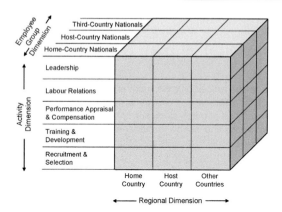

Source: Adapted from Morgan 1986, p. 44.

Increased Complexity of IHRM

The main difference between HRM for purely domestic companies and IHRM stems from the enhanced complexity (Dowling 1999, pp. 30-35; Zentes/Swoboda/Morschett 2004, p. 854):

Reasons for Increased Complexity

■ The *extent* of the activities of IHRM is broader. For instance, relocating employees to a foreign country has to be prepared and organised. Questions of international taxation have to be considered for compensation issues. MNCs have to provide certain administrative services to their employees abroad. Given the geographical dispersion of activities in an MNC, deployment, i.e., getting employees with the right qualifications to the geographic location where the company needs them, is a key challenge.

■ IHRM focuses on different and heterogeneous *groups of employees* with a different cultural background. Different national cultures affect employees' expectations and values and the effectiveness of different leadership styles.

■ *Norms* and *laws* strongly influence HRM in different countries. Regulations concerning labour rights, wages, participation of employees in company decisions, or terminating a labour contract, are strongly heterogeneous between different countries. Other external factors exert a strong influence as well.

- Central HRM decisions have an impact on employees from different nations. *Perceived fairness* and *equal treatment* of employees in different locations require an international perspective of HRM.

- IHRM is more strongly involved in employees' *private sphere*. For example, the families of employees are an important factor in the case of international assignments. They have to be considered in the selection process as well as in the administrative work in the host country.

- *Risks* and *costs* of IHRM are usually higher than for purely domestic operations. If candidates for international assignments are not optimally chosen, the financial and personal consequences are often more severe than in a purely domestic setting.

IHRM Activities

Recruitment and Selection

Recruitment refers to searching for and obtaining potential job candidates. *Selection* is the process of evaluating the candidates and deciding who should be employed for a particular job (Griffin/Pustay 2013, pp. 541-543). The first decision for IHRM is where employees for the various positions should come from. Taking the example of a French MNC with the need to fill an executive position in a subsidiary in Romania, there are three alternatives: a French national, a Romanian national or a manager from a third country. The general *staffing options*, thus, are:

- *Parent-country nationals* (or home-country nationals), in this case French employees, frequently have the advantage of knowing the MNC and the headquarters' strategies, values and procedures very well. They share a common national culture with the staff at the corporate headquarters and have been socialised into the corporate culture. They often have technical competence and experience in the specific function for which they are sent abroad. They facilitate communication between the foreign subsidiary and the corporate headquarters. They support the implementation of the corporate strategy in the host country. On the other hand, they usually do not know the host country very well and might have difficulties in adapting to the new environment. The procedures learned in the home country might not be efficient in the host country and cultural adjustment can be difficult. Furthermore, home-country nationals are a very expensive option since in addition to their usual salaries they receive substantial additional payments during their assignment abroad.

Parent-Country Nationals

Parent-country nationals are the typical case for *expatriates*, who are discussed in more detail later in this Chapter.

Host-Country Nationals

■ A second option is to employ a *host-country national*. In this case, a Romanian manager would be used to staff the position in the Romanian subsidiary. Host-country nationals have detailed market knowledge as well as local relations. They understand the culture of employees and of customers better and are capable of adapting the company's strategy to the specific requirements of a local market. However, in some host countries, candidates with adequate qualifications and experience might be hard to find. Also the reduced cultural conflicts in the host-country might be offset by an increased number of cultural conflicts between the subsidiary and the HQ.

Third-Country Nationals

■ As a third option, an MNC may also hire *third-country nationals*. In the above example, this could be a Hungarian manager who would be selected to work for the French MNC in the Romanian subsidiary. Reasons for this might be that the third-country national is expected to adapt faster to the new environment than a home-country national or that he has gathered experience in a certain function that is needed in the host-country. The MNC might have a pool of internationally experienced managers from different countries that are used to fill positions in its different subsidiaries regardless of nationality. Third-country nationals might also be a compromise for the costs of the assignment, since they still receive foreign service premiums and other additional payments but might have a lower base salary than a home-country national. The third-country national is a specific type of *expatriate*.

EPRG Staffing Philosophies

The use of these three different staffing options is related to the different *staffing philosophies* from the EPRG concept (see Chapter 2). For HRM, an *ethnocentric staffing model* considers parent-country nationals as the most adequate for higher-level positions in foreign countries, based on the assumption that home-country nationals are most effective in implementing corporate strategies in foreign locations and are better educated, trained and more competent. The *polycentric staffing model* emphasises the heterogeneity between different locations and, thus, prefers the use of host-country nationals. One disadvantage of this model, i.e. staffing each country with local managers, is that employees generally only have limited opportunities to gain international experience. In a *geocentric staffing model*, MNCs select the best person available, regardless of his/her nationality. However, even in this model, cultural aspects of adaptability should be considered when evaluating candidates. In a *regiocentric staffing model*, staffing is performed within each region, e.g., countries from Eastern Europe are staffed with managers from Eastern Europe but not necessarily the same country. The assumption is that adaptation within regions is easier than globally.

Part VI

In addition to the geographic aspect of recruitment, MNCs have to decide on the *source of candidates*: should they be internal or external to the company? The need to fill a position with an internal candidate is linked to promoting or relocating employees. Internal recruitment has several benefits which include relatively low cost and less time needed to introduce the candidate into the new position, existing general knowledge about the company and its strategy and pre-socialisation into the corporate culture. The MNC can evaluate the abilities and personality of the candidate very well. In addition, the selection of an internal candidate is often part of a long-term career planning and *personnel development strategy*. It usually increases motivation and employee loyalty if promotions and international assignments are used as rewards for high performance (Dessler 2008, p. 176). But the internal pool of candidates is limited and sometimes MNCs cannot find employees with the needed qualification among their current staff. In this and other cases, external sources are used. Job postings in newspapers, head-hunters, etc., are frequently employed to fill management positions in foreign subsidiaries but – compared with internal candidates – the identification of suitable candidates and their evaluation is a challenge. Studies show that *expatriates* are usually recruited from internal sources (Zentes/Swoboda/Morschett 2004, pp. 858-859). The main reason for selecting expatriates from within the MNC is that the main benefits of home-country nationals (e.g. knowledge of the company culture and strategy) are more likely to apply if internal candidates are chosen.

As *selection criteria* for a position in an MNC, in particular in a foreign subsidiary, it has to be noted that a candidate must have two sets of competences (Griffin/Pustay 2013, pp. 543-544): The skills and abilities necessary *to do the job* (i.e. functional, technical and managerial skills) and the skills and abilities necessary *to work in a foreign location* and/or with employees from different countries. This includes adaptability to new situations, location-specific skills (most notably the language of the host country) and personal characteristics such as cultural sensitivity, self-reliance, motivation to work abroad, stable family situation, etc.

Training and Development

Each of an MNC's employees must be provided with *training*, i.e. instruction in specific job-related skills and abilities, and *development*, a more general education concerned with preparing employees for new assignments and/or higher-level positions. More generally, when considering employees and their capabilities as a critical part of the resources of a company, training and development are part of how MNCs enhance their stock of human capital (Dowling/Festing/Engle 2013, p. 175).

Approaches to
Intercultural
Training

In MNCs, employees must learn more than purely technical or managerial skills. Employees must be prepared for the particularities of an international assignment or for working with colleagues with different nationalities. Given the high cost and risk of an international assignment, sufficient pre-departure *intercultural training* is crucial for success. This aims at ensuring that the manager understands the host-country culture and can behave accordingly. The chosen *training methods* depend, among other factors, on the duration of the foreign assignment (Zentes/Swoboda/Morschett 2004, pp. 871-875; Dowling/Festing/Engle 2013, pp. 175-177). For short-term stays abroad (i.e. a month or less), short training programmes are sufficient. In the *information giving approach*, providing information to the manager is the priority and area briefings and cultural briefings, via lectures, videos, books or interactive media, are the appropriate measures. For longer assignments, interaction with the foreign culture will be common. Thus, in addition to information-giving, the *affective approach* focuses on transmitting the necessary sensitivity to the foreign culture, e.g., via culture-assimilation training in which the participants are exposed to the kind of intercultural interactions that they are likely to encounter in the host country. If the employee is to stay for more than a year in a culturally very different host country, the training period should ideally be at least one month. Systematic sensitivity training, field experiences and intercultural experiential workshops might be appropriate as a type of *immersion approach*. Also, preliminary visits to the host country (with family) can help to facilitate adjustment to the new environment.

Management
Development

Another aspect of training and development is that the international assignment also develops the international skills of specific managers. As part of management development, individuals gain international experience, establish a better cultural awareness and become better connected with the diverse organisational units of the MNC (Dowling/Festing/Engle 2013, pp. 186-187). With increasing globalisation of companies, and in particular in transnational organisations, this type of *management development* is not only offered to home-country nationals, but increasingly to managers from other locations. There are an increasing number of *inpatriates*, i.e., employees from other countries that work in corporate headquarters for a period of time to develop their skills, become socialised into the corporate culture and develop informal relationships within the organisation. Eventually, these managers are relocated to the host-country and combine some of the advantages of expatriates (in particular the close knowledge of the corporate strategy and culture) with the advantages of host-country nationals (in particular the close knowledge of the host country including cultural awareness).

Career
Paths

These career paths also increase the options in the HR selection process. As well as the factors mentioned above – nationality of the candidate and internal or external recruitment – previous experience (within or outside the company) is obviously considered in the evaluation. If, for example, the position as managing director of a foreign subsidiary needs to be filled, the MNC can choose between a host-country national who has always worked in this host country, or a parent country national who has only worked in the home country before. But there is also the option to select a host country candidate who has been working as an inpatriate in headquarters for a few years (combining country knowledge with familiarity with the corporate headquarters culture), or a home country manager who has previously occupied mid-level positions in the host country or in third countries and thus has previous international experience in combination with home country familiarity. Other combinations of international experience and company experience are possible; thus, the combinations for adequate career paths are manifold.

Performance Appraisal and Compensation

Another IHRM activity involves the evaluation of employee performance as well as determining their compensation. The main purposes of *performance measurement* are coordination (since linking incentives to certain performance measures will lead the manager to put more effort into improving these performance measures), feedback on performance and rewarding certain performance.

An early decision is the level of uniformity in the MNC's performance appraisal systems across different countries (Zentes/Swoboda/Morschett 2004, p. 885). Should the performance appraisal follow a *global model*, with a standardised approach worldwide, or a *multinational model*, with performance measurement and appraisal being tailored to the country-specific context? As will be discussed in more detail in Chapter 23, it might be difficult to compare the performance of managers across countries. External factors (e.g. different market growth) or a subsidiary's specific situation (e.g. age or size) influence a subsidiary's results and render attributing certain outcome measures, like sales growth, to the manager's performance difficult. Thus, setting the same objectives for each manager might not adequately evaluate their performance.

Global or Multinational Model

In addition, different subsidiaries have different roles and different tasks to fulfil (see Chapter 3). Thus, using the same performance indicators for each subsidiary might not adequately support these specific objectives. On the other hand, incentive systems are an important component in developing a strong corporate culture. If the same performance indicators are measured worldwide, coherence within the MNC will improve. Different motivational structures in different countries that might otherwise lead to divergence in the MNC can be partially overcome through common incentive systems. Furthermore, breaking down the corporation's overall objectives into individual performance goals is more consistent with a standardised approach. Eventually, the complexity of customised performance appraisal systems might exceed their benefits.

Elements of Expatriate Compensation

A second aspect of compensation in MNCs is the compensation of expatriates. Here, the typical *compensation scheme* consists of several elements (Rugman/Collinson 2012, pp. 441-444):

- *Base salary.*

- *Cost-of-living allowance,* which is intended to compensate for differences in the cost of living between the home country and the foreign location. International organisations, statistical offices and consulting companies provide information on the cost of living in different locations. To maintain the manager's standard of living, the MNC will usually adjust their base salary to offset this difference. In addition, relocation costs, enhanced rental expenses, medical care, private schools for the manager's children, additional costs to travel to the home country, membership of a country club or a golf club, etc., may be compensated.

- A *foreign service premium* to induce the manager to accept the international assignment. In particular, this payment – which is also called a *hardship premium* – is necessary in the case of unattractive assignments. For instance, accepting a position in Mozambique, Bangladesh, or the rural areas of India or China may often be rewarded with up to an additional 40% on base salary.

- Finally, different tax regimes and the absence of tax agreements, potentially doubling the taxation on the manager's income, might make *tax equalisation* necessary. Here, the objective is to ensure that the expatriate's *after-tax income* allows a similar standard of living as in the home country.

Overall, costs for an expatriate are often twice as high as for a local manager. Expatriates often earn substantially more than their local colleagues. This may lead to *perceived unfairness*. Because expatriates often originate from the MNC's home country, host-country nationals might see this as an expression of an ethnocentric attitude by the MNC.

Labour Relations

Relations with workers, in particular with organised labour, have to be managed. This is part of IHRM, but sometimes manages from a separate department. Different countries have highly diverse legislation concerning employees' rights. For instance, in many European countries, workers play an active role in companies' decisions. As part of *industrial democracy*, employees have the right to influence a company's management. In Germany, firms above a certain size have to establish a supervisory board (similar to the board of directors of a US company) and half of the members are appointed by the workforce, known as *co-determination*. While this model is the most extreme in industrial democracy, other countries like the Scandinavian states, the Netherlands or Austria, use similar models (Rugman/Collinson 2012, pp. 444-449). In many cases, *trade unions* have a tremendous influence in industrial democracy, which is traditionally guaranteed by legislation.

Another aspect of labour relations includes *collective bargaining*, where agreements between labour unions and the management are negotiated. Often, an umbrella agreement for an entire industry, e.g. on wages, is the result (Griffin/Pustay 2013, pp. 559-560). In addition, trade unions or other labour representatives might influence MNCs' strategic choices by constraining their ability to vary employment levels in different countries and by imposing barriers to the integration of MNCs' operations. For example, plant closures and production relocation are heavily influenced by trade unions – both directly and indirectly via their influence on local governments (Dowling/Festing/Engle 2013, pp. 246-248). To manage labour relations, most MNCs follow a mixed approach with some *level of centralisation* and some *level of decentralised negotiations* via subsidiary managers.

Collective Bargaining

Leadership

Leading employees is another facet of IHRM. Here, as has been discussed in Chapter 9, heterogeneity between different country cultures exerts a strong influence on effective and efficient management. For example, work ethics, job satisfaction, intrinsic motivation, etc., are all related to culture. As the cultural models by *Hofstede* and *GLOBE* reveal, work-related cultural traits are widely divergent between countries. Research has consistently shown that no single leadership style works equally well in all situations, e.g., because the *motivation* in different cultures depends on different features. This *contingency perspective* advocates adapting leadership styles at least partially to the host country. For instance, in countries with high individualism, employees are more strongly motivated by *individual incentives* than by incentives linked to group performance. In countries with high acceptance of power distance, clear *hierarchical orders* are accepted and expected from a superior while the same behaviour might cause frustration in countries with low power distance. Conversely, employees in countries with low individualism might strongly favour *teamwork* and an atmosphere in which *interaction* with their colleagues is promoted. In countries with strong uncertainty avoidance, employees might be better motivated by secure jobs and long-

Cultural Influence on Effectiveness of Leadership Styles

term employment than by high salaries. A *participative leadership style* is preferred in some countries (e.g. the USA, the Netherlands, or the UK) while a *hierarchical leadership style* is preferred by employees in others (e.g. Arab countries, Greece, South America). In general, the lower the perceived discrepancy between the expected leadership style and the actual leadership style, the higher the motivation, performance and satisfaction of employees (see Zentes/Swoboda/Morschett 2004, p. 890). These few examples serve to illustrate that, from the perspective of motivational power, tailoring the leadership style to the host country may be beneficial. But, as a counter argument, the unity of the MNC has to be considered and a coherent leadership style across the MNC is one of the strongest determinants of a uniform corporate culture across all subsidiaries.

International Assignments

Reasons to Deploy Expatriates

There are many reasons to deploy expatriates to a foreign subsidiary various (Miller 1989; Zentes/Swoboda/Morschett 2004, pp. 877-878; Dowling/Festing/Engle 2013, pp. 116-117; Griffin/Pustay 2013, p. 541):

■ Supporting the subsidiary operations by *filling a position* with a competent candidate that might not be available among current host country staff.

■ *Coordinating* the MNC: Expatriates are often the *linchpins* between the HQ and the subsidiary. They help to implement the corporate strategy in the host country. They are a means of coordination by *direct supervision* and help to transfer the corporate culture from the HQ to the subsidiary and, upon their return, *vice versa*. *Informal relations* are established between the expatriate and host country employees.

■ *Knowledge transfer*: Expatriates are a knowledge transfer mechanism, particularly for tacit knowledge. They give knowledge that they have gained via personal experience in the HQ to their colleagues and subordinates in the foreign subsidiary. When returning to the home country, they transfer knowledge that they have gathered in the subsidiary back to the HQ.

■ Expatriate assignments can be an important *incentive* in the *career path* of executives. In this case expatriates are selected for *management development* and as a reward for high performance. The expatriate enhances his managerial skills, learns how to lead people from different cultural backgrounds, develops a tolerance for ambiguity and learns to accept different perspectives.

Phases in Expatriate Assignments

After the candidate has been selected for an international assignment and been send abroad, the expatriate has to adjust to the new environment to work effectively. Research has shown that *cultural adjustment* of expatriates to the host country typically proceeds through four different phases (see Figure 22.2) (Hofstede 2001; Dowling/Festing/Engle 2013, pp. 130-131):

Phases in Cultural Adjustment   *Figure 22.2*

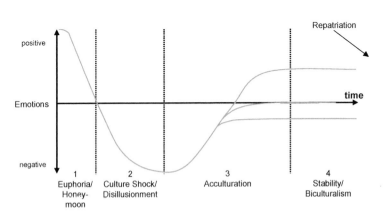

Source: Adapted from Hofstede 2001, p. 259; Griffin/Pustay 2013, p. 547.

■ In the first stage, the *honeymoon phase*, the excitement of working in the new environment is high. The manager sees the new culture as exotic and stimulating and underestimates the challenges of adjusting. This stage usually lasts a few weeks or months.

■ In the second stage, many expatriates become disillusioned and the differences between the old and the new environment are perceived in a magnified perspective. The challenges of everyday living become apparent for the expatriate and his family. A *culture shock* occurs, which may lead to feelings of disorientation, helplessness and self-doubt. Adequate pre-departure training and careful consideration of personal characteristics of potential expatriates mitigate this phase. However, expatriates may remain stuck in this phase and it is here that a premature termination of the assignment is most likely.

■ After a certain critical point, the expatriate often overcomes the problems and *acculturation* to the new environment can be observed. The employee begins to understand the patterns of the new culture, improves his language competence and adjusts to everyday living. However, this improvement might not be sufficient and various outcomes to this stage are possible (see Figure 22.2).

■ In the fourth phase, the situation stabilises and the employee adapts to the new culture. Anxiety has ended and confidence in a successful assignment is gained. The expatriate might even develop a *bicultural perspective*. In this phase, he or she might even prefer some of the environmental influences of the host country over the situation in the home country.

Repatriation | The average expatriate stays three to five years on an international assignment before returning to the home country. Reasons for *repatriation* are also manifold. Ideally, an expatriate is repatriated after the predetermined assignment period is completed. Other reasons include the expatriate's dissatisfaction with the situation abroad, poor performance, an HQ decision that considers the expatriate too expensive for the specific position or an open position at the HQ or somewhere else that needs to be filled (Rugman/Collinson 2012, p. 436). In addition, it has been shown that the inability of an expatriate's spouse to adapt to the foreign culture as well as other family related factors are among the major reasons for *expatriate failure*, indicating the importance of including employees' families in an MNC's considerations (Hill 2013, p. 480).

Reverse Culture Shock | In any case, an expatriate assignment is only successful if it ends with successful *repatriation*, and MNCs should therefore pay as much attention to *repatriation* as to *expatriation*. If managers and their families have been successfully expatriated, they become comfortable with living and working in the foreign culture. Returning home can be almost as challenging as the original relocation abroad. A *reverse culture shock* might occur for many reasons (Rugman/Collinson 2012, p. 436). The home office job often lacks the high degree of authority and responsibility the expatriate enjoyed in the overseas job. Sometimes, the employee might feel that the company does not value international experience. Frequently, employees may no longer be well connected to people at the HQ and often, their old job may have been eliminated or drastically changed. In terms of their long-term career, an adequate position might not be available at the time of re-entry. Their overall financial situation might worsen.

Given the high cost and relevance of expatriates, MNCs must attempt to minimise the potential effects of reverse culture shock because otherwise the management development related to the expatriate assignment is not successfully completed and in the long run fewer managers will be willing to take international assignments. In this regard, adequate *career planning* for the time after expatriation is a prerequisite for long-term success (Rugman/Collinson 2012, pp. 436-437).

Conclusion and Outlook

Considering the complex challenges of International Management and the dual requirements of local responsiveness and global integration, the employees of the MNC – non-managers and managers – are crucial to developing and implementing effective and efficient international strategies. Locally customised HRM practices and performance measures reflect the *differentiated network*; however, the increasing necessity of normative integration within the MNC produces in unifying approaches.

As a basic trend, the number of ethnocentrically oriented companies is permanently decreasing and the enhanced relevance of foreign subsidiaries – in terms of percentage of sales or their contribution to MNC strategy – is accompanied by an enhanced relevance of managers from foreign countries. Thus, MNCs are developing more competence within their subsidiaries. Management development is not only relevant for home-country nationals but increasingly for managers, regardless of their nationality. *Expatriates* and *inpatriates* have become a common phenomenon.

Due to the increased relevance of foreign markets for the sustainable competitiveness of MNCs, top management is increasingly composed of executives from different nations to incorporate multiple perspectives in strategic decisions. MNCs like *Nestlé, ABB* or *Unilever* all have top management in which home country nationals are the minority. Even in the case of home country nationals, the typical career path of top managers in MNCs includes long assignments abroad, usually in different foreign locations. This way, either as parent country national or as third country national, executives of MNCs are increasingly socialised and developed in different parts of the world and learn to accept, understand and exploit international diversity.

Internationalisation of Top Management

Further Reading

DOWLING, P.; FESTING, M.; ENGLE, A. (2013): International Human Resource Management, 6th ed., London, Cengage Learning Services.

Case Study: Google[*]

Profile, History and Status Quo

Google Inc. is an MNC of American origin. It is a global technology company that builds products and provides services to organise information. It is the biggest search engine in the world, handling over 70% of global online search requests (Britannica 2014). *Google's* main focus is around key areas such as search, operating systems and platforms, advertising and hardware products. As of May 2014, *Google* is divided into two segments: *Google* (which consists of an advertising and non-advertising business) and *Motorola Mobile* (which comprises the company's mobile devices business), which was acquired in 2012. However, the company has already announced in January 2014 that it will sell *Motorola Mobile* to *Lenovo*. However, *Google* will keep *Motorola's* Advanced Technologies & Projects unit and most of the patents it acquired in the deal, presumably the most valuable part of the acquisition. *Google's* main source of income is online advertising (Reuters 2014).

Google's headquarters are based in Mountain View, California. The company has offices in over 40 countries worldwide. *Google* had more than 47,700 employees in 2013. It offers more than 50 products and Internet services (see Table 22.1 for examples). Its wide selection of products and services places the company among the top four most influential high tech companies, together with *Apple*, *IBM*, and *Microsoft*.

History

Google was co-founded by two Ph.D. students, Larry Page and Sergey Brin. The *google.com* domain was registered in 1997, and a year later, Page and Brin filed for incorporation in California. The name *Google* is a play on the word "googol", a mathematical term for the number represented by a 1 followed by 100 zeroes. The name reflects the mission to organise the nearly infinite amount of information on the web. As with many innovative companies, *Google's* first workspace was set up in a garage. Just two years after the company registered its domain, its first press release announced that *Google* had received 25 million USD in equity funding. *Google* at that time was processing as many as 500,000 queries per day; by 2004 this had increased to 200 million per day and in 2011 it reached 3 billion per day. By 2006, the term *Google* was so popular that it was added as a verb to the Oxford English Dictionary and is defined as *"to search for information about (someone or something) on the Internet using the search engine Google"* (Oxford Dictionaries 2014).

---

[*] Sources used for this case study include the corporate websites (mainly http://www.google.com), various annual and interim reports, investor-relations presentations and explicitly cited sources.

By 2000, *Google* was already available in 15 language versions (as of 2014 there are more than 150 languages available). The first international office in Tokyo, Japan, was opened in 2001. In 2004, the popular e-mail account known as *Gmail* was launched. At that time it was only available on invite basis, but it enjoys more than 425 million users. *Google* became a public company in 2004, and in 2006 it bought the *Youtube* online video service. In 2007, *Fortune* named *Google* the No. 1 Best Company to Work For.

Selected Products and Services of Google   *Table 22.1*

Google Search	YouTube	Google Maps
Gmail	Google News	Google Places
Google Chrome	Google Scholar	Google AdWords
Google Calendar	Google Translate	Google Code
Google+	Google Wallet	Google Insights for Search
Google Groups	Google Glass	Google Docs
Google Play (Store)	Google Nexus	Google Chromecast

Source: Google 2014.

Google has a simple yet very ambitious mission statement, which is *"to organise the world's information and make it universally accessible and useful"*. The company is also well known for its corporate philosophies, including *"don't be evil"*. In the words of Larry Page (the co-founder of *Google*): *"don't be evil, [...] is to do the best things we know how for our users, for our customers, for everyone. So I think if we were known for that, it would be a wonderful thing"* (Farfan 2014).

Mission and Vision

Human Resource Management - People Operations at Google

Find Them, Grow Them, Keep Them

Google's HR department is unique and innovative (and claims to re-invent the field of HR). It is referred to as People Operations (POPS), to distinguish it from administrative functions. POPS consists of HR professionals, former consultants and analysts. The department takes a data-driven approach. At *Google* HR treated more like scientific work rather than the traditional HR. Everything can be measured. *"Data is central to everything we do — even when we choose a paint color for a conference room wall or plan a lunch menu. Laszlo*

People Operations

Bock, SVP of People Operations, and David Radcliffe, VP of Real Estate and Work-place Services, explain our data-centric approach to creating work environments that help Googlers live longer, healthier and more productive lives" (Google 2014).

POPS focuses on finding the world's most innovative people, creating training programmes and ensuring that employees are satisfied with their work. *Google* is very international and it prides itself on diversity and inclusion. It aspires to be a *"workplace that works for everyone, in every country, and in every culture in which [it] operates"* (Google 2014). The main activities at POPS are divided into three broad areas which can be summarised in the phrase: *Find them, keep them, grow them*. *"Find them"* deals with recruiting and hiring practices at *Google*. The main objective is to find people who have a lifelong dedication to learning, inquisitive minds, are passionate about their work and are open to evolution and change. *"Grow them"* deals with training and other activities, which create and preserve the best in their employees (employees are referred to as *Googlers* by the company). Lastly, *"keep them"* deals with Googlers' commitment, satisfaction and retention (Albert 2013).

Find Them

Google is very international and has offices around the world. They take a geocentric approach to hiring staff (finding the best talent is crucial). A closer look, however, reveals that top management positions (such as managing director) in many country locations are held by host-country nationals (e.g. in the United Kingdom, Poland and the United States).

The primary objective of POPS is to hire the right people. The work changes frequently and so do the requirements – few Googlers do what they were originally hired for. The potential Googler must be good at many things, be passionate about the challenges and be open to major changes. *Google* hires people who are competent in the long term, not just the current time, and a so-called "Noogler" (this is what *Google* calls new hires) should be *"someone who's good for the role, good for Google and good at lots of things"* (Google 2014).

Attracting Diverse Talent at Different Locations

Google understands that looking for the best talent is not restricted to age, gender, nationality or even to individual experience, but stems from diversity and individuals' abilities. Hence, it is important for *Google* to support *diversity of norms* throughout its offices worldwide and to embrace the local expressions of each location, ensuring there are differences between offices and employees across countries. For example, in *Google's* global headquarters (also known as the *Googleplex*) in Mountain View, USA, the company implemented its garage roots into the metal, wood, welding and electronics workshops. In this location the main focus is on changing the world at *Google*. In Dublin, Ireland (the European headquarters), the company included the culture of the city in its four modern buildings, including music rooms and kitchens which look like a traditional Irish pub. The walls have pictures of Irish folklore, street art graffiti and panoramic photos. The complex also has a Father Ted themed cafeteria (Father Ted is a popular sitcom set in Ireland). *Google Ireland* employs Googlers from 65 countries. In this location – which serves customers not only in Ireland but across Europe, the Middle East and Africa – a special emphasis is put on recruitment and selection of individuals who speak diverse languages; for example individuals who can speak Swedish, Danish or Finnish are currently in high demand in the Irish *Google* office. In Tokyo, Japan, the interior has traditional Japanese design components. The cafeteria offers local specialities and tatami-style seating (in order to eat, the Googlers must take off their shoes) and the subsidiary mainly seeks Googlers with diverse backgrounds. Zurich, Switzerland, has a different colour theme on every floor and one of the unique features is the old-style gondola ski lifts, where Googlers can find some privacy. The office is extremely diverse as it brings together 75 nationalities. One of *Google Switzerland*'s integration activities, as is typical for *Google* around the world, is to hold TGIF (Thank God it's Friday) meetings in a very informal way to discuss all relevant issues with all employees. In Zurich, each meeting has a theme based on a different European, Middle Eastern or African country.

Moreover, *Google* ensures that it is an attractive location to work and that it not only contributes to philanthropic activities worldwide but in the particular locations where it operates. For example, in the United States the company highlights the fact that it participates in beach clean ups and helps out local schools; in Ireland, the company promotes the Age Engage programme, in which Googlers create digital awareness among older people; in Poland Googlers donate time to painting schools, planting community gardens and cleaning neighbourhood playgrounds; in Japan, after the earthquake of 2011, the company created and implemented *Person Finder* within two hours; in China it offered financial support for Sichuan, which suffered an earthquake in 2005; in Switzerland Googlers volunteer to work at pet shelters, etc.

Attracting Local Talent by Helping Local Communities

Google looks for its employees not only from outside of the organisation but also from within. For example, when *Google* wanted to introduce a new vertical market based structure in Europe in order to attract more business advertisers, the company internally promoted Jeff Levick (originating from the American office) from its financial services group to vertical markets director for Europe. The promotion was tantamount to a relocation requirement to the United Kingdom, where Levick was responsible for implementing a vertical management structure similar to the US structure (Econsultancy 2005).

Selection Process

The way *Google* hires its employees had to change, as within a few years the numbers of new hires increased dramatically across the world. In the original hiring process the candidate had to go through as many as 25 interviews, and the entire hiring process could take between 6 and 12 months (Levy 2011). This process not only slowed down the hiring but also harmed *Google*'s reputation among candidates. Hence, a change was necessary. A study was conducted by *Google*'s staffing director Todd Carlisle, who investigated the optimal number of interviews a candidate should go through. The answer was four. Nowadays, the hiring process consists of few steps; usually it starts with a conversation with a recruiter, a phone interview, followed by an onsite interview at one of *Google*'s offices. The hiring decisions are made by the group, as opposed to individuals (which avoids opportunistic behaviour by managers). In 2011, the hiring time was drastically decreased and ranged from between 40 and 60 days (from beginning till the end). In that year, over 75,000 job applications were submitted in a single week, resulting in the hiring of 8,000 Googlers (Levy 2011; Womack 2011; Walker 2012; Sullivan 2013). This enormous amount of applications is a result of *Google*'s strong appeal for highly qualified candidates. In fact, in 2014, *Google* is seen by students across Europe (and, as other studies show, the world) as the most attractive employer for business students and among the top by engineering students (see Table 22.2). In a survey by another organisation carried out in 2014 in Switzerland, *Google* is listed as the No. 1 favourite employer for both business and engineering students (Steinhoff 2014, pp. 24-25.).

Table 22.2 | *Europe's Most Attractive Employers in 2014*

Rank	Business Ranking	Engineering Ranking
1	**Google**	Siemens
2	L'Oréal Group	IBM
3	PwC (PriceWaterhouseCoopers)	BMW Group
4	EY (Ernst & Young)	**Google**
5	Microsoft	Microsoft
6	McKinsey & Company	Nestlé
7	Unilever	General Electric
8	KPMG	Bosch
9	Procter & Gamble	Daimler Mercedes-Benz
10	The Boston Consulting Group	EADS (Airbus)

Source: Universum 2014.

Grow Them

It is essential for *Google* to develop employees so they can learn rapidly and stay innovative. To provide time for learning, *Google* utilizes a 70/20/10 time allocation model. 70% of time is spent on normal work tasks, 20% is for *"personal development that will ultimately benefit the company"* and 10% of work time is allowed for *"innovation, creativity and freedom to think"*. This leaves as much as 30% of an employee's time to his or her discretion (Sullivan 2007). At *Google* development is very important and so is the on-the-job learning. There are various types of training which can occur, e.g. new-hire mentors, "tech talks" or inspiring talks (Sullivan 2007).

70/20/10 Time Allocation Model

A particularly interesting type of training is so-called *Googler-to-Googler (g2g)*. The training programmes put 3,500 employees (most of them are volunteers who use the 20% of their personal development time to do so) from different departments into the role of teachers. The development programmes are not compulsory and are divided into different categories, e.g. for Nooglers (orientation programme), for early career Googlers (e.g. teamwork, presenting and receiving feedback), for mid-career Googlers (e.g. strategic thinking), etc. *Google*'s idea behind such training is firstly to ensure that a culture of learning is promoted by employees themselves rather than imposed on them. Second it puts employees into a teaching mindset (and lets them teach something they are passionate about). The content of the courses is reviewed by managers in order to ensure quality. The employees who take the courses assess the performance of their teacher, which comparable to the performance assessment of the professional teachers (Kessler 2013; Hughes 2014).

Googler-to-Googler Training Process

The topics for the courses come from learning and development, from employees themselves and from POPS. The course instructors are encouraged to think outside the box; for example, courses vary from engineering for non-engineers to body awareness and fire breathing. The g2g is offered personally or with the use of virtual tools such as *Google+* Hangout, which allows Googlers from diverse offices around the globe to be brought into a dynamic and interactive conversation. This ensures that training is available for all Googlers. As a result, 55% of the company's official classes are taught by in-house staff (Albert 2013; Hughes 2014).

Another particularly interesting training program, which aims to develop global mangers at *Google*, is very unusual to say the least. *Google* created an associate product managers (APMs) group, which consists of extraordinary students, hired for important positions, without job experience. *Google* sends the group on a trip around the world to enhance their cultural awareness. APMs visited such locations as a village in India (where many people had never heard of *Google*, and had neither Internet access nor computers);

Global Understanding and Expertise Training

Japan (where the group was familiarised with the local market, fellow Googlers and local customers); China (the group was faced with the realities of doing business in this country) and Israel (Steers/Sanchez-Runde/Nardon 2010, pp. 24-25).

Keep Them

Perks

Google aims to keep employees' passion and motivation high. They do so by making sure that employees' receive quick approval for their ideas (within days not months). Furthermore, *Google* also ensures that the benefits the employees obtain are very attractive (this is also part of the *find them* strategy). The average pay at *Google* is 107,000 USD (above the industry average). The company also offers a wide range of perks, for example the employees get free gourmet meals (3 times a day), receive purchase grants for hybrid cars, have five months of paid maternity leave, have a workout room, massage room and snack rooms with free snack foods, fruit and drinks as well as a laundry room and free on-site medical doctor. It is also important to note that, despite *Google*'s effort to standardise these perks and financial benefits, across all countries, it is not fully possible due to international taxation issues and international laws (Sullivan 2007; Hernandez 2013; Farfan 2014).

Furthermore, *Google* believes that in order to keep employee motivation high, the voice of all Googlers must be heard (including the newest employees). They hold weekly meetings (every Friday) where all the Googlers from across the company meet and get an opportunity to ask any questions they want. *Google* prides itself on its transparency. Employees also get an opportunity to work on a range of projects and can completely re-qualify if desired.

Motivation

The way Googlers are motivated varies slightly between countries, e.g. different famous guest speakers are invited to different locations. For example, in 2007 the headquarters in the USA welcomed such important public figures as Barack Obama (who at the time was presidential hopeful), who shared his innovative agenda and entered into a discussion with *Google*'s employees, or John McCain (another presidential hopeful in 2008 election) who spent a lot of time answering *Google* employees' questions. The London office was even visited by Queen Elizabeth II, where her Majesty launched the Royal Channel on *YouTube* (which belongs to *Google*) and uploaded her first video. Of course, the different offices are also visited by other famous people, for example Lady Gaga and David Beckham in Mountain View, USA. In Zurich, Swiss *Googlers* got an opportunity to host Alice Cooper (several conference rooms in the Swiss office are named after him), and for this occasion some employees dressed up like his stage persona and performed his songs on stage.

But despite all of *Google*'s efforts, the retention of talent in the company is rather low. This seems paradoxical because *Google* has regularly been rated as one of the best companies to work for. 84% of employees are satisfied with their work. POPS scientifically measures employee satisfaction and looks for ways in which it can be improved. Yet the median length of time that employees stay with the company at Mountain View California is only a little over a year (according to PayScale ranking). It is, however important to note that the number of employees at *Google* has risen drastically in recent years; between 2010 and 2013 the number increased from 24,400 to 43,862 (excluding *Google*'s employees at Motorola), meaning that many did not yet have the opportunity to serve a long tenure. Furthermore, *Google* mainly hires young people, who are described as generation Y. Generation Y is perceived as rather disloyal and young (the median age is just 29), hence they have not worked anywhere for long. Because *Google* only hires top talents, their employees are very attractive for other companies in this very competitive market. Hence, *Googles* employees are offered very attractive packages to join competing firms. Lastly, high turnover also comes with the territory for knowledge based industries (e.g. *Amazon's* medium tenure is one year and *Yahoo's* median tenure is only 2.4 years) (Bershidsky 2013; Hernandez 2013).

Summary and Outlook

Google is one of the best companies to work for. The company faces many challenges not only in attracting new employees but also in their retention. The fact that *Google* is a great place to work has been recognised not only in the United States but also across Europe and, for example, in Japan. The company promotes their employees as their *greatest asset* and attributes part of *Google*'s success to them. Different locations have different tasks, resulting in a different selection of employees. However, in most cases they come from a wide range of countries. In the hiring process POPS focuses on ensuring non-discrimination and emphasises individuals' abilities rather than experiences. Hence, *Google* aims to ensure the company has the best talent, which is equivalent to a diverse workforce.

Questions

1. What are the challenges *Google* faces in managing a globally diverse top talent workforce?

2. Can you recommend *Google* any strategies to ensure top talent retention worldwide?

3. What main international challenges faced by People Operations can you identify?

Hints

1. Look at websites dealing with management of top talent.

2. Check for websites dealing with the turnover rates of knowledge-based industries.

References

ALBERT, M. (2013): Growing Googlers, NYU SIG On-Site Practitioners June 2013 Event, http://www.astdny.memberlodge.org, accessed on May 20, 2014.

BERSHIDSKY, L. (2013): Why Are Google Employees So Disloyal?, http://www.bloombergview.com, accessed on May 20, 2014.

BRITANNICA (2014): Google Inc., http://www.britannica.com, accessed on May 20, 2014.

DESSLER, G. (2008): Human Resource Management, 11th ed., Upper Saddle River, New Jersey, Prentice Hall.

DOWLING, P. (1999): Completing the Puzzle: Issues in the Development of the Field of International Human Resource Management, in: Management International Review, Vol. 39, No. 3, pp. 27-43.

DOWLING, P.; FESTING, M.; ENGLE, A. (2013): International Human Resource Management, 6th ed., London, Cengage Learning Services.

ECONSULTANCY (2005): Google Brings Vertical Structure to Europe, https://econsultancy.com/nma-archive/30495-google-brings-vertical-structure-to-europe, accessed on May 20, 2014.

FARFAN, B. (2014): Google Profile - Mission Statement, History, Founders, Name, Culture & Quotes, http://retailindustry.about.com, accessed on July 16, 2014.

GOOGLE (2014): Google, http://www.google.com/about/, accessed on May 20, 2014.

GRIFFIN, R.; PUSTAY, M. (2013): International Business: A Managerial Perspective, 7th ed., Upper Saddle River, New Jersey, Pearson.

HERNANDEZ, B. (2013): Despite Employee Perks, Google Has High Turnover, http://www.nbcbayarea.com, accessed on May 20, 2014.

HILL, C.W.L. (2013): Global Business Today, 8th ed., Boston, McGraw-Hill.

HOFSTEDE, G. (2001): Lokales Denken, globales Handeln: Interkulturelle Zusammenarbeit und globales Management, 2nd ed., Munich, DTV-Beck.

HUGHES, S. (2014): Employee-to-Employee (E2E) Learning: Bring Google's g2g Program to Your Team, https://www.udemy.com/, accessed on May 20, 2014.

KESSLER, S. (2013): Here's a Google Perk any Company Can Imitate: Employee-to-Employee Learning, http://www.fastcompany.com, accessed on May 20, 2014.

LEVY, S. (2011): In the Plex: How Google Thinks, Works, and Shapes Our Lives, New York, Simon & Schuster.

MILLER, E. (1989): Auslandseinsatz, in: MACHARZINA, K.; WELGE, M. (Eds.): Handwörterbuch Export und Internationale Unternehmungen, Stuttgart, Schäffer-Poeschel, col. 73-83.

MORGAN, P. (1986): International Human Resource Management: Fact or Fiction?, in: Personnel Administrator, Vol. 31, No. 9, pp. 43-47.

OXFORD DICTIONARIES (2014): Google, http://www.oxforddictionaries.com, accessed on May 20, 2014.

REUTERS (2014): Profile Google Inc. (GOOG.O), http://www.reuters.com, accessed on July 10, 2014.

RUGMAN, A.M.; COLLINSON, S. (2012): International Business, 6th ed., Harlow, Pearson.

STEERS, R.; SANCHEZ-RUNDE, C.; NARDON, L. (2010): Management across Cultures: Challenges and Strategies, Cambridge, Cambridge University Press.

STEINHOFF, I. (2014): Zuversichtliche Job-Einsteiger, Handelszeitung, May 28, 2014, pp. 24-25.

SULLIVAN, J. (2007): Search Google for Top HR Practices, http://www.workforce.com, accessed on May 22, 2014.

SULLIVAN, J. (2013): How Google Became the #3 Most Valuable Firm by Using People Analytics to Reinvent HR, http://www.ere.net, accessed on May 15, 2014.

UNIVERSUM (2014): Europe's Most Attractive Employers 2014, http://www.universumglobal.com, accessed on May 28, 2014.

WALKER, J. (2012): School's in Session at Google, in: Wall Street Journal, July 05, 2012.

WOMACK, B. (2011): Google Gets Record 75,000 Job Applications in a Week, Bloomberg News, February, 2011.

ZENTES, J.; SWOBODA, B.; MORSCHETT, D. (2004): Internationales Wertschöpfungsmanagement, Munich, Vahlen.

Chapter 23

International Control

Control is a fundamental management task, with the primary aim of providing adequate information to decision makers at different levels of the company. This Chapter introduces the functions of international control, discusses the particularities of control within an MNC and describes several control concepts, methods and instruments.

Introduction

Control is a fundamental management task. It involves developing plans for a company, including budgets, monitoring the results and deciding on corrective actions in case the actual results differ from the planned results (Rugman/Collinson 2012, p. 524; Boddy 2014, p. 22).

The typical *control process* for an MNC subsidiary consists of three steps: First, HQ and the subsidiary jointly plan the subsidiary's objectives for the coming year. The influence the subsidiary management has in this process differs strongly between different MNCs. Second, throughout the year, the HQ monitors the subsidiary's performance against the set objectives. Third, if the subsidiary fails to achieve its objectives, the HQ intervenes to learn why the problems occurred and reacts accordingly when necessary (Hill 2013, p. 648). In addition, at the level of corporate controlling, the plans and budget proposals of diverse subsidiaries or divisions have to be *consolidated* into an overall plan and budget.

Control Process

More concretely, the first stage of the control process involves defining the performance dimensions. *"What you measure is what you get"* and, thus, the selection of performance indicators and specific targets give a *sense of direction* and clarity of purpose to managers and employees at the different levels of the MNC. It also serves to *align their activities* with the corporate strategy and exerts a *motivational influence*. The objectives for the subsidiary should be challenging but realistic (Merchant/Stede 2012, p. 33; Boddy 2014, p. 595).

Defining Performance Dimensions

Traditionally, the most important criterion for evaluating the performance of a foreign subsidiary is the subsidiary's actual *profits* compared with budgeted profits. Other commonly used criteria include the subsidiary's actual *sales* (compared with the objectives) and its *return on investment* (ROI) (Hill 2013, p. 648).

Effectiveness and Efficiency

More generally, controls can take many forms. A major distinction is drawn between effectiveness and efficiency measures:

- *Effectiveness* is a measure of how well the outcome of an activity relates to the objectives. For example, sales, profits, the number of customers or of produced units could be measures of the effectiveness of a subsidiary unit. Effectiveness reflects *"doing the right things"*.

- *Efficiency* is a measure of output divided by the input needed to produce the output. For example, sales per salesperson or produced units per machine hour are efficiency measures. Efficiency means *"doing things right"*.

Objective and Subjective Measures

Some aspects of performance can be measured *objectively* (e.g. sales or ROI) while other performance indicators, which might be equally important, depend more on *subjective evaluation* (e.g. innovativeness, company reputation, service quality) (Boddy 2014, p. 595). However, some level of quantification is necessary to compare actual results with pre-set standards.

Principal-Agent Problem

Considering the HQ-subsidiary relationship from a principal-agent perspective (see Chapter 10), with the subsidiary acting on behalf of the HQ, *information asymmetry* is a major problem, since the subsidiary ("the agent") usually knows substantially more about its activities and its external environment than the HQ ("the principal"). The aim of controlling is to reduce this information asymmetry without causing information overload at the HQ. Thus, providing the right amount of necessary information is crucial.

Controlling as Staff Function

It has to be noted that controllership is usually a staff function. Controlling assists management in making decisions by providing adequate information. Thus, the controller delivers information and monitors performance, but the use of this information remains the *responsibility of line management* (Gowthorpe 2011, pp. 412-414). As a consequence, establishing and running a system to collect and provide information regularly, i.e. an *information and control system*, is part of the controlling task (Boddy 2014, p. 25).

Particularities of International Control

When controlling an MNC, a set of heterogeneous factors, both from the external environment and the internal relationship between subsidiary and headquarters, increases the quantitative and qualitative challenges. Some measures are *uniform* across the MNC while others are *unique* to a certain situation or country. A number of particularities of international control are given below (Zentes/Swoboda/Morschett 2004, pp. 802-806).

An MNC usually has to consider a *greater number of "control objects"* (e.g. divisions, countries, subsidiaries) than domestic companies. In addition, these are usually characterised by a greater degree of *heterogeneity* than in a purely domestic context. Furthermore, the separate organisational units are often interdependent, e.g. due to intra-company product flows. Fluctuations in *currency exchange rates* may cause substantial distortions in the comparison between subsidiaries and in the performance measurement. For example, the US subsidiary of a German MNC may fail to achieve its profit goals in Euro not because of performance problems but merely because of a decline in the value of the US Dollar against the Euro. Due to different currencies, the control of cross-border transactions (including internal product flows) is also more complex. The *comparability* of data is not guaranteed. Different subsidiaries operate in different external environments, thus comparing profits or ROI may not be an adequate measure to compare the performance of the subsidiary's management (Hill 2013, p. 651).

Currency Exchange Rates

Different *legal systems, taxation systems* and *accounting practices* have long required the compliance of MNCs with heterogeneous reporting standards for their external financial reporting. While external financial reporting and internal control are two separate systems with different objectives and purposes, they are usually based on the same databases. Since IFRS (*International Financial Reporting Standards*) have been introduced as a legal standard in many countries (Boddy 2014, p. 633; Gowthorpe 2011, pp. 161-162), a convergence of internal control is likely. International control concerns people from different cultural backgrounds, and *cultural differences* will affect how people respond to control systems (Boddy 2014, p. 588). Problems and misunderstandings between the HQ in one country and a subsidiary in a foreign country are more likely. Cultural differences have an impact, e.g. on the expected and accepted time horizon for planning and reporting, on the use of quantitative or qualitative performance measures or on the degree of precision and detail in planning and monitoring.

Different Accounting Practices

Gathering *information* in an international context is more difficult and more costly; in addition, the information is often *more uncertain*. External data for foreign markets, in particular in less developed or emerging countries, might not be easily available. The resulting information advantage held by local management might be exploited to manipulate information, which obviously limits its reliability. It also increases the problems of performance measurement (which is a type of agency problem). Finally, as has been pointed out in Chapters 1-3 of this book, the tasks and roles of subsidiaries in different countries vary, along with other characteristics like age or value-added activities (manufacturing plants, sales subsidiaries, etc.). This has to be considered when measuring that subsidiary's *performance*.

Gathering External Data

Currency Issues

MNCs have subsidiaries in different countries and usually do business in different currency areas. As a consequence, MNCs are usually exposed to three kinds of *exchange risks* (Rugman/Collinson 2012, pp. 513-514):

Transaction Risk

■ When specific contracts are denominated in a foreign currency, the MNC faces *transaction risk*. This is the risk that a financial loss occurs due to an unanticipated exchange rate change which affects fixed future cash flows when exchanged in the home country currency. For example, accounts receivable in US Dollars from the sale of a machine today that is being paid by the foreign customer in one year might not result in the planned Euro value then. Instruments to reduce this risk (e.g. *futures* or *options*) are costly.

Translation Risk

■ *Translation risk*, or *accounting risk*, is the risk of losses on the MNC's balance sheet through value changes in foreign currency assets and liabilities. For example, the plant and equipment of a Japanese subsidiary that is consolidated in the British MNCs' financial statement is subject to devaluation if the Yen loses value versus the British Pound.

Economic Risk

■ *Economic risk* is the risk of unexpected changes to potential future cash flows from foreign operations that result from exchange rate changes. This can be caused by changes in sales, prices or costs. In recent years the Swiss Franc's gain in value has led to major challenges for numerous companies, because the translation of falling currency values decreased revenues. For example, the falling value of currencies in the USA, Brazil and India gave *Schindler*, a Swiss escalator and elevator manufacturer, cause to issue its second consecutive profit warning in 2013. Competitors like the German *ThyssenKrupp*, the US *Otis* or the Finnish *Kone* were not affected by this problem to such an extent, so *Schindler's* competitive position was weakened.

A strategy of so-called *"natural hedging"* tries to reduce this risk by spreading costs over different currency areas. For example, *Mercedes* and *BMW* have built factories in the USA that allow production to be shifted between countries as a response to a shift in exchange rates.

To avoid costly and unnecessary risk reducing mechanisms by separate subsidiaries that do not oversee the MNC's *overall risk exposure* and can usually not evaluate its *net effects*, a certain level of centralisation of financial management of MNCs is required. As a general trend, MNCs today use a centralised structure to manage currency and financial issues.

Particularities of Control in Multi-Level Organisations

MNCs are not only international, they are typically also *multi-level organisa-tions*, composed at least of a headquarters, divisions (regional, product, or functional) and usually also country subsidiaries (see Chapter 11).

"Quite simply, [...] information is produced because people need it. The reasons why they need it vary from one group of people to another" (Gowthorpe 2011, p. 14). It is evident that, particularly in an MNC, the needs of these different groups of people differ strongly, for example when comparing the information needs of corporate management, subsidiary management, a production manager or the marketing manager of a subsidiary. Since setting performance standards, monitoring them and providing information to the decision-makers in the organisation is the main task of controlling, the different decisions made at the different levels in the organisation and the related information requirements have to be considered.

Heterogeneous Information Needs

Decision and Information Requirements at Different Levels in an MNC

Table 23.1

Decision Type	Decisions	Information Requirements	Infor-mation
Strategic	Corporate Management		External
	• basic long-term strategic decisions for company • resource allocation to divisions • coordination of divisions (incl. selecting and appraising division management)	• opportunities/threats and strengths/weaknesses info on coporate level • info across divisions (and performance) • long-term developments (highly aggregated)	
	Division Management		
	• basic targets for subsidiaries • mid-term planning • resource allocation to subsidiaries • coordination of subsidiaries (incl. selecting and appraising subsidiary management)	• targets from HQ • long-term, mid-term, rather speculative data • specific product and/or region related coordination and evaluation data • quantitative monetary info on division results	
	Subsidiary Management		
Ope-rational	• development of country-specific strategies • coordination of operational issues in subsidiary	• targets from division management • operative data from internal accounting • only immediate info on external environment • supportive data from division or HQ	Internal

Source: Adapted from Zentes/Swoboda/Morschett 2004, p. 806.

As the overview, Table 23.1 suggests the proportion of *strategic decisions* increases with the hierarchy level in the organisation, usually requiring more aggregated information about the *external environment* and comparatively *long-term, future-oriented* information. An attempt to fully capture the heterogeneity and cross-relationships within the MNC can even lead to information overload at the HQ, which would reduce decision effectiveness.

At the level of subsidiary management, a preoccupation with *operational decisions* requires more *internal information*.

Level of Detail for Performance Targets

As another consequence of multi-level organisation, the corporate management and subsequently the division managers have to decide on the level of detail for the subordinate unit's performance objectives. This decision is related to the basic attitude toward *centralisation* or *decentralisation* (Merchant/Stede 2012, pp. 15, 309-312; Gowthorpe 2011, pp. 414-415; Boddy 2014, p. 180):

■ The upper hierarchy level can decide to set performance targets only through *bottom-line figures*, i.e. rough outcome figures such as ROI, etc. In this case, the subsidiary manager has the autonomy to decide *how* to achieve the desired results. These outcome figures are like a compass and give loose guidance – leading managers in the right direction but not dictating specific actions. Thus, this system permits the flexibility to adapt to the specific host country or to unexpected changes.

■ On the other hand, top management can set *unambiguous targets* about a *comprehensive set of performance indicators* which guarantees tight control over the subsidiary's operational behaviour. This systems acts like a "roadmap" which provides clear guidance to subsidiary managers on exactly how to achieve the specified objectives. The caveat is that superiors in the HQ might not fully understand the subsidiary's specific and thus might not really know which decisions are best suited to reaching the objectives. It also severely limits the subsidiary management's flexibility when responding to unexpected situations. The advantage of this approach is coherence in subsidiary behaviour.

Subsidiary Participation in the Process

The multi-level organisation also has to decide on subsidiaries' *level of participation* in the planning and budgeting process (Zentes/Swoboda/Morschett 2004, pp. 813-815; Merchant/Stede 2012, pp. 317-318; Amann/Petzold 2014, p. 143):

■ In a *top-down planning process*, top management starts the planning process and, in a cascading fashion, each subsequent management level uses this plan as an obligatory input and merely concretises the objectives for its organisational unit. The objective of plans at lower hierarchy levels (e.g. the subsidiary) is only to fulfil the present objectives of the superordinate plans. The main advantage of this procedure is the strong coherence of the organisation's plans; the main disadvantage is a negative impact on the motivation of subsidiaries, particularly if the current performance objectives are not considered adequate by the subsidiary management.

- Pure *bottom-up processes* hardly exist in reality. Here, subsidiary management (or division management) set their own performance targets and take decisions for their own organisational units. At the top management level, plans are merely acknowledged and maybe consolidated. The advantages of this procedure are that subsidiary managers are highly motivated to reach their self-set objectives and the targets are fully aligned to each local context.

- By far the most common procedure is an integrated *top-down, bottom-up process* that attempts to combine the advantages of both approaches. Here, top management issues *guidelines* and rough performance objectives for all divisions/subsidiaries. Then, each subsidiary develops concrete plans and performance targets for its organisational unit, e.g. budgets for the coming year. These plans and budgets are proposed to the HQ. After consolidation and analysis, the HQ might request modifications which are then carried out by the subsidiary in new proposals. These steps might be repeated several times; for an annual budgeting process, the whole procedure may last about three to four months. Despite the time and effort required, this procedure has many advantages. Since the process starts with HQ guidelines, coherence is guaranteed and corporate priorities are clearly communicated to the subsidiaries. Interdependencies among organisational units are considered by the top-down approach. But, the subsidiaries are also involved in the process which leads to better acceptance of the targets and subsequent commitment to achieving them.

Most Common Participation Process

In addition, in a multi-level organisation, the *consolidation* of reports, financial indicators, financial statements, etc., becomes important. While the typical MNC comprises a parent company and a number of subsidiaries located in different countries and often organised as separate legal entities, most of which are wholly owned by the parent, economically, all the companies in the MNC are interdependent. Thus, the purpose of consolidation is to provide information about the group of companies in the MNC by excluding the transactions among the members of this group (i.e. eliminating sales figures resulting from intra-company product flows or netting out the amount of money owed between MNC units) (Pratt 2011, p. 140).

Consolidation on the Corporate Level

Organisational Issues

Another concern in multi-level organisations is that the organisational relation within the controlling function (which is usually a staff function) exerts a strong influence on the role and principal tasks of the controller (Merchant/Stede 2012, pp. 617-619). This can be explained by using the example of a corporate controller and a divisional controller. The organisational challenge arises from the two main responsibilities of a *divisional controller*: On the one hand, he provides a certain *support function* for the division management. On the other hand, the divisional controller has a *responsibility* towards the corporate controller to ensure that the internal control practices in the division conform to the corporate objectives and standards and that the information provided by his division to HQ is accurate. He therefore acts partly as a *corporate guardian* over the division activities.

In each case, the division controller has to serve two different organisational units. Which of the two functions is dominant is largely dependent on the controller's organisational attachment (Merchant/Stede 2012, p. 620). If the divisional controller has a *"solid line"* relationship with the division management, reflecting that the division management has functional and hierarchical authority and the division controller a direct reporting responsibility to the division management, and only a *"dotted line"* relationship with the corporate controller (i.e. an indirect reporting responsibility), then the division support task prevails. Controllership function is in this case comparatively decentralised and the divisional controller perceived to be a *"division ally"* and a trusted supporter. If, however, the solid line is between the divisional controller and the corporate controller and the dotted line between the divisional controller and the division management, the direct reporting responsibility is focused on the internal and financial control responsibility. In the case of a centralised controllership function, the division controller is often seen as a *"corporate spy"*, or at least more as a representative of HQ.

Performance Measurement

As has already been shown, profits, ROI, and other performance indicators for foreign subsidiaries are strongly influenced by the external environment in which they operate. Thus, using standardised quantitative criteria to assess the performance of subsidiary managers might be inadequate. However, this might make it necessary to separate the evaluation of the subsidiary itself from the evaluation of the subsidiary management (Hill 2013, pp. 650-651):

■ When *comparing subsidiaries*, it may be sufficient to compare ROI, sales, profits, etc. Ultimately, it is the task of HQ to invest its resources in those countries that generate the highest returns. Whether the low returns of a foreign subsidiary are due to strong competition, a negative exchange rate development or other influences are not of primary interest. Still, the MNC may want to reduce its investment in a low-performing country.

■ When evaluating the *performance of managers* from different subsidiaries, the economic, political and social conditions have to be considered. For example, the manager of a subsidiary that has grown by 3% might have performed better than the manager of another subsidiary that has grown by 8%, depending on the average market growth in the two countries. Furthermore, it is reasonable to evaluate the management on the basis of their results in the local currency and after considering financial effects which they cannot directly influence (e.g. interest rates, taxes, inflation, transfer prices, etc.).

Evaluating Subsidiary Managers

Transfer Pricing

One characteristic of most modern MNCs is substantial intra-company transactions, e.g. sales of components that are produced by one foreign subsidiary to a subsidiary in another country which uses those components to assemble a final product, which might then be sold by another subsidiary in a third country. As already mentioned, about a third of world trade consists of these *intra-company sales*.

Intra-Company Sales

The price at which an exchange of products, services or rights between different units in the MNC occurs is referred to as the *transfer price*. Obviously, the choice of transfer price strongly affects the performance of the two subsidiaries engaged in the exchange. Using the *arm's length principle*, the price the buyer pays would be the *market price* under conditions of perfect competition. Thus, it would be openly negotiated between the foreign subsidiaries, which would also require the free choice for the buyer to choose another, external supplier. This would also perfectly make use of *market mechanisms* as a coordination instrument for internal resource allocation. However, transfer prices are *not* only a bilateral issue between the subsidiaries, and not a zero-sum game since they also influence the overall profits of the MNC. For instance, raising the sales price of a certain component will raise the profit of the selling subsidiary at the expense of the buying subsidiary. If the selling subsidiary is located in a low-tax country, this will reduce the overall *worldwide tax liability* of the MNC. A similar influence is exerted by *custom tariffs*. Since these are often a percentage of the value of the goods, lowering transfer prices lowers the *import duties* to be paid. In addition, transfer prices might be set in order to avoid *government restrictions on capital flows*. For example, transfer prices between a foreign subsidiary and the headquarters can be used as a hidden mechanism to repatriate profits from this subsidiary (Rugman/Collinson 2012, pp. 503-504; Hill 2013, pp. 660-662).

Influence of Transfer Prices

However, given the strong impact of transfer prices, *government regulations* usually keep tight restriction on the range for manipulation. Also, the MNC's overall interest in setting certain transfer prices obviously has to be considered when evaluating the subsidiary management, since this important profit determinant is outside their direct responsibility. It must also be noted that flexibility is drastically reduced in the case of a *joint venture* (as buyer or seller) where each of the joint venture partners might have different strategic objectives linked to the transfer price.

Selected Control Instruments

On the strategic level, relatively broad and highly aggregated plans concerning missions, goals and general strategies are developed (Merchant/Stede 2012, pp. 307-308). On the operational level, short-term financial planning is the major concern of control and operational optimisation, with a strong emphasis on quantitative data. The tactical level is the intermediate level between the strategic and operational levels. From strategic control to operational control, the level of detail and specificity increases while the planning and control period decreases. Control instruments can roughly be attributed to the three levels. *Operational control instruments* include short-term budgets, cost control, inventory control, break-even analysis or contribution margin analysis and short-term budgets. *Tactical instruments* include ABC analysis, industry analysis, benchmarking and financial ratio systems (like the *Dupont pyramid*). Typical examples of *strategic control instruments* are portfolio analysis, scenario planning, balanced scorecard and shareholder value.

Budget

A *budget* is a plan, expressed in financial terms (or, more generally, in quantitative terms), which extends for a certain period (often one year) into the future (Gowthorpe 2011, p. 359).

Usually, particularly in complex organisations, a number of budgets are prepared, e.g. for sales, production, labour, etc. The sales budget usually provides a reasonable starting point. With this as input, the production budget can be prepared. This is likewise usually directly linked to a materials budget, a labour budget, etc. The outcome of the budget process then is a *full set of interrelated budgets* (Gowthorpe 2011, p. 362). Part of international control involves ensuring the coherence of these budgets.

Portfolio Analysis

One principal task of MNC top management is to develop a corporate strategy that defines the businesses in which the company should be active and to thereby structure the *portfolio* of businesses. Closely related to this task, the MNC management has to ensure an *effective resource allocation* across business fields, countries and value-added functions. Portfolio models offer a framework that allows an overall assessment of the given portfolio of business units and the determination of the desired composition of the future portfolio (see Grünig/Kühn 2011, pp. 161-187; Grünig/Morschett 2012, pp. 65-68 with a detailed overview of such models).

Most portfolio models position objects (mostly business units) in a two-dimensional space, i.e. a *matrix* created from two criteria. Usually, they also suggest *norm strategies* for the overall portfolio as well as for business units in a specific position in that portfolio. The main differences between the portfolio models are the chosen dimensions:

- Traditionally, the term "portfolio" has its origins in *investment optimisation models*. Here, the portfolio dimensions (which can also be applied to business units or country subsidiaries if they are seen as investment objects which have to yield a certain return on investment) are *risk* and *return*, with the implication that diversification helps to reduce overall risk and that the optimal diversification depends on the correlation of risks across the diverse business units.

  Investment Optimisation Models

- In the well-known *Boston Consulting Group* portfolio matrix, the *relative market share* of the business unit and the *market growth rate* are used to group business units into categories such as *cash cows* (high market share but low growth) or *question marks* (low market share but high growth). It is assumed that cash expenditure and cash inflows depend on the two dimensions and, thus, a balance in the portfolio between cash-generating business units and cash-requiring (but high growth) business units should be chosen to ensure the long-term competitiveness of the company.

  BCG Matrix

- Another commonly used portfolio matrix is the *General Electric* matrix which uses the *industry attractiveness* and the *competitive strength* of the business unit as dimensions.

Balanced Scorecard

The control instrument that has arguably attracted the most attention in recent decades is the *balanced scorecard* (BSC) proposed by Kaplan and Norton (1996). This is a specific, four-dimensional performance measurement system that comprises *financial objectives* as well as *non-financial measures* (see Figure 23.1). "The balanced scorecard translates an organization's mission and strategy into a comprehensive set of performance measures that provides the framework for a strategic measurement and management system. [...] The BSC enables companies to track financial results while simultaneously monitoring progress in building the capabilities and acquiring the intangible assets they need for future growth" (Kaplan/Norton 1996, p. 2). More specifically, the BSC is built on the assumption of leading and lagging indicators with financial indicators considered to be "lagging" and other indicators (like learning & growth) seen as "leading" indicators that are closer to the root of long-term company success.

Figure 23.1	*The Balanced Scorecard*

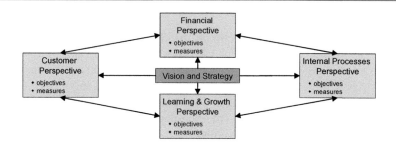

Source: Kaplan/Norton 1996, p. 9; Gowthorpe 2011, p. 425.

With regards to international control within an MNC, the BSC offers the opportunity to break down superordinate strategies and detailed performance measures on the corporate level into specific and clear objectives for subunits (see Figure 23.2).

Implementing the Balanced Scorecard in Multi-Level Organisations

Figure 23.2

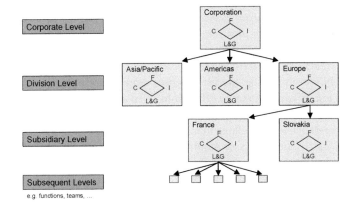

Source: Adapted from Rieg/Gleich 2002, p. 697; Zentes/Swoboda/Morschett
    2004, p. 830.

Thus, a detailed set of performance indicators comprising both financial and non-financial measures is produced for each subunit, guaranteeing coherence in the organisation.

Shareholder Value

From the shareholder perspective, one major objective of management is to increase the value of the company for its owners. Thus, company decisions should be based on their expected influence on *shareholder value*. Translating this to MNC management, the performance of a subsidiary or investment project is measured in terms of its contribution to the value of the MNC (Zentes/Swoboda/Morschett 2004, pp. 839-844).

This dynamic investment perspective investigates expected future cash flows and is calculated, e.g., based on *discounted cash flow* (i.e. the net present value of future free cash flows). An example of value-based performance measurement is presented in the *Henkel* case study to this Chapter.

One of the most frequently applied models of *value management* is the *economic value added* (EVA) developed by *Stern Stewart* (Stern/Shiely/Ross 2001). EVA is calculated according to formula (1) (Merchant/Stede 2012, pp. 427-428):

Economic Value Added (EVA)

(1) EVA = net operating profit (after taxes) - WACC x capital

Cost of Equity Capital

Thus, EVA considers not only the company's profit but also whether this profit is sufficient to appropriately compensate its capital providers. It is calculated as profit (using an adjusted profit measure) minus the *cost of capital*, thus, as a kind of *residual income* over the required rate of return for the capital investment (which also considers the *opportunity costs* for the investor). One problem is in defining the *weighted average cost of capital (WACC)*, which is averaged across the costs of debt and the costs of equity capital. The costs of debt are simply the interest expenses required to serve the debt. But the cost of equity capital is more difficult to calculate, because it depends on uncertain factors such as overall stock market risk, return expectations and the *risk-free rate of return* available to investors (Merchant/Stede 2012, pp. 418-419). Particularly for MNCs, a required rate of return that includes a *risk premium* can differ for investments in different countries or different investment projects that carry different risks. For each investment project in a subsidiary, this project creates shareholder value if EVA is greater than zero; but if EVA is below zero, the project destroys shareholder value (Estrada 2005, p. 286). Across potential investment projects or subsidiaries, capital should be invested in the one with the greatest expected EVA.

EVA as Evaluation Criterion

Conclusion and Outlook

International control covers not only operational performance monitoring but also strategic control, which is mainly future oriented. In an international setting, the complexity of control enhances dramatically, due to, e.g., currency issues, different external environments and cross-border interdependencies. Within an MNC, the multi-level structure adds to the complexity, resulting in highly heterogeneous information requirements at different organisational levels and units. A very comprehensive set of control instruments is available to handle this complexity. Their application depends not only on objective and rational decisions but also on subjective attitudes and corporate values.

Polycentric, Ethnocentric and Geocentric Orientation

The general "orientation" of the MNC will influence its response to the challenges for international control. With a *polycentric orientation*, the MNC will leave many decisions to the subsidiary, determine only rough objectives and merely control the output level, e.g. profits. With an *ethnocentric orientation*, the foreign operations are treated as extensions of domestic operations, leading to comparatively uniform planning and control systems and tight integration into the control system, with detailed performance indicators and objectives which might neglect the particularities of each foreign country. The *geocentric solution* tries to handle control on a global basis with an adequate level of centralised decisions and uniform control instruments and performance objectives while considering the heterogeneity of subsidiaries

(Rugman/Collinson 2012, pp. 501-502). This would include, for example, comparing performance of subsidiaries in a generally uniform way as an input for decisions on resource allocation but considering a more complex set of performance criteria for the evaluation of subsidiary managers.

As a general trend it can be observed that control is moving increasingly from *"looking back"* to *"looking forward"* to better support management (Nurdin 2009, p. 11). Related to this trend is the development that financial performance measures are increasingly being supplemented with non-financial performance measures (like customer or employee satisfaction). The widespread application of the BSC clearly reflects this trend to monitor a comprehensive set of performance indicators.

Further Reading

KAPLAN, R.; NORTON, D. (1996): The Balanced Scorecard: Translating Strategy into Action, Boston, McGraw-Hill.

MERCHANT, K.; STEDE, W. van der (2012): Management Control Systems: Performance Measurement, Evaluation and Incentives, 3rd ed., Harlow, Prentice Hall.

Case Study: Henkel[*]

Profile, History and Status Quo

Henkel is a German manufacturing company which operates worldwide with leading brands and technologies in the fields of detergents and adhesives. The *DAX*-listed company generated revenues of 16,355 million EUR and an adjusted operating profit of 2,516 million EUR in 2013.

The company has a strong presence in emerging countries. 44% of sales are generated there, while 34% of sales are attributed to Western Europe, 18% came from North America and a further 3% came from Japan, Australia and New Zealand. Besides the headquarters in Düsseldorf, Germany, there are seven regional centres in China, the UAE, Austria, Brazil, Mexico and the USA. Even the 18 major R&D sites are spread all over the world. Around 47,000 employees from more than 120 nations work in over 75 countries.

---

[*] Sources used for this case study include the web sites http://www.henkel.com, and various annual and interim reports, investor-relations presentations as well as sources explicitly cited sources.

Consequently, 80% of employees work outside the home country. The company's products, which are produced at 164 sites in 54 countries, are available worldwide. These facts show that *Henkel* is one of the most internationally oriented companies in Germany.

The company dates back to 1876 when Fritz Henkel and his two partners Otto Dicker and Otto Scheffen founded *Henkel & Cie* in Aachen, Germany. At the same time, *Henkel's* first brand-name product *"Universal-Waschmittel"* (Universal Detergent) appeared, and two years later the rollout of *"Bleich-Soda"* (Bleaching Soda) began. To take advantage of better transport and sales opportunities, *Henkel* relocated its headquarters to Düsseldorf, Germany. After Otto Dicker and Otto Scheffen left the company, Fritz Henkel was entered as the sole owner in the Commercial Register in 1879. In 1907, the laundry detergent *Persil* was launched, and is still available today. A few years later the first production subsidiary abroad was opened in Pratteln, Switzerland. In 1950, *Henkel* set up a new business sector by acquiring *TheraChemie* and its liquid hair colorant *Poly Color*. After a range of acquisitions and new market entries outside Europe, e.g. in South Africa and the USA, big steps in the company's history ensued in 1995 and 1997 when *Hans Schwarzkopf GmbH* and *Loctite Corp.* were obtained. Throughout its history, the company has been predominantly owned by descendants of Fritz Henkel.

Business Units — *Henkel* is structured into three business units: laundry and home care, beauty care and adhesive technologies. It is currently the world No. 1 adhesive producer according to its own account. *Henkel* has also reached globally leading market positions in consumer and industrial businesses e.g. with well-known brands like *Persil*, *Schwarzkopf* or *Loctite*.

Organisational Structure and Performance

Henkel remains true to its origins. As mentioned earlier, as well as the laundry and home care sector, beauty care and adhesive technologies form the *cornerstone* of the company. Figure 23.3 shows the business units and a range of respective brands.

Laundry and Home Care

Somat	Pril	Persil	Vernel	Spee	Perwoll

Beauty Care

Fa	Aok	Theramed	syoss	got2b	Schwarzkopf

Adhesive Technologies

Loctite	Pattex	Technomelt	Pritt	Metylan	Sista

Source: Henkel 2014.

- The laundry and home care business unit generated sales of 4,580 million EUR in 2013, 28% of total company sales. 70% came for laundry while 30% was attributed to home care. This unit comprises the top brands *Persil*, *Purex* and *Pril*, which together with another seven top brands make up about 85% of total laundry and home care sales. Strong competition in this field comes from huge players like *Procter&Gamble*, *Unilever* or *Reckitt Benckiser*. This business area is characterised by a high level of internationalisation. Large customers include German retail companies like *Edeka*, *Rewe* or *Metro* as well as French *Carrefour* and US *Walmart*.

- The beauty care sector is divided into three sub fields: hair care, body care and skin/oral. This business unit generated sales of 3,510 million EUR in 2013, 21% of total company sales. The strongest sector is hair care, which is responsible for two-thirds of the quoted sales. This is thanks to the strong brand *Schwarzkopf*, one of the world's leading suppliers of hair salon products thanks to its professional line. Other representative brands are *Syoss*, *Dial* and *got2b*. Major competitors in this field include *L'Oréal*, *Procter&Gamble*, *Unilever*, *Beiersdorf* and *KAO*.

- The adhesive technologies business unit supplies different target groups like end-consumers, craftsmen and industrial business under various brands. *Henkel* is the world market leader in adhesives, sealants and functional coatings. Sales of 8,117 million EUR were generated here in 2013, which equals 50% of company sales. Key competitors in the three customer groups of industry, consumers and craftsmen are *Bostik*, *Sika* and *BASF*.

Performance and financial key figures for the *Henkel* business units are presented in Table 23.2.

Table 23.2 *Selected Performance and Financial Key Figures for the Henkel Business Units (2013)*

	Laundry & Home Care	Beauty Care	Adhesive Technologies
Sales (in million EUR)	4,580	3,510	8,117
EBIT (in million EUR)	682	474	1,271
Adjusted Return on Sales (EBIT)	15.6%	15.0%	16.9%
Capital Employed (in million EUR)	2,321	2,007	6,752
Weighted Average Cost of Capital (WACC)	7.5%	7.5%	10.5%
Return on Capital Employed (ROCE)	29.4%	23.6%	18.8%
Economic Value Added (EVA; in million EUR)	507	323	562

Source: Henkel 2014.

International Control at Henkel

Value-Based Management

Henkel, especially its controlling, is influenced by *shareholder value*. This is particularly reflected by its values, where the pursuit of sustainable financial performance is noted. "We are a performance-driven company committed to growing the value of business and providing a competitive return to our shareholders" (Henkel 2011). Even *Henkel's corporate governance* is dedicated to achieving a long-term increase in shareholder value (Henkel 2014, p. 25). As a consequence, *Henkel* pursues the value-based management approach. "The objective of value-based management is to create, maintain, and deliver growth, and thereby deliver a long-term increase in shareholder value" (Häntsch/Huchzermeier 2013, p. 126). Combining traditional accounting-based measures of company performance with shareholder expectations is the main function of performance indicators (Rapp et al. 2010, p. 172). The key elements of value-based management are the creation of shareholder value, the identification of value drivers, the connection of performance measurement, target setting and rewards for value creation or value drivers as well as the connection of decision making and action planning (strategic and operational) to value creation or value drivers (Malmi/Ikäheimo 2003, p. 251).

Associated with the growing acceptance of the shareholder value principle, value-based management has attracted increasing interest among mangers, consultancy firms and the financial press (Rapp et al. 2010, p. 172).

Value-Based Performance Measurement at Henkel

"Performance Measurement is one of the critical factors how individuals in an organization behave" (Jensen/Meckling 1999, p. 8).

The key part of a value-based management system is a performance metric which is able to measure a company's value. Its function is to increase the informational content so that the management and its investors are supported in their strategic and operational decision-making. This leads to an alignment of managerial behaviour and shareholder targets. To reach this goal it is necessary for the performance metric to be consistently adopted across organisational functions and hierarchical levels. Traditionally used measures like earnings do not suit the requirements of value-based management, because they do not show the shareholder wealth which has been created. Non-financial performance measures do not meet the criteria of being available and comparable between different businesses.

Performance Metrics

To overcome these disadvantages it is necessary to use value-based metrics which draw on cash flows or earnings after the cost of equity. Frequently used *value-based performance measures* derived from cash flows include: discounted cash flow, shareholder value added and total business return. By using these measures, difficulties may arise if the value creation of a single period has to be measured. In this case *residual income metrics*, which refer to earnings instead of cash flow, are appropriate. The most common are: residual income, economic value added, economic profit and cash value added (Holler 2009, pp. 28-31).

Achieving a sustainable increase in shareholder value is of crucial importance for *Henkel*'s corporate management and control activities. Assessment of growth to date and appraisal of future plans are carried out on the basis of the economic value added (EVA), a central performance management parameter. Achieving sustainable EVA has a huge influence on all operating and strategic decisions like acquisitions or divestments. This concept helps with value-added decisions or the assessment of current or future profitable growth. An operation will be divested or discontinued if it yields consistently negative value contributions and future positive EVA cannot be expected.

Economic Value Added

EVA allows the measurement of additional financial value or net wealth that has been created by a company over a certain period. It is positive when the company's operating result outvalues the weighted average cost of capital. If the return on capital employed outvalues the cost of capital, then value is generated.

Elements of Economic Value Added

The operational profit measure at *Henkel* is *EBIT* (earnings before interest and taxes). This key figure allows the earning power of the operating business activities of a company to be assessed, which are independent of the company's financial structure. Thereby different entities can be compared, even if they are financed by varying levels of debt capital.

Capital employed describes the capital which has been invested in company assets and operations. Consequently this figure references the assets side of balance sheet. Its calculation is based on the total of operating assets, like goodwill at book value or inventories, of which operating liabilities are subtracted (resulting in net operating assets). After withdrawal of goodwill at book value and the addition of goodwill at cost the result is capital employed.

The costs of capital employed are calculated as a *weighted average cost of capital* (WACC). This value constitutes the minimum return of a company which is expected by its lenders for financing assets. Its calculation is based on the weighted average of the cost of debt and equity. The result is stated in percentage terms. Because of the dependence on the business sector involved, WACC rates differ for every business unit.

By using the information provided in Table 23.2, Figure 23.4 illustrates the calculation of the *economic value added* for *Henkel's* business unit adhesive technologies.

Figure 23.4

Economic Value Added of the Business Unit Adhesive Technologies in 2013 (in million EUR)

Source: Adapted from Henkel 2014, p. 109.

The business units vary in size, so comparisons among them is limited if only EVA is used. As a consequence, *Henkel* also applies another measurement which refers to a return ratio, the *return on capital employed* (ROCE).

Figure 23.5 shows how *Henkel* calculates ROCE.

Calculation of Return on Capital Employed of the Laundry and Home Care Business Unit

Figure 23.5

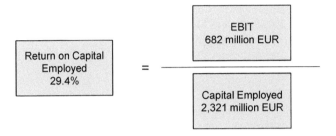

Source: Adapted from Henkel 2014, p. 109.

Summary and Outlook

Henkel's strategic goal is to achieve sustainable profitable growth across all divisions and to increase the value of the group. By 2016, the company aims to reach ambitious targets like sales of 20 billion EUR, of which 10 billion EUR should be generated in emerging markets. Furthermore, a 10% average annual growth in earnings per share should be realised. To meet these objectives, rigorous international controlling is inevitable. *Henkel's* overall aim of increasing shareholder value is the most important factor of value-based management.

Questions

1. *Henkel* heavily emphasises the shareholder value concept. Compare and discuss the shareholder value approach with the alternative concept known as the "stakeholder approach".

2. The shareholder value is established in *Henkel's* vision and values. Which other areas are affected by this approach?

3. This case study highlights the usage of economic value added (EVA) as a measure in value-based management. Explain why traditional account-

ing measures like earnings or earnings growth are inappropriate value-based management measures.

4. Which other value-oriented approaches except EVA exist? List their advantages and disadvantages.

Hints

1. See *Henkel's* annual report for 2013.

2. See Holler 2009 as well as Merchant and Stede 2012.

References

AMANN, K.; PETZOLD, J. (2014): Management und Controlling: Instrumente – Organisation – Ziele, Wiesbaden, Springer Gabler.

BODDY, D. (2014): Management: An Introduction, 6th ed., Harlow, Pearson.

ESTRADA, J. (2005): Finance in a Nutshell, London, FT Press.

GOWTHORPE, C. (2011): Business Accounting and Finance, 3rd ed., Hampshire, South-Western Cengage Learning.

GRÜNIG, R.; KÜHN, R. (2011): Process-based Strategic Planning, 6th ed., Berlin et al., Springer.

GRÜNIG, R.; MORSCHETT, D. (2012): Developing International Strategies: Going and Being International for Medium-sized Companies, Berlin-Heidelberg, Springer.

HÄNTSCH, M.; HUCHZERMEIER, A. (2013): Identifying, Analyzing, and Assessing Risk in the Strategic Planning of a Production Network: The Practical View of a German Car Manufacturer, in: Journal of Management Control, Vol. 24, No. 2, pp. 125-158.

HENKEL (2011): Vision and Values, Düsseldorf.

HENKEL (2013): Annual Report 2012, Düsseldorf.

HENKEL (2014): Annual Report 2013, Düsseldorf.

HILL, C.W.L. (2013): International Business: Competing in the Global Marketplace, 9th ed., New York, McGraw-Hill.

HOLLER, A. (2009): New Metrics for Value-Based Management, Wiesbaden, Gabler.

JENSEN, M.C.; MECKLING, W.H. (1999): Specific Knowledge and Divisional Performance Measurement, in: Journal of Applied Corporate Finance, Vol. 12, No. 2, pp. 8-17.

KAPLAN, R.; NORTON, D. (1996): The Balanced Scorecard: Translating Strategy into Action, Boston, McGraw-Hill.

MALMI, T.; IKÄHEIMO, S. (2003): Value Based Management Practices: Some Evidence From the Field, in: Management Accounting Research, Vol. 14, No. 3, pp. 235-254.

MERCHANT, K.; STEDE, W. van der (2012): Management Control Systems: Performance Measurement, Evaluation and Incentives, 3rd ed., Harlow, Prentice Hall.

NURDIN, G. (2009): International Business Control, Reporting and Corporate Governance, Amsterdam, Elsevier Books.

PRATT, J. (2011): Financial Accounting in an Economic Context, 8th ed., Hoboken, John Wiley & Sons.

RAPP, M.S.; SCHELLONG, D.; SCHMIDT, M.; WOLFF, M. (2010): Considering the Shareholder Perspective: Value-based Management Systems and Stock Market Performance, in: Review of Managerial Science, Vol. 5, No. 2, pp. 171-194.

RIEG, R.; GLEICH, R. (2002): Strategische Steuerung des internationalen Unternehmensverbunds, in: MACHARZINA, K.; OESTERLE, M.-J. (Eds.): Handbuch Internationales Management, 2nd ed., Wiesbaden, Gabler, pp. 677-703.

RUGMAN, A.M.; COLLINSON, S. (2012): International Business, 6th ed., Harlow, Pearson.

STERN, J.; SHIELY, J.; ROSS, I. (2001): The EVA Challenge: Implementing Value Added Change in an Organization, New York, Wiley&Sons.

WOYKE, W. (2002): The European Union after Nice: A Community Facing a New Century, in: SCHOLZ, C.; ZENTES, J. (Eds.): Strategic Management: A European Approach, Wiesbaden, Gabler, pp. 3-21.

WTO (2014): Understanding the WTO: Principles of the Trading System, http://www.wto.org/english/thewto_e/whatis_e/tif_e/fact2_e.htm, accessed on July 17, 2014.

ZENTES, J.; SWOBODA, B.; MORSCHETT, D. (2004): Internationales Wertschöpfungsmanagement, Munich, Vahlen.

Index

Mehr wissen – weiter kommen
↗

Retail management in 18 lessons –

Each lesson includes key issues and a comprehensive case study

This is not a traditional textbook or collection of case studies, but is intended to demonstrate the complex and manifold questions of retail management in the form of 18 lessons that provide a thematic overview of key issues and illustrate them with the help of comprehensive case studies.

In the second edition, all chapters were revised and updated. Three new chapters were added to treat topics like online-retailing and multi-channel-strategies as well as the so called verticals in specific chapters. All case studies were replaced by new ones to reflect the most recent developments. Eighteen well-known retail companies from different countries, like Best Buy, IKEA,TK Maxx, Tesco and Decathlon, are now used to illustrate particular aspects of retail management.

Contents

Functions, Formats and Players in Retailing

Strategic Marketing in Retailing

Marketing Mix in Retailing

Buying, Logistics and Performance Measurement

Joachim Zentes/Dirk Morschett/
Hanna Schramm-Klein
Strategic Retail Management
Text and International Cases
2nd ed. 2012. VIII, 445 p.
€ (D) 39,95 | € (A) 41,07
ISBN 978-3-8349-2536-7

Abraham-Lincoln-Straße 46 . D-65189 Wiesbaden
Tel. +49 (0)6221/ 3 45 - 4301 . springer-gabler.de

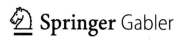 **Springer** Gabler

9783658078836